EDUGORILLA
PUBLICATION

AFCAT

Indian Air Force

Latest Edition
Practice Kit

10 Tests
10 Mock Test

Based On Real Exam Pattern

✓ Thoroughly Revised and Updated

✓ Detailed Analysis of all MCQs

Title	: AFCAT Indian Air Force
Author Name	: Mr. Rohit Manglik
Published By	: EduGorilla Community Pvt. Ltd.
Publishers Address	: 12/651, First Floor Opp. Arvindo Park, Near Jama Masjid, Indira Nagar, Lucknow, Uttar Pradesh-226016, India

Copyright EduGorilla

ISBN : 978-93-55562-52-4

Second Edition

No part of this book may be reproduced, distributed, or transmitted in any form by any means, without the prior written permission of the publisher.

All Right Reserved

© by EduGorilla Community Pvt. Ltd

Disclaimer EduGorilla

Although the author and publisher have made every effort to ensure the accuracy of information in this book, we do not assume any responsibility to errors and hereby disclaim any liability to any party for any loss, damage, or disruption caused by errors or omissions, whether such errors or omissions result from negligence, accident, or any other cause.

Compiled and created by EduGorilla Community Pvt. Ltd

Printed By EduGorilla Community Pvt. Ltd.

ROHIT MANGLIK
CEO, EduGorilla

Dear Applicants,

People say *"Success comes to those who work hard."* But I've seen people working hard for their exams day in and day out for marginal success. While others succeed in their examinations by putting in just half the work. So are they God Gifted? No! I believe that it's because they work *smart* and not just *hard*. Similarly, for your exams, you should strategize your preparation so as to increase the likelihood of success. Well with EduGorilla get ready to increase your *chances of selection* in your exam by *16x*.

EduGorilla helps you in not only working *hard* but also working in a *smart and strategic* manner. With EduGorilla's preparation package, you get a chance to make your exam preparation easy, and a fun learning path towards selection. Finding the right path to your preparations can be difficult if you don't know in which direction to head. Don't worry, we have you covered! EduGorilla will be your guide to success in your journey. With our Preparation Package, you can prepare strategically and beat the exam in just one attempt.

EduGorilla's Preparation Package includes-

- **Test Series**   • **Books**

Our preparation package is handcrafted as per the latest changes, expert opinions, and students' discretion. Thus, enabling you to get through each stage of the selection process for your exam.

Our Books are designed by the teachers and experts of the respective exam with a combined 150+ years of experience; to provide you with easy, efficient, and effective learning. Our books are smart, in the sense that not only do they give you the answers to the questions but also provide similar questions for practice.

EduGorilla's competent Test Series gives you real-time experience and confidence through which you can clear your offline or online exam in just one attempt. We currently host 83,000+ mock tests for 1,440+ competitive and academic exams.

Thus, EduGorilla misses no chance to assist you in your preparation and covers all stages of the exam, so that you don't have to look anywhere else.

We provide complete preparation packages for defense, banking, teaching, and other National & State-Level exams. Hence, it doesn't matter which exam you aspire to because you will reach your success.

ALL THE BEST !

Let EduGorilla be your Guide to Success.

Rohit Manglik,
Founder and CEO, EduGorilla

INTRODUCTION

EduGorilla focuses on guiding students to succeed in their examinations. With that in mind, our book, titled "AFCAT : Indian Air Force", has been drafted through the collective efforts of our distinguished experts with 150+ years of combined experience. This book consists of questions that are created following the latest changes in the syllabus and exam pattern. We compiled the book on the basis of questions that are most likely to appear in the AFCAT. Through EduGorilla's "AFCAT : Indian Air Force" your chances of success will increase 16x.

EduGorilla does this through our Complete Preparation Package. This package consists of well-conceptualized and structured content in the form of questions that are tailor-made according to your needs and will help you practice for exams in a smart way by pinpointing all the necessary information. It also provides hints and solutions, along with a smart answer sheet for your self-evaluation. You can assess your shortcomings and work accordingly on areas that may require more of your attention.

EduGorilla promises to help you succeed in your examination and accomplish your dream goals. We believe in our aspirants and see them at the top of the merit list. And the first step towards the top is to start preparing with us. EduGorilla's "AFCAT : Indian Air Force" includes the following attributes.

➤ Well-Researched Content

➤ Top-Notch Quality

➤ Detailed Answers and Analysis

➤ Smart Answer Sheet

➤ Exam Relevant Questions

Therefore, EduGorilla fortifies your preparation and makes it durable enough to help you stand tall and beat the examination.

AFCAT
Scan QR code for Eligibility, Exam Pattern, Syllabus and more.

Book ID: 0534

TABLE OF CONTENTS

Mock Test 01

Q.1 The Union Government has authorised which bank for issue and encash Electoral Bonds through its 29 Authorized Branches from 1–10 th of July 2022?

A. State Bank of India   **B.** Axis Bank

C. ICICI Bank   **D.** HDFC Bank

Q.2 Who has been appointed as the new Director-General of the Sashastra Seema Bal on June 2022?

A. Sujoy Lal Thaosen   **B.** Sanjay Arora

C. Sanjeev Sharma   **D.** Ranjeet Singh Rana

Q.3 Who has been appointed as the new CEO of Data Security Council of India in September 2022?

A. Anurag Thakur   **B.** Tushar Mehta

C. Sudha Murti   **D.** Vinayak Godse

Q.4 A special meeting of the UN Security Council's (UNSC) Counter-Terrorism Committee hosted on 28th and 29th of October, 2022, was held in which place?

A. Mumbai   **B.** Delhi

C. Jaipur   **D.** Both (A) and (B)

Q.5 Which country was host the 44th FIDE Chess Olympiad 2022?

A. Russia   **B.** France   **C.** Italy   **D.** India

Q.6 The rate of interest for the first 2 years is 6% p.a., for the next 3 years is 10% p.a. and for the period beyond 5 years is 12% p.a. If a person gets $Rs.\,12,771$ as simple interest after 7 years, then how much money did he invest?

A. $Rs.\,19,350$ **B.** $Rs.\,19,450$

C. $Rs.\,19,300$ **D.** $Rs.\,20,000$

Q.7 Interest obtained on a sum of Rs. 5000 for 3 years is Rs. 1500. Find the rate percent.

A. 8%   **B.** 9%   **C.** 10%   **D.** 11%

Q.8 The simple interest on some amount is $\dfrac{7}{8}$ of the principal for 5 years. What is the rate (in percentage) of interest per annum?

A. 15   **B.** 17.5   **C.** 14   **D.** 22.5

Ques (9-13):Direction: For the following question, you have one brief passage with 5 questions. Read the passage carefully and choose the best answer to each question out of the four alternatives.

Buddha was one of the world's great religious teachers. His real name was Gautam Siddharth. He was born in the year 500 B.C. He was born a prince. His father was the King of Kapilavastu. But he did not want to become a king. He wanted to find out the meaning of life. He left his place as a young man. He went out to seek the truth. For years he lived the hard life of poverty. He went to many teachers. But they could not help him. At least, the light came to him. He was thinking deeply under a Bodhi tree near Gaya. He became the 'Buddha' or the 'Enlightened One'.

Q.9 Who was Buddha?

[MPTET Paper I - Varg 3, 2012]

A. Buddha was God

B. Buddha was a saint

C. Buddha was a great religious teacher

D. Buddha was a great political leader

Q.10 What was the real name of Buddha?

[MPTET Paper I - Varg 3, 2012]

A. Gautam Siddhartha   **B.** Mahatma Gautam

C. Hiuen Tsang   **D.** Vardhaman

Q.11 Buddha was:

[MPTET Paper I - Varg 3, 2012]

A. Born a Muslim

B. Born in a poor family

C. Born a teacher

D. Born a prince

Q.12 Buddha was born:

[MPTET Paper I - Varg 3, 2012]

A. After the death of Christ

B. Before the birth of Christ

C. Two thousand years ago

D. At the same time as Mahavir

Q.13 The land of Buddha's birth is:

[MPTET Paper I - Varg 3, 2012]

A. Gaya   **B.** India

C. The palace   **D.** Kapilavastu

Q.14 What will come in place of the question mark in the following question?

$$120 \div 40 \text{ of } \frac{1}{4} + \frac{2}{5} \times 3\frac{1}{4} = ?$$

A. $13\frac{3}{10}$ **B.** $11\frac{1}{9}$ **C.** $3\frac{1}{10}$ **D.** $32\frac{3}{11}$

Q.15 How many quarters are there in $12\frac{1}{4}$?

A. 49   **B.** 12   **C.** 48   **D.** 50

Q.16 The 'Swadeshi' and 'Boycott' were adopted as methods of struggle in Bengal at the same time Vande Mataram Movement was in which place?

A. Tamil Nadu   **B.** Punjab

C. Andhra Pradesh   **D.** Poona

Q.17 Direction: Choose the correct alternative which appropriately describes the given idioms and phrases.

Goes to dogs

A. Goes mad   B. Is insulted

C. Is ruined   D. Becomes brutal

Q.18 Direction: Some proverb/idiom is given below together with their meanings. Choose the correct meaning of proverb/idiom.

To cry wolf

A. To listen eagerly

B. To give false alarm

C. To turn pale

D. To keep off starvation

Q.19 What are 'the camel', 'the mongoose', 'kaboom' and 'aluminum' that have been in news recently?

A. Cricket bats   B. Military codes

C. Squadrons   D. Chess moves

Q.20 A sentence has been given in Active/Passive Voice. Out of the four alternatives suggested, select the one which best expresses the same sentence in Passive/Active Voice.

By whom was this window broken? Five packets of milk were delivered by the milkman.

[SSC Sub Inspector (CPO), 2019]

A. Who broke this window? The milkman delivered five packets of milk.

B. Who had broke this window? The milkman had delivered five packets of milk.

C. Whom was break this window? The milkman will deliver five packets of milk.

D. Who is breaking this window? The milkman is delivering five packets of milk.

Q.21 Choose the option that is the active form of the sentence.

The politician's speech was loudly cheered.

[SSC Sub Inspector (CPO), 2019]

A. The audience cheer the politician's loud speech.

B. The audience was loudly cheered by the politician's speech.

C. The audience loudly cheered the politician's speech.

D. The audience had been loudly cheered by the politician.

Q.22 Find out the odd one from the given alternatives.

A. 676   B. 841   C. 1089   D. 728

Q.23 Which of the following combination is not correct?

A. Albania – Algiers   B. Brazil – Brasilia

C. Canada – Ottawa   D. Angola – Luanda

Q.24 Find out the odd one from the given alternatives.

A. BWAISAK   B. UNTIB

C. RICHDBQB   D. UBMUI

Q.25 Find odd word from the four given alternatives.

A. Deenar   B. Yen   C. Franc   D. Pound

Q.26 Pick out the odd one from the following:

A. Zoology   B. Botany

C. Entomology   D. Lobotomy

Q.27 If $25a + 25b = 115$, what is the average of a and b?

A. 2.5   B. 2.0   C. 3.5   D. 2.3

Q.28 The average age of 6 members of a family is 20 years. If the age of the servant is included, then the average age increase by 25%. What is the age (in years) of the servant?

A. 30   B. 35   C. 50   D. 55

Q.29 The average of 33 numbers is 74. The average of the first 17 number is 72.8 and that of the last 17 number is 77.2. If the 17th number is excluded, then what will be the average of the remaining numbers (correct to one decimal place)?

A. 72.9   B. 73.4   C. 71.4   D. 70.8

Q.30 A can do a work in 4 days and B can do the same work in 5 days. The contract for the work is $Rs.\,9000$. What will be the share of B if they will work together?

A. $Rs.\,4000$ B. $Rs.\,5000$

C. $Rs.\,1000$ D. $Rs.\,4500$

Q.31 Either 6 men or 18 women can paint a wall in 33 days. The number of days required to paint 3 such walls by 22 men and 33 women working at the same rate?

A. 21.5   B. 18   C. 27   D. 25

Q.32 Select the word which means the same as the group of words given.

One who plans the steps and moves in a dance

[SSC Sub Inspector (CPO), 2019]

A. Composer   B. Choreographer

C. Producer   D. Director

Q.33 Select the word which means the same as the group of words given.

An arrangement of events or dates in the order of their occurrence.

[SSC Sub Inspector (CPO), 2019]

A. Chronometry   B. Charter

C. Chronology   D. Calendar

Q.34 Bronze is an alloy of copper and:

[UPSC Central Armed Police Forces AC, 2017]

A. Nickel   B. Iron

C. Tin   D. Aluminium

Q.35 Which one of the following instruments is used for measuring moisture content of air?

[UPSC Central Armed Police Forces AC, 2017]

A. Hydrometer   B. Hygrometer

C. Hypometer   D. Pycnometer

Q.36 Which one of the following is not correct about organic farming?

A. It does not use genetically modified seeds

B. Synthetic pesticides or fertilizers are not used

C. It uses minimal crop rotation

D. It uses ecologically protective practices

Q.37 Which one of the following elements is present in the green pigment of leaves?

[UPSC Central Armed Police Forces AC, 2017]

A. Magnesium **B.** Iron
C. Calcium **D.** Copper

Q.38 Leakage of which one of the following gases had caused Bhopal Gas Tragedy in the year 1984.

[UPSC Central Armed Police Forces AC, 2017]

A. Methyl isocyanate
B. Hexamethylene diisocyanate
C. Isophorone diisocyanate
D. Isothitxyanate

Q.39 India's first self-made fighter jet is ________.
A. LCA Tejas
B. MiG-21
C. Dassault Rafale
D. Dassault Mirage 2000

Q.40 Which answer figure will complete the pattern in the question figure?

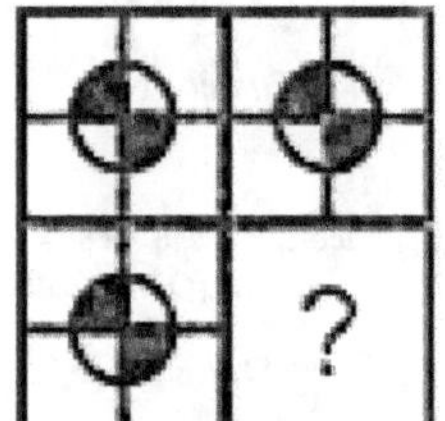

[UP Police Constable, 2019]

A. 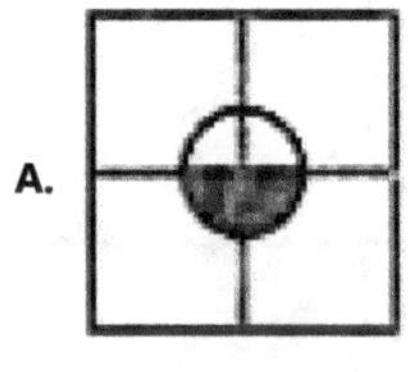 B. 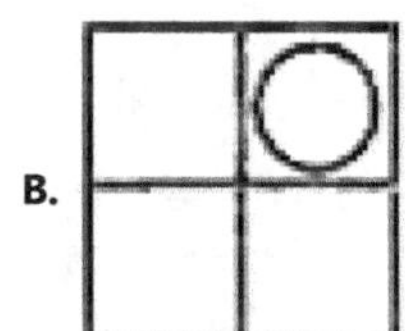

C. 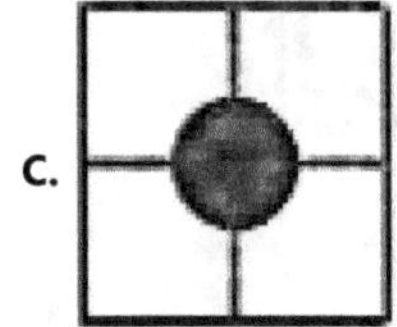 D. 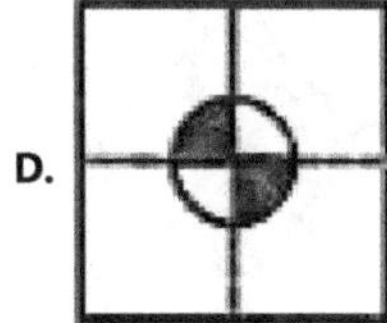

Q.41 Direction: Which answer figure will complete the pattern in the following question figure?

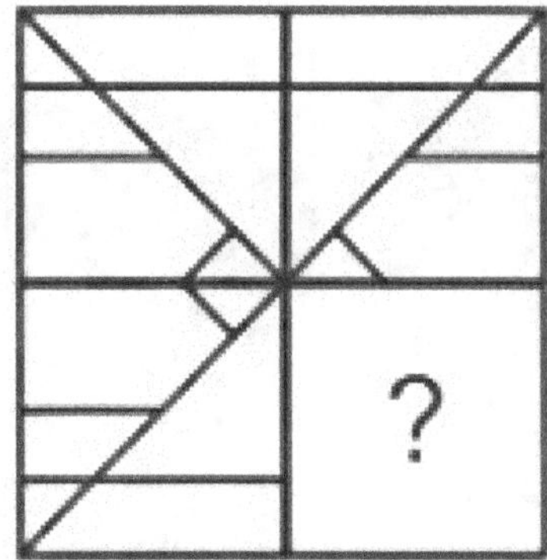

[AFCAT, 2021]

A. 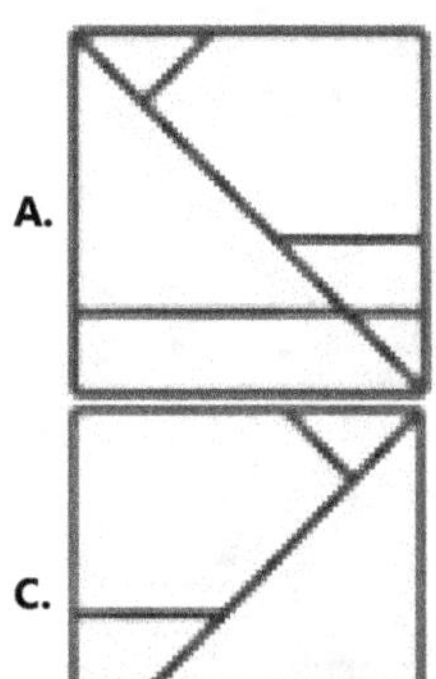 B. 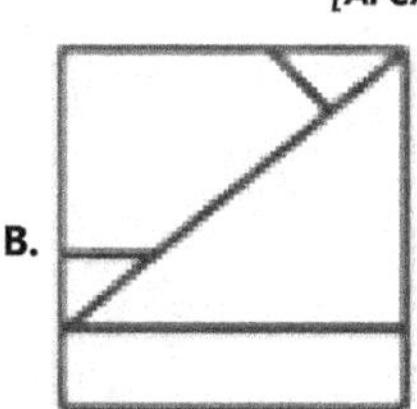

C. 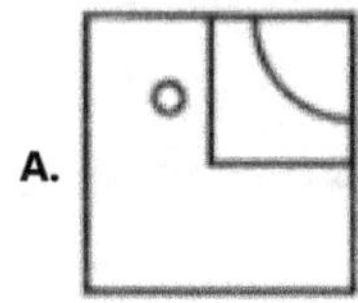 D. 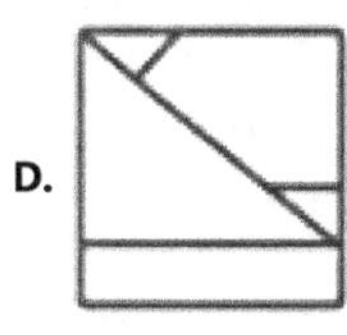

Q.42 Select the figure which complete the pattern.

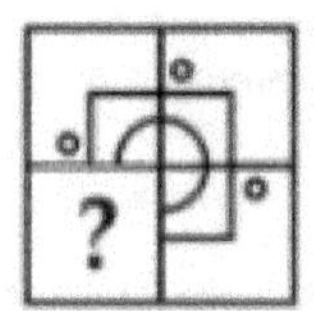

A. 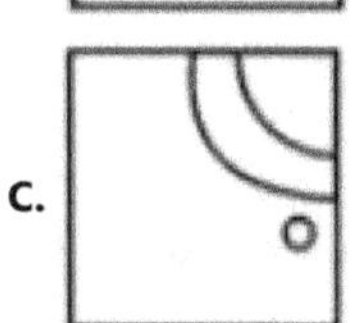 B. 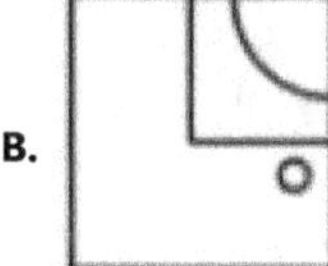

C. 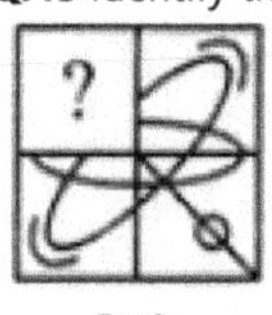 D. 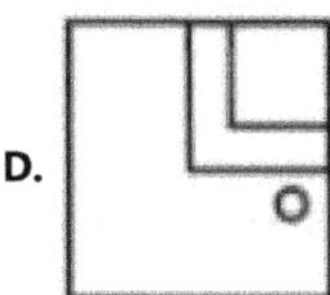

Q.43 Identify the figure that completes the pattern.

(X)

A.  B.  C.  D. 

Q.44 Which answer figure will complete the pattern in the following question figure?

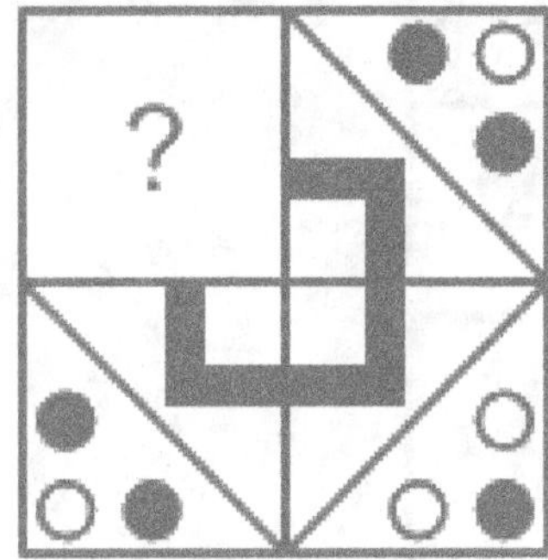

[AFCAT, 2021]

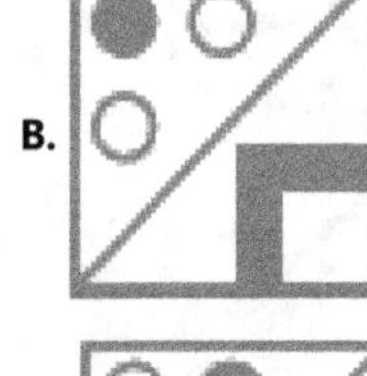

A. 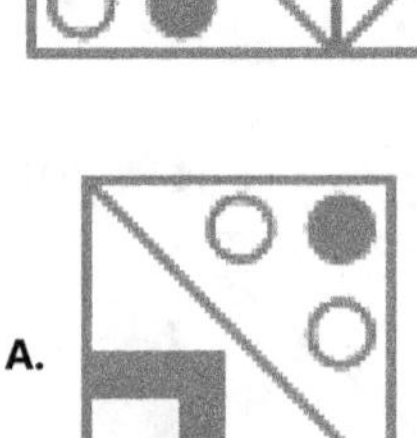

B. 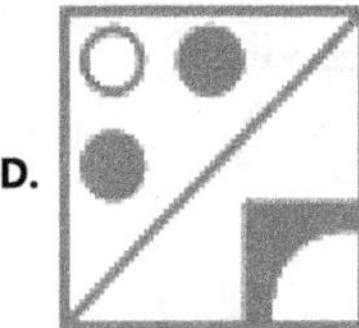

C.

D.

Q.45 Identify the segment in the sentence, which contains the grammatical error.

Prema is the girl in my class who write beautiful poems.

[SSC Sub Inspector (CPO), 2019]

A. Prema is the girl
C. beautiful poems

B. who write
D. in my class

Q.46 Identify the segment in the sentence, which contains the grammatical error.

Rahul was ready for accept any job, even a part-time one.

[SSC Sub Inspector (CPO), 2019]

A. Rahul was ready
B. even a part-time one
C. any job
D. for accept

Q.47 Yamini Krishnamurti is associated with which classical dance?

A. Bharatanatyam
C. Odyssey

B. Kathakali
D. Kuchipudi

Q.48 Leela Samson is associated with which classical dance form?

A. Bharatanatyam
C. Odyssey

B. Kuchipudi
D. Kathakali

Ques (49-53):Direction: Each of the following sentences in this section has a blank space with four-word or a group of words given. Select whichever word or group of words you consider the most appropriate for the blank space and indicate your response on the answer sheet accordingly.

The difficult thing about (1)________the science of habits is that most people when they hear about this field of research (2)_____ to know the secret formula for quickly changing any habit. If scientists have discovered how (3)_____ patterns work, then it stands to reason that they (4)_______ have also found a recipe for rapid change, right? if only it (5)________ that easy.

Q.49 What would come in place of blank (1)?
[Indian Military Academy (IMA), 2020], [Officers Training Academy (OTA), 2020]

A. studying
C. studies

B. study
D. are studying

Q.50 What would come in place of blank (2)?
[Indian Military Academy (IMA), 2020], [Officers Training Academy (OTA), 2020]

A. wanting
B. wanted
C. wants
D. want

Q.51 What would come in place of blank (3)?
[Indian Military Academy (IMA), 2020], [Officers Training Academy (OTA), 2020]

A. those
B. this
C. these
D. that

Q.52 What would come in place of blank (4)?
[Indian Military Academy (IMA), 2020], [Officers Training Academy (OTA), 2020]

A. must
B. will
C. would
D. might

Q.53 What would come in place of blank (5)?
[Indian Military Academy (IMA), 2020], [Officers Training Academy (OTA), 2020]

A. are
B. were
C. was
D. will be

Q.54 Select the related figure from the given alternatives.

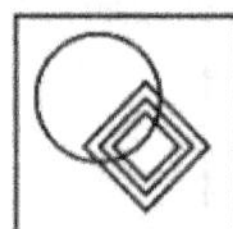 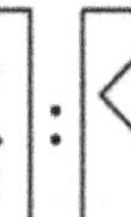 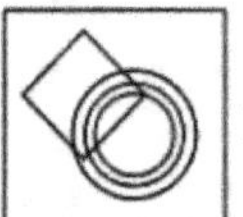 : 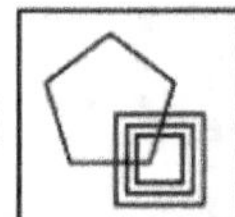 : 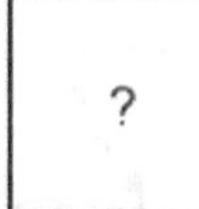

A. 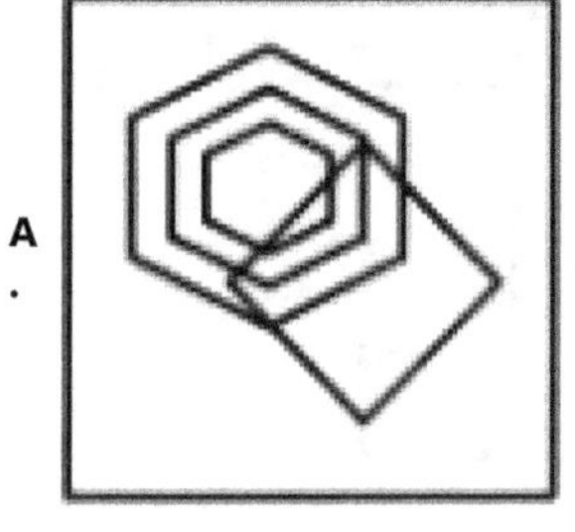

B. 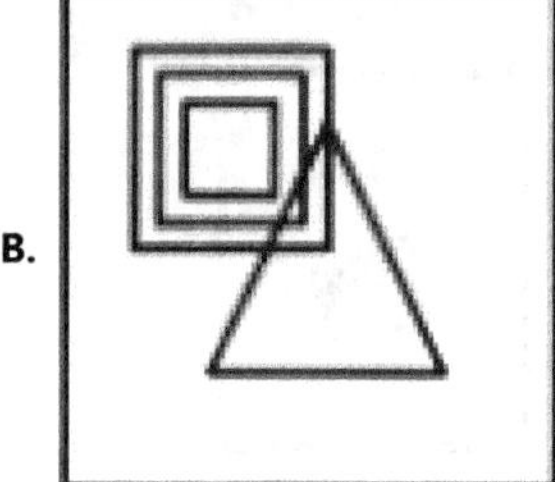

C. 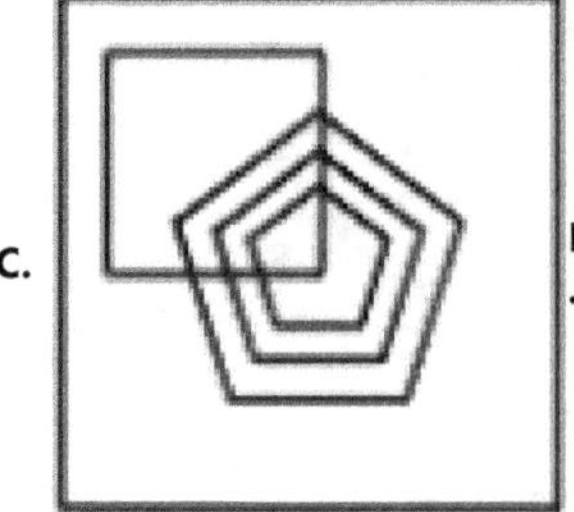

D. 

Q.55 Choose from the alternatives the figure that best completes the pattern given below.

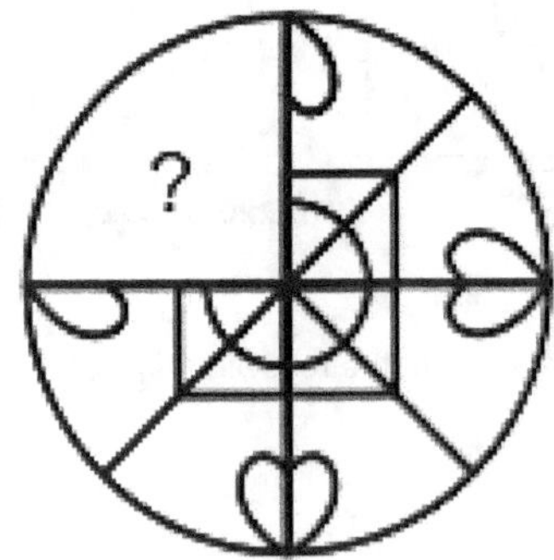

[AFCAT, 2021]

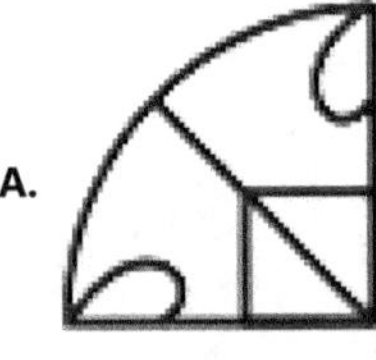
A.

B.

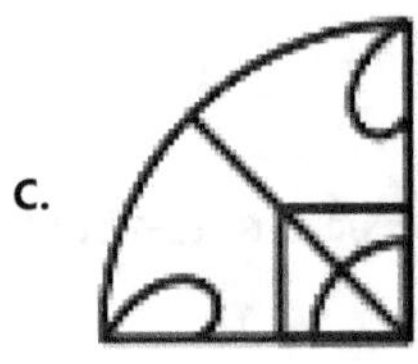
C.

D.

Q.56 How many triangles are there in the given figure?

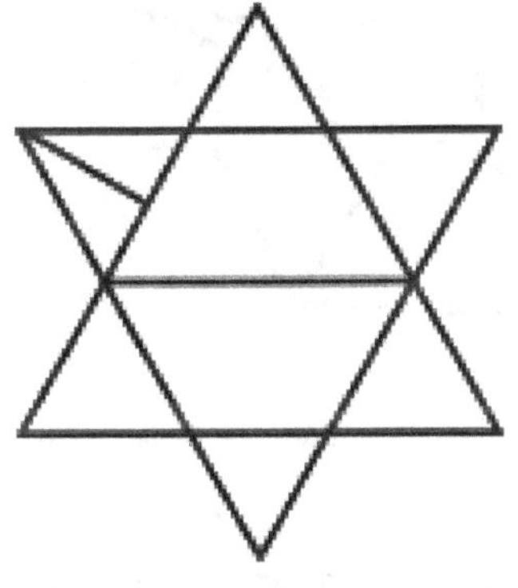

A. 16   B. 18   C. 12   D. 14

Q.57 How many squares are there in the given figure?

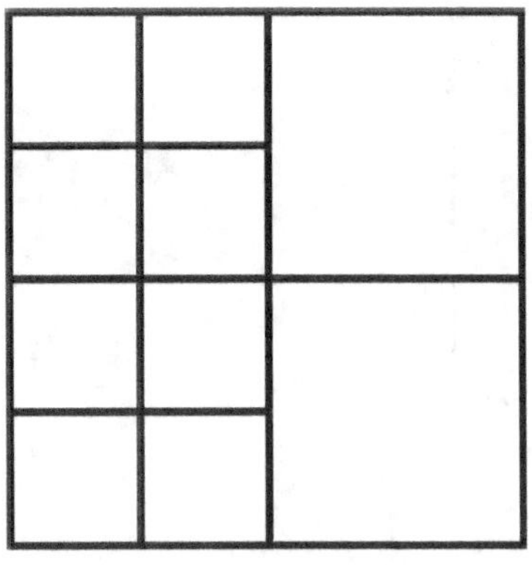

A. 16   B. 12   C. 14   D. 15

Q.58 Choose the correct figure which will replace the question mark?

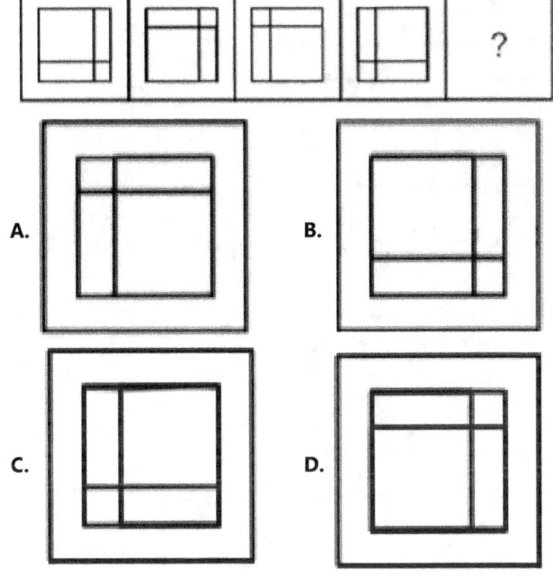

Q.59 In an alloy, the ratio of copper and zinc is $5:2$. If 1.250 kg of zinc is mixed in 17 kg 500 gm of alloy, then the ratio of copper and zinc will be?

A. $2:1$ B. $2:3$ C. $3:2$ D. $1:2$

Q.60 The ratio of a number of coins of 50 paise, 1 rupee, and 2 rupees is $2:3:4$. If the total amount is $Rs.240$ then how many 1 rupee coins are present?

A. 20   B. 80   C. 40   D. 60

Q.61 The ratio of incomes of Manish and Pankaj is 11 : 7. If pankaj gets Rs. 6000 less than Manish, then what is the total income (in Rs) of Manish and Pankaj?

A. 18000   B. 27000   C. 36000   D. 28000

Q.62 From the given answer figures, select the one in which question figure is hidden/embedded. (rotation is not allowed).

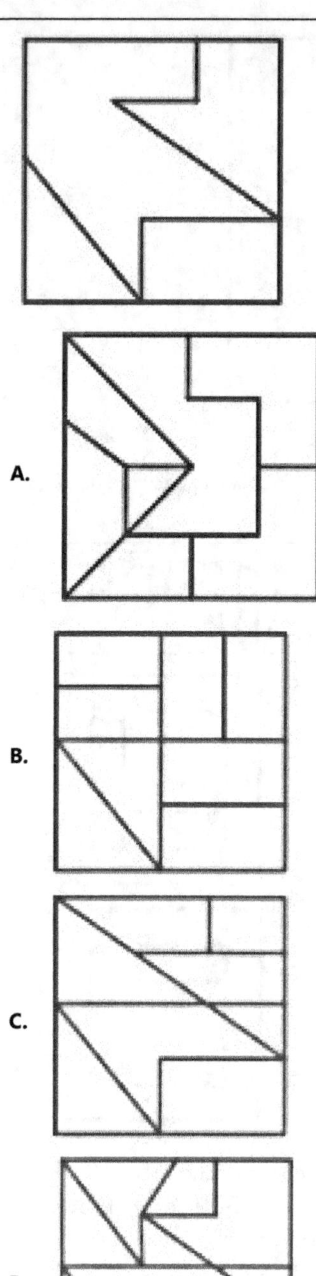

A.

B.

C.

D.

Q.63 Direction: Which of the answer figures is formed from the shapes given the problem figure?

Question figure:

Answer figure:

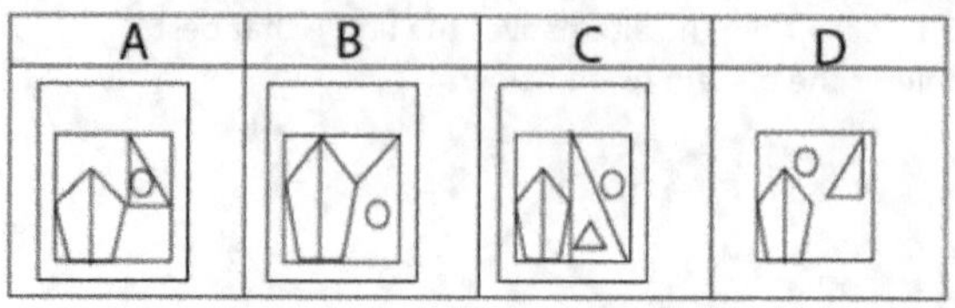

[RRB/RRC Group D, 2018]

A. A   **B.** C   **C.** B   **D.** D

Q.64 How many triangles are there in the following figure?

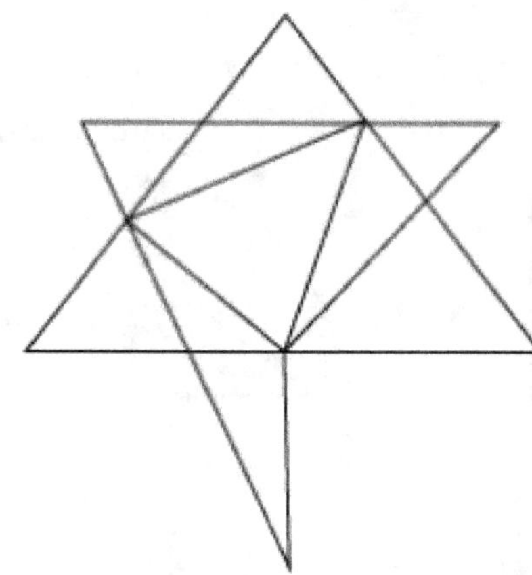

[RRB/RRC Group D, 2018]

A. 8   **B.** 12   **C.** 11   **D.** 17

Q.65 How many triangles are there in the below figure?

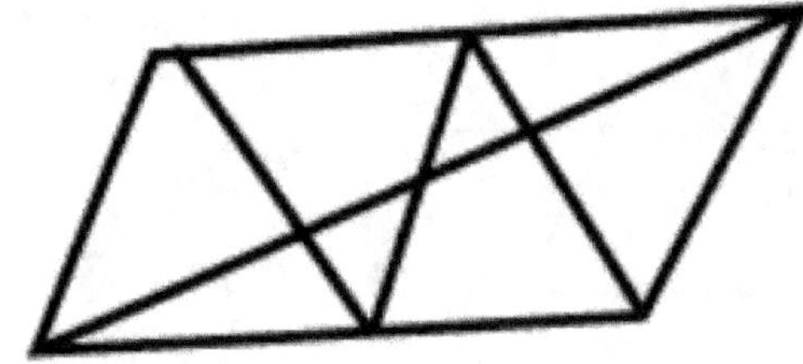

[RRB/RRC Group D, 2018]

A. 6   **B.** 13   **C.** 10   **D.** 8

Q.66 Which of the shapes in the options are combined to form the given shape?

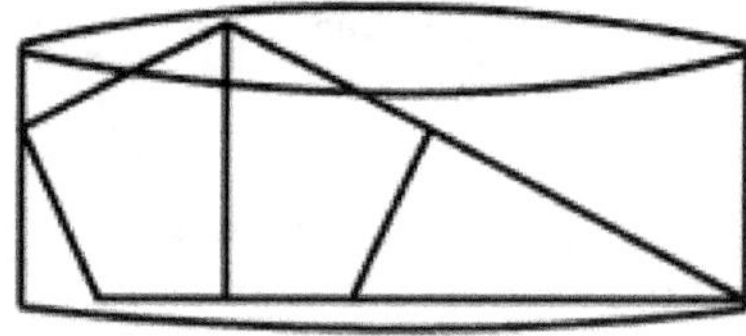

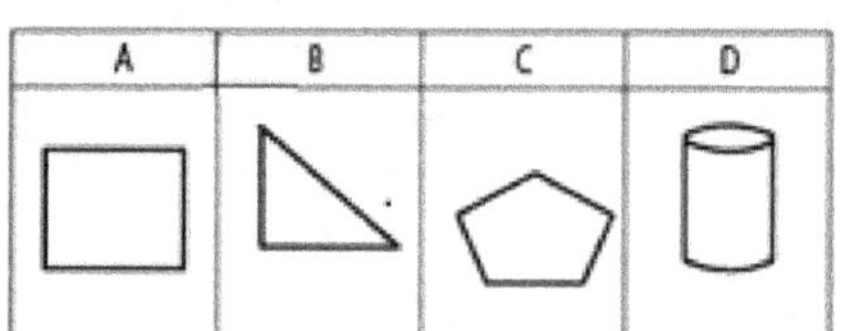

[RRB/RRC Group D, 2018]

A. A, B and D

C. D and A

B. B, C and D

D. C and D

Q.67 A person bought two bicycles for Rs. 1600 and sold the first at 10% profit and the second at 20% profit. If he sold the first at 20% profit and the second at 10% profit, he would get more. The difference in the cost price of the two bicycles was:

A. Rs. 25   **B.** Rs. 75   **C.** Rs. 50   **D.** Rs. 40

Q.68 To dispose of the old stocks, a person sold a tea-set for Rs 3540, which was 41% below the cost price. To make a profit of 11%, the seller should have sold the set for ___ more.

[RRB/RRC Group D, 2018]

A. 2664.42   **B.** 2460   **C.** 1812.60   **D.** 3120

Q.69 Rahul buys a Car worth Rs. $5,50,000$. He sells it to Vipul at a loss of 10%. Vipul then sells it to Yash at a profit of 5%. Yash sells it to Shubham at a profit of 2%. Shubham spends Rs. $10,000$ on the refurbishing of Car and add it to cost of the car and then he sold it to Shivansh at 5% profit. Find what amount Shivansh will pay to Shubham (in approximate).

A. Rs. 576800

C. Rs. 567150

B. Rs. 568180

D. Rs. 498070

Q.70 Direction: In the following figure small square represents the persons who know English, triangle to those who know Marathi, a big square to those who know Telugu, and a circle to those who know Hindi. In the different regions of the figures from 1 to 12 are given.

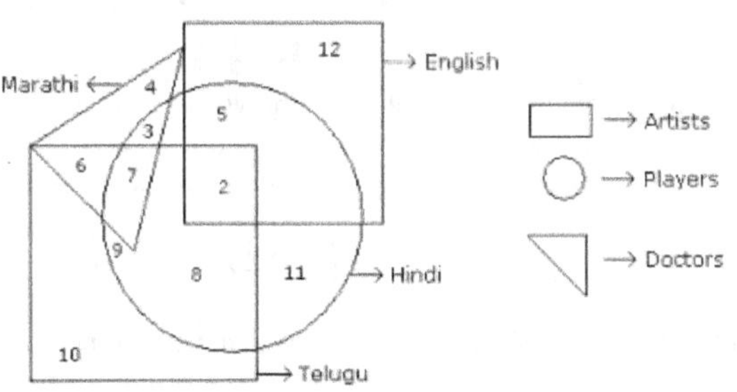

How many persons can speak English and Hindi both languages only?

A. 5   **B.** 8   **C.** 7   **D.** 18

Ques (71-74):Direction: Study the following figure and answer the questions given below.

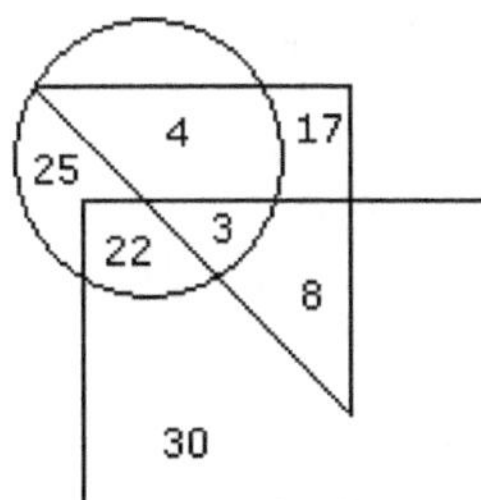

Q.71 How many doctors are neither artists nor players?

A. 17   **B.** 5   **C.** 10   **D.** 30

Q.72 How many doctors are both players and artists?

A. 22   **B.** 8   **C.** 3   **D.** 30

Q.73

How many artists are players?

A. 5   **B.** 25   **C.** 22   **D.** 16

Q.74

How many players are neither artists nor doctors?

A. 25   **B.** 17   **C.** 5   **D.** 10

Q.75 Direction: Write the following words according to the sequence in the dictionary-

(1) Bale

(2) Blade

(3) Balls

(4) Balance

(5) Balancing

A. 24135   **B.** 42135   **C.** 45132   **D.** 54213

Q.76 In total how many letters in the word, 'TIGER' will remain in the same position even when the letters are set in the ascending order of the English alphabets?

A. 4

C. 2

B. 3

D. None of these

Q.77 Which of the following is/are correct about the removal of a Supreme Court Judge?

1. A judge may be removed from office through a motion adopted by Parliament on grounds of 'proven misbehaviour or incapacity'.

2. He can be removed by a majority of at least one-third of the members of that House present and voting.

A. 1 only

C. Both 1 and 2

B. 2 only

D. Neither 1 nor 2

Q.78 Direction: The following sentence consists an underlined word(s) followed by four options. Select the option that is nearest in meaning to the underlined word and mark your response accordingly.

Having got excited she opened up the Pandora's Box which led to lot of <u>commotion</u>.

[Officers Training Academy (OTA), 2021], [Indian Military Academy (IMA), 2021]

A. uproar   **B.** peace   **C.** sound   **D.** furious

Q.79 Direction: The following sentence consists an underlined word(s) followed by four options. Select the option that is nearest in meaning to the underlined word and mark your response accordingly.

The <u>inherent</u> danger in the problem is that it would lead to many more problems.

[Officers Training Academy (OTA), 2021], [Indian Military Academy (IMA), 2021]

A. outward   **B.** difficult   **C.** hallow   **D.** inbuilt

Q.80 Direction: The following sentence consists an underlined word(s) followed by four options. Select the option that is nearest in meaning to the underlined word and mark your response accordingly.

The officer was <u>reprimanded</u> by the court for delaying the case.

[Officers Training Academy (OTA), 2021], [Indian Military Academy (IMA), 2021]

A. admonished   B. appreciated
C. praised   D. disliked

Q.81 Which of the following statement is true about the tropical convergence?

1. It is called ITCZ in short
2. It is a low-pressure zone between tropic of Cancer and tropic of Capricorn
3. Seasonal changes in position are found

A. 1, 2 and 3   B. 1 and 2
C. 2 and 3   D. 1 and 3

Q.82 In a town the ratio of men, women, and children is 9 : 8 : 3. 80% men are literate and 30% women are illiterate. If 90% of children are literate, then the illiteracy rate of that town is:

A. $22\frac{1}{2}\%$ B. $25\frac{1}{2}\%$ C. 27%   D. 30%

Q.83 In a college election for Ladies representative 60% girls and 80% of boys voted for Anushka. There are 45% girls in the college. How many percentage votes Anushka got?

A. 65%   B. 52%   C. 71%   D. 55%

Q.84 If the height of a cone is increased by 50% then what is the percentage increase in the volume of cone?

A. 25%   B. 50%   C. 75%   D. 100%

Q.85 The estimated percentage of the forest land that ideally India should have is:

A. 50%   B. 15%   C. 33%   D. 44%

Q.86 Direction: Select the most appropriate option to fill in the blank.

I was late________the cab was not on time.

A. because   B. though   C. if   D. yet

Q.87 During the freedom struggle in 1940s, he ________ a novel for 10 months.

A. Has been writing   B. Wrote
C. Had been writing   D. Was writing

Q.88 Fill in the blanks with the most appropriate word choosing from the options given below

The fun __________ reduced significantly when mom decided to tag along.

A. Mark   B. Sign   C. Quotient   D. Moment

Q.89 Direction: From the given option choose the correct word suitable to fill in the blank space.

I can't quite ________ if it is beauty or simply monstrous.

A. break   B. decide   C. take   D. dither

Q.90 Direction: Select the related number from the given alternatives.

49 : 343 :: 324 : ?

A. 5832   B. 1728   C. 4913   D. 4096

Q.91 Direction: Select the related word from the given alternatives.

Eskimo : Igloo :: Pig : ?

A. Sty   B. Kennel   C. Stable   D. Asylum

Q.92 Direction: Select the related word from the given alternatives.

Botany : Plants :: Entomology : ?

A. Words   B. Insects   C. Soils   D. Fungi

Ques (93-94):Direction: Select the related number from the given alternatives.

Q.93 245 : 40 :: 413 : ?

A. 12   B. 10   C. 20   D. 60

Q.94 122 : 6 :: 408 : ?

A. 5   B. 8   C. 10   D. 15

Q.95 In what time will a train 100 meters long cross an electric pole, if its speed be 144 kmph?

A. 2.5 seconds   B. 12.5 seconds
C. 3 seconds   D. 5 seconds

Q.96 A train is 120 m long and travels at the speed of 54 km/h. How long will it take for the train to cross a platform of 150 m in minutes?

A. 0.3   B. 0.4   C. 0.5   D. 0.9

Q.97 A person starts travelling from one place to another at 90 km/hr and returns at 120 km/hr. If the total time taken by him is 7 hours, then find the distance travelled during the return.

A. 300 km   B. 360 km   C. 350 km   D. 320 km

Q.98 A motor car moves from point A to B at 30 km/h and returns from there at a speed of 20 km/h. What is the average speed of the journey?

A. 50 km/h   B. 25 km/h   C. 24 km/h   D. 60 km/h

Q.99 B and C can complete the work in $\frac{60}{7}$ days. A and C can complete work in $\frac{20}{3}$ days. A, B and C together can complete the work in $\frac{60}{13}$ days. Find the number of days in which C alone can complete the work.

A. 20   B. 15   C. 10   D. 5

Q.100 Find the value of:

$$\frac{\sqrt{529} \div \sqrt{676}}{\sqrt{2116} \div \sqrt{169}} \text{ of } 400 \times \frac{3}{2} + \frac{1}{2}$$

A. 150.5   B. 160.5   C. 151.5   D. 145.5

// Smart Answer Sheet //

Correct — Percentage of students who answered correctly. **Skipped** — Percentage of students who skipped.

Q.	Ans.	Correct / Skipped	Q.	Ans.	Correct / Skipped	Q.	Ans.	Correct / Skipped	Q.	Ans.	Correct / Skipped	Q.	Ans.	Correct / Skipped	Q.	Ans.	Correct / Skipped
1	A	25.49 % / 16.67 %	18	B	64.71 % / 5.88 %	35	B	39.22 % / 12.74 %	52	A	10.78 % / 13.73 %	69	C	21.57 % / 8.82 %	86	A	72.55 % / 13.72 %
2	A	10.78 % / 19.61 %	19	A	14.71 % / 13.72 %	36	C	29.41 % / 17.65 %	53	B	14.71 % / 13.72 %	70	A	46.08 % / 10.78 %	87	C	31.37 % / 11.77 %
3	D	11.76 % / 12.75 %	20	A	57.84 % / 3.92 %	37	A	43.14 % / 15.68 %	54	C	62.75 % / 18.62 %	71	A	59.8 % / 16.67 %	88	C	24.51 % / 10.78 %
4	D	16.67 % / 16.66 %	21	C	47.06 % / 15.69 %	38	A	54.9 % / 14.71 %	55	C	78.43 % / 12.75 %	72	C	63.73 % / 16.66 %	89	B	42.16 % / 5.88 %
5	D	22.55 % / 17.65 %	22	D	32.35 % / 10.79 %	39	A	49.02 % / 12.74 %	56	C	55.88 % / 12.75 %	73	C	40.2 % / 14.7 %	90	A	44.12 % / 13.72 %
6	A	19.61 % / 1.96 %	23	A	34.31 % / 12.75 %	40	D	87.25 % / 7.85 %	57	C	49.02 % / 17.65 %	74	A	62.75 % / 15.68 %	91	A	36.27 % / 7.85 %
7	C	47.06 % / 12.74 %	24	C	16.67 % / 11.76 %	41	A	69.61 % / 11.76 %	58	B	56.86 % / 18.63 %	75	C	64.71 % / 12.74 %	92	B	56.86 % / 14.71 %
8	B	30.39 % / 16.67 %	25	B	4.9 % / 11.77 %	42	B	58.82 % / 12.75 %	59	A	10.78 % / 12.75 %	76	D	57.84 % / 8.83 %	93	A	22.55 % / 7.84 %
9	C	67.65 % / 13.72 %	26	D	50.98 % / 16.67 %	43	A	70.59 % / 13.72 %	60	D	32.35 % / 12.75 %	77	A	15.69 % / 13.72 %	94	A	17.65 % / 7.84 %
10	A	75.49 % / 13.73 %	27	D	48.04 % / 13.72 %	44	B	81.37 % / 8.83 %	61	B	38.24 % / 9.8 %	78	A	24.51 % / 15.69 %	95	A	45.1 % / 14.7 %
11	D	70.59 % / 13.72 %	28	D	32.35 % / 9.81 %	45	B	47.06 % / 16.67 %	62	C	75.49 % / 7.84 %	79	D	52.94 % / 12.75 %	96	A	38.24 % / 8.82 %
12	B	52.94 % / 13.73 %	29	A	10.78 % / 8.83 %	46	D	54.9 % / 13.73 %	63	C	37.25 % / 13.73 %	80	A	44.12 % / 14.7 %	97	B	32.35 % / 18.63 %
13	D	65.69 % / 13.72 %	30	A	35.29 % / 6.87 %	47	D	2.94 % / 12.75 %	64	D	39.22 % / 11.76 %	81	A	19.61 % / 13.72 %	98	C	34.31 % / 12.75 %
14	A	29.41 % / 13.73 %	31	B	13.73 % / 14.7 %	48	A	14.71 % / 13.72 %	65	B	46.08 % / 11.76 %	82	A	9.8 % / 16.67 %	99	A	8.82 % / 14.71 %
15	A	35.29 % / 13.73 %	32	B	72.55 % / 7.84 %	49	A	59.8 % / 13.73 %	66	B	62.75 % / 11.76 %	83	C	35.29 % / 7.85 %	100	A	30.39 % / 17.65 %
16	C	16.67 % / 5.88 %	33	C	40.2 % / 16.66 %	50	D	21.57 % / 13.72 %	67	C	1.96 % / 14.71 %	84	B	27.45 % / 8.82 %			
17	C	27.45 % / 8.82 %	34	C	39.22 % / 13.72 %	51	C	41.18 % / 13.72 %	68	D	20.59 % / 7.84 %	85	C	29.41 % / 14.71 %			

//Hints and Solutions//

1. The Union Government has authorized the State Bank of India to issue and encashes Electoral Bonds through its 29 Authorized Branches from 1–10 th of July 2022.

The Electoral Bonds will be valid for fifteen calendar days from the date of issue and no payment will be made to any payee Political Party if the Electoral Bond is deposited after the expiry of the validity period.

Hence, the correct option is (A).

2. Sujoy Lal Thaosen has been recently appointed as the new Director-General of the Sashastra Seema Bal.

New Delhi, June 2022 (PTI) IPS officer Sujoy Lal Thaosen took charge as the new director-general (DG) of the Sashastra Seema Bal (SSB), which guards Indian frontiers with Nepal and Bhutan. Thaosen, a 1988-batch Indian Police Service (IPS) officer of the Madhya Pradesh cadre, was handed over the baton by officiating DG and ITBP chief Sanjay Arora at the headquarters of the force in R K Puram.

Hence, the correct option is (A).

3. Premier industry body Data Security Council of India (DSCI) established by NASSCOM, has appointed its senior vice president Vinayak Godse as the new CEO.

- Godse will be taking over from Rama Vedashree who led DSCI for more than six years.
- Godse will be taking over as the CEO from 1 Oct 2022.
- DSCI Founded: 2008
- Founder: NASSCOM
- Current Chairman: Rajendra S Pawar
- HQ: Noida, Uttar Pradesh

Hence, the correct option is (D).

4. A special meeting of the UN Security Council's (UNSC) Counter-Terrorism Committee was hosted in Mumbai and Delhi on 28th and 29th of October, 2022.

Theme of the meting was 'Countering the use of new and emerging technologies for terrorist purposes'. India is currently the Chair of the UN Security Council Counter-Terrorism Committee for the year 2022.

Hence, the correct option is (D).

5. India was host the 44th FIDE Chess Olympiad 2022. It was originally scheduled to be hosted in Russia. FIDE has recently announced that it pulled out from Russia following the Ukraine invasion. After the announcement, Tamil Nadu government and All-India Chess Federation made a joint bid to host the tournament It is the first time that India is hosting FIDE Chess Olympiad since its inception in 1927.

Hence, the correct option is (D).

6. Given:

Total interest after 7 years $= Rs. 12,771$

We know that,

$$\text{Simple Interest} = \frac{(P \times R \times T)}{100}$$

Let the principal be ' P '.

For the first 2 years,

$$\text{Simple interest} = \frac{(P \times 6 \times 2)}{100} = \frac{3P}{25}$$

For the next 3 years,

$$\text{Simple interest} = \frac{(P \times 10 \times 3)}{100} = \frac{3P}{10}$$

For the next 2 years,

$$\text{Simple interest} = \frac{(P \times 12 \times 2)}{100} = \frac{6P}{25}$$

Total Interest in 7 years $= Rs. 12,771$

$$\left(\frac{3P}{25}\right) + \left(\frac{3P}{10}\right) + \left(\frac{6P}{25}\right) = 12771$$

$$\Rightarrow \frac{33P}{50} = 12771$$

$$\Rightarrow P = 19350$$

∴ The amount invested is $Rs. 19,350$.

Hence, the correct option is (A).

7. Let rate is $R\%$

We have,

$$I = \frac{PTR}{100}$$

Here,

$$1500 = \frac{5000 \times 3 \times R}{100}$$

Thus,

$$R = 10\%$$

Hence, the correct option is (C).

8. ($SI =$ Simple interest, $p =$ Principle amount, $r =$ Rate, $t =$ Time)

Let the principal amount $= 8x$

And simple interest $= 7x$

We know,

$$\Rightarrow SI = \frac{(p \times r \times t)}{100}$$

$$\Rightarrow 7x = \frac{(8x \times r \times 5)}{100}$$

$$\Rightarrow r = 17.5\%$$

Hence, the correct option is (B).

9. The given passage is all about one of the world's great religious teachers- The Gautam Buddha.

The first line or sentence of the passage says "Buddha was one of the world's great religious teachers".

Hence, the correct option is (C).

10. Real name of Buddha was Gautam Siddhartha.

The second line or sentence of the passage says "His real name was Gautam Siddhartha". Here, the possessive pronoun 'his' is used for the 'Buddha'.

Hence, the correct option is (A).

11. Buddha was born a prince.

The fourth line or sentence of the passage says "He was born a prince". Here, the personal pronoun 'he' is used for the 'Buddha'.

Hence, the correct option is (D).

12. Buddha was born before the birth of Christ.

The third line or sentence of the passage says "He was born in the year 500 B.C". Here, the personal pronoun 'he' is used for the 'Buddha'.

In the sentence, the term "B.C" means "Before the birth of Jesus Christ".

Hence, the correct option is (B).

13. The land of Buddha's birth is Kapilavastu.

The fifth line or sentence of the passage says "His father was the King of Kapilavastu". Here, the possessive pronoun 'his' is used for the 'Buddha'.

Hence, the correct option is (D).

14. Given:

$$? = 120 \div 40 \text{ of } \frac{1}{4} + \frac{2}{5} \times 3\frac{1}{4}$$

$$\Rightarrow ? = 120 \div 40 \times \frac{1}{4} + \frac{2}{5} \times \frac{13}{4}$$

$$\Rightarrow ? = 120 \div 10 + \frac{2}{5} \times \frac{13}{4}$$

$$\Rightarrow ? = 12 + \frac{13}{10}$$

$$\Rightarrow ? = 13\frac{3}{10}$$

Hence, the correct option is (A).

15. We know that a quarter means $\frac{1}{4}$

$$12\frac{1}{4} = \frac{49}{4}$$

So, quarters in $12\frac{1}{4} = \frac{49}{4} \div \frac{1}{4}$

$$= 49$$

Hence, the correct option is (A).

16. The 'Swadeshi' and 'Boycott' were adopted as methods of struggle in Bengal at the same time the Vande Matram Movement was in Andhra Pradesh.

Vande Matram Movement:

The movement against the Partition of Bengal was launched in 1906 by Indian nationals, known as the Vande Mataram movement. It was one of the campaigns against British rule that was most successful. Swadeshi was a major focus of Mahatma Gandhi, who described it as the soul of Swaraj (self-rule).

Hence, the correct option is (C).

17. Goes to dog describes something on the downgrade, something that is worse than it used to be, something that is deteriorating.

Hence, the correct option is (C).

18. To keep asking for help when you do not need it, with the result that people think you do not need help when you really need it: If you cry wolf too often, people will stop believing you.

Hence, the correct option is (B).

19. These terms were mentioned in the news recently to indicate the different the cricket bats used. "The Camel" bat was recently used by Afghanistan's Rashid Khan. Mangoose, Kaboom and Aluminium are some of the other names used to describe different cricket bats.

Hence, the correct option is (A).

20. The sentence becomes: Who broke this window? The milkman delivered five packets of milk.

The sentence is given in passive voice to convert it into active:

- While converting the voice, the subject and the object change their place:
- 'Who' becomes the subject. ('Whom' works as the object in the interrogative statement).
- In an assertive statement: 'The milkman' becomes the subject and 'Five packets of the milk' becomes the object.
- Preposition 'by' before the object is removed.
- 'was/were + V_3' in passive voice is changed into 'V_2' in active voice.

Hence, the correct option is (A).

21. The correct answer is:

'The audience loudly cheered the politician's speech.'

In the active form, the subject and the object will get interchanged. So, 'the politician's speech' will become the object. The passive form contains 'was' which means the active form must be in the past tense.

Option (A) is in the present tense.

Option (B) changes the meaning.

Option (D) is in the past perfect tense.

Rules of Conversion from Passive to Active Voice:

1. Identify the subject, the verb and the object: S+V+O.
2. Change the subject into object.

3. Omit the suitable helping verb or auxiliary verb.

4. Change the past participle to simple past tense form of the verb.

5. Omit the preposition "by".

6. Change the object into subject.

Hence, the correct option is (C).

22. $(26)^2 = 676$

$(29)^2 = 841$

$(33)^2 = 1089$

Except 728 all others are square.

Hence, the correct option is (D).

23. Except Albania — Algiers, the list of all other countries and their capital is in the correct order.
Hence, the correct option is (A).

24. Except RICHDQB, the sum of all letters in each option is 66.
Hence, the correct option is (C).

25. Deenar, Franc, and pound are the currencies of more than, country while yen is only of the country that is Japan.
Hence, the correct option is (B).

26. Zoology, botany, entomology fall in the field of biological science. Lobotomy is a surgical procedure.
Hence, the correct option is (D).

27. The given equation is:

$$25a + 25b = 115$$

$$\Rightarrow 25(a + b) = 115$$

$$\Rightarrow a + b = \frac{115}{25}$$

$$\Rightarrow a + b = \frac{23}{5}$$

$\therefore$ Average of a and $b = \dfrac{a+b}{2}$

$$= \frac{23}{5} \times \frac{1}{2}$$

$$= \frac{23}{10}$$

$$= 2.3$$

Hence, the correct option is (D).

28. Given:

Average age of a family of 6 members $= 20$ years

Total age of the family $= 6 \times 20 = 120$ years

Let the age of servant $= x$ years

Average age of family including servant,

$$20 \times \frac{125}{100} = 25 \text{ years}$$

$$\Rightarrow \frac{120+x}{7} = 25$$

$$\Rightarrow 120 + x = 25 \times 7$$

$$\Rightarrow 120 + x = 175$$

$$\Rightarrow x = 175 - 120$$

$$\Rightarrow x = 55 \text{ years}$$

Hence, the correct option is (D).

29. According to the question,

$$17\text{th number} = 17(72.8 + 77.2) - 33 \times 74$$

$$= 2550 - 2442$$

$$= 108$$

New Average $= \dfrac{2442-108}{32} = 72.9$

Hence, the correct option is (A).

30. Given:

Time taken by $A = 4$ days

Time taken by $B = 5$ days

Contract of work $= Rs.\,9000$

Total work $=$ Efficiency $\times$ days

A's one-day work $= \dfrac{1}{4}$

B's one-day work $= \dfrac{1}{5}$

The ratio of their wages $= \dfrac{1}{4} : \dfrac{1}{5} = 5 : 4$

B's share $= (9000) \times \dfrac{4}{9} = Rs.\,4000$

$\therefore$ The share of B is $Rs.\,4000$.

Hence, the correct option is (A).

31. 6 men $= 18$ women

1 man $= \dfrac{18}{6}$ women

Men= M and Women= W

Efficiencies: $\dfrac{M}{W} = \dfrac{3}{1}$

We know that,

Total work $\Rightarrow \dfrac{M_1 \times D_1}{W_1} = \dfrac{M_2 \times D_2}{W_2}$

$$\Rightarrow \frac{18 \times 33}{1} = \frac{(22 \times 3 + 33)D}{3}$$

$$\Rightarrow D = 18 \text{ days}$$

Hence, the correct option is (B).

32. Choreographer - one who plans the steps and moves in a dance. For Example: Lea Anderson is a choreographer who believes in making dance accessible.

Let's look at the meaning of the other options:

Composer: a person who writes music, especially as a professional occupation. For Example: The composer expresses his sorrow in his music.

Producer: a person, company, or country that makes, grows, or supplies goods or commodities for sale. For Example: a film producer.

Director: a person who is in charge of an activity, department, or organization. For Example: The director resigned in protest at the decision.

Hence, the correct option is (B).

33. Chronology is an arrangement of events or dates in the order of their occurrence.

Let's look at the meaning of the other options:

Chronometry - the science of accurate time measurement. For Example - An analogue to mineral chronometry is O isotope geothermometry.

Charter- a written grant by the sovereign or legislative power of a country, by which a body such as a city, company, or university is founded or its rights and privileges defined. For Example - This new law amounts to a tax evader's charter.

Calendar- a chart or series of pages showing the days, weeks, and months of a particular year, or giving particular seasonal information. For Example - Do you have next year's calendar?

Hence, the correct option is (C).

34. Bronze is an alloy of copper but consists 12-12.5% tin in that.

So, it is an alloy of both copper and tin.
Hence, the correct option is (C).

35. Hygrometer is the instrument which is used to measure the humidity. This instrument is also known as psychrometer.
Hence, the correct option is (B).

36. Organic farming is an agricultural process that uses biological fertilizers and pest control derived from animal or plant waste such as compost manure, green manure, and bone meal. So, statements 1, 2, and 4 are correct.

Organic farming lays emphasis on crop rotation and composting. So, statement 3 is incorrect.

- Sikkim has become India's first fully organic state by converting around 75,000 hectares of agricultural land into sustainable cultivation.
- Madhya Pradesh has the highest area of agriculture under organic certification among states.

Hence, the correct option is (C).

37. In the green pigment of leaves magnesium is present. Magnesium is needed during photosynthesis for chlorophyll to capture sun energy, i.e., magnesium is required to give green colour to leaves.

Hence, the correct option is (A).

38. Bhopal gas tragedy happened due to leakage of Methyl Isocyanate gas. It was the deadliest gas tragedy in the history of India. It destroyed the life of many generations of people.

The Bhopal disaster, also referred to as the Bhopal gas tragedy, was a gas leak incident on the night of 2–3 December 1984 at the Union Carbide India Limited (UCIL) pesticide plant in Bhopal, Madhya Pradesh, India. It is considered among the world's worst industrial disasters. Over 500,000 people were exposed to methyl isocyanate (MIC) gas. The highly toxic substance made its way into and around the small towns located near the plant.

Hence, the correct option is (A).

39. India's first self-made fighter jet is LCA Tejas.

The LCA Tejas is an Indian single-engine multi role light fighter designed by the Aeronautical Development Agency (ADA) in collaboration with Aircraft Research and Design Centre (ARDC) of Hindustan Aeronautics Limited (HAL) for the Indian Air Force and Indian Navy. It came from the Light Combat Aircraft (LCA) programme, which began in the 1980s to replace India's ageing MiG-21 fighters. In 2003, the LCA was officially named "Tejas".

The first endogenously-built Tejas Light Combat Aircraft (LCA) was handed over by Defense Minister Manohar Parrikar to the Indian Air Force on 17 January 2015. It marked the beginning of a 4.5th generation aircraft, being built at indigenous in India. The entire project of LCA Tejas was taken care of by the Defense Research and Development Organization (DRDO) and Hindustan Aeronautics Limited (HAL) jointly.

Hence, the correct option is (A).

40. By observing the incomplete image of the question, the missing part is:

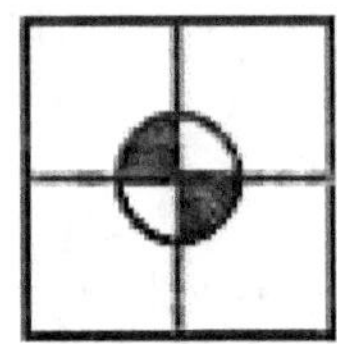

Therefore, the complete diagram is:

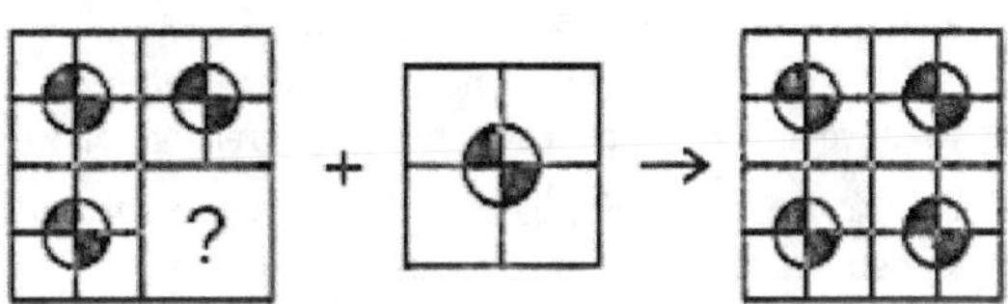

Hence, the correct option is (D).

41. The answer figure which will complete the pattern in the given question figure is as follows:

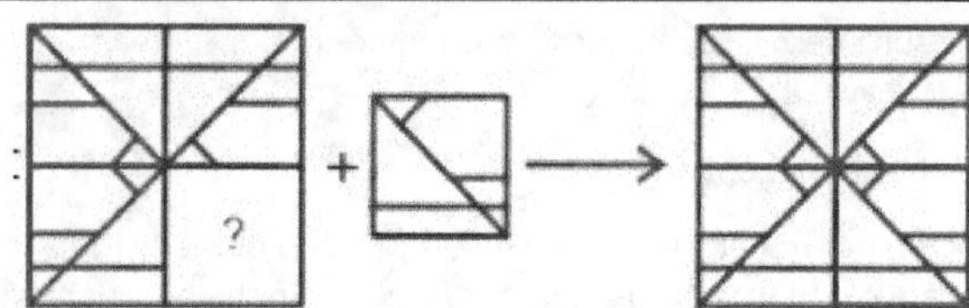

Hence, the correct option is (A).

42. Figure in option (B) will complete the question figure as:

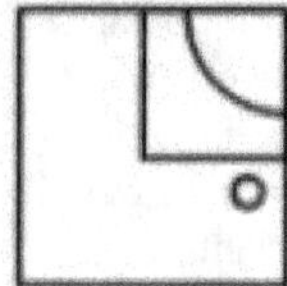

Hence, the correct option is (B).

43. We can see clearly that figure in option (A) is the correct pattern that will complete the question figure as:

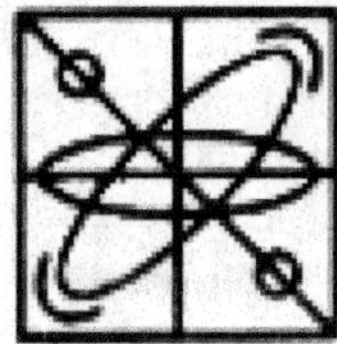

Hence, the correct option is (A).

44.

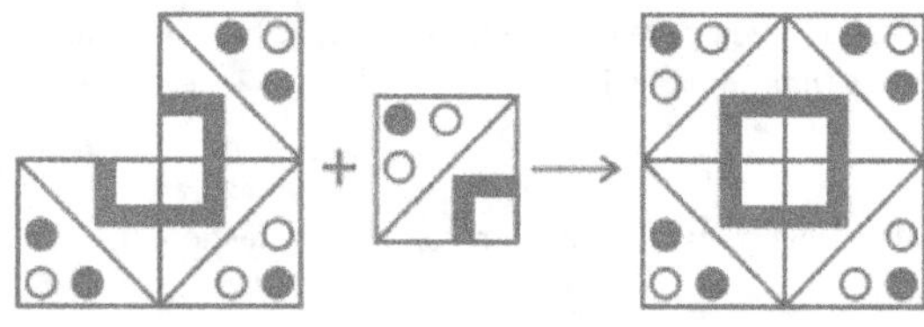

As you can see, the figure in option (B) is the right one to complete the pattern.

Hence, the correct option is (B).

45. The correct sentence will be: "Prema is the girl in my class who writes beautiful poems."

- Relative pronouns introduce relative clauses. The most common relative pronouns are who, whom, whose, which, that. The relative pronoun we use depends on what we are referring to and the type of relative clause.

- We use who in relative clauses to refer to people, and sometimes to pet animals. We use it to introduce defining and non-defining relative clauses.

Here, the speaker is referring to a third person i.e., Prerna, so we will use 'writes' instead of 'write'.

'Writes' is used with third person singular nouns.

Hence, the correct option is (B).

46. The correct sentence will be- "Rahul was ready "to" accept any job, even a part-time one."

Option (D) should use 'to' instead of 'for'.

In option (A) 'was' is correct as the sentence is in the past tense.

In option (B) the article 'a' is correct as it is used with indefinite things.

Option (C) is also grammatically meaningful.

'To' is used to indicate the relation between the person and the job.

'For' is used to indicate a purpose.

Hence, the correct option is (D).

47. Kuchipudi is an indigenous dance form of Andhra Pradesh that originated and flourished in a village of the same name, its original name was Kuchelapuri or Kuchelapuram, a town in the Krishna district.

Hence, the correct option is (D).

48. It is a famous dance of classical dance. Bharatanatyam is one of the famous dances of India and belongs to the state of Tamil Nadu in South India. The name is derived from the word 'Bharata' and is related to 'Nritya Shastra'.

Hence, the correct option is (A).

49. The correct answer is 'studying'.

A preposition is a word that shows direction (a letter to you), location (at the door), or time (by noon), or that introduces an object (a basket of apples).

Prepositions are typically followed by an object, which can be a noun (noon) or a gerund acting as a noun (falling), a noun phrase (the door), or a pronoun (you).

Let's look at the examples given below:

- I have been waiting for you since 2014. (preposition followed by a pronoun)

- He was excited about going to a hill station. (preposition followed by a gerund)

In the given sentence, the preposition 'about' must be followed by a noun, pronoun, or gerund.

Of the given options, we find that the gerund 'studying' is the most suited for the first blank.

The rest of the options are various verb forms.

Hence, the correct option is (A).

50. The correct answer is 'want'.

- The simple present tense is used when an action is happening right now, to state or ask about things in general, or when it happens regularly or unceasingly.

- The structure is given below:

  - Subject + V1 + object.

- The verb will take 's/es' if the given noun/pronoun (3rd person) is singular.

- Example: He plays badminton daily.

- Since the given sentence is in the present tense (as indicated by the earlier verbs), the plural verb 'want' will be used in the second blank as per the plural noun 'people'.

Hence, the correct option is (D).

51. The correct answer is 'these'.

The pronouns that connect a clause or phrase to a noun or a pronoun, is called a relative pronoun.

A demonstrative pronoun represents a thing or things. The most common demonstrative pronouns are:

this, that, these, those.

'This/that' are used with singular countable nouns and 'these/those' are used with plural countable nouns.

Example:

- This is my bag.
- Those were the days!

Since the patterns of habits (which is a plural countable noun) have already been discussed in the cloze test before, the demonstrative pronoun 'these' will be the correct choice in the third blank.

Hence, the correct option is (C).

52. The correct answer is 'must'.

An auxiliary verb is a verb that adds functional or grammatical meaning to the clause in which it occurs, so as to express tense, aspect, modality, voice, emphasis, etc.

A modal or a modal auxiliary is a word such as 'can' or 'would' which is used with the main verb (the 1st form of the verb) to express ideas such as possibility, intention, or necessity.

Example:

- I have taken my breakfast. (have- auxiliary verb)
- One should obey one's elders. (should- modal)

The former part of the given sentence talks about the scientists discovering the mechanism of patterns and the latter part talks about them certainly finding a recipe for rapid change.

In the given condition, the modal verb 'must' will be used in the fourth blank of the cloze test as it provides the required conclusive tone.

Hence, the correct option is (A).

53. The correct answer is 'were'.

Conditional sentences are statements discussing known factors or hypothetical situations and their consequences.

One of the structures is mentioned below:

This particular type is followed when we talk about something in the past which is purely imaginary.

- If + Simple Past, Subject + Would + V1 + Object.

In the case of imaginary sentences, 'were' is used with all subjects irrespective of their number.

Example:

- If I had wings, I would fly like a bird.
- He shouted at me as if he were my coach.

Thus, in the fifth blank of the given cloze test, 'were' will be used as the given clause of the sentence is conditional/imaginary in nature.

Hence, the correct option is (B).

54. The pattern followed here is:

The upper element becomes lower element and the lower element becomes upper element.

Hence, the correct option is (C).

55. The figure that best completes the pattern given is shown below:

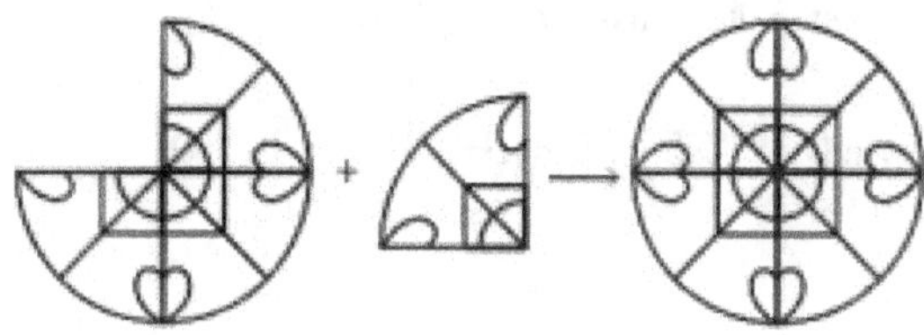

Hence, the correct option is (C).

56. The number of triangles in the figure is shown below:

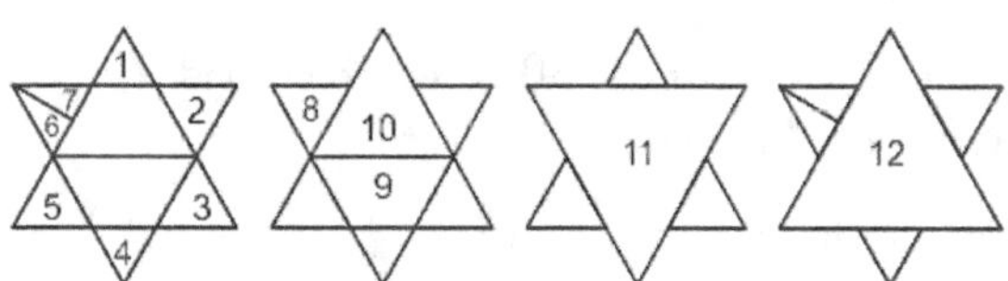

So, '12' is the correct answer.

Hence, the correct option is (C).

57.

Number of squares = ADRO, ABFE, BCGF, EFIH, FGJI, HIML, IJNM, LMPO, MNQP, CDKJ, JKRQ, ACJH, HJQO, EGNL

Hence, the correct option is (C).

58. In the problem figure, the small square in the right lower corner of the image moves one step backward so that it is shifted to the next corner.

Hence, the correct option is (B).

59. Given,

The ratio of copper and zinc is $5:2$.

Let the quantity of copper $= 5x$

And the quantity of zinc $= 2x$

Quantity of initial mixture $= 17.5$ kg

$\therefore 5x + 2x = \dfrac{35}{2}$

$\Rightarrow x = \dfrac{5}{2}$

Quantity of Copper in initial mixture $= \dfrac{5}{2} \times 5$

$= \dfrac{25}{2}$ kg

Quantity of Zinc in initial mixture $= \dfrac{5}{2} \times 2$

$= 5\ kg$

Now after adding $1.250\ kg$ of zinc $= 5 + 1.250$

$= 6.250$ kg

$= \dfrac{25}{4}$ kg

$\therefore$ New Ratio of copper : zinc $= \dfrac{25}{2} : \dfrac{25}{4}$

$= 2:1$

Hence, the correct option is (A).

60. Let the number of coins of 50 paise, 1 rupee and 2 rupees be $2x, 3x$ and $4x$ respectively.

It is given that the total sum $= 240$

Therefore,

$$2x \times \left(\dfrac{1}{2}\right) + 3x \times (1) + 4x \times (2) = 240$$

$$\Rightarrow x + 3x + 8x = 240$$

$$\Rightarrow x = 20$$

So, the number of 1 rupee coins $= 3 \times 20 = 60$

Hence, the correct option is (D).

61. Given,

The ratio of incomes of Manish and Pankaj is 11 : 7 and pankaj gets Rs. 6000 less than Manish.

Let the income of Manish and Pankaj be 11x and 7x respectively.

11x - 7x = 6000

$\Rightarrow$ 4x = 6000

$\Rightarrow$ x = 1500

Total income of Manish and Pankaj = (11x + 7x) = 18 × 1500 = Rs. 27000

Hence, the correct option is (B).

62. Shape in option (C) is embedded in given figure.

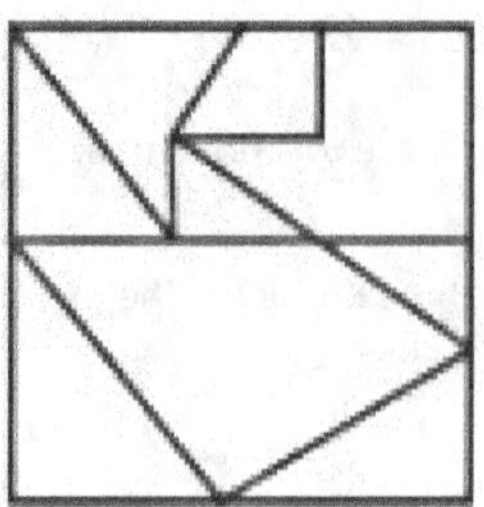

Hence, the correct option is (C).

63. The shapes from the problem figure can be used to create the below figure:

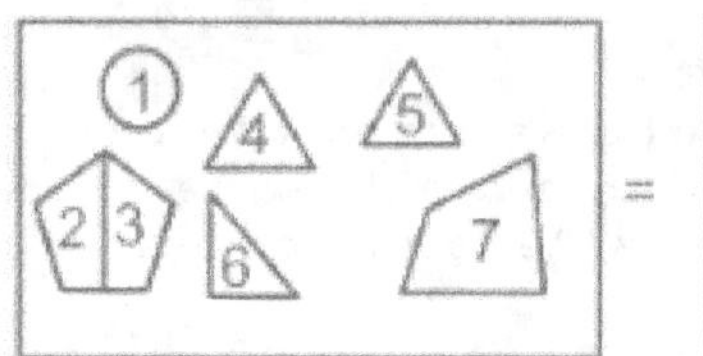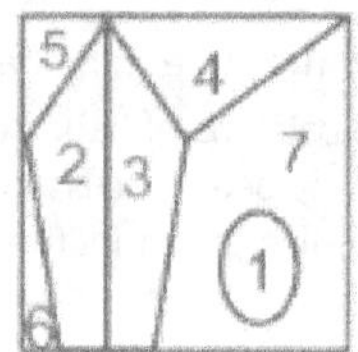

Hence, the correct option is (C).

64.

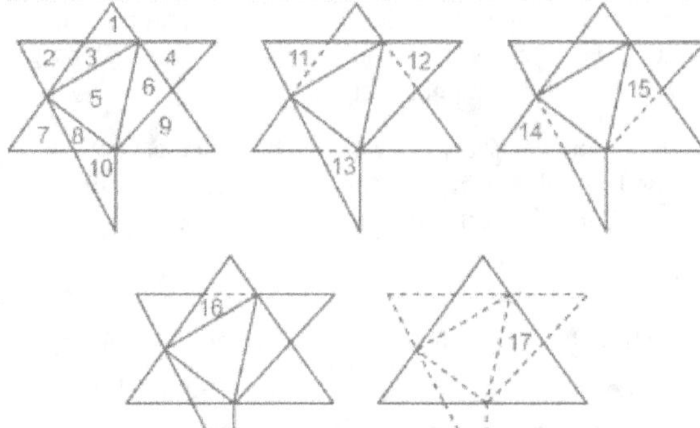

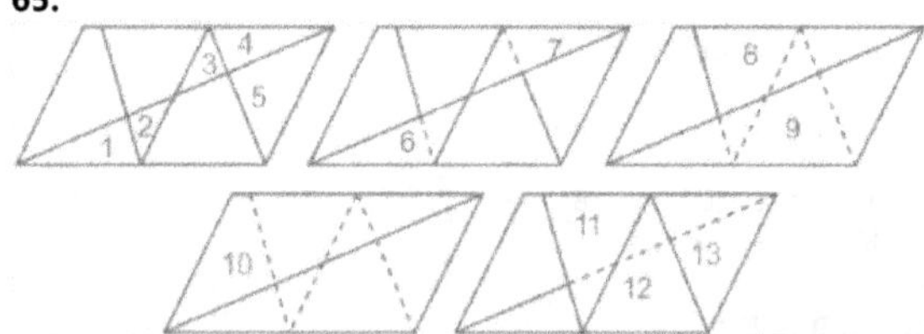

Therefore, there are 17 triangles in the figure.

Hence, the correct option is (D).

65.

Therefore, there are 13 triangles in the figure.

Hence, the correct option is (B).

66.

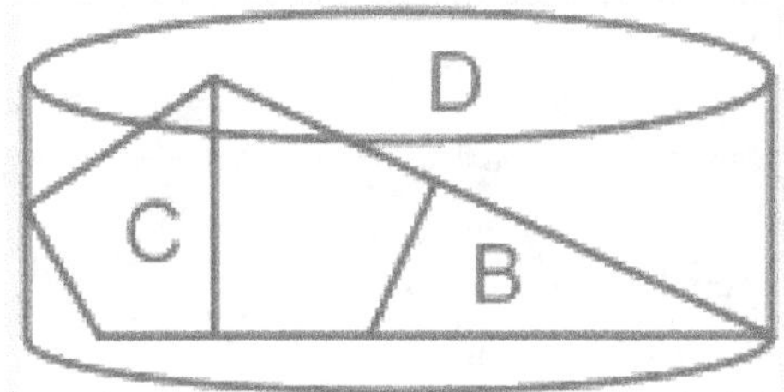

Therefore, 'B, C and D' is the correct answer.

Hence, the correct option is (B).

67. Total cost price Rs. $= 1600$ Let CP $_1 = 600$ and CP $_2 = 1000$

Case I, When he sells first at 10% profit and second at 20% profit:

∴ Profit on CP $_1 = 10\%$ on $600 =$ Rs. 60

Profit on CP $_2 = 20\%$ on $1000 =$ Rs. 200

Total Profit = Rs.260 ...(i) Case II, When he sells first at 20% profit and second at 10% profit:

∴ Profit on CP $_1 = 20\%$ on $600 =$ Rs. 120

Profit on $_2 = 10\%$ on $1000 =$

Rs. 100

Total Profit $=$ Rs. $220 \dots (ii)$

Difference in Profit $[(i) - (ii)\} = Rs.\,260 - Rs.\,220$

$=$ Rs. 40

When difference in profit is Rs. 40, then difference in cost price would be Rs. $(1000 - 600) =$ Rs. 400.

When difference in profit is Rs. 5, then difference in cost price would be:

Rs. $= \left(\dfrac{400}{40} \times 5\right)$

$=$ Rs. 50.

Hence, the correct option is (C).

68. Given,

SP of the tea-set $=$ Rs 3540

Let the cost price of the tea-set be Rs x

According to the question

$\Rightarrow x + \dfrac{(100-41)}{100} = 3540$

$\Rightarrow x = 3540 \times \left(\dfrac{100}{59}\right) =$ Rs 6000

To make 11% profit seller should have sold the set for $=$ Rs $6000 \times \left(\dfrac{111}{100}\right) =$ Rs 6660

The seller should have sold the set more by $=$ Rs $(6660 - 3540) =$ Rs 3120

Hence, the correct option is (D).

69. Given:

C.P. for Rahul $=$ Rs. $5,50,000$

He sells it to Vipul at a loss of 10%. Vipul then sells it to Yash at a profit of 5%. Yash sells it to Shubham at a profit of 2%.

Shubham spends Rs. $10,000$ on the refurbishing of Car and add it to cost of the car and then he sold it to Shivansh at 5% profit.

C.P. for Shubham $= 550000 \times 0.9 \times 1.05 \times 1.02 =$ Rs. 530145

Total Cost after Refurbishing $=$ Rs. $530145 + 10000 =$ Rs. 540145

C.P. for Shivansh $= 540145 \times 1.05 =$ Rs. 567150 (approximate)

Hence, the correct option is (C).

70. Number of persons who can speak English and Hindi both only is 5.
Hence, the correct option is (A).

71. The number of doctors who are neither artists nor players is 17.
Hence, the correct option is (A).

72. The number of doctors who are both players and artists is 3.
Hence, the correct option is (C).

73. From the Venn diagram,

The number of artists who are players is = 22

Hence, the correct option is (C).

74. The number of players who are neither artists nor doctors is 25.
Hence, the correct option is (A).

75. (4) Balance, (5) Balancing, (1) Bale, (3) Balls, (2) Blade

Hence, the correct option is (C).

76. According to the question,

TIGER – EGIRT

Therefore, none of the letters in the alphabet have the same position.

Hence, the correct option is (D).

77. A judge may be removed from office through a motion adopted by Parliament on grounds of 'proven misbehaviour or incapacity'. The Constitution provides that a judge can be removed only by an order of the President, based on a motion passed by both Houses of Parliament. The procedure for the removal of judges is elaborated in the Judges Inquiry Act, 1968. Under the Act, an impeachment motion may originate in either House of Parliament. To initiate proceedings at least 100 members of Lok Sabha may give a signed notice to the Speaker, or at least 50 members of Rajya Sabha may give a signed notice to the Chairman. The Speaker or Chairman may consult individuals and examine relevant material related to the notice. Based on this, he or she may decide to either admit the motion or refuse to admit it. If the motion is admitted, the Speaker or Chairman will constitute a three-member committee to investigate the complaint. It will comprise a Supreme Court judge Chief Justice of a High Court and a distinguished jurist. The committee will frame charges based on which the investigation will be conducted. A copy of the charges will be forwarded to the judge who can present a written defense. After concluding its investigation, the Committee will submit its report to the Speaker or Chairman, who will then lay the report before the relevant House of Parliament. If the report records a finding of misbehaviour or incapacity, the motion for removal will be taken up for consideration and debated. So, statement 1 is correct.

The motion for removal is required to be adopted by each House of Parliament by a majority of the total membership of that House, and a majority of at least two-thirds of the members of that House present and voting. So, statement 2 is not correct.

If the motion is adopted by this majority, the motion will be sent to the other House for adoption. Once the motion is adopted in both Houses, it is sent to the President, who will issue an order for the removal of the judge.

Hence, the correct option is (A).

78. The correct answer is **uproar**.

commotion: a state of confused and noisy disturbance

uproar: a loud and impassioned noise or disturbance

Let's look at the meanings of the other given options:

- peace- freedom from disturbance; tranquility
- sound- vibrations that travel through the air or another medium and can be heard when they reach a person's or animal's ear
- furious- extremely angry

Thus, from the given meanings, we find that commotion and uproar are synonyms.

Hence, the correct option is (A).

79. The correct answer is **inbuilt**.

inherent: existing in something as a permanent, essential, or characteristic attribute

inbuilt: existing as an original or essential part of something or someone

Let's look at the meanings of the other given options:

- outward- of, on, or from the outside

- difficult- needing much effort or skill to accomplish, deal with, or understand
- hallow- honor as holy

Thus, from the given meanings, we find that inherent and inbuilt are synonyms.

Hence, the correct option is (D).

80. The correct answer is **admonished**.

reprimanded: rebuke (someone), especially officially

admonished: warn or reprimand someone firmly

Let's look at the meanings of the other given options:

- appreciated- recognize the full worth of
- praised- express warm approval or admiration of
- disliked- feel distaste for or hostility toward

Thus, from the given meanings, we find that reprimanded and admonished are synonyms.

Hence, the correct option is (A).

81. The southeast trade winds in the southern hemisphere and the northeast trade winds in the northern hemisphere meet each other near the equator. The meeting place of these winds is known as the Inter-Tropical Convergence Zone (ITCZ).

Characteristics features related to ITCZ:

- The Intertropical Convergence Zone (ITCZ) lies in the equatorial trough.
- It is a permanent low-pressure feature where surface trade winds, laden with heat and moisture, converge to form a zone of increased convection, cloudiness, and precipitation.
- It is a low-pressure zone between tropic of Cancer and tropic of Capricorn
- This is the region of ascending air, maximum clouds, and heavy rainfall.
- The location of ITCZ shifts north and south of the equator with the change of season.
- In the summer season, the sun shines vertically over the Tropic of Cancer, and the ITCZ shifts northwards.

Therefore, all the statements are correct about ITCZ or tropical convergence zone.

Hence, the correct option is (A).

82. Given,

The ratio of men, women, and children $= 9:8:3$

Suppose, Men $= 90$, Women $= 80$, Children $= 30$

Total population $= 200$

Now, the number of literate men $= \dfrac{90 \times 80}{100} = 72$.....(i)

The number of literate women $= \dfrac{80 \times 70}{100} = 56$.....(ii)

The number of literate children $= \dfrac{30 \times 90}{100} = 27$ .....(iii)

Total literate $= 155$

Total illiterate $200 - 155 = 45$

So, illiteracy rate $= \dfrac{45}{200} \times 100$

$\Rightarrow 22\dfrac{1}{2}\%$

Hence, the correct option is (A).

83. Given:

Percentage of girls in the college = 45%

Percentage of girls who voted for Anushka = 60%

Percentage of boys who voted for Anushka = 80%

Let the number of students be 100.

Then according to the question,

Number of girls = 45% of 100 = 45

Number of boys = 100 – 45 = 55

Now, Votes cast by girls = $\dfrac{60}{100} \times 45 = 27$

Votes cast by boys = $\dfrac{80}{100} \times 55 = 44$

Votes cast by both = (27 + 44) = 71

% of votes cast by both = $\left(\dfrac{71}{100}\right) \times 100 = 71\%$

$\therefore$ Votes obtained by Anushka is 71%.

Hence, the correct option is (C).

84. Let h and r be the height and radius of the cone respectively.

Volume $= \dfrac{1}{3}\pi r^2 h$

New height $= \dfrac{h \times 150}{100} = \dfrac{3h}{2}$

New volume of the cone $= \dfrac{1}{3}\pi r^2 \cdot \dfrac{3h}{2} = \dfrac{1}{2}\pi r^2 h$

Change in volume $= \dfrac{1}{2}\pi r^2 h - \dfrac{1}{3}\pi r^2 h = \dfrac{1}{6}\pi r^2 h$

Percentage increase $= \dfrac{\frac{1}{6}\pi r^2 h}{\frac{1}{3}\pi r^2 h} \times 100$

$= 50\%$

Hence, the correct option is (B).

85. The estimated percentage of the forest land that ideally India should have is 33%.

The ideal forest land area is 33%, while in hills and mountains it is around 45%. It means the estimated forest land in mountains and hills should be two-third. Thus, India needs to increase the forest land to increase the forest cover.

Hence, the correct option is (C).

86. The subordinating conjunction 'because' is used to give reasons.

Thus, 'because' is the correct answer.

The sentence should be 'I was late **because** the cab was not on time.'

Hence, the correct option is (A).

87. The mentioned action was taken in past and it continued for a certain period. Therefore Past perfect continuous tense should be chosen.

Hence, the correct option is (C).

88. Quotient: a degree or amount of a specified quality or characteristic.

So, for the given fill in the blank 'Quotient" is the most suitable word.

Hence, the correct option is (C).

89. The correct word suitable for fill in the blank space is 'decide'.

Decide - come or bring to a resolution in the mind as a result of consideration.

I can't quite <u>decide</u> if it is beauty or simply monstrous.

Hence, the correct option is (B).

90. The logic follows here is:

$(\text{Number})^2 : (\text{Number})^3 :: (\text{Number})^2 : (?)^3$

$49 : 343$

$(7)^2 : (7)^3$

Similarly,

$324 : ?$

$(18)^2 : (18)^3$

$324 : 5832$

Thus $? = 5832$

Hence, the correct option is (A).

91. The logic followed is:

As Igloo is the Dwelling place of Eskimo.

Similarly,

Sty is the Dwelling Place of Pig.

Hence, the correct option is (A).

92. The logic followed is:

As the scientific study of plants is called Botany.

Similarly,

The study of the insects is called Entomology.

Hence, the correct option is (B).

93. The logic followed is:

The second number = multiplication of all the digits of the first number

245 : 40

40 = 2 × 4 × 5

40 = 40

Similarly,

413 : ?

? = 4 × 1 × 3

? = 12

Hence, the correct option is (A).

94. The logic followed is:

(First two digits of the first number together) ÷ third digit of the first number = second number

122 : 6

12 ÷ 2 = 6

6 = 6

Similarly,

408 : ?

40 ÷ 8 = ?

? = 5

Hence, the correct option is (A).

95. Given,

Length of the train = 100 meters

Speed of the train = 144 km/hr

$$\text{Time} = \frac{\text{Distance}}{\text{Speed}}$$

$$\text{Time in second} = \frac{100}{\left(144 \times \left(\frac{5}{18}\right)\right)}$$

$$\Rightarrow \frac{100}{40} = 2.5$$

∴ A train will take time 2.5 second to cross an electric pole.

Hence, the correct option is (A).

96. Given,

The length of the train = 120 m.

The speed of the train = 54 km/h.

The length of the platform = 150 m.

$$\text{Time} = \frac{\text{Distance}}{\text{speed}}$$

$$1 \text{ km/h} = \frac{5}{18} \text{ m/s}$$

Speed = 54 km/h

$$\Rightarrow 54 \times \frac{5}{18} \text{ m/s}$$

$$\Rightarrow 15 \text{ m/s}$$

Total distance = 120 + 150

⇒ 270 m

$$\text{Time required} = \frac{270}{15} \Rightarrow 18 \text{ s}$$

$$\frac{18}{60} \text{ min} = \frac{3}{10} \text{ min} \Rightarrow 0.3 \text{ min}$$

∴ The time required to cross the platform is 0.3 min.

Hence, the correct option is (A).

97. Given,

A person starts travelling from one place to another at 90 km/hr.

Person returns at the speed of 120 km/hr.

The total time taken is 7 hours.

If the distance is constant then, the time taken will be inversely proportional to the speed.

Ratio of Speed = 90 : 120 = 3 : 4

∵ Distance traveled is constant, the ratio of Time taken will be 4 : 3.

We can say that the total time taken is 7 unit.

According to the question,

The total time taken is 7 hours.

7 unit → 7 hours

$$\Rightarrow 4 \text{ unit} \rightarrow \frac{7 \times 4}{7} = 4$$

$$\Rightarrow 3 \text{ unit} \rightarrow \frac{7 \times 3}{7} = 3$$

Time taken while going is 4 hours and returning is 3 hours.

Distance travelled = 90 × 4 = 360 km.

∴ Distance travelled is 360 km.

Hence, the correct option is (B).

98. Given,

Speed of motor car while travelling from A to B = 30 km/h

Speed of motor car while travelling from B to A = 20 km/h

$$\text{Average speed} = \frac{\text{Total distance}}{\text{Total time}}$$

Let the distance between A and B is x km

$$\text{Time taken from A to B} = \frac{x}{30} \text{ hr.}$$

Time taken from B to A = $\dfrac{x}{20}$ hr.

Total time = $\dfrac{x}{30} + \dfrac{x}{20}$

$\Rightarrow \dfrac{(3x+2x)}{60} = \dfrac{5x}{60}$ hr.

Total distance = $2x$ km

Average speed = $\dfrac{2x}{\left(\frac{5x}{60}\right)}$

$\Rightarrow \dfrac{(2\times 60)}{5} = 24$

$\therefore$ The average speed of journey is 24 km/h

Hence, the correct option is (C).

99. Given,

$\dfrac{1}{B} + \dfrac{1}{C} = \dfrac{7}{60}$

$\dfrac{1}{A} + \dfrac{1}{C} = \dfrac{3}{20}$

$\dfrac{1}{A} + \dfrac{1}{B} + \dfrac{1}{C} = \dfrac{13}{60}$

Solving,

$\Rightarrow \dfrac{1}{B} = \dfrac{13}{60} - \dfrac{3}{20} = \dfrac{1}{15}$

Then,

$\Rightarrow \dfrac{1}{C} = \dfrac{7}{60} - \dfrac{1}{15} = \dfrac{1}{20}$

$\therefore$ In 20 days, C alone can complete the work.

Hence, the correct option is (A).

100. $\dfrac{\sqrt{529} \div \sqrt{676}}{\sqrt{2116} \div \sqrt{169}}$ of $400 \times \dfrac{3}{2} + \dfrac{1}{2}$

$\Rightarrow \dfrac{1}{4} \times 400 \times \dfrac{3}{2} + \dfrac{1}{2}$

$\Rightarrow 100 \times \dfrac{3}{2} + \dfrac{1}{2}$

$\Rightarrow 150 + 0.5$

$\Rightarrow 150.5$

$\therefore 150.5$

Hence, the correct option is (A).

Mock Test   02

Q.1 Who among the followings has been elected as the 15 th President of India in July 2022 ?

A. Nirmala Sitharaman

B. Swati Piramal

C. Hima Kohli

D. Droupadi Murmu

Q.2 The Ministry of Women and Child Development had extended the PM Cares for Children Scheme till 28th __________.

A. February 2022

B. March 2022

C. February 2022

D. December 2022

Q.3 Recently which place has Bihar got invor the ongoing cleanliness survey 2021?

[Delhi Forest Guard, 2021], [UPSSSC Rajasva Lekhpal, 2015]

A. 1st **B.** 10th **C.** 12th **D.** 13th

Q.4 Where has the only Genome Sequencing Lab in the Bihar started?

[Delhi Forest Guard, 2021]

A. Patna

B. Darbhanga

C. Gaya

D. Vaishali

Q.5 Tarkari Express was started from which of the following cities in Bihar?

A. Darbhanga

B. Patna

C. Gaya

D. Munger

Q.6 A sum of money becomes 5 times at simple interest in 16 years. What is the rate of interest?

A. 33.33%   **B.** 25%   **C.** 20%   **D.** 30%

Q.7 The difference between the simple interest and the compound interest compounded annually at the rate of 12% per annum on Rs.5000 for two years will be:

A. 17   **B.** 36   **C.** 45   **D.** 72

Q.8 The compound interest on a sum of money for 2 years at 10% per annum is Rs. 16800. Find the simple interest for 3 years at the same rate of interest and the same sum.

A. 24000   **B.** 12000   **C.** 22000   **D.** 14000

Q.9 Which among the following is the motto of "Indian Army"?

A. Shano Varuna

B. Nabhah Sprsham Diptam

C. Service Before Self

D. Protection and Security

Q.10 The closest meaning of the word "Claustrophobia" is:

A. Fear of clouds

B. Fear of closed spaces

C. Fear of clowns

D. Fear of nothing

Q.11 Direction: Which of the given words describe Yashpal's state most appropriately?

"I am feeling under the weather, today," said Yashpal.

[Allahabad High Court Review Officer (RO), 2019]

A. Brightness

B. Hardness

C. Wellness

D. Illness

Q.12 Which of the following was an outcome of Alexander's invasion of India?

1. Development of important geographical accounts of India.

2. The decrement in trade facilities with Greece.

3. Expansion of the Mauryan empire.

Select the correct answer using the codes:

A. 1,2 and 3 only

B. 1 and 2 only

C. 2 and 3 only

D. 1 and 3 only

Ques (13-17):Direction: Complete the sentence with the most appropriate word.

Q.13 Making pies and cakes _____ Mr. Kumar's specialty.

A. have

B. is

C. has

D. are being

Q.14 I always arrive at class twenty minutes _____ so that I have time to prepare.

A. late

B. early

C. later

D. behind time

Q.15 A _______ man is certain to be prosperous.

A. diligent   **B.** inactive   **C.** indolent   **D.** lethargic

Q.16 Students are not expected to leave without _____.

A. tolerance

B. indulgence

C. permission

D. freedom

Q.17 Laxmi's sons are the most _____ thing in her life.

A. importancy

B. importance

C. importantly

D. important

Q.18 Select the most appropriate meaning of the underlined idiom in the given sentence.

I will not go to work today as I am feeling <u>under the weather.</u>

[SSC Stenographer Grade C & D, 2019]

A. Bad weather

B. Too hot to go out

C. Being sick

D. Rainy weather

Q.19 Direction: Select the most appropriate for the phrase.

Hard-nosed attitude

A. Quality to forgive

B. Protective

C. Aggressive

D. Calm

Q.20 What are Jowar, Bajra and Ragi together known as?

A. Millets

B. Pulses

C. Horticulture

D. Paddy

Q.21 Choose the option that is the passive form of the sentence.

The child tore the page of the book.

[SSC Sub Inspector (CPO), 2019]

A. The page of the book was torn by the child.
B. The page of the book tore by the child.
C. The book's page is torn by the child.
D. The page of the book is tearing by the child.

Q.22 Choose the option that is the passive form of the sentence.

Shyam saw Abhishek starting the car.

[SSC Sub Inspector (CPO), 2019]

A. Abhishek has seen Shyam starting the car.
B. Abhishek can be seen starting the car by Shyam.
C. Abhishek was seen starting the car by Shyam.
D. Abhishek was saw by Shyam starting the car.

Q.23 A train moving at the rate of 72 kmph crosses a pole in 20 seconds. How much time will the train require to cross car moving at speed of 18 kmph in opposite direction?
A. 20 s   B. 16 s   C. 10 s   D. 12 s

Q.24 A river flows at 4 km/hr. The speed of a boat in downstream is thrice the speed of that boat in upstream. Find out the speed of the boat in still water?
A. 8 km/hr   B. 4 km/hr   C. 6 km/hr   D. 12 km/hr

Q.25 A is twice as fast as B and B is thrice as fast as C. If some distance is covered by C in 54 minutes, then in how much time will B cover?
A. 9 minutes   B. 18 minutes
C. 12 minutes   D. 15 minutes

Q.26 A person has to cover a distance of 150 km in 15 hours. If he traveled with the speed of 11.8 km/hr for 10 hours. At what speed he has to travel to cover the remaining distance in the remaining time?

[SSC CGL, 2020]

A. 6 km/hr   B. 8 km/hr
C. 6.5 km/hr   D. 6.4 km/hr

Q.27 Pick the odd one out.
A. 3   B. 7   C. 9   D. 11

Q.28 Pick the odd one out
A. Lion   B. Tiger   C. Hen   D. Cow

Q.29 Pick the odd one out.
A. English   B. Hindi   C. Urdu   D. Sanskrit

Q.30 Pick the odd one out.
A. 671   B. 352   C. 561   D. 211

Q.31 Pick the odd one out.
A. 857 : 21   B. 259 : 16   C. 718 : 16   D. 679 : 22

Q.32 The average weight of A, B and C is 72 kg. If the average weight of A and B is 78 kg and the average weight of A and C is 71 kg, then what is the weight of A? (in kg)

[Delhi Forest Guard, 2021]

A. 83   B. 82   C. 81   D. 80

Q.33 The captain of a cricket team of 11 members is 26 years old and the wicket-keeper is 3 years older. If the ages of these two are excluded, the average age of the remaining players is one year less than the average age of the whole team. What is the average age of the team?
A. 23 years   B. 24 years
C. 25 years   D. None of these

Q.34 There are 5 consecutive odd numbers. The average of the second and fifth number is 16. Find the average of all 5 consecutive odd numbers.
A. 17.5   B. 17   C. 15   D. 18

Q.35 Direction: The following question consists of some Problem Figures followed by other figures marked 1, 2, 3, 4 called the Answer Figures.
Find out the correct answer figure that should come next in the sequence of problem figures.

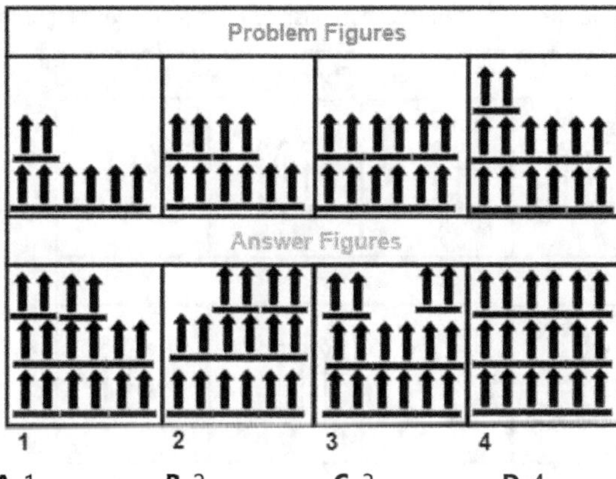

A. 1   B. 2   C. 3   D. 4

Q.36 Direction: In the following question consists of figures marked A, B, C, D called the Problem Figures followed by other figures marked 1, 2, 3, 4 called the Answer Figures. Select a figure from amongst the Answer Figures which will continue the same series as established by the Problem Figures.

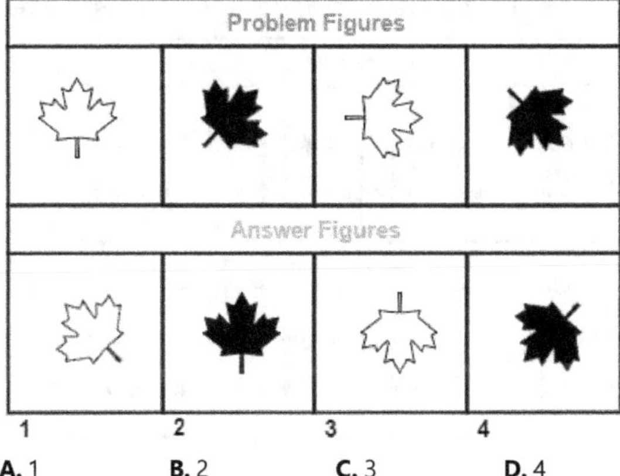

A. 1   B. 2   C. 3   D. 4

Q.37 Direction: The following questions consists of figures marked A, B, C, D called the Problem Figures followed by other figures marked 1, 2, 3, 4 called the Answer Figures.
Select a figure from amongst the Answer Figures which will continue the same series as established by the Problem Figures.

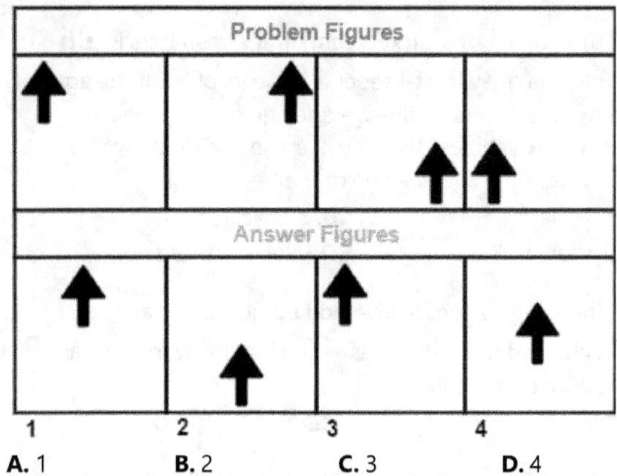

A. 1   B. 2   C. 3   D. 4

Q.38 Direction: Each of the following questions consists of figures marked A, B, C, D called the Problem Figures followed by other figures marked 1, 2, 3, 4 called the Answer Figures. Select a figure from amongst the Answer Figures which will continue the same series as established by the Problem Figures.

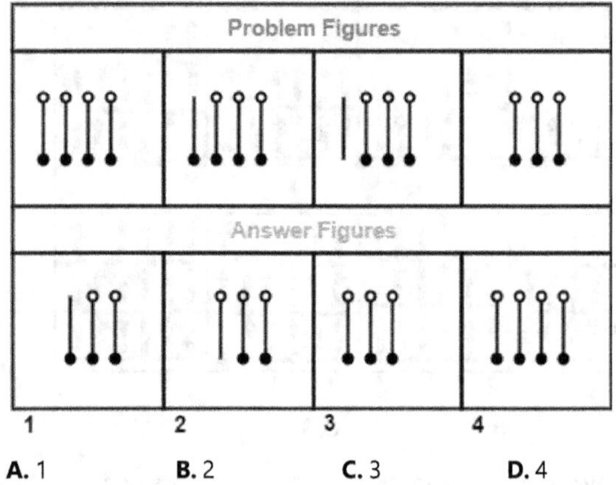

A. 1   B. 2   C. 3   D. 4

Q.39 Direction: In the following question consists of figures marked A, B, C, D called the Problem Figures followed by other figures marked 1, 2, 3, 4 called the Answer Figures.
Select a figure from amongst the Answer Figures which will continue the same series as established by the Problem Figures.

A. 1   B. 2   C. 3   D. 4

Q.40 Write four more rational numbers in the following pattern

$$\frac{1}{-6}, \frac{2}{-12}, \frac{3}{-18}, \frac{4}{-24}$$

[RRB/RRC Group D, 2018]

A. $\frac{5}{6}, \frac{7}{8}, \frac{9}{10}, \frac{11}{12}$

B. $\frac{5}{30}, \frac{6}{36}, \frac{7}{42}, \frac{8}{48}$

C. $\frac{5}{-6}, \frac{6}{-12}, \frac{7}{-18}, \frac{8}{-24}$

D. $\frac{5}{-30}, \frac{6}{-36}, \frac{7}{-42}, \frac{8}{-48}$

Q.41 $\frac{3.8}{1.25}$, written as a pure decimal, will be:

[RRB/RRC Group D, 2018]

A. 3.14   B. 3.04   C. 3.06   D. 3.08

Q.42 Simplify the following expression:

$$\left(\frac{3}{11} \times \frac{33}{6}\right) - \left(\frac{9}{4} \times \frac{12}{3}\right) + \left(\frac{5}{11} \times \frac{22}{10}\right)$$

[RRB/RRC Group D, 2018]

A. $\frac{-2}{9}$ B. $\frac{-13}{2}$ C. $\frac{13}{2}$ D. $\frac{9}{2}$

Q.43 Why are metals good conductors of electricity?
A. Because they contain free electrons
B. Because the atoms are lightly packed
C. Because they have high melting point
D. All of these

Q.44 For which reason does the crystal of diamond shine?
A. High density
B. Total internal reflection
C. Crystal lattice
D. None of these

Q.45 What do we get on dividing the total distance travelled by the total time taken?
A. Average speed   B. Displacement
C. Acceleration   D. Velocity

Q.46 In the equation v=u+at, what does u represent?
A. Initial velocity of the body
B. Final velocity of the body
C. Acceleration of the body
D. None of these

Q.47 For which of the following substances, the resistivity decreases with an increase in temperature?
A. Pure Silicon   B. Copper
C. Nichrome   D. Platinum

Q.48 'Amphan' made landfall in a part of West Bengal and Orissa in May 2020. It is an example of:
A. Tropical cyclone
B. Temperate cyclone
C. Extra-tropical cyclone
D. Anticyclone

Ques (49-53):Directions: In the following question, select the related word/letters/numbers from the given alternatives.

Q.49 86 : 62 : : 49 : ?
A. 29   B. 49   C. 35   D. 42

Q.50 $62 : 155 : : 58 : ?$
A. 131   B. 148   C. 145   D. 256

Q.51 $21:3::574:?$

A. 23 **B.** 82 **C.** 97 **D.** 113

Q.52 $LNPQ:TVXY::CEGH:?$

A. JLNP **B.** FHJM **C.** KMPT **D.** KMOP

Q.53 CEMQ : BFNP : : FBSV : ?

A. IYRV **B.** ECTU **C.** YJSW **D.** YJVS

Q.54 How many triangles are there in the given figure?

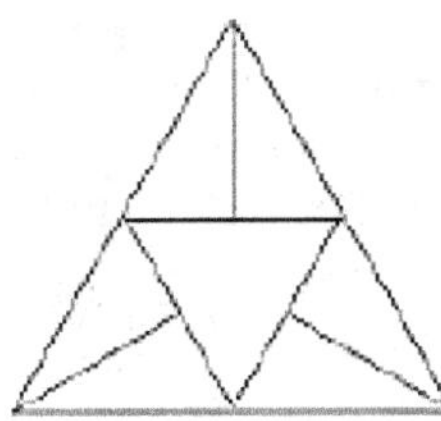

[SSC CGL, 2021]

A. 10 **B.** 11 **C.** 12 **D.** 14

Q.55 Which of the answer figure is embedded in the question figure?

Question Figure:

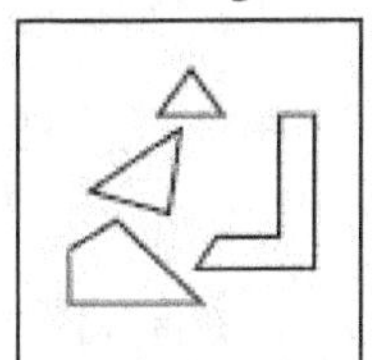

Answer Figures:

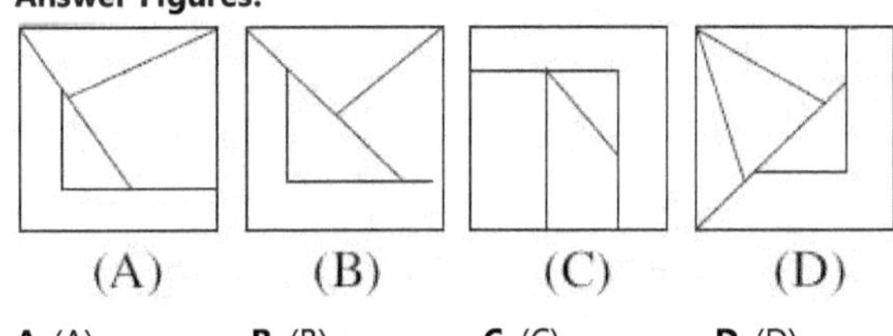

(A) (B) (C) (D)

A. (A) **B.** (B) **C.** (C) **D.** (D)

Q.56 Which of the answer figure is embedded in the question figure?

Question Figure:

Answer Figures:

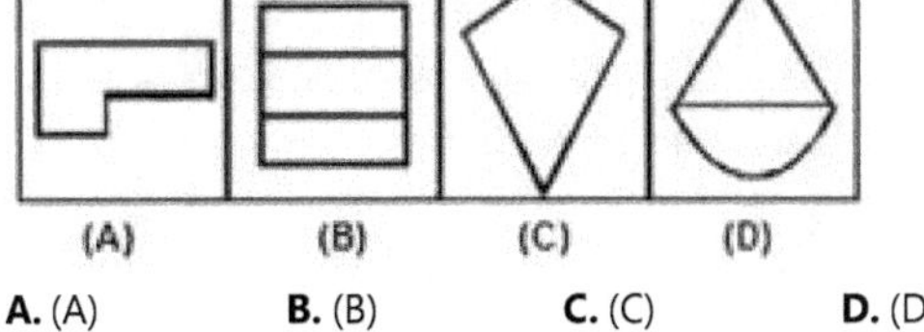

(A) (B) (C) (D)

A. (A) **B.** (B) **C.** (C) **D.** (D)

Q.57 Which of the answer figure is not made up only by the components of the question figure?

Question figure :

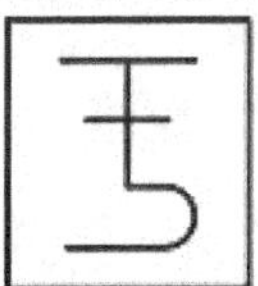

Answer figures :

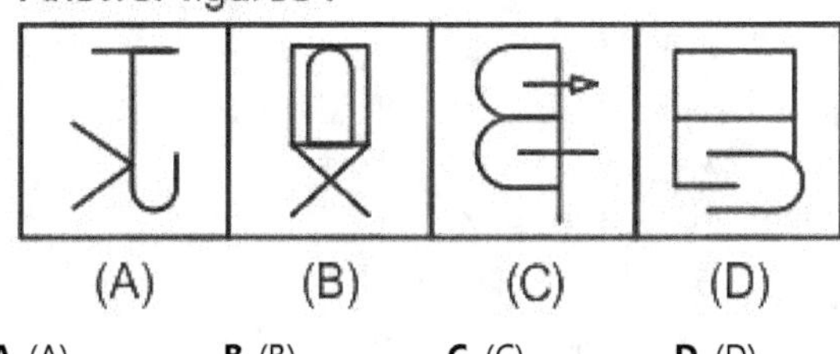

(A) (B) (C) (D)

A. (A) **B.** (B) **C.** (C) **D.** (D)

Q.58 Which answer figure will complete the pattern in the following question figure?

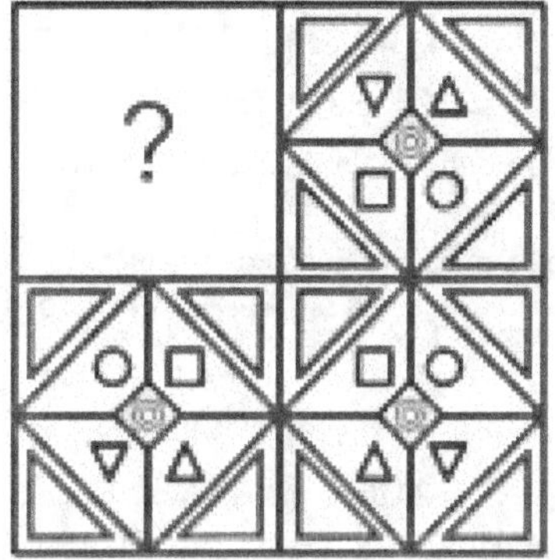

[AFCAT, 2021]

A. 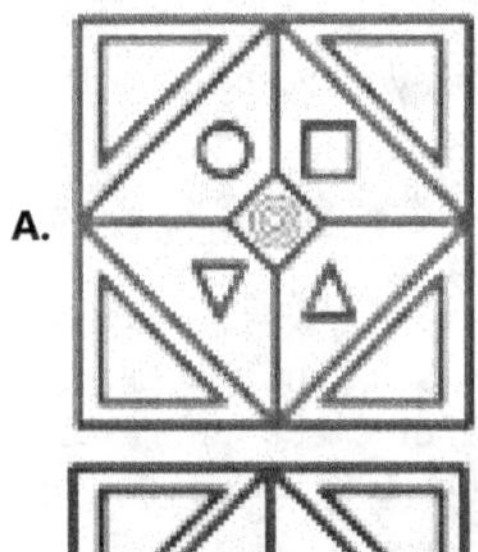 **B.** 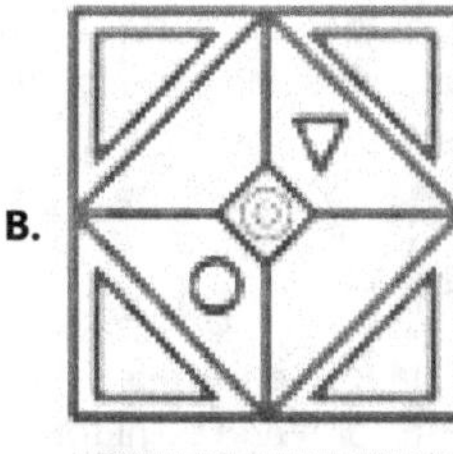

C. 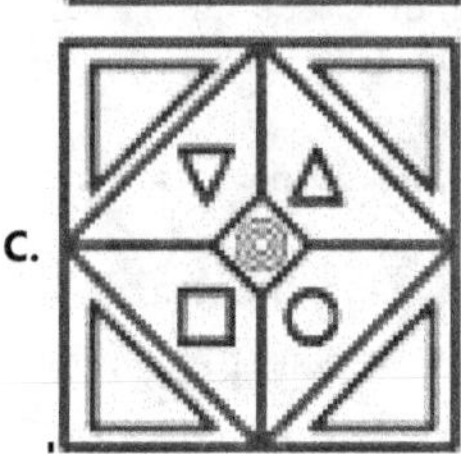 **D.** 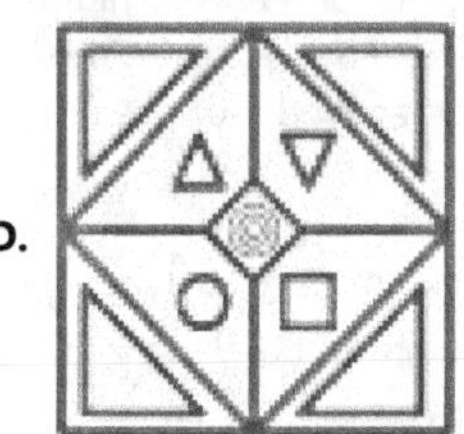

Q.59 With reference to cultural history of India, consider the following statements :

1. Kabir Das' writings had a great influence on the Bhakti movement.

2. The major part of Kabir's work was collected by the Guru Hargobind.

3. Kabir Das' ideologies were greatly influenced by Vaishnava saint Swami Ramananda.

4. Kabir Das and Data Ganj Bakhsh are contemporaries.
Which of the statements given above are correct?

A. 1 and 3 only   **B.** 2 and 4 only
C. 1, 2 and 3   **D.** 1, 2, 3 and 4

Q.60 Which of the following animals are represented on the seals and terracotta art of the Harappan Culture?

1. Unicorn bull
2. Elephant
3. Tiger
4. Cow

Select the correct answer code:

A. 1, 2, 3   **B.** 1, 2   **C.** 1, 3, 4   **D.** 1, 2, 3, 4

Q.61 Identify the segment in the sentence, which contains the grammatical error.

The box of paper clips are kept in the drawer.
[SSC Sub Inspector (CPO), 2019]

A. are kept   **B.** The box
C. of paper clips   **D.** in the drawer

Q.62 Direction: Identify the segment in the sentence, which contains the grammatical error.

Each student will have to carry his own lunch on the picnic.
[SSC Sub Inspector (CPO), 2019]

A. Each student   **B.** his own lunch
C. on the picnic   **D.** will have to carry

Q.63 If 10 men can do a work in 20 days, then how many men can do the same work in 4 days?

A. 60 men   **B.** 20 men   **C.** 50 men   **D.** 40 men

Q.64 A is thrice as good as a workman as B so A takes 60 days less than B to complete work. In how many times they will do it together.

A. 20 days   **B.** $22\frac{1}{2}$ days
C. 25 days   **D.** 30 days

Q.65 Distance between Surat and Delhi is 324 km. Two bikes start from Surat and Delhi towards each other at a same time and meet after 4 hours. Speed of one bike is 9 km/hr faster than other. Find the speed of slower bike.

A. 45 km/hr   **B.** 36 km/hr   **C.** 30 km/hr   **D.** 24 km/hr

Q.66 In a mixture 60 liters, the ratio of milk and water $2:1$. If this ratio is to be $1:2$, then the quantity of water to be further added is:

A. 20 litres   **B.** 30 litres   **C.** 40 litres   **D.** 60 litres

Q.67 Three numbers are in the ratio $\frac{1}{2}:\frac{2}{3}:\frac{3}{4}$. The difference between the greatest and the smallest number is 27. The smallest number is :

A. 81   **B.** 40   **C.** 72   **D.** 54

Q.68 The income of A is 60% less than that of B, and the expenditure of A is equal to 60% of $B's$ expenditure. If A's income is equal to 70% of B's expenditure, then what is the ratio of the savings of A and B?

A. 4:7   **B.** 2:15   **C.** 3:8   **D.** 5:9

Q.69 Which of the following clubs was declared the winner of the second-tier Women's Championship by England's Football Association (FA) in June 2020?

A. Aston Villa   **B.** Birmingham City
C. Liverpool   **D.** West Ham

Q.70 A TV set is being sold for Rs. X in Delhi. A dealer went to Chandigarh and bought the TV at 20% discount (from the price of Delhi). He spends Rs. 600 on transport. Thus, he sold the set in Delhi for Rs. X making (100/7) % profit what is the value of X?

A. Rs. 7200   **B.** Rs. 8000   **C.** Rs. 8800   **D.** Rs. 9600

Q.71 In 1998, the price of an article increased by 25% with respect to that in 1997. In 1999 the price of the article is reduced by 10% with respect to that in 1998 and sold at 7200 rupees then what is the price of the article in 1996 if the price of the article in 1996 and 1997 are in a ratio 3 : 2?

A. 5200   **B.** 9600   **C.** 1800   **D.** 5800

Q.72 A dishonest shopkeeper makes cheating of 14.28% at the time of selling the goods and 28.57% at the time of buying the goods and he promised to sell his goods at 12.5% loss. Find the profit % of the shopkeeper.

A. 31.25   **B.** 31.75   **C.** 33   **D.** 33.5

Q.73 Identify the diagram that best represents the relationship among classes given below.

Examination, School, College

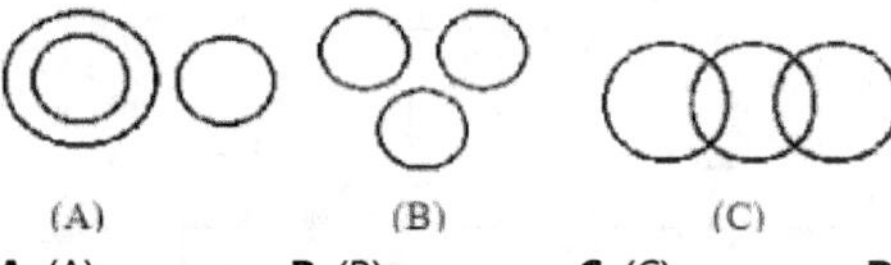

A. (A)   **B.** (B)   **C.** (C)   **D.** (D)

Q.74 In the given figure, how many people like billiards and chess?

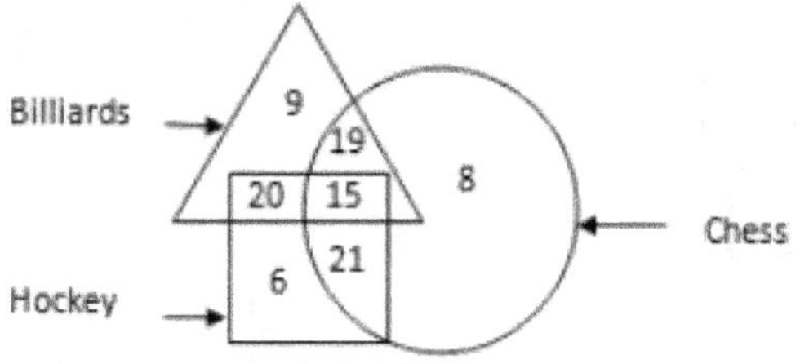

A. 17   **B.** 19   **C.** 15   **D.** 27

Q.75 Which of the following diagrams, shows the relationship between preparation, writing, and results.

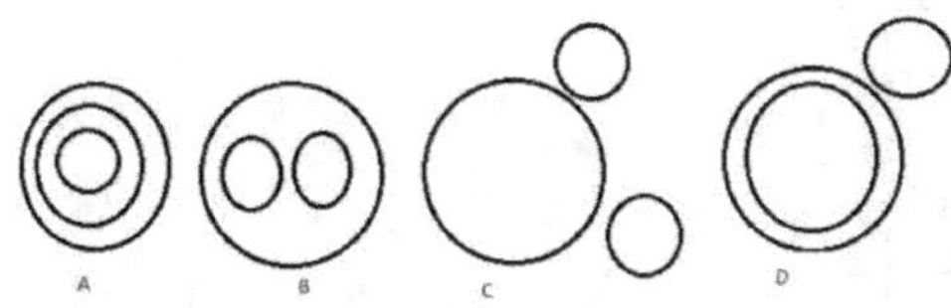

A. A   **B.** B   **C.** C   **D.** D

Q.76 Direction: In the question given below contains three elements. These elements may or may not have some inter linkage. Each group of elements may fit into one of these diagrams at (A), (B), (C), (D).

Which of the following diagrams indicates the best relation between Women, Mothers, and Engineers?

A.    **B.** 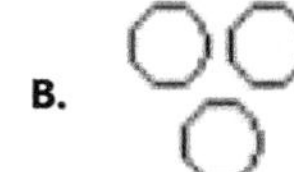

C. 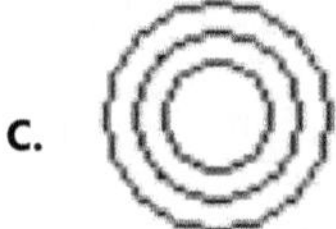   **D.** 

Q.77 Direction: If the following words will arrange in the sequence as they appear in the dictionary, then what will be the sequence as per the dictionary order?

1. HEARER
2. ERASER
3. SHARE
4. ERASE
5. RACER

A. 42153   **B.** 41253   **C.** 24153   **D.** 21354

Q.78 Direction: Arrange the given words in the sequence in which they occur in the dictionary.

1. Lieutenant
2. Light
3. Limit
4. Lines

A. 1342   **B.** 1234   **C.** 1423   **D.** 2143

Q.79 Which of the following is/are correct concerning Department related standing committees (DRSC)?

1. It comprises of 45 members: 30 from Lok Sabha and 15 from the Rajya Sabha.
2. All the members are elected.
3. They are appointed for a maximum period of one year.

A. 1 and 2 only   **B.** 3 only

C. 1 only   **D.** 2 and 3 only

Q.80 Direction: The following sentence consists an underlined word(s) followed by four options. Select the option that is nearest in meaning to the underlined word and mark your response accordingly.

Some people think that their strength is <u>perpetual.</u>

[Officers Training Academy (OTA), 2021], [Indian Military Academy (IMA), 2021]

A. temporary   **B.** powerful

C. everlasting   **D.** all persuasive

Q.81 Direction: The following sentence consists an underlined word(s) followed by four options. Select the option that is nearest in meaning to the underlined word and mark your response accordingly.

One's actions <u>exemplify</u> one's attitude and values.

[Officers Training Academy (OTA), 2021], [Indian Military Academy (IMA), 2021]

A. Devise   **B.** Sympathize

C. Asks for   **D.** Demonstrate

Q.82 Direction: The following sentence consists an underlined word(s) followed by four options. Select the option that is nearest in meaning to the underlined word and mark your response accordingly.

The <u>crux</u> of the issue was that there was no evidence to prove the accused guilty of the act.

[Officers Training Academy (OTA), 2021], [Indian Military Academy (IMA), 2021]

A. core   **B.** part   **C.** idea   **D.** tip

Q.83 $6\frac{1}{4}$% of 1600 + $12\frac{1}{2}$% of 800 equals:

A. 100   **B.** 200   **C.** 300   **D.** 400

Q.84 In a class of 135 students, the numbers of boys is twice that of girls. One-sixth of the boys and one-third of the girls failed in the final examination. Find the percentage of students who passed the examination.

A. 75%   **B.** 71.45%   **C.** 77.78%   **D.** 81.23%

Q.85 3% of 5% of 10% of 20% of 100,000 is equal to:

A. 3   **B.** 250   **C.** 300   **D.** 400

Q.86 Direction: Choose the appropriate word to fill in the blank.

A _______ of seagulls flew over the ship screeching raucously.

[Allahabad High Court Review Officer (RO), 2017]

A. drove   **B.** fleet   **C.** bunch   **D.** flock

Q.87 Direction: Choose the appropriate word to fill in the blank.

She was the _____ of all eyes at the party.

[Allahabad High Court Review Officer (RO), 2017]

A. pride   **B.** limelight   **C.** star   **D.** cynosure

Q.88 Direction: Choose the appropriate word to fill in the blank.

Ghaziabad is the _____ city in India.

[Allahabad High Court Review Officer (RO), 2017]

A. fast growing   **B.** more fast growing

C. most fast growing   **D.** fastest growing

Q.89 Direction: Choose the appropriate word to fill in the blank.

She _______ for a walk every morning to the park.

[Allahabad High Court Review Officer (RO), 2017]

A. is going   **B.** goes   **C.** has gone   **D.** gone

Ques (90-94):Direction: Select a suitable figure from the four alternatives that would complete the figure matrix.

Q.90

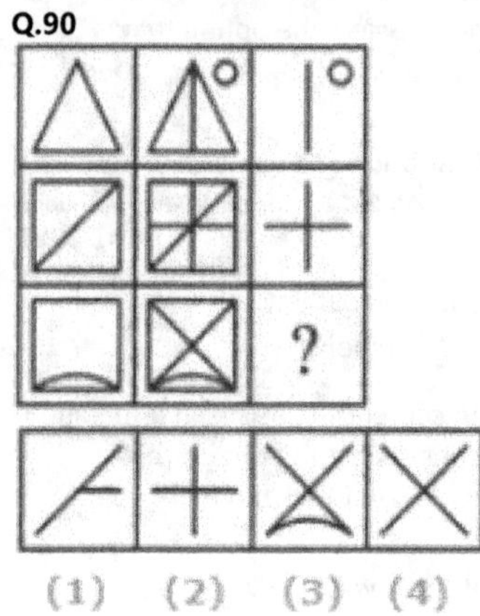

[SSC Sub Inspector (CPO), 2020]

A. 1   **B.** 2   **C.** 3   **D.** 4

Q.91

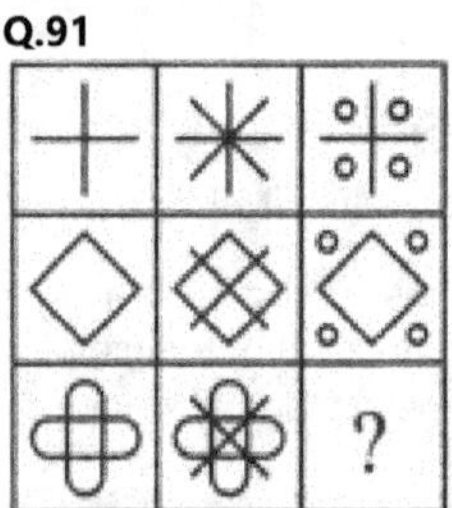

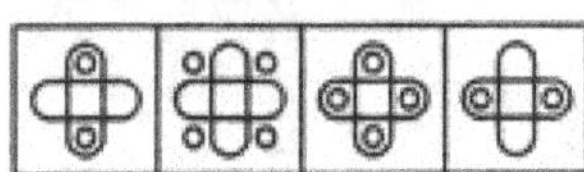

A. 1   **B.** 2   **C.** 3   **D.** 4

Q.92

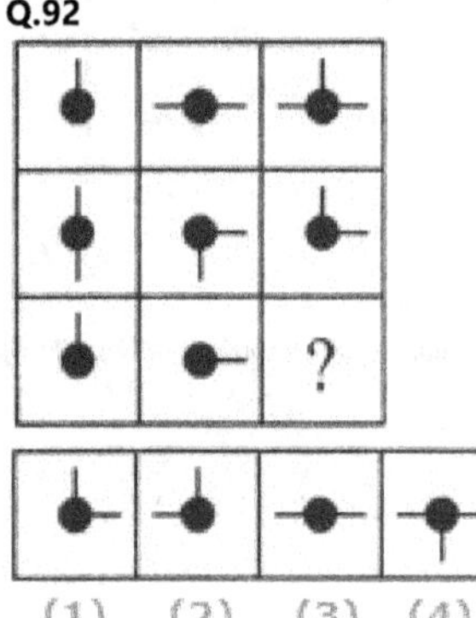

[UP Police Sub Inspector, 2021]

A. 1   **B.** 2   **C.** 3   **D.** 4

Q.93

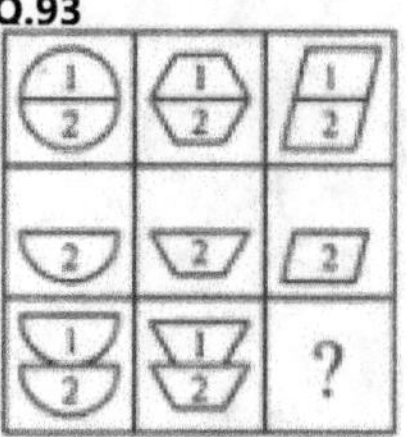

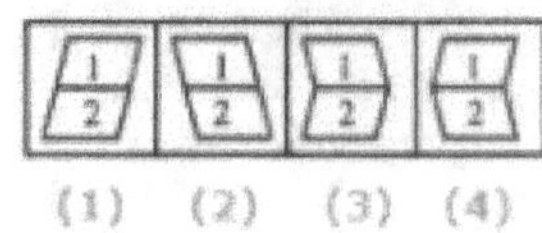

[Telangana Police Constable, 2015]

A. 1   **B.** 2   **C.** 3   **D.** 4

Q.94

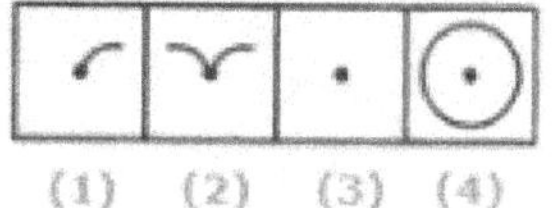

[Telangana Police Constable, 2015]

A. 1   **B.** 2   **C.** 3   **D.** 4

Ques (95-99):Direction: A passage is given with 5 questions following it. Read the passage carefully and choose the best answer to each question out of the four alternatives.

Food and drinks are an integral part of marking Goa's vibrant culture. Meals bring families together, and a staple is the combination of Goan fish curry and rice. Apart from this staple, Goa is also famous for its mixed bag of freshly caught seafood. Another festive favourite for the Goans is their beef and pork roasts that are a must on their Christmas men's which is best paired with Goa's famous brew Feni, made with fermented cashews. Reaping the benefits of its location, the most common occupation of locals is fishing. Owing to the fertile land and abundant water supply, often locals practice farming and grow common food items like cashew, coconuts, jackfruit and other grains. In an area where tourism is the core economy booster, small handicrafts and souvenir jewellery are popular items found in the local markets. Skilled artisans reuse shells and coconut skins found on the beach to make stunning jewellery, frames, and showpieces for home decor. The folk dances and music in the state are performed for both religious festivals and cheerful events. Dekhni dance is performed while wearing a ghumat. The Dekhni dance is performed by only the women of the community and is one of the best-known traditions of Goa. Goff Tolgadi and Shigmo are a couple of dance forms that are very local to the Goan community and are usually performed during the months of Spring, as an offering and jubilation which the season brings to the peasants and their crops. The

Goff consists of weaving braids with various tints of colours and is often performed by the people residing in the Canacona Taluka of Goa. The Shigmo is marked by traditional dances that are performed by wearing colourful dresses accompanied by beats of dhol, Tasha or that of cymbals.

Q.95 How artisans reuse shells and coconut skins?
A. By weaving braids
B. As food ingredient
C. By making jewellery
D. In local farming

Q.96 How is Feni made?
A. With fermented rice
B. With fermented cashew
C. Grown in farming
D. With fermented potatoes

Q.97 What is the most common occupation of the Goans?
A. Fishing
B. Weaving
C. Cattle farming
D. None of these

Q.98 What is the characteristic of Goff tolgadi?
A. Performed only by women
B. Wearing Ghumat
C. Weaving colourful braids
D. None of these

Q.99 What is the staple food of Goans?
A. Feni
B. Beef and pork roast
C. Cashew and jackfruit
D. Goan fish curry and rice

Q.100 Direction: Identify the diagram that best represents the relationship among the given classes.

Cricketer, Male, Actor

A. 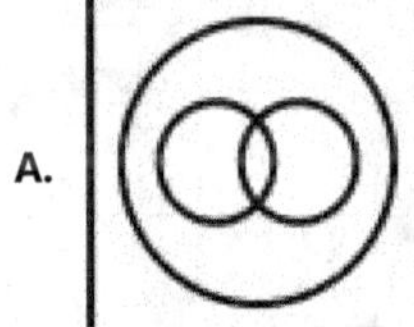

B. 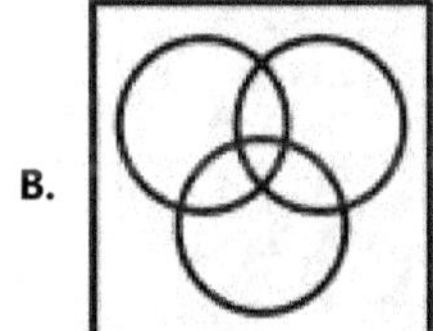

C. 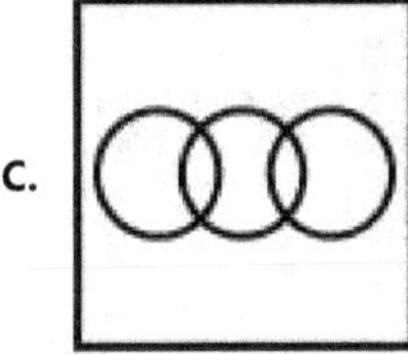

D. 

// Smart Answer Sheet //

Correct — Percentage of students who answered correctly. **Skipped** — Percentage of students who skipped.

Q.	Ans.	Correct	Skipped
1	D	83.7 %	12.64 %
2	A	49.03 %	49.05 %
3	D	52.24 %	35.02 %
4	A	54.28 %	45.42 %
5	B	62.45 %	32.8 %
6	B	25.52 %	70.2 %
7	D	57.32 %	35.35 %
8	A	89.01 %	10.2 %
9	C	89.13 %	10.7 %
10	B	64.01 %	30.53 %
11	D	77.14 %	18.38 %
12	D	18.05 %	69.17 %
13	B	77.44 %	13.2 %
14	B	89.93 %	10.05 %
15	A	77.82 %	11.18 %
16	C	79.69 %	14.3 %
17	D	80.13 %	11.46 %

Q.	Ans.	Correct	Skipped
18	C	60.59 %	30.53 %
19	C	79.5 %	18.69 %
20	A	68.22 %	31.45 %
21	A	25.89 %	70.03 %
22	C	26.69 %	70.43 %
23	B	55.04 %	31.99 %
24	A	43.2 %	35.32 %
25	B	54.3 %	30.24 %
26	D	89.46 %	10.02 %
27	C	88.98 %	10.18 %
28	C	59.14 %	33.7 %
29	C	62.78 %	32.35 %
30	D	52.4 %	36.97 %
31	A	51.42 %	41.31 %
32	B	61.87 %	35.87 %
33	A	49.19 %	35.94 %
34	C	50.45 %	39.11 %

Q.	Ans.	Correct	Skipped
35	A	65.07 %	31.92 %
36	C	43.52 %	55.96 %
37	C	68.94 %	30.68 %
38	A	57.01 %	31.22 %
39	D	44.21 %	53.9 %
40	D	80.46 %	18.84 %
41	B	45.32 %	50.7 %
42	B	69.3 %	30.04 %
43	A	54.72 %	35.15 %
44	B	46.48 %	31.94 %
45	A	89.86 %	10.05 %
46	A	83.38 %	10.73 %
47	A	41.04 %	57.33 %
48	A	46.18 %	31.53 %
49	B	55.95 %	37.35 %
50	C	23.53 %	67.44 %
51	B	78.44 %	19.52 %

Q.	Ans.	Correct	Skipped
52	D	78.02 %	16.34 %
53	B	84.05 %	12.8 %
54	B	67.47 %	30.57 %
55	A	62.62 %	32.7 %
56	C	63.98 %	32.94 %
57	C	88.08 %	11.21 %
58	D	47.96 %	51.03 %
59	A	41.78 %	54.17 %
60	A	78.54 %	16.67 %
61	A	87.27 %	11.45 %
62	C	41.99 %	34.14 %
63	C	86.63 %	11.18 %
64	B	45.51 %	32.34 %
65	B	48.1 %	42.99 %
66	D	67.24 %	31.29 %
67	D	64.35 %	35.03 %
68	B	48.46 %	43.15 %

Q.	Ans.	Correct	Skipped
69	A	16.0 %	67.18 %
70	B	81.59 %	12.9 %
71	B	16.96 %	74.47 %
72	A	67.4 %	31.33 %
73	D	56.42 %	36.74 %
74	B	42.87 %	52.02 %
75	A	76.94 %	17.38 %
76	A	89.85 %	10.04 %
77	A	42.9 %	35.6 %
78	B	80.29 %	16.7 %
79	B	78.83 %	14.08 %
80	C	31.65 %	67.47 %
81	D	51.34 %	36.97 %
82	A	48.58 %	49.81 %
83	B	53.68 %	34.91 %
84	C	44.0 %	33.23 %
85	A	59.16 %	39.27 %

Q.	Ans.	Correct	Skipped
86	D	51.35 %	43.63 %
87	D	62.76 %	33.84 %
88	D	81.18 %	12.7 %
89	B	47.55 %	42.73 %
90	D	61.2 %	38.62 %
91	B	49.52 %	36.06 %
92	A	63.49 %	33.85 %
93	C	43.64 %	49.07 %
94	C	50.91 %	38.07 %
95	C	62.02 %	37.91 %
96	B	41.06 %	41.62 %
97	A	61.82 %	34.95 %
98	C	64.94 %	35.05 %
99	D	47.74 %	34.05 %
100	B	46.53 %	34.9 %

//Hints and Solutions//

1. Former Jharkhand Governor and National Democratic Alliance candidate Droupadi Murmu has been elected as the 15th President of India on 21 July 2022.

She is the first tribal woman to be elected to the position & the youngest as well.

She defeated opposition candidate Yashwant Sinha by bagging 64.03% of the electoral college votes.

Hence, the correct option is (D).

2. The Ministry of Women and Child Development had extended the PM Cares for Children Scheme till 28th February 2022. Earlier the scheme was valid till 31st December 2021. The scheme covers all children who have lost both parents, surviving parents, or legal guardian/adoptive parents/single adoptive parent due to COVID 19 pandemic, starting from 11 March 2020.

Hence, the correct option is (A).

3. The Central Government released the State Ranking of Swachhta Survekshan 2021, in which Bihar is ranked 13th among the states with more than 100 municipal bodies, while Gaya district has been ranked 289th out of 659 districts across the country in the district ranking of all India. The same Supaul has got 300th, Patna 313th and Muzaffarpur 351st.

Hence, the correct option is (D).

4. Patna has the only Genome Sequencing Lab of the state started. Bihar's first and only genome-sequencing facility at Patna-based Indira Gandhi Institute of Medical Sciences (IGIMS), has become non-operational since last week due to a lack of reagents. No samples are being tested in the state at the moment to ascertain the omicron variant of COVID- 19.

Hence, the correct option is (A).

5. Bihar Cooperation Minister Subhash Singh launched Tarkari Express on August 24,2021. It is a service to deliver vegetables to the residents of Patna at their doorstep at half prices. The vegetables are obtained directly from farmers' fields and reaches all the neighbourhoods of Patna on e-rickshaws.

Hence, the correct option is (B).

6. Given:

The Sum of money becomes 5 times of itself in 16 years

Formula used:

(i) $SI = \dfrac{PRT}{100}$

Where P = principal

R = rate

T = time

(ii) A = SI + P

Where, A = Amount

SI = simple interest

Let the principal be P.

For 16 years,

$$SI = \dfrac{(P \times R \times 16)}{100}$$

$$\Rightarrow \dfrac{16PR}{100}$$

A = SI + P

$$\Rightarrow 5P = \dfrac{16PR}{100} + P$$

$$\Rightarrow 4P = \dfrac{16PR}{100}$$

$$\Rightarrow R = \dfrac{400}{16}$$

$$\Rightarrow R = 25\%$$

$\therefore$ The rate of interest is 25%.

Hence, the correct option is (B).

7. $SI = \dfrac{(P \times R \times T)}{100}$

$$CI = P\left[\left(1 + \dfrac{R}{100}\right)^{n} - 1\right]$$

According to question,

$$\left[5000\left(1 + \dfrac{12}{100}\right)^{2} - 5000\right] - \dfrac{5000 \times 12 \times 2}{100}$$

$$= 5000\left(\dfrac{28}{25} \times \dfrac{28}{25} - 1\right) - 1200$$

$$= 5000\left(\dfrac{784 - 625}{625}\right) - 1200 = Rs.\,72$$

Hence, the correct option is (D).

8. Given,
Compound interest in 2 years = 16800
Rate = 10%
Simple interest for Time = 3 years
As we know,

Compound interest = principal $\{(1 + \dfrac{rate}{100})^{time} - 1\}$

$$\Rightarrow 16800 = P \times \{(1 + \dfrac{10}{100})^{2} - 1\}$$

$$\Rightarrow 16800 = P \times \{(\dfrac{11}{10} \times \dfrac{11}{10}) - 1\}$$

$$\Rightarrow 16800 = P \times \dfrac{(121 - 100)}{100}$$

$$\Rightarrow 16800 = P \times (\dfrac{21}{100})$$

$$\Rightarrow P = Rs.\ 80,000$$

Simple interest

$$= \dfrac{(principal \times rate \times time)}{100} = \dfrac{(80000 \times 10 \times 3)}{100} = Rs.\ 24,000$$

∴ The simple interest is Rs. 24,000.
Hence, the correct option is (A).

9. The motto of "Indian Army" is Service Before Self.

Motto	Defence
Shano Varuna	Indian Navy
Nabhah Sprsham Diptam	Indian Airforce
Service Before Self	Indian Army
Protection and Security	CISF

Hence, the correct option is (C).

10. Claustrophobia (noun): Fear of being in closed spaces.

Example: He suffers from claustrophobia so he never travels on underground trains.

Hence, the correct option is (B).

11. If someone is or feels under the weather, they feel ill.

For example: I'm feeling a bit under the weather - I think I'm getting a cold.

Therefore, the word that describes Yashpal's state most appropriately is illness.

Hence, the correct option is (D).

12. The Greek invasion paved the way for the expansion of the Mauryan empire in North-west India as the petty local states were destroyed by the Greeks.

- Chandragupta Maurya also acquired knowledge about the working of Alexander's military tactics which helped him in destroying the power of the Nandas.

So, Statement 3 is correct.

- Invasion paved the way for Greek merchants and craftsmen to trade with India and increase the trade facilities.

So, Statement 2 is incorrect.

- These historical creations provide us with valuable information about the socio-economic conditions of that time.

So, Statement 1 is correct.

Hence, the correct option is (D).

13. In the above-given sentence, 'is' will be used.

It is so because it is a reverse-order sentence. The subject of the sentence is a specialty, which is singular and therefore the verb should also be singular.

Complete Sentence:

Making pies and cakes **is** Mr. Kumar's specialty.

Hence, the correct option is (B).

14. In the above-given sentence, 'early' will be used.

It is so because 'early' is an adverb meaning before the usual or expected time. The sentence tells the fact that the person goes before the usual class timing so that he can prepare for the class.

All the other options are antonyms of early.

Complete Sentence:

I always arrive at class twenty minutes **early** so that I have time to prepare.

Hence, the correct option is (B).

15. In the above-given sentence, 'diligent' will be used.

It is so because 'diligent' is an adjective meaning having or showing care and conscientiousness in one's work or duties; hard-working.

The other options are antonyms of diligence.

The sentence tells the fact that a hard-working man is certain to become successful and flourish financially.

Complete Sentence:

A **diligent** man is certain to be prosperous.

Hence, the correct option is (A).

16. In the above-given sentence, 'permission' will be used.

It is so because 'permission' is a noun meaning the action of officially allowing someone to do a particular thing; consent or authorization.

The sentence is trying to convey the idea that the students are not expected to leave without official consent.

The correct answer is because permission in the given sentence expresses consent which is required before taking leave.

Complete Sentence:

Students are not expected to leave without **permission**.

Hence, the correct option is (C).

17. In the above-given sentence, 'important' will be used.

It is so because 'important' is an adjective meaning of great significance or value.

The blank should be filled by an adjective because here in the given sentence we need an adjective to tell about the quality of a noun i.e. thing.

Complete Sentence:

Laxmi's sons are the most **important** thing in her life.

Hence, the correct option is (D).

18. The idiom 'under the weather' means 'slightly unwell or in low spirits.'

Therefore, 'being sick' is the correct answer.

Hence, the correct option is (C).

19. Hard nose attitude: being tough, stubborn, or uncompromising

For example, That guy seems so hard-nosed that I'm afraid to say hi to him.

Thus, 'aggressive' is the most suitable meaning.

Hence, the correct option is (C).

20. Jowar, Bajra and Ragi are together known as Millets.

Millets are a group of highly variable small-seeded grasses.

Millets can see everywhere as cereal crops or grains for fodder and human food.

The most widely grown millet is pearl millet.

In 2016, global production of millet was 28.4 million tonnes, led by India with 36% of the world total.

Hence, the correct option is (A).

21. The above-given sentence is in the active voice.

We need to change it in the passive voice.

The following steps are required to change the given sentence into passive voice:-

- The subject 'the child' of the active voice will become the object of the passive voice.
- The object 'the page of the book' of the active voice will become the subject of the passive voice.
- The tense(simple past tense) will change according to the following structure:-
    - Active Voice - Subject + did + V_1 or V_2 (tore) + Object.
    - Passive Voice - Object + was/were + V_3 (torn) + by + Object.

Therefore, the correct passive voice is The page of the book was torn by the child.

Hence, the correct option is (A).

22. The correct answer is:

'Abhishek was seen starting the car by Shyam.'

In the passive form, the subject and the object get interchanged.

'Abhishek' will become the subject in the passive form.

The sentence is in the past continuous tense.

So, the passive form will be- subject+ was + past participle form of verb + continuous form of verb + object.

Hence, the correct option is (C).

23. Given:

Speed of train = 72 kmph

Time = 20 seconds

Speed of car = 18 kmph

$$\text{Speed} = \frac{\text{Distance}}{\text{Time}}$$

$$1 \text{ kmph} = \frac{5}{18} \text{ m/s}$$

Calculating length of train

$$\Rightarrow 72 \text{ kmph} = \frac{72 \times 5}{18} \text{ m/s}$$

$\Rightarrow$ Speed of train = 20 m/s

$\Rightarrow$ length of train = Speed × Time

$\Rightarrow$ length = 20 × 20

$\Rightarrow$ Length of train = 400 m

Now, calculate relative speed

$\Rightarrow$ car is moving in opposite direction as train hence relative speed = 72 + 18

$\Rightarrow$ Relative speed = 90 kmph

$\Rightarrow$ Relative speed = 25 m/s

$$\Rightarrow \text{Time taken to cross car} = \frac{400}{25}$$

$\Rightarrow$ Time taken = 16 sconds

$\therefore$ Train takes 16 seconds to cross the car

Hence, the correct option is (B).

24. Let the speed of boat in still water be 'x' km/hr

Let the speed of boat in downstream and upstream be 'd' km/hr and 'u' km/hr respectively

Then, as per question

d = 3 × u

$\Rightarrow$ x + 4 = 3×(x - 4)

$\Rightarrow$ x + 4 = 3x - 12

$\Rightarrow$ x = 8

$\therefore$ Speed of boat in still water is 8 km/hr.

Hence, the correct option is (A).

25. Given,

A is twice as fast as B and B is thrice as fast as C.

C covered some distance in 54 min.

$$\text{Speed} = \frac{\text{Distance}}{\text{Time}}$$

Let the time taken by B be t min.

$\Rightarrow$ A : B = 2 : 1, B : C = 3 : 1

$\Rightarrow$ A : B : C = (2 × 3) : (1 × 3) : (1 × 1)

$\Rightarrow$ A : B : C = 6 : 3 : 1

$\Rightarrow$ Ratio of speed between A, B and C = 6 : 3 : 1

$\Rightarrow$ Ratio of time = $\left(\dfrac{1}{6}\right) : \left(\dfrac{1}{3}\right) : 1$

$\Rightarrow$ Ratio of time between A, B and C = 1 : 2 : 6

$\Rightarrow$ 6 unit = 54 min

$\Rightarrow$ 1 unit = 9 min

$\Rightarrow$ 2 unit = 18 min

$\Rightarrow$ So, time taken by B = t = 18 min

∴ Time taken by B = 18 min.

Hence, the correct option is (B).

26. Given:

Total distance = 150 km

Total time is taken = 15 hours

Formula used:

$$Speed = \frac{Distance}{Time}$$

For starting 10 hours travelled with 11.8 km/hr.

Distance = Speed × Time

⇒ 11.8 × 10

⇒ 118 km

Remaining distance

⇒ 150 – 118 = 32 km

Remaining Time

⇒ 15 – 10 = 5 hours

Speed to travel 32 km in 5 hours

$$⇒ \frac{32}{5}$$

⇒ 6.4 km/hr

∴ Speed to travel remaining distance is 6.4 km/hr.

Hence, the correct option is (D).

27. 3,7 and 11 are prime numbers. But 9 is not a prime number. 9 is square of 3.

Hence, the correct option is (C).

28. All the animals have 4 legs except for hen.

Hence, the correct option is (C).

29. All the languages except Urdu are written from left to right, While Urdu is written from right to left

Hence, the correct option is (C).

30. Middle Number is addition of First and Third Number.

⇒ 6 + 1 = 7

⇒ 3 + 2 = 5

⇒ 5 + 1 = 6

⇒ 2 + 1 = 3

Thus, 211 is odd one.

Hence, the correct option is (D).

31. Second number is the sum of all digits of first number except for option (A).

As shown:

8 + 5 + 7 = 20

2 + 5+ 9 = 16

7 + 1 + 8 = 16

6 + 7 +9 = 22

Hence, the correct option is (A).

32. Given,

The average weight of A, B and $C = 72kg$

The average weight of A and $B = 78kg$

The average weight of A and $C = 71kg$

$$Average = \frac{Sum\ of\ data}{Number\ of\ data}$$

Total weight of A, B and $C = (A + B + C) \times 3 = 72 \times 3 = 216kg$

Total weight of A and $B = (A + B) \times 2 = 78 \times 2 = 156kg$

Total weight of A and $C = (A + C) \times 2 = 71 \times 2 = 142kg$

Weight of $C =$ Total weight of A, B and $C -$ Total weight of A and $B = 216 - 156 = 60$

Weight of $A =$ Total weight of A and $C -$ Weight of $C = 142 - 60 = 82kg$

∴ The Weight of A is $82kg$.

Hence, the correct option is (B).

33. Given:

The age of the captain is 26 years and the wicket keeper's age is 29 years.

Let the average age of the whole team be x years.

According to the question,

$$∴ 11x - (26 + 29) = 9(x - 1)$$

$$⇒ 11x - 9x = 46$$

$$⇒ 2x = 46$$

$$⇒ x = 23$$

So, the average age of the team is 23 years.

Hence, the correct option is (A).

34. Let the five consecutive odd number be $a - 4, a - 2, a, a + 2, a + 4$

Sum of second and fifth number $= (a - 2 + a + 4)$

$$2a + 2 = 16 \times 2$$
$$a = 15$$

The average of 5 consecutive odd number is the middle number
$$= a = 15$$

Hence, the correct option is (C).

35. Elements are added one by one from left to right. The correct answer should be figure 1.
Hence, the correct option is (A).

36. The leaf is rotated through 45 degrees in clockwise order with alternating shallow and filled leaf. The answer figure should be figure 3.
Hence, the correct option is (C).

37. The element is moving from corner to corner in a clockwise order. The answer figure should be figure 3.
Hence, the correct option is (C).

38. Elements are deleted one by one beginning from top-left bar. Each line has two elements (circle) attached to it and each element is deleted one by one from left to right. The answer figure should be figure 1.
Hence, the correct option is (A).

39. The movement of arrows is from right to left in a set order. In the next step, it is inverted vertically and moves one step forward as shown.

The answer figure should be figure 4.
Hence, the correct option is (D).

40. $\dfrac{1}{-6}, \dfrac{2}{-12}, \dfrac{3}{-18}, \dfrac{4}{-24}, \dfrac{5}{-30}, \dfrac{6}{-36}, \dfrac{7}{-42}, \dfrac{8}{-48}$

Numerators are consecutive natural numbers and denominators are successive multiples of 6.

Hence, the correct option is (D).

41. Given that,

$$\frac{3.8}{1.25}$$

Multiplying by $\dfrac{8}{8}$ to make 10 in the denominator,

$$\Rightarrow \frac{3.8}{1.25} \times \frac{8}{8}$$

$$\Rightarrow \frac{30.4}{10}$$

$$\Rightarrow 3.04$$

Hence, the correct option is (B).

42. Given:

$$\left(\frac{3}{11} \times \frac{33}{6}\right) - \left(\frac{9}{4} \times \frac{12}{3}\right) + \left(\frac{5}{11} \times \frac{22}{10}\right)$$

$$= \left(\frac{3}{2}\right) - 9 + 1$$

$$= \left(\frac{3}{2}\right) - 8$$

$$= \left(\frac{3-16}{2}\right)$$

$$= \frac{-13}{2}$$

Hence, the correct option is (B).

43. Metals are good conductors of electricity and heat because the atoms in the metals form a matrix through which outer electrons can move freely. Instead of orbiting in their respective atoms, they form a huge collection of electrons that surround the positive nuclei of the interacting metal ions.

Hence, the correct option is (A).

44. The crystal of diamond shines due to total internal reflection. The faces of diamond are cut in such a way that whenever light falls on any of the face, the angle of incidence is greater than the critical angle. So, when light falls on diamond, repeated internal reflections occur. When this reflected light emerges out, diamond sparkles.

Hence, the correct option is (B).

45. We get average speed on dividing the total distance travelled by the total time taken. Average speed is a scalar quantity because it is obtained by dividing total distance travelled by total time taken which are scalar. The standard unit of average speed is meters/second.

Hence, the correct option is (A).

46. In the first equation of accelerated motion v=u+at, u represents the initial velocity of the body. Initial velocity is the velocity at time interval t=0 at which the motion of a body starts.

Hence, the correct option is (A).

47. Resistivity of a semiconductor decreases with an increase in temperature. This is because of the electrons in the valence band which gain sufficient thermal energies to reach the conduction band. As the number of electrons in the conduction band increases, conductivity increases and resistivity decreases.

For pure Silicon, the resistivity decreases with an increase in temperature.

Hence, the correct option is (A).

48.

- 'Amphan' made landfall in a part of West Bengal and Orissa in May 2020. It is an example of a Tropical cyclone.

- A tropical cyclone is a rapidly rotating storm system characterized by a low-pressure center, a closed low-level atmospheric circulation, strong winds, and a spiral arrangement of thunderstorms that produce heavy rain and/or squalls.

- It caused widespread damage in Eastern India, specifically West Bengal, Odisha, and in Bangladesh in May 2020.

Hence, the correct option is (A).

49. Here, the pattern is,

$$86 = (8 \times 6) + (8 + 6) = 48 + 14 = 62$$

Similarly,

$49 = (4 \times 9) + (4 + 9) = 36 + 13 = 49$

Thus, 49 is related to 49.

'Hence, the correct option is (B).

50. The pattern here is:

$62 = \dfrac{62}{2} = 31$

$31 \times 5 = 155$

Similarly,

$58 = \dfrac{58}{2} = 29$

$29 \times 5 = 145$

Thus, 58 is related to 145.

Hence, the correct option is (C).

51. Here, $21 : 3$ is given in the form of $7x : x$.

So, $574 = 7 \times ?$

$\Rightarrow ? = \dfrac{574}{7} = 82$

Hence, the correct option is (B).

52. Here, the pattern is:

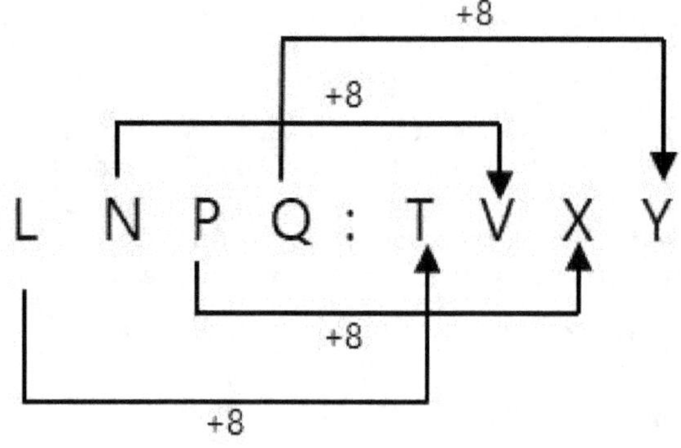

Similarly,

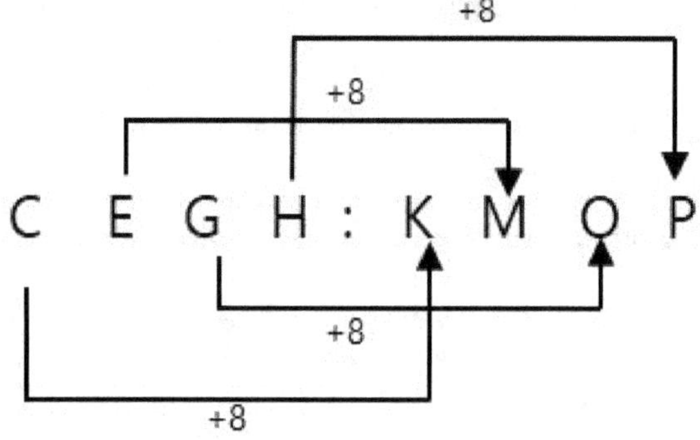

Thus, $CEGH$ is related to $KMOP$.

Hence, the correct option is (D).

53. Here, the pattern is:

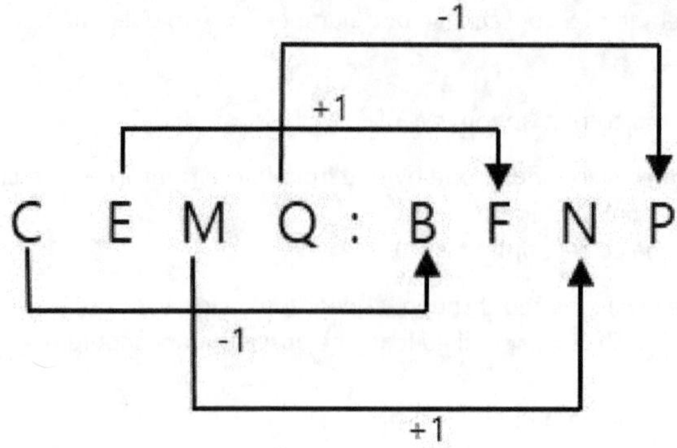

Similarly,

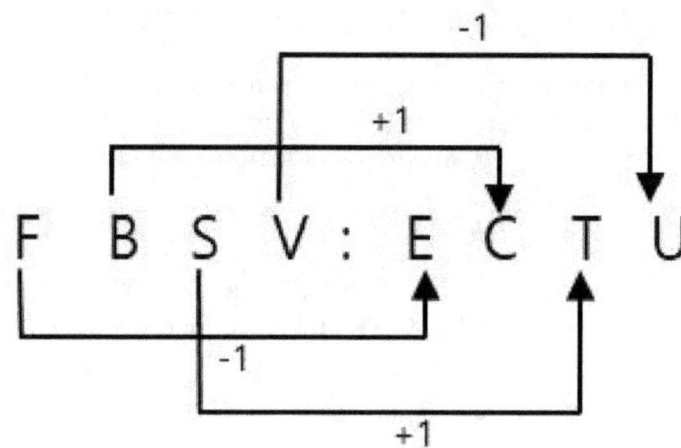

Thus, FBSV is related to ECTU.

Hence, the correct option is (B).

54. On counting the number of triangles in the given figure we find that there are 11 triangles in the given figure.

Hence, the correct option is (B).

55. Answer figure (A) in which question figure is hidden/embedded.

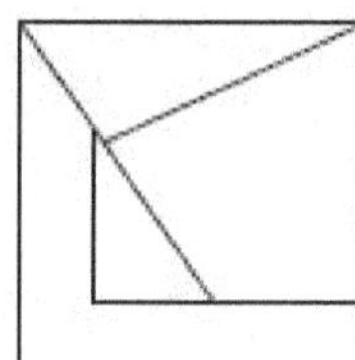

Hence, the correct option is (A).

56. The answer figure (C) is embedded in the question figure.

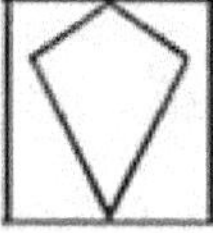

Hence, the correct option is (C).

57. The answer figure is not made up only by the components of the question figure is '(C)'.

Clearly, an arrow symbol is there in figure (C) which is not present in the question figure.

Hence, the correct option is (C).

58.

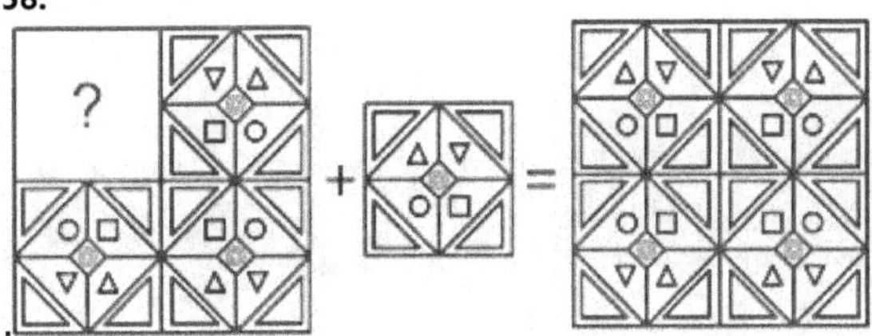

Hence, the correct option is (D).

59. Statement 1: Kabir Das' writings had a great influence on the Bhakti movement and include titles like Kabir Granthawali, Anurag Sagar, Bijak, and Sakhi Granth.

Statement 3: Kabir Das' ideologies were greatly influenced by Vaishnava saint Swami Ramananda who accepted Kabir as his disciple.

Statement 2: The major part of his work was collected by the fifth Sikh guru–Guru Arjan Dev.

Statement 4: Data Ganj Bakhsh was an 11th-century Persian Sunni Muslim mystic and theologian. While Kabir Das was a 15th-century Indian mystic poet.
Hence, the correct option is (A).

60. Archaeologists have discovered thousands of seals, mostly made of steatite, and occasionally of agate, chert, copper, faience, and terracotta, with beautiful figures of animals, such as unicorn bull, rhinoceros, tiger, elephant, bison, goat, and buffalo.
Hence, the correct option is (A).

61. The correct sentence is: "The box of paper clips "is" kept in the drawer."

Here, the box of clips is referred to as a single thing so we will use 'is' instead of 'are'.

We are referring to a specific box, so the use of 'the' before box is correct.

'Of' is used to define a relation.

'In' is used to define the location.

Hence, the correct option is (A).

62. The correct sentence will be: "Each student will have to carry his own lunch to the picnic."

In option (C), the preposition 'on' is incorrect and should be replaced with 'to' as 'to' is used to refer to a destination which is the picnic.

In option (A), 'each' is correct as it refers to each and every student.

In option (B), the pronoun 'his' is appropriately placed.

In option (D), 'will' is correct as it refers to an action in the future.

Hence, the correct option is (C).

63. Given,

$M_1 = 10$, $D_1 = 20$ days

$D_2 = 4$ days

Here M is number of men, and D is number of days.

As we know,

$M_1 \times D_1 = M_2 \times D_2$

$\Rightarrow 10 \times 20 = M_2 \times 4$

$\Rightarrow M_2 = \dfrac{200}{4} = 50$

$\therefore$ 50 men can complete the same work in 4 days.

Hence, the correct option is (C).

64. The ratio of times taken by A and $B = 1 : 3$

The time difference is $(3 - 1) = 2$ days while B take 3 days and A takes 1 day.

If the difference of time is 2 days, B takes 3 days.

If difference of time is 60 days, B takes $\left(\dfrac{3}{2} \times 60\right) = 90$ days.

So, A takes 30 days to do the work.

A's 1 day's work $= \dfrac{1}{30}$

B's 1 day's work $= \dfrac{1}{90}$

$(A + B)'s\,1$ day's work $= \left(\dfrac{1}{30} + \dfrac{1}{90}\right) = \dfrac{4}{90} = \dfrac{2}{45}$

$\therefore A$ and B together can do the work in $\dfrac{45}{2} = 22\dfrac{1}{2}$ days.

Hence, the correct option is (B).

65. Let the speed of slower bike be x km/hr.

Speed of faster bike $= x + 9$

Relative speed $= 2x + 9$

$\Rightarrow 2x + 9 = \dfrac{324}{4}$

$\Rightarrow 2x + 9 = 81$

$\Rightarrow x = 36$ km/hr

$\therefore$ The speed of slower bike be 36 km/hr.

Hence, the correct option is (B).

66. Quantity of milk $= \left(60 \times \dfrac{2}{3}\right)$ litres $= 40$ litres

Quantity of water in it $= (60 - 40)$ litres $= 20$ litres
New ratio $= 1 : 2$

Let quantity of water to be added further be x litres
Then, milk :
$= \dfrac{40}{20 + x}$

Now, $\dfrac{40}{20 + x} = \dfrac{1}{2}$

$\Rightarrow 20 + x = 80$

$\Rightarrow x = 60$

∴ Quantity of water to be added $= 60$ litres.
Hence, the correct option is (D).

67. Ratio of numbers $= \dfrac{1}{2}:\dfrac{2}{3}:\dfrac{3}{4}$

Difference between largest and smallest number $= 27$

Let The numbers are $\dfrac{x}{2}:\dfrac{2x}{3}:\dfrac{3x}{4}$

$= \dfrac{6x}{12}:\dfrac{8x}{12}:\dfrac{9x}{12}$

The difference:

$\left(\dfrac{9x}{12}-\dfrac{6x}{12}\right) = 27$

$\Rightarrow \dfrac{3x}{12} = 27$

$\Rightarrow x = 12 \times 9 = 108$

Smaller number $= \dfrac{6x}{12} = \dfrac{6\times108}{12} = 54$

Larger number $= \dfrac{9x}{12} = \dfrac{9\times108}{12} = 81$

So, the smaller number is 54

Hence, the correct option is (D).

68. Given the income of A is 60% less than that of B.

$\Rightarrow 60\% = \dfrac{3}{5}$

Let income of $B = 5x$

Income of $A = 5x - 3x = 2x$

Expenditure of A is equal to 60% of B's expenditure.

Now, $60\% = \dfrac{3}{5}$

Let Expenditure of $B = 5y$

Expenditure of $A = 3y$

A's income is equal to 70% of B's expenditure:

$\Rightarrow 2x = \left(\dfrac{7}{10}\right) \times 5y$

$\Rightarrow \dfrac{x}{y} = \dfrac{7}{4}$

Saving of $B = 5x - 5y = 5(x - y)$

Saving of $A = 2x - 3y$ Ratio of saving of B to A

$= \dfrac{5(x-y)}{2x-3y} = \dfrac{5\left(\frac{7}{4}y-y\right)}{2\left(\frac{7}{4}y\right)-3y}$

$= \dfrac{15y}{2y} = \dfrac{15}{2}$

So, $A:B = 2:15$.

Hence, the correct option is (B).

69. Chelsea has been awarded the Women's Super League title.

Aston Villa was declared the winner of the second-tier Women's Championship by England's Football Association (FA) on 5 June 2020.

Bottom-placed Liverpool, whose men's team are two wins away from securing a first top-flight crown in 30 years, will be relegated to the second-tier for the 2020-21 season.

Hence, the correct option is (A).

70. Selling price of car (SP)$= xRs$

Cost price of Car (CP) $= (0.8\text{x} + 600)\textbf{Rs}$

Profit percentage ($P\%$) $= 14\dfrac{2}{7}\%$

$SP = \dfrac{CP(100+P\%)}{100}$

$x = \dfrac{(0.8x+600)\left(100+\frac{100}{7}\right)}{100}$

$x = \dfrac{(0.8x+600)(800)}{7\times100}$

$700x = 640x + 480{,}000$

$x = 8{,}000$

Hence, the correct option is (B).

71. Given:

The price of the article in 1999 is 7200.

Profit and loss:

$\Rightarrow$ Price of the article in 1999 = 7200

$\Rightarrow$ Price of the article in 1998 $= Price \times \left(\dfrac{100}{100-loss}\right)$

$= (7200) \times \left(\dfrac{100}{90}\right) = 8000$

$\Rightarrow$ Price of the article in 1997 = (8000) $\times \left(\dfrac{100}{125}\right) = 6400$

$\Rightarrow$ Price of article in 1996 = (6400) $\times \left(\dfrac{3}{2}\right) = 9600$

∴ The required result will be 9600.

Hence, the correct option is (B).

72. Cheating at the time of selling = 14.28% = $\dfrac{1}{7}$

The shopkeeper gives 6 units instead of 7 units

Cheating at the time of buying = 28.57% = $\dfrac{2}{7}$

The shopkeeper gets 9 units instead of 7 units

Loss of the shopkeeper = 12.5% = $\dfrac{1}{8}$

The shopkeeper suffered loss of 1 unit in 8 units

The shopkeeper invested for (6 × 7 × 8) units and got (7 × 7 × 9) units

Profit % = $\left\{\dfrac{(441-336)}{336}\right\} \times 100 = 31.25$

∴ The Profit % of the shopkeeper is 31.25%.

Hence, the correct option is (A).

73.

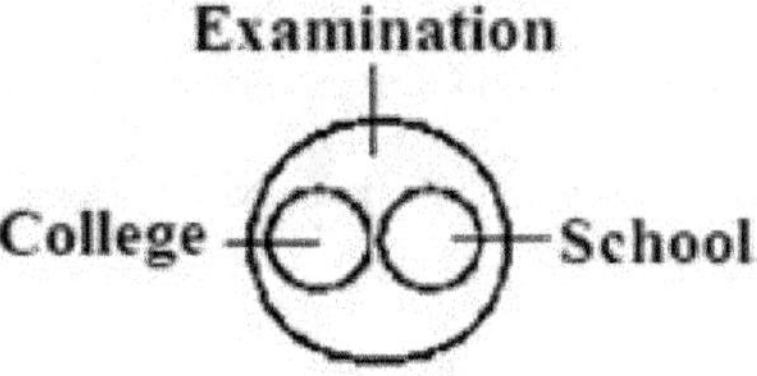

Hence, the correct option is (D).

74. The number of people who like billiards and chess can be represented by the numbers common to the triangle and the circle, Such numbers are 19.

Hence, the correct option is (B).

75. First, we do the preparation, then write the things according to it, and at the end, we get the results.

Option (A) includes all of the three.

Hence, the correct option is (A).

76. From the information, given in the question, we analyse,

All mothers are women and some mothers and some women may be engineers.

Hence, the correct option is (A).

77. The sequence followed is:

4. ERAS<u>E</u>

2. ERASE<u>R</u>

1. <u>H</u>EARER

5. <u>R</u>ACER

3. <u>S</u>HARE

Hence, the correct option is (A).

78. According to the dictionary:

1. L<u>i</u>eutenant

2. L<u>ig</u>ht

3. L<u>im</u>it

4. L<u>in</u>es

Hence, the correct option is (B).

79. The Reports of Rules Committees of the 10th Lok Sabha and Rajya Sabha adopted by the two Houses on 29 March 1993 paved the way for the setting up of the 17 departmentally related standing committees covering under their jurisdiction all the Ministries/Departments of the Union Government. The 17 departmentally related standing committees were formally constituted with effect from April 1993. Till 13th Lok Sabha, each of these standing committees used to consist of 45 members 30 nominated by the Speaker from amongst the members of Lok Sabha and 15 members nominated by the Chairman, Rajya Sabha from amongst the members of Rajya Sabha. So, statement 2 not correct. With re-structuring of DRSCs in July 2004, each DRSC consists of 31 members—21 from Lok Sabha and 10 from Rajya Sabha. So, statement 1 is not correct. There are 24 department-related standing committees (DRSCs). They are appointed for a maximum period of one year and the committees are reconstituted every year cutting across party lines. So, statement 3 is correct.

Functions:

- To consider the Demands for Grants of the related Ministries/Departments and report thereon.

- The report shall not suggest anything of the nature of cut motions.

- To examine Bills, pertaining to the related Ministries/Departments, referred to the Committee by the Chairman or the Speaker, as the case may be, and report thereon.

- To consider the annual reports of the Ministries/Departments and report thereon.

- To consider national basic long term policy documents presented to the Houses, if referred to the Committee by the Chairman or the Speaker, as the case may be, and report thereon.

- Provided that the Standing Committees shall not consider matters of day-to-day administration of the related Ministries/Departments.

Hence, the correct option is (B).

80. The correct answer is **everlasting**.

perpetual: never-ending or changing

everlasting: lasting forever or a very long time

Let's look at the meanings of the other given options:

- temporary- lasting for only a limited period of time; not permanent

- powerful- having great power or strength

- persuasive- good at persuading someone to do or believe something through reasoning or the use of temptation

Thus, from the given meanings, we find that perpetual and everlasting are synonyms.

Hence, the correct option is (C).

81. The correct answer is **demonstrate**.

exemplify: be a typical example of

demonstrate: give a practical exhibition and explanation of (how a machine, skill, or craftworks or is performed)

Let's look at the meanings of the other given options:

- devise- plan or invent (a complex procedure, system, or mechanism) by careful thought
- sympathize- feel or express sympathy
- ask for- put a question or seek an answer from someone

Thus, from the given meanings, we find that exemplify and demonstrate are synonyms.

Hence, the correct option is (D).

82. The correct answer is core.

crux: the decisive or most important point at issue

core: the central or most important part of something

Let's look at the meanings of the other given options:

- part- an element or constituent that belongs to something and is essential to its nature
- idea- a thought or suggestion as to a possible course of action
- tip- the pointed or rounded end or extremity of something slender or tapering

Thus, from the given meanings, we find that crux and core are synonyms.

Hence, the correct option is (A).

83. Let

$$X = 6\frac{1}{4}\% = 6\frac{1}{4}\% \text{ of } 1600$$

$$X = \frac{25}{4} \times \frac{1}{100} \times 1600 = 100$$

And $Y = 12\frac{1}{2}\% = \frac{25}{2} \times \frac{1}{100}$ of 800

$$Y = 100$$

According to the question:

$$X + Y = 200$$

Hence, the correct option is (B).

84. Let the number of girls be x.

∴ Number of boys = 2x

Total number of students = x + 2x = 3x

⇒ 135 = 3x

$$\therefore x = \frac{135}{3} = 45$$

Number of girls = 45

Number of boys = 45 × 2 = 90

Number of girls who failed in the examination = $45 \times \frac{1}{3} = 15$

Number of boys who failed in the examination = $90 \times \frac{1}{6} = 15$

Total number of students who failed in the examination = 15 + 15 = 30

Percentage of students who failed in the examination = $\frac{30}{135} \times 100 = 22.22\%$

∴ Percentage of students who passed the examination = (100 - 22.22)% = 77.8%

Hence, the correct option is (C).

85. According to the question:

$$\frac{3}{100} \times \frac{5}{100} \times \frac{10}{100} \times \frac{20}{100} \times 1,00,000$$

$$= 3$$

Hence, the correct option is (A).

86. The meaning of the given words:

- Flock: a number of birds of one kind feeding, resting, or travelling together.
- Drove: a herd or flock of animals being driven in a body.
- Fleet: a marshland creek, channel, or ditch.
- Bunch: a number of things, typically of the same kind, growing or fastened together.

Use of Collective Noun 'Flock' in the blank space of the sentence is appropriate.

Hence, the correct option is (D).

87. She was the **cynosure** of all eyes at the party.

The word 'cynosure' means- something that strongly attracts attention by its brilliance, interest, etc. The cynosure of all eyes, something serving for guidance or direction; a person or thing that is the center of attention or admiration.

Use of Noun 'cynosure' (attraction point) in the blank space of the sentence is appropriate.

Hence, the correct option is (D).

88. Ghaziabad is the **fastest growing** city in India.

The use of 'fastest growing' (Superlative degree) in the blank space of the sentence is appropriate.

Hence, the correct option is (D).

89. She **goes** for a walk every morning to the park.

As per the rule of subject-verb agreement, singular verb is used with singular subject.

The use of the singular verb 'goes' is appropriate in the space of the sentence.

Hence, the correct option is (B).

90.

The third figure in each row comprises parts that are not common to the first two figures.

Hence, the correct option is (D).

91.

In each row, the second figure is obtained from the first figure by adding two mutually perpendicular line segments at the centre and the third figure is obtained from the first figure by adding four circles outside the main figure.

Hence, the correct option is (B).

92.

In each row, the third figure comprises a black circle and only those line segments which are not common to the first and the second figures.

Hence, the correct option is (A).

93.

In each column, the second figure (middle figure) is obtained by removing the upper part of the first figure (uppermost figure) and the third figure (lowermost figure) is obtained by vertically inverting the upper part of the first figure.

Hence, the correct option is (C).

94.

The third figure in each row comprises the parts common to the first two figures.

Hence, the correct option is (C).

95. The above passage highlights the culture of goa.

Let us refer to the passage, "Skilled artisans reuse shells and coconut skins found on the beach to make stunning jewellery, frames, and showpieces for home decor".

From this line, it is clear that the coconut skins and shells are reused to make jewellery.

Hence, the correct option is (C).

96. Lets us refer to the passage, " Another festive favourite for the Goans is their beef and pork roasts that are a must on their Christmas men's which is best paired with Goa's famous brew Feni, made with fermented cashews".

From this line, it is clear that Feni is made with fermented cashew.

Hence, the correct option is (B).

97. Let us refer to the passage, " Reaping the benefits of its location, the most common occupation of locals is fishing".

From this line, it is clear that fishing is the common occupation of goans.

Hence, the correct option is (A).

98. Let us refer to the passage, "Goff Tolgadi and Shigmo are a couple of dance forms that are very local to the Goan community and are usually performed during the months of Spring, as an offering and jubilation which the season brings to the peasants and their crops. The Goff consists of weaving braids with various tints of colours and is often performed by the people residing in the Canacona Taluka of Goa".

From these lines, it is clear that weaving colourful braids is the characteristic of Goff tolgadi.

Hence, the correct option is (C).

99. Let us refer to the passage, "Food and drinks are an integral part of marking Goa's vibrant culture. Meals bring families together, and a staple is the combination of Goan fish curry and rice".

From these lines, it is clear that the staple food of goans is fish curry and rice.

Hence, the correct option is (D).

100. A male can be a cricketer or an actor, but an actor cannot be a cricketer.

Thus, the Venn diagram that best describes the above relationship is:

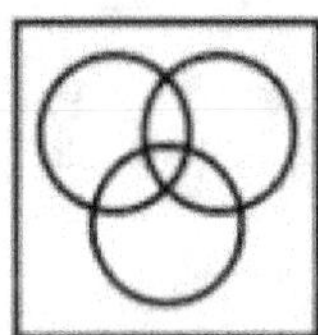

Hence, the correct option is (C).

Q.1 As on March 2018, which of the following is the India's fastest supercomputer?

[Super TET Paper - I, 2019]

A. Summit **B.** Sierra **C.** Mihir **D.** Pratyush

Q.2 Who has been appointed as the Principal Director General of the Press Information Bureau (PIB) in August 2022?

A. Ravi Semwal **B.** Anand Pandey
C. Priya Chaudhary **D.** Satyendra Prakash

Q.3 For the first time in its 100-year-old history, Dehradun's Rashtriya Indian Military College (RIMC) will induct girls. How many girls cadets are set to join Rashtriya Indian Military College in July 2022?

A. 3 **B.** 5 **C.** 7 **D.** 9

Q.4 Who has been appointed as the new brand ambassadors for My11Circle, fantasy sports platform, in March 2022?

A. Shubman Gill and Shreyas Iyer
B. Devdutt Padikkal and Mayank Agarwal
C. Shreyas Iyer and Ruturaj Gaikwad
D. Shubman Gill and Ruturaj Gaikwad

Q.5 Which of the following has launched its Digital Exchange Traded Fund in March 2022?

A. Axis Mutual Fund
B. Kotak Mutual Fund
C. ICICI Prudential Mutual Fund
D. Tata Mutual Fund

Q.6 Shikha invested a total of Rs. 1500 in two different schemes offering simple interest of 6% and 4% respectively. In two years' time, the scheme offering higher interest rate gives Rs. 100 more interest than the scheme offering the lower rate. What was the ratio of amount invested at higher interest rate to the other amount?

A. 4 : 15 **B.** 11 : 4 **C.** 4 : 11 **D.** 4 : 15

Q.7 A amount at the simple interest at $\dfrac{27}{2}\%$ per annum amounts to Rs 2502.50 after 4 years. Find the sum?

A. Rs. 1345 **B.** Rs. 1625 **C.** Rs. 2502 **D.** Rs. 1825

Q.8 A person owned ₹ 800 from the bank for 2 years at a rate of compound interest 5% per annum. The amount he would pay to bank would be

A. ₹ 8820 **B.** ₹ 8800 **C.** ₹ 8810 **D.** ₹ 8815

Q.9 Select the word which means the same as the group of words given.

A solution for all difficulties or diseases.

[SSC Sub Inspector (CPO), 2019]

A. Medication **B.** Treatment
C. Remedy **D.** Panacea

Q.10 Select the word which means the same as the group of words given.

Branch of physics dealing with the properties of sound.

[SSC Sub Inspector (CPO), 2019]

A. Mechanics **B.** Radiation
C. Acoustics **D.** Audition

Q.11 Choose the option that is the passive form of the sentence.

The little puppy chewed my new slippers.

[SSC Sub Inspector (CPO), 2019]

A. My new slippers were chewing the little puppy.
B. My new slippers can be chewed by the little puppy.
C. My new slippers were chewed by the little puppy.
D. My new slippers are being chew by the little puppy.

Q.12 Choose the option that is the passive form of the sentence.

Give the command.

[SSC Sub Inspector (CPO), 2019]

A. Let the command be given.
B. You can give the command.
C. The command can be given.
D. The command should be give by you.

Q.13 Which country is to play host to the ICC Under -19 World Cup 2020 tournament?

A. England **B.** New Zealand
C. South Africa **D.** Zimbabwe

Q.14 Ramsar Convention refers to the conservation of __________.

A. Deserts **B.** Wetlands
C. Agriculture lands **D.** Forest land

Q.15

Direction: Arrange the words given below in a meaningful sequence.

1. Key 2. Door 3. Lock 4. Room 5. Switch on

A. 5, 1, 2, 4, 3 **B.** 4, 2, 1, 5, 3
C. 1, 3, 2, 4, 5 **D.** 1, 2, 3, 5, 4

Q.16 Direction: Arrange the words given below in a meaningful sequence.

1. Income 2. Status 3. Education 4. Well-being 5. Job

A. 3, 1, 5, 2, 4 **B.** 1, 3, 2, 5, 4
C. 1, 2, 5, 3, 4 **D.** 3, 5, 1, 2, 4

Q.17 The market price of a car was Rs. 9,40,000. Mr. Suman bought the same for Rs. 8,46,000. What was the discount?

A. Rs. 12,000 **B.** Rs. 13,000
C. Rs. 94,000 **D.** Rs. 84,000

Q.18 Raghavan purchase a scooter at $\dfrac{13}{15}$ of its selling price and sold it at 12% more than its selling price. His gain is:

A. 20%   **B.** $29\frac{3}{13}\%$ **C.** 30%   **D.** $38\frac{1}{13}\%$

Q.19 The cost price of 20 articles is the same as the selling price of x articles. If the profit is 25%, then the value of x is:

A. 15   **B.** 16   **C.** 18   **D.** 25

Q.20 It takes 10 hours for a person to travel a distance. If he reduces his speed by 20%, then what is the percentage increase in the time taken to cover the same distance?

[UP Police Sub Inspector, 2017]

A. 33.33%

B. 20%

C. 25%

D. Can not be determined

Q.21 A helicopter covers a certain distance at a speed of 180 km/h in 6 hours. To cover the same distance in $\dfrac{10}{3}$ hours, at what speed will it has to travel?

[UP Police Sub Inspector, 2017]

A. 360 km/h   **B.** 344 km/h
C. 315 km/h   **D.** 324 km/h

Q.22 Two trains run simultaneously, one of which is traveling from place C to B and the other is traveling from place B to C. After meeting, the two trains arrive at their destinations in 4 hours and 9 hours respectively. Find the ratio of their speed.

[UP Police Sub Inspector, 2017]

A. 4 : 3   **B.** 4 : 5   **C.** 3 : 2   **D.** 3 : 4

Q.23 A train is moving at a speed of 72 km/h. If the length of the train is 220 meters, then how long will it take to cross the 330 metre long platform?

[UP Police Sub Inspector, 2017]

A. 48.5 seconds   **B.** 11 seconds
C. 16.5 seconds   **D.** 27.5 seconds

Q.24 Three of the following four letter-clusters are alike in a certain way and one is different. Pick the odd one out.

A. TGL   **B.** DWB   **C.** UFK   **D.** KQU

Q.25 Four pairs of numbers have been given, out of which three are alike in some manner, while one is different. Choose out the odd one.

A. 17 : 306   **B.** 21 : 420   **C.** 13 : 182   **D.** 19 : 380

Q.26 Four words are given in the given question, three of them are similar in some way and one is different. Find the odd one.

A. Lion   **B.** Dog   **C.** Buffalo   **D.** Cow

Q.27 Pick the odd one out:

A. 257   **B.** 358   **C.** 224   **D.** 116

Q.28 Three of the following four words are alike in a certain way and one is different. Pick the odd word out.

A. Wheel   **B.** Bat
C. Cricket Ball   **D.** Compact Disc

Q.29 The average of 17 numbers is 7. If one number is excluded, the average becomes 4. What is the excluded number?

A. 21   **B.** 55   **C.** 24   **D.** 20

Q.30 The average height of a family of three members is 140 cm and when two more members A and B added to that family, the average height is increased by 8 cm. If A is 36 cm taller than B, then what is the height of B?

A. 138 cm   **B.** 142 cm   **C.** 140 cm   **D.** 144 cm

Q.31 The sum of marks obtained by Aniket in Mathematics and Science is 100 more than his English marks. The average score of all three subjects is 60. How many marks does she get in English?

A. 60

B. 40

C. 80

D. Statistics are incomplete

Q.32 Worker A takes 8 hours to do a job. Worker B takes 10 hours to do a job. How long should it take both A and B, working together to do the same job?

A. $\dfrac{4}{9}$ **B.** $2\frac{4}{9}$ **C.** $3\frac{4}{9}$ **D.** $4\frac{4}{9}$

Q.33 Ragini and Raghav can make a carpet respectively in 3 days and 12 days more than the time taken if both of them worked together. In how many days can Ragini alone make the carpet.

A. 7   **B.** 10   **C.** 9   **D.** 18

Q.34 If 24 men and 6 women can complete a work in 10 days while 6 men and 6 women can complete the same work in 12 days. In how many days 4 men and 1 women will complete the work?

[AFCAT, 2021]

A. 45 days   **B.** 18 days   **C.** 60 days   **D.** 48 days

Q.35 A person spends $\dfrac{2}{7}$th of his salary on rent, $\dfrac{1}{4}$th of the salary on education, and the remaining on food. If he spends Rs. 2800 on his rent then what is the amount he spends on food?

A. 4550   **B.** 4200   **C.** 4500   **D.** 4000

Q.36 What is the value of 2047.235+231+21.2323?

A. 2299.4673   **B.** 2199.4673
C. 2219.4673   **D.** 2200.4673

Q.37 Which of the following is the least?

$$\frac{17}{13},\ \frac{18}{15},\ \frac{15}{9},\ \frac{12}{7}$$

A. $\dfrac{17}{13}$ **B.** $\dfrac{18}{15}$ **C.** $\dfrac{15}{9}$ **D.** $\dfrac{12}{7}$

Q.38 Which of the following diseases are caused by the consumption of water contaminated by mercury and nitrate?

[UPSC Central Armed Police Forces AC, 2017]

A. Minamata disease and Osteoporosis
B. Osteoporosis and Blue Baby Syndrome
C. Minamata disease and Blue Baby Syndrome
D. Osteoporosis and Minamata disease

Q.39 Which one of the following polymers is made of protein?
[UPSC Central Armed Police Forces AC, 2017]

A. Rubber   **B.** Cotton   **C.** Wool   **D.** Jute

Q.40 Which one of the following artificial sweeteners is modified sugar?
[UPSC Central Armed Police Forces AC, 2017]

A. Aspartarne   **B.** Saccharin
C. Sucralose   **D.** Alitame

Q.41 Which of the following helps in blood clotting?
A. Vitamin A   **B.** Vitamin D
C. Vitamin K   **D.** Folic acid

Q.42 Which of the following aquatic animals does NOT have gills?
A. Octopus   **B.** Squid
C. Clown fish   **D.** Whale

Q.43 Who is the supreme Commander of the Indian Armed Forces ?
A. President
B. Prime Minister
C. Defense Minister
D. Longest serving Chief to Staff

Q.44 Arrange the layer of the atmosphere from top to bottom.
A. Troposphere - Stratosphere - Mesosphere - Ionosphere
B. Ionosphere - Troposphere - Stratosphere - Mesosphere
C. Ionosphere - Mesosphere - Stratosphere - Troposphere
D. Troposphere - Stratosphere - Ionosphere - Mesosphere

Ques (45-46):Direction: In the following question, the given sentence has four parts marked P, Q, R, and S. Choose the part of the sentence with the error and mark it as your answer. If there is no error, mark 'No error (S)' as your answer.

Q.45 We have issued (P) / a order seeking immediate (Q) / printing of revised price tag. (R) / No error (S)
[SSC Sub Inspector (CPO), 2018], [SSC Sub Inspector (CPO), 2017]

A. P   **B.** Q   **C.** R   **D.** S

Q.46 Earth's deserts (P) / is a land of extremes,(Q) / constantly pushing life to the limit. (R) / No error (S)
[SSC Sub Inspector (CPO), 2018], [SSC Sub Inspector (CPO), 2017]

A. P   **B.** Q   **C.** R   **D.** S

Q.47 Priyamvada Mohanty is associated with which classical dance form?
A. Kathakali   **B.** Bharatanatyam
C. Odissi   **D.** Koodiyattam

Q.48 Mrinalini Sarabhai is associated with which classical dance form?
A. Kathakali   **B.** Bharatanatyam

C. Koodiyattam   **D.** Kutti Attam

Q.49 With reference to Ashokan inscriptions, consider the following statements:
1. Rummindei pillar edict mentioned about the tax exemption of Lumbini.
2. Kandhar inscription was carved in Aramaic language.
3. The second rock edict mentioned names of the Kerelaputras.
Which of the statement given above is/are correct?
A. 1,2 and 3   **B.** 3 only
C. 1 and 2 only   **D.** 1 and 3 only

Q.50 Which answer figure will complete the pattern in the following question figure?

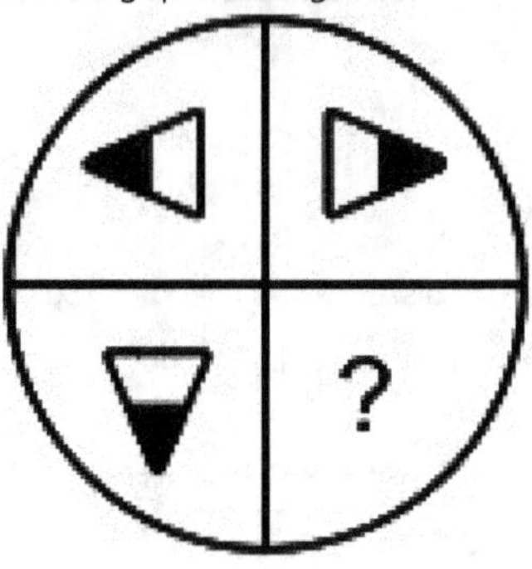

[AFCAT, 2021]

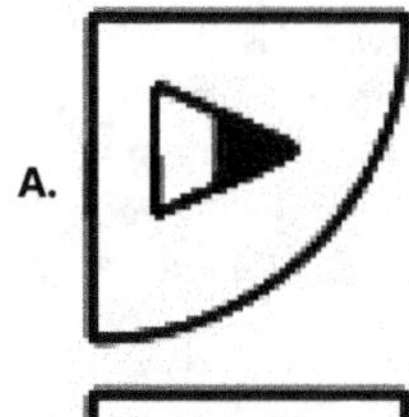
A.

B.

C.

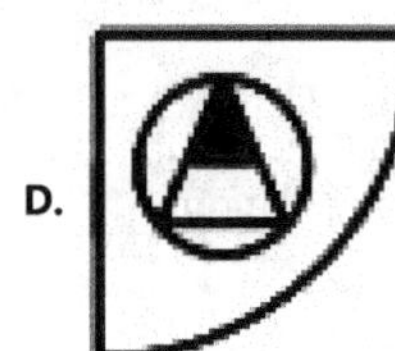
D.

Q.51 Select the option in which the given figure is embedded.

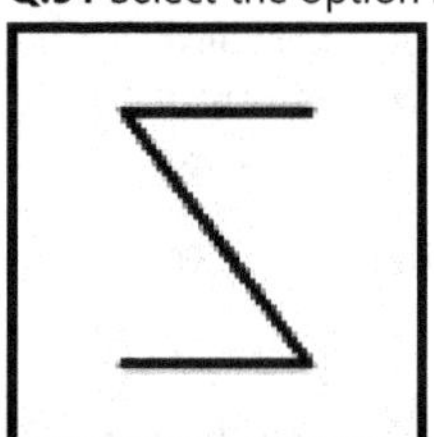

[SSC MTS, 2019], [SSC Constable (GD), 2019], [SSC Stenographer Grade C & D, 2019]

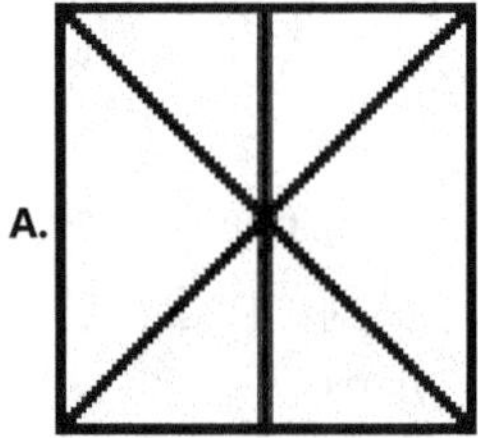
A.

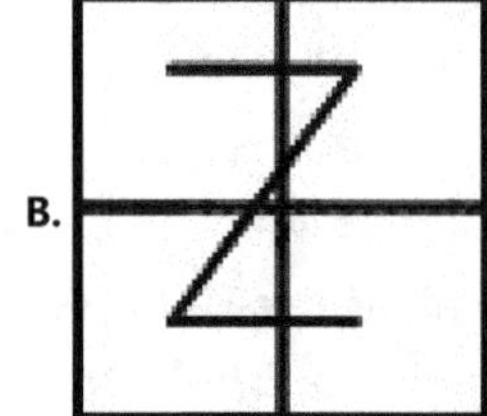
B.

C.

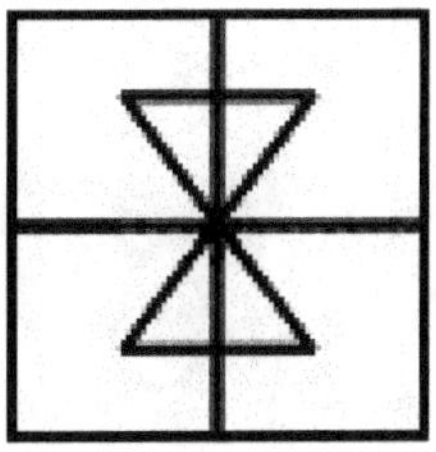

D.

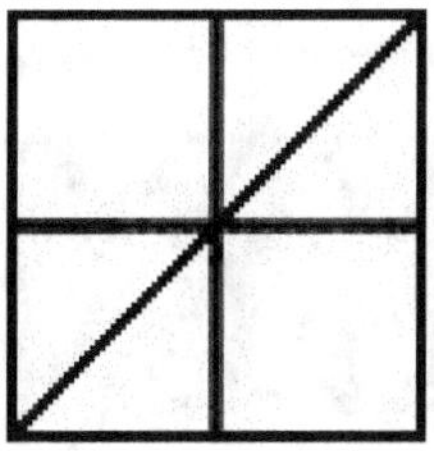

Q.52 Find out the alternative figure which contains question figure as its part.

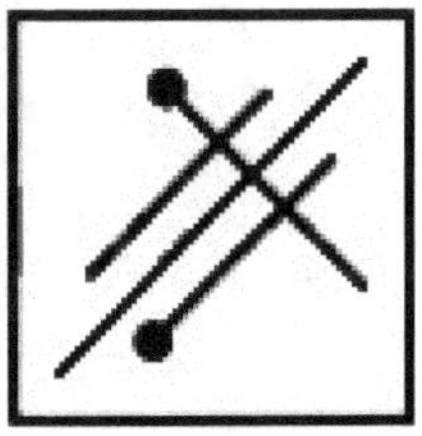

A.

B.

C.

D.

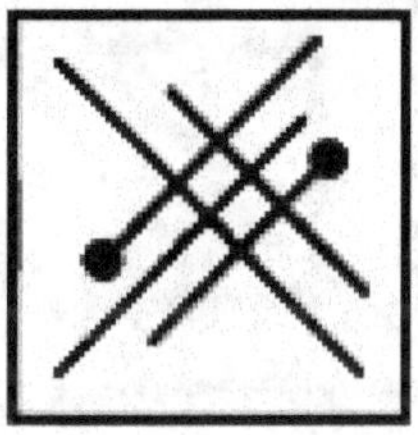

A.

B.

C.

D.

Q.53 From the given answer figures, select the one in which the question figure is hidden/embedded? (rotation is not allowed)

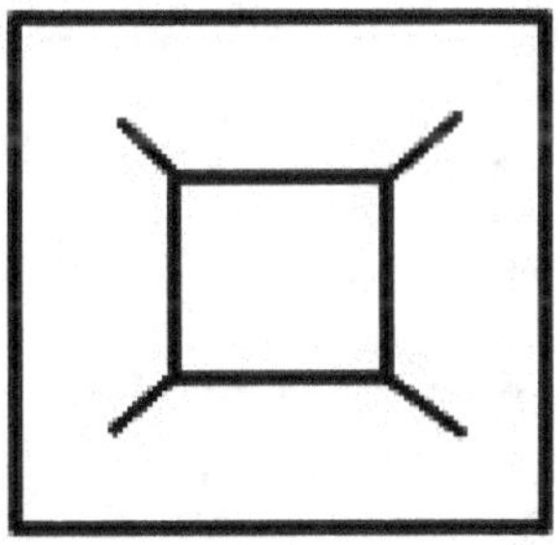

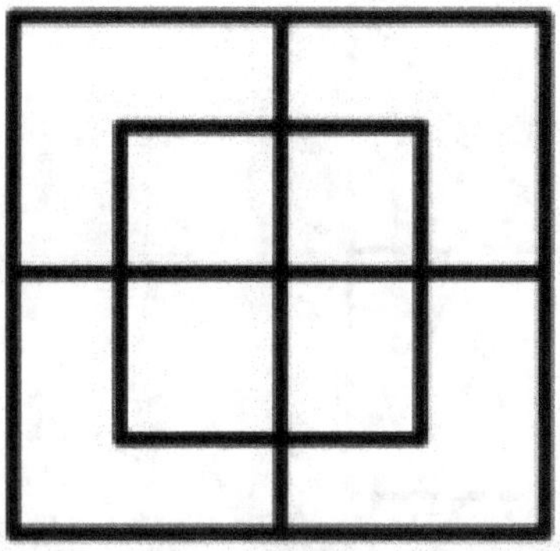

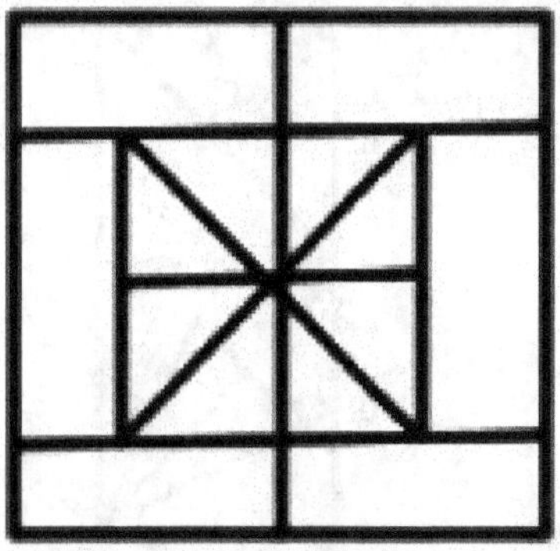

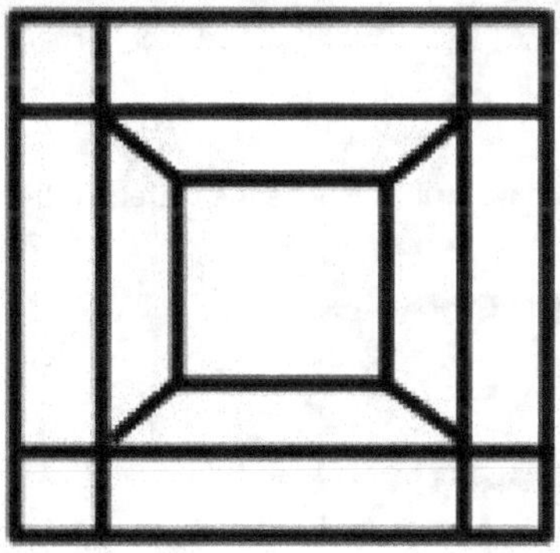

Q.54 Which answer figure will complete the pattern in the question figure?

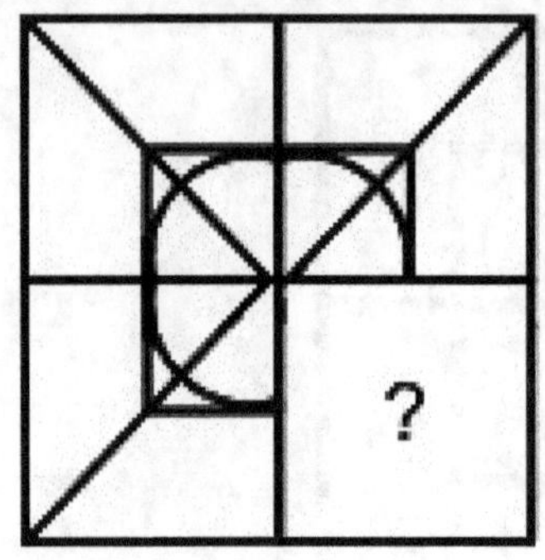

[UP Police Constable, 2019]

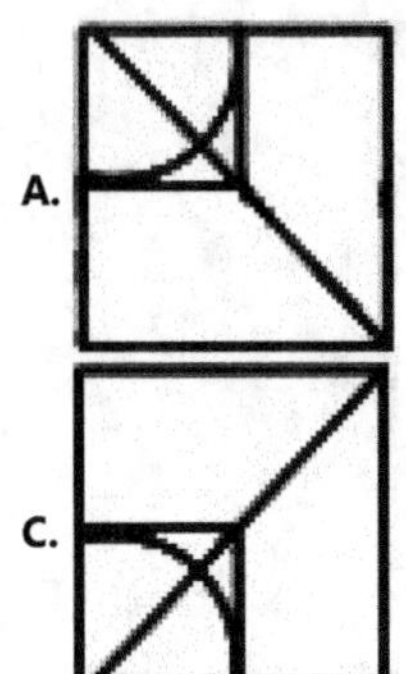

A.

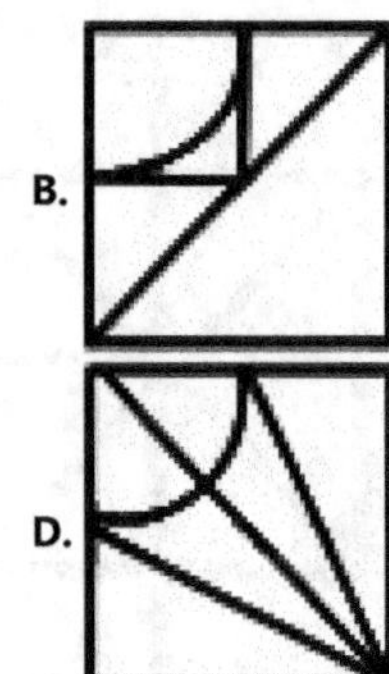

B.

C.

D.

A.

B.

C.

D.

Q.55 If the numerator and denominator of a fraction are decreased by 2 then the ratio becomes $2:1$ and if the numerator is increased by 4 and the denominator by 3 then the ratio becomes $5:3$ then what is the original fraction?

A. $256:81$ **B.** $16:9$ **C.** $4:3$ **D.** $2:1$

Q.56 A 48 litres solution contains liquids water and milk in the ratio $3:5$. How much amount of milk is to be added so that amount of milk is 70% of the new solution?

A. 12   **B.** 18   **C.** 20   **D.** 52

Q.57 The ratio of the father's age to his son's age is 8 : 5. The product of their age is 1440. The ratio of their ages after 6 years will be:

A. 2 : 1   **B.** 3 : 2   **C.** 11 : 6   **D.** 13 : 9

Q.58 Which answer figure will complete the pattern in the question figure?

[UP Police Constable, 2019]

Q.59 Find out the alternative figure which contains figure (X) as its part.

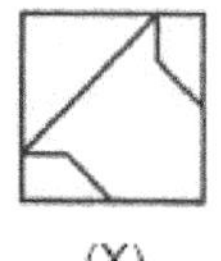

A. A   **B.** B   **C.** C   **D.** D

Q.60 From the given answer figures, select the one in which the question figure is hidden/embedded.

Question figure:

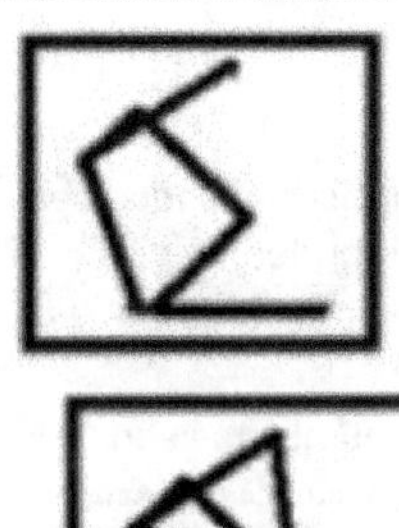

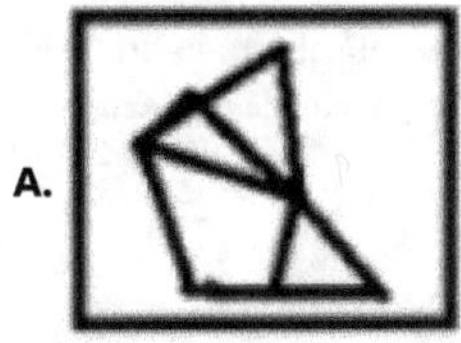

A. 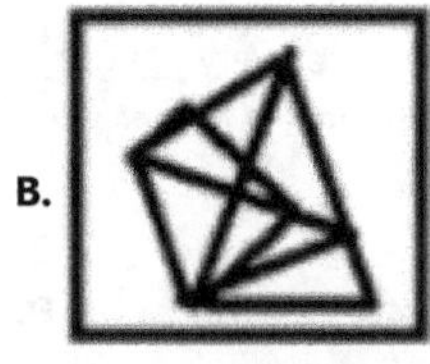

B.

C. **D.** 

Q.61

Direction: Find out the alternative figure which contains figure (X) as its part.

   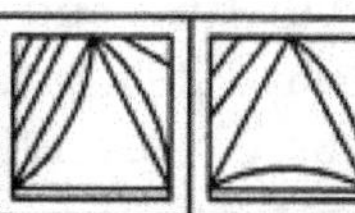

A. 1 **B.** 2 **C.** 3 **D.** 4

Q.62

Find out the alternative figure which contains figure (X) as its part.

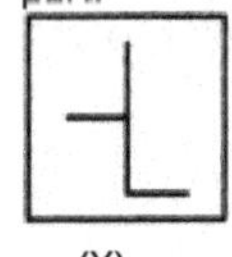 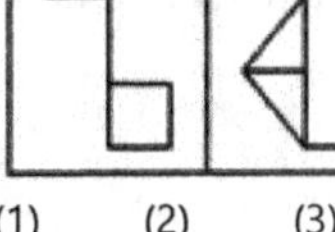 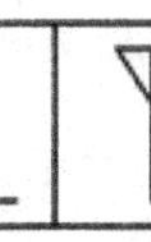 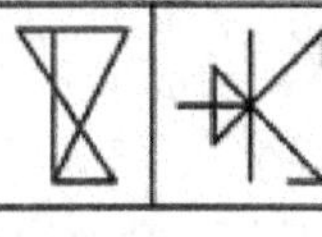

(X) (1) (2) (3) (4)

A. 1 **B.** 2 **C.** 3 **D.** 4

Q.63 Which one of the following venn diagrams correctly illustrates the relationship among the classes: Carrot, Food, Vegetable?

A. 

B. 

C. 

D. 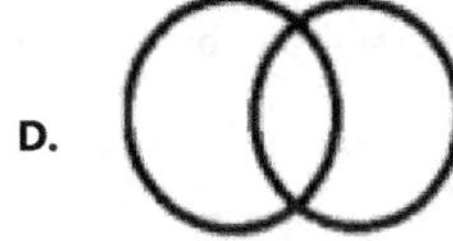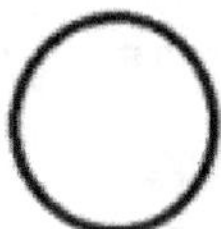

Q.64 Direction: Based upon the items given, logically draw the venn diagrams according to the relation between them.

Men, Authors, Teachers:

A.  **B.** 

C.  **D.** 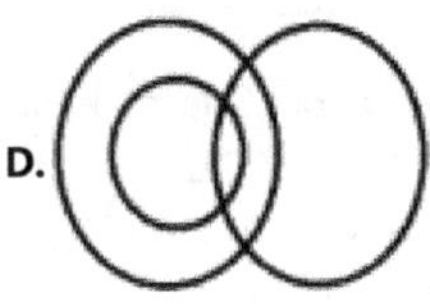

Q.65 Identify the diagram that best represents the relationship among classes given below:

Apple, Fruit, Banana

A. 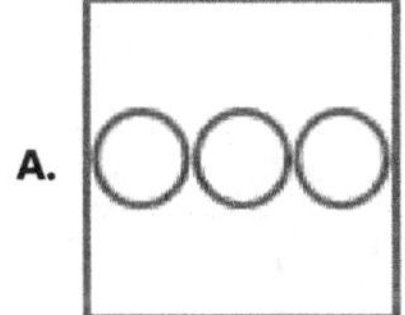 **B.** 

C. 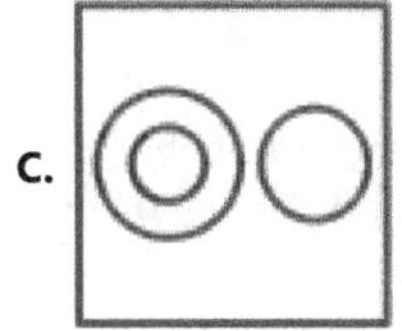 **D.** 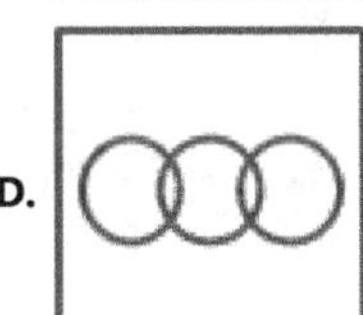

Q.66 Select the option that correctly represents the relationship among the following:

Politician, Officer, Woman

A. 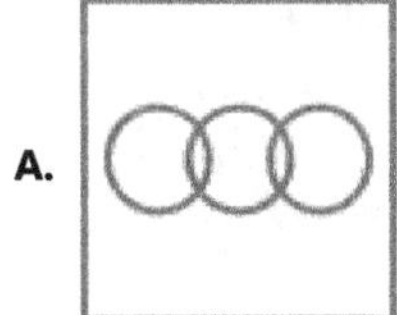 **B.** 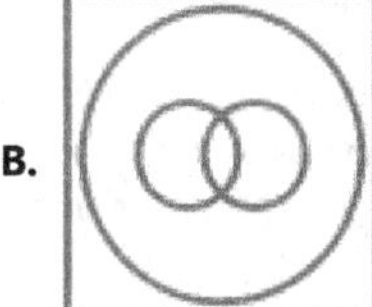

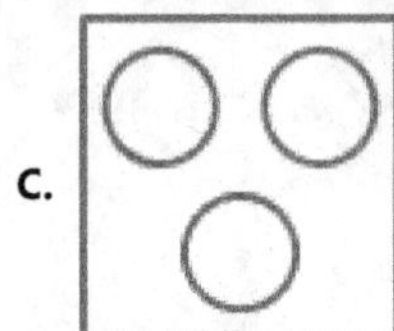

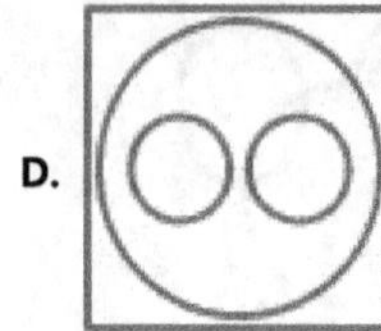

Q.67 Select the option that correctly represents the relationship among the following:

Nitrogen, Liquid, Non-metal

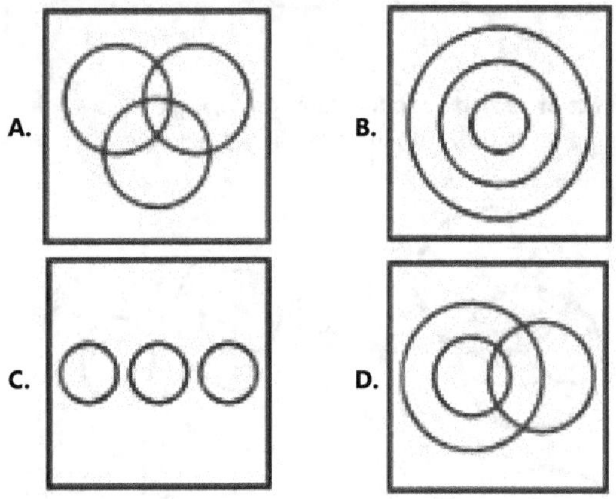

Q.68 Direction: Select the most appropriate meaning of the given idiom.

Why must you look a <u>gift horse in the mouth</u>?

A. Welcome a gift

B. Find fault with a gift

C. Be fastidious

D. Examine a gift carefully

Q.69 Direction: Select the most appropriate meaning of the given idiom.

Dowry is a <u>burning question</u> of the day.

A. A widely debated issue

B. A dying issue

C. A relevant problem

D. An irrelevant issue

Q.70 Consider the following statements:

1. The 7th Justice Ministers' Meeting of Shanghai Cooperation Organisation (SCO) the Member States to be hosted by Union Law Minister.

2. The SCO Secretariat, based in Shanghai, is the main permanent executive body of the SCO.

Which of the following statements is/are correct?

A. 1 only

B. 2 only

C. Both 1 and 2

D. Neither 1 nor 2

Q.71 Direction: The following sentence consists an underlined word(s) followed by four options. Select the option that is nearest in meaning to the underlined word and mark your response accordingly.

Each child develops his/her <u>competency</u> based on the contexts and the inputs for learning.

[Officers Training Academy (OTA), 2021], [Indian Military Academy (IMA), 2021]

A. capability

B. thinking

C. knowledge

D. ideal

Q.72 Direction: The following sentence consists an underlined word(s) followed by four options. Select the option that is nearest in meaning to the underlined word and mark your response accordingly.

He appears to be very <u>haughty</u>, but he is a humble person.

[Officers Training Academy (OTA), 2021], [Indian Military Academy (IMA), 2021]

A. tough

B. modest

C. arrogant

D. knowledgeable

Q.73 Direction: The following sentence consists an underlined word(s) followed by four options. Select the option that is nearest in meaning to the underlined word and mark your response accordingly.

The newly appointed secretary is <u>industrious.</u>

[Officers Training Academy (OTA), 2021], [Indian Military Academy (IMA), 2021]

A. diligent

B. knowledgeable

C. indolent

D. insincere

Q.74 800 is first increased by 10% and then it is again increased by 20%. What is the final value?

A. 1034   **B.** 1140   **C.** 1056   **D.** 1086

Q.75 Find the approximate value of the following question.

$$67\% \text{ of } 801 - 231.17 = ? - 23\% \text{ of } 789$$

A. 490   **B.** 440   **C.** 540   **D.** 590

Q.76 A discount of 8% on the marked price of a bat enables a man to get a ball of worth Rs. 256 for free. how much did the man pay for the bat?

A. Rs. 3200   **B.** Rs. 2856   **C.** Rs. 2944   **D.** Rs. 3000

Ques (77-80):Direction: Choose an appropriate word from the options to suitably fill the blank in the sentence below so that the sentence makes sense, both grammatically and contextually.

Q.77 He currently resides in Raipur with his wife, daughter, and a mighty _______ of cats.

A. flock   **B.** clowder   **C.** sloth   **D.** pack

Q.78 Do you have ____ books focusing on this war?

A. some

B. any

C. the

D. None of these

Q.79 The new laws are ________ and will not solve the real crime issue.

A. Rational

B. Preposterous

C. Inventive

D. Perceptive

Q.80 Select the most appropriate option to fill blank number (3).

[SSC Stenographer Grade C & D, 2019]

A. mistake   **B.** crime   **C.** problem   **D.** mischief

Ques (81-85):Direction: Select a suitable figure from the four alternatives that would complete the figure matrix.

Q.81

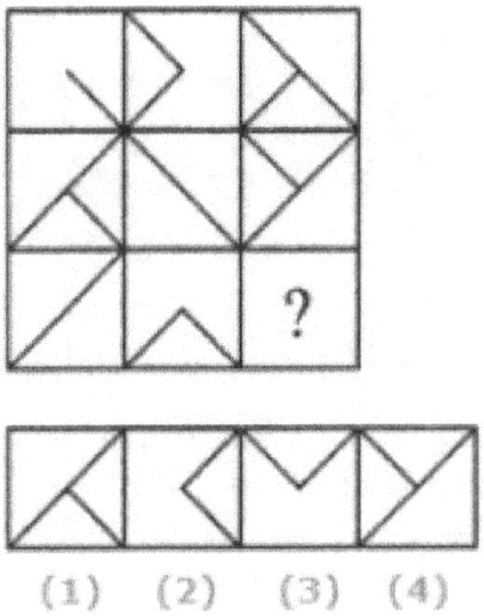

(1) (2) (3) (4)

A. 1   **B.** 2   **C.** 3   **D.** 4

Q.82

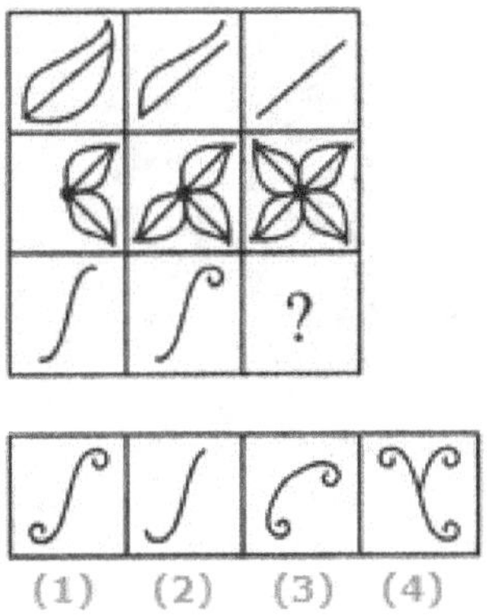

(1) (2) (3) (4)

[UP Police Sub Inspector, 2021]

A. 1   **B.** 2   **C.** 3   **D.** 4

Q.83

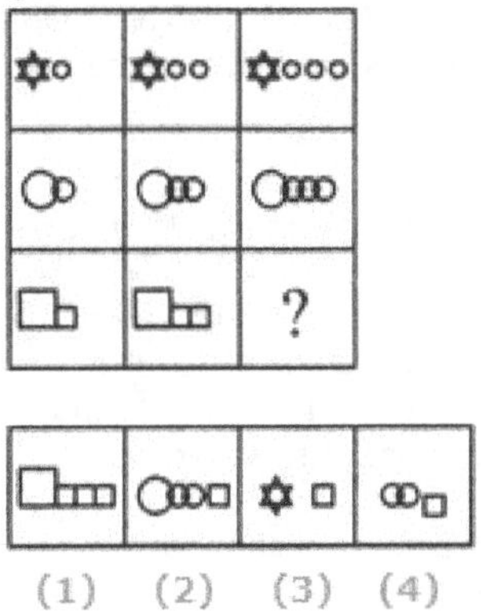

(1) (2) (3) (4)

[UP Police Sub Inspector, 2021]

A. 1   **B.** 2   **C.** 3   **D.** 4

Q.84

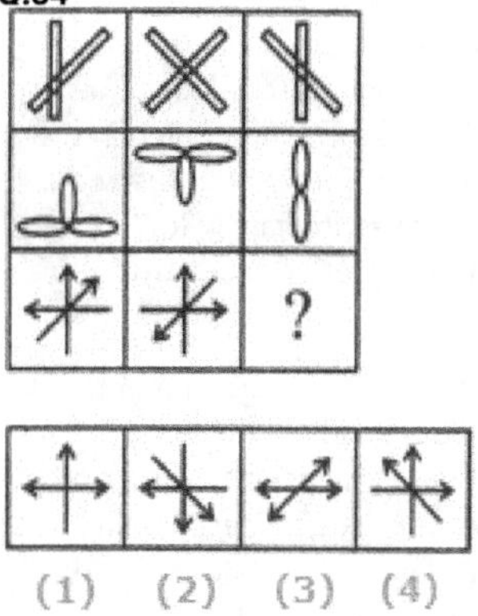

(1) (2) (3) (4)

[Telangana Police Constable, 2015]

A. 1   **B.** 2   **C.** 3   **D.** 4

Q.85

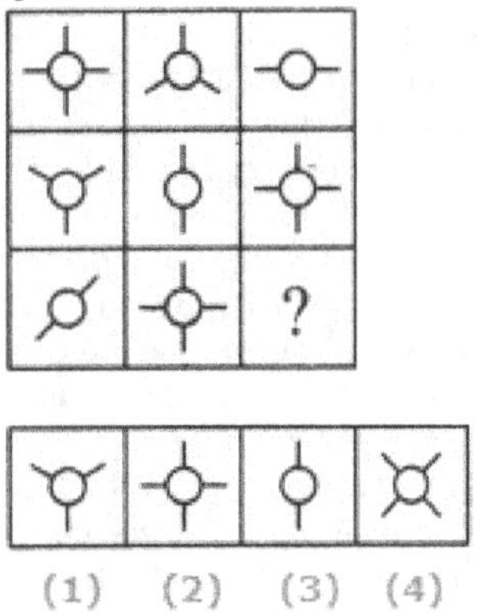

(1) (2) (3) (4)

[UP Police Sub Inspector, 2021]

A. 1   **B.** 2   **C.** 3   **D.** 4

Ques (86-90):Direction: In each of the following questions, select the related word from the given alternatives.

Q.86 Soldier : Regiment : : Horse : ?
A. Navy   **B.** Fleet   **C.** Cavalry   **D.** Herd

Q.87 Unfeign : Scrupulous :: Recompense : ?
A. Pillage   **B.** Peculiar
C. Vehemence   **D.** Restoration

Q.88 Predict : Forecast :: Postpone : ?
A. Adjourn   **B.** Expedite   **C.** Hasten   **D.** Maintain

Q.89 Myopia : Eyes :: Pyorrhea : ?
A. Nose   **B.** Ears   **C.** Teeth   **D.** Skin

Q.90 Pillage : Redeem
A. Palpable : Intangible
B. Emerge : Leak
C. Modesty : Diffidence
D. Inferior : Trivial

Ques (91-95):Direction: Read the passage and answer the following questions.

Born to Vladimir Aksyonovich Tereshkova, a sergeant in the Soviet Army, and Yelena Fyodorovna Tereshkova in Yaroslavl Oblast, Russia, on March 6, 1937, Valentina Tereshkova was the second among three children. Tereshkova's father died in the Finnish Winter War during World War II, when she was two years old. After that, her mother moved the family to Yaroslavl, seeking better employment opportunities and took up a job at the Krasny Perekop cotton mill.

Tereshkova enrolled at school in 1945 at the age of eight. In 1953, she left school and began working but continued education by correspondence courses. Later, she lived with her grandmother in Yaroslavl and worked as a trainee in a tire factory. In 1955, to help her family further, she started working as a loom operator in a nearby textile mill. During that time, she graduated from the Light Industry Technical School. Tereshkova developed an interest in parachuting quite early and trained in skydiving at the local aeroclub, making her first jump at age 22, on May 21, 1959.

While still working as a textile worker, she trained as a competitive parachutist. She also joined the local Komsomol (a Communist Youth League) in Yaroslavl and served as its secretary in 1960 as well as in 1961. She became a member of the Communist Party in 1962. Thanks to her training in parachuting, Tereshkova was among the five women who were selected for the cosmonaut programme in 1961. After Yuri Gagarin's historic space trip, the Soviet government was keen to send women to space. Tereshkova fitted the bill despite the lack of any training for the space programme. In 1963, Tereshkova was part of a second double flight that involved handling spacecraft like Vostok 5 and Vostok 6. She attended an extensive 18-month programme wherein the candidates learned the nuances of space travel. She was chosen to pilot Vostok 6. Cosmonaut Valery Bykovsky took off on Vostok 5 on June 14, 1963, and two days later, Tereshkova too blasted off.

She logged more than 70 hours in space and made 48 orbits of the Earth. On June 19, 1963, Tereshkova's spacecraft re-entered the Earth's atmosphere and she successfully parachuted for 20,000 feet. After her tryst with space, she studied at Zhukovsky Air Force Academy. She graduated as a cosmonaut engineer and earned a doctorate in engineering. From 1966 and 1991, she remained an active member of the USSR Supreme Soviet. Tereshkova worked for the Soviet Women's Committee for many years and then was a member of the Supreme Soviet Presidium.

Tereshkova was honoured with the titles Hero of the Soviet Union, Order of Lenin and the Gold Star Medal. She received the United Nations Gold Medal of Peace and was made the honorary citizen of many countries.

Q.91 According to the passage, the word 'honored' refers to:

A. Paid no attention to or ignored someone.

B. Regarded with great respect.

C. A state of shame or disgrace.

D. Received what one deserves.

Q.92 What events occurred after Tereshkova's father died?

1. Her mother moved the family to Yaroslavl

2. Her mother sought better employment opportunities

3. Her mother took up a job at the Krasny Perekop cotton mill

4. Her mother passed away soon after

5. Her mother remarried

A. 1, 2 and 5   **B.** 4, 5 and 2

C. 2, 3 and 4   **D.** 1, 2 and 3

Q.93 What did Tereshkova do while living with her grandmother?

1. Worked as a trainee in a tire factory

2. Left her studies and started working

3. Started working as a loom operator in a nearby textile mill

4. Graduated from the Light Industry Technical School

5. Handled spacecraft like Vostok 5 and Vostok 6

A. 2, 4 and 1   **B.** 1, 3 and 4

C. 3, 4 and 5   **D.** 3, 4 and 2

Q.94 What were some of the honours that Tereshkova received?

1. Hero of the Soviet Union Title

2. Order of Lenin

3. Nobel Prize for Aerospace

4. Silver Star Medal

5. United Nations Gold Medal of Peace

A. 3, 4 and 5   **B.** 4, 5 and 2

C. 1, 2 and 5   **D.** 2, 3 and 1

Q.95 What was the Soviet keen about after Yuri Gagarin's space trip?

A. Sending women to space

B. Sending animals to space

C. Exploring the surface of the moon

D. Setting up space stations

Ques (96-100):Direction: Below, a passage is given with five blanks labelled (A)-(E). Below the passage, four options are given for each blank. Choose the word that fits each blank most appropriately in the context of the passage, and mark the corresponding answer.

One of the greatest figures of wisdom and knowledge in the Indian history is Chanakya. He is estimated to have lived from 350 - 283 B.C. Chanakya is touted as the " __ (A) __ Economist of India". Chanakya was the adviser and Prime Minister of Emperor Chandragupta. Chanakya was a professor at the University of Takshila (located in present day Pakistan) and was an expert in commerce, warfare, economics, etc. His famous works include Chanakya Neeti, Arthashastra and Neeti shastra. Chanakya is also known by the name of Kautilya and Vishnugupta as is mentioned in his text.

His famous work called Arthashastra is a classic example of statecraft and politics and is read in Europe even today. It basically consists of the __ (B) __ of politics and how the state works. As such, he is considered the pioneer of the field of political science and economics in India, and his work is thought of as an important __ (C) __ to classical economics. An able ruler has to be a __ (D) __ leader to make sure that the state works smoothly and efficiently. Chanakya was thrown out of the court of King Nanda as he was a blunt man and spoke

his mind clearly. Chanakya swore he would take revenge. Chanakya comes across Chandragupta as a young child. He was the guiding force behind Chandragupta and the vital person who made him an able Emperor.

Chanakya assisted the first Mauryan emperor Chandragupta in his rise to power. He is widely credited for having played an important role in the establishment of the Maurya Empire. Chanakya served as the chief advisor to both emperors Chandragupta and his son Bindusara. The __ (E) __ associated with Chanakya are very interesting and provide a testimony of his greatness.

Q.96 Which of the following words most appropriately fits the blank labeled (A)?

A. Native   **B.** Inheritor   **C.** Pioneer   **D.** Heir

Q.97 Which of the following words most appropriately fits the blank labeled (B)?

A. Principles   **B.** Doubts

C. Confusions   **D.** Denials

Q.98 Which of the following words most appropriately fits the blank labeled (C)?

A. Successor   **B.** Precursor

C. Descendant   **D.** Offspring

Q.99 Which of the following words most appropriately fits the blank labeled (D)?

A. Ruthless   **B.** Merciful   **C.** Gentle   **D.** Loving

Q.100 Which of the following words most appropriately fits the blank labeled (E)?

A. Legends   **B.** Truths   **C.** Histories   **D.** Novels

// Smart Answer Sheet //

Correct — Percentage of students who answered correctly.   **Skipped** — Percentage of students who skipped.

Q.	Ans.	Correct / Skipped	Q.	Ans.	Correct / Skipped	Q.	Ans.	Correct / Skipped	Q.	Ans.	Correct / Skipped	Q.	Ans.	Correct / Skipped	Q.	Ans.	Correct / Skipped
1	D	55.9 % / 34.79 %	18	B	64.0 % / 35.37 %	35	A	55.7 % / 33.85 %	52	A	49.67 % / 32.92 %	69	A	77.0 % / 16.16 %	86	D	40.41 % / 40.12 %
2	D	19.33 % / 78.89 %	19	B	58.94 % / 31.4 %	36	A	85.66 % / 11.77 %	53	D	43.99 % / 50.79 %	70	A	59.34 % / 38.76 %	87	D	44.46 % / 34.68 %
3	B	49.06 % / 39.0 %	20	C	18.91 % / 69.16 %	37	B	86.68 % / 10.16 %	54	A	50.36 % / 47.13 %	71	A	10.2 % / 85.64 %	88	A	87.16 % / 12.79 %
4	D	58.92 % / 36.68 %	21	D	66.26 % / 30.37 %	38	C	79.05 % / 11.05 %	55	B	50.17 % / 40.51 %	72	C	76.36 % / 13.05 %	89	C	50.02 % / 37.81 %
5	D	60.32 % / 38.04 %	22	C	81.29 % / 12.77 %	39	C	59.51 % / 30.98 %	56	D	56.58 % / 42.14 %	73	A	88.46 % / 10.51 %	90	A	50.71 % / 45.51 %
6	B	19.71 % / 73.34 %	23	D	44.64 % / 32.51 %	40	C	82.67 % / 15.63 %	57	B	83.74 % / 13.17 %	74	C	77.0 % / 17.56 %	91	B	50.96 % / 43.99 %
7	B	41.35 % / 36.33 %	24	D	45.67 % / 52.33 %	41	C	65.98 % / 32.35 %	58	C	47.03 % / 35.78 %	75	A	67.15 % / 31.27 %	92	D	57.07 % / 32.28 %
8	A	69.91 % / 30.01 %	25	B	51.13 % / 38.87 %	42	D	60.68 % / 31.75 %	59	D	40.1 % / 30.31 %	76	C	49.07 % / 44.44 %	93	A	45.18 % / 37.28 %
9	D	30.15 % / 68.38 %	26	A	84.2 % / 11.71 %	43	A	76.46 % / 10.12 %	60	A	40.36 % / 54.9 %	77	B	62.88 % / 35.43 %	94	C	54.48 % / 36.79 %
10	C	61.02 % / 31.57 %	27	D	59.58 % / 35.95 %	44	C	77.66 % / 12.09 %	61	D	42.13 % / 34.17 %	78	B	78.86 % / 18.52 %	95	A	50.5 % / 37.05 %
11	C	44.09 % / 33.27 %	28	B	80.39 % / 13.48 %	45	B	66.22 % / 31.52 %	62	B	86.42 % / 10.99 %	79	B	58.01 % / 37.59 %	96	C	57.1 % / 40.19 %
12	A	80.06 % / 17.43 %	29	B	69.24 % / 30.55 %	46	B	65.78 % / 33.58 %	63	A	45.52 % / 45.67 %	80	B	87.34 % / 10.21 %	97	A	57.29 % / 36.85 %
13	C	49.43 % / 50.11 %	30	B	43.67 % / 55.77 %	47	C	53.71 % / 43.56 %	64	A	49.31 % / 35.04 %	81	B	51.94 % / 39.54 %	98	B	65.72 % / 31.17 %
14	B	77.29 % / 20.55 %	31	B	57.41 % / 37.52 %	48	A	52.53 % / 31.37 %	65	B	87.64 % / 11.56 %	82	A	52.72 % / 39.22 %	99	A	66.39 % / 31.68 %
15	C	43.33 % / 42.06 %	32	D	68.84 % / 31.1 %	49	A	19.73 % / 78.58 %	66	A	50.2 % / 39.19 %	83	A	40.25 % / 31.2 %	100	A	41.84 % / 36.97 %
16	D	47.7 % / 46.6 %	33	C	56.73 % / 32.46 %	50	B	55.44 % / 40.72 %	67	D	65.43 % / 31.45 %	84	C	66.9 % / 32.38 %			
17	C	78.21 % / 19.89 %	34	C	65.76 % / 31.01 %	51	C	81.89 % / 12.31 %	68	B	77.16 % / 15.49 %	85	A	52.62 % / 45.45 %			

//Hints and Solutions//

1. As on March 2018, Pratyush is the India's fastest supercomputer.

Pratyush is set up at the Indian Institute of Tropical Meteorology (IITM) in Pune and is used for weather and climate predictions.

India's most powerful supercomputer Pratyush, the first multi-petaflop device in the country which is being used to improve weather and climate predictions, has made it to the 39th spot on the Top 500 List of supercomputers in the world.

- The 4 petaflop supercomputer has improved India's ranking in the list from high 300s to under 50 for the first time.
- One petaflop is a million billion floating-point operations per second and is a reflection of the computing capacity of a system
- Pratyush will be used to do more accurate weather and climate forecasting, including the all-important monsoon predictions.

Hence, the correct option is (D).

2. Satyendra Prakash has been appointed as the Principal Director General of the Press Information Bureau (PIB) in August 2022.

He is an Indian Information Service officer of the 1988 batch. He succeeded Jaideep Bhatnagar who superannuated on 31 July 2022. Prior to this, Mr Prakash held the position of Principal DG, Central Bureau of Communication.

Hence, the correct option is (D).

3. For the first time in its 100-year-old history, Dehradun's Rashtriya Indian Military College (RIMC) will induct girls.

The premier institute for the armed forces, admits students from Class 8 onwards. Five girls cadets are set to join Rashtriya Indian Military College in July 2022. The institution was opened by the Prince of Wales on March 13, 1922.

Originally christened as the Prince of Wales's Royal Indian Military College, after Independence, it was renamed the Rashtriya Indian Military College, popularly called RIMC.

Hence, the correct option is (B).

4. Games24x7, an online skill gaming company has appointed cricketers, Shubman Gill and Ruturaj Gaikwad as the new brand ambassadors for My11Circle, its fantasy sports platform. Both the cricketers will feature in multimedia campaigns by the company spanning across TV, digital and social media platforms. My11Circle is also the official title sponsor of the new IPL team Lucknow Super Giants.

Hence, the correct option is (D).

5. Tata Mutual Fund has launched Tata Nifty India Digital Exchange, Traded Fund. It is an open-ended exchange-traded fund (ETF) replicating/tracking Nifty India Digital Index. The minimum subscription amount is ₹5,000 and in multiples of ₹1 thereof.

The Nifty India Digital Index aims to track the performance of a portfolio of stocks that broadly represent the digital theme.

Tata India Tax Savings Fund is an open-ended Equity Linked Tax Saving Scheme (ELSS) with a compulsory lock-in period of 3 years. The fund offers dual advantage of Tax Benefit of Rs.1,50,000 u/s 80C of the Income Tax Act and the long-term upside potential of the Indian equity market.

Hence, the correct option is (D).

6. Let the sum invested by Shikha in the Scheme offering a higher interest rate be 'x'

So, Sum invested by Shikha in another scheme = (1500-x)

Thus, $\dfrac{(x\times6\times2)}{100} - \dfrac{[(1500-x)\times4\times2]}{100}$

$= 100$

$\left(\dfrac{12x}{100}\right) + \left(\dfrac{8x}{100}\right) - 120$

$= 100$

On solving,

x = Rs 1100

Another amount = 1500 – 1100

= Rs 400

Thus, the required ratio = 11 : 4
Hence, the correct option is (B).

7. Let principal be x.

$r = \dfrac{27}{2}\%$

$t = 4$

Then,

$S.I = \dfrac{x.r.t}{100}$

$S.I = \left(x \times \dfrac{27}{2} \times 4 \times \dfrac{1}{100}\right)$

$= \dfrac{27x}{50}$

So, Amount $= \left(x + \dfrac{27x}{50}\right)$

$= \dfrac{77x}{50}$

$\dfrac{77x}{50} = 2502.5$

$x = \dfrac{2502.50\times50}{77}$

$= 1625$

Hence, the correct option is (B).

8. Principal $=$ Rs 800

Time $= 2$ years

Rate $= 5\%$

$A = P\left(1 + \dfrac{R}{100}\right)^{T}$

$$A = 800 \left(1 + \frac{5}{100}\right)^2$$

$$A = \frac{800 \times 105 \times 105}{100 \times 100}$$

$A = $ Rs 8820

Hence, the correct option is (A).

9. Let's look at the meaning of the correct answer:

Panacea - a solution or remedy for all difficulties or diseases. For Example - There is no panacea for the country's economic problems.

Let's look at the meaning of the other options:-

Medication - a drug or other form of medicine that is used to treat or prevent disease. For Example - The medication should ease the suffering.

Treatment - medical care given to a patient for an illness or injury. For Example - She is responding well to treatment.

Remedy - medicine or treatment for a disease or injury. For Example - The remedy is worse than the disease.

Hence, the correct option is (D).

10. Acoustics is the correct answer.

Acoustics means the branch of physics concerned with the properties of sound.

Mechanics means the branch of applied mathematics dealing with motion and forces producing motion.

Radiation means the emission of energy as electromagnetic waves or as moving subatomic particles, especially high-energy particles which cause ionization.

Audition means an interview for a role or job as a singer, actor, dancer, or musician, consisting of a practical demonstration of the candidate's suitability and skill.

Hence, the correct option is (C).

11. The correct answer is 'My new slippers were chewed by the little puppy'.

The instructions given below should be followed while changing an assertive sentence to a passive voice.

- Find the subject and object of the sentence and exchange their places; make changes in their cases as well if subject and object are pronouns.
- Use preposition 'by' before the agent.
- Use an appropriate helping verb in passive form according to the tense of the active form.
- Always use the third form of the main verb in passive form.
- At last line up the remaining part.

Now let us look at the question:

The subject will become "my new slippers".

The active form contains the past participle form of verb i.e. chewed so the passive form will be in past tense form.

Option (A) is in past continuous form.

Option (B) contains 'can' which is incorrect.

Option (D) is in present continuous form.

Hence, the correct option is (C).

12. The given sentence is an imperative sentence.

The instructions given below should be followed while changing an imperative sentence to passive voice.

Find the subject and object of the sentence and exchange their places; make changes in their cases as well if subject and object are pronouns.

The passive form will be:

Let + object(the command) + be + past participle form (given). For Example:

Active Voice: Open the door.

Passive Voice: Let the door (object) be opened (be + past participle or V_3).

Active Voice: Please calculate the bill.

Passive Voice: Let the bill (object) be calculated (be + past participle or V_3).

Hence, the correct option is (A).

13. The ICC Under-19 World Cup 2020 tournament will be hosted by South Africa. Indian U-19 Cricket Team is led by Priyam Garg. India is the defending champion of the U-19 World cup and winner of the championship for four times.

Many IPL 2020-fame players are to play for India, including Yashasvi Jaiswal and Ravi Bishnoi. India's first match is against Sri Lanka on January 19. India is placed in Group A with Sri Lanka, Japan and New Zealand. Recently the India U-19 team has won the U-19 Asia Cup and a Tri-Nations Tournament with Bangladesh and England.

Hence, the correct option is (C).

14. The Ramsar Convention on Wetlands of International Importance especially as Waterfowl Habitat is an international treaty for the conservation and sustainable use of wetlands.

It is also known as the Convention on Wetlands. It is named after the city of Ramsar in Iran, where the Convention was signed in 1971.
Hence, the correct option is (B).

15. The correct order is:
Key, Lock, Door, Room, Switch on
$\Rightarrow$ 1, 3, 2, 4, 5
Hence, the correct option is (C).

16. The correct order is:
Education, Job, Income, Status, Well-being
$\Rightarrow$ 3, 5, 1, 2, 4
Hence, the correct option is (D).

17. Given:

Market price = Rs. 9,40,000

Selling price = Rs. 8,46,000

For formula, Discount = market price – selling price

Discount = Rs. 9,40,000 – Rs. 8,46,000

=Rs. 94,000

Hence, the correct option is (C).

18. According to the question,

Cost price $= \dfrac{13}{15}$ Selling price

$\dfrac{Cost\ price}{Selling\ price} = \dfrac{13}{15}$

If they sold 12% more then it's the old selling price.

So, the new selling price is:

$= 15 + \dfrac{12}{100} \times 15$

$= 16.8$

$\therefore Profit = Selling\ price - Cost\ price$

$= 16.8 - 13$

$= 3.8$

$Profit\% = \dfrac{3.8}{13} \times 100$

$= 29\dfrac{3}{13}\%$

Hence, the correct option is (B).

19. Let the cost price of each article be Rs. 1.

The cost price of x articles $=$ Rs. x

The selling price of x articles $=$ Rs. 20

Profit $=$ Rs. $(20 - x)$

$\therefore \dfrac{20-x}{x} \times 100 = 25$

$\Rightarrow 2000 - 100x = 25x$

$\Rightarrow 125x = 2000$

$\Rightarrow x = 16$

Hence, the correct option is (B).

20. Given:

Let, speed be x km/hour

It takes 10 hours to travel the distance.

That means total distance = 10x km

Latter speed $= x\left\{\dfrac{(100-20)}{100}\right\} = \left(\dfrac{4x}{5}\right)$ km/hour

Time taken to cover the whole distance at this speed

is $\dfrac{10x}{\left(\frac{4x}{5}\right)}$ = 12.5 hour

Time increase = (12.5 – 10) hours = 2.5 hours

Percentage increase in time taken = $\left(\dfrac{2.5}{10}\right) \times 100 = 25\%$

Hence, the correct option is (C).

21. Given:

The helicopter covers a certain distance at a speed of 180 km/h in 6 hours.

We know that distance covered = speed × time

The helicopter covers a certain distance at a speed of 180 km/h in 6 hours.

Total distance = 180 × 6 = 1080 km

Now, the helicopter needs to cover the same distance in $\dfrac{10}{3}$ hours.

Then the speed will be $= \left(1080 \div \dfrac{10}{3}\right)$

$\Rightarrow \left(1080 \times \dfrac{3}{10}\right) = 324$

$\therefore$ It has to travel at 324 km/hour speed.

Hence, the correct option is (D).

22. When the time taken by 2 vehicles after the meeting is given, the ratio of their speeds is

$v_1 : v_2 = \sqrt{t_2} : \sqrt{t_1}$

$\Rightarrow v_1 : v_2 = \sqrt{9} : \sqrt{4}$

$\Rightarrow v_1 : v_2 = 3 : 2$

$\therefore$ The ratio of speeds of 2 trains is 3: 2.

Hence, the correct option is (C).

23. Given:

Speed of train = 72 km/h

Length of train = 220 metre

Length of platform = 330 metre

Formula used: Speed $= \dfrac{Distance}{Time}$

Speed (in m/s) = Speed (in km/h) × $\left(\dfrac{5}{18}\right)$

Speed = 72 × $\left(\dfrac{5}{18}\right)$ = 4 × 5 = 20 m/s

Total distance to travel = 220 + 330 = 550 m

Time taken to cover the distance $= \dfrac{Distance}{Speed}$

$\Rightarrow \dfrac{550}{20}$ = 27.5 seconds

∴ The train takes 27.5 seconds to cross the 330 m long platform.

Hence, the correct option is (D).

24. The logic followed here is:

The first two letters are reverse positional of each other.

The 3rd letter is obtained by shifting the 2nd letter to 5 places.

Option (D) does not follow the pattern.

Hence, the correct option is (D).

25. The pattern followed is,

Option (A) → 17 : 306 → 17 : 17^2 + 17

Option (B) → 21 : 420 → 21 : 21^2 - 21

Option (C) → 13 : 182 → 13 : 13^2 + 13

Option (D) → 19 : 380 → 19 : 19^2 + 19

All follow the same pattern, except 21 : 420.

Hence, the correct option is (B).

26. Dog, Buffalo and Cow all are domestic animal but Lion is wild animal.

Hence, the correct option is (A).

27. Here, the pattern followed is,

(First Digit) + (Second Digit) = Third Digit

257 → 2 + 5 = 7

358 → 1 + 2 = 8

224 → 2 + 2 = 4

116 → 1 + 1 = 2 ≠ 6

Hence, the correct option is (D).

28. All options except Bat are circular in shape.

Hence, the correct option is (B).

29. Let the excluded number be x.

Average of 17 number $= 7$

∴ Sum of 17 number $= 17 \times 7 = 119$

According to the questions,

$\Rightarrow 119 - x = (17 - 1) \times 4$

$\Rightarrow 119 - x = 64$

$\Rightarrow x = 55$

∴ The excluded number $= 55$

Hence, the correct option is (B).

30. Sum of heights of three persons = 140 × 3 = 420 cm

Sum of heights of five persons = 5 × (140 + 8) = 740 cm

Let the height of A and B be x and (x - 36) respectively.

Sum of heights of A and B = x + (x - 36) = 740 - 420

⇒ 2x - 36 = 320

⇒ x = 178

Hence height of B = x - 36 = 142 cm

Hence, the correct option is (B).

31. Suppose Aniket's marks obtained in Mathematics = M

Scores obtained in Science = S, and marks obtained in English = E

M + S = E + 100

According to question,

(M + S) + E = 180

E + 100 + E = 180

2E = 80

E = 40

Hence, the correct option is (B).

32. In this type of question, first we need to calculate 1 hours work, then their collective work as,

A's 1 hour work is $\dfrac{1}{8}$

B's 1 hour work is $\dfrac{1}{10}$

(A+B)'s 1 hour work $= \dfrac{1}{8} + \dfrac{1}{10} = \dfrac{9}{40}$

So both will finish the work in $\dfrac{40}{9}$ hours

$= 4\dfrac{4}{9}$

Hence, the correct option is (D).

33. Given that:

Time taken by Ragini alone = 3 days more than both of them worked together

Time taken by Raghav alone = 12 days more than both of them worked together

Let the time both of them took to make the carpet be x.

Time taken by Ragini alone = x + 3

Time taken by Raghav alone = x + 12

∴ One day of work when they both work together = Sum of their individual per day work

$$\Rightarrow \frac{1}{x} = \frac{1}{(x+12)} + \frac{1}{(x+3)}$$

$$\Rightarrow \frac{1}{x} = \frac{(2x+15)}{(x^2+15x+36)}$$

$$\Rightarrow x^2 + 15x + 36 = 2x^2 + 15x$$

$$\Rightarrow x = 6$$

∴ Time taken by Ragini alone = 6 + 3

⇒ 9 days

Hence, the correct option is (C).

34. Given:

24 Men and 6 women can complete the work in 10 days

6 men and 6 women can complete the work in 12 days

(24M + 6W) × 10 = (6M + 6W) × 12

⇒ 240M + 60W = 72M + 72W

⇒ 168M = 12W

⇒ M : W = 1 : 14

Total work = (24 × 1 + 6 × 14) × 10 = 1080 units

Time in which 4 men and 1 women will complete the work

$$= \frac{1080}{(4\times1+14)} = 60 \text{ days}$$

∴ 4 men and 1 woman can complete the work in 60 days

Hence, the correct option is (C).

35. Let the total salary be x

Given that, salary spent on rent $= \frac{2x}{7}$

According to the question,

$$\frac{27}{x} = 2800$$

$$x = 9800$$

The portion of salary spent on food $= x - \left(\frac{2x}{7}\right) - \frac{x}{4}$

$$= x - \left(\frac{15x}{28}\right)$$

$$= \frac{13x}{28} \quad .....(i)$$

Putting the value of x in equation (i)

$$= \frac{13}{28} \times 9800$$

$$= 4550$$

Hence, the correct option is (A).

36. By adding we get,

⇒ 2278.235+21.2323

⇒ 2299.4673

Hence, the correct option is (A).

37. L.C.M of $13,\ 15,\ 9,$ and 7 is $4095.$

So,

$$\frac{17}{13} \times 4095 = 5355$$

$$\frac{18}{15} \times 4095 = 4914$$

$$\frac{15}{9} \times 4095 = 6825$$

$$\frac{12}{7} \times 4095 = 7020$$

Hence, the correct option is (B).

38. Minamata disease caused by the mercury contaminated water. It was first discovered in Minamata city of japan that's why it is called as Minamata Disease.

Blue baby syndrome caused by the nitrate contaminated water. Hence, the correct option is (C).

39. Wool is a polymer which is made up of protein. Wool is extracted from sheep. Rubber, cotton, and Jute do not make up of protein.
Hence, the correct option is (C).

40. Sucralose is an artificial sweetener and sugar substitute. The majority of ingested sucralose is not broken down by the body, so it is noncaloric.
Hence, the correct option is (C).

41. Vitamin K is a vitamin found in leafy green vegetables, broccoli, and Brussels sprouts.

In the body, vitamin K plays a major role in blood clotting. So it is used to reverse the effects of "blood-thinning" medications when too much is given; to prevent clotting problems in newborns who don't have enough vitamin K, and to treat bleeding caused by medications.

Hence, the correct option is (C).

42. Gills are respiratory organs found in most aquatic organisms.

Gills can extract dissolved oxygen from water and excrete carbon dioxide.

Gills can be found in Octopus, Squid, Clownfish, Tadpole, Prawn, etc.

Lungs are the breathing organ of Whales.

Hence, the correct option is (B).

43. The Supreme Commander of the Indian Armed Forces is the President.

Indian Armed Forces:

- The military forces of the Republic of India. It consists of three professional uniformed services: the Indian Army, Indian Navy, and Indian Air Force.

- Supported by the Indian Coast Guard and paramilitary organizations (Assam Rifles, and Special Frontier Force) and various inter-service commands and institutions such as the Strategic Forces Command, the Andaman and Nicobar Command and the Integrated Defense Staff.

- The President of India is the Supreme Commander of the Indian Armed Forces under the management of the Ministry of Defense (MoD).

Hence, the correct option is (A).

44. The order of the layers of the atmosphere from top to bottom: Ionosphere - Mesosphere - Stratosphere - Troposphere

The space in which the air surrounds the earth is called the atmosphere.

The lower part of the atmosphere (which usually extends from four to eight miles) is called the troposphere, the upper part of it is called the stratosphere, and the part above it is called the mesosphere and the upper part from the mesosphere is called the ionosphere.

Hence, the correct option is (C).

45. The given sentence is grammatically incorrect.

- Here, 'an order seeking immediate' should be used instead of 'a order seeking immediate'.

- The article 'an' should be used before singular, countable nouns which begin with vowel sounds.

- In the given sentence, 'order' is preceded by 'a' which is erroneous.

- Here, 'an' should be used instead.

Hence, the correct option is (B).

46. The given sentence is grammatically incorrect.

- Here, 'are a land of extreme temperature' should be used instead of 'are a lamd of extremes'.

- Here, in the given sentence 'deserts' is plural. Therefore, it should be followed by a plural helping verb that is 'are'.

- Here, 'Extremes' is also incorrect.

- Rather it should be 'extreme temperature' to form a grammatically correct sentence.

Hence, the correct option is (B).

47. Priyamvada Mohanty is associated with Odissi classical dance form.

Priyambada Mohanty Hejmadi is an Indian classical dancer of Odissi, art writer, a biologist and a former vice chancellor of Sambalpur University. Odissi is considered to be one of the oldest surviving classical dance forms based on archaeological evidence.

The traditional dance of Odisha, Odissi was born from the dance of the devadasis who danced in the temple.

Hence, the correct option is (C).

48. The tradition of Kathakali, a rich and thriving classical dance of the southwestern state of Kerala, is here. Kathakali means a story drama or a dance drama. Katha means story, here actors portray characters drawn from the Ramayana and Mahabharata epics and Puranas.

Hence, the correct option is (A).

49. Kandhar Inscription deals with Ashoka's policies.

- The inscription was carved in Aramaic & Greek language.

- It is bilingual and specifies that fisherman and hunters gave up hunting.

So, statement 2 is correct.

Minor Pillar inscriptions:

- Rummindei Pillar Inscription: It mentioned the exemption of Lumbini (the birth place of Buddha) from tax.

- Ashoka visited Lumbini in the 29th year of his coronation.

- It is the only inscription which makes a precise reference to taxation.

So, statement 1 is correct.

Hence, the correct option is (A).

50.

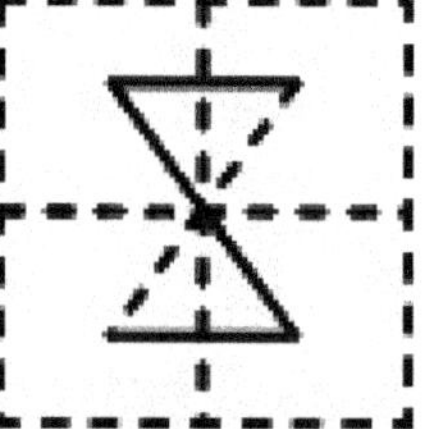

Therefore, the figure in option (B) will complete the pattern. Hence, the correct option is (B).

51. The given figure is embedded in the answer figure shown below:

Hence, the correct option is (C).

52. On close observation, we find that the problem figure is embedded in figure (A) as shown below.

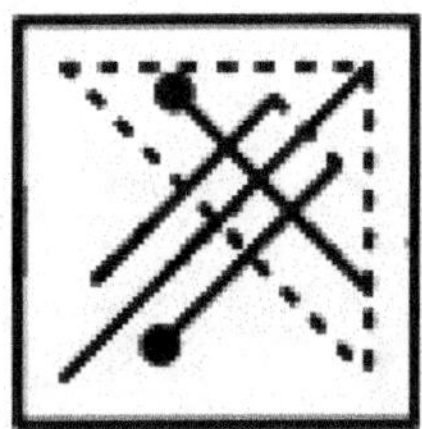

Hence, the correct option is (A).

53. On close observation, we find that the problem figure is embedded in figure (D) as shown below:

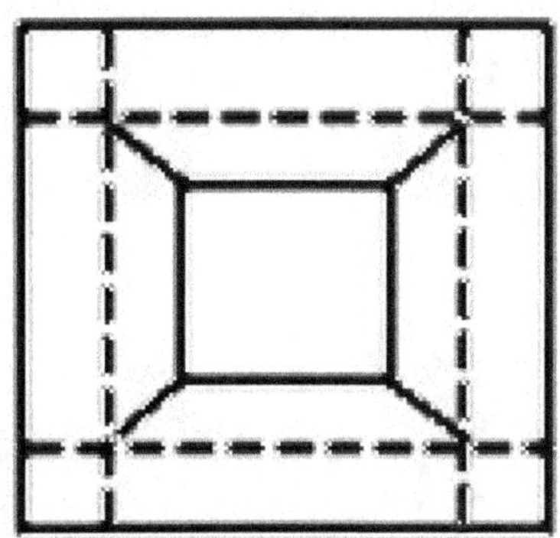

Hence, the correct option is (D).

54.

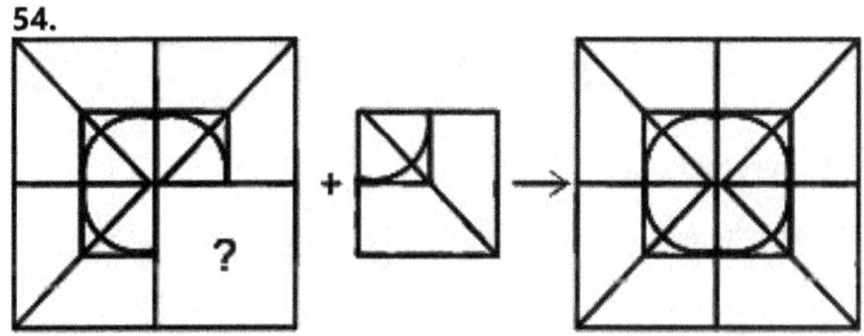

Therefore, given figure in option (A) will complete the pattern. Hence, the correct option is (A).

55. Let the fraction be $\dfrac{x}{y}$

$\dfrac{(x-2)}{(y-2)} = 2:1$

$x - 2 = 2y - 4$

$x - 2y = -2$

$\dfrac{(x+4)}{(y+3)} = 5:3$

$3x + 12 = 5y + 15$

$3x - 5y = 3$

$3x - 6y = -6$

$y = 9$

$x = 16$

$\dfrac{x}{y} = \dfrac{16}{9}$

Hence, the correct option is (B).

56. Water present in solution $= \dfrac{3}{8} \times 48 = 18$ lit.

Milk present in solution $= \dfrac{5}{8} \times 48 = 30$ lit.

Let x liters of milk to be added

Milk is 70% of the new solution, so water is to be 30% of the new solution.

For the new solution

$18 + x = 70\%$ of $(48 + x)$ Amount of milk

$30 = 30\%$ of $(48 + x)$ Amount of water

$x = 52$ liters.

Hence, the correct option is (D).

57. Given, ratio of the father's age to his son's age is $8:5.$
Let their ages be $8x$ and $5x$ respectively.
Given, product of their age is 1440.
$\therefore 8x \times 5x = 1440$
$\Rightarrow x^2 = 36$
$\Rightarrow x = 6$
Father's present age $= 8 \times 6 = 48$
Son's present age $= 5 \times 6 = 30$
Ratio of their ages after 6 years $= \dfrac{(48+6)}{(30+6)} = \dfrac{54}{36} = 3:2$
Hence, the correct option is (B).

58. When we observe carefully, we find that figure given in option (C) will complete the question figure.

Hence, the correct option is (C).

59. "D" is the correct embedded figure which contains figure (X) as its part.

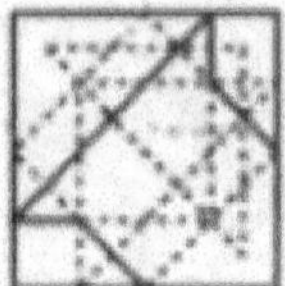

Hence, the correct option is (D).

60. After observing the given diagram carefully, option figure A has the given embedded figure

Hence, the correct option is (A).

61.

Hence, the correct option is (D).

62.

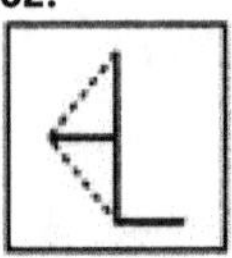

Hence, the correct option is (B).

63. All carrots are vegetables. All vegetables are foods.

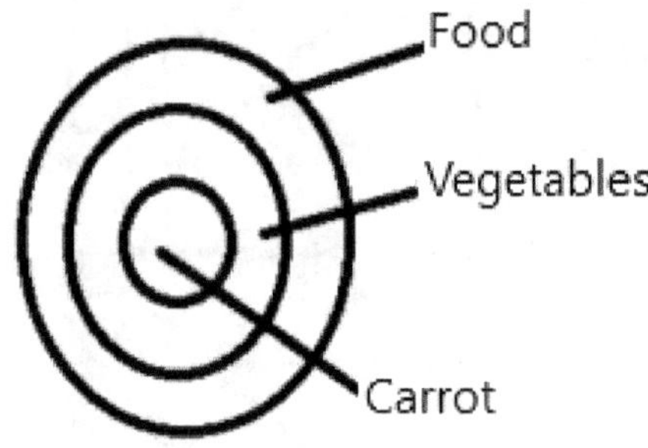

Hence, the correct option is (A).

64. Some authors can be teachers. Some teachers can be men. Some authors can be men. So, the given items are partly related to each other.

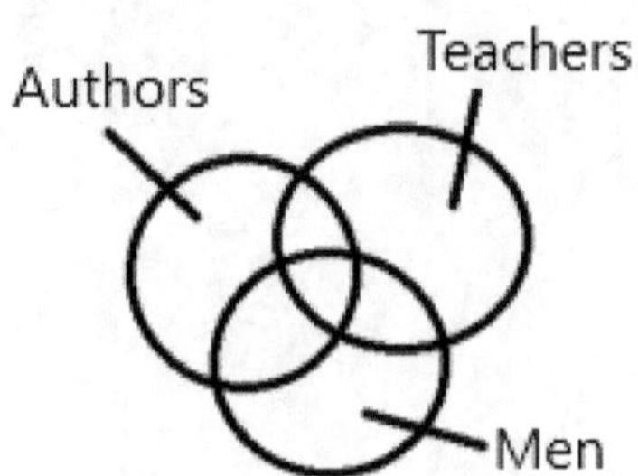

Hence, the correct option is (A).

65. The Logic here is as follows:

Apple and Bananas come under the type of Fruits.

So the diagram which shows the best relationship between the given variables is:

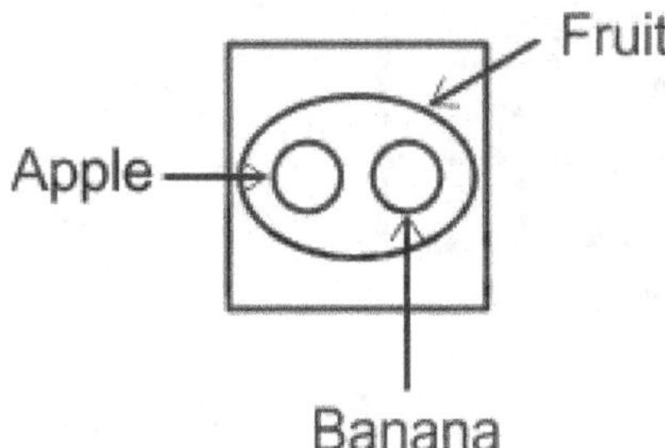

Hence, the correct option is (B).

66. A woman can be a politician as well as an officer.

The correct Venn diagram is:

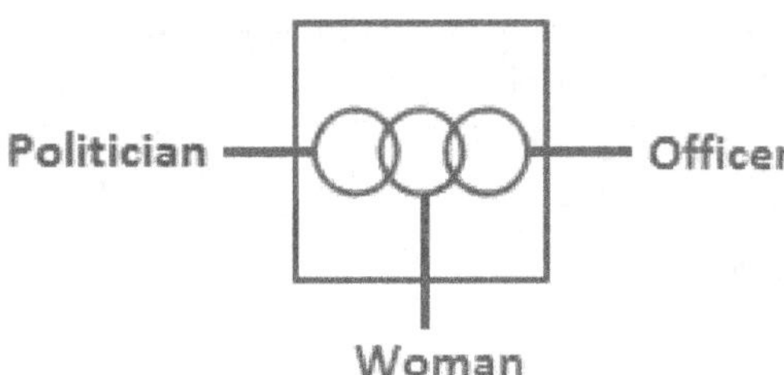

Hence, the correct option is (A).

67. All nitrogen are non-metals but some non-metals and some nitrogen can be liquid.

The correct Venn diagram representation is,

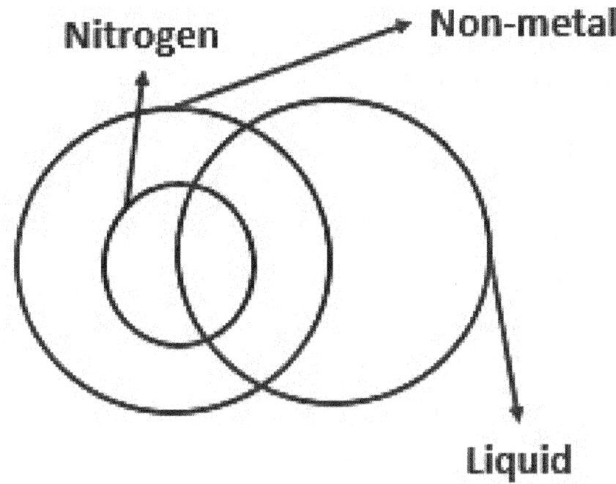

Hence, the correct option is (D).

68. Gift horse in the mouth: to show a lack of appreciation or gratitude when receiving a gift.

Find fault with something that has been received as a gift or favour.

Hence, the correct option is (B).

69. Burning question: an important question that requires an answer.

Hence, the correct option is (A).

70. The 7th Justice Ministers' Meeting of Shanghai Cooperation Organisation (SCO) the Member States to be hosted by Union Law Minister. So, statement 1 is correct.

The Shanghai Cooperation Organisation (SCO) is a permanent intergovernmental international organization, the creation of which was announced on 15 June 2001 in Shanghai (China) by the Republic of Kazakhstan, the People's Republic of China, the Kyrgyz Republic, the Russian Federation, the Republic of Tajikistan, and the Republic of Uzbekistan. It was preceded by the Shanghai Five mechanism.

The SCO Secretariat, based in Beijing, is the main permanent executive body of the SCO. So, statement 2 is incorrect.

SCO's main goals are as follows :

- Strengthening mutual trust and neighborliness among the member states;

- Promoting their effective cooperation in politics, trade, the economy, research, technology, and culture, as well as in education, energy, transport, tourism, environmental protection, and other areas.

- Making joint efforts to maintain and ensure peace, security, and stability in the region and moving towards the establishment of a democratic, fair, and rational new international political and economic order.

Hence, the correct option is (A).

71. The correct answer is **capability**.

competency: the ability to do something successfully or efficiently

capability: the ability or power to do, experience, or understand something

Let's look at the meanings of the other given options: thinking- the process of using one's mind to consider or reason about something

- knowledge- what is known in a particular field or in total; facts and information
- ideal- satisfying one's conception of what is perfect; most suitable

Thus, from the given meanings, we find that competency and capability are synonyms.

Hence, the correct option is (A).

72. The correct answer is **arrogant**.

haughty: arrogantly superior and disdainful

arrogant: having or revealing an exaggerated sense of one's own importance or abilities

Let's look at the meanings of the other given options:

- tough- (of a substance or object) strong enough to withstand adverse conditions or rough or careless handling
- modest- unassuming or moderate in the estimation of one's abilities or achievements
- knowledgeable- intelligent and well informed

Thus, from the given meanings, we find that haughty and arrogant are synonyms.

Hence, the correct option is (C).

73. The correct answer is **diligent**.

industrious: diligent and hard-working

diligent: having or showing care and conscientiousness in one's work or duties

Let's look at the meanings of the other given options:

- knowledgeable- intelligent and well informed
- indolent- wanting to avoid activity or exertion; lazy
- insincere- not expressing genuine feelings

Thus, from the given meanings, we find that industrious and diligent are synonyms.

Hence, the correct option is (A).

74. When 800 is first increased by 10%

$$\Rightarrow 800 + 800 \times \frac{10}{100} = 880$$

And it is again increased by 20%

$$\Rightarrow 880 + 880 \times \frac{20}{100} = 1056$$

Hence, the correct option is (C).

75. Given,

67% of $801 - 231.17 = ? - 23\%$ of 789

Take the approximate value of each numbers,

$? \approx \frac{(67 \times 800)}{100} - 231 + \frac{(23 \times 790)}{100}$

$\Rightarrow ? \approx 536 - 231 + 181.7$

$\Rightarrow ? \approx 490$

Hence, the correct option is (A).

76. Given:

Discount = 8% and Ball's worth = Rs. 256

We know that,

Discount % = $\frac{Discount}{M.P.} \times 100$

Let M.P be Rs. x

∴ 8% of x = 256

$x = \left(\frac{256}{8}\right) \times 100$

x = Rs. 3200

Price paid for bat = 3200 - 256 = Rs. 2944

Hence, the correct option is (C).

77. A collective noun is a noun that represents a collection of animals and people.

Example: Even litters of puppies specially bred by Customs risked exposure to disease.

Therefore, a group of cats is called 'clowder'.

Complete sentence:

He currently resides in Raipur with his wife, daughter, and a mighty **clowder** of cats.

Hence, the correct option is (B).

78. The correct determiner to be used is 'any'. 'Any' is the determiner used in negative sentences as well as in interrogative sentences.

Example: There isn't any milk in the fridge.

Was there any problem at the shop?

Complete sentence:

Do you have **any** books focusing on this war?

Hence, the correct option is (B).

79. The new laws are _preposterous_ and will not solve the real crime issue.

preposterous means absurd, not logical, it is the only option that fits in the given blank.

Hence, the correct option is (B).

80. In the previous sentence, it is given that Billington was the first murderer, and murder is considered a crime.

So, here **crime** is the most appropriate word.

Hence, the correct option is (B).

81.

The third figure in each row comprises parts that are not common to the first two figures.

Hence, the correct option is (B).

82.

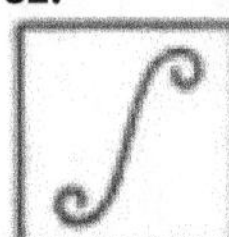

The number of components in each row either increases or decreases from left to right. In the third row, it increases.

Hence, the correct option is (A)

83.

In each row, the second figure is obtained from the first figure by increasing the number of smaller elements by one and the third figure is obtained from the second figure by increasing the number of smaller elements by one.

Hence, the correct option is (A).

84.

The third figure in each row comprises of parts that are not common to the first two figures.

Hence, the correct option is (C).

85.

Each row (as well as each column) contains a figure consisting of a circle and two line segments, a figure consisting of a circle and three line segments and a figure consisting of a circle and four line segments.

Hence, the correct option is (A).

86. A large group of soldiers is called a regiment.

Similarly,

Herd refers to a group of animals, Here are horses.

Hence, the correct option is (A).

87. 'Unfeign' is a synonym of 'Scrupulous'.

Unfeign, Scrupulous - guided by or in accordance with one's sense of right and wrong.

Similarly, 'Recompense' is synonym of 'Restoration'.

Restoration, Recompense - the act or an instance of bringing something damaged or worn back to its original state.

1. Pillage - Plunder

2. Peculiar - Unusual

3. Vehemence - Passion

Hence, the correct option is (D).

88. Here Predict and Forecast both have the somewhat same meaning. Similarly, the word which has the same meaning to Postpone is "Adjourn".

Hence, the correct option is (A).

89. Myopia is an eyes disease.

Similarly, Pyorrhea is teeth disease

Hence, the correct option is (C).

90. The pattern followed here is:

Pillage and Redeem are antonyms of each other where pillage means valuables stolen or taken by force and redeem means to do what is required by the terms.

Similarly,

Palpable and Intangible are antonyms where palpable means able to be perceived by a sense or by the mind and intangible means not capable of being perceived by the sense of touch.

2. Emerge Leak – they are synonyms of each other which means to become known.

3. Modesty: Diffidence – they are synonyms of each other which means the absence of any feelings of being better than others.

4. Inferior: Trivial – they are synonyms of each other which means one who is of lower rank and typically under the authority of another.

Hence, the correct option is (A).

91. The passage speaks about one of the famous cosmonauts Valentina Tereshkova.

It speaks of her life, education and journey to space.

Let us look at the 1st sentence of the last paragraph:

"Tereshkova was honoured with the titles Hero of the Soviet Union, Order of Lenin and the Gold Star Medal."

Based on the context, the word honoured refers to Tereshkova being regarded with great respect through various titles and medals.

Example: She was honoured for her bravery.

Hence, the correct option is (B).

92. The passage speaks about one of the famous cosmonauts Valentina Tereshkova.

It speaks of her life, education and journey to space.

The 2nd sentence in the 1st paragraph containing the above read the following:

"Tereshkova's father died in the Finnish Winter War... After that, her mother moved the family to Yaroslavl, seeking better employment opportunities and took up a job at the Krasny Perekop cotton mill."

Tereshkova's father died when she was 2 years old.

Hence, the correct option is (D).

93. The passage speaks about one of the famous cosmonauts Valentina Tereshkova.

It speaks of her life, education and journey to space.

The 3rd and 4th sentences in the 2nd paragraph containing the above read the following:

"Later, she lived with her grandmother in Yaroslavl and worked as a trainee in a tire factory. In 1955, to help her family further, she started working as a loom operator in a nearby textile mill. During that time, she graduated from the Light Industry Technical School."

Tereshkova enrolled at school in 1945 at the age of eight. In 1953, she left school and began working but continued education by correspondence courses.

Hence, the correct option is (A).

94. The passage speaks about one of the famous cosmonauts Valentina Tereshkova.

It speaks of her life, education and journey to space.

The sentences in the last paragraph containing the above reads the following:

"Tereshkova was honoured with the titles Hero of the Soviet Union, Order of Lenin and the Gold Star Medal. She received the United Nations Gold Medal of Peace and was made the honorary citizen of many countries."

Thanks to her training in parachuting, Tereshkova was among the five women who were selected for the cosmonaut programme in 1961.

She logged more than 70 hours in space and made 48 orbits of the Earth. On June 19, 1963, Tereshkova's spacecraft re-entered the Earth's atmosphere and she successfully parachuted for 20,000 feet.

Hence, the correct option is (C).

95. The passage speaks about one of the famous cosmonauts Valentina Tereshkova.

It speaks of her life, education and journey to space.

The 5th sentence in the 3rd paragraph containing the above reads the following:

"After Yuri Gagarin's historic space trip, the Soviet government was keen to send women to space."

Tereshkova developed an interest in parachuting quite early and trained in skydiving at the local aeroclub, making her first jump at age 22, on May 21, 1959.

Thanks to her training in parachuting, Tereshkova was among the five women who were selected for the cosmonaut programme in 1961.

Hence, the correct option is (A).

96. It has been mentioned in the second paragraph of the passage that Chanakya is considered the pioneer of the field of political science and economics 'Pioneer' means 'a person who starts a new trend/an explorer/discoverer'. Given that Chanakya lived in ancient India (350 - 283 B.C), he can be said to be the first one to have discovered the organised form of the economics 'discipline' as we know it today. 'Inheritor' means a person who possesses some property left after the death of a relative;'Native' means 'a person born in a specified place or associated with a place by birth';'Successor' means the person who is in charge after the demise of a relative.

Hence, the correct option is (C).

97. It has been the told in the concerned sentence that Arthashastra is a classic example of statecraft and politics. Thus, a written work on statecraft and politics would contain 'principles' or 'theories or concepts'. Since the work of Chanakya has been praised here, it cannot be said to consist of 'doubts', 'confusions', 'denials'

Hence, the correct option is (A).

98. It has already been established that Chanakya was a pioneer of economics in India. Thus, it can be said that even his work was a pioneer or forerunner to 'classical economics'. This meaning is conveyed by the word 'precursor' which means 'a predecessor; forerunner; someone who acts before anyone else does'.'Successor' and 'descendant' refer to people who follow someone next in line;'Offspring' is a 'descendant';All the words other than 'precursor' convey an idea opposite to the one intended in the passage.

Hence, the correct option is (B).

99. The next sentence says that 'Chanakya was thrown out of the court of King Nanda as he was a blunt man and spoke his mind'. This means that Chanakya's idea about an 'able ruler' would have been something which was not accepted in general and had offended the king. To say that a king should be 'merciful', 'gentle' and 'loving' is not offensive. Thus, 'ruthless' which means 'merciless' aptly fits the context.

Hence, the correct option is (A).

100. The given passage talks about Chanakya who became a significant figure in the history of India. So a lot of stories must have been associated with him. 'Legend' which means 'a traditional story sometimes popularly regarded as historical but not authenticated', thus suits best in the blank space.

Correct sentence: The Legends associated with Chanakya are very interesting and provide a testimony of his greatness.

Hence, the correct option is (A).

Mock Test 04

Q.1 L&T collaborated with _____ to develop Green Hydrogen Technology.

A. IIT Bombay   **B.** IIT Delhi

C. IIT Kanpur   **D.** IIT Madras

Q.2 Which organization has produced the "The Global Report on Food Crises 2020"?

A. UNESCO   **B.** ILO

C. GNAFC   **D.** IMF

Q.3 National Science and Technology Entrepreneurship Development Board (NSTEDB) works under the aegis of which Ministry?

A. Ministry of Education

B. Ministry of Skill Development and Entrepreneurship

C. Ministry of Science and Technology

D. Ministry of Commerce and Industry

Q.4 Which financial services company has partnered with USAID to launch 'Project Kirana' for women entrepreneurs in India?

A. VISA   **B.** Mastercard

C. American Express   **D.** Rupay

Q.5 Which country has signed a $ 2.25 billion deal with a Russian state-run nuclear energy company 'ASE' in August 2022?

[RBI Assistant, 2020], [UPSSSC Rajasva Lekhpal, 2015]

A. India   **B.** China

C. Japan   **D.** South Korea

Q.6 At what time will Rs. 1000 amounts to Rs. 1331 at 20% per annum compounded half-yearly?

A. $1\frac{1}{2}$ years   **B.** 2 years

C. 1 years   **D.** $2\frac{1}{2}$ years

Q.7 ₹ 67,200 are invested in ₹ 100 (nominal value) shares which are quoted at ₹ 120 (market value). If 12% dividend is declared on the shares, then the income would be

[Joint Entrance Examination (Polytechnic), 2017]

A. ₹ 8,064   **B.** ₹ 8,032   **C.** ₹ 7,064   **D.** ₹ 6,720

Q.8 If the simple interest for 6 years is equal to 30% of the principal, it will be equal to the principal after:

A. 10 years   **B.** 20 years   **C.** 22 years   **D.** 30 years

Q.9 Joint exercises between the Air Forces of India and France are called:

A. Yama   **B.** Garuda   **C.** Varuna   **D.** Vajra

Q.10 The Kalinga war caused guilt and huge penitence to Ashoka, because of which he started to used "Dhammaghosha" instead of "Bherighosha". Here, the term "Dhammaghosha" signifies which of the following?

A. Military conquest

B. Cultural annihilation

C. Conquest by regional tribes

D. Conquest by Brahmanical traditions

Ques (11-15):Direction: Complete the sentence with the most appropriate word.

Q.11 I work very _____ and am decisive and accurate in my judgement.

A. anxious   **B.** elaborate

C. efficiently   **D.** precise

Q.12 I don't have much energy these days. After a short stroll, I am quite _____.

A. relieved   **B.** eager

C. uplifted   **D.** exhausted

Q.13 Sanjay found the unchanging rhythm of the musical piece to be annoyingly _____.

A. irreverent   **B.** recusant

C. monotonous   **D.** coherent

Q.14 Bengaluru is a beautiful city which _____ the modern with the traditional.

A. breaks   **B.** blends   **C.** grows   **D.** shares

Q.15 The nationalists followed a policy of non-violence to make their _____ successful.

A. encounter   **B.** struggle

C. politics   **D.** speeches

Q.16 Choose the option that is the passive form of the sentence.

The class teacher was taking the children to the zoo.

[SSC Sub Inspector (CPO), 2019]

A. The children will go to the zoo by their class teacher.

B. The children can be taking to the zoo by their class teacher.

C. The children being taken to the zoo by their class teacher.

D. The children were being taken to the zoo by their class teacher.

Q.17 Choose the option that is the passive form of the sentence.

The manager permitted women employees to leave the office early on that day.

[SSC Sub Inspector (CPO), 2019]

A. Women employees permitted the manager to leave the office early on that day.

B. Women employees had to leave the office early on that day.

C. Women employees should leave the office early on that day.

D. Women employees were permitted to leave the office early on that day.

Q.18 Which of the following causes soil pollution?
A. Ozone   B. Aerosol
C. Acid rain   D. None of these

Q.19 The purchase value of 4 items are equal to sales value of 3 items. The % profit is

[Joint Entrance Examination (Polytechnic), 2018]

A. $33\frac{1}{3}\%$ B. $11\frac{1}{9}\%$ C. $66\frac{2}{3}\%$ D. $9\frac{1}{11}\%$

Q.20 The cost price of item A is equal to the cost price of item B. If the market price of item A is Rs____ after increased by 60% of its cost price and the market price of B is Rs 600 after increased by 50% of its cost price. The difference between the selling price of item B and item A is Rs____ if a 10 % of discount given on the market price of both the items.
A. 680, 80   B. 640, 36   C. 540, 28   D. 720, 240

Q.21 The difference between the selling prices obtained after a single discount of 45% and two successive discounts of 30% and 15% on an article marked at Rs 12000 is:
A. Rs. 440   B. Rs. 560   C. Rs. 520   D. Rs. 540

Q.22 In the following question, select the related word from the given alternatives.
Butterfly : Lepidopterology : : Map : ?
A. Hematology   B. Phycology
C. Cartography   D. Numismatics

Q.23 In the question, select the related word from the given alternatives.
Country : President :: State:?
A. Chief Minister   B. Prime Minister
C. Speaker   D. Governor

Q.24 Direction: Select the word which means the same as the group of words given.
Embarrassed is to humiliated as frightened is to:
A. Terrified   B. Agitated
C. Courageous   D. Reckless

Q.25 In the following question find out the alternative which will replace the question mark.
Peacock : India :: Bear : ?
A. Australia   B. America   C. Russia   D. England

Q.26 In the following question find out the alternative which will replace the question mark.
South : North-West :: West : ?
A. North   B. South-West
C. North-East   D. East

Q.27 A person crosses a 455-meter long distance in 35 minutes. What is his speed in km/hr?

[UP Police ASI, 2018]

A. 0.52   B. 0.95   C. 0.62   D. 0.78

Q.28 A train running at a speed of 72 km/hr takes 25 seconds to cross an electric pole. What is the length of the train?

[UP Police ASI, 2018]

A. 250 metres   B. 750 metres
C. 500 metres   D. 1000 metres

Q.29 Ramesh travels from "A" to "B" at a speed of $40\ km/hr$ and returns back from "B" to "A" by same route at a speed of $60\ km/hr$. Total time taken by him is 10 hours. How far is "A" from "B"?
A. 120 km B. 240 km C. 480 km D. 180 km

Q.30 A train passes two persons moving at the speeds 26 m/s and 42 m/s in the opposite direction to that of the train in 9 sec and 7 sec respectively. The length of the train is:

[UP Police ASI, 2018]

A. 504 m   B. 449 m   C. 479 m   D. 443 m

Q.31 Select the answer figure which is embedded in the given figure.

A. 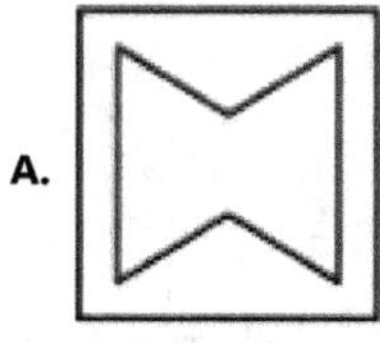

B. 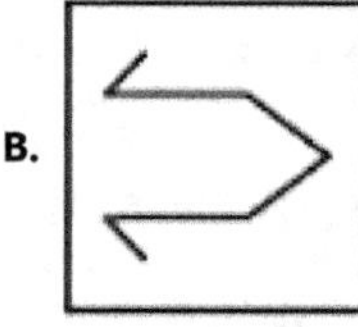

C. 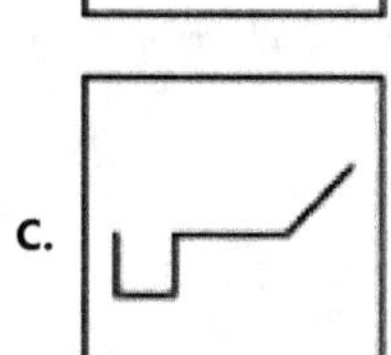

D. 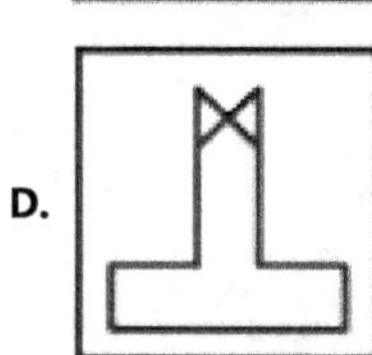

Q.32 Find the embedded figure given below from the options:

A. 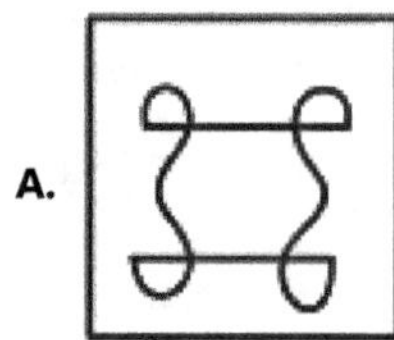

B. 

C.

D.

 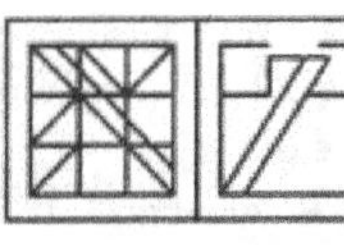 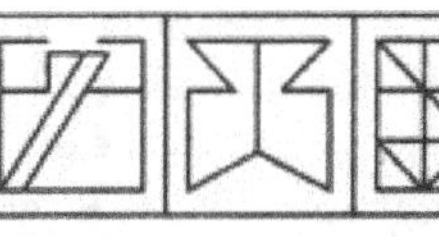

(X)   (1)   (2)   (3)   (4)

A. (1)   **B.** (2)   **C.** (3)   **D.** (4)

Q.33 Direction: From the given options, select the one in which the given question figure is embedded. (Rotation is not allowed)

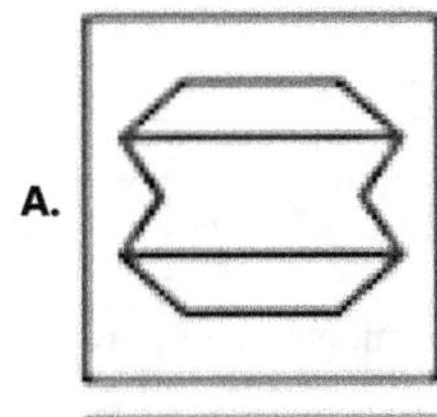
A.

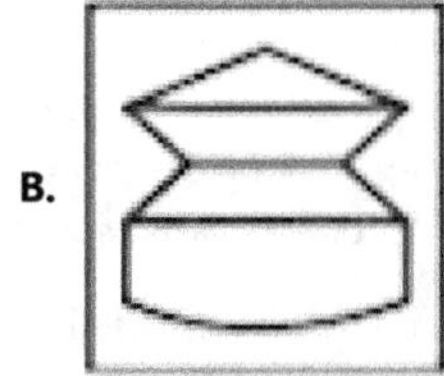
B.

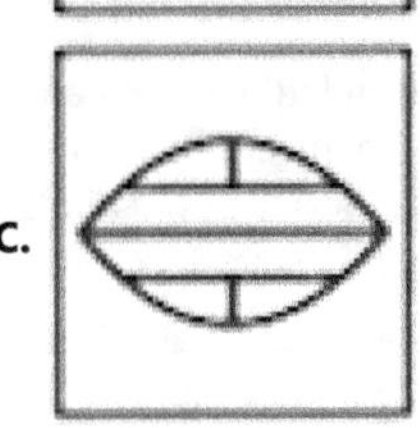
C.

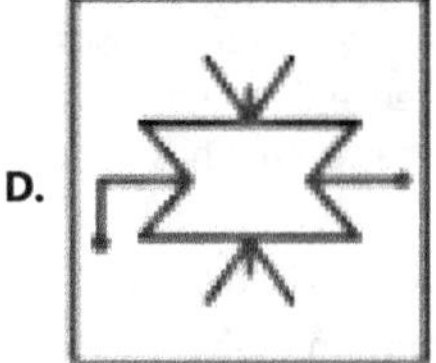
D.

Q.34 Direction: Which one of the option figures can be formed from the pieces given in the question figure below?

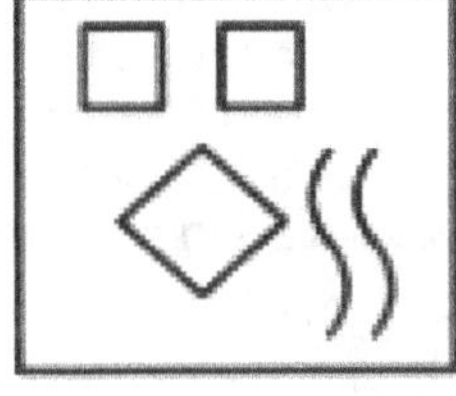

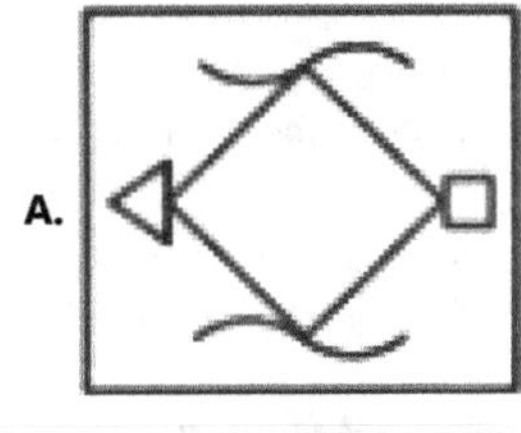
A.

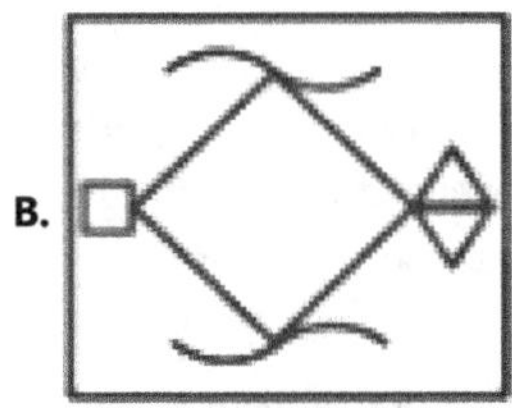
B.

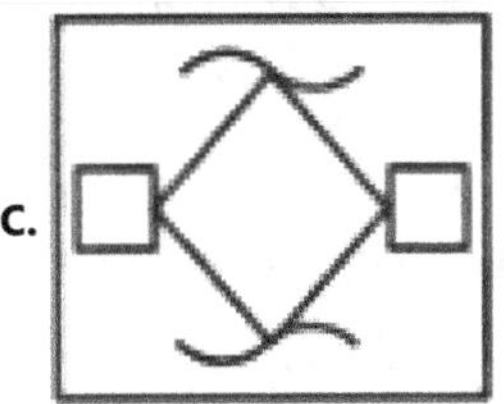
C.

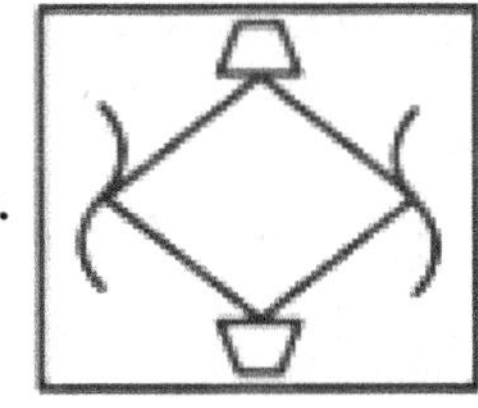
D.

Q.35

Direction: Find out the alternative figure which contains figure (X) as its part.

Q.36 40% of the employees in a factory are workers. All the remaining employees are executives. The annual income of each worker is Rs. 390. The annual income of each executive is Rs. 420. What is the average annual income of all the employees in the factory together?

A. 390   **B.** 405   **C.** 408   **D.** 415

Q.37 A batsman makes a score of 87 runs in the 17th match and thus increases his average by 3. Find his average after the 17th match:

A. 36   **B.** 37   **C.** 38   **D.** 39

Q.38 The average of three numbers is 6. The average of the first two is 5 while the average of the last two is 8. What are the three numbers?

A. 2, 8, 8   **B.** 3, 7, 8   **C.** 2, 6, 10   **D.** 2, 7, 9

Q.39 Ganesh and Bhima can complete a work in 6 days. If Ganesh alone can finish it in 10days, in how many days Bhima can complete the work?

A. 18   **B.** 14   **C.** 12   **D.** 15

Q.40 A can do a piece of work in 10 days and B can do it in 15 days. Number of days to complete the work if they work together is:

A. 6 days   **B.** 9 days   **C.** 7 days   **D.** 5 days

Q.41 A, B, and C can do a work in 24, 16 and 12 days respectively. How many days will it take them to complete the work, if the three of them decide to work together?

A. $5\frac{1}{3}$ days   **B.** $5\frac{2}{3}$ days   **C.** $5\frac{1}{2}$ days   **D.** $5\frac{3}{4}$ days

Ques (42-43):Direction: Choose from the four options, the word that best defines/substitutes the given phrase.

Q.42 A speech or piece of writing praising somebody
[SSC Sub Inspector (CPO), 2018], [SSC Sub Inspector (CPO), 2017]

A. Angiology   **B.** Etymology
C. Eulogy   **D.** Arcology

Q.43 "A person or animal that eats all kinds of food"
[SSC Sub Inspector (CPO), 2018], [SSC Sub Inspector (CPO), 2017]

A. Omnivorous   **B.** Herbivorous
C. Insectivorous   **D.** Carnivorous

Q.44 Find the odd one out from the given options:
A. BEIN   **B.** LOSX   **C.** DGJN   **D.** HKOT

Q.45 Direction: In each of following question, four words have been given of which three are alike in some way and one is different. Choose the odd one out.

A. Dollar   **B.** Peso   **C.** Ounce   **D.** Euro

Q.46 Direction: In each of following question, four words have been given of which three are alike in some way and one is different. Choose the odd one out.

A. Geometry
B. Algebra
C. Calculus
D. Thermodynamics

Q.47 Direction: In each of following question, four words have been given of which three are alike in some way and one is different. Choose the odd one out.

A. Square
B. Triangle
C. Rectangle
D. Cuboid

Q.48 Direction: In each of following question, four words have been given of which three are alike in some way and one is different. Choose the odd one out.

A. Fish
B. Snake
C. Crocodile
D. Whale

Q.49 Which of the following statements is/are correct about Lysosome?

1. It is called the "suicidal bags" of the cell.

2. The lysosomal membrane is rich in Cardiolipin.

3. They are absent in Erythrocytes.

4. They are basic in nature.

A. 1 and 3 only
B. 2 and 4 only
C. 1, 2 and 4 only
D. 2, 3 and 4 only

Q.50 Which of the following statements is/are correct concerning Ozone gas?

1. Good ozone is found in the upper part of the atmosphere called the Troposphere.

2. The thickness of the ozone in a column of air from the ground to the top of the atmosphere is measured in terms of Dobson units (DU).

A. 1 only
B. 2 only
C. Both 1 and 2
D. Neither 1 nor 2

Q.51 Which of the following is/are correct concerning Bharat Stage norms?

1. Bharat stage (BS) emission standards are laid down by the government to regulate the output of air pollutants from the internal combustion engines and spark-ignition engine equipment.

2. The central government has mandated that vehicle makers must manufacture, sell, and register only BS-VI (BS6) vehicles from April 1, 2020.

3. The first emission norms were introduced in India in 1992 for petrol and in 1994 for diesel vehicles.

A. 1 and 2 only
B. 2 and 3 only
C. 1 and 3 only
D. All of the above

Q.52 Which of the following statements is/are correct?

1. Eutrophication is the natural ageing of a lake by nutrient enrichment of its water.

2. The prime contaminants are nitrates and phosphates, which act as plant nutrients.

A. 1 only
B. 2 only
C. Both 1 and 2
D. Neither 1 nor 2

Q.53 Consider the following statements regarding electrostatic precipitator.

1. An electrostatic precipitator can remove over 60 per cent particulate matter present in the exhaust from a thermal power plant.

2. It has electrode wires that are maintained at several thousand volts, which produce a corona that releases electrons.

A. 1 only
B. 2 only
C. Both 1 and 2
D. Neither 1 nor 2

Q.54 Which of the following is a erosional feature by river?

A. Loess
B. U-shaped valley
C. V-shaped valley
D. Natural levee

Q.55 Select the option that means the same as the given idiom.
To pull oneself together

[SSC Constable (GD), 2019]

A. To hide important facts and reasons
B. To put necessary matters on the table
C. To keep working constantly with attention
D. To calm oneself and begin to think or act

Q.56 Direction: Read the following information carefully and answer the question given below-

In the given question, a word or phrase is underlined. Beneath each sentence, four alternative meanings are given. Select the best alternative that has the closest meaning to the underlined phrase.

Readers are advised to take this information with a grain of salt.

A. Taking something under consideration.
B. Taking responsibility to maintain privacy.
C. Not taking something too seriously.
D. Not taking something easily.

Q.57 Identify the segment in the sentence, which contains the grammatical error.

My father did never have an opportunity to go to a University.

[SSC Sub Inspector (CPO), 2019]

A. an opportunity
B. a University
C. to go to
D. did never have

Q.58 Select the alternative that will improve the underlined part of the sentence in case there is no improvement select "No improvement".

Kalidasa was a greater classical Sanskrit poet of India.

[SSC Sub Inspector (CPO), 2019]

A. No improvement
B. was a great classical
C. was the greater classic
D. was a greatest classical

Q.59 The concept of the Eight-fold path forms the theme of:

A. Parinirvana
B. Divyavadana
C. Dipavamsa
D. Dharma Chakra Pravartana Sutra

Q.60 Consider the following statements regarding Dhamma Chakra Day.

1. The day marks Buddha's first teaching after attaining Enlightenment.

2. This day is considered the only sacred day for Buddhists.

3. The teaching of Dharma chakra Pravartana Sutra is also known as the First Turning of Wheels of Dharma.

Which of the above statements is/are correct?

A. 1 only   **B.** 1, 2   **C.** 1, 3   **D.** 1, 2, 3

Q.61 From the given answer figures, select the one in which the question figure is hidden/embedded. (Rotation is not allowed)

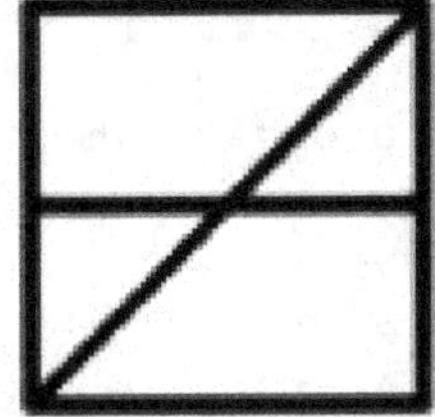

[AFCAT, 2021]

A.

B.

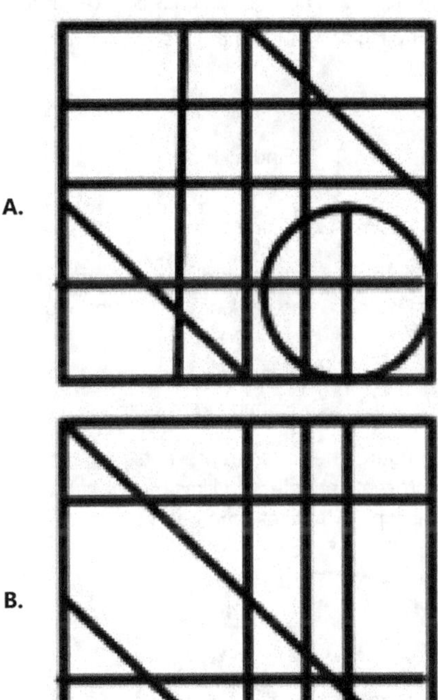

C.

D.

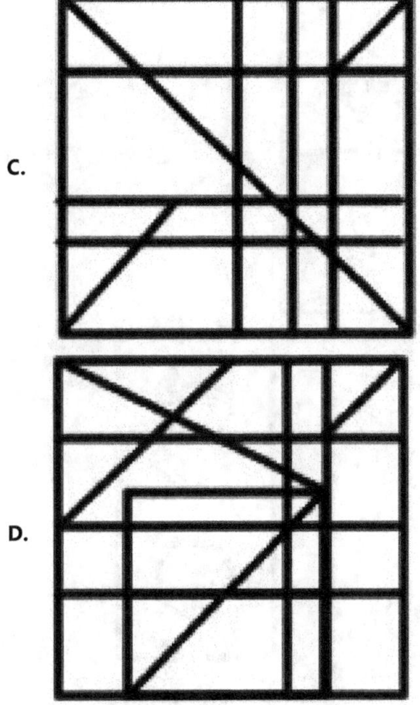

Q.62 From the given answer figures, select the one in which the question figure is hidden/embedded.

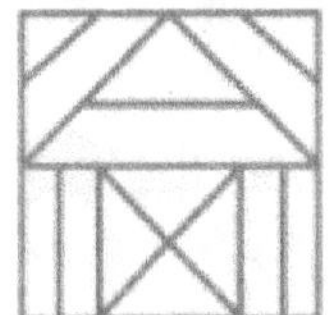

[SSC Constable (GD), 2019], [UP Police Constable, 2019], [SSC MTS, 2017]

A.   **B.**

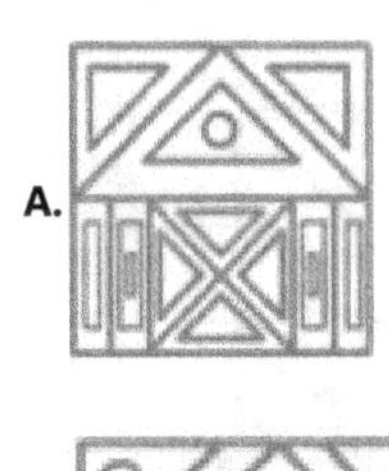
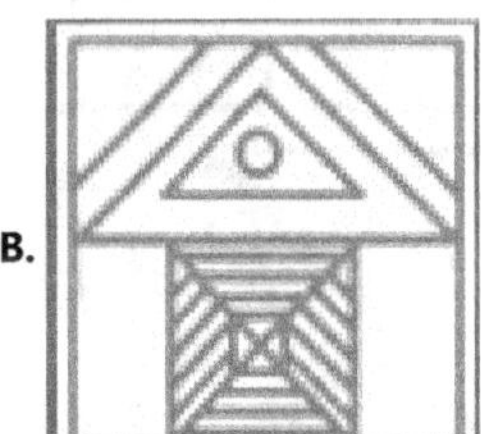

C.   **D.**

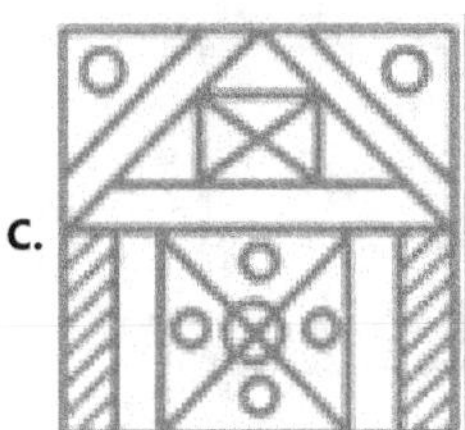

Q.63 Direction: In which answer, the figure will complete the pattern in the following question figure?

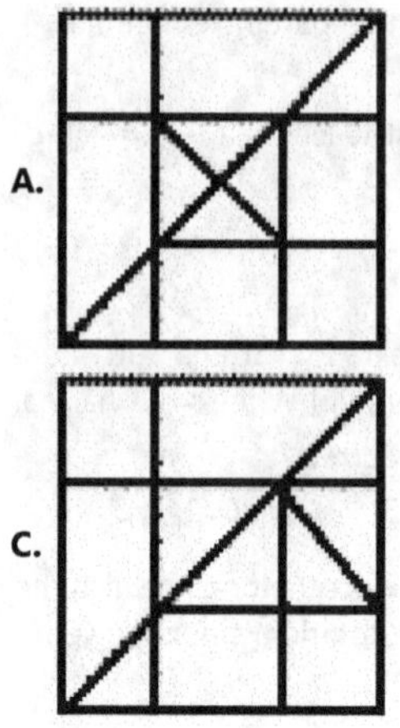

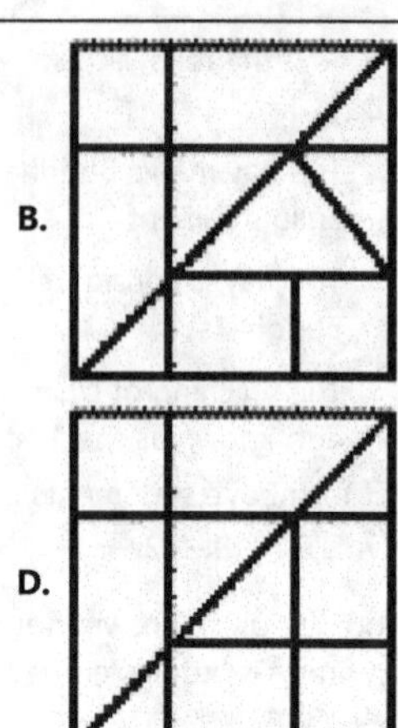

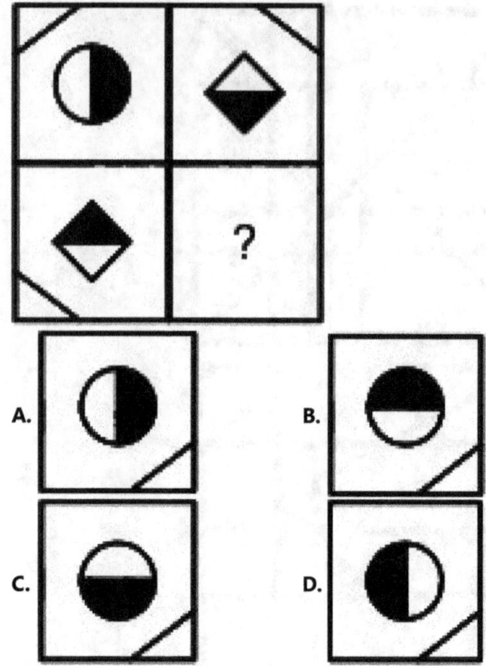

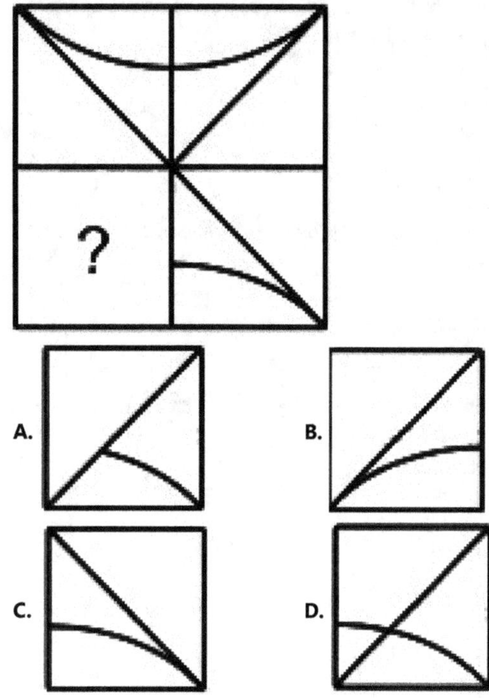

Q.64 Direction: Select a suitable figure from the four alternatives that would complete the figure matrix.

Q.65 Direction: From the given answer figures, select the one in which question figure is hidden/embedded (Rotation not allowed).

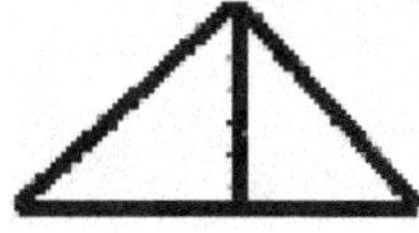

Q.66 If $a:b = 3:2, b:c = 5:7$ and $d:c = 3:4$. Then find $a:b:c:d$

A. 17: 20: 28: 13   **B.** 28: 20: 22: 21

C. 30: 20: 28: 21   **D.** 30: 25: 28: 27

Q.67 A got twice as many marks in English as in Science. His total marks in English, Science, and Mathematics is 180. If the ratio of his marks in English and Mathematics is $2:3$, what is his marks in Science?

A. 20   **B.** 60   **C.** 30   **D.** 40

Q.68 a : b = 2 : 3 and b : c = 4 : 7. Find a : b : c.

A. 4 : 3 : 7   **B.** 2 : 4 : 7

C. 8 : 12 : 21   **D.** None of these

Q.69 Who remained the highest-placed Indian batsman at the fourth position in the latest ICC Test rankings issued in January 2021?

A. David Warner   **B.** Kane Williamson

C. Virat Kohli   **D.** Rishabh Pant

Q.70 In the following figure, the square represents people who likes cricket, circle represents people who likes basket ball, rectangle represents people who likes tennis and triangle represents people who likes hockey.

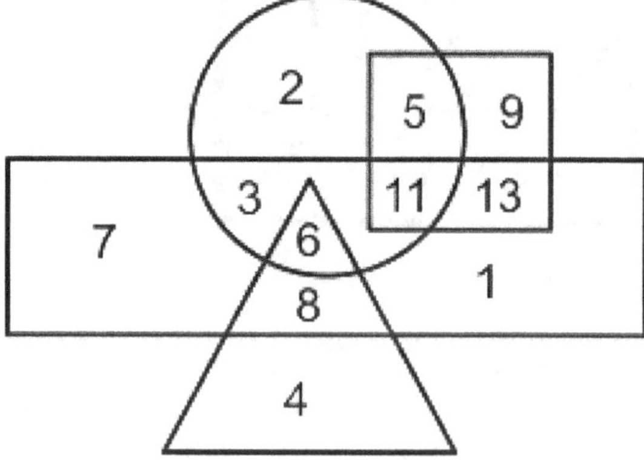

The people who likes basket ball, tennis, and hockey but not cricket?

A. 14   **B.** 18   **C.** 11   **D.** 6

Q.71 Identify the diagram that best represents the relationship among classes given below:

Shirt, pants, and cloth

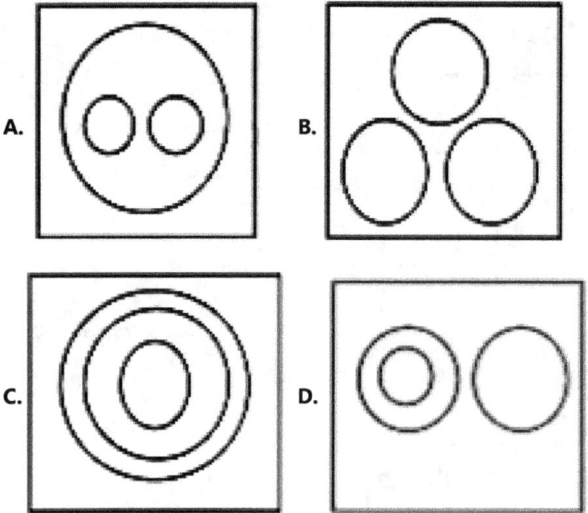

Q.72 Select the Venn diagram that best represents the given set of classes.

Infant, Boys, humans

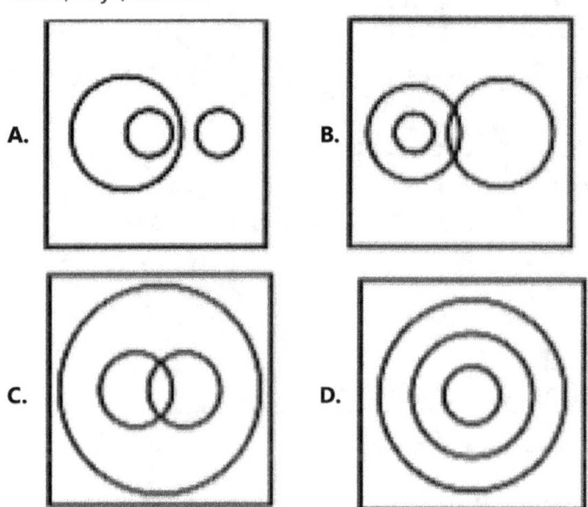

Ques (73-74):Direction: In the following figure, rectangle, square, circle and triangle represent the regions of wheat, gram, maize and rice cultivation, respectively. On the basis of the figure, answer the following question:

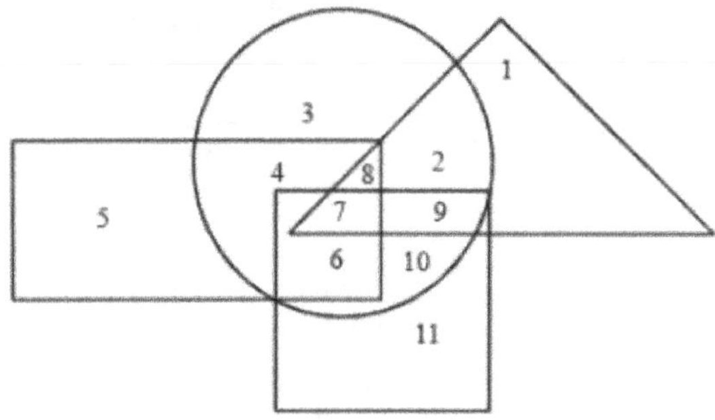

Q.73 Which area is cultivated by all four commodities?

A. 7   **B.** 8   **C.** 9   **D.** 2

Q.74 Which area is cultivated by wheat and maize only?

A. 8   **B.** 6   **C.** 5   **D.** 4

Q.75 Direction: Arrange the given words in the sequence in which they occur in the dictionary.

1. Dutch
2. Dust
3. Dump
4. Dummy

A. 4312   **B.** 4213   **C.** 4132   **D.** 4321

Q.76 Direction: Arrange the given words in the sequence in which they occur in the dictionary.

1. Education
2. Election
3. Earliest
4. Edition
5. Eclipse

A. 3 4 2 5 1   **B.** 5 4 2 3 1   **C.** 5 3 1 2 4   **D.** 3 5 4 1 2

Q.77 Consider the following statements:

1. The office of Chief Justice of India comes under the purview of the Right to Information (RTI) Act.

2. The Chief Information Commissioner and an Information Commissioner shall hold office for such term as prescribed by the Central Government or until they attain the age of 65 years, whichever is earlier.

Which of the above statements is/are correct?

A. 1 only   **B.** 2 only

C. Both 1 and 2   **D.** Neither 1 nor 2

Q.78 Direction: The following sentence consists an underlined word(s) followed by four options. Select the option that is nearest in meaning to the underlined word and mark your response accordingly.

The underlined attitude of the speaker made the groups unhappy.

[Officers Training Academy (OTA), 2021], [Indian Military Academy (IMA), 2021]

A. resentful   **B.** congenial

C. unruly   **D.** supportive

Q.79 Direction: The following sentence consists of an underlined word followed by four options. Select the option that is opposite in meaning to the underlined word and mark your response accordingly.

His arguments are not valid. People consider it bombastic.

A. Outdated   **B.** Straightforward

C. Verbose   **D.** Untrue

Q.80 Direction: The following sentence consists an underlined word followed by four options. Select the option that is opposite in meaning to the underlined word and mark your response accordingly.

The decision was absurd for many of the members of the team.

[Officers Training Academy (OTA), 2021], [Indian Military Academy (IMA), 2021]

A. bizarre
B. meaningless
C. reasonable
D. thoughtful

Q.81 Srinivas works and earns Rs. 14,500 per month, out of which, he saves only 20% and spends the remaining amount on other deeds. Find the amount spent?

[RRB/RRC Group D, 2018]

A. Rs. 11,500
B. Rs. 11,400
C. Rs. 11,000
D. Rs. 11,600

Q.82 In an examination, 80% of candidates passed in English, and 85% of candidates passed in Mathematics. If 73% of candidates passed in both these subjects, then what percent of candidates failed in both the subjects?

A. 8
B. 15
C. 27
D. 35

Q.83 What is the value of 19% of 23% of 560?

A. 24.472
B. 23.572
C. 25.762
D. 27.342

Q.84 Direction: Choose the appropriate word to fill in the blank.

They did not want to leave ________ to chance while deciding on the trip.

[Allahabad High Court Review Officer (RO), 2017]

A. something
B. nothing
C. anything
D. someone

Q.85 Direction: Choose the appropriate word to fill in the blank.

Keep your friends close and your enemies ______.

[Allahabad High Court Review Officer (RO), 2017]

A. closer
B. farther
C. far away
D. closest

Q.86 Direction: Choose the correct 'sound' word to describe.

The_____ of strange and unfamiliar dialects at the market held my interest.

[Allahabad High Court Review Officer (RO), 2017]

A. racket
B. rumble
C. clanging
D. babble

Q.87 Direction: Choose the appropriate word to fill in the blank.

There are ____ takers for animal fur today, while ___ of the yesteryear stars were proud owners of mink coats.

[Allahabad High Court Review Officer (RO), 2017]

A. few, quite a few
B. quite a few, a few
C. few, a few
D. a few, few

Ques (88-92):Direction: Select a suitable figure from the four alternatives that would complete the figure matrix.

Q.88

(1) (2) (3) (4)

[UP Police Sub Inspector, 2021]

A. 1
B. 2
C. 3
D. 4

Q.89

(1) (2) (3) (4)

A. 1
B. 2
C. 3
D. 4

Q.90

(1) (2) (3) (4)

[Telangana Police Constable, 2015]

A. 1
B. 2
C. 3
D. 4

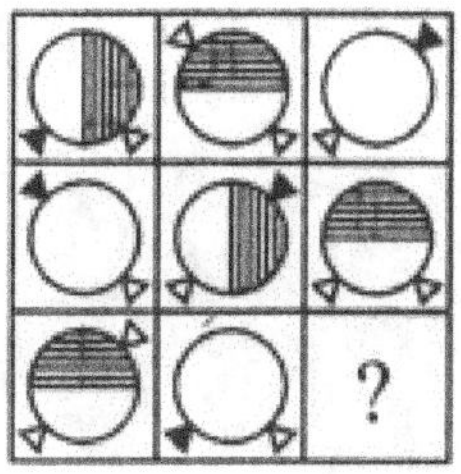

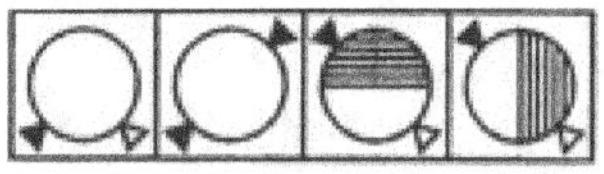

Q.91 (1) (2) (3) (4)

[SSC Sub Inspector (CPO), 2020]

A. 1 **B.** 2 **C.** 3 **D.** 4

Q.92

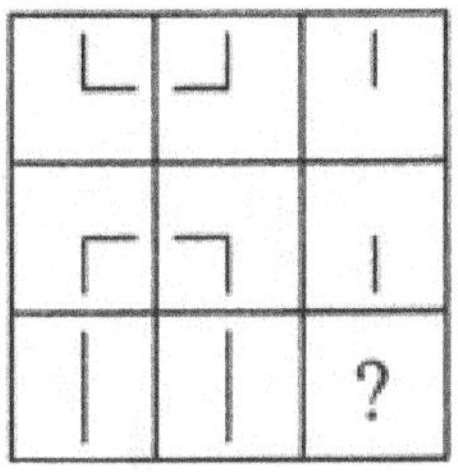

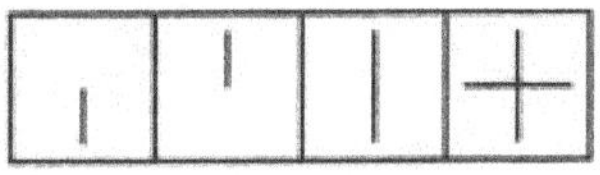

(1) (2) (3) (4)

[Telangana Police Constable, 2015]

A. 1 **B.** 2 **C.** 3 **D.** 4

Ques (93-97):Direction: Read the passage and answer the questions based on it.

RICHARD WRIGHT, the father figure of African American literature, both nurtured and was rejected by his two most conspicuous heirs, Ralph Ellison and James Baldwin. Wright, who took Ellison under his wing in New York in the late 1930s, told his acolyte to stop copying him, that he was mimicking, not cultivating his own style. Ellison responded that he was trying to learn to write well by imitating his mentor. That was when they were close. Baldwin, too, started out as a pupil and an admirer who saw Wright poised to be the greatest Black writer in the United States.

Though it happened slowly, by 1941, Ellison betrayed signs of feeling that Wright, affiliated off and on with the Communist Party, wrote fiction that was too ideological and not sensitive enough to nuance: Wright wanted to testify to the monstrosities of white supremacy, rather than the power of Black resilience. Ellison grew committed to the poetry of American democracy, despite how badly it was sullied; he swore by the virtues of individualism. Calling Wright "Poor Richard," Baldwin joined Ellison in lamenting their mentor's failure to see the beauty of Black people. The two of them never ceased to love Wright's prose, but they came to reject his perspective.

I admit I've been inclined to share their verdict, based on Wright's first novel, Native Son, published in 1940, which I read again and again in classes before and during college. I've parroted the notes I took in lectures, and I've taught a version of those lectures myself: Bigger Thomas was a protagonist stripped of any redeeming qualities, so distorted by the conditions of racism that he became an avatar more than a character, and an unsettling representation of Blackness.

My assessment of Wright has begun to shift over the past couple of years. I've read 12 Million Black Voices (1941)—his reflections on the Great Migration, accompanied by Farm Security Administration photographs taken during the Depression—and been struck by his broad sympathy. And I've reread Black Boy (1945), a memoir I hadn't touched since my final year of high school in the Northeast, in a writing seminar led by a teacher born, like me, in Birmingham, Alabama. Wright reached for the very core of the human condition in his portrait of growing up destitute in the Deep South during the early 20th century and then making his way north: abundance everywhere and terrible hunger, tragedy mixed with the quotidian in the most disorienting ways. The experience he evoked might not have been every Black life, but it was indeed a part of Black life. In Mississippi, the land could swallow you whole. In Chicago, a rat might bite you, because after all, you were made to live in slums no different from rattraps. Wright was showing us something true, if not absolute—how, with the plantation breathing at your back and deferred dreams before you, a tragedy happened. Now I'm even more convinced that Wright deserves to be looked at with fresh eyes.

Q.93 All of the following statements can be inferred from the passage EXCEPT that:

A. The protagonist, Bigger Thomas, is portrayed as a pessimistic character who is an unsettling reflection of Blackness

B. Wright grew up extremely poor in the Deep South in the early twentieth century and then moved north

C. Bigger Thomas, a character devoid of any negative traits, was the protagonist in Wright's first book, Native Son

D. The author was moved by Wright's broad sympathy after reading his book 12 Million Black Voices

Q.94 Why does the author claim that "In Mississippi, the land could swallow you whole. In Chicago, a rat might bite you, because after all, you were made to live in slums no different from rattraps?"

A. The author was trying to emphasize how blacks faced horrible hunger and disaster, were suppressed, and were denied their dreams

B. The author was reading lines from Wright's novel 12 Million Black Voices (1941), which was about the Great Migration

C. The author was referring to Black Protestantism, which provided believers with psychic refuge while still recommending submission to the cruelty of the world

D. The author was explaining how Wright came across all of the blacks' misery while growing up destitute in the early 21st century

Q.95 Which of the following statements WEAKENS the author's argument that said: "RICHARD WRIGHT, the father figure of

African American literature, both nurtured and was rejected by his two most conspicuous heirs, Ralph Ellison and James Baldwin"?

A. Ellison and Baldwin both opposed and chastised Wright for his intermittent affiliation with the Communist Party.

B. Ellison was attempting to learn to write well by imitating Wright, and Baldwin, too, respected Wright, who was on the verge of becoming the greatest Black writer in the United States.

C. Ellison and Baldwin criticized Wright's viewpoint, claiming that he failed to acknowledge the beauty of Black people.

D. Ellison and Baldwin chastised Wright for his insistence on dramatising inevitability of subjugation and saw Wright as submitting to Black supremacy.

Q.96 Which of the following best represents the author's change of opinions about Richard Wright?

A. ideological and non sensitive works of Wright, American democracy, virtues of individualism

B. Wright's first novel, Native Son, Wright's reflections on the Great Migration, Black Boy (1945)

C. Black resilience, virtues of individualism, 12 Million Black Voices

D. Communist Party, fiction, ideological and non sensitive works

Q.97 Which of the following can be reasonably inferred from the passage?

A. Despite his reputation as a father and figure in African American literature, Richard Wright nurtured and rejected his own children.

B. In the late 1930s, Richard Wright expelled his son Ellison in New York for imitating and mimicking him rather than developing his own style.

C. The author, who is from New York, has changed his opinion of Richard Wright after reading one of his novels.

D. Richard Wright's sons believed that instead of depicting the endurance of Blacks, Richard wanted to show only evil of whites in his novels.

Q.98 Compare: $\dfrac{3}{4} \ and \ \dfrac{-5}{6}$

A. $\geq$ **B.** $<$ **C.** $>$ **D.** $=$

Q.99 Which one of the followings will be the correct ascending order?

A. 30.003, 300.03, 30.030, 030.30, 3.033

B. 3.033, 30.03, 30.003, 030.30, 300.03

C. 3.033, 30.003, 30.030, 030.30, 300.03

D. 3.033, 030.30, 30.030, 30.003, 300.03

Q.100 Find the value of:

$$\frac{[(1.569\times1.569\times0.431)+(1.569\times0.431\times0.431)]}{[(1.569+0.431)^2-(1.569-0.431)^2]}$$

A. 1.5   **B.** 2   **C.** 0.5   **D.** 1

// Smart Answer Sheet //

Correct Percentage of students who answered correctly. **Skipped** Percentage of students who skipped.

Q.	Ans.	Correct / Skipped	Q.	Ans.	Correct / Skipped	Q.	Ans.	Correct / Skipped	Q.	Ans.	Correct / Skipped	Q.	Ans.	Correct / Skipped	Q.	Ans.	Correct / Skipped
1	A	43.23 % / 37.26 %	18	C	84.15 % / 12.77 %	35	A	66.3 % / 31.5 %	52	C	69.75 % / 30.05 %	69	C	89.51 % / 10.26 %	86	D	68.34 % / 31.6 %
2	C	42.29 % / 33.37 %	19	A	50.13 % / 35.56 %	36	C	24.02 % / 72.0 %	53	B	78.69 % / 16.3 %	70	D	58.26 % / 36.94 %	87	A	76.12 % / 14.31 %
3	C	65.59 % / 31.7 %	20	B	28.13 % / 71.23 %	37	D	65.15 % / 31.79 %	54	C	49.69 % / 32.49 %	71	A	88.05 % / 10.15 %	88	A	44.49 % / 53.56 %
4	B	51.05 % / 33.66 %	21	D	76.45 % / 17.05 %	38	A	68.13 % / 30.76 %	55	D	17.92 % / 81.48 %	72	C	62.08 % / 35.83 %	89	B	25.98 % / 72.74 %
5	D	88.77 % / 11.03 %	22	C	66.27 % / 33.44 %	39	D	79.1 % / 14.24 %	56	C	50.01 % / 38.0 %	73	A	79.98 % / 12.84 %	90	C	45.49 % / 30.67 %
6	A	52.2 % / 30.03 %	23	D	81.13 % / 16.76 %	40	A	79.8 % / 18.93 %	57	D	18.06 % / 67.37 %	74	D	64.57 % / 32.23 %	91	D	49.45 % / 33.01 %
7	D	46.26 % / 39.51 %	24	A	46.65 % / 43.23 %	41	A	84.99 % / 13.85 %	58	B	13.5 % / 83.39 %	75	D	79.14 % / 15.65 %	92	C	43.37 % / 32.06 %
8	B	63.51 % / 36.11 %	25	C	87.58 % / 11.91 %	42	C	67.51 % / 32.01 %	59	D	85.36 % / 14.6 %	76	D	44.13 % / 49.58 %	93	C	83.94 % / 13.31 %
9	B	78.78 % / 15.07 %	26	C	52.77 % / 35.99 %	43	A	82.34 % / 11.8 %	60	C	29.31 % / 70.14 %	77	A	42.2 % / 45.56 %	94	A	66.19 % / 31.45 %
10	B	56.01 % / 34.22 %	27	D	40.98 % / 57.88 %	44	C	77.59 % / 11.7 %	61	D	78.79 % / 10.32 %	78	A	40.33 % / 51.7 %	95	B	68.9 % / 30.12 %
11	C	81.44 % / 11.51 %	28	C	40.33 % / 34.76 %	45	C	67.06 % / 30.93 %	62	C	87.86 % / 11.97 %	79	B	79.56 % / 17.96 %	96	B	47.48 % / 49.61 %
12	D	85.45 % / 10.28 %	29	B	46.76 % / 46.14 %	46	D	64.2 % / 32.35 %	63	D	86.04 % / 11.19 %	80	C	87.06 % / 12.8 %	97	D	64.47 % / 34.02 %
13	C	52.55 % / 31.8 %	30	A	64.8 % / 32.48 %	47	D	67.93 % / 30.46 %	64	B	77.9 % / 21.47 %	81	D	84.17 % / 15.43 %	98	C	69.04 % / 30.73 %
14	B	79.28 % / 18.64 %	31	C	53.05 % / 35.9 %	48	D	76.14 % / 21.23 %	65	C	76.44 % / 20.42 %	82	A	64.98 % / 30.65 %	99	C	13.02 % / 84.63 %
15	B	42.33 % / 53.08 %	32	D	76.61 % / 17.72 %	49	A	44.99 % / 30.22 %	66	C	67.32 % / 30.32 %	83	A	58.93 % / 39.13 %	100	C	77.08 % / 17.73 %
16	D	40.06 % / 53.79 %	33	B	48.69 % / 38.01 %	50	B	27.09 % / 67.93 %	67	C	84.02 % / 15.45 %	84	C	66.95 % / 31.04 %			
17	D	87.15 % / 10.67 %	34	C	31.65 % / 67.44 %	51	A	87.74 % / 10.87 %	68	C	58.69 % / 33.35 %	85	A	16.14 % / 81.78 %			

//Hints and Solutions//

1. Larsen & Toubro (L&T) signed a pact with the Indian Institute of Technology in Bombay, Maharashtra to co-research and develop green hydrogen technology. Under this partnership, L&T will utilize its engineering expertise, product scale-up, and commercialization know-how, while IIT Bombay will use its cutting-edge research in hydrogen technologies and world-class technologists to develop indigenous globally-competitive technologies.

Hence, the correct option is (A).

2. "The Global Report on Food Crises 2020" has been released recently, which is produced by the Global Network against Food Crises. It is an international alliance working to address the root causes of extreme hunger.

The report analyses the factors which contribute to food crises across the globe, and explains how COVID pandemic could worsen the crisis.

Hence, the correct option is (C).

3. The National Science & Technology Entrepreneurship Development Board (NSTEDB) works under the aegis of Department of Science and Technology (DST), Ministry of Science and Technology.

DST has launched a report on the journey of the National Science and Technology Entrepreneurship Development Board (NSTEDB) in catalysing innovation, entrepreneurship, and incubation.

Hence, the correct option is (C).

4. Global financial services and payment technology company Mastercard has partnered with USAID to launch a programme called 'Project Kirana'.

Under the programme, the organisations aim to expand financial inclusion and encourage women who own or operate kirana shops to adopt digital payments, thereby helping to increase their revenue. Around 3000 women are to be enrolled across Uttar Pradesh, in a pilot step.

Hence, the correct option is (B).

5. South Korea has signed a $ 2.25 billion deal with a Russian state-run nuclear energy company 'ASE'in August 2022.

- It has been signed to provide components for Egypt's first nuclear power plant.
- ASE is a subsidiary of Rosatom, a state-owned Russian nuclear conglomerate.
- South Korea has also signed a $ 20 billion contract to build nuclear power reactors in the UAE.

Hence, the correct option is (D).

6. Given:

$$P = \text{Rs. } 1000, A = \text{Rs. } 1331$$

Let the required time be t years.

Interest is compounded half-yearly

$\therefore$ Time $= 2t$ half years and rate $= \dfrac{20}{2} = 10\%$

$$\therefore 1000 \left(1 + \frac{10}{100}\right)^{2t} = 1331$$

$$\Rightarrow \left(\frac{11}{10}\right)^{2t} = \frac{1331}{1000}$$

$$\Rightarrow \left(\frac{11}{10}\right)^{2t} = \left(\frac{11}{10}\right)^{3}$$

$$\Rightarrow 2t = 3$$

$$\therefore t = \frac{3}{2} \text{ years or } 1\frac{1}{2} \text{ years}$$

Hence, the correct option is (A).

7. Investment = Market value $\times$ number of shares

According to the question:

$$\text{Number of shares} = \frac{67200}{120}$$

$$\text{Number of shares} = 560$$

$$\text{Dividend} = \frac{\text{Dividend\%}}{100} \times \text{Nominal value} \times \text{Number of shares}$$

$$\text{Dividend} = \frac{12}{100} \times 100 \times 560$$

$$\text{Dividend} = 12 \times 560$$

$$\text{Dividend} = 6720 \text{ i.e., the income}$$

Hence, the correct option is (D).

8. We know that,

$$SI = \frac{P \times R \times T}{100}$$

According to the question,

$$\frac{30}{100}P = \frac{P \times R \times 6}{100}$$

$$R = 5\%$$

It will be equal to the principal after,

$$P = \frac{P \times R \times T}{100}$$

$$P = \frac{P \times 5 \times T}{100}$$

$$T = 20 \text{ years}$$

Hence, the correct option is (B).

9. Joint exercises between the Air Forces of India and France are called Garuda.

This year, the Garuda VI exercise took place from 1st to 12th July 2019 at Mont de Marsan in France. This tactical bilateral Indo-French exercise aims at enhancing the interoperability level of the French and Indian crews in air defense and ground attack missions.

The exercise is alternately held in France and India.

Hence, the correct option is (B).

10.

- After Ashoka's coronation, he fought only a major war known as the Kalinga war.

- The massacre in this war filled him with grief.

- This war caused great suffering to the people of Kalinga, the priests, monks who filled Ashoka with great penitence.

- He, then started to use "Dhammaghosha" instead of "Bherighosha" & adopted the policies of cultural annihilation rather than attacking kingdoms physically.

- This step became one of the causes responsible for the decline of the Mauryan empire.

Hence, the correct option is (B).

11. In the above-given sentence, 'efficiently' will be used.

It is so because 'efficiently' is an adverb meaning in a well-organized and competent way or in a way that achieves maximum productivity with minimum wasted effort or expense. The sentence tells the fact that the person is well-organized and competent and therefore his judgment is accurate.

Complete Sentence:

I work very **efficiently** and am decisive and accurate in my judgment.

Hence, the correct option is (C).

12. In the above-given sentence, 'exhausted' will be used.

It is so because 'exhausted' is an adjective meaning very tired. The sentence tells the fact that the person gets tired by a short stroll as he/she is lacking energy.

Complete Sentence:

I don't have much energy these days. After a short stroll, I am quite **exhausted**.

Hence, the correct option is (D).

13. In the above-given sentence, 'monotonous' will be used.

It is so because 'monotonous' is an adjective meaning dull, tedious, and repetitious; lacking in variety and interest or (of a sound or utterance) lacking in variation in tone or pitch.

The sentence tells the fact that the sound lacked variation in tone and pitch and therefore Sanjay found it monotonous.

Complete Sentence:

Sanjay found the unchanging rhythm of the musical piece to be annoyingly **monotonous**.

Hence, the correct option is (C).

14. In the above-given sentence, 'blends' will be used.

It is so because 'blends' is a verb meaning 'to form a harmonious combination'.

The sentence talks about the harmonious combination of modern and traditional culture/concepts in the city of Bangalore.

Complete Sentence:

Bengaluru is a beautiful city which **blends** the modern with the traditional.

Hence, the correct option is (B).

15. The most appropriate word is 'struggle'.

The sentence talks about the task or the movement which is made successful by the policy of non-violence.

Complete Sentence:

The nationalists followed a policy of non-violence to make their **struggle** successful.

Hence, the correct option is (B).

16. The correct answer is:

The children were being taken to the zoo by their class teacher.

The above-given sentence is in the active voice.

We need to change it into passive voice.

We need to follow the given steps for converting the sentence into passive voice:-

- The subject 'the class teacher' of the active voice becomes the object of the passive voice.

- The object 'the children' of the active voice becomes the subject of the passive voice.

- The tense(past continuous tense) will be changed according to the following structure:-
    - Active Voice - Subject + was/were + V_{ing} + Object.
    - Passive Voice - Object + was/were + being + V_3 + Subject.

- Thus, 'was taking' will be replaced by 'were being taken'.

- The rest of the sentence remains the same.

Hence, the correct option is (D).

17. The correct answer is:

Women employees were permitted to leave the office early on that day.

The above-given sentence is in the active voice.

We need to change it in the passive voice.

The following steps are required to change the given sentence into passive voice:

- The subject 'the manager' of the active voice will become the object of the passive voice.

- The object 'women employees' of the active voice will become the subject of the passive voice.

- The tense(simple past tense) will change according to the following structure:-

- Active Voice - Subject + did + V₁ or V₂ + Object.
- Passive Voice - Object + was/were + V₃ + by + Object.

- Thus, 'permitted' will be replaced by 'were permitted'.
- The rest of the sentence remains the same.

Hence, the correct option is (D).

18. Soil pollution is defined as the contamination of a part of land due to the presence of xenobiotics or other alteration in the natural soil environment. The major causes of soil pollution are- Industrial activities, agricultural activities, waste disposal, accidental oil spills, acid rain.

Hence, the correct option is (C).

19. Let cost price of 4 items be $= x$

Cost price of 1 item be $= \dfrac{x}{4}$

According to question:

Sellingt price of 3 times = x

Selling price of 1 item = $= \dfrac{x}{3}$

$$\text{Profit} = \dfrac{x}{3} - \dfrac{x}{4}$$

$$= \dfrac{4x-3x}{12} = \dfrac{x}{12}$$

$$\text{Profit\%} = \dfrac{\frac{x}{12}}{\frac{x}{4}} \times 100$$

$$= \dfrac{4}{12} \times 100$$

$$= 33\dfrac{1}{3}\%$$

Hence, the correct option is (A).

20. Given:

Cost price of item A is equal to the cost price of item B

MP of item $A = 160\%$ of CP

MP of item $B = 150\%$ of CP

Calculation:

Marked price of item B is 600 after increased by 50%

CP of item B,

$$\Rightarrow CP \times \dfrac{150}{100} = 600$$

Cost price of item $B = Rs.\,400$

CP of $A = CP$ of B

$$\Rightarrow \text{Marked price of item } A = 400 \times \dfrac{160}{100}$$

MP of item $A = $ Rs. 640

MP of item $B = $ Rs. 600

Selling price of item A and item B after giving 10% discount

SP of Item $A = 640 \times \dfrac{90}{100} = 576$

SP of Item $B = 600 \times \dfrac{90}{100} = 540$

$\Rightarrow$ Difference between selling price of item A and item $B = $ $576 - 540$

$\Rightarrow$ Rs. 36

Hence, the correct option is (B).

21. SP1 $= 12000 \times \dfrac{55}{100} = $ Rs. 6600

SP1 $= 12000 \times \dfrac{70}{100} \times \dfrac{85}{100}$ Rs. 7140

Therefore, reqd. difference=7140−6600= Rs. 540

Hence, the correct option is (D).

22. The study of butterflies is known as Lepidopterology. Similarly, the study of maps is known as Cartography.

Hence, the correct option is (C).

23. President is the highest officer of Country and Governor is the highest officer of State.

Hence, the correct option is (D).

24. If someone has been humiliated, they have been greatly embarrassed. If someone is terrified, they are extremely frightened.

Hence, the correct option is (A).

25. As Peacock is the national bird of India, similarly Bear is the national animal of Russia.

Hence, the correct option is (C).

26. As North-West is 135º clockwise from South in the same were North-East is 135º clockwise from the West.

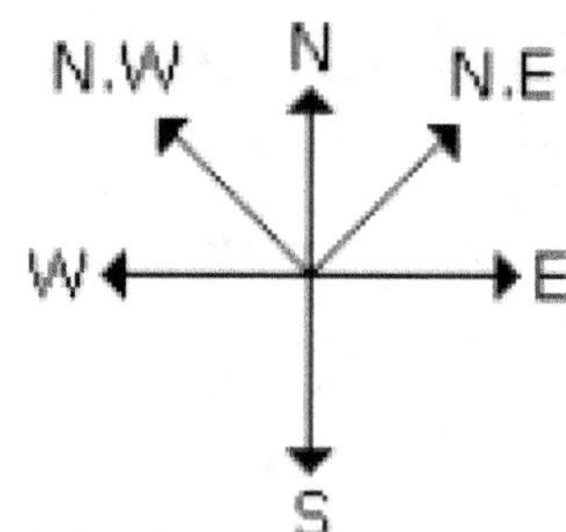

Hence, the correct option is (C).

27. Given:

Covers 455 meters in 35 minutes

$$\text{Speed} = \dfrac{Distance}{Time}$$

Speed = 455 meters / 35 minutes

But we need speed in km/hr

We know that,

1 km = 1000 meters

1 hour = 60 minutes

$$\Rightarrow \text{Speed} = \frac{\left(\frac{455}{1000}\right)}{\left(\frac{35}{60}\right)}$$

$$\Rightarrow \text{Speed} = \frac{(455 \times 60)}{(1000 \times 35)}$$

$\Rightarrow$ Speed = 0.78 km/hr

$\therefore$ Speed of a person is 0.78 km/hr.

Hence, the correct option is (D).

28. Formula used:

Distance = speed × time

$1 \text{ m/sec} = \dfrac{18}{5} \text{ km /hr}$

Length of train = distance

Speed convert km/hr to m/sec

$$\Rightarrow 72 \times \left(\frac{5}{18}\right)$$

$\Rightarrow$ Speed = 20 m/sec

Distance = 20 × 25

$\Rightarrow$ 500 metres

$\therefore$ The length of the train is 500 metres.

Hence, the correct option is (C).

29. Formula Used:

$$\text{Average Speed} = \frac{\text{Total dis tance}}{\text{Total time taken}}$$

Let the distance be xkm.

Time taken from city A to city B $= \dfrac{x}{40} = \dfrac{x}{40}$ hours

Time taken from city B to city A $= \dfrac{x}{60} = \dfrac{x}{60}$ hours

Total time $= 10$ hours

$$\Rightarrow \frac{x}{40} + \frac{x}{60} = 10$$

$$\Rightarrow x \times \frac{3x+2x}{120} = 10$$

$$\Rightarrow \frac{5x}{120} = 10$$

$$\Rightarrow x = 240 \; km$$

The distance between A and B is $240 \; km.$

Hence, the correct option is (B).

30. Let the speed of train be S_T.

Distance = length of train(L)

Speed(S_1) of first person be 26 m/s, Speed(S_2) of second person be 42 m/s

Relative speed, person moving opposite direction,

First person passes

$$\Rightarrow (S_T + S_1) = \frac{L}{9}$$

$$\Rightarrow S_T = \left(\frac{L}{9}\right) - 26 \quad \text{----(1)}$$

Second person passes

$$\Rightarrow (S_T + S_2) = \frac{L}{7}$$

$$\Rightarrow S_T = \left(\frac{L}{7}\right) - 42 \quad \text{----(2)}$$

Substitute the value of S_T in equation (1)

$$\Rightarrow \frac{L}{9} - 26 = \frac{L}{7} - 42$$

$$\Rightarrow \frac{L}{7} - \frac{L}{9} = 16$$

$$\Rightarrow L = 16 \times \frac{63}{2}$$

$$\Rightarrow L = 504 \text{ m}$$

$\therefore$ The length of the train is 504 m.

Hence, the correct option is (A).

31.

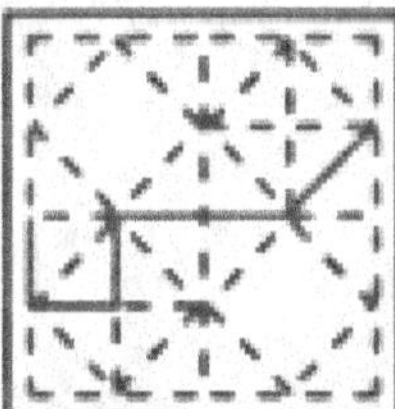

Therefore, the correct answer is 'option (C)'.

Hence, the correct option is (C).

32. The embedded part of this image is:

Hence, the correct option is (D).

33. From the given options, we can see that the question figure is embedded in option (B).

Hence, the correct option is (B).

34. Only option (C) can be formed by the given pieces in the question figure.

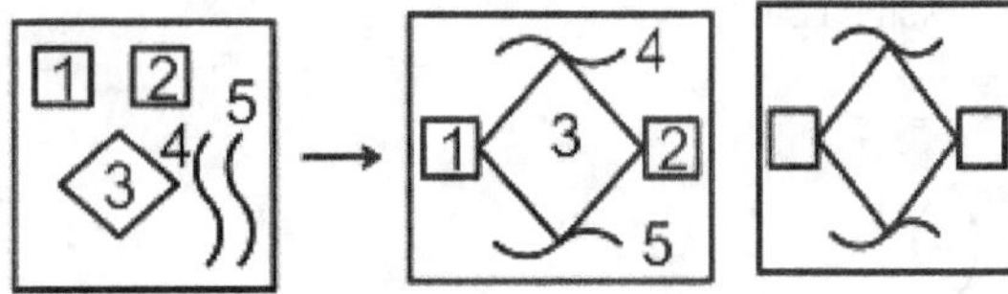

Hence the correct option is (C).

35.

The figure (X) given in the question is embodied in the alternative figure (1).

Hence, the correct option is (A).

36. Let X be the number of employees.

We are given that 40% of the employees are workers.

Now, 40% of X is $\dfrac{40}{100} \times X = 0.4X$

Therefore, the number of workers is $\dfrac{2X}{5}$

All the remaining employees are executives,

So the number of executives equals,

(The number of Employees) $-$ (The number of Workers)

$$= X - \dfrac{2X}{5}$$

$$= \dfrac{3X}{5}$$

The annual income of each worker is Rs. 390.

Therefore, the total annual income of all workers together is

$$= \dfrac{2X}{5} \times 390 = 156X$$

Also, the annual income of each executive is Rs. 420.

So, the total income of all the executives together is,

$$= \dfrac{3X}{5} \times 420 = 252X$$

Therefore, the total income of the employees is,

$$= 156X + 252X = 408X$$

The average income of all the employees together equals.

Hence, the correct option is (C).

37. Let the average after the 17th match is x

Then, the average before the 17th match is x-3

So,

16(x-3) + 87 = 17x

$\Rightarrow$ x = 87 - 48

= 39

Hence, the correct option is (D).

38. Let the three numbers be a, b and c.

Given average of three numbers $= 6$

$$\Rightarrow \dfrac{(a + b + c)}{3} = 6$$

$$\Rightarrow a + b + c = 18 \quad \text{.....(i)}$$

Given average of the first two number $= 5$

$$\Rightarrow \dfrac{(a + b)}{2} = 5$$

$$\Rightarrow a + b = 10 \quad \text{.....(ii)}$$

Given average of the last two numbers $= 8$

$$\Rightarrow \dfrac{(b + c)}{2} = 8$$

$$\Rightarrow b + c = 16 \quad \text{.....(iii)}$$

From equation (i) & (ii)

$$\Rightarrow c = 8$$

$$\Rightarrow b + c = 16$$

$$\Rightarrow b = 16 - 8 = 8$$

and $a = 18 - 8 - 8 = 2$

$\therefore$ The numbers are 2, 8 and 8.
Hence, the correct option is (A).

39. As we know,

If a person completes a piece of work in 'n' days, then work of 1 day is $\dfrac{1}{n}$ part of work.

Time taken by Ganesh and Bhima complete a work $= 6$ days

The part of the work that is completed by Ganesh and Bhima in 1 day $= \dfrac{1}{6}$

Time taken by Ganesh to complete a work $= 10$ days

The part of work that is completed by Ganesh in 1 day $= \dfrac{1}{10}$

Now, we first find the part of work completed by Bhima in 1 day

$= \dfrac{1}{6} - \dfrac{1}{10}$

$= \dfrac{(10-6)}{60}$

$= \dfrac{4}{60}$

$= \dfrac{1}{15}$

$\therefore$ Bhima completes the whole work in 15 days.

Hence, the correct option is (D).

40. Given,

A can do work in 10 days.

A's 1 day's work $= \dfrac{1}{10}$

B can do work in 15 days.

B's 1 day's work $= \dfrac{1}{15}$

(A + B)'s 1 day's work $= \dfrac{1}{10} + \dfrac{1}{15}$

$= \dfrac{(3+2)}{30}$

$= \dfrac{1}{6}$

$\therefore$ Together they can complete work in 6 days.

Hence, the correct option is (A).

41. Given,

A can do the work in 24 days.

B can do the work in 16 days.

C can do the work in 12 days.

$\text{Efficiency} = \dfrac{\text{Total work}}{\text{Time taken}}$

LCM of $24, 16$ and $12 = 48 = $ Total work

Efficiency of $A = \dfrac{48}{24} = 2$ units/day

Efficiency of $B = \dfrac{48}{16} = 3$ units/day

Efficiency of $C = \dfrac{48}{12} = 4$ units/day

Total efficiency of A, B and C together $= (2 + 3 + 4) = 9$ units/day

Time taken by A, B and $C = \dfrac{48}{9} = \dfrac{16}{3} = 5\dfrac{1}{3}$ days

$\therefore$ Time taken if all of them work together is $5\dfrac{1}{3}$ days.

Hence, the correct option is (A).

42. One word for the given phrase is '**Eulogy**'.

Eulogy: a speech or piece of writing that praises someone or something highly, especially a tribute to someone who has just died.

Angiology: the branch of anatomy dealing with blood vessels and lymphatics.

Etymology: the study of the origin of words and the way in which their meanings have changed throughout history.

Arcology: a type of architecture concerned with the design of enormous vertical cities.

Hence, the correct option is (C).

43. One word for the given phrase is '**Omnivorous**'.

Omnivorous: person or animal eats all kinds of food, including both meat and plants.

Herbivorous: an animal that eats only plants.

Insectivorous: an animal or plant that feeds mainly on insects.

Carnivorous: an animal that eats the meat of other animals, or a plant that traps and digests insects or other small animals.

Hence, the correct option is (A).

44. The pattern followed here is:

1) BEIN → B + 3 = E; E + 4 = I; I + 5 = N

2) LOSX → L + 3 = O; O + 4 = S; S + 5 = X

3) DGJN → D + 3 = G; G + 3 = J; J + 4 = N

4) HKOT → H + 3 = K; K + 4 = O; O + 5 = T

Thus, DGJN does not fulfil the above condition. So, it is the odd one out from the given options.

Hence, the correct option is (C).

45. All except Ounce are names of currencies, while Ounce is a unit of weight.

Hence, the correct option is (C).

46. All except Thermodynamics are topics of Mathematics.

Hence, the correct option is (D).

47. All except Cuboids are 3 dimensional figures.

Hence, the correct option is (D).

48. All except Whale lay eggs.

Hence, the correct option is (D).

49. Lysosomes:

- It is called the "suicidal bags" of the cell. Therefore statement 1 is correct.

- It is also known as the is called the perinuclear dense bodies.

- The lysosomal membrane is rich in Sialic acid. Therefore statement 2 is not correct.

- They are absent in Erythrocytes. Therefore statement 3 is correct.

- They are acidic in nature due to the presence of anabolic enzymes. Therefore statement 4 is not correct.

- Acid phosphatase (Enzyme) is used as a marker for the lysosomes.

- Sucrose density gradient centrifugation is used in the isolation of Liposomal fractions.

Functions of lysosomes:

- Autolysis

- Autophagy

- Digestion (intracellular and extracellular)

Gamori staining techniques are used to locate the lysosomes.

Phosphate esters and nucleases are the components of lysosomes.

They are considered the "garbage trucks" of a cell because they remove all unwanted cellular materials.

White blood cells contain the most active lysosomes.

They are involved in Secretion.

They are found in Leukocytes.

Hence, the correct option is (A).

50. Good ozone is found in the upper part of the atmosphere called the stratosphere, and it acts as a shield absorbing ultraviolet radiation from the sun. Therefore, statement 1 is incorrect.

UV rays are highly injurious to living organisms since the DNA and proteins of living organisms preferentially absorb UV rays, and it's high energy breaks the chemical bonds within these molecules.

The thickness of the ozone in a column of air from the ground to the top of the atmosphere is measured in terms of Dobson units (DU). Therefore, statement 2 is correct.

Ozone gas is continuously formed by the action of UV rays on molecular oxygen and also degraded into molecular oxygen in the stratosphere.

There should be a balance between the production and degradation of ozone in the stratosphere. Of late, the balance has been disrupted due to the enhancement of ozone degradation by chlorofluorocarbons (CFCs).

CFCs find wide use as refrigerants. CFCs discharged in the lower part of the atmosphere move upward and reach the stratosphere.

In the stratosphere, UV rays act on them releasing Cl atoms.

- Cl degrades ozone releasing molecular oxygen, with these atoms acting merely as catalysts;

- Cl atoms are not consumed in the reaction.

Therefore, whatever CFCs are added to the stratosphere, they have permanent and continuing effects on Ozone levels.

Although ozone depletion is occurring widely in the stratosphere, the depletion is particularly marked over the Antarctic region.

This has resulted in the formation of a large area of the thinned ozone layer, commonly called the ozone hole.

UV radiation of wavelengths shorter than UV-B is almost completely absorbed by Earth's atmosphere, given that the ozone layer is intact.

But, UV-B damages DNA and mutation may occur. It causes ageing of the skin, damage to skin cells, and various types of skin cancers. In the human eye, the cornea absorbs UV-B radiation, and a high dose of UV-B causes inflammation of the cornea, called snow-blindness, cataracts, etc. Such exposure may permanently damage the cornea.

Recognizing the deleterious effects of ozone depletion, an international treaty, known as the Montreal Protocol, was signed at Montreal (Canada) in 1987 (effective in 1989) to control the emission of ozone-depleting substances.

Subsequently, many more efforts have been made and protocols have laid down definite roadmaps, separately for developed and developing countries, for reducing the emission of CFCs and other ozone-depleting chemicals.

Hence, the correct option is (B).

51. Bharat stage (BS) emission standards are laid down by the government to regulate the output of air pollutants from the internal combustion engines and spark-ignition engine equipment. Therefore, statement 1 is correct.

The first emission norms were introduced in India in 1991 for petrol and in 1992 for diesel vehicles. Therefore, statement 3 is incorrect.

- Followed these, the catalytic converter became mandatory for petrol vehicles and unleaded petrol was introduced in the market.

The central government has mandated that vehicle makers must manufacture, sell, and register only BS-VI (BS6) vehicles from April 1, 2020. Therefore, statement 2 is correct.

- As per BS-VI emission norms, petrol vehicles will have to effect a 25% reduction in their NOx, or nitrogen oxide emissions.

- Diesel engines will have to reduce their HC+NOx (hydrocarbon + nitrogen oxides) by 43%, their NOx levels by 68%, and particulate matter levels by 82%.

- The emission norms of all models of two-wheelers in India are ahead of Europe (2021) and Japan (2022).

- India is the first country to adopt this level of emission norms. (BS-VI norms).

Hence, the correct option is (A).

52. Eutrophication is the natural ageing of a lake by nutrient enrichment of its water. Therefore, statement 1 is correct.

- In a young lake, the water is cold and clear, supporting little life.

- With time, streams draining into the lake introduce nutrients such as nitrogen and phosphorus, which encourage the growth of aquatic organisms.

- As the lake's fertility increases, plant and animal life burgeons, and organic remains begin to be deposited on the lake bottom.

- Over the centuries, as silt and organic debris pile up, the lake grows shallower and warmer, with warm-water organisms supplanting those that thrive in a cold environment.

Marsh plants take root in the shallows and begin to fill in the original lake basin. Eventually, the lake gives way to large masses of floating plants (bog), finally converting into the land.

Depending on the climate, the size of the lake, and other factors, the natural ageing of a lake may span thousands of years.

However, pollutants from man's activities like effluents from the industries and homes can radically accelerate the ageing process. This phenomenon has been called Cultural or Accelerated Eutrophication.

During the past century, lakes in many parts of the earth have been severely eutrophied by sewage and agricultural and industrial wastes.

The prime contaminants are nitrates and phosphates, which act as plant nutrients. Therefore statement 2 is correct.

They overstimulate the growth of algae, causing unsightly scum and unpleasant odours, and robbing the water of dissolved oxygen vital to other aquatic life.

At the same time, other pollutants flowing into a lake may poison whole populations of fish, whose decomposing remains further deplete the water's dissolved oxygen content.

In such a fashion, a lake can literally choke to death.

Hence, the correct option is (C).

53.

- Air pollutants cause injury to all living organisms.

- They reduce the growth and yield of crops and cause the premature death of plants.

- Air pollutants also deleteriously affect the respiratory system of humans and of animals.

- Harmful effects depend on the concentration of pollutants, duration of exposure, and the organism.

- Smokestacks of thermal power plants, smelters, and other industries release particulate and gaseous air pollutants together with harmless gases, such as nitrogen, oxygen, etc.

- These pollutants must be separated/ filtered out before releasing the harmless gases into the atmosphere.

Hence, the correct option is (B).

54. The landscape is being continuously worn away by two processes – weathering and erosion. Erosion is the wearing away of the landscape by different agents like water, wind, and ice.

- At higher gradients, downward, vertical erosion is more dominant. This produces V-shaped valleys

- The V-shaped valley is typical of one that has been carved by flowing water.

- The erosion is more pronounced when the water flow is a heavy one, and the water carries suspended particles (sedimentary load).

Hence, the correct option is (C).

55. Let's look at the meaning of the given idiom:

To pull oneself together - To calm oneself and begin to think or act and recover control of one's emotions.

Example:

I blew my nose and tried to pull myself together.

Hence, the correct option is (D).

56. The meaning of the phrase "take with a grain of salt" means not taking something too seriously.

Example: The Indian players took the issue of racism with a grain of salt.

Hence, the correct option is (C).

57. The correct sentence would be:

My father never did have an opportunity to go to a University.

In the above-given sentence, the error is related to adverb placement.

An adverb must come before the auxiliary verb in a sentence. For Example: I never was a fan of hers.

The structure of the sentence is incorrect.

Thus, 'did never' will be replaced by 'never did'.

Hence, the correct option is (D).

58. The correct sentence will be:

Kalidasa was a great classical Sanskrit poet of India.

The word 'Greater' is a comparative adjective that is used while comparing two things. Example: He was a greater dancer than his sister.

In the given sentence, there is no comparison so we will use the basic form of the adjective i.e., great.

The article 'the' is used with specific objects and 'a' is used with unspecific objects. Here 'a' is most appropriate.

Hence, the correct option is (B).

59. The teaching of Dhamma Cakka Pavattana Sutta (Pali) or Dharma Chakra Pravartana Sutra (Sanskrit) is also known as the First Turning of Wheels of Dharma and comprised the Four Noble Truths and Noble Eightfold Path.
Hence, the correct option is (D).

60. Statement 1: Dhamma Chakra Day marks Buddha's first teaching after attaining Enlightenment to the first five ascetic disciples (pañcavargika) on the full-moon day of Asadha at 'Deer Park', Rishipatana in modern-day Sarnath, near Varanasi.

Statement 3: This teaching of Dhamma Cakka Pavattana Sutta (Pali) or Dharma Chakra Pravartana Sutra (Sanskrit) is also known as the First Turning of Wheels of Dharma and comprised the Four Noble Truths and Noble Eightfold Path.

Statement 2: The day is also known as Esala Poya in Sri Lanka and Asanha Bucha in Thailand. It is the second most sacred day for Buddhists after the Buddha Poornima or Vesak.
Hence, the correct option is (C).

61. The question figure is embedded in,

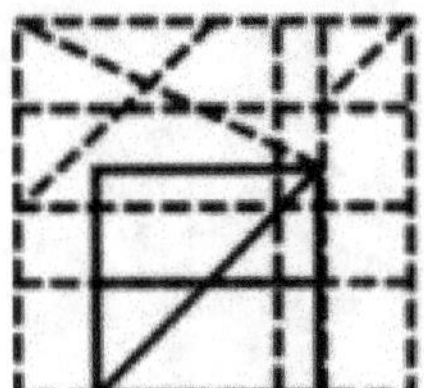

Hence, the correct option is (D).

62.

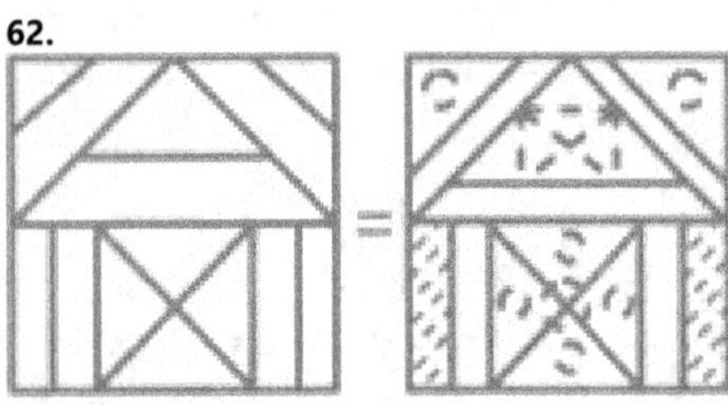

Hence, the correct option is (C).

63.

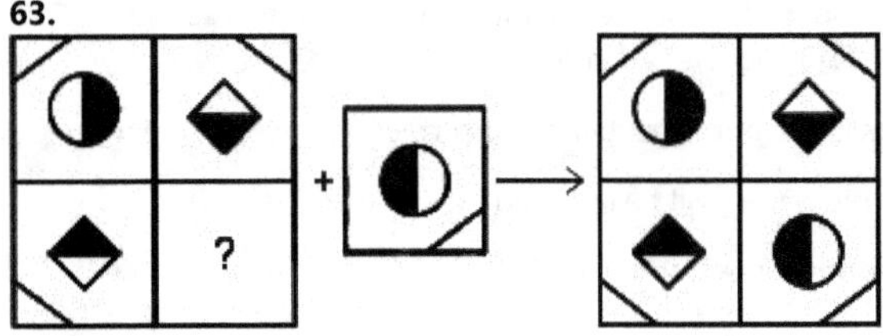

As you can see, the figure in option (D) is the right one to complete the pattern.
Hence, the correct option is (D).

64. The given pattern can be completed as shown below:

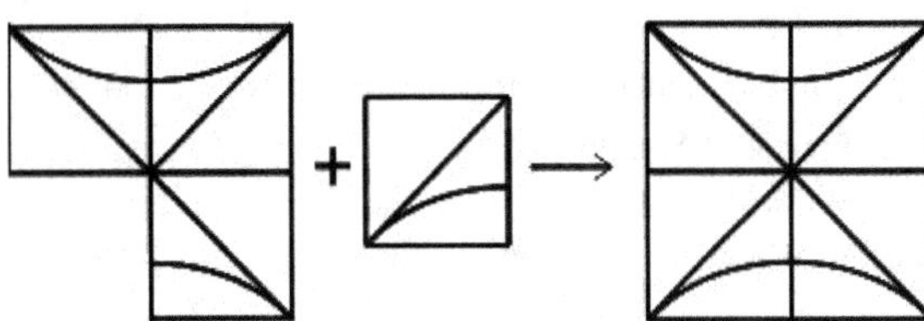

Hence, the correct option is (B).

65. The question figure is embedded in,

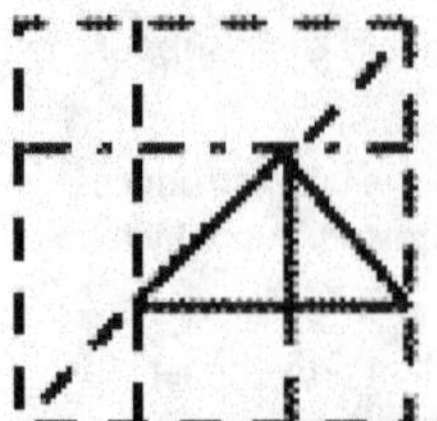

Hence, the correct option is (C).

66. Given:

$$a:b = 3:2$$

$$b:c = 5:7$$

$$c:d = 4:3$$

Now, $a:b:c:d$ will be,

$=3:2:2:2$

$=5:5:7:7$

$=4:4:4:3$

$\Rightarrow (3 \times 5 \times 4) : (2 \times 5 \times 4) : (2 \times 7 \times 4) : (2 \times 7 \times 3)$

$\Rightarrow 60:40:56:42$

$\Rightarrow 30:20:28:21$

$\therefore a:b:c:d = 30:20:28:21$

The correct option is 3 i.e. 30: 20: 28: 21

Hence, the correct option is (C).

67. English: Mathematics $= 2:3$
English: Science $= 2:1$
English : Mathematics: Science $= 2:3:1$
Given,
English $+$ Mathematics $+$ Science $= 180$

$$\text{Marks} = \frac{\text{Science}}{(\text{Science + Maths + English})} \times \text{Total marks}$$

$$\text{Marks in Science} = \left(\frac{1}{6}\right) \times 180 = 30$$

Hence, the correct option is (C).

68. Given,

A :B = 2:3

B : C = 4 : 7

$\therefore$ A : B : C = 2 × 4 : 3 × 4 : 3 × 7

= 8 : 12 : 21

Hence, the correct option is (C).

69. Virat Kohli remained the highest-placed Indian batsman at the fourth position in the latest ICC Test rankings issued on 30 Jan 2021.

Cheteshwar Pujara moved up one place to 6th.

Test vice-captain Ajinkya Rahane is the other Indian batsman in the top-10 on the eighth spot.

New Zealand captain Kane Williamson continued to lead the batting charts.

Hence, the correct option is (C).

70.

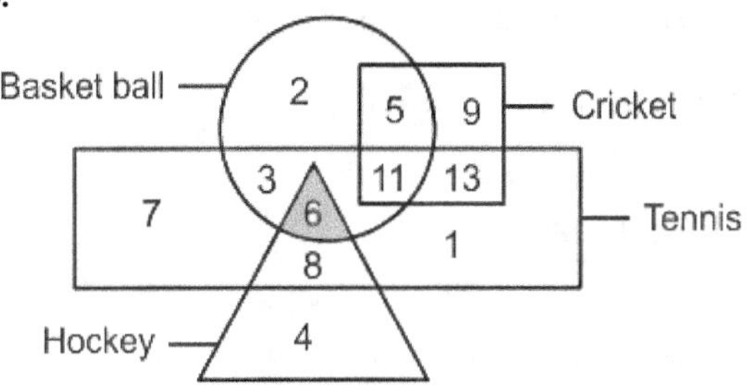

Here the numbers in,

Circle represents person who likes basket ball: 2, 3, 5, 6, 11

Rectangle represents person who likes tennis: 1, 3, 6, 7, 8, 11, 13

Triangle represents person who likes hockey: 4, 6, 8

The person who likes basket ball, tennis, and hockey but not cricket will lie in the intersection of rectangle, triangle, and circle.

6 people who likes basket ball, tennis, and hockey but not cricket.

Hence, the correct option is (D).

71. As shirt and pants are made of cloth, but shirts and pants do not have any relationship they are the opposite.

Hence, the Venn diagram which shows the relationship between shirt, pants, and cloth would be:

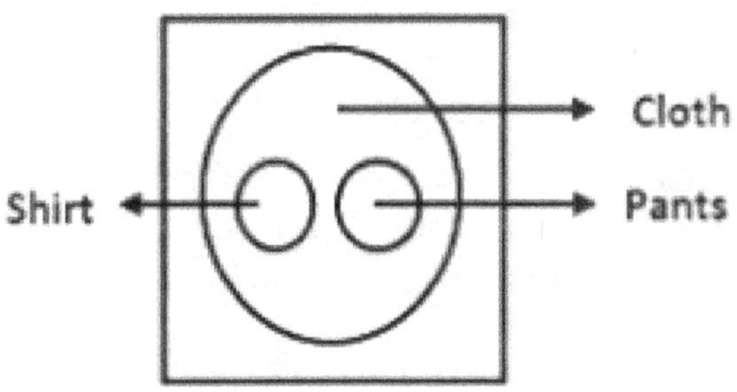

Hence, the correct option is (A).

72. Some boys can be infants. All the boys and infants are humans.

The correct Venn diagram representation is,

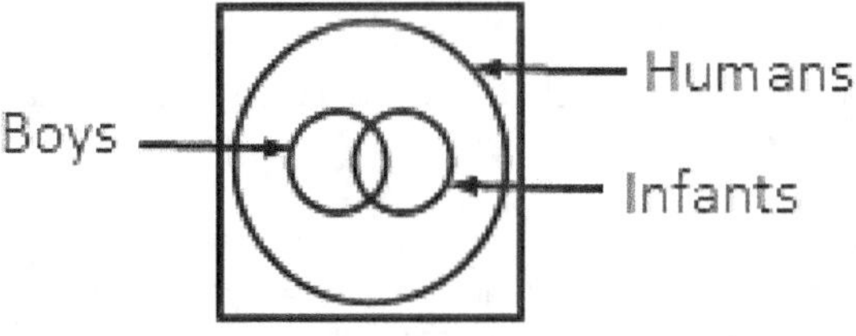

Hence, the correct option is (C).

73. The required region is the one common to the rectangle, square, circle and the triangle i.e. 7.

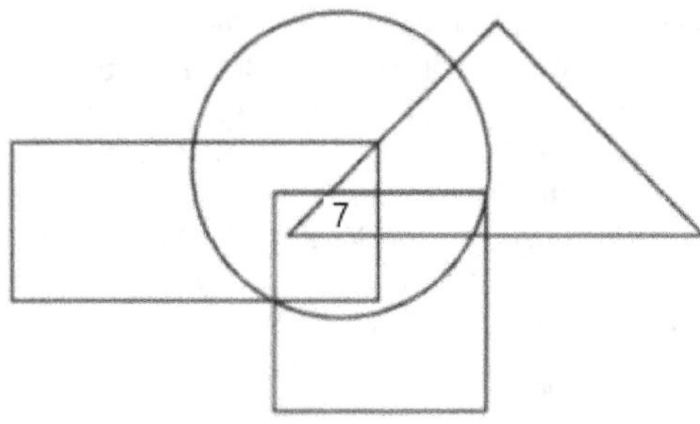

Hence, the correct option is (A).

74. The required region is the one which is common to only the rectangle and the circle and is not a part of either the triangle or the square i.e. 4.

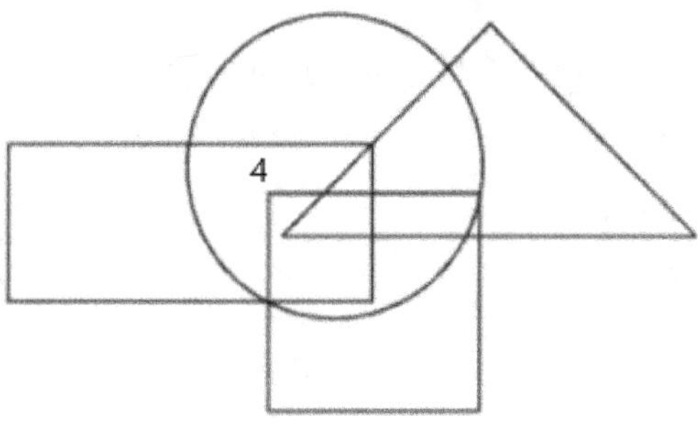

Hence, the correct option is (D).

75. According to the dictionary,

4. **Dumm**y

3. **Dump**

2. **Dus**t

1. **Dut**ch

So, "4321" is the correct sequence.

Hence, the correct option is (D).

76. According to the sequence in the dictionary,

3. **Earl**iest

5. **Ecl**ipse

4. **Edi**tion

1. **Edu**cation

2. **Ele**ction

So, "3 5 4 1 2" is the correct sequence.

Hence, the correct option is (D).

77. RTI applicable to the Supreme Court of India in 2019, upheld the decision of the Delhi High Court bringing the office of Chief Justice of India under the purview of the Right to Information

(RTI) Act. So, statement 1 is correct. Currently, Political parties are not under the ambit of the RTI act.

The Central Information Commission was established by the Central Government in 2005. It was constituted through an Official Gazette Notification under the provisions of the Right to Information Act (2005). Hence, it is not a constitutional body. The Central Information Commission is a high-powered independent body that inter alia looks into the complaints made to it and decides the appeals. The Chief Information Commissioner/Information Commissioner shall hold office for a term of 5 (five) years or till he attains the age of 65 years. Therefore, statement 2 is not correct.

Hence, the correct option is (A).

78. The correct answer is **resentful**.

resentful: feeling or expressing bitterness or indignation at having been treated unfairly

indignant: feeling or showing anger or annoyance at what is perceived as unfair treatment

Let's look at the meanings of the other given options:

- congenial- (of a person) pleasant because of a personality, qualities, or interests that are similar to one's own
- unruly- disorderly and disruptive and not amenable to discipline or control
- supportive- providing encouragement or emotional help

Thus, from the given meanings, we find that resentful and indignant are synonyms.

Hence, the correct option is (A).

79. The correct answer is straightforward.

- Bombastic: high-sounding but with little meaning; inflated
- Straightforward: uncomplicated and easy to do or understand

Thus, from the given meanings, we find that bombastic and straightforward are antonyms.

Hence, the correct option is (B).

80. The correct answer is **reasonable**.

absurd: wildly unreasonable, illogical, or inappropriate

reasonable: (of a person) having sound judgment; fair and sensible

Let's look at the meanings of the other given options:

- bizarre- very strange or unusual, especially so as to cause interest or amusement
- meaningless- having no meaning or significance
- thoughtful- absorbed in or involving thought

Thus, from the given meanings, we find that absurd and reasonable are antonyms.

Hence, the correct option is (C).

81. Srinivas works and earns $= Rs. \ 14,500$

He saves $= 20\%$

He spent $= 100\% - 20\% = 80\%$

He spent $= 14,500 \times \dfrac{80}{100} = Rs. \ 11,600$

Hence, the correct option is (D).

82. Students passed in English = 80%

Students passed in Math's = 85%

Students passed in both subjects = 73%

Then, the number of students passed in at least one subject

= (80+85)-73

= 92%

Thus, students failed in both subjects = 100 - 92

= 8%

Hence, the correct option is (A).

83. By simplification we get,

$$\Rightarrow 19\% \text{ of } 23\% \text{ of } 560$$

$$\Rightarrow \left(\frac{19}{100}\right) \times \left(\frac{23}{100}\right) \times 560$$

$$\Rightarrow 24.472$$

Hence, the correct option is (A).

84. They did not want to leave **anything** to chance while deciding on the trip.

The meaning of the given words:

- Anything: used to refer to a thing, no matter what.
- Something: a thing that is unspecified or unknown.
- Nothing: not anything. no single thing.
- Someone: an unknown or unspecified person, some person.

The use of Pronoun 'anything' is appropriate in the blank space of the sentence.

Hence, the correct option is (C).

85. Keep your friends close and your enemies **closer**.

It is appropriate to use the Comparative Degree 'closer' of Noun 'close' in the blank space of the sentence.

Hence, the correct option is (A).

86. The **babble** of strange and unfamiliar dialects at the market held my interest.

The meaning of the given words:

- Babble: talk rapidly and continuously in a foolish, excited, or incomprehensible way.

- Racket: a loud unpleasant noise; a din.
- Rumble: make a continuous deep, resonant sound.
- Clanging: a pattern of speech observed in some types of mental illness.

The use of the word 'babble (sound word)' in the blank space of the sentence is appropriate.

Hence, the correct option is (D).

87. There are **few** takers for animal fur today, while **quite a few** of the yesteryear stars were proud owners of mink coats.

- Few: a small number of.
- Quite a few: being of a large but indefinite number.

It is appropriate to use 'few' and 'quite a few' respectively in the blanks of the sentence.

Hence, the correct option is (A).

88.

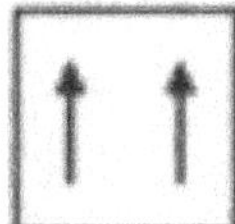

In each row, the second figure is obtained from the first figure by reversing the direction of the RHS arrow and the third figure is obtained from the second figure by reversing the direction of both the arrows.

Hence, the correct option is (A).

89.

In each row, the figures are getting laterally inverted in each step. The number of components or the quantities are either increasing or decreasing from left to right sequentially.

Hence, the correct option is (B).

90.

The second figure is obtained from the first figure by moving the line segment to the opposite side of the square boundary and replacing it with two similar line segments. Also, the element in the lower-left corner gets replaced by two similar elements - one placed in the upper-left and the other placed in the lower-right corner.

Hence, the correct option is (C).

91.

In each row, there are 3 types of shadings of circles - a circle is unshaded, another circle has its right half shaded with vertical lines and yet another circle has its upper half shaded with horizontal lines. There are three specified positions of the two triangles each of which is used only once in a row. Also, two of the figures in each row have one triangle shaded.

Hence, the correct option is (D).

92.

In each row, the third figure is a collection of the common elements (line segments) of the first and the second figures.

Hence, the correct option is (C).

93. The correct answer is 'Bigger Thomas, a character devoid of any negative traits, was the protagonist in Wright's first book, Native Son.'

The given passage is talking about Richard Wright, an American author of novels, and his concerns on racial themes, especially related to the plight of African Americans who suffered discrimination and violence.

Let's refer to the line "Bigger Thomas was a protagonist stripped of any redeeming qualities, so distorted by the conditions of racism that he became an avatar more than a character, and an unsettling representation of Blackness." It means he lacked good qualities, while the given sentence says 'he is devoid of negative traits,' which means that he lacked bad qualities.

From the given explanation, it can be understood that option C cannot be inferred from the given passage.

Hence, the correct option is (C).

94. The correct answer is 'The author was trying to emphasize how blacks faced horrible hunger and disaster, were suppressed and were denied their dreams.'

Let's refer to the passage "Wright reached for the very core of the human condition in his portrait of growing up destitute in the Deep South during the early 20th century and then making his way north: abundance everywhere and terrible hunger, tragedy mixed with the quotidian in the most disorienting ways. The experience he evoked might not have been every Black life, but it was indeed a part of Black life. In Mississippi, the land could swallow you whole. In Chicago, a rat might bite you, because after all, you were made to live in slums no different from rattraps. Wright was showing us something true, if not absolute".

Hence, the correct option is (A).

95. The correct answer is 'Ellison was attempting to learn to write well by imitating Wright, and Baldwin, too, respected Wright, who was on the verge of becoming the greatest Black writer in the United States.'

Option 2 discusses his sons admiring and loving him and imitating his father to write well.

Hence, the correct option is (B).

96. The correct answer is 'Wright's first novel, Native Son, Wright's reflections on the Great Migration, Black Boy (1945)'.

From the given explanation, it can be understood that option 2 best represents the author's change of opinions about Richard Wright.

Hence, the correct option is (B).

97. The correct answer is 'Richard Wright's sons believed that instead of depicting the endurance of Blacks, Richard wanted to show only evil of whites in his novels.'

The above line means that Ellison expressed his ill feelings about Richard's literary works. He felt that instead of depicting the endurance of Blacks, Richard wanted to show only the evil of whites in his novels. The above line means that Ellison expressed his ill feelings about Richard's literary works. He felt that instead of depicting the endurance of Blacks, Richard wanted to show only the evil of whites in his novels.

Hence, the correct option is (D).

98. In these types we try make the denominators equal then compare them

Now,

$$\frac{-3}{4} = \frac{-9}{12}$$

$$\frac{-5}{6} = \frac{-10}{12}$$

As the base of both the numbers are equal.

So, we can easily compare the numbers

$$\frac{-9}{12} > \frac{-10}{12}$$

$$\frac{3}{-4} > \frac{-5}{6}$$

Hence, the correct option is (C).

99. Given numbers are 30.003, 300.03, 30.030, 030.30, 3.033

The correct ascending order will be

3.033 < 30.003 < 30.030 < 030.30 < 300.03

Hence, the correct option is (C).

100. Given,

$$\Rightarrow ? = \frac{[(1.569\times1.569\times0.431)+(1.569\times0.431\times0.431)]}{[(1.569+0.431)^2-(1.569-0.431)^2]}$$

$$\Rightarrow ? = \frac{[(1.569\times1.569\times0.431)+(1.569\times0.431\times0.431)]}{[4\times1.569\times0.431]}$$

$$\Rightarrow ? = \frac{[(1.569\times0.431)\times(1.569+0.431)]}{[4\times1.569\times0.431]}$$

$$\Rightarrow ? = \frac{(1.569+0.431)}{4}$$

$$\Rightarrow ? = \frac{2}{4} = 0.5$$

Hence, the correct option is (C).

Q.1 In March 2022, who has launched TEJAS (Training for Emirates Jobs And Skills) programme?

A. Prem Kumar Dhumal
B. Jai Ram Thakur
C. Jyotiraditya Scindia
D. Anurag Thakur

Q.2 In 2022, India's equity market has broken into the world's top five club in terms of market capitalization for the first time. The country's total market cap stands at how many trillion dollars?

A. 3.21   **B.** 3.78   **C.** 4.12   **D.** 4.65

Q.3 Which of the following has become the 1st company in the world to have its product linear alkylbenzene (LAB) conferred with IS12795:2020 certification?

A. Manali Petrochemical
B. Tamilnadu Petroproducts Ltd
C. Andhra Petrochemicals Ltd
D. Godawari Power And Ispat

Q.4 The term "2-deoxy-D-glucose" was in news recently, is related to which of the following?

A. Anti-septic cream
B. Anti-Covid drug
C. Some cosmetic product
D. Agriculture pesticide

Q.5 Tamil Nadu Assembly Election 2021 was won by which political party?
[UPSSSC Preliminary Eligibility Test, 2021]

A. DMK   **B.** BJP
C. AIADMK   **D.** PMK

Q.6 In how much time will a sum of Rs.1600 amount to Rs.1852.20 at 5% per annum compound interest?

A. 3 years   **B.** 2.5 years   **C.** 3.5 years   **D.** 4 years

Q.7 What will Rs. 40,000 amount to in 2 years at the rate of 20% p.a., if interest is compounded yearly?

A. Rs. 48,620   **B.** Rs. 58,564
C. Rs. 57,600   **D.** Rs. 60,000

Q.8 Raghu has invested Rs 1000 and received Rs 1300 at 6% per annum simple interest after X years. Find the value of X.
[RRB/RRC Group D, 2018]

A. 4 years   **B.** 3 years   **C.** 2 years   **D.** 5 years

Q.9 Which of the following missiles of India is a "Supersonic Cruise Missile"?

A. BrahMos   **B.** Agni
C. Trishul   **D.** Nag

Ques (10-11):Directions: In each of the following questions, choose the most suitable word for the given expression.

Q.10 One who is present everywhere.
[NCHM JEE (Hotel Mgmt & Catering), 2018]

A. Omnipresent   **B.** Omnipotent
C. Omnivorous   **D.** Eternal

Q.11 One who does not believe in the existence of God.
[Sainik School Entrance Class VI, 2020]

A. Atheist   **B.** Agnostic   **C.** Arboreal   **D.** Acoustic

Q.12 Ms. Sonia Lather is associated with which of the following sports?
[Haryana Primary Teacher (PRT), 2020]

A. Wrestling   **B.** Kabaddi
C. Atheletics   **D.** Boxing

Ques (13-17):Direction: A passage is given below with ten blanks labelled (1)-(5). From the given options, select whichever word or group of words you consider the most appropriate for the blank space and indicate your response accordingly.

It sounds like _____(1) great idea. People getting instantly excited when they hear _____(2) phrase 'education for peace' or the title of a course that calls itself 'peace Education'. About a decade ago, I proposed such _____(3) course in my institute. The idea of a course _____(4) 'peace education' had occurred to me on the way back from one of the neighbouring countries where I met students of class IX. I could not find _____(5) difference between Indian students and their counterparts in the other country on peace and living together.

Q.13 Choose the correct response for blank no. (1).
[Officers Training Academy (OTA), 2021], [Indian Military Academy (IMA), 2021]

A. a   **B.** an   **C.** the   **D.** some

Q.14 Choose the correct response for blank no. (2).
[Officers Training Academy (OTA), 2021], [Indian Military Academy (IMA), 2021]

A. a   **B.** the   **C.** that   **D.** some

Q.15 Choose the correct response for blank no. (3).
[Officers Training Academy (OTA), 2021], [Indian Military Academy (IMA), 2021]

A. any   **B.** the   **C.** some   **D.** a

Q.16 Choose the correct response for blank no. (4).
[Officers Training Academy (OTA), 2021], [Indian Military Academy (IMA), 2021]

A. to   **B.** in   **C.** for   **D.** on

Q.17 Choose the correct response for blank no. (5).
[Officers Training Academy (OTA), 2021], [Indian Military Academy (IMA), 2021]

A. any   **B.** the   **C.** that   **D.** this

Q.18 The species restricted to be present in one region and nowhere else in the world are called-

A. Invasive species   **B.** Endemic species
C. Endangered species   **D.** None of these

Q.19 Choose the option that is the active form of the sentence. An award was given to the film 'Andhaa Dhund.'

[SSC Sub Inspector (CPO), 2019]

A. The jury had given the film 'Andhaa Dhund' an award.
B. The jury gave the film 'Andhaa Dhund' an award.
C. The jury was gave the film 'Andhaa Dhund' an award.
D. The jury will give the award to the film 'Andhaa Dhund'.

Q.20 Choose the option that is the passive form of the sentence.

I burnt my hand yesterday while cooking.

[SSC Sub Inspector (CPO), 2019]

A. My hand was burning yesterday while cooking.
B. My hand could be burnt yesterday while cooking.
C. My hand was burnt yesterday while cooking.
D. My hand will be burnt yesterday while cooking.

Q.21 Select the option that is related to the third number in the same way as the second number is related to the first number.

$12 : 60 :: 16 : ?$

A. 210   **B.** 121   **C.** 112   **D.** 201

Q.22 Select the option that is related to the fourth number in the same way as the first number is related to the second number and the fifth number is related to the sixth digit.

$17 : 293 :: ? : 488 :: 21 : 445$

A. 22   **B.** 20   **C.** 28   **D.** 24

Q.23 Select the option in which the words share the same relationship as that shared by the given pair of words.

Resistance : Ohm

A. Force: Watt   **B.** Force: Ampere
C. Density: Joule   **D.** Angle: Radians

Q.24 Select the option that has the same relation to the third word as the second word to the first word.

Golden Wattle: Australia :: Iris:?

A. Spain   **B.** Canada   **C.** Japan   **D.** France

Q.25 Select the related number from the given alternatives.

$122 : 6 : 408 : ?$

A. 5   **B.** 8   **C.** 10   **D.** 15

Q.26 Vinod can row a certain distance downstream in 4 hours and return the same distance in 6 hours. If the stream flows at the rate of $3\ km/hr$, then find the speed of Vinod in still water?

A. $20\ km/hr$ **B.** $15\ km/hr$
C. $30\ km/hr$ **D.** $45\ km/hr$

Q.27 How many minutes Raman's will take to cover a distance of 400 meters. if he runs at a speed of 20 km/hr?

A. 2 minute   **B.** 1.5 minute
C. 1.2 minute   **D.** 2.5 minute

Q.28 The length of two trains are 450 m and 620 m respectively and speed of the trains are 72 kmph and 90 kmph respectively. Find the difference in the time taken by the trains to cross each other moving in the same direction and opposite direction.

A. 23.78 sec   **B.** 190.22 sec
C. 214 sec   **D.** 237.78 sec

Q.29 A person travelled $132 km$ by auto, $852 km$ by train and $248 km$ by bike. It took 21 hours in all. If the speed of train is 6 times the speed of auto and 1.5 times speed of bike, what is the speed of train?

A. $78\ kmh^{-1}$ **B.** $104\ kmh^{-1}$
C. $96\ kmh^{-1}$ **D.** $88\ kmh^{-1}$

Q.30 Select the one which is different from the other three responses.

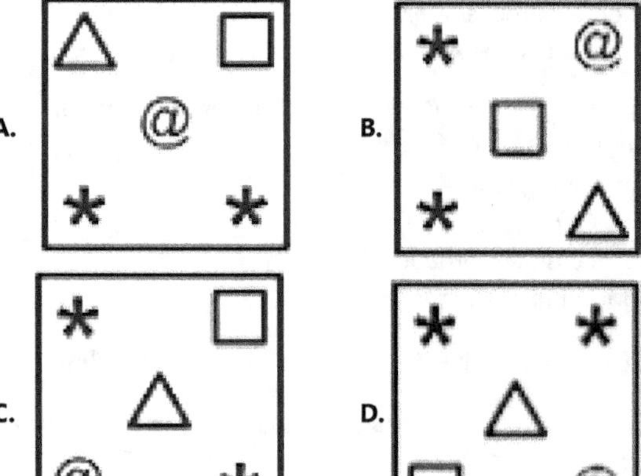

Q.31 From the given options, find the ODD one out.

A. PV   **B.** TW   **C.** LO   **D.** EH

Q.32 Find the odd one out.

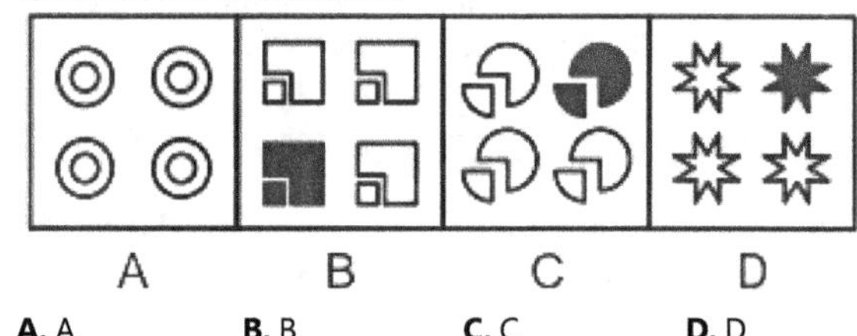

A. A   **B.** B   **C.** C   **D.** D

Q.33 Choose the odd one out of the given options.

A. Legs   **B.** Stomach   **C.** Heart   **D.** Kidneys

Q.34 Find the odd set of letters from the given alternatives.

A. GEC   **B.** MKI   **C.** YWU   **D.** OQS

Q.35 The average of 10 numbers is calculated as 15. It is discovered later on that while calculating the average one number namely 36 was wrongly read as 26. The correct average is:

A. 20   **B.** 18   **C.** 16   **D.** 14

Q.36 The average age of 30 students is 20 years and that of 20 other students is 30 years. The average age of total students is:

A. 20   **B.** 22   **C.** 12   **D.** 24

Q.37 What is the average of first 31 multiples of 19?

A. 304   **B.** 430
C. 280   **D.** None of these

Q.38 A and B together can complete a work in 3 days. They start together but after 2 days, B left the work. If the work is completed after two more days, B alone could do the work in:

A. 5 days   **B.** 6 days   **C.** 9 days   **D.** 10 days

Q.39 A and B can finish a work in 30 days and 20 days, respectively. If they worked together for 6 days and A leaves the job abruptly; then, how many days will B take to complete the remaining task?

A. 15 days   **B.** 10 days   **C.** 12 days   **D.** 18 days

Q.40 A and B together complete work in 20 days. B alone can complete the same work in 60 days. They took Rs. 36000 to complete the work. What will be the share of A (in Rs.)?

A. Rs. 18000   **B.** Rs. 24000
C. Rs. 26000   **D.** Rs. 22000

Q.41 Simplify:

$$\frac{.009}{?} = .01$$

A. .0009   **B.** .09   **C.** .9   **D.** 9

Q.42 Simplify:

$$3889 + 12.952 - ? = 3854.002$$

A. 47.095   **B.** 47.752   **C.** 47.932   **D.** 47.95

Q.43 When $0.232323.....$ is converted into a fraction, then the result is:

A. $\frac{1}{5}$ **B.** $\frac{1}{5}$ **C.** $\frac{23}{99}$ **D.** $\frac{23}{100}$

Q.44 Electron affinity of noble gases is-

A. Low   **B.** High
C. Very high   **D.** Almost zero

Q.45 Which of the following gases is heavier than oxygen?

A. Carbon dioxide   **B.** Ammonia
C. Methane   **D.** Helium

Q.46 What is the chemical name of Vinegar?

A. Citric acid   **B.** Acetic acid
C. Pyruvic acid   **D.** Malic acid

Q.47 Which of the following is used in making pencils?

A. Graphite   **B.** Cobalt
C. Tungsten   **D.** None of these

Q.48 The major components in LPG are-

A. Methane   **B.** Butane

C. Propane   **D.** Both (B) and (C)

Q.49 Direction: Choose the correct meaning of the idiom and mark the answer.

Be in eclipse

[Officers Training Academy (OTA), 2021], [Indian Military Academy (IMA), 2021]

A. Less successful   **B.** Feeling happy
C. Very successful   **D.** Being defeated

Q.50 Direction: Choose the correct meaning of the idiom and mark the answer.

Ways and means

[Officers Training Academy (OTA), 2021], [Indian Military Academy (IMA), 2021]

A. A technique
B. Methods of achieving something
C. Norms and regulations of doing something
D. Improving one's way of doing

Ques (51-52):Direction: In the following question, the given sentence has four parts marked P, Q, R, and S. Choose the part of the sentence with the error and mark it as your answer. If there is no error, mark 'No error (S)' as your answer.

Q.51 King penguins (P) / are active throughout (Q) / the long summer days. (R) / No error (S)

[SSC Sub Inspector (CPO), 2018], [SSC Sub Inspector (CPO), 2017]

A. P   **B.** Q   **C.** R   **D.** S

Q.52 The behaviour of resident spiders (P) / towards pirate spiders and their own prey (Q) / are quite different. (R) / No error (S)

[SSC Sub Inspector (CPO), 2018], [SSC Sub Inspector (CPO), 2017]

A. P   **B.** Q   **C.** R   **D.** S

Q.53 Which Veda is the primary source of classical music?

A. Rigveda   **B.** Yajurveda
C. Samveda   **D.** Atharvaveda

Q.54 When is 'Raag Bhairav' or 'Raag Bhairavi' sung?

A. First stroke of the night
B. Second stroke of night
C. Night's third stroke
D. Morning

Q.55 Who of the following was/were economic critic/ critics of colonialism in India?

1. Dadabhai Naoroji

2. G. Subramania Iyer

3. R. C. Dutt

A. 1 only   **B.** 1 and 2 only
C. 2 and 3 only   **D.** 1,2 and 3

Q.56 Direction: Choose the figure which is different from the rest.

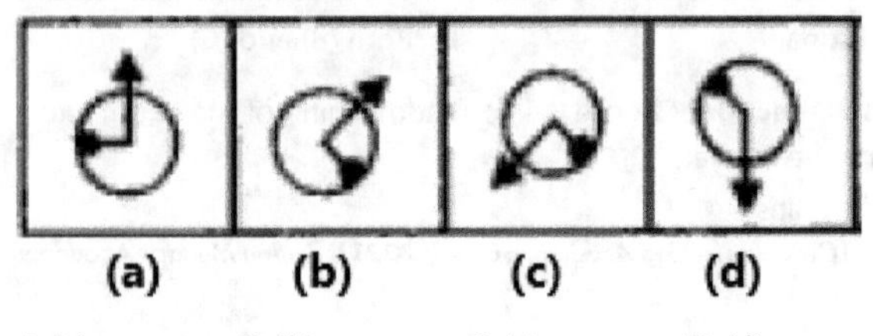

(a)   **(b)**   **(c)**   **(d)**

A. (a)   **B.** (b)   **C.** (c)   **D.** (d)

Q.57 G The first two figures in the given Problem Set bear a relationship. Select that figure. from the Answer Set which bears the same relationship to the third figure in the Problem Set as the second one bears to the first in the Problem Set.

Problem Set

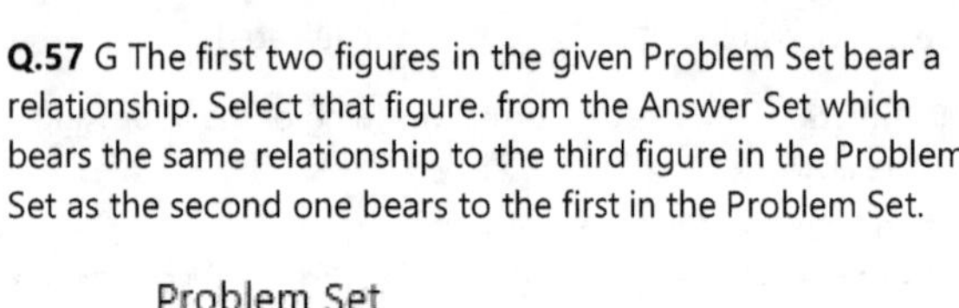

Answer Set

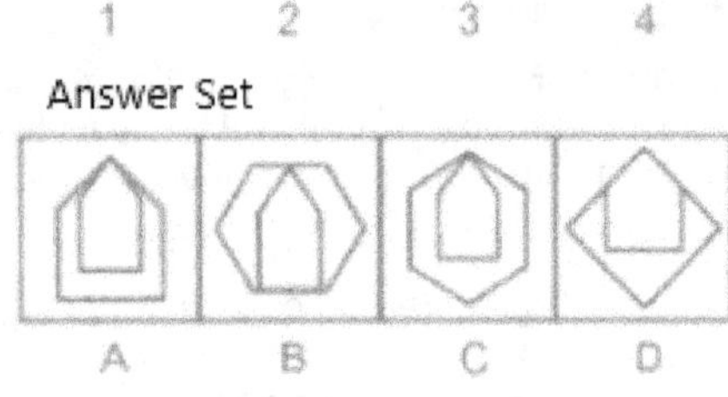

[UP Police Constable, 2018]

A. Figure A   **B.** Figure B   **C.** Figure C   **D.** Figure D

Q.58 The first two figures in the Problem Figure bear a relationship. Select the figure from the Answer Figure which bears the same relationship to the third Problem Figure as the second bears to the first Problem Figure.

Problem Figure:

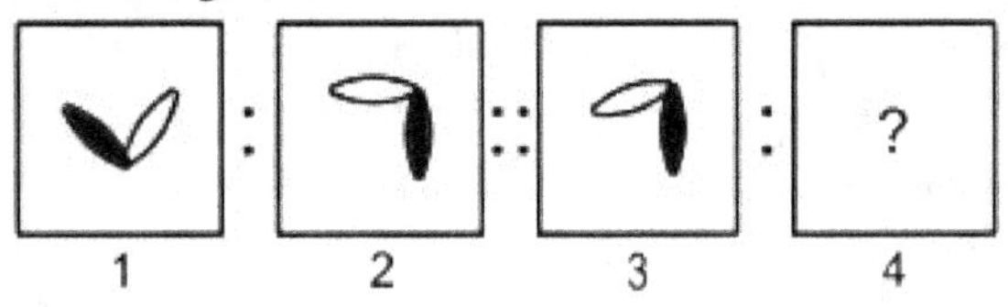

Answer Figure:

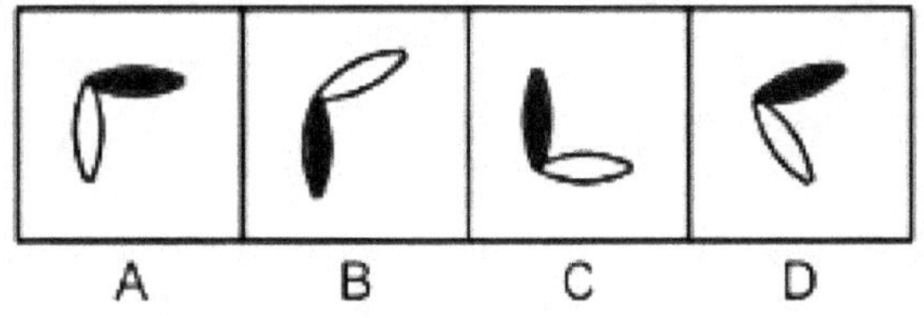

[UP Police Constable, 2018]

A. Figure A   **B.** Figure B   **C.** Figure C   **D.** Figure D

Q.59 Select a suitable figure from the answer figures that would replace the question mark

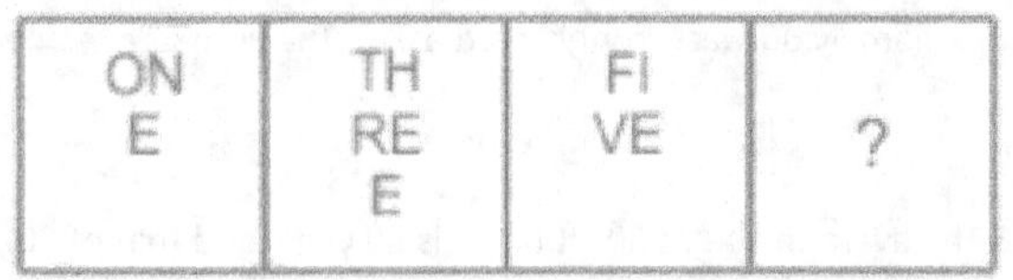

ON E	TH RE E	FI VE	?

[UP Police Constable, 2018]

A. 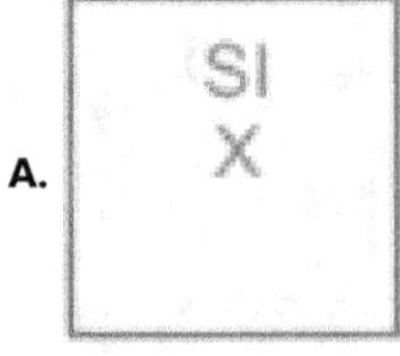
SI
X

B. 
SE
VE
N

C. FO
UR

D. TE
N

Q.60 Select a suitable figure from the Answer Figures that would replace the question mark.

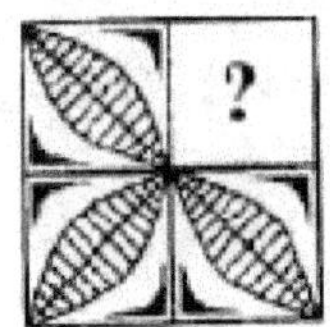

[UP Police Constable, 2018]

A. 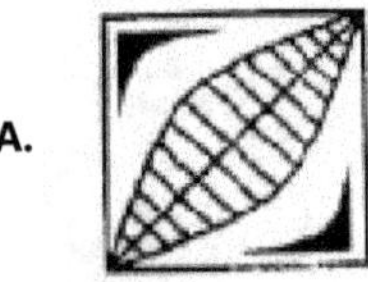   **B.** 

C. 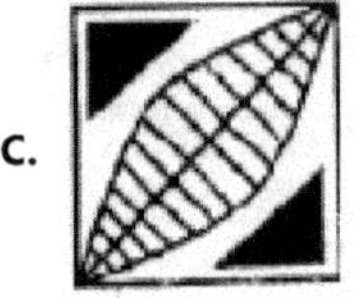   **D.** 

Q.61 If $6A = 11B = 7C$, find $A : B : C$.

A. $66 : 42 : 77$ **B.** $77 : 42 : 66$

C. $42 : 77 : 66$ **D.** $7 : 11 : 6$

Q.62 Rs. 6400 are divided among three workers in the ratio $\dfrac{3}{5} : 2 : \dfrac{5}{3}$. The share (in Rs) of the second worker is:

A. 3000   **B.** 2000   **C.** 25000   **D.** 2700

Q.63 The income of R, S and T are in the ratio of 4 : 2 : 3 respectively and their expenses are in the ratio of 2 : 1 : 3 respectively. If R saves Rs. 12000 out of an income of Rs. 20000, then what will be the savings of S?

[Delhi Forest Guard, 2021]

A. Rs. 2000   **B.** Rs. 4000   **C.** Rs. 8000   **D.** Rs. 6000

Q.64 Find out the alternative figure which contains figure (X) as its part.

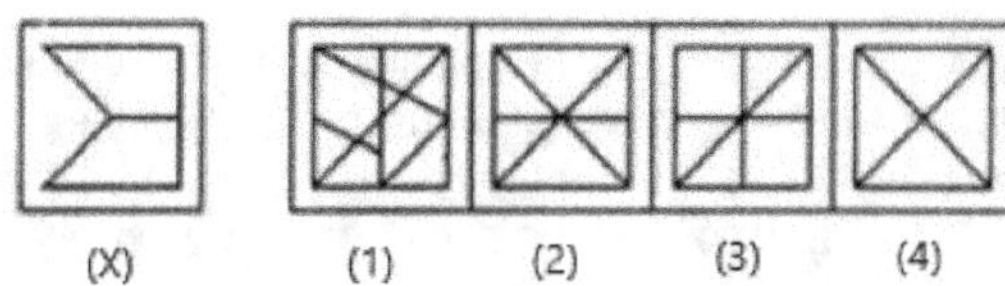

A. 1   **B.** 2   **C.** 3   **D.** 4

Q.65 Choose the figure which is different from the rest.

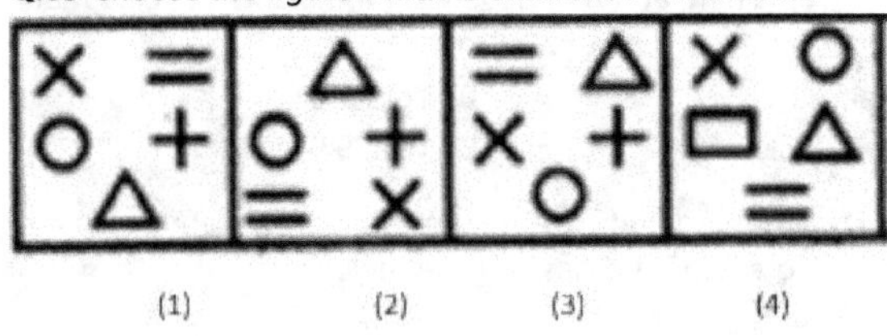

A. 1   **B.** 2   **C.** 3   **D.** 4

Q.66 From the option figures, select the one in which the question figure is hidden/embedded.

Question Figure:

A.

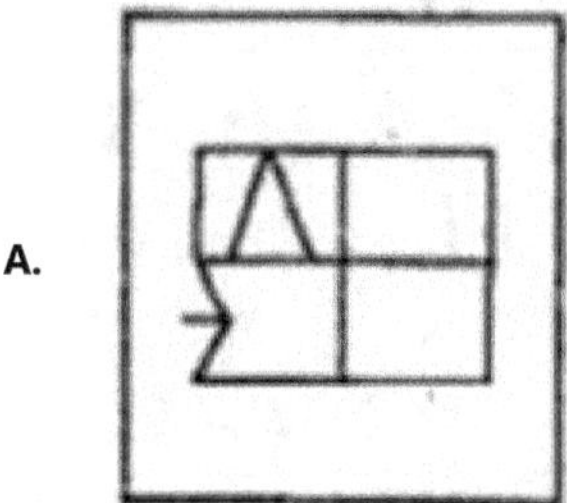

B.

C.

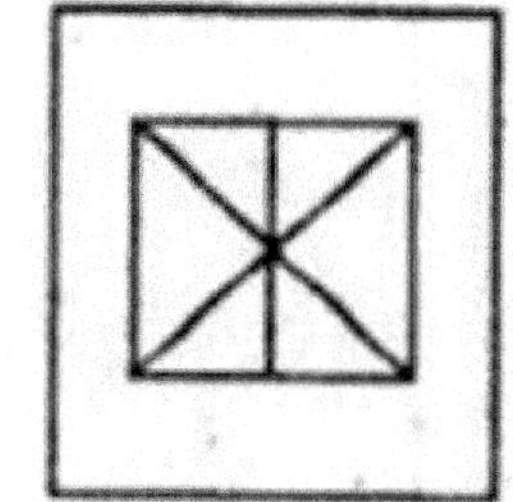

D.

Q.67 In which of the following answer figures, the given question figure is hidden/embedded.

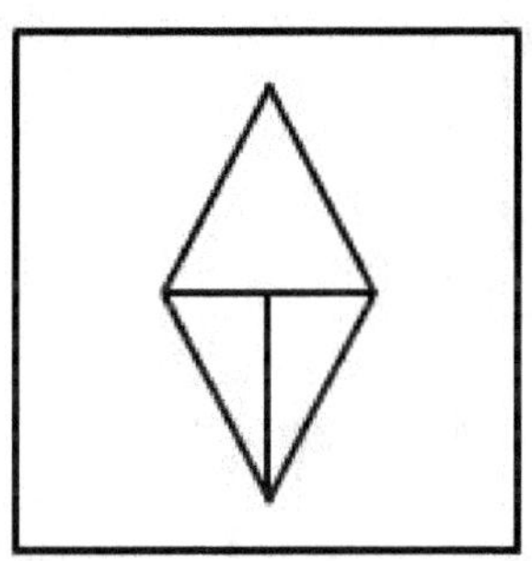

A.

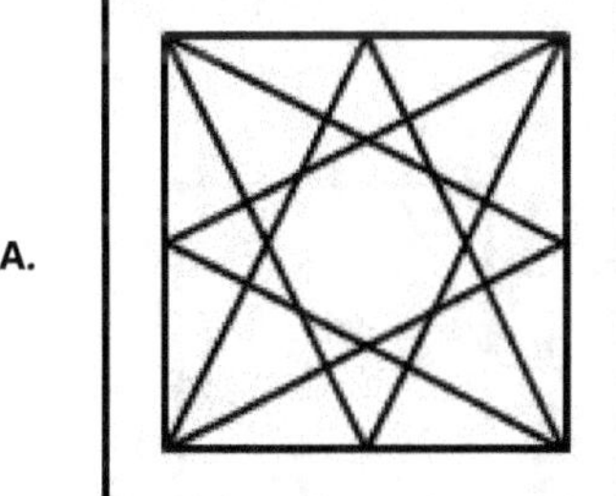

B.

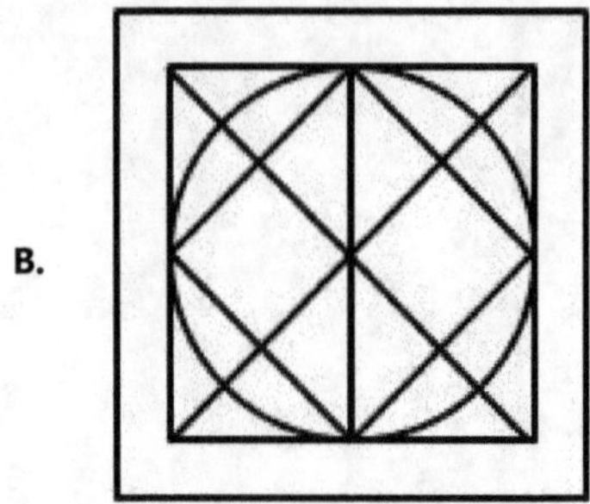

C.

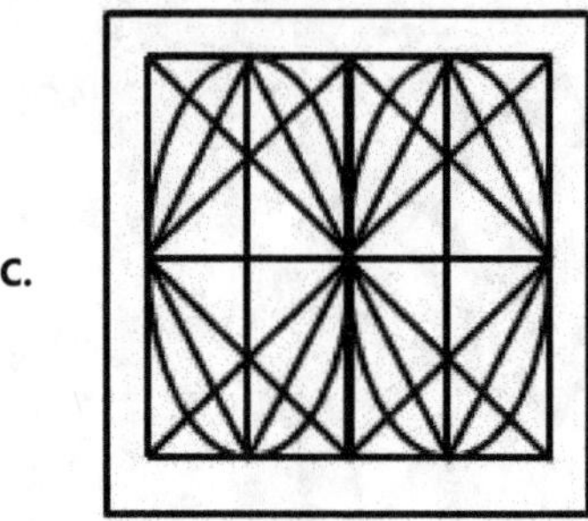

D.

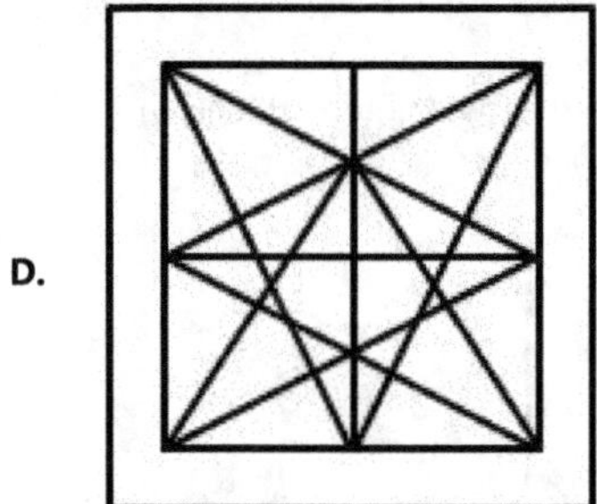

Q.68 Which option figure will complete the question figure?

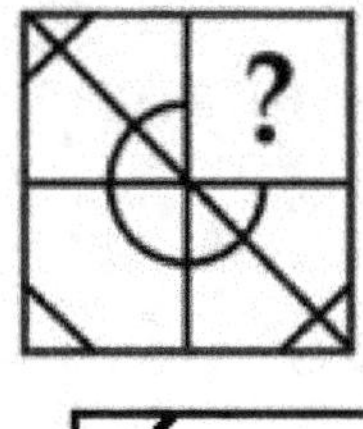

A.

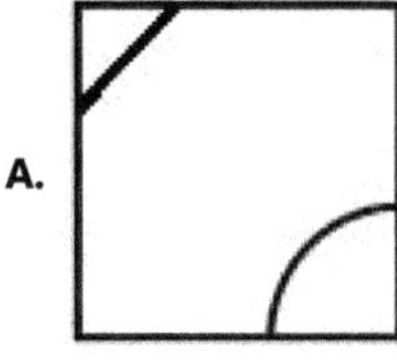

C.

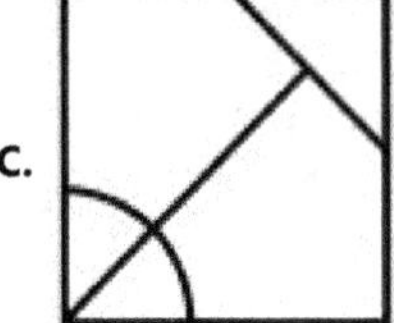

B.

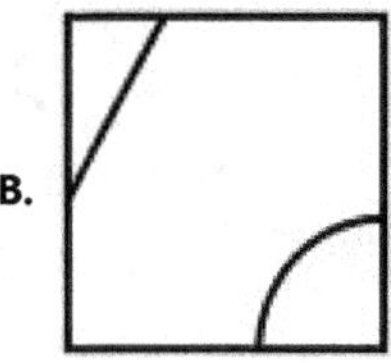

D.

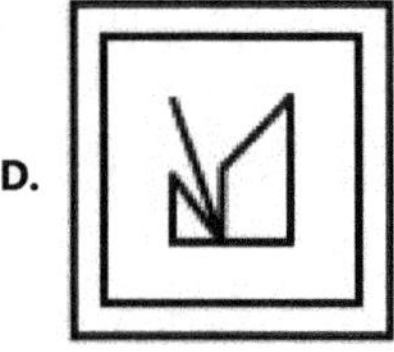

Q.69 A man purchases a car for $1,35,000$ and spent $25,000$ on repairs. At what price was the car sold if he suffered a 10% loss on it?

A. 1,50,000   **B.** 1,76,000

C. 1,44,000   **D.** 1,21,500

Q.70 Vishnu sells an article at 25% profit. Had he sold it for Rs. 51 more, he would have gained 28%. The cost price of the article will be:

A. 1500   **B.** 1700   **C.** 2100   **D.** 2500

Q.71 A shopkeeper marks his goods at 20% above the cost price. He sells three - fourth of the goods at the marked price and the remaining at 30% discount on the marked price. What is his gain/loss percentage?

A. Gain 11%   **B.** Loss 9%

C. Loss 11%   **D.** Gain 9%

Q.72 Direction: Identify the diagram which best represents the relationship among the classes given below -

student, teacher, school

A.

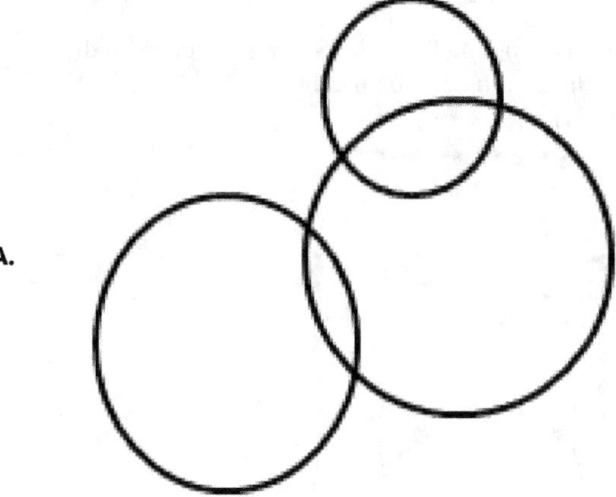

B.

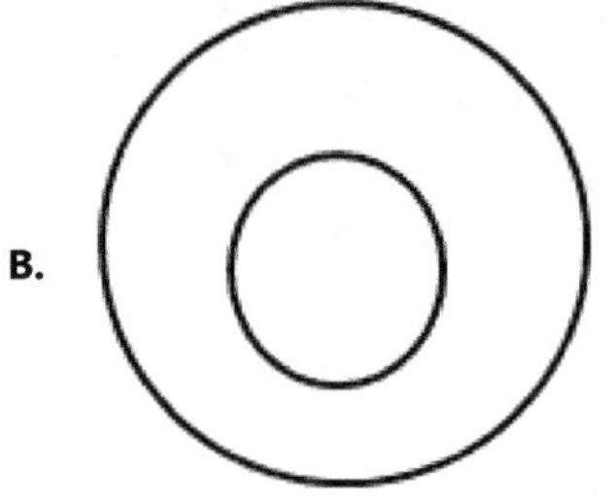
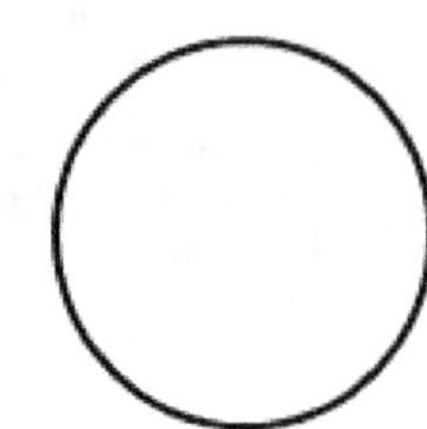

C.

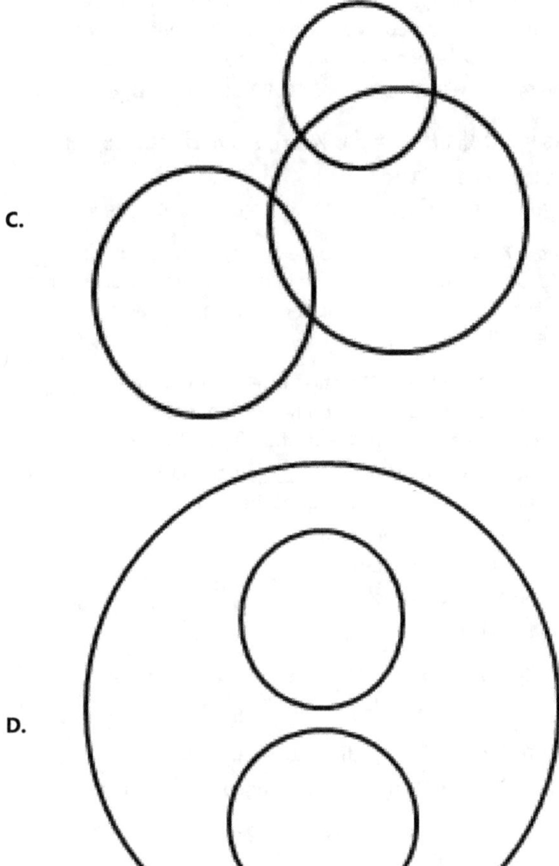

C.

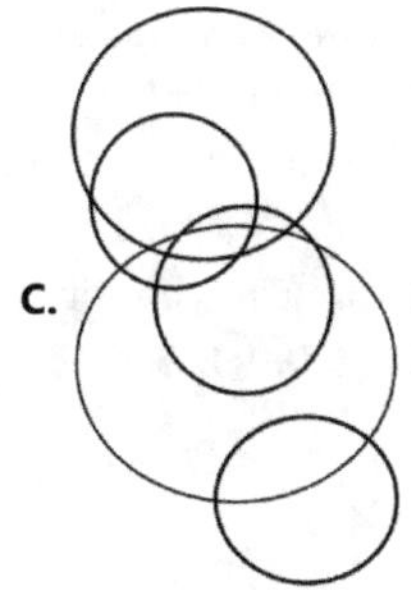

D.

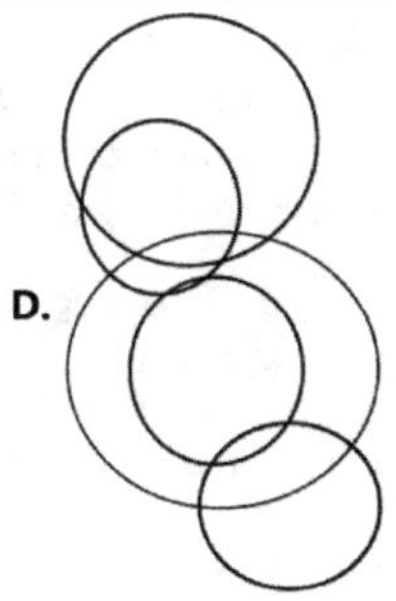

Q.74 Which of the following diagrams the relationship among Husband, Wife, Family?

A.

B.

C.

D.
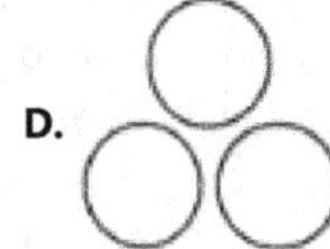

Q.75 Which of the following number is present only in a circle and the triangle?

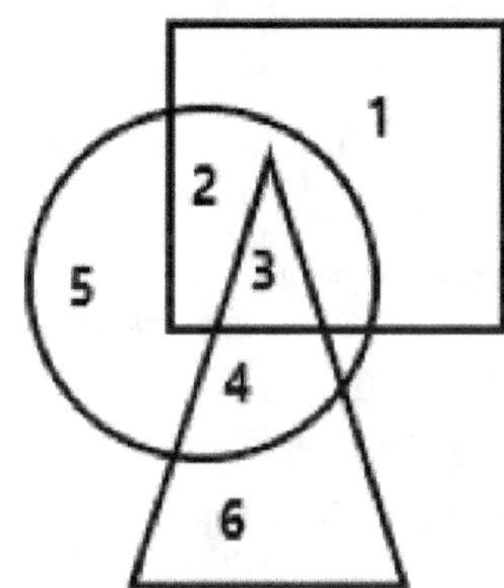

A. 5   **B.** 3   **C.** 4   **D.** 6

D.

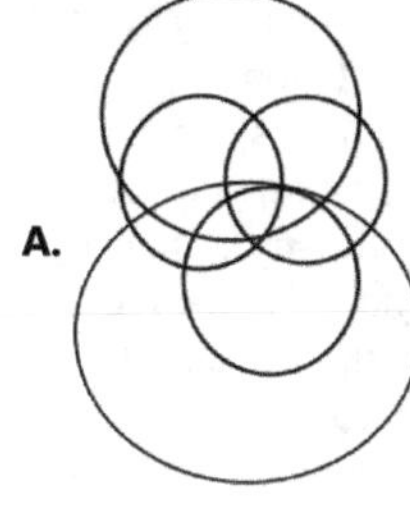

Q.73 Direction: Choose the option which correctly captures the relationship between the following things.

1. Doctor
2. Teacher
3. Male
4. Student
5. Engineer

A.
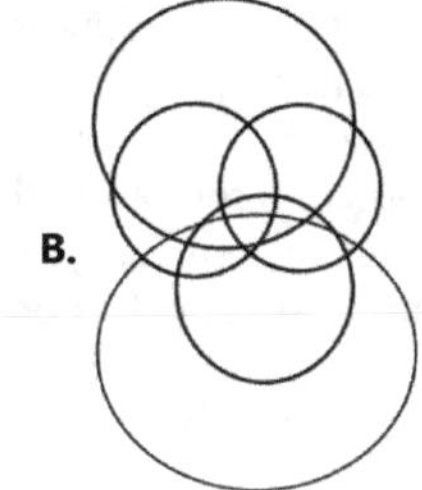

B.

Q.76 Find out the number of all those people who can speak Tamil and Telugu?

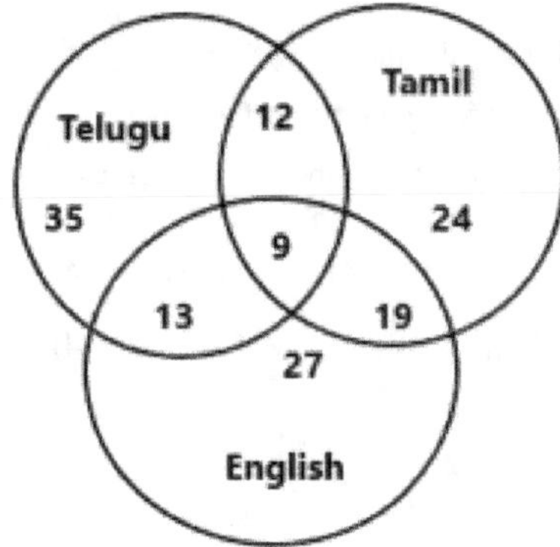

A. 3   **B.** 59   **C.** 21   **D.** 112

Ques (77-78):Direction: In the following question, arrange the given words in a meaningful sequence and then choose the most appropriate sequence from amongst the alternatives provided below the question;

Q.77 1. Bowling 2. Defending 3. Appealing 4. Umpire's decision
A. 4, 3, 1, 2   **B.** 2, 3, 1, 4   **C.** 1, 2, 4, 3   **D.** 1, 2, 3, 4

Q.78 1. Game 2. Class 3. School 4. Recess 5. Home 6. Prayer
A. 3, 6, 2, 4, 1, 5   **B.** 6, 1, 5, 2, 4, 3
C. 1, 2, 4, 5, 3, 6   **D.** 2, 3, 4, 1, 5, 6

Q.79 Which of the following statements is/are correct regarding the Central Vigilance Commission (CVC)?
1. The CVC comes under the Ministry of Home.
2. The Central Vigilance Commissioner or any Vigilance Commissioner can be removed from his office only by order of the Prime Minister.
3. The Central Vigilance Commission has amended the Standard Operating Procedure (SOP) on the adoption of the "Integrity Pact" in government organizations for procurement activities.
A. 1 only   **B.** 2 and 3 only
C. 3 only   **D.** None of the above

Ques (80-82):Direction: Each item in this section consists of a sentence with an underlined word followed by four options. Select the option that is nearest in meaning to the underlined word.

Q.80 He is always <u>anxious</u>.
A. worried   **B.** dispassionate
C. sluggish   **D.** torpid

Q.81 The poems of Kabir are <u>ecstatic</u> in nature.
[UPSC NDA, 2019]

A. efficacious   **B.** eerie
C. rapturous   **D.** reverential

Q.82 Ravi loves <u>seclusion</u>. Therefore, he lives in the mountains.
[UPSC NDA, 2019]

A. nature   **B.** scripture
C. seafaring   **D.** solitariness

Q.83 Which of the following is true about the Indian ocean currents:
1. It is mostly driven by the monsoon wind
2. Seasonal reversal is found in the northern part
3. Agulhas is a cold current near the east African coast
A. 1,2 and 3   **B.** 1 and 2
C. 2 and 3   **D.** 1and 3

Q.84 If an item costs Rs. 3 in 1999 and Rs. 203 in 2000. What is the $\%$ increase in price?
A. $\frac{200}{3}$ **B.** $\frac{200}{6}$
C. 100 **D.** None of these

Q.85 If a number is increased by 10% and then reduced by 50%, further increased by 50%, the resulting number would be what percentage of an original number?
A. 80 %   **B.** 82.5 %   **C.** 90.5 %   **D.** 85 %

Q.86 If 90% of $A = 30\%$ of B and $B = 2x\%$ of A, then the value of x is:
A. 150   **B.** 300   **C.** 400   **D.** 450

Ques (87-89):Direction: Choose an appropriate word from the options to suitably fill the blank in the sentence below so that the sentence makes sense, both grammatically and contextually.

Q.87 Direction: In the Question given below a statement consists of one/two blank. You have to choose the option which provides the correct word that fits in the blanks.
The government must now _______ its seriousness by moving away from the _______ policies of the past.
A.   ensconce, conscientious
B.   masquerade, equitable
C.   shelter, scrupulous
D.   demonstrate, flawed

Q.88 Keep away from that dog, he can be <u>vicious</u>.
A. Cruel   **B.** Gentle   **C.** Evil   **D.** Wicked

Q.89 The servant ______ the picture on the wall.
A. Hang   **B.** Hung   **C.** Hanged   **D.** Hunged

Ques (90-94):Direction: Read the passage and answer the question based on it.

Woodrow Wilson, the 28th president of the United States of America was referring to the much-touted liberal idea of the economic market when he said that the free enterprise system backed by a laissez-faire political setup is the most efficient economic system. Maximum freedom means maximum productiveness which leads to maximum social benefits; our "openness" is to be the measure of our stability with the open free enterprises forming pillars of our economy.

The general public's fascination with this ideal has made Americans defy the "Old World" categories of stalled possessiveness versus unsettling deprivation, the cupidity of retention versus the cupidity of seizure, a "status quo" defended or attacked. The United States cherished the notion that there was no status quo ante. Our only "station & motivation" was the turning of a stationary wheel, spinning faster and faster irrespective of the spinning capacity of the wheel. We did not base our system on the property or stability or a fixed income but on the opportunity and willingness to take risks - which meant we based it not on stability but on mobility. There was a reward for out-of-the-box thinking whereas conventional ideas were looked down upon. The more things changes, be it in the field of economy, technology, etc., that is, the more rapidly the wheel turned, the steadier we would be irrespective of the direction the wheel was moving in.

"Reform" in America has been sterile and sometimes counter-productive because it can imagine no change except through the extension of this metaphor of a race with the trophy being placed at the end of the finishing line, wider inclusion of competitors,' a piece of the action", as it were, for the disenfranchised. There is no attempt to call off the race or make it equal for all the participants. There is, in our legends, no heroism of the office clerk who does all the sundry tasks, no stable industrial workforce who are the backbone of an economy. There has been no boasting about our social workers- they are merely signs of the system's failure, of opportunity, denied or not taken, of things to be eliminated

We have no pride in our growing interdependence nor do we cherish our social well-being. The fact that our system can serve others, that we are able to help those in need doesn't instill a sense of confidence in us. There is no honor but in the Wonderland race we must all run, all trying to win with sometimes too many competitors, none winning in the end(for there is no end).

Q.90 What is the primary purpose of the passage?

A. Highlight the drawback of the one-dimensional American economic and political setup

B. Champion those Americans whom the author deems to be neglected

C. Suggest a substitute for the traditional metaphor of race which would benefit the Americans

D. Contrast the "New World" and "Old World" economic ideology and criticize the former

Q.91 What can we infer from the author's use of word "Reform" in the first line of the third paragraph?

A. Emphasize its departure from the concept of settled progressiveness

B. Highlight that the American political system does not prefer reforms

C. Assert that the reform in the United States has not been fundamental

D. Suggest what reforms should be undertaken to improve the economic system

Q.92 It can be inferred from the passage that the author most probably thinks that giving the 'disenfranchised "a piece of action" is

A. Duty of the state on compassionate grounds

B. United State's inherent resistance to profound and fundamental change

C. An innovative program from genuine social change which would end the race

D. A surprising 'Old World' remedy for social needs which America needs

Q.93 Which of the following would be the correct inference regarding Woodrow Wilson's idea of an ideal economic market?

A. Encourage equal distribution of wealth through free enterprises

B. Encourage people to think out of the box

C. Encourage the growth of free enterprise at the cost of ordinary social workers

D. Promote the growth of free enterprises sans any political intervention

Q.94 What does the author imply by "station and motivation" as mentioned in the second paragraph of the passage?

A. Free enterprising getting a free which led to several problems

B. Creating an atmosphere of rat race where only risk takers were rewarded and others looked down upon

C. Americans fascination with keeping on focusing on mobility and taking risks irrespective of the outcome

D. America's fascination with pushing for changes backed by free enterprises

Ques (95-99):Direction: Select a suitable figure from the four alternatives that would complete the figure matrix.

Q.95

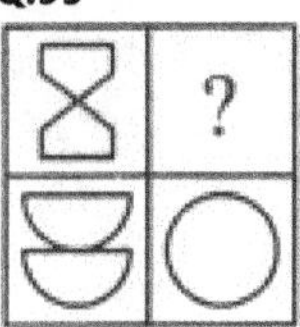

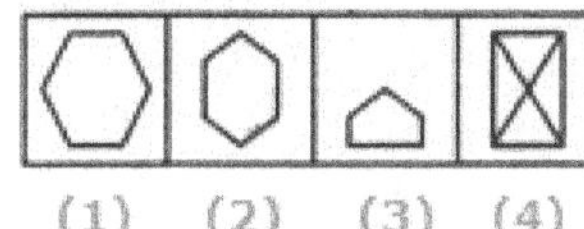

A. 1   B. 2   C. 3   D. 4

Q.96

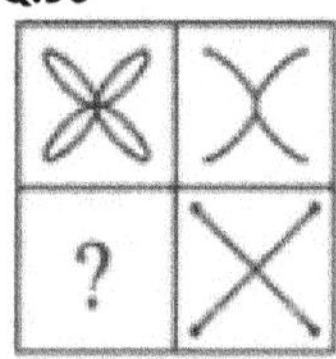

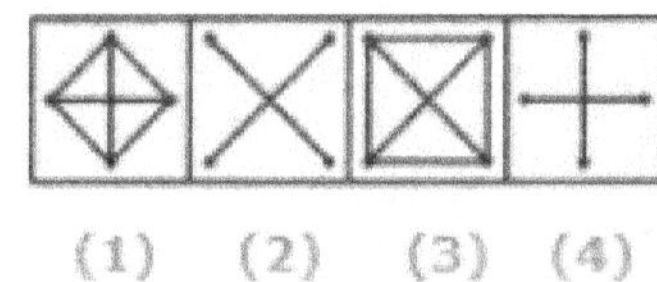

[Telangana Police Constable, 2015]

A. 1   B. 2   C. 3   D. 4

Q.97

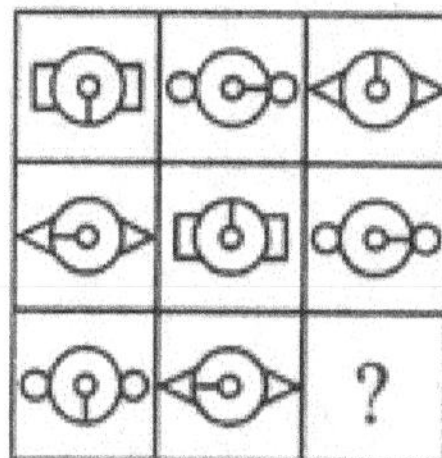

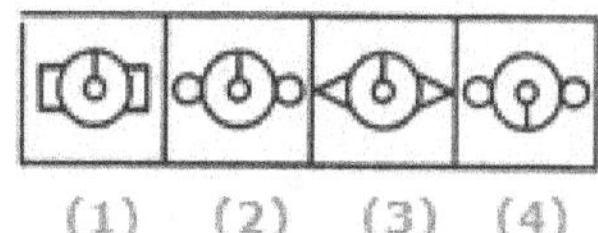

[UP Police Sub Inspector, 2021]

A. 1   **B.** 2   **C.** 3   **D.** 4

Q.98

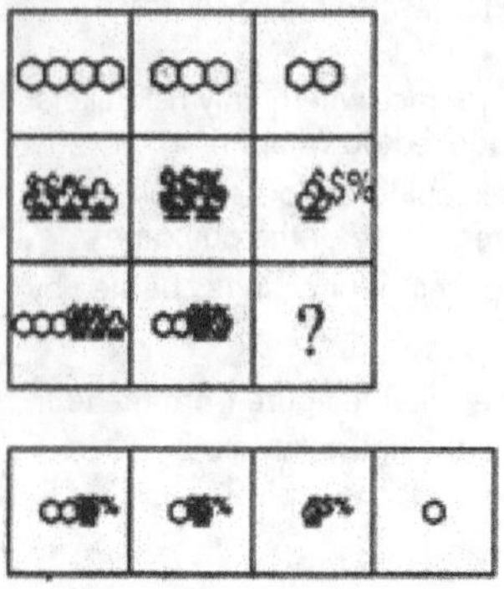

(1)   (2)   (3)   (4)

A. 1   **B.** 2   **C.** 3   **D.** 4

Q.99

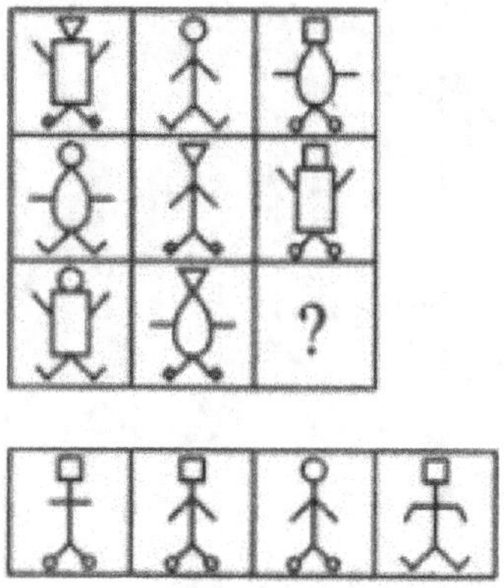

(1)   (2)   (3)   (4)

A. 1   **B.** 2   **C.** 3   **D.** 4

Q.100 Fill in the blank with the words given below.

Inspite__________ we got there on time.

A. of heavy traffic being there

B. of having heavy traffic

C. of the heavy traffic

D. the heavy traffic

// Smart Answer Sheet //

Correct — Percentage of students who answered correctly. **Skipped** — Percentage of students who skipped.

Q.	Ans.	Correct	Skipped	Q.	Ans.	Correct	Skipped	Q.	Ans.	Correct	Skipped	Q.	Ans.	Correct	Skipped	Q.	Ans.	Correct	Skipped	Q.	Ans.	Correct	Skipped
1	D	44.43 %	54.29 %	18	B	43.73 %	32.27 %	35	C	60.5 %	37.35 %	52	C	80.81 %	11.27 %	69	C	59.31 %	37.25 %	86	A	67.79 %	30.1 %
2	A	28.5 %	70.7 %	19	B	14.65 %	73.9 %	36	D	84.47 %	13.79 %	53	A	50.13 %	39.18 %	70	B	61.82 %	30.86 %	87	D	66.79 %	30.0 %
3	B	27.13 %	71.93 %	20	C	67.69 %	31.69 %	37	A	23.76 %	69.23 %	54	D	58.37 %	38.53 %	71	A	54.79 %	30.81 %	88	B	86.68 %	13.19 %
4	B	88.79 %	10.29 %	21	C	56.31 %	30.44 %	38	B	68.05 %	30.38 %	55	D	83.16 %	15.15 %	72	D	58.14 %	33.66 %	89	B	76.14 %	23.25 %
5	A	11.72 %	68.81 %	22	A	63.34 %	34.9 %	39	B	42.81 %	43.8 %	56	D	59.68 %	34.48 %	73	B	25.54 %	73.42 %	90	A	51.85 %	30.01 %
6	A	85.99 %	11.27 %	23	D	58.29 %	38.98 %	40	B	46.22 %	31.37 %	57	B	51.88 %	32.03 %	74	A	60.89 %	36.01 %	91	C	51.47 %	43.91 %
7	C	53.27 %	33.45 %	24	D	49.99 %	37.39 %	41	C	56.8 %	35.42 %	58	D	28.13 %	68.86 %	75	C	55.2 %	39.04 %	92	B	56.37 %	41.64 %
8	D	87.87 %	11.14 %	25	A	54.48 %	39.09 %	42	D	60.76 %	38.32 %	59	B	53.57 %	36.55 %	76	C	42.08 %	55.09 %	93	D	67.04 %	31.32 %
9	A	86.68 %	10.74 %	26	B	40.59 %	44.48 %	43	C	46.35 %	51.22 %	60	A	24.7 %	73.6 %	77	D	85.33 %	14.11 %	94	C	64.03 %	35.47 %
10	A	83.45 %	14.76 %	27	C	47.32 %	39.31 %	44	D	46.13 %	43.92 %	61	B	40.6 %	57.95 %	78	A	81.35 %	13.17 %	95	B	65.19 %	32.75 %
11	A	64.29 %	30.17 %	28	B	30.17 %	67.44 %	45	A	63.24 %	33.12 %	62	A	30.1 %	69.61 %	79	C	88.8 %	10.29 %	96	C	56.18 %	37.65 %
12	D	49.96 %	37.75 %	29	C	29.26 %	68.79 %	46	B	79.43 %	16.12 %	63	D	63.19 %	30.36 %	80	A	85.12 %	10.18 %	97	A	53.1 %	32.84 %
13	A	53.56 %	42.46 %	30	C	42.63 %	37.85 %	47	A	44.18 %	31.2 %	64	B	85.94 %	11.18 %	81	C	44.58 %	45.49 %	98	B	66.91 %	30.89 %
14	B	63.69 %	31.33 %	31	A	65.82 %	30.21 %	48	D	48.73 %	49.69 %	65	D	46.29 %	43.91 %	82	D	66.57 %	31.36 %	99	B	55.82 %	32.97 %
15	D	41.42 %	49.69 %	32	A	27.77 %	69.03 %	49	A	55.09 %	41.41 %	66	B	79.76 %	19.14 %	83	B	48.71 %	32.47 %	100	C	64.05 %	33.94 %
16	D	26.38 %	70.92 %	33	A	49.65 %	39.03 %	50	B	44.72 %	33.39 %	67	C	81.82 %	12.88 %	84	D	56.22 %	30.21 %				
17	A	78.41 %	14.18 %	34	D	42.88 %	33.58 %	51	D	69.37 %	30.01 %	68	C	43.26 %	32.81 %	85	B	46.87 %	42.98 %				

//Hints and Solutions//

1. Union Minister Shri Anurag Thakur on 27 March 2022 has launched TEJAS (Training for Emirates Jobs And Skills) programme. It is a Skill India International Project to train overseas Indians.

The project is aimed at skilling, certification and overseas employment of Indians. Tejas is aimed at creating pathways to enable the Indian workforce to get equipped for skill and market requirements in UAE.

Hence, the correct option is (D).

2. The country's total market cap stands at $3.21 trillion, which is higher than that of the UK ($3.19 trillion), Saudi Arabia ($3.18 trillion), and Canada ($3.18 trillion). In 2022, India has climbed two positions, despite a 7.4 percent drop in its market cap.

Hence, the correct option is (A).

3. Tamilnadu Petroproducts Ltd (TPL) has become the 1st company in the world to have its product linear alkylbenzene (LAB) conferred with IS12795:2020 certification. It has been certified by the Department of Chemicals and Petrochemicals, Ministry of Chemicals and Fertilizers.

With the Bureau of Indian Standards certification, TPL emerges as the only authorized seller of LAB in the Indian market.

TPL is a part of the petrochemicals division of AM International, the Singapore-headquartered diversified, multinational group of companies with a federated operating architecture.

Hence, the correct option is (B).

4. Dr. Reddy's Laboratories has announced the commercial launch of the drug 2-deoxy-D-glucose (2-DG). It is an anti-Covid drug developed by the Defence Research and Development Organisation (DRDO).

The drug is approved for emergency use as an adjunct therapy to the standard of care in the treatment of coronavirus patients in hospital settings.
Hence, the correct option is (B).

5. Tamil Nadu Assembly Election 2021 was won by DMK political party.

- The Dravida Munnetra Kazhagam (DMK) won the election, ending the decade-long reign of the All India Anna Dravida Munnetra Kazhagam (AIADMK).

- The DMK's leader M. K. Stalin became the eighth Chief Minister of Tamil Nadu and the 12th Chief Minister since the 1956 reorganization.

- He replaced Edappadi K. Palaniswami of the AIADMK.

- The poll was Tamil Nadu's first assembly election after the demises of the two most prominent Chief Ministers in the state's modern history, J. Jayalalithaa—general secretary of the AIADMK, and M. Karunanidhi—president of the DMK, who died in 2016 and 2018 respectively.

Hence, the correct option is (A).

6. We know that,

$$A = P\left(1 + \frac{r}{100}\right)^t$$

According to the question,

$$1852.20 = 1600\left(1 + \frac{5}{100}\right)^t$$

$$\frac{18522}{16000} = \left(\frac{21}{20}\right)^t$$

$$\frac{9261}{8000} = \left(\frac{21}{20}\right)^t$$

$$\left(\frac{21}{20}\right)^3 = \left(\frac{21}{20}\right)^t$$

$$t = 3 \text{ years}$$

Hence, the correct option is (A).

7. Given:

$$P = 40000 \text{ Rs.,} \quad r = 20\% \text{ and } n = 2 \text{ years}$$

If P amount compounded yearly at $r\%$ rate of interest for n years, then amount become

$$A = P\left(1 + \frac{r}{100}\right)^n$$

$$= 40000\left(1 + \frac{20}{100}\right)^2$$

$$= 40000(1.2)^2$$

$$= 40000 \times 1.44$$

$$= 57600$$

Hence, the correct option is (C).

8. Simple interest $= \dfrac{(Principal Amount \times time \times rate)}{100}$

$$= \frac{(1000 \times 6 \times X)}{100}$$

$$= 60X$$

Amount $=$ Interest $+$ Principal Amount

$$= 1000 + 60X$$

According to question,

$$1000 + 60X = 1300$$

$$60X = 300$$

$$X = 5$$

Hence, the correct option is (D).

9. The BrahMos is a medium-range supersonic cruise missile in India.

BrahMos is the world's fastest anti-ship cruise missile in operation. It's developed as a joint venture between Russia and India.

- It was developed by the Defense Research and Development Organization (DRDO) of India and the Federal State Unitary Enterprise NPO Mashinostroyenia(NPOM) of Russia.
- It was named after two rivers, the Brahmaputra of India and the Moskva of Russia. It can be launched against ships and land-based targets.
- It has a flight range of up to 290 km and can reach a maximum speed of Mach 3.

Hence, the correct option is (A).

10. One who is present everywhere - **Omnipresent**

Example:

God is not only omnipotent but also **omnipresent**.

Hence, the correct option is (A).

11. One who does not believe in the existence of God- **Atheist**

Example:

Being an **atheist** he never went to a religious place.

Hence, the correct option is (A).

12. Sonia Lather is an Indian boxer.

She was a silver medallist at the 2016 AIBA Women's World Boxing Championships and a twice silver medallist at the Asian Amateur Boxing Championships.

Hence, the correct option is (D).

13. The correct answer is, 'It sounds like **a** great idea'.

Articles are words that define a noun as specific or unspecific. The definite article 'the' is used with the name of things that are unique or already mentioned before.

- The article 'a' is used with the name of things that are not specific.
- The article 'an' is used with the words starting with the sound of a vowel.
- If a word starts with a vowel but has the sound of a consonant, it will be preceded by the article 'a'.
- For example: a university, a union, a one rupee note, etc.

In the 1st blank part of the cloze test, the article 'a' will be used as the adjective 'great' starts with a consonant sound.

Hence, the correct option is (A).

14. The correct answer is, 'People getting instantly excited when they hear **the** phrase 'education for peace' or the title of a course that calls itself 'peace Education'.

Articles are words that define a noun as specific or unspecific. The definite article 'the' is used with the name of things that are unique or already mentioned before.

- The article 'a' is used with the name of things that are not specific.
- The article 'an' is used with the words having the first letter as a vowel and having the sound of a vowel.
- If a word starts with a vowel but has the sound of a consonant, it will be preceded by the article 'a'.
- For example: a university, a union, a one rupee note, etc.

In the given 2nd blank of the cloze test, the article 'the' will be used as a particular phrase (education for peace) has been talked about in the question.

Hence, the correct option is (B).

15. The correct answer is, 'About a decade ago, I proposed such **a** course in my institute'.

Articles are words that define a noun as specific or unspecific. The definite article 'the' is used with the name of things that are unique or already mentioned before.

- The article 'a' is used with the name of things that are not specific.
- The article 'an' is used with the words starting with the sound of a vowel.
- If a word starts with a vowel but has the sound of a consonant, it will be preceded by the article 'a'.
- For example: a university, a union, a one rupee note, etc.

In the 3rd blank part of the cloze test, the article 'a' will be used as the noun 'course' starts with a consonant sound.

Hence, the correct option is (D).

16. The correct answer is, 'The idea of a course **on** 'peace education' had occurred to me on the way back from one of the neighbouring countries where I met students of class IX'.

There are some fixed prepositional phrases given below:

- by dint of, out of jealousy, course on something, read between the lines, by car/bus/train, owing to, on a trip, for a change, etc.

For example: Hence according to the phrases given above, 'on' will be the correct choice in the 4th blank.

- Julie has signed up for **courses on** English and French this year.

The phrase 'course on something' means a series of lessons on a particular subject.

Hence, the correct option is (D).

17. The correct answer is, 'I could not find **any** difference'.

An adjective is any member of a class of words that modify nouns and pronouns.

- Any- used to refer to one or some of a thing or number of things, no matter how much or how many
- Few- a small number of (negligible)

- That- used to identify a specific person or thing observed by the speaker
- This- used to identify a specific person or thing close at hand or being indicated or experienced

The adjective 'few' is used with plural countable nouns, whereas 'any' is used with singular countable nouns.

The singular noun 'difference' used after the blank part of the sentence suggests that the adjective in the blank part must be a singular one.

Since no specific difference is being talked about here, we find that the option (A) i.e., any is the correct choice in the 5th blank.

Hence, the correct option is (A).

18. The species restricted to be present in one region and nowhere else in the world are called Endemic species. Some species are restricted to a continent while the others are restricted to an island.

Hence, the correct option is (B).

19. The correct answer is:

'The jury gave the film 'Andhaa Dhund' an award.'

In the active form, the subject and the object will get interchanged.

In the active form 'award' will become the object.

The passive form contains 'was' + past participle form of verb so the active form will contain the past participle form of the verb.

Option (A) is in past perfect tense.

Option (C) is grammatically incorrect. 'Was gave' is totally incorrect.

Option (D) is in future tense because the word 'will' is used.

Hence, the correct option is (B).

20. The correct answer is:

My hand was burnt yesterday while cooking.

In the passive form, the subject and the object will be interchanged. So, 'my hand' will become the subject. The sentence uses the past participle form of the verb i.e., burnt. The passive form will be in the past tense.

Option (A) is in past continuous tense.

Option (B) uses could which should be used only when 'can' is there in the active form.

Option (D) is in future tense.

Hence, the correct option is (C).

21. The logic is:

$$12 : 60 \rightarrow 12 \times [(12 \div 2) - 1] = 12 \times [6 - 1] = 12 \times 5 = 60$$

Similarly,

$$16 : ? \rightarrow 16 \times [(16 \div 2) - 1] = 16 \times [8 - 1] = 16 \times 7 = 112$$

Hence, the correct option is (C).

22. The logic followed here is:

$$17^2 + 4 = 289 + 4 = 293$$

$$21^2 + 4 = 441 + 4 = 445$$

Similarly,

$$?^2 + 4 = 488$$

$$?^2 = 488 - 4$$

$$?^2 = 484$$

$$? = 22$$

Hence, the correct option is (A).

23. The logic followed here is:

Ohm is the unit of resistance.

Similarly,

Radian is the unit of angle.

Watt is the unit of Power, not Force. Ampere is the unit of Current not Force. Joule is the unit of Energy, not Density.

Hence, the correct option is (D).

24. The logic follows here is:

Golden Wattle is the national flower of Australia.

Similarly,

Iris is the national flower of France.

France has the same relation to Iris as the second word to the first word.

Hence, the correct option is (D).

25. The logic followed is:

(First two digits of the first number together) ÷ third digit of the first number = the second number

$$122 : 6$$

$$12 \div 2 = 6$$

$$6 = 6$$

Similarly,

$$408 : ?$$

$$40 \div 8 = ?$$

$$? = 5$$

Hence, the correct option is (A).

26. As per the given data, we know

In one direction Vinod will go by down-stream and return with up-stream and in both cases the distance is same

$\Rightarrow$ Downstream distance $=$ Upstream distance

$\Rightarrow (U + 3)4 = (U - 3)6$

$\Rightarrow 4U + 12 = 6U - 18$

$\Rightarrow 30 = 2U$

$\Rightarrow U = 15\ km/hr$

$\therefore$ Speed of the Vinod in still water $= 15\ km/hr$

Hence, the correct option is (B).

27. Speed of Raman $= 20 km/hr$

After convert in km/hr to m/s, $= \dfrac{5}{18} \times 20 = \dfrac{50}{9} m/s$

We know that, Time $= \dfrac{distance}{speed}$

$\Rightarrow Time = \dfrac{400}{\frac{50}{9}}$

$\Rightarrow Time = 400 \times \dfrac{9}{50}$

$\Rightarrow Time = 8 \times 9$

$\Rightarrow Time = 72$ sec

$\Rightarrow 72$ sec $= \dfrac{72}{60} = \dfrac{6}{5} = 1.2$ minute

Hence, the correct option is (C).

28. The Lenght of the train $A = 450$ m

Speed of the train $A = 72$ kmph $= 72 \times \left(\dfrac{5}{18}\right) = 20$ m/sec

The Lenght of train $B = 620$ m

Speed of the train $B = 90$ kmph $= 90 \times \left(\dfrac{5}{18}\right) = 25$ m/sec

Distance covered to cross each other $= 450 + 620 = 1070$ m

For trains moving in same direction,

Relative speed $= 25 - 20 = 5$ m/s

Time taken $\dfrac{1070}{5} = 214$ sec

For train moving in opposite direction,

Relative speed $= 25 + 20 = 45$ m/s

Time taken $= \dfrac{1070}{45} = 23.78$ sec

Difference in time $= 214 - 23.78 = 190.22$ sec

$\therefore$ Required Difference $= 190.22$ sec

Hence, the correct option is (B).

29. Let the speed of auto be $x\ kmh^{-1}$.

So, the speed of the train will be $6x$ and that of bike will be

$= \dfrac{6x}{1.5} = 4x$

As per the given information,

Time taken by auto $+$ Time taken by train $+$ Time taken by bike $= 21$ hours

$\Rightarrow \dfrac{132}{x} + \dfrac{852}{6x} + \dfrac{248}{4x} = 21$

or, $\dfrac{132}{x} + \dfrac{142}{x} + \dfrac{62}{x} = 21$

or, $21x = 132 + 142 + 62 = 336$

$\therefore x = \dfrac{336}{21} = 16$

$\therefore$ Speed of the train $= 6x = 6 \times 16 = 96\ kmh^{-1}$

Hence, the correct option is (C).

30. In each figure both the "*" symbols are adjacent to each other whereas in the figure given below both are diagonally opposite to each other.

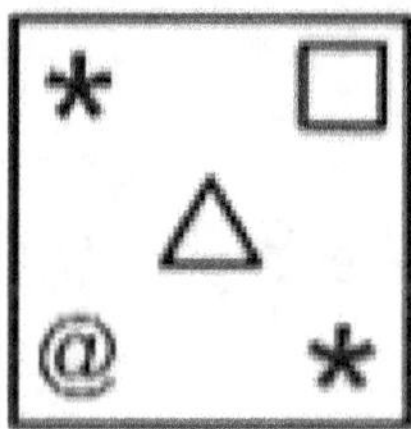

Hence, the correct option is (C).

31.

All follow the same pattern, except 'PV'.

Hence, the correct option is (A).

32. All option except '(A)' has one of the images shaded, while option (A) has no image shaded.

Hence, the correct option is (A).

33. Stomach, Heart and Kidneys are internal organs.

Whereas,

Legs are not internal organs.

Hence, "legs" is the odd one.

Hence, the correct option is (A).

34. (A)

$$G \xrightarrow{-2} E \xrightarrow{-2} C$$

(B)

$$M \xrightarrow{-2} K \xrightarrow{-2} I$$

$$Y \xrightarrow{-2} W \xrightarrow{-2} U$$

(C)

$$O \xrightarrow{+2} Q \xrightarrow{+2} S$$

(D)

So, 'OQS' is the odd one out.

Hence, the correct option is (D).

35. According to the question:

The average of 10 numbers is $=15$

Sum of 10 numbers $= 15 \times 10 = 150$

He mistakenly writes one number 26 instead of 36.

Difference $= 36 - 26 = 10$

Actual sum of 10 numbers is $= 150 + 10 = 160$

So, actual average of 10 numbers is $= \dfrac{160}{10} = 16$

Hence, the correct option is (C).

36. Average age of 30 students $= 20$

Sum of ages of 30 students $= 20 \times 30 = 600$

Average age of 20 students $= 30$

Sum of ages of 20 students $= 30 \times 20 = 600$

Average of total 50 students $= \dfrac{1200}{50} = 24$

Hence, the correct option is (D).

37. First 31 multiples of 19 are $19, 38, 57 \ldots 589$

Sum of all multiples $= 19 + 38 + 57 + \cdots + 589$

$\Rightarrow 19(1 + 2 + 3 + \cdots + 31)$

$\Rightarrow 19 \times 496 = 9424$

$\therefore$ Average $= \dfrac{9424}{31} = 304$

Hence, the correct option is (A).

38. $(A + B)$'s 1 day's work $= \dfrac{1}{3}$ part

$(A + B)$ works 2 days together $= \dfrac{2}{3}$ part

Remaining work $= 1 - \dfrac{2}{3} = \dfrac{1}{3}$ part

$\dfrac{1}{3}$ part of work is completed by A in two days

Hence, one day's work of A $= \dfrac{1}{6}$

Then, one day's work of B $= \dfrac{1}{3} - \dfrac{1}{6} = \dfrac{1}{6}$

So, B alone can complete the whole work in 6 days.

Hence, the correct option is (B).

39. Given:

A can finish the work in 30 days.

B can finish the work in 20 days.

they both worked for 6 day and A left the job.

By LCM method,

$\Rightarrow$ Let the total work $=$ LCM of (30, 20) $= 60$ unit

$\Rightarrow$ A's efficiency $= \left(\dfrac{60}{30}\right) = 2 \ \dfrac{unit}{day}$

$\Rightarrow$ B's efficiency $= \left(\dfrac{60}{20}\right) = 3 \ \dfrac{unit}{day}$

$\Rightarrow$ Both work for 6 days,

$\Rightarrow$ work done in 6 days $= (2 + 3) \ \dfrac{unit}{day} \times 6$ day $= 30$ unit

$\Rightarrow$ remaining work $= 60 - 30 = 30$ unit

$\Rightarrow$ remaining work done by B $= \left(\dfrac{30}{3}\right) = 10$ days.

$\therefore$ B completed the remaining work in 10 days.

Hence, the correct option is (B).

40. B's one-day work $= \dfrac{1}{60}$

Let A can complete the work in x days

Let A's one-day work $= \dfrac{1}{x}$

Total time taken by A and B to complete the work $= 20$

A and B's one-day work $= \dfrac{1}{20}$

$\dfrac{1}{60} + \dfrac{1}{x} = \dfrac{1}{20} \Rightarrow x = 30$

A can complete the work in 30 days.

A's one-day work $= \dfrac{1}{30}$

Total work done by A in 20 days $= 20 \times \dfrac{1}{30} = \dfrac{2}{3}$

Total work done by B in 20 days $= 20 \times \dfrac{1}{60} = \dfrac{1}{3}$

Money earned by person $=$ Total money $\times$ Work done by the person

Share of A $= 36000 \times \dfrac{2}{3} =$ Rs. 24000

Hence, the correct option is (B).

41. Let $\dfrac{.009}{x} = .01$

Then $x = \dfrac{.009}{.01}$

$\Rightarrow x = \dfrac{.9}{1}$

$\Rightarrow x = .9$

Hence, the correct option is (C).

42. Let $3889 + 12.952 - x = 3854.002$

Then $x = (3889 + 12.952) - 3854.002$

$\Rightarrow x = 3901.952 - 3854.002$

$\Rightarrow x = 47.95$

Hence, the correct option is (D).

43. As given,

$0.232323\ldots$

$\Rightarrow 0.\overline{23}$

$\Rightarrow \dfrac{23}{99}$

Hence, the correct option is (C).

44. Electron affinity is defined as the change in energy of a neutral atom (in the gaseous phase) when an electron is added to the atom to form a negative ion.

Electron affinity of noble gases is almost zero. Noble gases have completely filled valence shells and stable octets. They do not accept electrons easily as they have no deficiency, also adding electrons produces repulsion between the electrons.

Hence, the correct option is (D).

45. Carbon dioxide has one carbon atom and two oxygen atoms and a molecular weight of 44. The oxygen in the air is actually two atoms of O with a molecular weight of 32. So, carbon dioxide has a higher density and is heavier than oxygen.

Hence, the correct option is (A).

46. The chemical name of Vinegar is Acetic acid. Vinegar is an aqueous solution of Acetic acid and trace compounds that may include flavorings. Vinegar typically contains 5% to 8% Acetic acid by volume.

Hence, the correct option is (B).

47. Graphite is used in making pencils.

Graphite, also referred to as plumbago, is a crystalline form of Carbon with its atoms arranged in a hexagonal structure. It occurs naturally in this form and is the most stable form of Carbon under standard conditions. In high pressure and temperature, it converts to diamond.

Hence, the correct option is (A).

48. LPG stands for Liquefied Petroleum Gas. Like all fossil fuels, it is a non-renewable source of energy. It is extracted from crude oil and natural gas. Normally, the gas is stored in liquid form under pressure in a steel container, cylinder or tank.

LPG is composed of hydrocarbons containing three or four carbon atoms. The major components in LPG are Butane and Propane.

Hence, the correct option is (D).

49. The correct answer is **Less successful**.

Be in eclipse: much less successful and important than before

For example: Even when her career was temporarily **in eclipse** she had no financial worries.

Hence, the correct option is (A).

50. The correct answer is '**Methods of achieving something.**'

Ways and means: The methods by which something is accomplished or attained, especially in relation to finances

For example: We're here to discuss the goals of the project, not the **ways and means**.

Hence, the correct option is (B).

51. King penguins are active throughout the long summer days.

- The given sentence is grammatically correct.
- Here, 'King penguins' is plural.
- The king penguin (Aptenodytes patagonicus) is the second-largest species of penguin, smaller, but somewhat similar in appearance to the emperor penguin.
- Therefore, a plural helping verb that is 'are' is used.

Hence, the correct option is (D).

52. The given sentence is grammatically incorrect.

- Here, 'is quite different' should be used instead of 'are quite different'.

- 'Behaviour' is a singular noun, hence, the verb must also be singular to maintain the subject-verb agreement. Therefore, 'are' must be replaced with 'is' to form a grammatically correct sentence.

Hence, the correct option is (C).

53. The Rigveda is the source of Sanatana Dharma or Hinduism. There are 1028 suktas in which the deities are praised. In this scripture, there are mantras to invoke the Gods in the Yajna. This is the first Veda. The Rigveda is considered by all historians of the world to be the first creation of the Indo-European language-family.

Hence, the correct option is (A).

54. The origin of 'Raag Bhairav' or 'Raag Bhairavi' is believed to be from Chic Bhairavi. In this Re, Ga, Dha, and Ni seem soft and M is considered as a vadi and Sa is a conversational tone. Singing time is morning.

Hence, the correct option is (D).

55. Dadabhai Naoroji, G. Subramania Iyer, R. C. Dutt were famous economic critique.

- Amongst the famous economic critique Dadabhai Naoroji, G. Subramania Iyer, R. C. Dutt who studied the economic relationship between the British Empire and India, Dadabhai Naoroji was the most prominent.

- He popularized the drain theory in his book "Poverty and Un-British Rule in India".

- They explained the colonial structure in all its three aspects of domination through trade, industry and finance.

Hence, the correct option is (D).

56. In all figures, the arrow and the pin are at right angles to each other.

Hence, the correct option is (D).

57. In the first figure of the question figure, the triangle is given and in the second figure, the triangle is placed within the square.

Similarly,

The pentagon is given in the 3rd figure of the question figure, so the Pentagon will be placed within the hexagon in the 4th figure.

When the figure is completed it will appear like:-

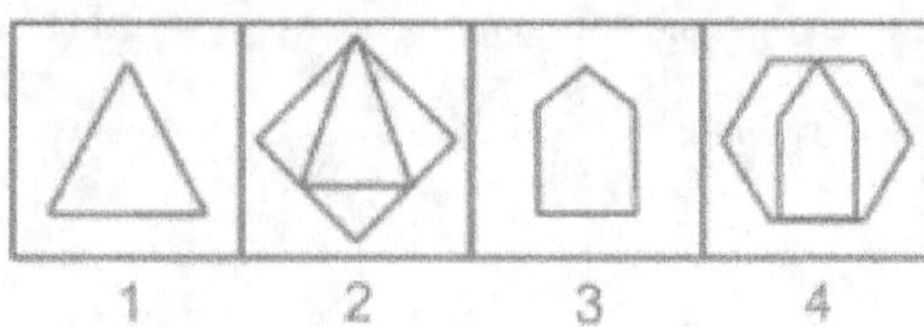

Hence, the correct option is (B).

58. When the first image is rotated 135° anticlockwise to get the second image which appear like.

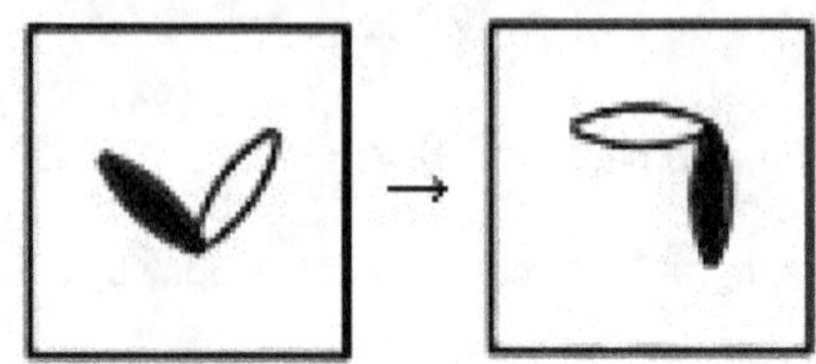

Similarly,

The third image is rotated 135° anticlockwise to get the fourth image which appear like.

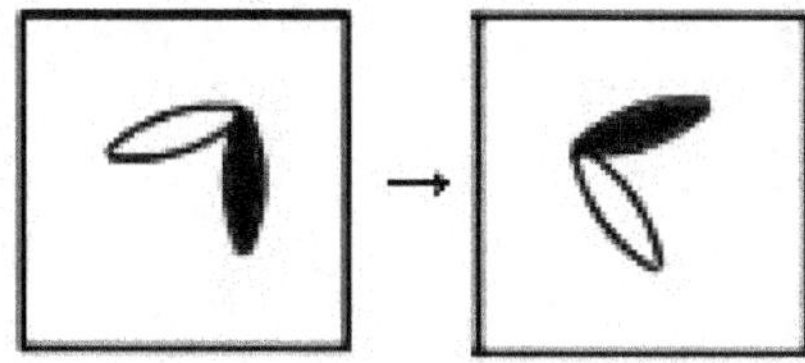

Hence, the correct option is (D).

59. Logic:- Odd number in each of the figure of the question figure.

When the figure is completed it will appear like:-

ON E	TH RE E	FI VE	SE VE N

The first three figures of the question figure have odd numbers.

So, the fourth will also have an odd number.

Hence, the correct option is (B).

60. When the figure is competed it will appear like:-

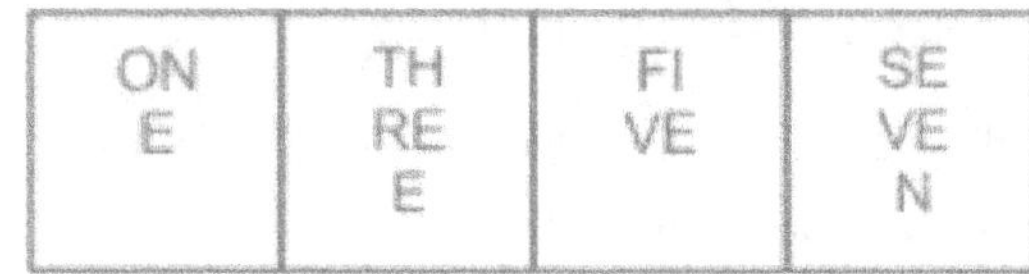

Hence, the correct option is (A).

61. Given:

$$6A = 11B = 7C$$

LCM of $6, 11$ and $7 = 462$

Required ratio

$$A:B:C = \frac{462}{6} : \frac{462}{11} : \frac{462}{7}$$

$$= 77:42:66$$

Hence, the correct option is (B).

62. Given:

Total amount $= 6400$

Let the first worker's share $= \frac{3}{5}x$

Second worker's share $= 2x$

Third worker's share $= \frac{5}{3}x$

Then, $\frac{3}{5}x + 2x + \frac{5}{3}x = 6400$

$\Rightarrow \frac{9x+30x+25x}{15} = 6400$

$\Rightarrow 64x = 6400 \times 15$

$\Rightarrow x = 1500$

$\therefore$ Second worker's share $1500 \times 2 = 3000$

Hence, the correct option is (A).

63. Given,

Income of R, S and T = 4 : 2 : 3

Expense of R, S and T = 2 : 1 : 3

Income = Expenditure + saving

Let the income of R, S and T be 4x, 2x and 3x

Let the expense of R, S and T be 2y, y and 3y

Income of R = Rs.20000

$\Rightarrow$ 4x = 20,000

$\Rightarrow$ x = 5,000

Expenditure of R = Rs. 8000

$\Rightarrow$ 2y = 8000

$\Rightarrow$ y = 4000

Saving of S = 2x - y = 2(5000) - 4000 = Rs. 6000

$\therefore$ Saving of S is Rs. 6000

Hence, the correct option is (D).

64.

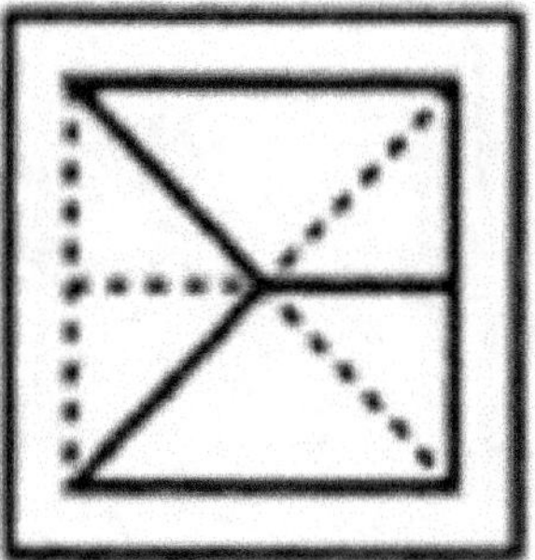

Hence, the correct option is (B).

65.

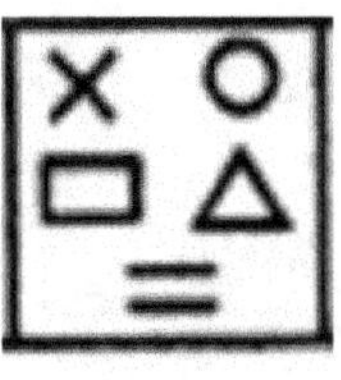

(4)

Figure (4) has a rectangle in place of a '+' sign.

Hence, the correct option is (D).

66. The question figure is embedded in the option figure (B).

Hence, the correct option is (B).

67.

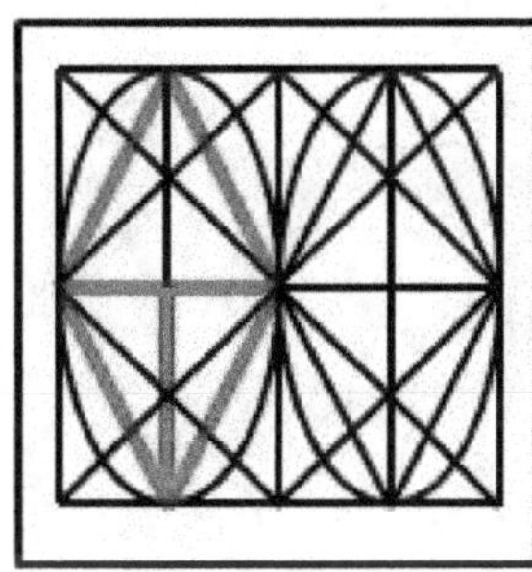

Hence, the correct option is (C).

68. On observing all the above figures, we see that figure 3 will complete the question figure.

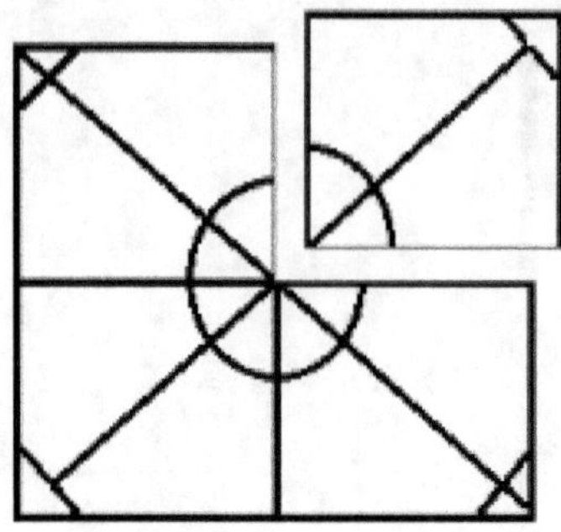

Hence, the correct option is (C).

69. According to the question

Cost Price $=$ Rs. 135000

Repairing Cost $= 25000$

Total Cost Price $= 160000$

$$\text{Selling Price} = \text{Cost Price} \times \frac{100 - \text{loss}}{100}$$

$$= 160000 \times \frac{90}{100} = 1,44,000$$

Hence, the correct option is (C).

70. Given

On selling article for Rs 51 more, Vishnu is getting 3% more profit.

Formula

$$\text{Selling price} = \text{Cost price} \times \left[\frac{(100 + Profit\%)}{100} \right]$$

Let CP be 100x.

$$SP_1 = 100x \times \left(\frac{125}{100} \right) = 125x$$

$$SP_2 = 100x \times \left(\frac{128}{100} \right) = 128x$$

According to question

$128x - 125x = 51$

$\Rightarrow 3x = 51$

$\Rightarrow x = 17$

$\therefore$ Cost price = $100x = 100 \times 17 = 1700$.

Hence, the correct option is (B).

71. Given:

A shopkeeper marks his goods at 20% above the cost price.

He sells three - fourth of the goods at the marked price and the remaining at 30% discount on the marked price.

$$MP \left(1 - \frac{D}{100} \right) = SP$$

MP = Marked Price

SP = Selling Price

D = Discount

Let CP be Rs. x.

$\Rightarrow$ MP = 1.2x

$\Rightarrow$ SP of $\frac{3}{4}$ goods = $\left(\frac{3}{4} \right) \times 1.2x$

$\Rightarrow$ 0.9x

$\Rightarrow$ SP of remaining $\frac{1}{4}$ goods = $\left(\frac{70}{100} \right) \times \left(\frac{1}{4} \right) \times 1.2x$

$= 0.21x$

$\Rightarrow$ Total SP = 0.9x + 0.21x = 1.11x

$\Rightarrow$ Gain = 1.11x - x = 0.11x

$\Rightarrow$ Gain% = $\frac{.11x}{x} \times 100$

$\therefore$ Gain% is 11%

Hence, the correct option is (A).

72. Both teachers and students are part of the school. Also, no student can be a teacher.

Hence, the correct option is (D).

73. A doctor can be a teacher, student as well as an engineer. The same is true for each of the other professionals. Moreover, some of each of these types can be males.

Therefore, option B best captures the relationship between the given things.

Hence, the correct option is (B).

74. Husband and Wife are entirely different. But, both are parts of a family.

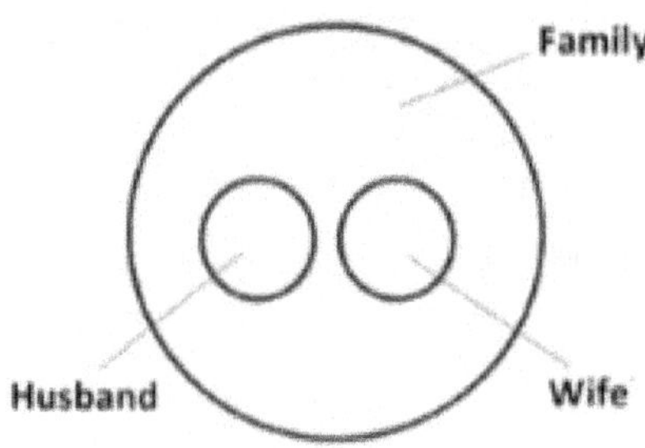

75. From the figure, we can observe that the 4 is the only number that is present in the triangle and circle.

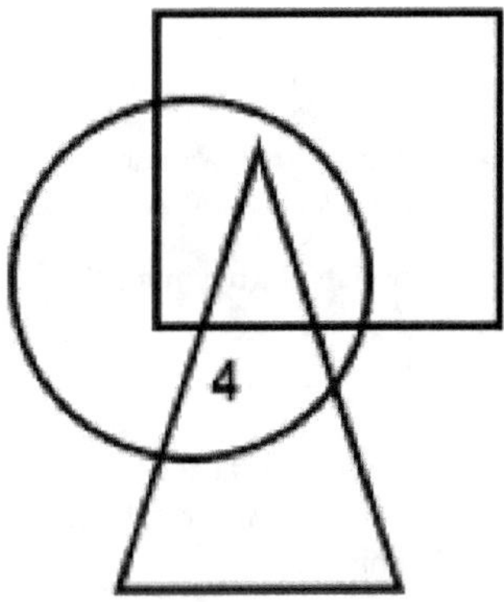

Hence, the correct option is (C).

76. From the figure, we can observe 9 + 12 people can speak Tamil and Telugu i.e. 21.

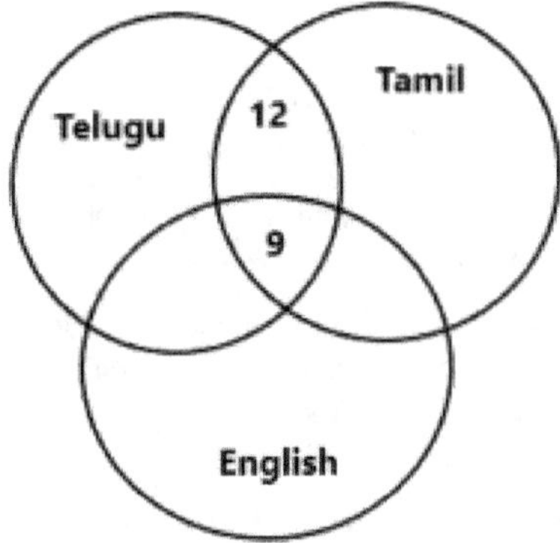

Hence, the correct option is (C).

77. At first a bowler will bowl then batsman will defend then the bowler will appeal and wait for umpire's decision.

Hence, the correct option is (D).

78. First we will go to school, then attend prayer, after that class, then recess, then normally game period takes place then finally we will come to home.

Hence, the correct option is (A).

79. The CVC is a multi-member body consisting of a Central Vigilance Commissioner (chairperson) and not more than two vigilance commissioners. They are appointed by the president by warrant under his hand and seal.

On the recommendation of a three-member committee consisting of

- The prime minister as its head,
- The Union minister of home affairs and
- The Leader of the Opposition in the Lok Sabha.

The president can remove the Central Vigilance Commissioner or any vigilance commissioner from the office. (So, Statement 2 is not correct)

The CVC is not controlled by any Ministry/Department. It is an independent body that is only responsible to the Parliament. (Therefore, Statement 1 is not correct)

The Central Vigilance Commission has amended the Standard Operating Procedure (SOP) on the adoption of the "Integrity Pact" in government organizations for procurement activities. So, statement 3 is correct. The Central Vigilance Commission (CVC) is the main agency for preventing corruption in the Central government. It was established in 1964 by an executive resolution of the Central government.

Hence, the correct option is (C).

80. Anxious means feeling or showing worry, nervousness, or unease about something.

Worried means anxious or troubled about actual or potential problems.

The option that is nearest in meaning to the underlined word 'anxious' is 'worried'.

Hence, the correct option is (A).

81. Ecstatic means feeling or expressing overwhelming happiness or joyful excitement.

Rapturous means characterized by, feeling, or expressing great pleasure or enthusiasm.

The option that is nearest in meaning to the underlined word ' ecstatic' is 'rapturous'.

Hence, the correct option is (C).

82. Seclusion means the state of being private and away from other people.

Solitariness means a person who lives alone or in solitude.

The option that is nearest in meaning to the underlined word 'seclusion' is solitariness'.

Hence, the correct option is (D).

83. The ocean current is a general movement of a mass of water in a fairly defined direction over great distances. Base on the temperature characteristics it can be categorized as warm and cold current. It can be broadly categorized into Atlantic ocean current, Pacific ocean current, and Indian ocean current. The currents in the northern portion of the Indian Ocean differ entirely from the general pattern of circulation.

- The currents in the northern portion of the Indian Ocean differ entirely from the general pattern of circulation.

- They change their direction from season to season in response to the seasonal rhythm of the monsoons.

- In the northern section of the Indian Ocean, there is a clear reversal of currents between winter and summer.

- In winter, the north equatorial current and the south equatorial current flow from east to west.

- The northeast monsoons drive the water along the coast of the Bay of Bengal to circulate in an anti-clockwise direction.

- Similarly, along the coasts of the lands bordering the Arabian Sea, an anticlockwise circulation of currents develops.

Therefore, statements 1 and 2 are correct.

Hence, the correct option is (B).

84. Given:

Price in 1999 = Rs. 3

Price in 2000 = Rs. 203

Percentage increase in price $= \dfrac{\text{Price in 2000} - \text{Price in 1999}}{\text{Price in 1999}} \times 100\%$

$= \dfrac{203-3}{3} \times 100\% = \dfrac{2000}{3}\%$

Hence, the correct option is (D).

85. Let the original number be 100, then

First, it is increased by 10%,

$\Rightarrow 100 \times \dfrac{110}{100} = 110$

Further, it is decreased by 50%,

$\Rightarrow 110 \times \dfrac{50}{100} = 55$

Now, it is increased by 50%,

$\Rightarrow 55 \times \dfrac{150}{100} = 82.5$

$\therefore$ Required % $= 100 \times \dfrac{82.5}{100} = 82.5\%$

Hence, the correct option is (B).

86. Given that:

90% of $A = 30\%$ of B and $B = 2x\%$ of A

90% of $A = 30\%$ of $2x\%$ of A

$\Rightarrow A \times \dfrac{90}{100} = A \times \dfrac{2x}{100} \times \dfrac{30}{100}$

$\Rightarrow 3 = \dfrac{x}{50}$

$x = 150$

Hence, the correct option is (A).

87. The government must now demonstrate its seriousness by moving away from the flawed policies of the past.

Demonstrate - give a practical exhibition and explanation of (how a machine, skill, or craftworks or is performed).

Flawed - having or characterized by a fundamental weakness or imperfection.
Hence, the correct option is (D).

88. Let us know the meanings of the given words:

Cruel- wilfully causing pain or suffering to others, or feeling no concern about it.

Gentle - having or showing a mild, kind, or tender temperament or character.

Evil - profoundly immoral and wicked.

Wicked - evil or morally wrong.

The underlined word 'vicious' means (of an animal) wild and dangerous to people.

From the given options, the most appropriate antonym for the given word is 'Gentle'.

Hence, the correct option is (B).

89. Hang means kill (someone) by tying a rope attached from above around their neck and removing the support from beneath them (often used as a form of capital punishment).

Forms- Hang, Hanged, Hanged.

He was hanged for murder.

Hang- to have been suspended in the air or placed on a wall

Forms- Hang, Hung, Hung.

He hung up his coat.

Hence, the correct option is (B).

90. To answer this question we have to analyze the common theme which links all the paragraph

First paragraph - The author mentions Woodrow Wilson's idea of economic setup for the Unites States. According to the Wilson, United States should follow the idea of free enterprise which are free from government interference

Wilson, according to the author, favoured giving maximum freedom to the enterprises as this would lead to higher productivity and economic benefits

The phrase,' free enterprise system backed by a laissez-faire political setup is the most efficient economic system', in the first line of the first paragraph, and the phrase,' Maximum freedom means maximum productiveness which leads to maximum social benefits, in the last line of the first paragraph mentions this fact.

Second paragraph- The author then highlights that the American public has by and large accepted this economic set up

The author highlights how America as a nation just want to run faster and faster without any regards for stability. The 'risk takers' are rewarded whereas those looking for a stable system are mocked upon

In the second paragraph, the author also highlights, how the USA just want to grow without any concern for the direction in which America is growing.

The phrase,' the more rapidly the wheel turned, the steadier we would be irrespective of the direction the wheel was moving in ' in the last line of the second paragraph captures these facts.

Third paragraph - The author highlights that due to this obsession with moving fast at any cost which is due to the rigid economic and political system, the reforms to the system have been more or less useless in the United States.

The phrase, ' sterile and sometimes counter-productive ', refers to the fact mentioned in the above point.

As per the author, there is no attempt to change the system. The more there is a notion to change the system, the more Unites States ends up reinforcing it. Given this rigidity, United States doesn't cherish its workers who prefer stability (like office clerks, social workers etc)

It highlights the one-dimensional and rigid nature of the political and economic setup mentioned in the first two paragraphs. The third paragraph in essence means that since the system has so many drawbacks, reforms have been useless.

The phrase,' There is no attempt to call off the race or make it equal for all the participants', mentions these facts.

Fourth paragraph- It sums up the passage, mentioning the implications of such a set-up and its impact on society.

Hence, the correct option is (A).

91. To answer this question we have to analyze the third paragraph.

Third paragraph - The author highlights that due to this obsession with moving fast at any cost which is due to the rigid economic and political system, the reforms to the system have been more or less useless in the United States.

The phrase, ' sterile and sometimes counter-productive ', refers to the fact mentioned in the above point that the reform is at best lip service and is not addressing the root of the problem.

As per the author, there is no attempt to change the system. The more there is a notion to change the system, the more United States ends up reinforcing it. Given this rigidity, United States doesn't cherish its workers who prefer stability (like office clerks, social workers, etc)

It highlights the one-dimensional and rigid nature of the political and economic setup mentioned in the first two paragraphs. The third paragraph in essence means that since the system has so many drawbacks, reforms have been useless.

The phrase,' There is no attempt to call off the race or make it equal for all the participants', mentions these facts.

Hence, the correct option is (C).

92. To answer this question we have to analyze the third paragraph.

Third paragraph - The author highlights that due to this obsession with moving fast at any cost which is due to the rigid economic and political system, the reforms to the system have been more or less useless in the United States.

The phrase, ' sterile and sometimes counter-productive ', refers to the fact mentioned in the above point that the reform is at best lip service and is not addressing the root of the problem.

As such, there is inherent inertia present in the United States set up which resists any fundamental change to its style of functioning

In the first line of the third paragraph, the phrase' can imagine no change', refers to this fact.

As per the author, there is no attempt to change the system. The more there is a notion to change the system, the more United

States ends up reinforcing it. Given this rigidity, United States doesn't cherish its workers who prefer stability (like office clerks, social workers, etc)

It highlights the one-dimensional and rigid nature of the political and economic setup mentioned in the first two paragraphs. The third paragraph in essence means that since the system has so many drawbacks, reforms have been useless.

The phrase,' There is no attempt to call off the race or make it equal for all the participants', mentions these facts.

Hence, the correct option is (B).

93. The answer to this question lies in the first paragraph.

First paragraph - The author mentions Woodrow Wilson's idea of economic setup for the Unites States. According to the Wilson, United States should follow the idea of free enterprise which are free from government interference

Wilson, according to the author, favored giving maximum freedom to the enterprises as this would lead to higher productivity and economic benefits

The phrase,' free enterprise system backed by a laissez-faire political setup is the most efficient economic system', in the first line of the first paragraph, and the phrase,' Maximum freedom means maximum productiveness which leads to maximum social benefits, in the last line of the first paragraph mentions this fact.

Hence, the correct option is (D).

94. The answer to this question lies in the 2nd paragraph.

Second paragraph- The author then highlights that the American public has, by and large, accepted this economic setup

The author highlights how America as a nation just wants to run faster and faster without any regard for stability. The 'risk takers' are rewarded whereas those looking for a stable system are mocked upon

In the second paragraph, the author also highlights, how the USA just wants to grow without any concern for the direction in which America is growing.

The phrase,' the more rapidly the wheel turned, the steadier we would be irrespective of the direction the wheel was moving in ' in the last line of the second paragraph captures these facts.

Hence, the correct option is (C).

95.

The two parts of the first figure are rearranged and joined along the longer sides. The common side is then lost to form the second figure.

Hence, the correct option is (B).

96.

The second figure is a part of the first figure (but is not exactly the same as the first figure).

Hence, the correct option is (C).

97.

In each row, the central part of the first figure rotates either 90o CW or 90o ACW to form the central part of the second figure and the central part of the first figure rotates through 180o to form the central part of the third figure. Also, in each row, there are 3 types of side elements - rectangles, circles and triangles.

Hence, the correct option is (A).

98.

In each column, the third figure (lowermost figure) contains one less number of hexagons as the first figure (uppermost figure) and the same number of trees as the second figure (middle figure).

Hence, the correct option is (B).

99.

There are 3 types of faces, 3 types of bodies, 3 types of hands and 3 types of legs, each of which is used only once in a single row. So, the features which have not been used in the first two figures of the third row would combine to produce the missing figure.

Hence, the correct option is (B).

100. 'Inspite' is followed by the fixed preposition 'of'.

We use 'inspite of' and 'despite' to express something that is unexpected or surprising.

'Inspite of' can be followed by a noun (Inspite of the heavy traffic) or verb (Inspite of the traffic being heavy).

Hence, the correct option is (C).

Q.1 The country's first-ever radio channel for the visually impaired, named 'Radio Aksh' has been launched in which city?

[Delhi Forest Guard, 2021]

A. Delhi
B. Nagpur
C. Allahabad
D. Agra

Q.2 Who clinched the gold medal in weightlifting at the ongoing Singapore International?

[Delhi Forest Guard, 2021]

A. Mirabai Chanu
B. Swati Singh
C. Kunjarani Devi
D. Karnam Malleswari

Q.3 The assembly of Haryana, which hasbeen constituted after the election ofOctober, 2019 :

[HTET PGT - Computer Science, 2020]

A. 12th
B. 13th
C. 14th
D. 15th

Q.4 Which among the following IN ship(s) participated in the SIMBEX-19?

1. INS Kolkata
2. INS Shakti
3. INS Vikrant

Select the correct answer using the code given below:

[Indian Military Academy (IMA), 2019], [Officers Training Academy (OTA), 2019]

A. 1, 2 and 3
B. 1 and 2 only
C. 2 and 3 only
D. 1 only

Q.5 Who is the first Indian to win four medals at World Wrestling Championships?

[HSSC Canal Patwari, 2021]

A. Vinesh Phogat
B. Bajrang Punia
C. Babita kumari
D. Gita Phogat

Q.6 A total amount of Rs. 12,000 is invested by Rachita at a rate of 5% compounded annually for three years. What amount will she get after three years?

A. Rs. 10,881.50
B. Rs. 11,981.50
C. Rs. 12,881.50
D. Rs. 13,891.50

Q.7 A certain sum of money yields an interest of Rs. 1050 at 10% per annum compound interest for 2 years. Find the sum.

A. Rs. 6000
B. Rs. 12000
C. Rs. 5000
D. Rs. 15000

Q.8 A sum of Rs. 725 is lent at the beginning of a year at a certain rate of interest. After 8 months, a sum of Rs. 362.50 more is lent but at a rate twice the former. At the end of the year, Rs. 33.50 is earned as interest from both the loans. What was the original rate of interest?

A. 3.6%
B. 4.5%

C. 5%
D. None of these

Q.9 What is the value of $\dfrac{11.2\times0.36+0.42\times3.2}{0.8\times4.2}$?

A. 2
B. 1.6
C. 3
D. $\frac{3}{2}$

Q.10 If $2994 \div 14.5 = 172$, then $29.94 \div 1.45 = ?$

A. 0.172
B. 1.72
C. 17.2
D. 172

Q.11 The value of $22.\overline{4} + 11.5\overline{67} - 33.5\overline{9}$ is:

A. $0.4\overline{12}$
B. $0.\overline{31}$
C. $0.\overline{412}$
D. $0.\overline{32}$

Q.12 Match the following:

Provinces	Capital
A. Central Province	1. Patliputra
B. Uttarapatha	2. Toshali
C. Prachya	3. Taxila
D. Dakshinapatha	4. Suvarnagiri
E. Avanti Rastra	5. Ujjain

A. $A(3), B(5), C(1), D(4), E(2)$
B. $A(1), B(4), C(3), D(5), E(2)$
C. $A(1), B(3), C(2), D(4), E(5)$
D. $A(4), B(3), C(4), D(2), E(5)$

Ques (13-17):Direction: Complete the sentence with the most appropriate word.

Q.13 Generally, people use _____ oils for their cooking.
A. cleared
B. refined
C. improved
D. washed

Q.14 The committee's suggestion was not acceptable to everyone as it was _____.
A. considerate
B. controversial
C. concrete
D. convenient

Q.15 During the nighttime, the express train picked up _____.
A. speed
B. distance
C. rate
D. quick

Q.16 _____ was present in the hall took part in the voting process.
A. Whoever
B. Whichever
C. Wherever
D. Whatever

Q.17 Bonsai gardening was first practiced in China but became _____ because of the Japanese.
A. frequent
B. prevailing
C. popular
D. customary

Q.18 Select the most appropriate meaning of the underlined idiom in the given sentence.

I told you not to play the prank but you didn't listen, now <u>face the music</u>.

[SSC Sub Inspector (CPO), 2019]

A. accept the consequences
B. put on earphones
C. listen to the songs
D. sing popular songs

Q.19 Select the most appropriate meaning of the underlined idiom in the given sentence.

Pradeep was so tired that he hit the sack as soon as possible.

[SSC Sub Inspector (CPO), 2019]

A. Left work   **B.** Went to bed
C. Accepted defeat   **D.** Kicked the sack

Q.20 An example of an abiotic component:
A. Plants   **B.** Soil   **C.** Animals   **D.** Bacteria

Q.21 Choose the option that is the passive form of the sentence.

The Municipal Corporation changed the manhole covers before the rainy season.

[SSC Sub Inspector (CPO), 2019]

A. The manhole covers is being changed before the rainy season.
B. The manhole covers are change before the rainy season.
C. The manhole covers were changed before the rainy season.
D. The manhole covers can be changed before the rainy season.

Q.22 Choose the option that is the passive form of the sentence.

Switch off the television.
A. Can you switch off the television?
B. May I switch off the television?
C. Let the television be switched off.
D. Let the television being switch off

Q.23 Select the option that is related to the third term on the same basis as the second term is related to the first term.

Badminton : shuttlecock :: Snooker : ?

[Delhi Forest Guard, 2021]

A. Billiard ball   **B.** Volleyball
C. Baseball   **D.** Golf ball

Q.24 Select the option that is related to the third number on the same basis as the second number is related to the first number.

12 : 312 :: 10 : ?
A. 218   **B.** 230   **C.** 226   **D.** 220

Q.25 In the following question, select the related number from the given alternatives.

39 : 156 :: ?
A. 61 : 244   **B.** 65 : 248   **C.** 67 : 250   **D.** 63 : 246

Q.26 Select the option that is related to the third number in the same way as the second number is related to the first number.

19 : 441 :: 17 : ?

A. 225   **B.** 144   **C.** 169   **D.** 361

Q.27 Select the option that is related to the third term on the same basis as the second term is related to the first term.

Sweater : Socks :: Raincoat : ?

[Delhi Forest Guard, 2021]

A. Cap   **B.** Umbrella
C. Jeans   **D.** Sunglasses

Q.28 A car travels a distance of 840 km at a uniform speed. If the speed of the car is 10 kmph more, it takes two hours less to cover the same distance. The original speed of the car is:
A. 80 kmph   **B.** 50 kmph   **C.** 75 kmph   **D.** 60 kmph

Q.29 Two trains are running at a speed of 30 km and 58 km/h in the same direction. A person who is sitting in a slow-moving train crosses the fast-moving train in 18 seconds. The length (in metres) of the faster train is :
A. 70   **B.** 100   **C.** 128   **D.** 140

Q.30 The speeds of 3 cars in the ratio 5 : 4 : 6. The ratio between the time taken by them to travel same distance is:
A. 12 : 15 : 10   **B.** 12 : 10 : 13
C. 10 : 20 : 30   **D.** 15 : 12 : 11

Q.31 Walking at 75% of his usual speed, Raghu is 80 minutes late to his office. What is his usual time in hours to cover the same distance?

[SSC Constable (GD), 2019]

A. $3\frac{1}{2}$ **B.** 5   **C.** 4   **D.** $4\frac{1}{2}$

Q.32 From the given answer figures select the one in which the question figure is hidden/embedded.

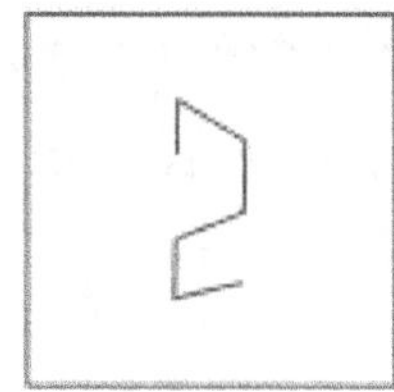

[SSC Constable (GD), 2019], [UP Police Constable, 2019], [SSC MTS, 2017]

A. 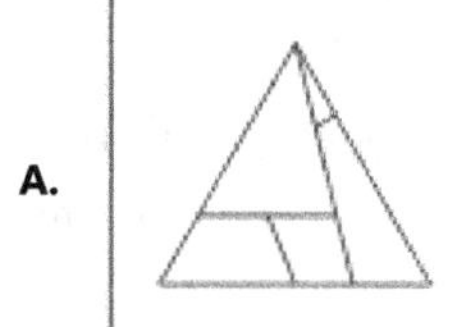   **B.** 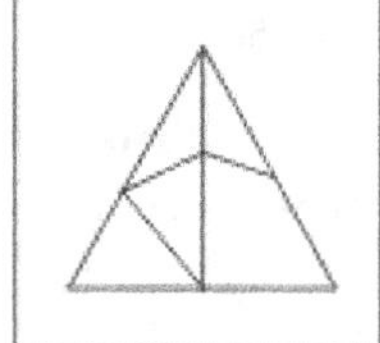

C. 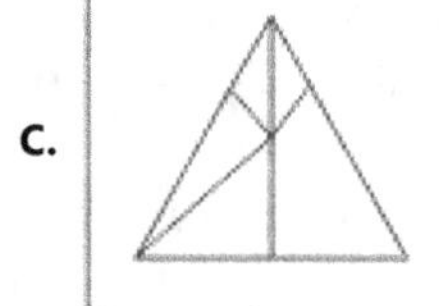   **D.** 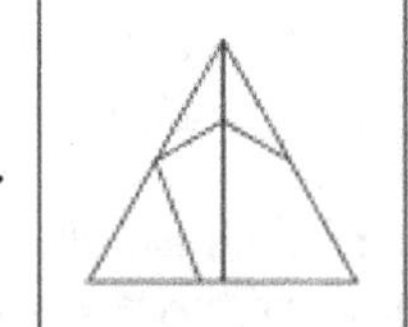

Q.33 If the following two squares shown below overlap, which one of the following options is formed.

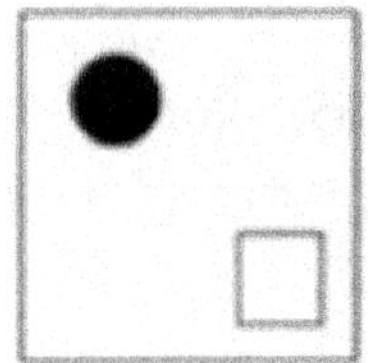 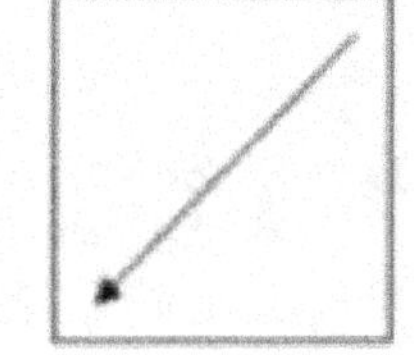

[MP Police (Constable), 2017]

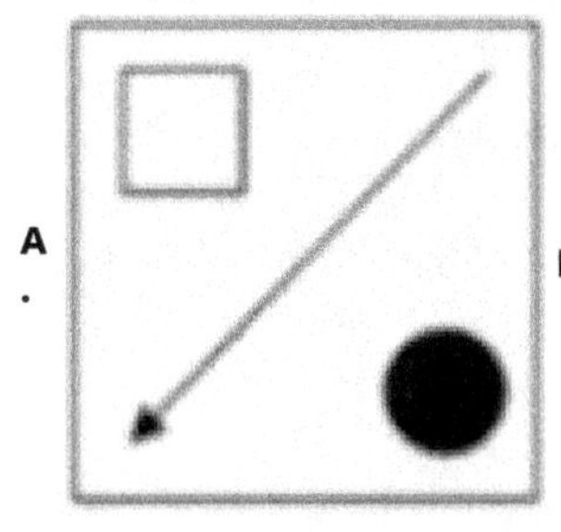 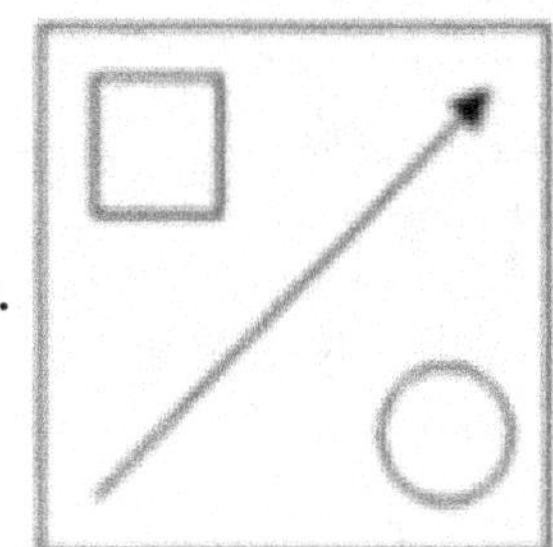

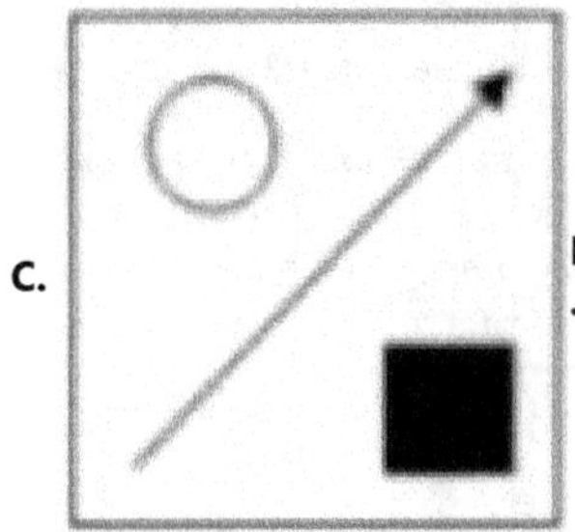 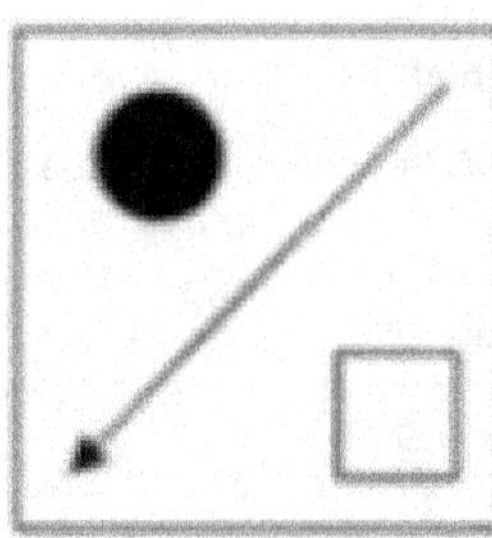

Q.34 Which answer figure will be complete the pattern in the question figure?

Question Figure:

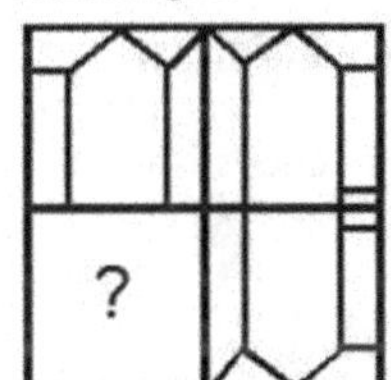

Answer Figures:

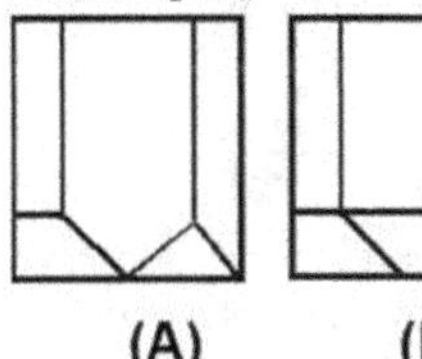  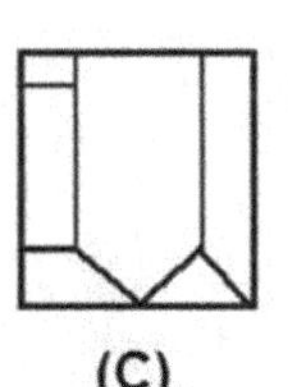 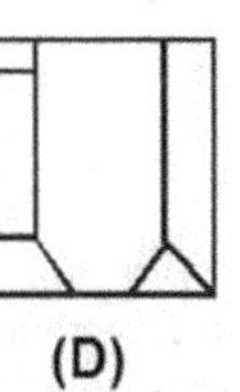

(A)   (B)   (C)   (D)

A. (A)   **B.** (B)   **C.** (C)   **D.** (D)

Q.35 Find out the alternative figure which contains figure (X) as its part.

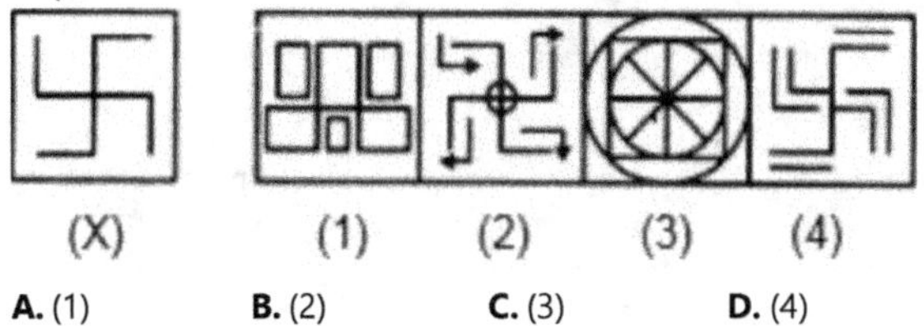

(X)   (1)   (2)   (3)   (4)

A. (1)   **B.** (2)   **C.** (3)   **D.** (4)

Q.36 Find out the alternative figure which contains figure (X) as its part.

 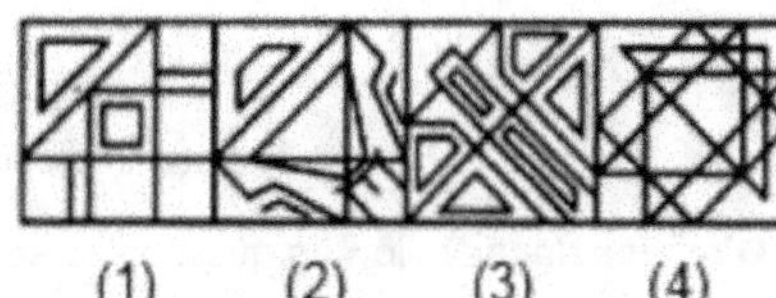

(X)   (1)   (2)   (3)   (4)

A. (1)   **B.** (2)   **C.** (3)   **D.** (4)

Q.37 In class IX, the average of marks in science for six students was 48. After result declared, it was found in case of one student, the marks 45 were misread as 54. The correct average is:

[SSC Constable (GD), 2019]

A. 46.40   **B.** 46.50   **C.** 76.50   **D.** 64.39

Q.38 The average of $5, 11, 16, x, 14$ is 12. Then find the value of x.

A. 10   **B.** 12   **C.** 14   **D.** 13

Q.39 A grocer has a sale of Rs. 6435, Rs. 6927, Rs. 6855, Rs. 7230 and Rs. 6562 for 5 consecutive months. How much sale must he have in the sixth month so that he gets an average sale of Rs. 6500?

A. Rs. 4991   **B.** Rs. 5991   **C.** Rs. 6001   **D.** Rs. 6991

Q.40 3 men or 5 women can complete the work in 12 days then in how many days 3 men and 7 women will complete the same work?

A. 5 days   **B.** 8 days   **C.** 10 days   **D.** 15 days

Q.41 A man and a woman received Rs. 1500 as wages for 20 days for the work they did together. If the efficiency of the man is double the women, then find daily wages of woman.

A. Rs. 25   **B.** Rs. 50   **C.** Rs. 500   **D.** Rs. 100

Q.42 A alone can complete a work in 12 days and B alone can complete the same work in 15 days. If they finish the work together and received Rs. 3600. Then find the share of A.

A. Rs. 1200   **B.** Rs. 3000   **C.** Rs. 1500   **D.** Rs. 2000

Q.43 Select the word which means the same as the group of words given.

Sound of horses

[SSC Sub Inspector (CPO), 2019]

A. Grunt   **B.** Screech   **C.** Squeak   **D.** Neigh

Q.44 Select the word which means the same as the group of words given.

An underground hole dug by a small animal as a dwelling.

[SSC Sub Inspector (CPO), 2019]

A. Drain   **B.** Pit   **C.** Cave   **D.** Burrow

Q.45 Direction: Select out the odd word/letters/number /number pair from the given alternatives.

A. 85431   **B.** 23870   **C.** 99300   **D.** 11559

Q.46 Direction: Select the odd word/letters/number /number pair from the given alternatives.

A. 256   **B.** 289   **C.** 343   **D.** 144

Q.47 Direction: In the following question, select the odd word from the given alternatives.

A. Nestle   **B.** Café Coffee Day
C. InMobi   **D.** Peter England

Q.48 Direction: In the following question, select the odd number pair from the given alternatives.

A. 130,26   **B.** 75,16   **C.** 35,7   **D.** 65,13

Q.49 Direction: Select the odd word/letters/number /number pair from the given alternatives.
A. Bismillah Khan
B. C. V. Raman
C. Homi Jehangir Bhabha
D. Vikram Sarabhai

Q.50 Brilliance of diamond is due to-
[UPSC Central Armed Police Forces AC, 2019]

A. Interference of light
B. Diffraction of light
C. Polarization of light
D. Total internal reflection of light

Q.51 Which one of the following is NOT an electromagnetic wave?
[UPSC Central Armed Police Forces AC, 2019]

A. Light wave   **B.** Radio waves
C. Sound waves   **D.** Microwave

Q.52 Which one of the following is NOT true for an electromagnetic wave?
[UPSC Central Armed Police Forces AC, 2019]

A. Electromagnetic wave transports energy and momentum
B. An electromagnetic wave can be polarized and reflected
C. An electromagnetic wave is longitudinal
D. Electromagnetic wave propagation is described by the varying electric and magnetic fields

Q.53 A snowboard pulled up by a tow rope travels at the rate of 5 m/s up a mountain. If 3000 watt of power is used, what force was applied to it?
[UPSC Central Armed Police Forces AC, 2019]

A. 50 N   **B.** 100 N   **C.** 600 N   **D.** 15000 N

Q.54 The number of neutrons inside the nucleus of the element Uranium 235 is-
[UPSC Central Armed Police Forces AC, 2019]

A. 235   **B.** 92   **C.** 143   **D.** 51

Q.55 _____ is India's largest military exercise with Nepal in terms of troop participation.
A. Indra   **B.** Surya Kiran
C. Varuna   **D.** Bold Kurukshetra

Q.56 Direction: Choose the incorrect spelling for the word given below in the alternatives.
A. Dulce   **B.** Dilce   **C.** Doolce   **D.** Dulse

Q.57 Choose the correctly spelt word.
A. Horizontal   **B.** Horezontal
C. Horizontel   **D.** Horezontel

Q.58 Consider the following statements regarding Zardozi Art.
1. Zardozi art prospered in India during the reign of the Mughal emperor Akbar.
2. Zardozi is the indigenous art of India.
3. The gold coils and beads are tucked into the fabric.

Which of the above statements is/are correct?
A. 1, 2   **B.** 1, 3   **C.** 1 only   **D.** 1, 2, 3

Q.59 Consider the following statements regarding Chindu Yakshagana.
1. It is a form of theatre practiced by members of the Chindu Madiga community.
2. It is a form of entertainment in villages across Tamil Nadu.

Which of the above statements is/ are correct?
A. 1 only   **B.** 2 only
C. Both 1 and 2   **D.** Neither 1 nor 2

Q.60 Direction: In the problem, out of the four figures marked (1), (2), (3) and (4) three are similar in a certain manner. However, one figure is not like the other four. Choose the figure which is different from the rest.

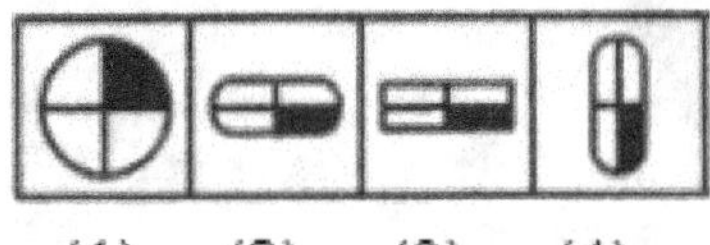

A. (1)   **B.** (2)   **C.** (3)   **D.** (4)

Q.61 Direction: In each problem, out of the four figures marked (1), (2), (3) and (4) three are similar in a certain manner. However, one figure is not like the other four. Choose the figure which is different from the rest.

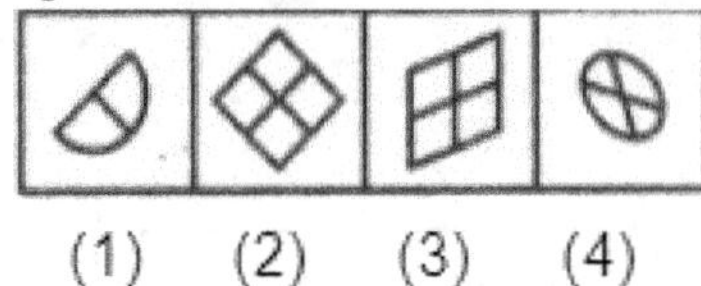

A. (1)   **B.** (2)   **C.** (3)   **D.** (4)

Q.62 Direction: In the given question figures, three out of four figures are similar in a particular manner. Find out the figure which is different from the rest three figure.

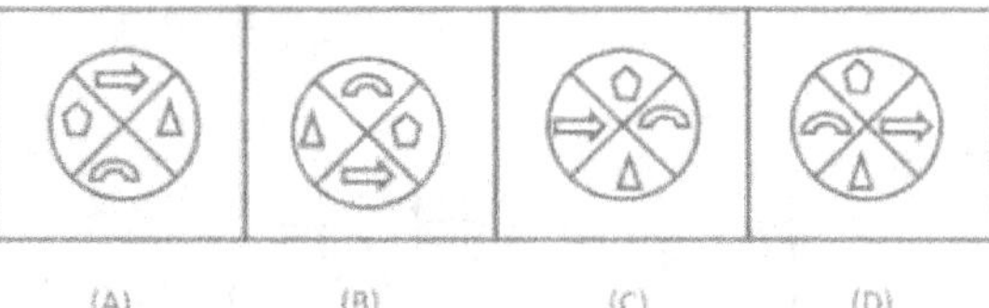

A. (D)   **B.** (C)   **C.** (A)   **D.** (B)

Q.63 Direction: Out of the four given figures, three figures are similar in certain way, one figure is not like the others. Find out the figure which doe not belongs the group.

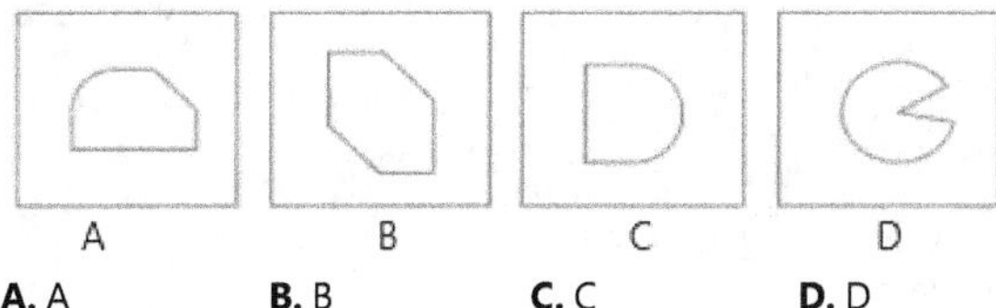

A. A   **B.** B   **C.** C   **D.** D

Q.64 Direction: Three of the given four figures are similar in a certain manner while one is different. Pick the odd one out.

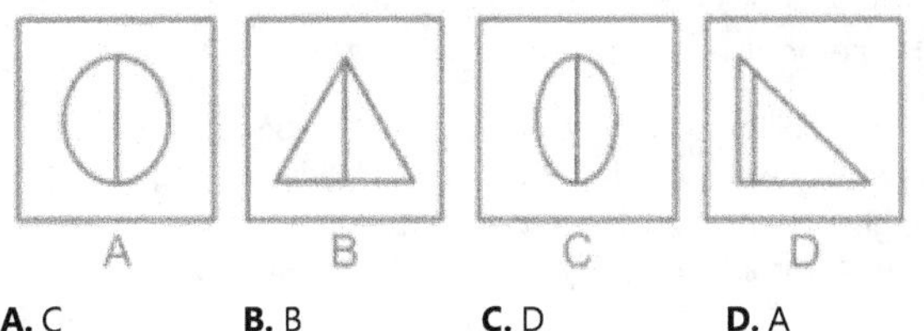

A. C   **B.** B   **C.** D   **D.** A

Q.65 The average height of 3 girls is 180 cm. If the ratio of their heights is 4 : 5 : 6, then find height of smallest girl.

A. 48 cm   **B.** 44 cm   **C.** 144 cm   **D.** 142 cm

Q.66 The present age of P and Q is 2 : 7. 18 yr ago, this ratio was 1 : 26. What is the sum of the present age of P and Q?

A. 70 yr   **B.** 80 yr   **C.** 90 yr   **D.** 60 yr

Q.67 In a mixture, the ratio of milk to water is $3 : 1$. After adding 20 litres another mixture, in which the ratio of milk to water was $2 : 3$, the concentration of water in the new mixture became 33.75%. What had become the quantity (in litres) of new mixture?

A. 60   **B.** 75   **C.** 80   **D.** 100

Q.68 Who among the following is NOT a recipient of Rajiv Gandhi Khel Ratna 2020?

A. Vinesh Phogat
B. Rohit Sharma
C. Mariyappan Thangavelu
D. Mirabai Chanu

Q.69 A shopkeeper sells 200 shirts and makes a profit equal to the selling price of 25 shirts. Find his profit percentage.

A. 13.35%   **B.** 12.50%   **C.** 14.28%   **D.** 15.08%

Q.70 An exhibition was organized by fruit exporters in Delhi. Kailash, a fruit vendor, purchases 300 mangoes at 5 for Rs. 8 and sells them at 2 for Rs. 5. Which of the following is correct about his returns?

A. Loss of Rs. 170   **B.** Profit of Rs. 270
C. Loss of Rs. 300   **D.** Profit of Rs. 300

Q.71 'A' sells an article to 'B' at a profit of 20% and 'B' sells it to 'C' at a profit of 25%. If 'C' pays Rs. 1,200, the cost price of the article originally (in Rs.) is:

A. 700   **B.** 600   **C.** 1,000   **D.** 800

Q.72 Which of the following diagram shows the relationship between all these.

Carnivores, lions, rabbits

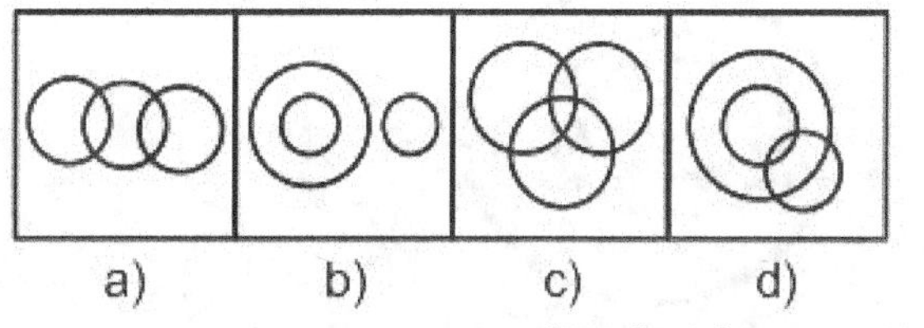

[UP Police Sub Inspector, 2017]

A. (a)   **B.** (b)   **C.** (c)   **D.** (d)

Q.73 Which of the following diagram shows the relationship between all these.

Ireland, Dublin, Greece

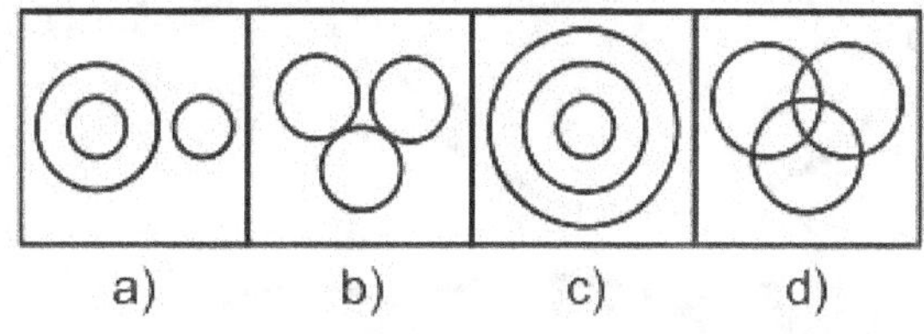

[UP Police Sub Inspector, 2017]

A. (a)   **B.** (b)   **C.** (c)   **D.** (d)

Q.74 Which of the following Venn diagrams shows the relation among

Engineer, Businessmen, Politician

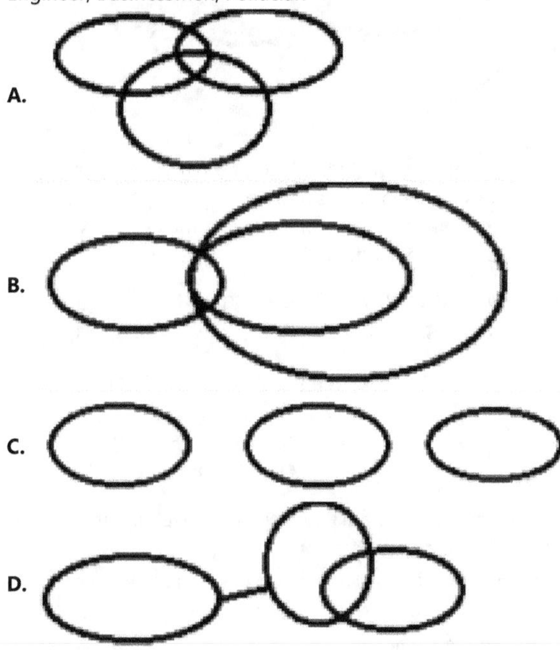

Q.75 Which of the following Venn diagrams shows the relation among

Diwali, Eid, Festival

A.

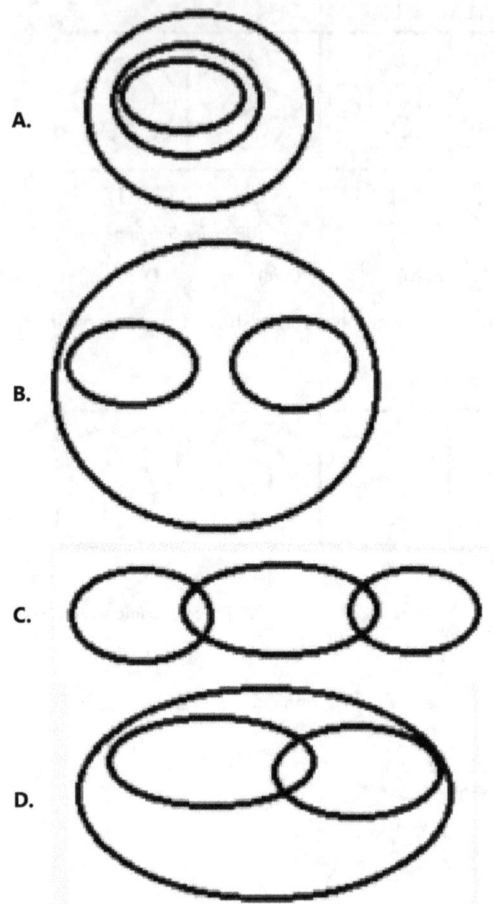

B.

C.

D.

Ques (76-77):Direction: In the following question, arrange the given words in a meaningful sequence and then choose the most appropriate sequence from amongst the alternatives provided below the question;

Q.76 1. Furniture 2. Wood 3. Tree 4. Carpenter

A. 3, 2, 4, 1   **B.** 1, 3, 2, 4   **C.** 4, 2, 3, 1   **D.** 3, 4, 1, 2

Q.77 1. 60 degree 2. 120 degree 3. 90 degree 4. Rounder 5. Line

A. 5, 4, 1, 2, 3   **B.** 1, 3, 2, 4, 5
C. 4, 3, 2 ,1, 5   **D.** 3, 2, 1, 4, 5

Q.78 With reference to the Parliamentary government, which of the following features is/are correct?

1. President is both the head of the State and the head of government

2. Double membership

3. Dissolution of the lower house

4. Collective responsibility

A. 1 only   **B.** 1 and 2 only
C. 2, 3 and 4 only   **D.** 1, 2, 3 and 4

Ques (79-81):Directions: Each item in this section consists of a sentence with an underlined word(s) followed by four words/group of words. Select the option that is nearest in meaning to the underlined word and mark your response accordingly.

Q.79 <u>Emboldened</u> by its success, the leader now plans to go ahead with the plan and implementation.
[Indian Military Academy (IMA), 2020], [Officers Training Academy (OTA), 2020]

A. Encouraged   **B.** Disgruntled
C. Succeeded   **D.** Failed

Q.80 It is encouraging to see India's <u>indigenous</u> cinema is going places.
[Indian Military Academy (IMA), 2020], [Officers Training Academy (OTA), 2020]

A. Homogenous   **B.** Classical
C. Home-grown   **D.** Non-native

Q.81 The ability to imagine and conceive a common good is inconsistent with what is known as '<u>pleonexia</u>' is a major struggle for a good democracy to realize.
[Indian Military Academy (IMA), 2020], [Officers Training Academy (OTA), 2020]

A.   Greed to grab everything for oneself
B.   Greed to accumulate more and more wealth
C.   Dislike for others
D.   Over-ambitious

Q.82 Which of the following are block mountains?
[CTET Paper-II (Social Science), 2019]

A. Himalayas   **B.** Appalachians
C. Ural   **D.** Vosges

Q.83 In an institute, 60% of the students are boys and the rest are girls. Further 15% of the boys and 7.5% of the girls are getting a fee waiver. If the number of those getting a fee waiver is $90,$ find the total number of students getting 50% concessions if it is given that 50% of those not getting a fee waiver are eligible to get half fee concession?

A. 360   **B.** 320   **C.** 330   **D.** 350

Q.84 In a factory there are three types of machine M1, M2 and M3 which produces 25%, 35% and 40% of the total products respectively. M1, M2 and M3 produces 2%, 4% and 5% defective products, respectively. What is the percentage of non-defective products ?

A. 89%   **B.** 97.1%   **C.** 96.1%   **D.** 86.1%

Q.85 A person spends 30% of his salary on rent, 20% of his salary on clothing, 15% of his salary on food and saves the rest. If he saves Rs.10500, then find his salary.

A. Rs.25000   **B.** Rs.30000
C. Rs.35000   **D.** Rs.40000

Q.86 Direction: Complete the sentence by filling in the blank with the best option from those given below.

I have bought a new ____.

A. spectacle   **B.** spectacles
C. pair of spectacle   **D.** pair of spectacles

Q.87 Direction: Fill in the blank with a suitable Adverb.

He will ______ hate her.

A. always   **B.** not

C. (A) and (B) both **D.** None of the above

Q.88 Direction: Choose the correct adverb from the options given.

Our Mathematics teacher __________ ever smiles.

A. Hardly **B.** Usually **C.** Always **D.** Mostly

Q.89 Direction: Select the suitable adverb of the manner in the sentence given below.

He talked so ______ that I could not grasp even a single word.

A. cleary **B.** fast
C. gracefully **D.** correctly

Ques (90-94):Direction: Read the given passage carefully and select the best answer to each question out of the four given alternatives.

Is my yellow the same as your yellow? Does your pain feel like my pain? The question of whether the human consciousness is subjective or objective is largely philosophical. But the line between consciousness and unconsciousness is a bit easier to measure. A research suggests that our experience of reality is the product of a delicate balance of connectivity between neurons - too much or too little and the consciousness slips away. "It's a very nice study," says neuroscientist Melanie Boly at the University of Wisconsin, Madison, who was not involved in the work. "The conclusions that they draw are justified." Previous studies of the brain have revealed the importance of "cortical integration" in maintaining consciousness, meaning that the brain must process and combine multiple inputs from different senses at once. Our experience of an orange, for example, is made up of sight, smell, taste, touch, and the recollection of our previous experiences with the fruit.

The brain merges all of these inputs - photons, aromatic molecules, etc. - into our subjective experience of the object in that moment

Q.90 Our experience of reality is the product of __________.

A. A delicate balance of connectivity between both hands
B. A delicate balance of connectivity between right hemisphere and left hemisphere
C. A delicate balance of connectivity between neurons
D. A delicate balance of connectivity between consciousness and subconsciousness

Q.91 How does our subjective experience of an object form?

A. With the help of sensation
B. The recollection of previous experiences with the help of sensory inputs
C. With the help of our eyesight only
D. The recollection of experience as dictated by other person

Q.92 What is "cortical integration"?

A. The process of mixing subconscious and conscious
B. The process of combining multiples inputs of senses at different time
C. The process of combining one input from different senses at once
D. The process of combining multiple inputs from different senses at once

Q.93 Which one is true, according to the passage?

A. Whether the human consciousness is subjective or objective is largely philosophical
B. Whether the human consciousness is subjective or objective is largely biological
C. Whether the human consciousness is subjective or objective is largely psychological
D. Wheather the human consciousness is subjective or objective is largely psychologicaly

Q.94 How can consciousness be slipped away?

A. Too much or too little connectivity between neurons
B. No connectivity between neurons
C. Too much connectivity between neurons
D. Too little connectivity between neurons

Q.95 Direction: Which answer figure will complete the pattern in the following question figure?

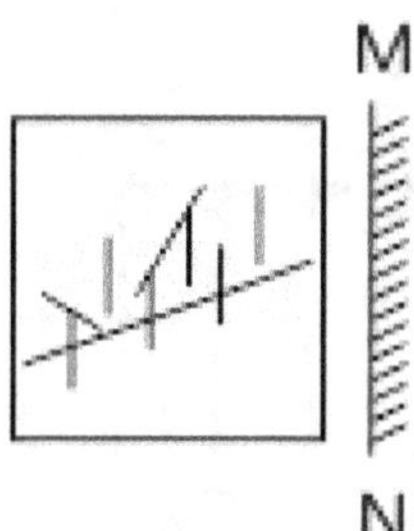

[Jawahar Navodaya Entrance Class VI, 2022], [SSC MTS, 2021],
[Jawahar Navodaya Entrance Class VI, 2021]

A. 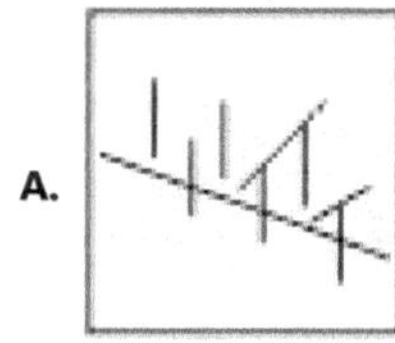 **B.** 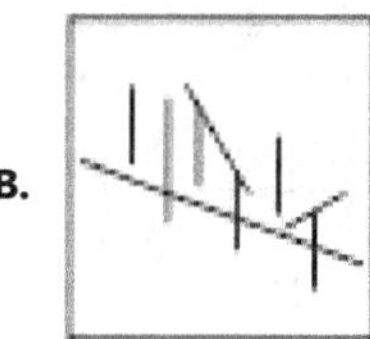

C. 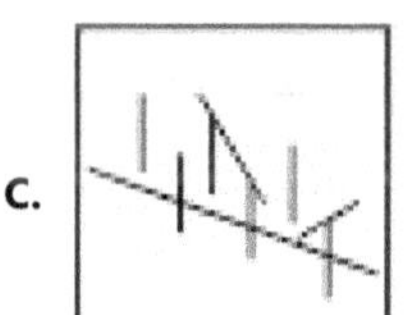 **D.** 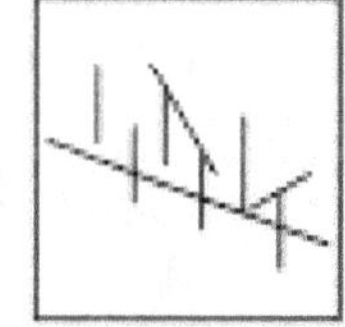

Q.96 Select a figure from the four alternatives, which when placed in the blank space of fig. (x).

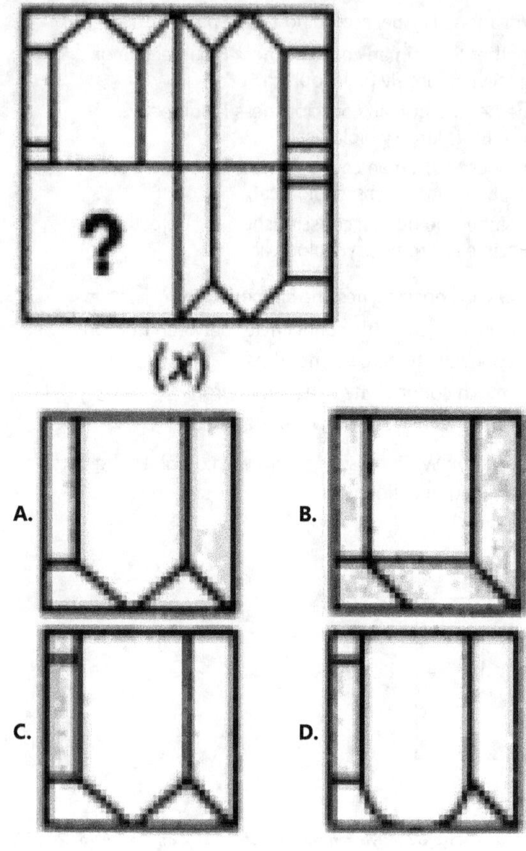

(x)

A.

B.

C.

D.

Q.97

Choose the figure which is different from the rest.

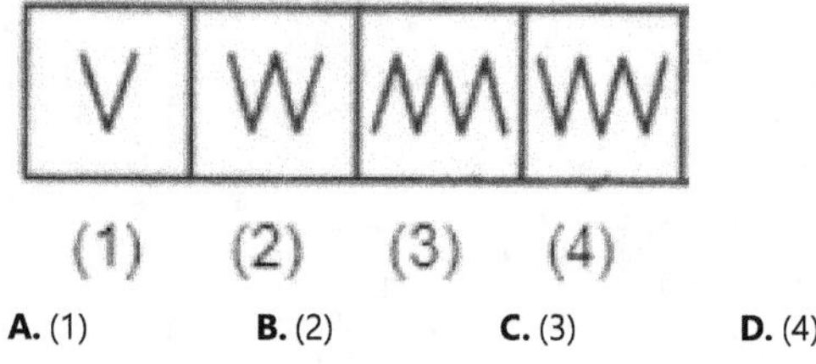

(1)   (2)   (3)   (4)

A. (1)   **B.** (2)   **C.** (3)   **D.** (4)

Q.98 Select a figure from the four alternatives, which when placed in the blank space of figure (x).

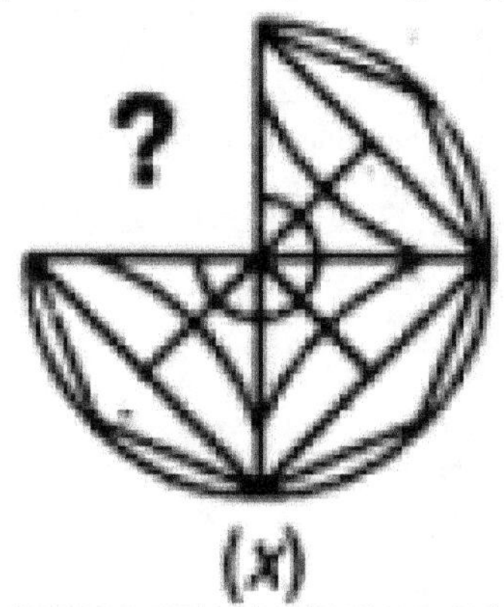

(x)

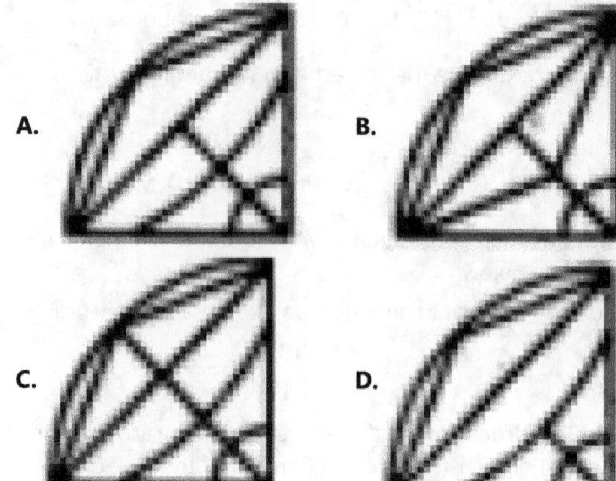

A.

B.

C.

D.

Q.99 What will come in the place of question mark (?).

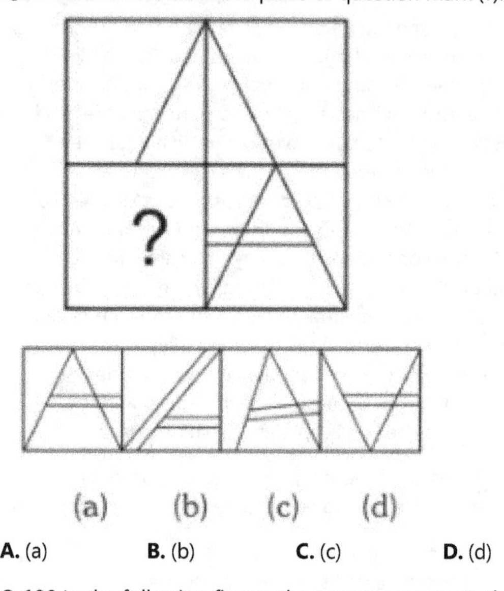

(a)   (b)   (c)   (d)

A. (a)   **B.** (b)   **C.** (c)   **D.** (d)

Q.100 In the following figure, the square represents the people who likes mango, rectangle represents the people who likes banana, circle represents the people who likes orange and the triangle represents the people who likes grapes.

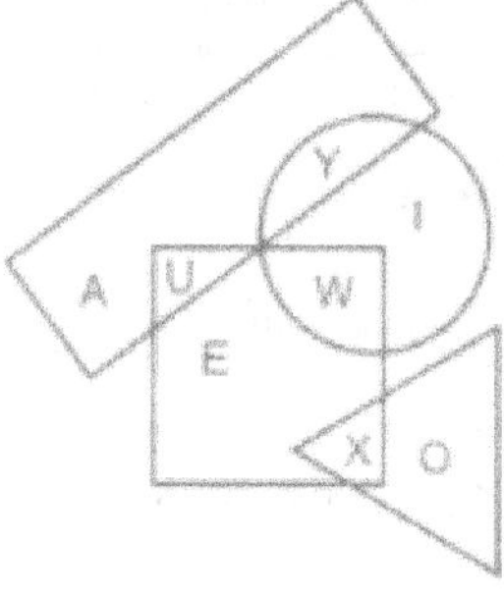

The people who likes mango and orange?

A. U   **B.** W   **C.** E   **D.** W, X

// Smart Answer Sheet //

Correct — Percentage of students who answered correctly. **Skipped** — Percentage of students who skipped.

Q.	Ans.	Correct / Skipped	Q.	Ans.	Correct / Skipped	Q.	Ans.	Correct / Skipped	Q.	Ans.	Correct / Skipped	Q.	Ans.	Correct / Skipped	Q.	Ans.	Correct / Skipped
1	B	53.02 % / 30.74 %	18	A	88.18 % / 10.22 %	35	C	65.67 % / 33.61 %	52	C	53.75 % / 36.34 %	69	C	78.48 % / 19.51 %	86	D	57.38 % / 33.26 %
2	A	48.39 % / 34.96 %	19	B	41.55 % / 36.68 %	36	D	63.27 % / 31.44 %	53	C	78.08 % / 18.83 %	70	B	53.02 % / 46.04 %	87	A	79.37 % / 15.62 %
3	C	67.99 % / 31.8 %	20	B	81.86 % / 11.49 %	37	B	68.52 % / 31.14 %	54	C	83.41 % / 12.59 %	71	D	65.87 % / 32.84 %	88	A	61.36 % / 30.21 %
4	B	26.2 % / 70.35 %	21	C	32.25 % / 67.37 %	38	C	47.26 % / 49.77 %	55	B	85.69 % / 10.78 %	72	B	40.99 % / 30.69 %	89	B	80.85 % / 16.96 %
5	B	41.64 % / 58.26 %	22	C	53.64 % / 46.02 %	39	A	48.26 % / 41.11 %	56	C	89.79 % / 10.19 %	73	A	89.58 % / 10.34 %	90	C	22.57 % / 72.92 %
6	D	42.05 % / 39.53 %	23	A	64.18 % / 30.43 %	40	A	89.95 % / 10.01 %	57	A	63.81 % / 31.44 %	74	A	88.12 % / 10.44 %	91	C	32.22 % / 67.18 %
7	C	80.05 % / 19.68 %	24	D	79.5 % / 19.38 %	41	A	55.63 % / 38.94 %	58	B	40.56 % / 57.84 %	75	B	32.92 % / 67.06 %	92	D	68.37 % / 30.62 %
8	D	24.14 % / 68.59 %	25	A	57.03 % / 33.96 %	42	D	43.69 % / 49.4 %	59	A	41.85 % / 51.57 %	76	A	68.44 % / 30.78 %	93	A	56.6 % / 38.03 %
9	B	46.38 % / 53.4 %	26	D	52.56 % / 33.65 %	43	D	85.03 % / 11.23 %	60	A	88.94 % / 10.53 %	77	A	61.53 % / 37.62 %	94	A	69.75 % / 30.01 %
10	C	30.98 % / 68.01 %	27	B	83.17 % / 14.38 %	44	D	61.83 % / 33.29 %	61	D	48.82 % / 40.51 %	78	C	80.83 % / 11.69 %	95	C	56.95 % / 42.53 %
11	C	50.51 % / 35.93 %	28	D	45.11 % / 39.53 %	45	B	61.52 % / 36.0 %	62	B	69.57 % / 30.25 %	79	A	51.94 % / 37.38 %	96	C	40.97 % / 30.59 %
12	C	61.55 % / 30.53 %	29	D	52.0 % / 46.31 %	46	C	80.73 % / 11.31 %	63	B	41.52 % / 48.1 %	80	C	16.62 % / 74.37 %	97	C	50.61 % / 44.41 %
13	B	80.51 % / 15.24 %	30	A	86.87 % / 12.65 %	47	A	20.76 % / 67.71 %	64	C	49.03 % / 30.62 %	81	B	83.41 % / 11.73 %	98	A	45.69 % / 32.02 %
14	B	66.38 % / 33.48 %	31	C	66.11 % / 33.61 %	48	B	50.79 % / 39.22 %	65	C	40.78 % / 50.87 %	82	D	86.36 % / 10.11 %	99	A	83.21 % / 14.23 %
15	A	69.69 % / 30.06 %	32	A	44.35 % / 45.2 %	49	A	84.0 % / 12.48 %	66	C	65.56 % / 33.15 %	83	C	52.59 % / 43.18 %	100	B	61.64 % / 32.74 %
16	A	25.97 % / 73.42 %	33	D	87.37 % / 12.6 %	50	D	47.31 % / 33.57 %	67	C	66.16 % / 30.68 %	84	C	12.27 % / 86.28 %			
17	C	58.43 % / 39.78 %	34	A	52.19 % / 33.82 %	51	C	54.26 % / 45.67 %	68	D	78.88 % / 13.59 %	85	B	53.09 % / 44.46 %			

//Hints and Solutions//

1. The country's first-ever radio channel for the visually impaired, named 'Radio Aksh' has been launched in Nagpur. The Blind Relief Association Nagpur and Samdrushti Kshamata Vikas Avam Anusandhan Mandal (Saksham) are the pioneers of the concept. It will help the visually-impaired gain seamless access to education resources and audiobooks.

Hence, the correct option is (B).

2. Mirabai Chanu clinched the gold medal in weightlifting at the Singapore International.

The 2020 Tokyo Olympics silver medallist in weightlifting, Mirabai Chanu, clinched the gold medal at the ongoing Singapore International on 25 February 2022. This win also helped her secure a slot at the upcoming 2022 Commonwealth Games in Birmingham. Competing in a new weight category- 55 kg, Chanu lifted a total of 191 kg- 86 kg in Snatch and 105 kg in Clean and Jerk, to clinch the gold.

Hence, the correct option is (A).

3. The 14th assembly of Haryana, which has been constituted after the election of October, 2019.

The results were announced on 24 October 2019. The Bharatiya Janata Party emerged as the single largest party and formed the government in a post-poll alliance with the Jannayak Janta Party and seven Independent MLAs.

Hence, the correct option is (C).

4. The Indian Navy deployed INS Kolkata and INS Shakti as a part of the SIMBEX-19

Singapore India Maritime Bilateral Exercise, also called the SIMBEX held its annual bilateral naval exercise from 16th May to 22nd May 2019.

- SIMBEX was started in 1993 and has been an annual affair since then.
- These are Kolkata Class Destroyers.
- The objective of SIMBEX to extend friendship between the countries of East and South-East Asia in domains like Maritime, Economy, and Culture.
- Along with the Kolkata Class destroyers mentioned above, Poseidon-8I (P8I) - Indian long-range maritime patrol aircraft will also take part.
- The Royal Singapore Navy Ships RSN Steadfast and RSN Valiant, along with F-16 fighter aircraft and Fokker-50 (F-50) Maritime Patrol Aircraft will participate.

Hence, the correct option is (B).

5. India's Bajrang Punia had won bronze in men's 65 kg category at World Wrestling Championships in Belgrade.

With this medal, Bajrang Punia becomes first Indian to win four medals at world wrestling championships. The 2022 World Wrestling Championships was the 17th edition of the World Wrestling Championships of combined events and was held between 10 and 18 September 2022 in Belgrade, Serbia.

Hence, the correct option is (B).

6. Given that:

Principal= Rs. 12,000

Rate = 5%

Time = 3 years

We know that,

$$\text{Amount} = \text{Principal} \left(1 + \frac{r}{100}\right)^t$$

$$\therefore \text{Amount after 3 years} = 12{,}000 \left(1 + \frac{5}{100}\right)^3$$

$$= 12{,}000 \times \frac{21}{20} \times \frac{21}{20} \times \frac{21}{20}$$

$$= 441 \left(\frac{63}{2}\right) = \text{Rs. } 13{,}891.50$$

Hence, the correct option is (D).

7. Let the principal be Rs. $100P$

Amount after 2 years at 10% per annum compound interest $= \frac{100+10}{100} \times \frac{100+10}{100} \times 100P$

$$= \text{Rs. } 121P$$

Interest $= \text{Rs. } 121P - \text{Rs. } 100P = \text{Rs. } 21P$

Given,

Rs. $21P = 1050$

$$\Rightarrow P = 50$$

Therefore, Principal $= 100P = 100 \times 50 = \text{Rs. } 5000$

Hence, the correct option is (C).

8. Let the original rate be $R\%$. Then, the new rate $= (2R)\%$.

Note:

Here, original rate is for 1 year(s); the new rate is for only 4 months i.e. $\frac{1}{3}$ year(s).

$$\therefore \frac{725 \times R \times 1}{100} + \frac{362.50 \times 2R \times 1}{100 \times 3}$$

$$= 33.50$$

$$\Rightarrow (2175 + 725)R = 33.50 \times 100 \times 3$$

$$\Rightarrow (2175 + 725)R = 10050$$

$$\Rightarrow (2900)R = 10050$$

$$\Rightarrow R = \frac{10050}{2900} = 3.46$$

$$\therefore \text{Original rate} = 3.46\%$$

Hence, the correct option is (D).

9. Given,

$$\frac{11.2 \times 0.36 + 0.42 \times 3.2}{0.8 \times 4.2}$$

$$\Rightarrow \frac{4.032 + 1.344}{3.36}$$

$$\Rightarrow \frac{5.376}{3.36}$$

$$\Rightarrow 1.6$$

Hence, the correct option is (B).

10. Given,

$$2994 \div 14.5 = 172$$

$$\frac{29.94}{1.45}$$

$$= \frac{299.4}{14.5}$$

$$= \frac{2994}{14.5} \times \frac{1}{10} \text{ [Here, Substitute 172 in the place of } \frac{2994}{14.5}]$$

$$= \frac{172}{10}$$

$$= 17.2$$

Hence, the correct option is (C).

11. Given,

$$22.\overline{4} + 11.5\overline{67} - 33.\overline{59}$$

$$= 22 + \frac{4}{9} + 11 + \frac{567 - 5}{990} - 33 - \frac{59 - 5}{90}$$

$$= \frac{4}{9} + \frac{562}{990} - \frac{54}{90}$$

$$= \frac{440 + 562 - 594}{990}$$

$$= \frac{408}{990}$$

$$= \frac{408 + 4}{990}$$

$$= \frac{412}{990}$$

$$= 0.4\overline{12}$$

Hence, the correct option is (C).

12.

- The Mauryan empire was one of the greatest empires which ruled on India.
- It has great historical significance.
- The rule of Mauryas ruled from 322-185 B.C. & under them, the majority of India remained united as a single state by the great founder emperor Chandragupta Maurya.

- With the help of Chanakya, Chandragupta Maurya laid the foundation of this great Mauryan empire.

Hence, the correct option is (C).

13. Refined oil is a kind of oil that has been purified.

'Cleared', 'improved', and 'washed' have meanings related to the word 'refined', but they are not appropriate in the given context.

Complete Sentence:

Generally, people use **refined** oils for their cooking.

Hence, the correct option is (B).

14. Considerate means to be careful not to inconvenience or harm others.

Concrete means existing in material or physical form.

Convenient means fitting in well with a person's needs and activities.

Controversial means giving rise to or likely to give rise to any controversy.

Complete Sentence:

The committee's suggestion was not acceptable to everyone as it was **controversial**.

Hence, the correct option is (B).

15. The distance can be covered up with the speed.

The rate refers to price or fare.

Quick refers to speed. An express train can pick up speed and not quick.

Complete Sentence:

During the nighttime, the express train picked up **speed**.

Hence, the correct option is (A).

16. Since we are referring to living people, we have to use 'who'

Whoever means the people who; any person(s) who. It is distinct from whoever is used as an object of a verb or preposition.

Complete Sentence:

Whoever was present in the hall taking part in the voting process.

Hence, the correct option is (A).

17. In the above-given sentence, 'popular' will be used.

It is so because 'popular' is an adjective meaning 'liked, enjoyed, or supported by many people'.

The sentence talks about a type of gardening that first started in China and the most appropriate word for the blank is 'popular' as it means that Bonsai gardening was liked by people because of the Japanese.

Complete Sentence:

Bonsai gardening was first practiced in China but became **popular** because of the Japanese.

Hence, the correct option is (C).

18. To face the music means <u>to accept the consequences</u>.

For eg- He would later have to face the music for his improper decisions.

Hence, the correct option is (A).

19. To Hit the sack means to go to bed.

Example: After the long journey, he hit the sack as soon as he reached home.

He wanted to hit the sack and did not feel like going out to party with his friends.

Hence, the correct option is (B).

20. Soil is often considered an abiotic factor since it is mostly made up of small particles of rock (sand and clay) mixed with decomposed plants and animals. Plants use their roots to get water and nutrients from the soil.
Hence, the correct option is (B).

21. The above-given sentence is in the active voice.

We need to change it in the passive voice.

The following steps are required to change the given sentence into passive voice:

- The subject 'the Municipal Corporation' of the active voice will become the object of the passive voice.
- The object 'the manhole covers' of the active voice will become the subject of the passive voice.
- The tense(simple past tense) will change according to the following structure:-
    - Active Voice - Subject + did + V_1 or V_2 + Object.
    - Passive Voice - Object + was/were + V_3 + by + Object.

Hence, the correct option is (C).

22. The passive voice of the given sentence is:

Let the television be switched off.

The given sentence is an imperative sentence.

The instructions given below should be followed while changing an imperative sentence to passive voice.

Find the subject and object of the sentence and exchange their places; make changes in their cases as well if subject and object are pronouns.

The passive form will be - Let + object (the command) + be + past participle form.

Hence, the correct option is (C).

23. The logic is:

Badminton: shuttlecock → Shuttlecock is a lightweight conical object with a rounded often rubber-covered nose that is used in badminton.

Similarly,

Snooker:? → A billiard ball is a small, hard ball used in cue sports, such as carom billiards, pool, and snooker.

Hence, the correct option is (A).

24. The pattern followed here is,

12: 312 :: 10 : ?

12 : 12 × (12 × 2 + 2)

Similarly,

10 : 10 × (10 × 2 + 2)

Hence, the correct option is (D).

25. The logic followed is:

Second number ÷ first number = 4

39 : 156

156 ÷ 39 = 4

Similarly,

244 ÷ 61 = 4

Hence, the correct option is (A).

26. The pattern follows here are:

First number: (First number $+2)^2$ = Second number

The 1st term $19 = (19 + 2)^2 = (21)^2 = 441$

Similarly,

The 2 nd term $17 = (17 + 2)^2 = (19)^2 = 361$

Hence, the correct option is (D).

27. The logic is:

Sweater: Socks → We use sweaters and socks in the winter season to protect ourselves from cold weather.

Similarly,

Raincoat: ? → We use raincoats and umbrella in the monsoon season to protect ourselves from rain.

Hence, the correct option is (B).

28. Let the original speed of the car is x km/hr.

Then, time taken in moving 840 km $= \dfrac{840}{x}$ hr

If speed is going 10 km/hr more $= x + 10$

Then, time taken in moving 840 km $= \dfrac{840}{x+10}$ hr

$\therefore \dfrac{840}{x} - \dfrac{840}{x+10} = 2$

$\Rightarrow 840(x + 10) - 840x = 2x(x + 10)$

$\Rightarrow 2x^2 + 20x - 8400 = 0$

$\Rightarrow x^2 + 70x - 60x - 4200 = 0$

$\Rightarrow (x + 70)(x - 60) = 0$

$\Rightarrow x = 60$ or $x = -70$

If $x = -70$ is not true because the speed is not negetive.

So, speed is 60 km/hr.

Hence, the correct option is (D).

29. In this question, it is given that A man who sits in the slower train cross the faster train it means faster train cross the man in 18 second

speed of the faster train and man in the same direction $=$ $58 - 30 = 28$ kmph

So distance covered by faster train in 18 seconds $= 28$ kmph $\times 18$ sec

$= \dfrac{28 \times 5}{18} \times 18 = 140$ metres

Hence, the correct option is (D).

30. The speeds of 3 cars in the ratio 5 : 4 : 6

When traveling the same distance, speed $\propto \dfrac{1}{time}$

Speed of the three cars = 5 : 4 : 6

Then, ratio of time of the three cars = $\dfrac{1}{5} : \dfrac{1}{4} : \dfrac{1}{6}$

Ratio of time = $\left(\dfrac{12}{60}\right) : \left(\dfrac{15}{60}\right) : \left(\dfrac{10}{60}\right) = 12 : 15 : 10$

$\therefore$ The required ratio is 12 : 15 : 10.

Hence, the correct option is (A).

31. Given,

Regular speed of Raghu = v km/hr

Reduced speed of Raghu = $\dfrac{75}{100} \times$ v

$\Rightarrow$ 0.75v km/hr

Delay in time due to reduced speed = 80 minutes

$\Rightarrow \dfrac{80}{60} = \dfrac{8}{6}$ hr

Distance = Speed × Time

Time to reach office with regular speed = t hr

Case 1:

Distance = v × t   ----(1)

Case 2:

Distance = 0.75v × (t + $\dfrac{8}{6}$)   ----(2)

Distance in both the cases is equal

$\Rightarrow$ vt = 0.75v × (t + $\dfrac{8}{6}$)

$\Rightarrow$ 6vt = 0.75v × 6t + 0.75v × 8

$\Rightarrow$ 6vt = 4.5vt + 6v

$\Rightarrow$ 1.5vt = 6v

$\Rightarrow$ 1.5t = 6

$\Rightarrow$ t = $\dfrac{6}{1.5}$

$\Rightarrow$ t = 4 hr

$\therefore$ With usual speed Raghu would take 4 hours to go to office.

Hence, the correct option is (C).

32. On close obeservation, we find that the question figure is embedded in option (A) as shown below:

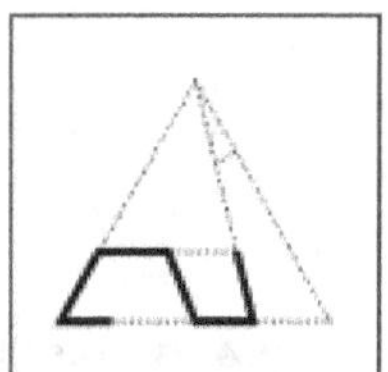

Hence, the correct option is (A).

33.

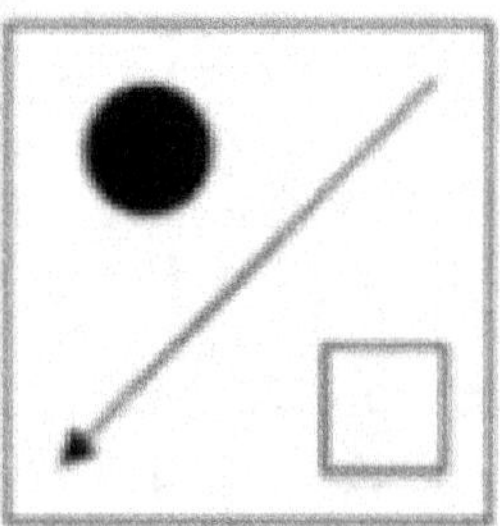

Hence, the correct option is (D).

34.

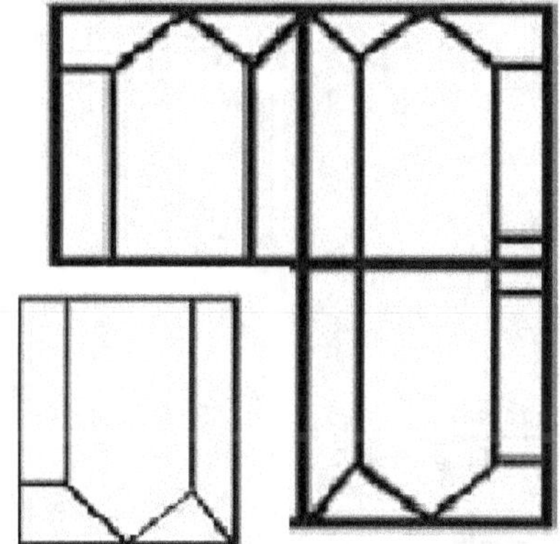

Hence, the correct option is (A).

35.

Hence, the correct option is (C).

36.

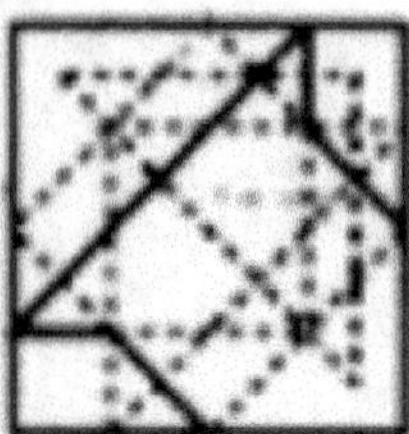

Hence, the correct option is (D).

37. Given,

The average marks of six students are 48. The mark 45 is misread as 54.

$$\text{Average} = \frac{\text{(Sum of all entry)}}{\text{(Number of total entry)}}$$

The average marks of six students are 48.

Total marks of six students = 48 × 6

⇒ 288

The mark 45 is misread as 54

Sum of numbers of five students is (288 – 54) = 234

Actual sum of marks of six students = (234 + 45)

⇒ 279

The correct average = $\frac{(279}{6})$

⇒ 46.5

∴ The correct average is 46.5

Hence, the correct option is (B).

38. Given:

Number $= 5, 11, 16, x, 14$

Average $= 12$

$$\text{Average} = \frac{Sum\ of\ element}{Number\ of\ element}$$

$\Rightarrow 12 = \frac{(5+11+16+x+14)}{5}$

$\Rightarrow 12 = \frac{(x+46)}{5}$

$\Rightarrow 12 \times 5 = (x + 46)$

$\Rightarrow 60 = (x + 46)$

$\Rightarrow x = 60 - 46 = 14$

∴ The value of x is 14.

Hence, the correct option is (C).

39. Total sale for 5 months

= Rs. (6435 + 6927 + 6855 + 7230 + 6562)

= Rs. 34009

Therefore Required sale

= Rs. [(6500 × 6) - 34009]

= Rs. (39000 - 34009)

= Rs. 4991

Hence, the correct option is (A).

40. Given,

3 men or 5 women can complete the work in 12 days.

Work done by 3 men = Work done by 5 women

1 men $= \frac{5}{3} \times$ women

Now, 3 men $+7$ women $= 3 \times \left(\frac{5}{3}\right) + 7$ women $= 12$ women

As we know,

$$W1 \times D1 = W2 \times D2$$

$$\therefore 5 \times 12 = 12 \times D2$$

$$\Rightarrow D2 = 5 \text{ days}$$

Hence, the correct option is (A).

41. Given,

Wages of 20 days of 1 man and 1 woman = Rs. 1500

Let efficiency of 1 woman be 1 unit/day

Efficiency of 1 man $= 2$ unit/day

According to the question,

$2 + 1 = 3$ unit

$\Rightarrow 3$ unit $= 1500$

$\Rightarrow 1$ unit $= \frac{1500}{3} = 500$

20 day's wages of 1 woman = Rs. 500

Daily wages of 1 woman $= \frac{500}{20} = $ Rs. 25

Hence, the correct option is (A).

42. Given,

A alone can complete a work in = 12 days

B alone can complete the same work in = 15 days

As we know,

Wages are distributed into efficiency ratio.

Efficiency is inversely proportional to time.

Time ratio of A and B = 12 : 15 = 4 : 5

Efficiency ratio of A and B = 5 : 4

According to the question,

5 + 4 = 9 units

⇒ 9 units = 3600

⇒ 1 unit = 400

⇒ 5 units = 5 × 400 = Rs. 2000

∴ Share of A is Rs. 2000.

Hence, the correct option is (D).

43. Let's look at the meaning of the correct answer:

Neigh - the sound of horses. For Example: With a wild neigh of terror the animal fell bodily into the pit, drawing the buggy and its occupants after him.

Hence, the correct option is (D).

44. The correct one word for the given descriptive sentence/words is Burrow.

Let's look at the meaning of the correct answer:

Burrow: An underground hole dug by a small animal as a dwelling. For Example: Two burrows were randomly selected for the addition of water to the sand.

Hence, the correct option is (D).

45. In the given question, the sum of all the options except option (B) is 21.

8 + 5 + 4 + 3 + 1 = 21

2 + 3 + 8 + 7 + 0 = **20**

9 + 9 + 3 + 0 + 0 = 21

1 + 1 + 5 + 5 + 9 = 21

Hence, the correct option is (B).

46. All are square of some number except '343', which is a cube of '7'.
$256 = 16^2$
$289 = 17^2$
$144 = 12^2$
$343 = 7^3$
Hence, the correct option is (C).

47. Café Coffee Day, InMobi, and Peter England are brands of Indian origin whereas Nestle is a brand from Switzerland.

Thus Nestle is the odd word.

Hence, the correct option is (A).

48. From options:

(A) $\dfrac{130}{26} = 5$

(B) $\dfrac{75}{16} = 4.6875$

(C) $\dfrac{35}{7} = 5$

(D) $\dfrac{65}{13} = 5$

Clearly, Except (B), in the rest of the pairs, after dividing the first number by the second number, we get to number 5 as quotient.

Hence, the correct option is (B).

49. All are scientists except 'Bismillah Khan', who was a musician.

Hence, the correct option is (A).

50. Refractive index of diamond is very much large and structure of the diamond is such that when light enters inside the diamond, there is a 'total internal reflection" which happens in the diamond, i.e., light gets reflected from one internal surface of the diamond and further reflect from other parts of the surface. This phenomenon gets repeated many times. It is because of this phenomenon the diamond shines.

Hence, the correct option is (D).

51. Sound waves are examples of the mechanical waves, while the light waves, Radio waves, and Microwaves are examples of electromagnetic waves. Electromagnetic waves are formed by the vibration of an electric charge. This vibration makes a wave that has both an electric and also a magnetic component. Sound waves are the longitudinal waves that require a medium to travel, and it can't travel through the vacuum. Light generally refers to the visible light, which is electromagnetic radiation that is seen to the human eye and is even responsible for the sense of sight.

Hence, the correct option is (C).

52. The electromagnetic waves (EM waves) are transverse in nature, not longitudinal.

Applications for the Electromagnetic waves:

• Electromagnetic waves get to accomplish the transmission of energy via a vacuum or using no medium.

• As EM waves transmit energy, it plays an essential role in our day to day lives, including communication technology.

• They are even used to transmit short/long-wavelength radio waves.

• They are also used to transmit TV or wireless signals and energies.

• EM waves are responsible for the transmission of energy in the forms of microwaves, visible light, ultraviolet light, infrared radiation, gamma rays, and also of X-rays.

• Electromagnetic radiation is the basis for working of radar, which in turn is used for directing and remote sensing the understanding of our planet Earth.

• UV rays are germicidal in nature, and they destroy bacteria, viruses, and molds from various surfaces, air/water.

• Ultraviolet rays are even used to detect the forged banknotes. Real banknotes do not turn fluorescent under the Ultraviolet light.

• UV rays have even sanitary and therapeutic properties.

Hence, the correct option is (C).

53. Given information:

Velocity of Snowboard =5 m/s

Power =3000 watt

Then,

Power = Force × Velocity

3000=Force × 5

Force =600 N

Hence, the correct option is (C).

54. Uranium-235 has 92 protons, so the proton number of 235U is 92. It has 92 protons plus 143 neutrons inside its nucleus, so it's total nucleon number is 235.

Uranium-235 (235U) is an isotope of Uranium forming up about 0.72 percent of natural Uranium. Unlike that of predominant isotope Uranium238, it is much fissile, i.e., it may sustain a fission chain reaction. This is the only fissile isotope that is primordial and is found in relatively sufficient quantities in nature. Uranium-235 possesses a half-life of 703.8 million years. It was first discovered in 1935 by Arthur Jeffrey Dempster. Its fission cross-section for slow thermal neutrons is almost about 584.994 barns. For quick neutrons, it is on the order of 1 barn. Mostly but not all neutron absorptions result in fission; a minority even results in neutron capture making uranium-236.

Hence, the correct option is (C).

55. Surya Kiran is India's largest military exercise with Nepal in terms of troop participation.

Some exercises by Indian Army:-

Name	Partner Nation
Hand in Hand	China
Sampriti	Bangladesh
Mitra Shakti	Sri Lanka
Yudh Abhyas	USA
Vajra Prahar	USA
IMBAX	Myanmar
Harimau Shakti	Malaysia
Garuda Shakti	Indonesia
Ekuverin	Maldives
Indra	Russia
Al Nagah	Oman
Dharma Guardian	Japan
Maitree	Thailand
Prabal Dostyk	Kazakhstan

Nomadic Elephant	Mongolia
Lamitiye	Seychelles
Bold Kurukshetra	Singapore
Khanjar	Kyrgyzstan

Hence, the correct option is (B).

56. Dolce is an Italian luxury fashion house founded in 1985 in Legnano.

Dulce sweet to the taste: soothing, agreeable.

Dilce is a small settlement west of Postojna in the Inner Carniola region of Slovenia.

Dulse is a type of seaweed. It is used as food in Ireland and Eastern parts of Canada.

Hence, the correct option is (C).

57. The correctly spelt word- Horizontal

Horizontal: Going from side to side, not up and down; flat or level

Hence, the correct option is (A).

58. Statement 1 and 2: Zardozi prospered in India during the 17th century during the reign of the Mughal emperor Akbar. It came to India from Persia. Its literal translation, 'Zar' means gold and 'dozi' meaning embroidery. Thus, Zardozi comes from the Persian term meaning 'embroidering with gold threads.'

Statement 3: In this embroidery, gold coils and beads are tucked into the fabric using a needle and thread. Metals like gold and silver are transformed into a zari (thin thread) that is used to adorn motifs onto rich fabrics like silk, velvet, organza, chiffon, etc.

In 2013 the Geographical Indication Registry (GIR) accorded the Geographical Indication (GI) registration to the Lucknow Zardozi. Hence, the correct option is (B).

59. Statement 1: Chindu Yakshaganam is a form of theatre practised by members of the Chindu Madiga community.

Statement 2: It is a form of entertainment in villages across Telangana, with the artists skilfully depicting classic tales from the epics and entertaining the masses. The art form probably started when people enacted acts of hunting, wars and other acts of valour. The Chindu community has traditionally been a nomadic community.
Hence, the correct option is (A).

60. In all other figures, the lower-right quarter portion is shaded.

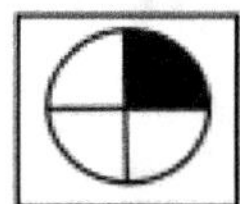

Hence, the correct option is (A).

61. All other figures are divided into equal parts.

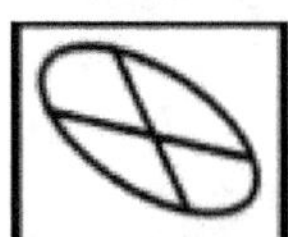

Hence, the correct option is (D).

62. Here, in all the figures except figure (C), positions of the elements will remain the same upon rotation.

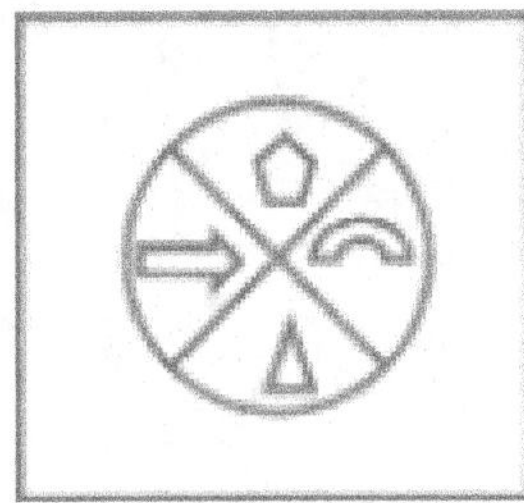

Hence, the correct option is (B).

63. In the given figures, one of the sides is curved except figure B which is made up of straight lines only.

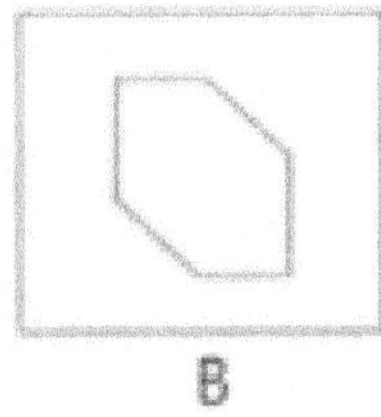

Hence, the correct option is (B).

64. In figure A, B, C, the inside line divided the figure into two equal half area,

But in figure D, the area is not equally divided by the line.

Hence, the correct option is (C).

65. Given:

Average height of 3 girls = 180 cm

Ratio of height of 3 girls = 4 : 5 : 6

Formula:

Average = Sum of all observations/Total number of all observations

Sum of height of 3 girls = 180 × 3 = 540

Height ratio of 3 girls = 4 : 5 : 6 = 4x : 5x : 6x

According to the question

4x + 5x + 6x = 540

$\Rightarrow 15x = 540$

$\Rightarrow x = 36$

Height of smallest girls = 4 × 36

$\Rightarrow 144$ cm

$\therefore$ The height of smallest girl is 144 cm.

Hence, the correct option is (C).

66. Given:

Present age of P and $Q = 2 : 7$

18 yrs ago age of P and $Q = 1 : 26$

Let the present age of P be $2x$.

Let the present age of Q be $7x$.

$\therefore$ According to the question

$$\Rightarrow \frac{(2x-18)}{(7x-18)} = \frac{1}{26}$$

$$\Rightarrow 26(2x - 18) = (7x - 18)$$

$$\Rightarrow 52x - 468 = 7x - 18$$

$$\Rightarrow 52x - 7x = -18 + 468$$

$$\Rightarrow 45x = 450$$

$$\Rightarrow x = \frac{450}{45}$$

$$\Rightarrow x = 10$$

P's present age $= 2 \times 10 = 20$ yr

Q's present age $= 7 \times 10 = 70$ yr

$\therefore$ The sum of the present age of P and $Q = 20 + 70 = 90$ yr

Hence, the correct option is (C).

67. In the mixture, let the quantity of milk $= 3a$ litres and the quantity of water $= a$ litres

In 20 litres another mixture, the quantity of milk $= \frac{20 \times 2}{5} = 8$ litres

The quantity of water $= \frac{20 \times 2}{5} = 12$ litres

The quantity of milk $= 3a + 8$ litres

The quantity of water $= a + 12$ litres

Total quantity of mixture $= 4a + 20$ litres

Therefore, according to the question,

$$\Rightarrow 33.75\% \text{ of } (4a + 20) = a + 12$$

$$\Rightarrow 1.35a - a = 12 - 6.75 = 5.25$$

$$\Rightarrow 0.35a = 5.25$$

$$\Rightarrow a = 15$$

Total quantity of mixture $= 4a + 20 = 80$ litres

Hence, the correct option is (C).

68. Among the options, only Mirabai Chanu is NOT a recipient of Rajiv Gandhi Khel Ratna 2020.

Mirabai Chanu is an Indian weightlifter.

- She was honored with the Rajiv Gandhi Khel Ratna in 2018.

Rajiv Gandhi Khel Ratna 2020 winners:

- Rohit Sharma (Cricket)
- Mariyappan Thangavelu (Paralympian)
- Manika Batra (Table Tennis)
- Vinesh Phogat (Wrestler)
- Rani Rampal (Hockey)

Hence, the correct option is (D).

69. Given:

A shopkeeper sells 200 shirts.

S.P. of 25 shirts = Rs.25

Profit = S.P of 25 shirts = Rs. 25

C.P. = S.P. – Profit

= Rs. 200 – Rs. 25 = Rs. 175

Profit % = $\left(\dfrac{Profit}{C.P}\right) \times 100$

= $\left(\dfrac{25}{175}\right) \times 100$

= $\dfrac{100}{7}\%$ = 14.28%

∴ The profit percentage is 14.28%.

Hence, the correct option is (C).

70. According to the question,

CP of each mango = Rs. $\dfrac{8}{5}$ = Rs. 1.60

SP of each mango = Rs. $\dfrac{5}{2}$ = Rs. 2.50

Profit per mango = 2.50 - 1.60 = Rs. 0.90

Total profit = 300 × 0.90 = Rs. 270

Hence, the correct option is (B).

71. Effective profit percent $= X + Y + \dfrac{XY}{100}$

Effective profit percent $= 20 + 25 + \dfrac{20 \times 25}{100} = 50\%$

Original C.P. $= \dfrac{100}{150} \times 1200 = 800$

Hence, the correct option is (D).

72. The carnivores are those animals who eat flesh and meat.

Lions eat flesh but rabbits do not eat flesh.

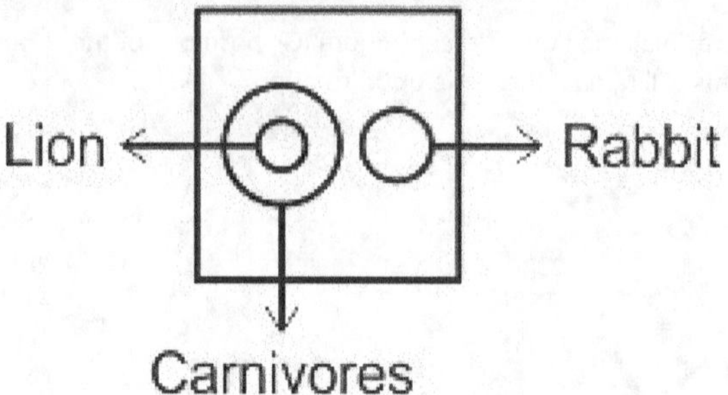

Hence, the correct option is (B).

73. Ireland is a country and Dublin is its capital, whereas Greece is a country.

So the possible relationship diagram would be:

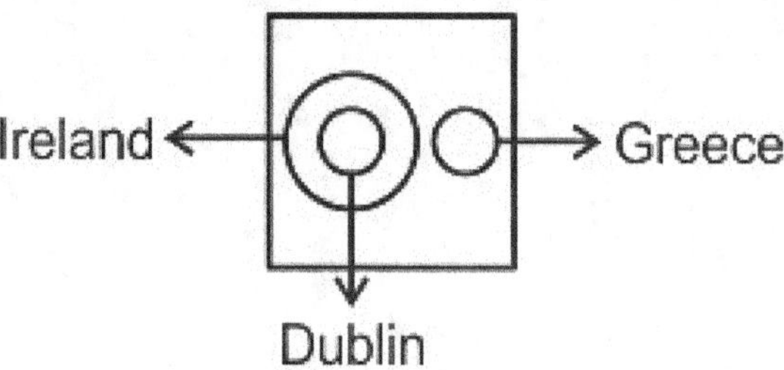

Hence, the correct option is (A).

74. A person can be engineer, businessmen and politician so following Venn diagram can be formed.

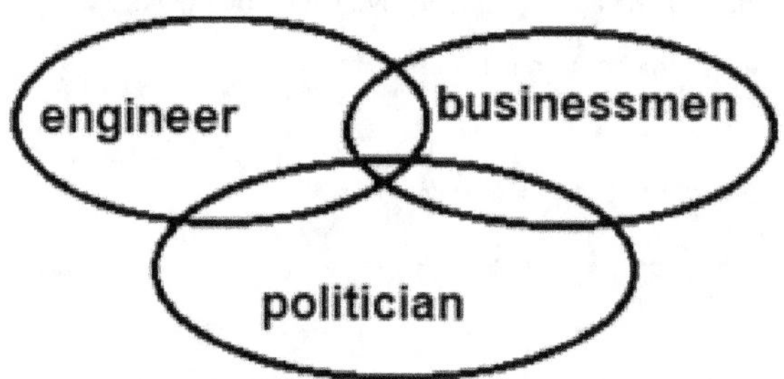

Hence, the correct option is (A).

75. Following figure shows the relation among Diwali, Eid, Festival.

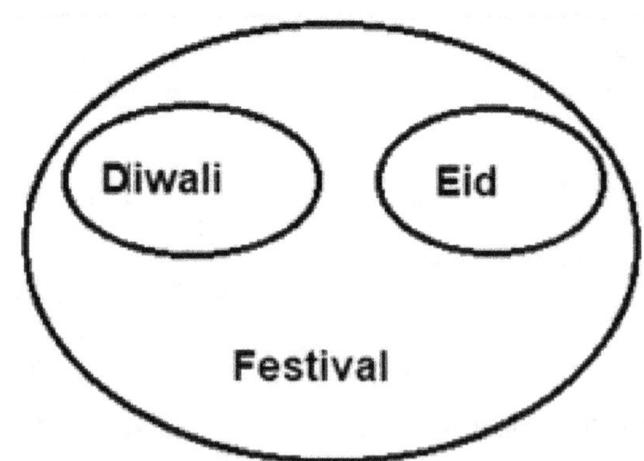

Hence, the correct option is (B).

76. First tree will be cut from which we can get wood which will go to carpenter who will make furniture for us.

Hence, the correct option is (A).

77. First we will draw a line. Then with the help of rounder, we will draw a 60 degree then 120 degree and finally we can draw a 90 degree.

Hence, the correct option is (A).

78. The features of parliamentary government in India:

Nominal and Real Executives -

- The President is the nominal executive (de jure executive or titular executive) while the Prime Minister is the real executive (de facto executive).

- Thus, the President is head of the State, while the Prime Minister is head of the government. So, Statement 1 is not correct.

Majority Party Rule -

- The political party which secures majority seats in the Lok Sabha forms the government.

Collective Responsibility

- This is the bedrock principle of parliamentary government.

- The ministers are collectively responsible to the Parliament in general and to the Lok Sabha in particular (Article 75).

- They act as a team, and swim and sink together.

- The principle of collective responsibility implies that the Lok Sabha can remove the ministry (i.e., the council of ministers headed by the prime minister) from office by passing a vote of no confidence.

Political Homogeneity

- Usually, members of the council of ministers belong to the same political party, and hence they share the same political ideology.

- In the case of a coalition government, the ministers are bound by consensus.

Double Membership

- The ministers are members of both the legislature and the executive.

- This means that a person cannot be a minister without being a member of Parliament.

- The Constitution stipulates that a minister who is not a member of the Parliament for a period of six consecutive months ceases to be a minister.

The Leadership of the Prime Minister

- The Prime Minister plays a leadership role in this system of government.

- S/He is the leader of the council of ministers, the leader of the Parliament, and the leader of the party in power.

Dissolution of the Lower House

- The lower house of the Parliament (Lok Sabha) can be dissolved by the President on the recommendation of the Prime Minister.

- In other words, the prime minister can advise the President to dissolve the Lok Sabha before the expiry of its term and hold fresh elections.

- This means that the executive enjoys the right to get the legislature dissolved in a parliamentary system.

Secrecy

- The ministers operate on the principle of secrecy of procedure and cannot divulge information about their proceedings, policies, and decisions.

- They take the oath of secrecy before entering their office.

- The oath of secrecy to the ministers is administered by the President.

Hence, the correct option is (C).

79. The correct answer is 'Encouraged'.

- The word 'Emboldened' means to give someone the courage or confidence to do something.

- The synonyms of the word 'Emboldened' are "encouraged, strengthened, inspired".

- From the synonym of the given word, we can say that the word 'Encouraged' has the same meaning.

- The word 'Encouraged' means to give support, confidence, or hope to someone.

Hence, the correct option is (A).

80. The correct answer is 'home-grown'.

- The word 'Indigenous' means originating or occurring naturally in a particular place; native.

- The synonyms of the word 'Indigenous' are "home-grown, domestic, endemic".

- From the synonym of the given word, we can say that the word 'Home-grown' has the same meaning.

- The word 'Home-grown' means belonging to one's own particular locality or country.

Hence, the correct option is (C).

81. The correct answer is 'Greed to accumulate more and more wealth'.

- The word 'Pleonexia' means greed to accumulate more and more wealth.

- The synonyms of the word 'Pleonexia' are "avarice, covetousness, greed".

- From the synonym of the given word, we can say that option (B) has the same meaning.

Hence, the correct option is (B).

82. Vosges are block mountains.

A mountain is any natural elevation of the earth's surface.

- Mountains are formed by enormous movements upon the earth's crust.
- These gigantic movements fold and break the crust into many layers and sometimes these movements raise the crust in the upward direction (dome-shaped).
- As a result, the changes in crust give rise to different types of mountains.

Hence, the correct option is (D).

83. Let us assume there are 100 students in the institute.

Then, number of boys $= 60$

And, number of girls $= 40$

Further, 15% of boys get fee waiver $= 9$ boys

7.5% of girls get fee waiver $= 3$ girls

Total $= 12$ students who gets fee waiver

But, here given 90 students are getting fee waiver. So we compare $12 = 90$

So, $1 = \dfrac{90}{12}$

$= 7.5$

Now number of students who are not getting fee waiver $= 51$ boys and 37 girls

50% concession $= 25.5$ boys and 18.5 girls (i.e. total 44)

So, required students $= 44 \times 7.5$

$= 330$

Hence, the correct option is (C).

84. Non-defective products $M^1 = 25 \times 0.98 = 24.5\%$

Non-defective products $M^2 = 35 \times 0.96 = 33.6\%$

Non-defective products $M^3 = 40 \times 0.95 = 38\%$

Percentage of non-defective products,

$= 24.5 + 33.6 + 38$

$= 96.1\%$

Hence, the correct option is (C).

85. Let the salary be Rs.100x

Amount spent on rent = 30% of 100x = Rs.30x

Amount spent on clothing = 20% of 100x = Rs.20x

Amount spent on food = 15% of 100x = Rs.15x

Then, His savings = 100x - (30x+20x+15x) = 100x - 65x = Rs.35x

Given,

35x = 10500

$\Rightarrow$ x = 300

Therefore,

His salary = 100x = 100×300 = Rs.30000

Hence, the correct option is (B).

86. In grammar, when we refer to something that exists in numbers of 'two' for e.g. legs and trousers, ears and earrings, glasses or spectacles, we use the word 'Pair' to indicate that they are singular in number but two of them make one item a Pair of spectacles where the word 'spectacles' indicates that there are two i.e., one for each eye but together they make one item so they are referred to as 'a' Pair. Since the subject is 'Pair' which is singular, we use the phrase 'Pair'.

Hence, the correct option is (D).

87. Option (A): 'Always' is an adverb of frequency. It indicates that some action is taking place 'all the time'.

Option (B): 'Not' is not an adverb of frequency. It's a tool used to convert a positive sentence to a negative. It has no relation to time and hence, frequency.

Option (C) is incorrect because 'not' is not a frequency adverb.

Option(D) is incorrect because the answer lies in (A).

Hence, the correct option is (A).

88. In order to fill in the blank, let's understand what adverbs of frequency are. Adverbs of frequency are words that explain how often something happens. For example, 'I often visit the museum.' Here, 'often' explains that the subject goes to the museum many times.

The word 'ever' explains that the idea of 'smiles' is negative. For example, 'Do he ever come to school?' which indirectly means that he never comes to school.

Option (B) - 'Usually' is an adverb, which means 'most of the times.' As we need an adverb that explains the negative idea of the sentence. 'Usually never' is used to give a negative idea and thus we can't use it with 'ever'.

Option (C) - 'Always' is an adverb, which means 'all the time'. It is clearly used to give a positive idea about a sentence, thus we can't use it here.

Option (D) - 'Mostly' is an adverb that means 'most of the time'. As explained above, we can't use an adverb that is used to give a positive idea about a sentence.

Option (A) - 'Hardly' is an adverb that means 'barely'. It also means 'rarely'. As it gives a negative idea about the adjective, we can use it here.

'Our Mathematics teacher hardly ever smiles.'

Hence, the correct option is (A).

89. Adverb of manner defines how something happens. The sentence is talking about someone's ability to talk. Options (A), (C), and (D) are opposite of what a sentence means to say.

Hence, the correct option is (B).

90. The answer to this question can be directly found in this statement:

A research suggests that our experience of reality is the product of a delicate balance of connectivity between neurons - too much or too little and the consciousness slips away.

Hence, the correct option is (C).

91. The answer to this question can be directly found in this statement:

The brain merges all of these inputs - photons, aromatic molecules, etc. - into our subjective experience of the object in that moment.

Hence, the correct option is (C).

92. The answer to this question can be directly found in this statement:

Previous studies of the brain have revealed the importance of "cortical integration" in maintaining consciousness, meaning that the brain must process and combine multiple inputs from different senses at once.

Hence, the correct option is (D).

93. The answer to this question can be directly found in this statement:

The question of whether the human consciousness is subjective or objective is largely philosophical.

Hence, the correct option is (A).

94. The answer to this question can be directly found in this statement:

A research suggests that our experience of reality is the product of a delicate balance of connectivity between neurons - too much or too little and the consciousness slips away.

Hence, the correct option is (A).

95.

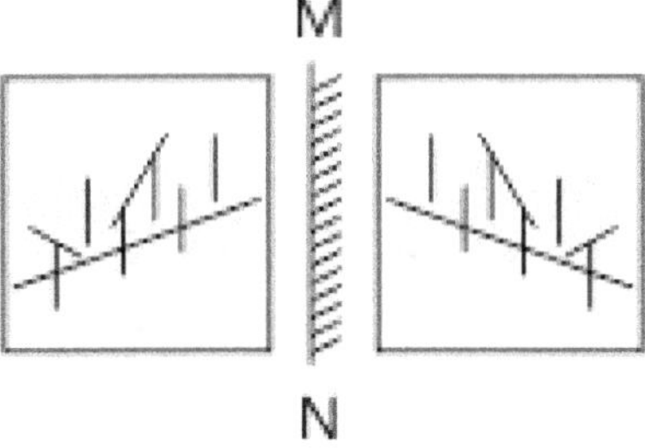

Hence, the correct option is (C).

96.

Hence, the correct option is (C).

97. Fig. (3) is formed by a combination of A-shaped elements while all other figures are formed by a combination of V-shaped elements.

Hence, the correct option is (C).

98.

Hence, the correct option is (A).

99.

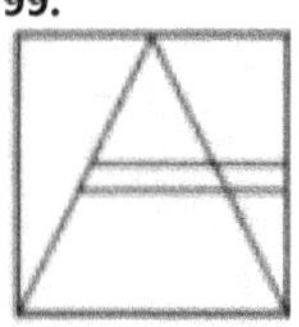

Right Side figure contains the complete triangle with double across. So the (a) option in the given figure will complete the figures.

Hence, the correct option is (A).

100.

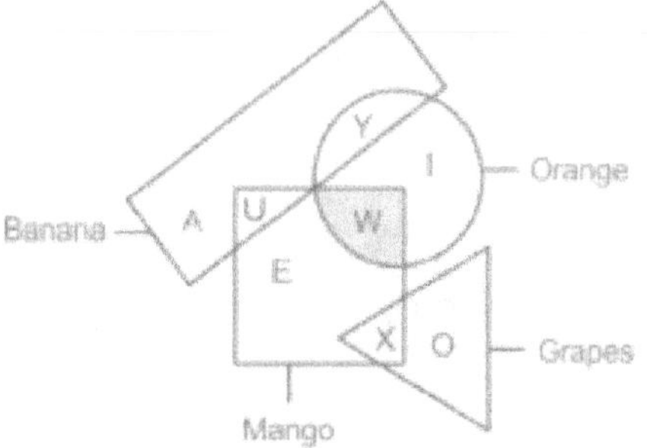

The circle represents people who like orange: I, W, Y

Square represents people who like mango: E, U, W, X

The people who like orange and mango will lie in the intersection of square and circle.

W likes mango and orange.

Hence, the correct option is (B).

Q.1 In April 2022, the Mazagon Dock Shipbuilders launched _______, the last of the six submarines under Project 75.

A. INS Vela   **B.** INS Vagsheer
C. INS Kalvari   **D.** INS Vagir

Q.2 The Indian Railways has placed a purchase order for 39,000 wheels for LHB coaches from the manufacturer of which of the following country in July 2022?

A. Ukraine   **B.** China
C. Russia   **D.** Germany

Q.3 What is the venue of the 'Semicon India Conference-2022'?

A. Mumbai   **B.** New Delhi
C. Chennai   **D.** Bengaluru

Q.4 Who among the following has been awarded the 'Changemaker Award' by the Bill and Melinda Gates Foundation for the year 2019?

[Rajasthan Police Constable, 2020]

A. Payal Jangid
B. Sumedha Kailash
C. Kailash Satyarthi
D. Apurvi Singh Chandela

Q.5 Who won a silver medal at the German Open 2022 in March 2022?

A. Srikanth Kidambi   **B.** Lakshya Sen
C. Prannoy HS   **D.** Chirag Shetty

Q.6 A person borrows certain amount of money at the rate of 2.5% per month. If he pays Rs. 13110 after 6 months to clear his dues then find the amount of interest paid by the person.

A. Rs. 1840   **B.** Rs. 1690   **C.** Rs. 1710   **D.** Rs. 1660

Q.7 A bank offers the business loan at simple interest, rate of interest for 1st 2 years is 8% for the next 3 years it is 10% and for the period beyond 5 years it is 12.5% per annum. If a person took the loan of Rs. $20\,L$ and paid Rs. $36.7\,L$ after some years. Find the number of years after which he repaid the loan:

A. 7 years   **B.** 9 years   **C.** 8 years   **D.** 10 years

Q.8 A sum of money was invested in a bank at 8% simple interest p.a. for 3 years. Had it been invested in a mutual fund at 8.5% p.a. simple interest for 4 years, the earning would have been Rs. 500 more. What is the sum invested?

A. 5000   **B.** 5500   **C.** 5550   **D.** 4500

Q.9 Who was India's first Chief of Defense Staff?
A. General Vijay Kumar Singh
B. General Manoj Mukund Naravane
C. General Arjan Singh
D. General Bipin Rawat

Q.10 Direction: Out of the following options, select the word that best substitutes the given sentence:
"Official prohibition or order to stop something"

[Allahabad High Court Review Officer (RO), 2019]

A. Ban   **B.** Bane   **C.** Curse   **D.** Ruin

Q.11 Choose the option that is closest in meaning to the word 'Quagmire'.
A. Buffoon   **B.** A traitor
C. An admirer   **D.** A predicament

Q.12 Choose the option that is the passive form of the sentence.
They considered it an impressive building.

[SSC Sub Inspector (CPO), 2019]

A. It was considered to be an impressive building.
B. It can be consider to be an impressive building.
C. It was considering to being an impressive building.
D. It is considered to be an impressive building.

Q.13 Choose the option that is the active form of the sentence.
By whom was this poem written?

[SSC Sub Inspector (CPO), 2019]

A. Who wrote this poem?
B. Who is wrote this poem?
C. Who write this poem?
D. This poem is wrote by whom?

Q.14 With reference to Stupas, consider the following statements:
1. There were four Chhatris on the top of Stupas, which directly touched the Harmika.
2. Sanchi stupa has Pradakshinapatha enclosed within a Vedika with many narrative sculptures depicted on it.
3. The Amravati stupa comprised of Buddha images symbolically presented.
Select the correct answer using the options given below:
A. 1 and 2 only   **B.** 1 and 3 only
C. 2 only   **D.** 1,2 & 3

Ques (15-19):Direction: Complete the sentence with the most appropriate word.

Q.15 You have traveled a long way. You ______ be tired.
A. should   **B.** must   **C.** can   **D.** could

Q.16 You will not be allowed in the Film Festival _______ you have a photo ID card.
A. whether   **B.** unless   **C.** in case   **D.** if

Q.17 By _____ was this done?
A. whose   **B.** why   **C.** whom   **D.** where

Q.18 I write _____ my sister every month.

A. in   B. of   C. to   D. at

Q.19 Manideep _______ in Kerala for four years when his parents came to visit.

A. had been living   B. had live

C. has live   D. has living

Q.20 Direction: Select the option that means the same as the given idiom.

Alive and kicking

A. To be dead inside   B. To excel

C. Lively and active   D. To participate

Q.21 Direction: Choose the option which best expresses the meaning of the idiom/phrase given below.

Be in the same boat

A. To ask someone to travel on the same boat

B. To be in the same difficult situation

C. Willing to do something immediately

D. To force an issue that has already ended

Q.22 Which of the following is a renewable source of energy?

A. Coal   B. Uranium

C. Wind   D. None of these

Q.23 A man sells an article at a 15% loss. If he had sold it for Rs. 450 more, he would have earned a profit of 10%. Find the cost price of this article.

A. 1800   B. 1600   C. 1700   D. 1500

Q.24 The selling price of glass is Rs 1965 and the loss percentage is 25%. If the selling price is Rs 3013, then what will be the profit percentage?

A. 13%   B. 10%   C. 15%   D. 20%

Q.25 A person bought some eggs at a rate Rs. 5 for 3 and sold them at a rate Rs. 12 for 5. If he got Rs. 143, the number of eggs was:

A. 210   B. 200   C. 193   D. 195

Q.26 Direction: In the following question, select the related word from the given alternatives.

Insult : Humiliation

A. Shoot : Death   B. Abuse : Happy

C. Dog : Bark   D. Injury : Pungent

Q.27 Direction: In the following question choose the set of numbers from the four alternative sets that is similar to the given set.

Given set: (246, 257, 358)

A. (233, 343, 345)   B. (273, 365, 367)

C. (143, 226, 237)   D. (145, 235, 324)

Q.28 Direction: In the following question choose the set of numbers from the four alternative sets that is similar to the given set.

Given set: (7, 27, 55)

A. (21, 35, 52)   B. (18, 42, 65)

C. (16, 40, 72)   D. (13, 30, 58)

Q.29 Direction: The following question consists of two words each that have a certain relationship to each other, followed by four lettered pairs of words. Select the lettered pair that has the same relationship as the original pair of words.

Parsing : Grammar

A. Running : Health

B. Praying : God

C. Para trooping : Air force

D. Cleaning : House

Q.30 Direction: In the following question, there is some relationship between the two terms to the left of (: :) and the same relationship holds between the two terms to the right of (: :) is missing which is given in one of the four alternatives given below the question. Find out the term from amongst the alternatives.

JDRC : GGOF : : SPKW : ?

A. KPRF   B. KKOV   C. PSHZ   D. TMUS

Q.31 A car travels a distance of 516 kms. Out of which it travels 50% at a speed of 12 kmph, 25% at a speed of 20 kmph, and the remaining 25% at the speed of 30 kmph. Find the average speed of the car.

A. 13 kmph   B. 15 kmph   C. 16 kmph   D. 18 kmph

Q.32 Travelling at $\frac{3}{4}$ of the normal speed, a person reaches his workplace 15 minutes late. How many minutes does he take usually to reach the workplace?

A. 60 minutes   B. 30 minutes

C. 42 minutes   D. 45 minutes

Q.33 A man walks from P to Q at the rate of 5 km/h and returns from Q to P at 3 km/h. What is his average speed for the whole journey?

A. 3.25 km/h   B. 3.75 km/h

C. 3.5 km/h   D. 8 km/h

Q.34 A boat covers a distance of 36 km in 3h running downstream. While returning, it covers the same distance in 9h. What is the speed of the boat in still water?

A. 8 km/h   B. 12 km/h   C. 14 km/h   D. 10 km/h

Q.35 Select the odd word from the given alternatives:

A. Spanish   B. Hindi   C. Urdu   D. France

Q.36 Find the odd word from the given alternatives.

A. BDGK   B. JLOS   C. NPSW   D. MORU

Q.37 Direction: In the following question, find the odd letters from the given alternatives.

A. DBGE   B. POSR   C. JHMK   D. OMRP

Q.38 Find out the odd number from the given alternatives.

A. 123   B. 727   C. 341   D. 218

Q.39 Find the odd word from the given alternatives.

A. Fire   B. Light   C. Gas   D. Water

Q.40 The average of 5 consecutive numbers is 62. Find the average of smaller and largest numbers.

A. 64   **B.** 60   **C.** 63   **D.** 62

Q.41 Which of the following exactly denotes the average price of all the goods together if, Ramesh buys 'a' number of goods of type 'A' at a price of Rs. 'E' each, 'b' number of goods of type 'B' at a price of Rs. 'F' each and 'c' number of goods of type 'C' at a price of Rs. 'G' each?

A. $\frac{(E+F+G)}{(a+b+c)}$ **B.** $\frac{(AE+BF+CG)}{(a+b+c)}$

C. $\frac{(aE+bF+cG)}{(a+b+c)}$ **D.** $\frac{(aA+bB+cC)}{(a+b+c)}$

Q.42 If a 32 year old man is replaced by a new man, then the average age of 42 men increases by 1 year. What is the age of the new man?

[SSC Constable (GD), 2019]

A. 72 years   **B.** 75 years   **C.** 74 years   **D.** 73 years

Q.43 Prabhat has done $\frac{1}{2}$ of a job in 12 days. Santhosh completes the rest of the job in 6 days. In how many days can they together do the job?

A. 12 days   **B.** 4 days   **C.** 8 days   **D.** 16 days

Q.44 A is 25% more efficient than B, and B takes 6 days more than A to complete a piece of work. How many days will B take to complete the same work?

A. 30 days   **B.** 20 days   **C.** 24 days   **D.** 28 days

Q.45 Two men and 7 women can complete a work in 28 days, whereas 6 men and 16 women can do the same work in 11 days. In how many days will 5 men and 4 women, working together, complete the same work?

[SSC CGL, 2020]

A. 22   **B.** 18   **C.** 14   **D.** 20

Q.46 What decimal of a day is a minute?

[Delhi Forest Guard, 2021]

A. 0.000778   **B.** 0.000727
C. 0.000694   **D.** 0.000667

Q.47 What is the value of 0.420420420... - 0.240240240...?

[Delhi Forest Guard, 2021]

A. $\frac{40}{111}$ **B.** $\frac{15}{111}$ **C.** $\frac{24}{111}$ **D.** $\frac{20}{111}$

Q.48 When 0.353535..... is converted to a fraction, what will be the result?

A. $\frac{35}{99}$ **B.** $\frac{35}{100}$ **C.** $\frac{15}{19}$ **D.** $\frac{1}{19}$

Q.49 Which rays are absorbed by the ozone layer?

A. Infrared rays   **B.** X-rays
C. γ-rays   **D.** Ultraviolet rays

Q.50 The acid injected into the skin when an ant bite is:

A. Nitric acid   **B.** Sulphuric acid
C. Formic acid   **D.** Acetic acid

Q.51 When CO_2 is passed through lime water, lime water becomes:

A. Milky   **B.** Silvery
C. Shiny   **D.** Golden yellow

Q.52 Gobar gas mainly contains which gas?

A. Carbon   **B.** Methane
C. Ethane   **D.** Natural air

Q.53 One of the following is the smallest organelle in a cell:

A. Lysosome   **B.** Spherosome
C. Peroxisome   **D.** Ribosome

Q.54 The invisible line joins the North pole to the South Pole is called:

A. Meridian   **B.** Latitude
C. Equator   **D.** Axial plane

Ques (55-56):Direction: In the following question, the given sentence has four parts marked P, Q, R, and S. Choose the part of the sentence with the error and mark it as your answer. If there is no error, mark 'No error (S)' as your answer.

Q.55 Suresh have never (P) / encouraged nor (Q) /condoned violence. (R) / No error (S)

[SSC Sub Inspector (CPO), 2018], [SSC Sub Inspector (CPO), 2017]

A. P   **B.** Q   **C.** R   **D.** S

Q.56 Scientists intended (P) / to reintroduce and conserve grey wolves (Q) / in their original habitats. (R) / No error (S)

[SSC Sub Inspector (CPO), 2017]

A. P   **B.** Q   **C.** R   **D.** S

Q.57 Where was 'Kheer Bhavani Mela' 2019 celebrated in India?

A. Manipur
B. West Bengal
C. Jammu and Kashmir
D. Jharkhand

Q.58 Bathukamma Utsav, 2019 was held in which state of India?

A. Arunachal Pradesh   **B.** Himachal Pradesh
C. Meghalaya   **D.** Telangana

Q.59 Find the answer figure in which the question figure is embedded?

Question figure:

Answer Figure:

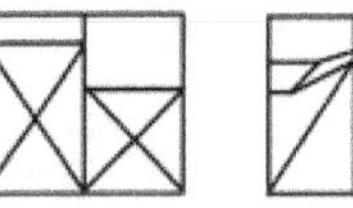 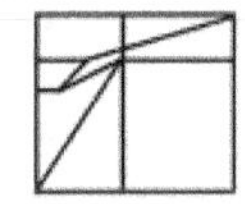 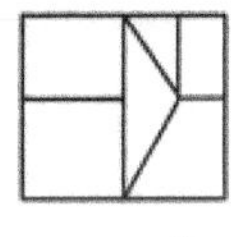 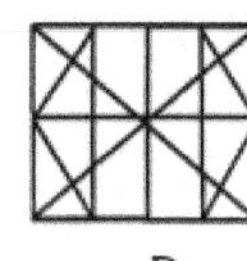

A   B   C   D

A. Figure A   **B.** Figure B   **C.** Figure C   **D.** Figure D

Q.60 Find the answer figure in which the question figure is embedded?

Question Figure:

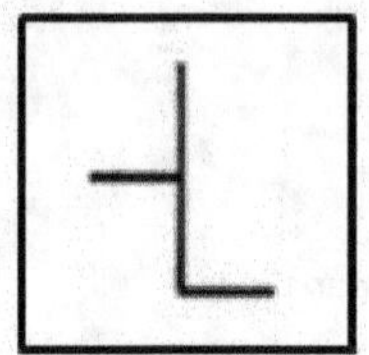

Answer Figure:

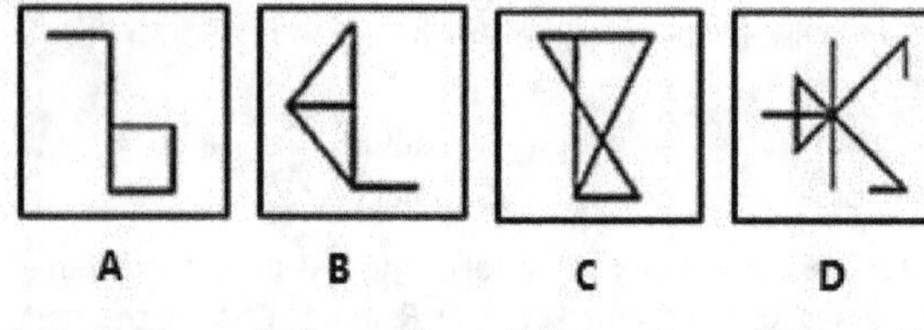

| A | B | C | D |

A. Figure A   **B.** Figure B   **C.** Figure C   **D.** Figure D

Q.61 From the given Answer Figures select the one in which the Question Figure is hidden/embedded.

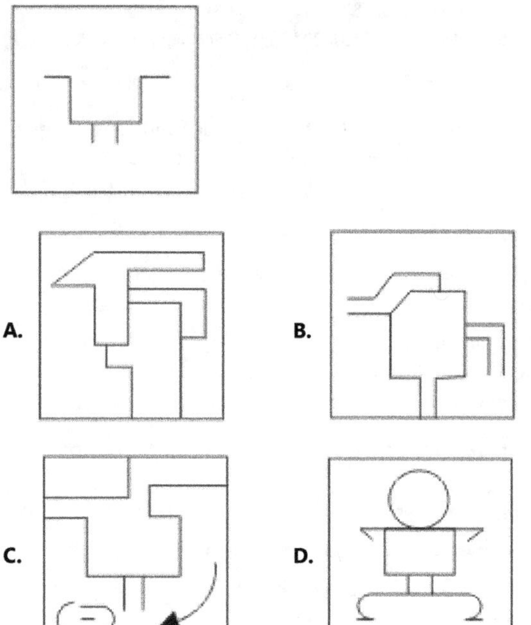

A.   **B.**

C.   **D.**

Q.62 Direction: From the given answer figures select the one in which the question figure is hidden/embedded.

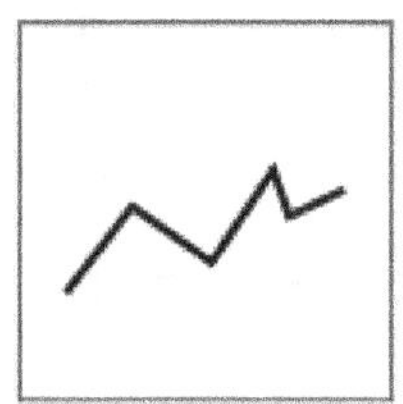

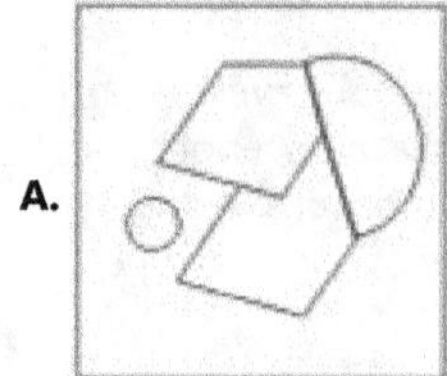
A.

B.

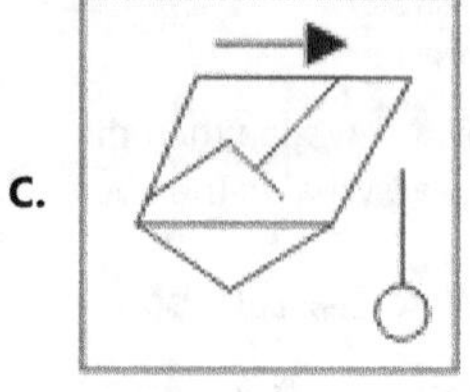
C.
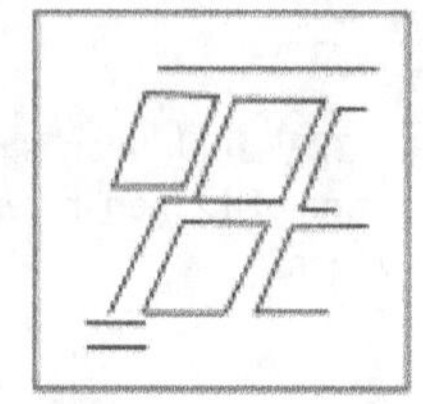
D.

Q.63 From the given answer figures, select the one in which the question figure is hidden/embedded.

Question Figure:

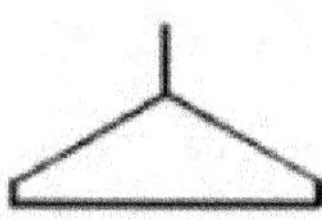

Answer Figure:

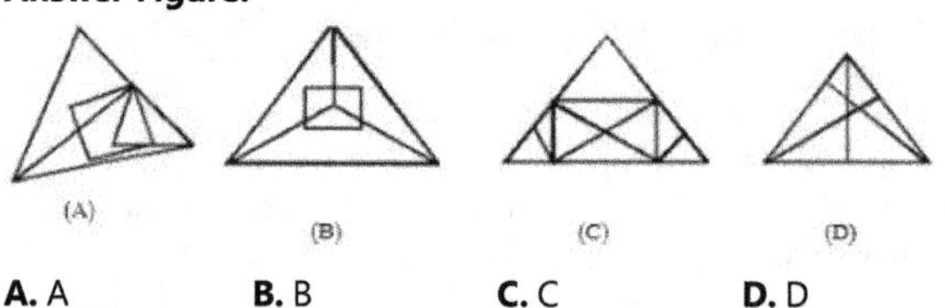

| (A) | (B) | (C) | (D) |

A. A   **B.** B   **C.** C   **D.** D

Q.64 Direction: In each problem, out of the four figures marked (1), (2), (3), and (4), three are similar in a certain manner. However, one figure is not like the other three. Choose the figure which is different from the rest.

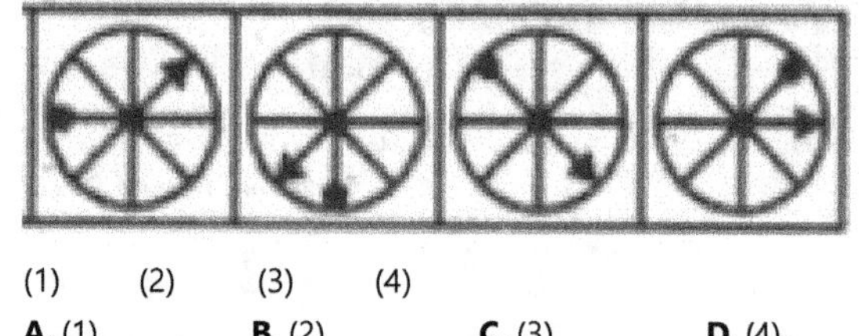

(1)   (2)   (3)   (4)

A. (1)   **B.** (2)   **C.** (3)   **D.** (4)

Q.65 Direction: In each problem, out of the four figures marked (1), (2), (3), and (4), three are similar in a certain manner. However, one figure is not like the other three. Choose the figure which is different from the rest.

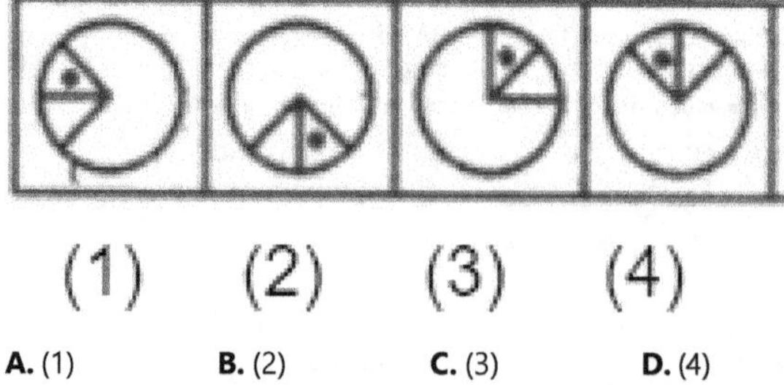

(1)   (2)   (3)   (4)

A. (1)   **B.** (2)   **C.** (3)   **D.** (4)

Q.66 Choose the figure that is different from the rest-

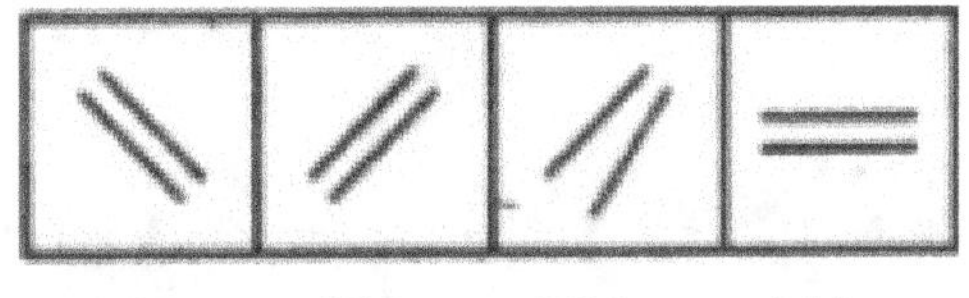

A. (1)   **B.** (2)   **C.** (3)   **D.** (4)

Q.67 Choose the figure that is different from the rest-

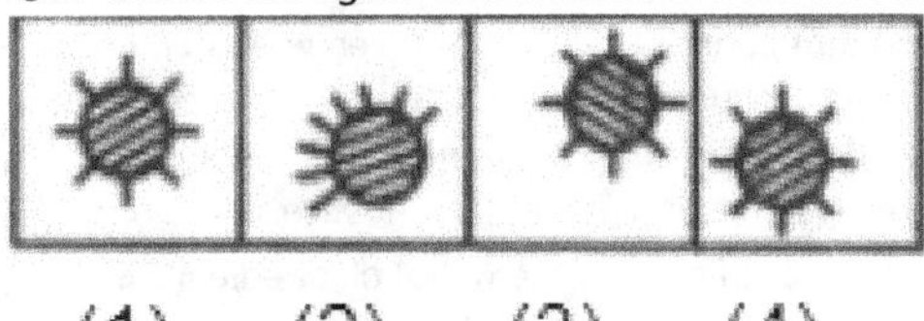

A. (1)   **B.** (2)   **C.** (3)   **D.** (4)

Q.68 Choose the figure that is different from the rest-

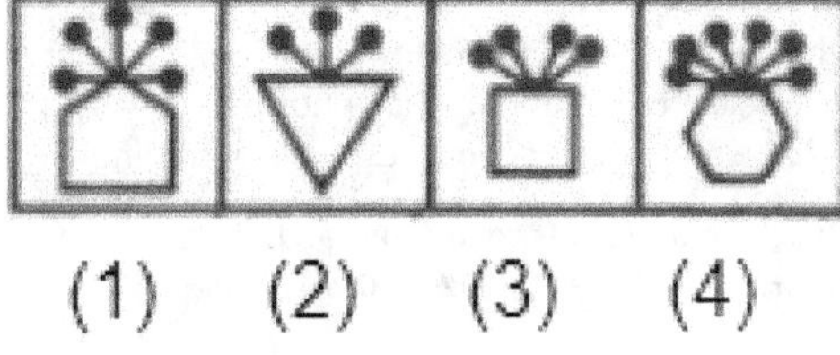

A. (1)   **B.** (2)   **C.** (3)   **D.** (4)

Q.69 A pot is filled with 3 parts fruit juice and 5 parts with water. By removing how much the amount of the mixture from it and filling the same amount of juice in it, the ratio of fruit juice and water will be 1: 1?

[UP Police Sub Inspector, 2017]

A. $\frac{13}{19}$ **B.** $\frac{1}{5}$ **C.** $\frac{11}{6}$ **D.** $\frac{7}{9}$

Q.70 A seller has some apples and oranges in the ratio of $7 : 5$. If 25 apples were rotten and he bought 25 new oranges, then the new ratio will be $1 : 5$. Find how many apples were left after the rotten apples?

A. 14   **B.** 8   **C.** 12   **D.** 10

Q.71 The ratio of the number of boys to the number of girls in a school of 640 students, is $5:3$. If 30 more girls are admitted in the school, then how many more boys should be admitted so that the ratio of boys to that of the girl? becomes $14:9$.

A. 20   **B.** 15   **C.** 25   **D.** 30

Q.72 Which badminton player recently clinched the 'Indonesia Masters title'?

A. Carolina Marin   **B.** Ratchanok Intanon
C. P V Sindhu   **D.** Nozomi Okuhara

Q.73 Select the option that correctly represents the relationship among the following:

Advocate, Gardener, Cook

A. 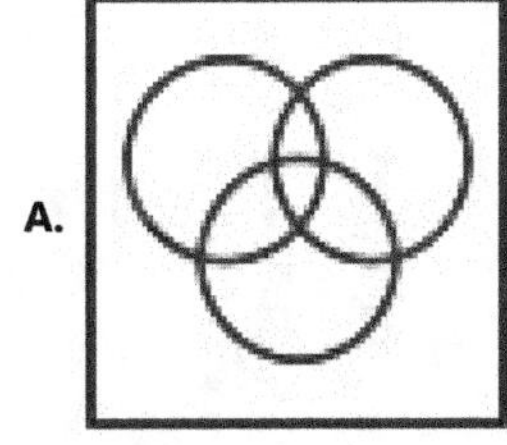   **B.** 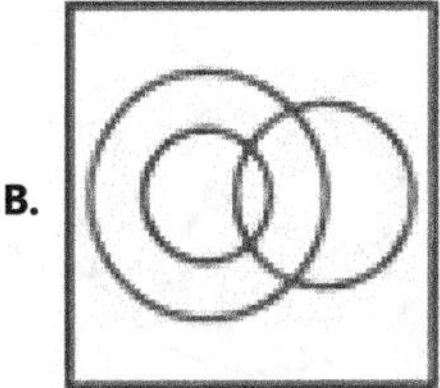

C. 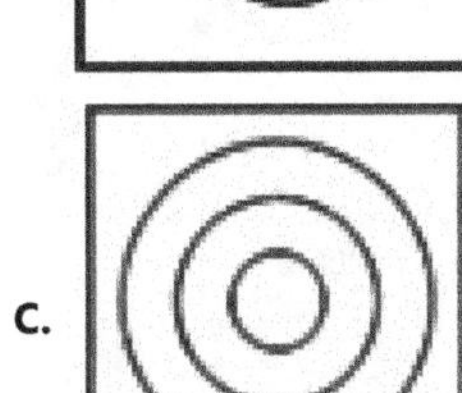   **D.** 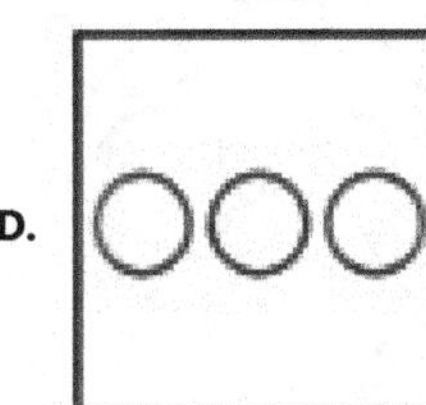

Q.74 Select the option that correctly represents the relationship among the following:

Summer, Winter, and Season

A. 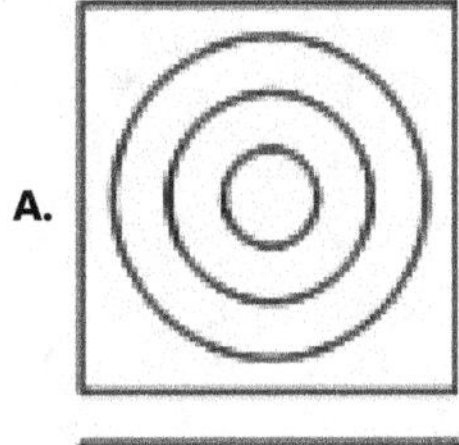   **B.** 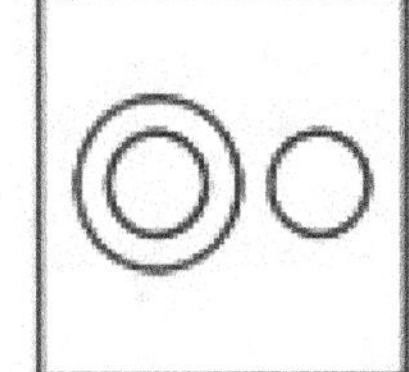

C. 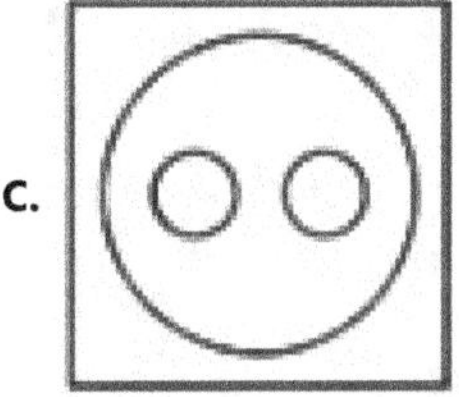   **D.** 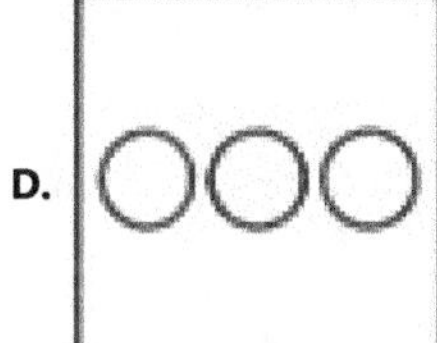

Q.75 Select the Venn diagram that best illustrates the relationship between the three given classes.

Engineers, Professionals and Doctors

A. 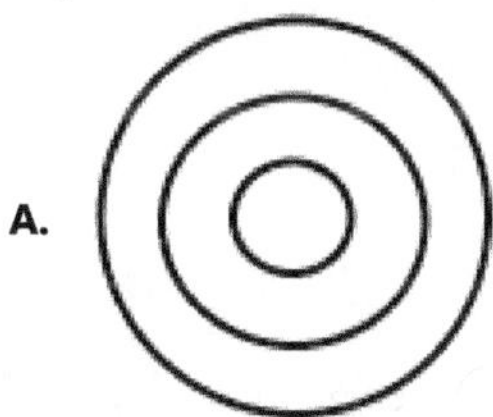

B. 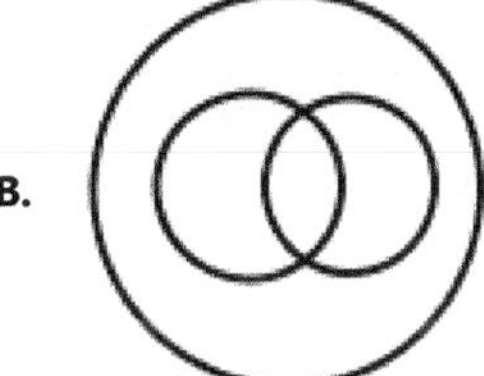

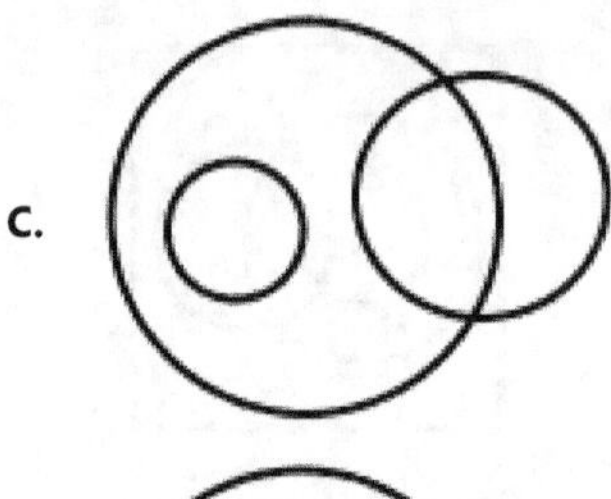

C.

D.

Q.76 Which of the following diagrams the relationship among Vegetable, Pumpkin, and Jackfruit

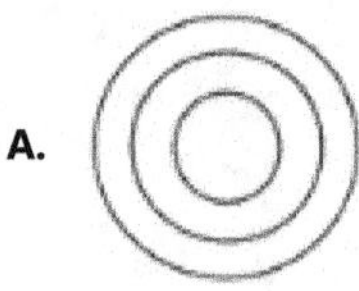

A.

B.

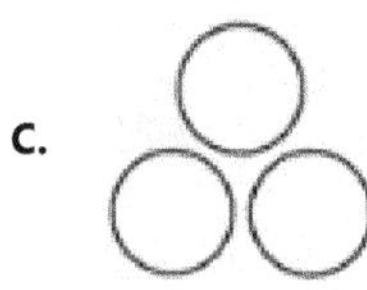

C.

D.

Q.77 Which of the following diagrams the relationship among Day, Week, Year.

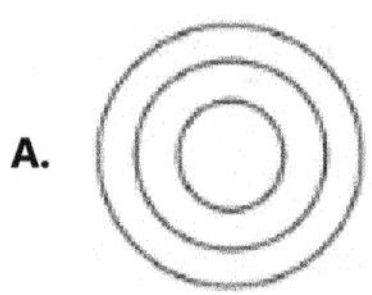

A.

B.

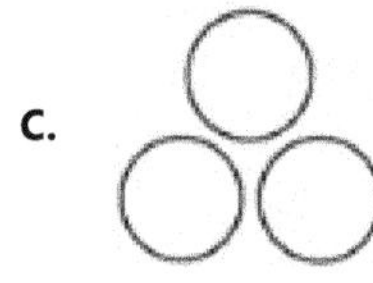

C.

D.

Q.78 Direction: Arrange the words given below in a meaningful sequence.

1. Interview

2. Preliminary examination

3. Form fill up

4. Mains examination

5. Final result

A. 3, 1, 2, 4, 5   **B.** 3, 2, 4, 1, 5

C. 1, 2, 4, 5, 3   **D.** 2, 5, 1, 4, 3

Q.79 Direction: In the following question, arrange the given words in meaningful sequence and then choose the most appropriate sequence from amongst the alternative provided below :

(A) Poverty

(B) Population

(C) Death

(D) Unemployment

(E) Disease

A. C, D, B, E, A   **B.** B, D, A, E, C

C. B, C, D, E, A   **D.** A, B, C, D, E

Q.80 Which of the following statements is/are incorrect?

1. Civil contempt of court is written or spoken words or any act that scandalizes the court or lowers its authority or prejudices or interferes with the due course of a judicial proceeding or interferes/obstructs the administration of justice.

2. Criminal contempt of court is the willful disobedience of a court order or judgment or willful breach of an undertaking given to a court.

A. 1 only   **B.** 2 only

C. Both 1 and 2   **D.** Neither 1 nor 2

Ques (81-83):Directions: Each item in this section consists of sentences with an underlined word followed by four words or a group of words. Select the option that is opposite in meaning to the underlined word and mark your response accordingly.

Q.81 The <u>archaic</u> thinking leads to unfounded beliefs.
[Indian Military Academy (IMA), 2020], [Officers Training Academy (OTA), 2020]

A. Antiquated   **B.** Outmoded

C. Beyond the times   **D.** Modern

Q.82 Police had to resort to tear gas to <u>diffuse</u> tension among the crowd.
[Indian Military Academy (IMA), 2020], [Officers Training Academy (OTA), 2020]

A. Concentrate   **B.** Scatter

C. Disperse   **D.** Strew

Q.83 <u>Unrest</u> in some pockets made the city dwellers confine themselves at home.
[Indian Military Academy (IMA), 2020], [Officers Training Academy (OTA), 2020]

A. Turbulence   **B.** Unease

C. Apprehension   **D.** Calm

Q.84 A shopkeeper sells an article at its marked price of Rs. 7,500 and charges sales-tax at the rate of 12% from the customer. If the shopkeeper pays a VAT of ₹ 180 on selling of an article, then the price inclusive of tax paid by the shopkeeper is
[Joint Entrance Examination (Polytechnic), 2017]

A. Rs. 6,720   **B.** Rs. 6,520

C. Rs. 6,000   **D.** Rs. 7,000

Q.85 If Ramesh gets 10% more salary than Mohan, then Mohan gets.

A. 10% less than Ramesh

B. 10% more than Ramesh

C. $9\frac{1}{11}$% less than Ramesh

D. $9\frac{9}{11}$% more than Ramesh

Q.86 A person got a 10 % increase in his salary. If his salary was Rs. 50000, then the new salary is:

A. Rs. 55000   **B.** Rs. 60000

C. Rs. 45000   **D.** Rs.65000

Q.87 Direction: Complete the given sentence using the appropriate pronoun from the following options:

This is the boy _____ scored the highest marks.

[Allahabad High Court Review Officer (RO), 2019]

A. it   **B.** whose   **C.** which   **D.** who

Q.88 Direction: Fill in the blank with the most appropriate option as given:

Giving money to the poor is a/an _____ act of service to the poor.

[Allahabad High Court Review Officer (RO), 2019]

A. benevolent   **B.** bemused

C. atrocious   **D.** bad

Q.89 Direction: Among the following options, select the word that can best complete the given sentence:

When I met Ram yesterday, it was the first time I _____ him since my graduation.

[Allahabad High Court Review Officer (RO), 2019]

A. met   **B.** had been meet

C. have meet   **D.** have been seeing

Q.90 Direction: Complete the given sentences using the correct form of the verb in the brackets. Choose present simple or present continuous tense.

a. What's your skirt made from? It _____ like wool.

b. I won't be coming to work today. I _____ very well. (feel)

[Allahabad High Court Review Officer (RO), 2019]

A. feels, not feeling   **B.** feels, don't feel

C. is feeling, feeling   **D.** feeling, feel

Ques (91-95):Direction: Read the following passage carefully and answer the questions given below it in the context of the passage.

The world is fast becoming a global village due to the increasing daily requirement of energy by all population across the world but, the earth in its form cannot change. The need for energy and its related services to satisfy human social and economic development, welfare, and health is increasing. Returning to renewables to help mitigate climate change is an excellent approach that needs to be sustainable in order to meet the energy demand of future generations. The study reviewed the opportunities associated with renewable energy sources which include: Energy Security, Energy Access, Social and Economic Development, Climate Change Mitigation, and reduction of environmental and health impacts.

Despite these opportunities, there are challenges that hinder the sustainability of renewable energy sources towards climate change mitigation. These challenges include Market failures, lack of information, access to raw materials for future renewable resource deployment, and our daily carbon footprint. The study suggested some measures and policy recommendations which when considered would help achieve the goal of renewable energy thus reducing emissions, mitigate climate change and provide a clean environment as well as clean energy for all and future generations.

Q.91 What is the magnificent perspective that needs to be maintained?

A. Challenging the requirements of energy

B. Looking back to renewable sources to reduce the changes in climate

C. Looking back to non- renewable sources to reduce the changes in climate

D. Looking back to renewable sources to increase the changes in climate

Q.92 What are Market failures, lack of information, access to raw materials for future renewable resource deployment, and our daily carbon footprint as used in the passage?

A. These are the challenges that create obstructions to reduce climatic changes

B. These are the factors that are necessary for uplifting energy consumption

C. These are the names of various studies

D. These are the challenges that helps to reduce climatic changes

Q.93 Why is energy required in our day to day life?

A. Because it is helpful for controlling population

B. Because it is helpful for the development of human beings that further leads to productivity

C. Because it is helpful for digesting foods

D. Because it is helpful for the development of science

Q.94 What are the opportunities which are connected to renewable sources of energy?

A. Fuel Security, Fuel Access, Political Development and an increase in environmental impacts

B. Market profits, abundance of knowledge and daily carbon traces

C. Market failures, lack of information, access to raw materials for future renewable resource deployment, and our daily carbon footprint

D. Energy Security, Energy Access, Social and Economic Development, Climate Change Mitigation, and reduction of environmental and health impacts

Q.95 The main purpose of the passage is to:

A. Inform   **B.** Apologize

C. Claim   **D.** Praise

Ques (96-100):Direction: Select a suitable figure from the four alternatives that would complete the figure.

Q.96

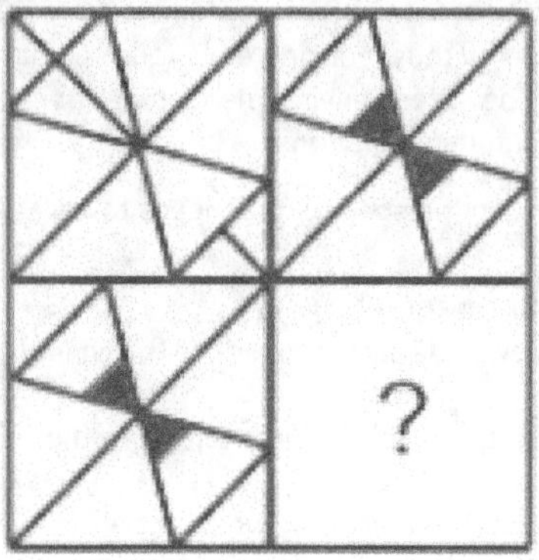

[Jawahar Navodaya Entrance Class VI, 2022], [SSC MTS, 2021],
[Jawahar Navodaya Entrance Class VI, 2021]

A.

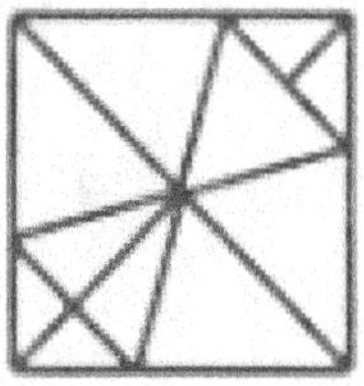

B.

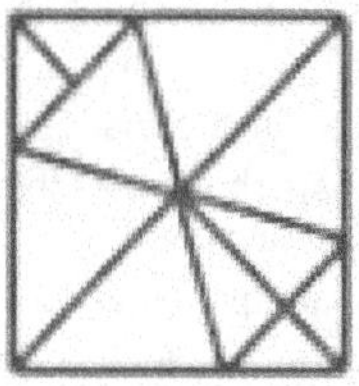

C.

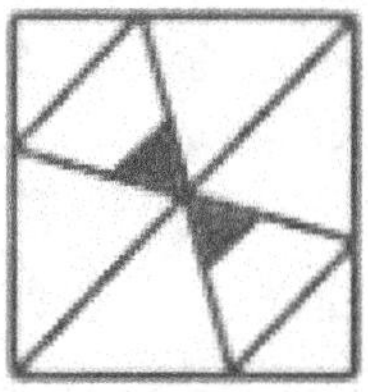

D.

Q.97

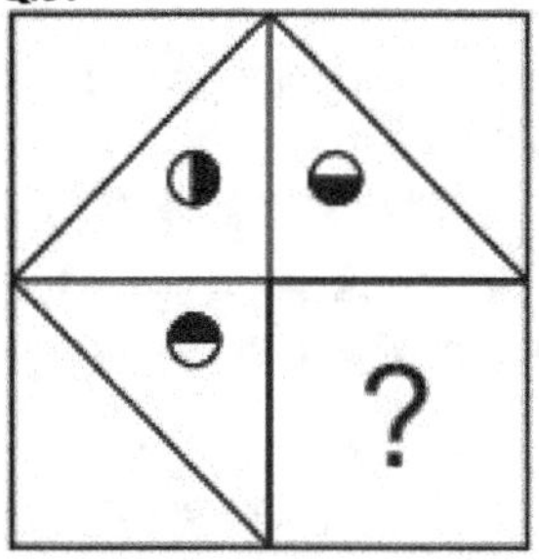

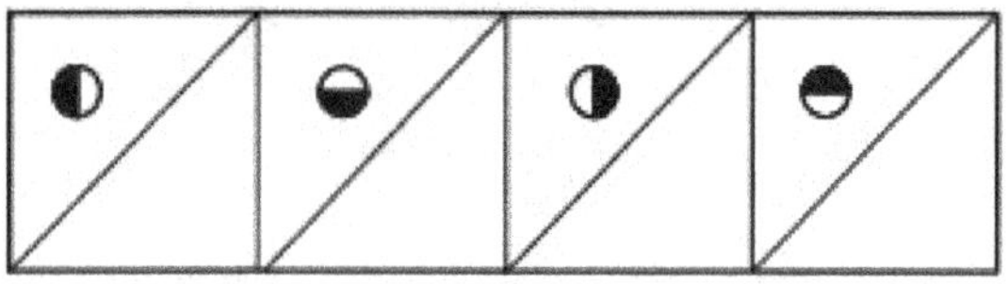

(a)   (b)   (c)   (d)

A. (a)   **B.** (b)   **C.** (c)   **D.** (d)

Q.98

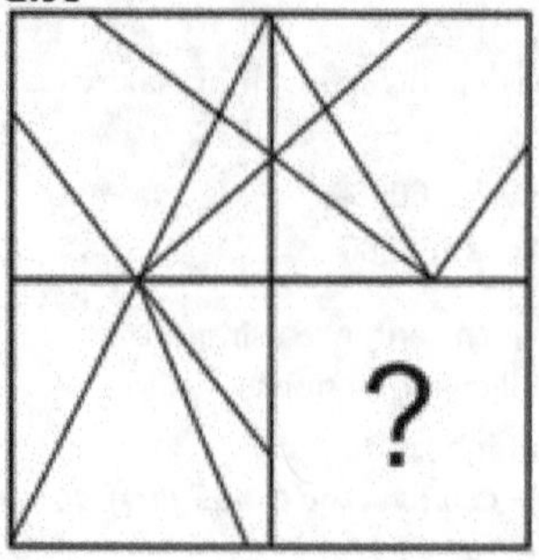

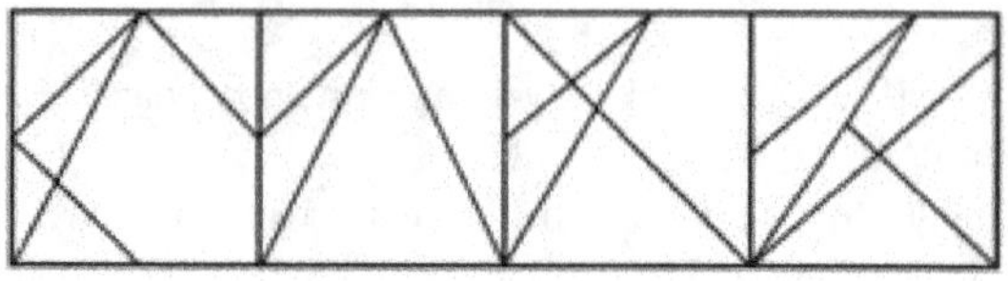

(a)   (b)   (c)   (d)

A. (a)   **B.** (b)   **C.** (c)   **D.** (d)

Q.99

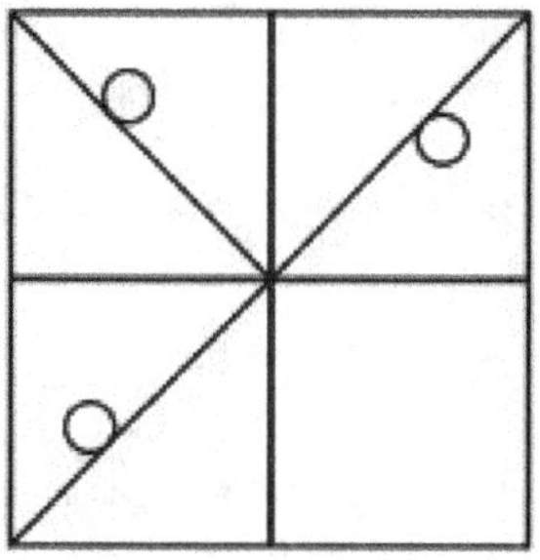

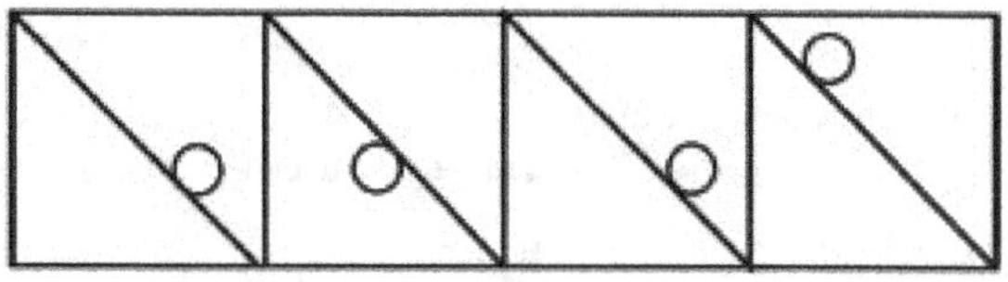

(a)   (b)   (c)   (d)

A. (a)   **B.** (b)   **C.** (c)   **D.** (d)

Q.100

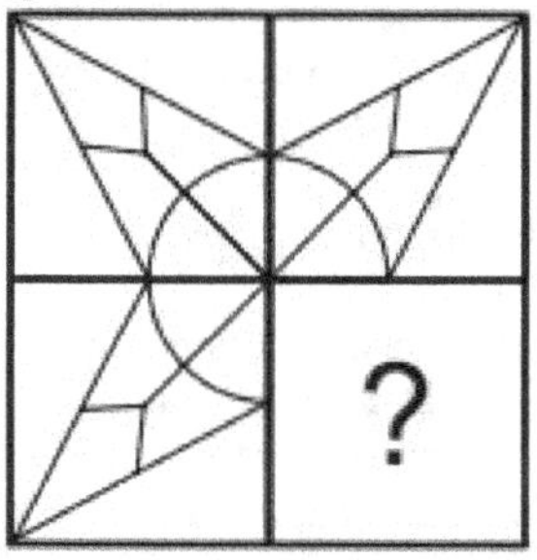

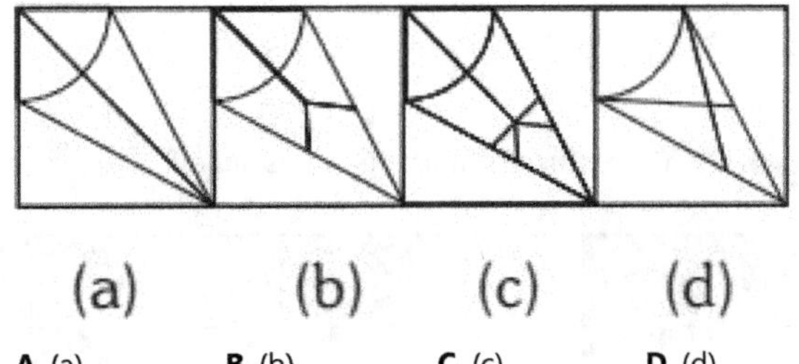

A. (a)

B. (b)

C. (c)

D. (d)

// Smart Answer Sheet //

Correct — Percentage of students who answered correctly. **Skipped** — Percentage of students who skipped.

Q.	Ans.	Correct / Skipped	Q.	Ans.	Correct / Skipped	Q.	Ans.	Correct / Skipped	Q.	Ans.	Correct / Skipped	Q.	Ans.	Correct / Skipped	Q.	Ans.	Correct / Skipped
1	B	68.21 % / 31.79 %	18	C	89.73 % / 10.01 %	35	D	76.19 % / 14.0 %	52	B	83.61 % / 13.68 %	69	B	45.19 % / 40.63 %	86	A	60.16 % / 32.33 %
2	B	65.41 % / 33.19 %	19	A	14.03 % / 84.03 %	36	D	43.11 % / 39.35 %	53	D	54.22 % / 43.04 %	70	D	66.29 % / 33.4 %	87	D	76.64 % / 20.14 %
3	D	64.96 % / 33.87 %	20	C	86.13 % / 10.26 %	37	B	29.0 % / 70.03 %	54	A	65.97 % / 32.14 %	71	A	41.86 % / 53.62 %	88	A	69.02 % / 30.29 %
4	A	57.85 % / 31.66 %	21	B	49.35 % / 47.05 %	38	D	53.52 % / 34.3 %	55	A	14.17 % / 74.71 %	72	B	68.93 % / 30.81 %	89	A	81.41 % / 10.2 %
5	B	88.15 % / 11.48 %	22	C	88.32 % / 11.22 %	39	D	48.97 % / 45.69 %	56	D	19.23 % / 79.0 %	73	A	50.65 % / 36.99 %	90	B	10.21 % / 75.87 %
6	C	63.98 % / 31.82 %	23	A	47.24 % / 52.15 %	40	D	20.47 % / 78.3 %	57	C	79.29 % / 16.02 %	74	C	81.53 % / 14.67 %	91	B	44.98 % / 38.44 %
7	C	68.47 % / 31.3 %	24	C	51.58 % / 32.1 %	41	C	53.9 % / 42.74 %	58	D	83.4 % / 13.98 %	75	D	84.45 % / 15.0 %	92	A	57.38 % / 41.72 %
8	A	65.47 % / 32.81 %	25	D	63.86 % / 31.01 %	42	C	40.55 % / 45.81 %	59	D	83.8 % / 15.52 %	76	B	49.14 % / 36.51 %	93	B	54.74 % / 34.52 %
9	D	83.36 % / 10.58 %	26	A	88.89 % / 10.33 %	43	C	63.71 % / 31.53 %	60	B	82.19 % / 11.53 %	77	A	78.16 % / 15.14 %	94	D	57.14 % / 42.15 %
10	A	83.65 % / 11.84 %	27	B	10.52 % / 69.81 %	44	A	65.67 % / 30.68 %	61	D	13.46 % / 82.6 %	78	B	45.55 % / 43.34 %	95	A	47.54 % / 51.96 %
11	D	66.27 % / 33.39 %	28	C	66.63 % / 32.31 %	45	A	50.42 % / 34.43 %	62	B	59.97 % / 34.84 %	79	B	46.66 % / 45.03 %	96	B	47.32 % / 42.0 %
12	A	48.97 % / 31.83 %	29	C	47.61 % / 31.87 %	46	C	48.61 % / 33.89 %	63	B	86.11 % / 11.45 %	80	C	55.24 % / 32.5 %	97	A	66.33 % / 31.2 %
13	A	79.42 % / 19.5 %	30	C	60.41 % / 31.44 %	47	D	80.23 % / 16.4 %	64	C	76.55 % / 18.5 %	81	D	24.31 % / 75.16 %	98	B	62.64 % / 30.94 %
14	C	19.04 % / 78.92 %	31	C	43.64 % / 38.91 %	48	A	86.51 % / 11.74 %	65	A	89.84 % / 10.01 %	82	A	83.89 % / 10.43 %	99	B	63.25 % / 31.16 %
15	B	42.64 % / 50.49 %	32	D	45.68 % / 45.14 %	49	D	64.39 % / 33.7 %	66	C	82.31 % / 14.85 %	83	D	48.4 % / 35.32 %	100	B	61.74 % / 35.68 %
16	B	13.1 % / 83.5 %	33	B	58.71 % / 38.88 %	50	C	54.02 % / 32.1 %	67	B	44.69 % / 35.06 %	84	A	46.17 % / 48.48 %			
17	C	79.08 % / 15.85 %	34	A	67.92 % / 30.96 %	51	A	61.78 % / 32.78 %	68	A	44.12 % / 48.74 %	85	C	53.92 % / 45.66 %			

//Hints and Solutions//

1. The Mazagon Dock Shipbuilders on 20 April 2022, launched INS Vagsheer, the last of the six submarines under Project 75. The submarine was launched by Defence Secretary Ajay Kumar.

Named after sandfish, a deadly deep water sea predator of the Indian Ocean, the first submarine 'Vagsheer' was commissioned in Indian navy December 1974. It was decommissioned in Indian navy April 1997.

Hence, the correct option is (B).

2. The Indian Railways has placed a purchase order for 39,000 wheels for LHB Coaches from the Chinese manufacturer Taiyuan against a global tender." Due to the ongoing war between Russia and Ukraine, the supplies against the ongoing contracts with the firms from Russia and Ukraine have been affected. The contract rate is 1.68% higher than the rate per wheel given in a Ukrainian firm's earlier Letter of Acceptance (LoA).

Hence, the correct option is (B).

3. Prime Minister Narendra Modi inaugurated Semicon India Conference-2022 in Bengaluru.

To make India a global hub for Semiconductor Design, Manufacturing, and Technology Development which will help propel the vision of the India Semiconductor Mission.

Semiconductors are materials with electrical conductivity values falling between a conductor and an insulator.

Hence, the correct option is (D).

4. Payal Jangid has been awarded the 'Changemaker Award' by the Bill and Melinda Gates Foundation for the year 2019.

Founded by Bill Gates and his wife Melinda Gates this organization help people lead healthy, productive lives. In developing countries, the organization focuses on improving people's health and providing them with the chance to lift themselves out of hunger and extreme poverty. Its headquarters is in Washington, USA.

Payal Jangid was awarded the 'Changemaker Award' at Goalkeepers Global Goals Awards 2019. She was awarded for her work towards the abolition of child marriage in her village. Her mentors were Nobel Peace Laureate Kailash Satyarthi and child rights activist Sumedha Kailash.

Hence, the correct option is (A).

5. India's Lakshya Sen won a silver medal at the German Open 2022 on 13 March 2022. He lost the men's singles final to Thailand's Kunlavut Vitidsarn. He lost 18-21, 15-21 in the final.

Lakshya Sen has become the 1st Indian to clinch a silver medal at the Badminton World Federation BWF Superseries 300 German Open 2022.

Hence, the correct option is (B).

6. Given:

Rate of interest $= 2.5\%$ per month

Amount paid after 6 months $=$ Rs. 13110

Amount, $A = P + SI$

Simple interest, $SI = \dfrac{P \times R \times T}{100}$

Where $P \rightarrow$ Principal, $R \rightarrow$ rate of interest, $T \rightarrow$ time

Suppose the sum borrowed be Rs. x

$$SI = \dfrac{x \times 2.5 \times 6}{100} = 0.15x$$
$$A = x + 0.15x = 1.15x$$
$$1.15x = 13110$$
$$\Rightarrow x = 11400$$
$$\Rightarrow \text{Amount of interest} = 0.15 \times 11400$$
$$= \text{Rs. } 1710$$

Hence, the correct option is (C).

7. Given:

The rate of interest for 1st 2 years is 8%

For the next 3 years it is 10%

For the period beyond 5 years it is 12.5%

Principal $= Rs\,20\,L$

Amoun paid $= Rs\,36.7\,L$

Amount $= P + SI$

Simple Interest, $SI = \dfrac{P \times R \times T}{100}$

Where $P \rightarrow$ Principal, $R \rightarrow$ rate of interest, $T \rightarrow$ time

Total $SI = A - P = 36.7\,L - 20L$

Total $SI = 16.7\,L$

SI for first 2 years $= 20\,L \times 2 \times \dfrac{8}{100} = 3.2\,L$

SI for next 3 years $= 20\,L \times 3 \times \dfrac{10}{100} = 6\,L$

So, total SI for the first 5 years $= 9.2\,L$

Then, the rest of the interest is obtained at the rate of 12.5%

Remaining interest $= 16.7\,L - 9.2\,L = 7.5\,L$

SI for next N years $= 20\,L \times N \times 12.5\% = 7.5\,L$

$$N = 7.5\,L \times \dfrac{8}{20}\,L \quad (12.5\% \rightarrow \tfrac{1}{8}\,in \text{ fraction })$$

$$N = 3$$

That is, total years $= 2 + 3 + 3 = 8$ years.

Hence, the correct option is (C).

8. Given:

Initial Rate $= 8\%$

Time $= 3$ years

Rate in mutual fund $= 8.5\%$ and time $= 4$ years

Simple interest $= \dfrac{P \times R \times T}{100}$

Let the sum be Rs. x

Simple interest from the bank $= \dfrac{x \times 8 \times 3}{100}$

$$\Rightarrow \dfrac{24x}{100}$$

Earnings in the form of interest from mutual fund $= \dfrac{(x \times 8.5 \times 4)}{100}$

$$\Rightarrow \frac{34x}{100}$$

According to question:

$$\frac{34x}{100} - \frac{24x}{100} = \text{Rs.}\,500$$

$$\Rightarrow 10x = 50000 \text{ or } x = 5000$$

$\therefore$ The sum invested $=$ Rs. 5000

Hence, the correct option is (A).

9. The first Chief of Defense Staff of India was General Bipin Rawat.

Chief of Defense Staff (CDS) is the head of Indian Armed forces and the head of the Department of Military Affairs, under the Ministry of Defense. The office was created in December 2019. He will serve the full three-year term.

Hence, the correct option is (D).

10. Ban: an official order that prevents something from happening.

Bane: a cause of continuous trouble or unhappiness.

Curse: magic words that are intended to bring bad luck to someone.

Ruin: the process or state of being spoiled or destroyed.

Therefore, the word that best substitutes the given sentence is 'Ban.'

Hence, the correct option is (A).

11. Quagmire (noun): An area of soft, wet ground that you sink into if you try to walk on it.

Predicament (noun): An unpleasant situation that is difficult to get out of.

For example:

1. At the end of the game, the pitch was a real quagmire.
2. She is hoping to get a loan from her bank to help her out of her financial predicament.

Therefore, the word Predicament is the most appropriate synonym for Quagmire.

Hence, the correct option is (D).

12. The above-given sentence is in the active voice.

We need to change it in the passive voice.

The following steps are required to change the given sentence into passive voice:

- In the passive form, the subject and the object will be interchanged. 'It' will become the subject.
- The tense(simple past tense) will change according to the following structure:-
    - Active Voice - Subject + did + V_1 or V_2 + Object.
    - Passive Voice - Object + was/were + V_3 + by + Object.

Option (B) and (D) are in the present tense.

Option (C) is in the past continuous tense.

Hence, the correct option is (A).

13. The above-given sentence is in the passive voice.

We need to change it into an active voice.

We need to follow the given steps for converting the given sentence into active voice:

- In sentences containing 'who', the passive starts with 'by whom'.
- The following structure is followed:-
    - Active Voice - Who + V_1 + Object?
    - Passive Voice - By whom + helping verb + Object + V_3?
- Thus, 'written' will be converted to 'wrote'.

Hence, the correct option is (A).

14. The three chatras were elevated from the Harmika with the help of Yasti.

These three chatras represented Triratna of Buddhism are:

- Buddha (enlightened).
- Dhamma (doctrine).
- Sangha (order).

So, statement 1 is incorrect.

- Like the Amravati stupa, Sanchi stupa also has a pradakshinapatha enclosed within vedika on which many narrative sculptures are depicted.

So, statement 2 is correct.

- Though the early phase of Buddhist architecture marks the absence of Buddha's images, nut during the later phase in 2nd and 3rd century CE, the Buddha images are carved on the drum slabs and many other places.
- Buddha is shown only symbolically as an empty throne, feet, chatras, stupas etc. in Sanchi stupa.

So, statement 3 is incorrect.

Hence, the correct option is (C).

15. Can is used to show a possibility.

Could is the past tense of can.

Should is used to give advice or logical answer.

Must is used when there is a certain obligation or an order. It is a modal verb most commonly used to express certainty.

In the given sentence, it is suggesting that traveling a long way has made the person tired. So, must be used here.

Complete Sentence:

You have traveled a long way. You **must** be tired.

Hence, the correct option is (B).

16. In case is used to give a certain case for an event.

Unless means except if or only if.

Whether is used to express a doubt.

If is a condition to any event.

Here, in the sentence, it is suggesting that only if one is having a photo card then he will be allowed. So unless will be the correct answer.

Complete Sentence:

You will not be allowed in the Film Festival **unless** you have a photo ID card.

Hence, the correct option is (B).

17. This is an interrogative pronoun. We generally use 'whom' when referring to a person.

Complete Sentence:

By **whom** was this done?

Hence, the correct option is (C).

18. In - Used to describe the position of someone or something in an enclosed area or place surrounding it.

Of - Used for belonging to, relating to, or connected with someone or something; to indicate the reference.

To - Used when there is a specific destination in mind.

At - Used for precise times.

With reference to the context, the letter is written to her sister. so, the preposition to should be used here.

Complete Sentence:

I write **to** my sister every month.

Hence, the correct option is (C).

19. From the given statement, it is clear that an action (living in Kerela) continued for some time in the past up to another moment (when parents came to visit) in the past. In these cases, the past perfects continuous tense is used which has the following format:

Subject + had been +V1 + ing + Object.

Complete Sentence:

Manideep **had been living** in Kerala for four years when his parents came to visit.

Hence, the correct option is (A).

20.

- The idiom, 'Alive and kicking' means continue to live or exist and be full of energy.

- For example, She hadn't met her younger sister after her marriage and was delighted to see her alive and kicking at a social event last weekend.

Hence, the correct option is (C).

21. The meaning of the idiom -"Be in the same boat" is 'To be in the same difficult situation'.

Example: When he lost his job he did not feel too bad as, after the company downsized, many others were in the same boat.

Hence, the correct option is (B).

22. Renewable sources of energy are the sources that get replenished after usage and consumption in a finite amount of time. Examples of renewable sources of energy are- Solar energy, Wind energy, Hydro energy, Tidal energy.

Hence, the correct option is (C).

23. According to the question,

Man when sells the article at loss,

Loss percentage = x% = 15%

Cost Price = 100

Selling Price = 100 - x = 100 - 15 = 85

Now, if he sells the article to earn the profit of 10%,

Profit percentage = x% = 10%

Cost Price = 100

Selling Price = 100 + x = 100 + 10 = 110

The difference in Selling price = 110 - 85 = 25

And the sentence in the question says "if the product was sold for Rs. 450 more" which means the difference in amount is Rs. 450.

Therefore, 25% = 450

And we need to determine the Cost Price which is 100%, So

100% = ?

The equation for calculation becomes

$$\frac{450}{25} \times 100 = 1800 \text{ (Cost Price)}$$

This method can be remembered in the form of formula as:

$$\text{Cost} = \frac{\text{More gain} \times 100}{\text{Difference in percentage}}$$

Hence, the correct option is (A).

24. According to the question,

Selling price of glass = Rs. 1965

And loss = 25%

$$\therefore CP = \frac{1965}{75} \times 100 = \text{Rs. } 2620$$

If selling price = Rs. 3013

$$\therefore \text{Profit } \% = \frac{(3013 - 2620)}{2620} \times 100$$

$$= \frac{3930}{262} = 15\%$$

Hence, the correct option is (C).

25. Let the number of eggs be x

Cost of 3 eggs = Rs. 5

Cost of 1 egg = $\frac{5}{3} \times x$

So, CP = $\frac{5}{3} \times x$

Eggs sold = 5

Price at which eggs are sold = Rs. 12

So, SP = $\frac{12}{5x}$

Profit = SP - CP

$$143 = \frac{12}{5x} - \frac{5}{3x}$$

(For Solving, take the LCM of 3 and 5 and solve through it)

x = 195

Thus, he purchased 195 eggs.

Hence, the correct option is (D).

26. As for insult results in humiliation, shooting results in death.

Hence, the correct option is (A).

27. The pattern followed in (246, 257, 358)

As in 246 → 2 + 4 + 6 = 12

257 → 2 + 5 + 7 = 14

358 → 3 + 5 + 8 = 16

Now we will check for given sets,

(233, 343, 345)

233 → 2 + 3 + 3 = 8

343 → 3 + 4 + 3 = 10

345 → 3 + 4 + 5 = 12

(273, 365, 367)

273 → 2 + 7 + 3 = 12

365 → 3 + 6 + 5 = 14

367 → 3 + 6 + 7 = 16

(143, 226, 237)

143 → 1 + 4 + 3 = 8

226 → 2 + 2 + 6 = 10

237 → 2 + 3 + 7 = 12

(145, 235, 325)

145 → 1 + 4 + 5 = 10

235 → 2 + 3 + 5 = 10

325 → 3 + 2 + 4 = 9

Thus (273, 365, 367) is the answer.

Hence, the correct option is (B).

28. The pattern followed in (7, 27, 55) is:

Sum of 1st and 3rd = 7 + 55 = 62 and ((27 × 2) + 8) = 54 + 8 = 62

Now we will check for given sets,

(21, 35, 52) → 21 + 52 = 73 and ((35 × 2) + 8) = 78

(18, 42, 65) → 18 + 65 = 83 and ((42 × 2) + 8) = 92

(16, 40, 72) → 16 + 72 = 88 and ((40 × 2) + 8) = 88

(13, 30, 58) → 13 + 58 = 71 and ((30 × 2) + 8) = 68

Hence, the correct option is (C).

29. Parsing means processing linguistic data in real-time as it is being spoken or read, in order to determine its linguistic structure and meaning whereas Grammar means the branch of linguistics that deals with syntax and morphology.

So Parsing is an essential part of grammar.

Based on a similar pattern Para trooping is an essential part of the Air force as Para trooping is the process of warfare in which troops parachuted into enemy territory to fight.

Running makes a person healthy and praying is done to God and cleaning is done in a house but in all these first is not essential to do to get the second one.

Hence, the correct option is (C).

30.

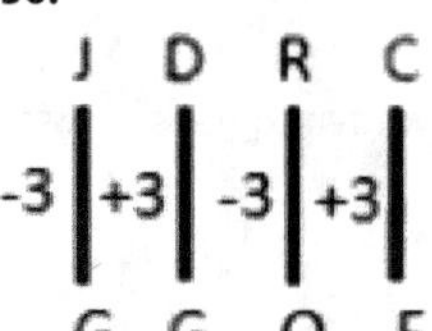

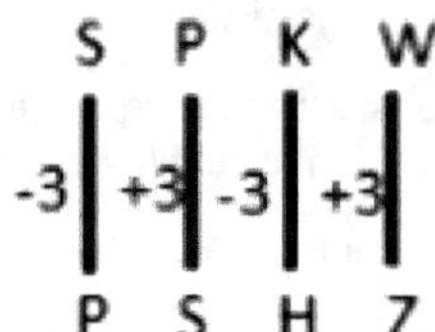

So, the correct answer would be PSHZ.

Hence, the correct option is (C).

31. Given:

A car travels a distance of $516 kms$.

We know that:

$$\text{Speed} = \frac{\text{Distance}}{\text{Time}}$$

We are finding the average thus we don't need to use the real value of distance as it will be canceled in the end.

We know that:

$$\text{Average speed} = \frac{\text{Total distance}}{\text{Total time}}$$

Let total distance be D.

For 50% journey time $= \dfrac{D}{(2 \times 12)}$

For 25% journey time $= \dfrac{D}{(4\times20)}$

For 25% journey time $= \dfrac{D}{(4\times30)}$

Total time $= \dfrac{D}{24} + \dfrac{D}{80} + \dfrac{D}{120} = \dfrac{D}{16}$

$\therefore$ Average speed of the car $= \dfrac{D}{\left(\frac{D}{16}\right)} = 16$ kmph

Hence, the correct option is (C).

32. Let the normal speed be 4 km/hr

Travelling speed $= 4 \times \left(\dfrac{3}{4}\right) = 3$ km/hr

Ratio of normal speed to travelling speed = 4x : 3x

As we know,

Time is inversely proportional to time.

Ratio of normal time to travelling time = 3x : 4x

4x – 3x = 15

$\Rightarrow$ x = 15

$\therefore$ Normal time = 3x = 3 × 15 = 45 min

Hence, the correct option is (D).

33. Let the distance between P and Q be x km, then

As we know,

Average speed = Total distance/Total time

$\therefore$ Average speed $= \dfrac{(x+x)}{\left[\left(\frac{x}{5}+\frac{x}{3}\right)\right]} = \dfrac{2x}{\left[\frac{(3x+5x)}{15}\right]} = \dfrac{(2x\times15)}{8x} = 3.75$ km/hr

Hence, the correct option is (B).

34. Let the speed of the boat in still water be c and that of the stream be v. Hence we have,

Downstream:

$c + v = \dfrac{36}{3} = 12$

Upstream:

$c - v = \dfrac{36}{9} = 4$

Solving the above obtained results by adding them eliminating v, we have

2c = 16

$\Rightarrow$ c = 8 kmph

Hence, the correct option is (A).

35.

Spanish	Language
Hindi	Language

Urdu	Language
France	Country

Therefore, France is odd one out.
Hence, the correct option is (D).

36. From options,

(D) M (+2) = O (+ 3) = R (+ 3) = U

(A) B (+2) = D (+ 3) = G (+ 4) = K

(B) J (+2) = L (+ 3) = O (+ 4) = S

(C) N (+2) = P (+ 3) = S (+ 4) = W

Thus, MOUR is the odd one.

Hence, the correct option is (D).

37. The pattern followed is that in each term 1st term – 2 = 2nd term;

2nd term + 5 = 3rd term;

3rd term – 2 = 4th term

From options,

(A) DBGE → D – 2 = B; B + 5 = G; G – 2 = E

(B) POSR → P – 1 = O; O + 4 = S; S – 1 = R

(C) JHMK → J – 2 = H; H + 5 = M; M – 2 = K

(D) OMRP → O – 2 = M; M + 5 = R; R – 2 = P

But POSR does not follow the pattern as shown above.

Thus, POSR is odd one.

Hence, the correct option is (B).

38. The logic followed is:

(A) 123 → 5^3 – 2

(B) 727 → 9^3 – 2

(C) 341 → 7^3 – 2

(D) 218 → 6^3 + 2

Thus, "218" is the odd one among the given alternatives.

Hence, the correct option is (D).

39. In this question, Fire, Light and Gas are luminous elements whereas water is non luminous and an inhibitor of fire and gas.

Thus, Water is odd one.

Hence, the correct option is (D).

40. Given,

The average of 5 consecutive numbers is 62.

Consecutive numbers are those numbers whose common difference is 1.

Let the numbers be $x, x + 1, x + 2, x + 3, x + 4$.

$\Rightarrow$ Sum of consecutive numbers are $x + x + 1 + x + 2 + x + 3 + x + 4$.

$\Rightarrow 5x + 10$

According to question,

$\Rightarrow \dfrac{(5x+10)}{5} = 62$

$\Rightarrow 5x + 10 = 310$

$\Rightarrow 5x = 300$

$\Rightarrow x = 60$

$\Rightarrow$ Numbers are $60, 61, 62, 63, 64$.

$\Rightarrow$ Smaller and largest numbers are 60 and 64.

$\therefore$ The average of smaller and largest umber $\dfrac{(60+64)}{2}$ is 62.

Hence, the correct option is (D).

41. Average $= \dfrac{\text{Sum of all observations}}{\text{Total number of observations}}$

$\therefore$ Total number of observations = Total goods bought $= a + b + c$

Here, the sum of all observations = Money spent for each type of goods.

Money spent for Type A = Number of type A goods x Price $= aE$

$\therefore$ Money spent for Type $B = bF$

$\therefore$ Money spent for Type $C = cG$

$\therefore$ Sum of all observations $= aE + bF + cG$

$\therefore$ Average $= \dfrac{\text{Sum of all observations}}{\text{Total number of observations}} = \dfrac{aE+bF+cG}{a+b+c}$

Hence, the correct option is (C).

42. Given,

A 32-year-old man is replaced by a new man, then the average age of 42 men increases by 1 year.

Average age × Number of Men = Total age

Let initially the average age of 42 men be x

$\Rightarrow$ Total age of 42 men = 42x

Now, a 32 year old man is replaced by a new man

$\Rightarrow$ New Total age = 42 × (x + 1)

$\therefore$ 42 × (x + 1) - 42x = Age of the New man - 32

$\Rightarrow$ 42x + 42 - 42x = Age of the New man - 32

$\Rightarrow$ Age of the New man - 32 = 42

$\therefore$ Age of the New man = 42 + 32 = 74 years

Hence, the correct option is (C).

43. Prabhat has done $\dfrac{1}{2}$ of job in 12 days.

Prabhat has done in $\dfrac{1}{24}$ part of job in 1 day.

Santhosh complete rest $\dfrac{1}{2}$ part of job in 6 days.

Santhosh has done in $\dfrac{1}{12}$ part of job in 1 days.

Santhosh and Prabhat complete part of job in 1 day = $\left(\dfrac{1}{24}\right) + \left(\dfrac{1}{12}\right) = \dfrac{1}{8}$

Santhosh and Prabhat complete $\dfrac{1}{8}$ part of job in 1 day.

Santhosh and Prabhat will complete job in 8 day.

Hence, the correct option is (C).

44. Ratio of efficiency of A and B = 125 : 100

Ratio of time taken by A and B = 100 : 125

Let A takes 100x days, and B takes 125x days to complete a piece of work.

Days taken by B – Days taken by A = 6

$\Rightarrow$ 125x – 100x = 6

$\Rightarrow$ 25x = 6

$\Rightarrow$ x = $\dfrac{6}{25}$

Days taken by A = 100x

$\Rightarrow$ 100 × $\dfrac{6}{25}$

$\Rightarrow$ 4 × 6

$\Rightarrow$ 24

And, days taken by B = 125x

$\Rightarrow$ 125 × $\dfrac{6}{25}$

$\Rightarrow$ 5 × 6

$\Rightarrow$ 30

$\therefore$ B will take 30 days to complete the same work.

Hence, the correct option is (A).

45. Let the efficiency of 1 man be M.

And the efficiency of 1 woman is W.

According to the question,

2 men and 7 women complete a work in 28 days = 6 men and 16 women complete the same work in 11 days

$\Rightarrow$ (2M + 7W) × 28 = (6M + 16W) × 11

$\Rightarrow$ 56M + 196W = 66M + 176W

$\Rightarrow 10M = 20W$

$\Rightarrow M = 2W$

2 men and 7 women = 2M + 7W

$\Rightarrow$ 2 men and 7 women = 4W + 7W

$\Rightarrow$ 2 men and 7 women = 11W

5 men and 4 women = 5M + 4W

$\Rightarrow$ 5 men and 4 women = 10W + 4W

$\Rightarrow$ 5 men and 4 women = 14W

$$\frac{M_1 D_1}{W_1} = \frac{M_2 D_2}{W_2}$$

$\Rightarrow$ 11W × 28 = 14W × D_2

$\Rightarrow D_2$ = 22 days

∴ 5 men and 4 women, working together, complete the same work in 22 days.

Hence, the correct option is (A).

46. 1 day = 24 hours

1 hours = 60 minutes

1 minute/1day

$\Rightarrow$ 1minute/24 hours

$\Rightarrow$ 1minute/(24 × 60) minutes

$\Rightarrow$ 0.000694

∴ The required answer is 0.000694.

Hence, the correct option is (C).

47. $0.420420420 \ldots - 0.240240240 \ldots$

$\Rightarrow \dfrac{420}{999} - \dfrac{240}{999}$

$\Rightarrow \dfrac{(420-240)}{999}$

$\Rightarrow \dfrac{180}{999}$

$\Rightarrow \dfrac{20}{111}$

∴ The value of $0.420420420 \ldots .0.240240240 \ldots \ldots$ is $\dfrac{20}{111}$.

Hence, the correct option is (D).

48. Given,

0.35353......

Let x = 0.35353535.............

Multiply by 100 the above expression, we get

$\Rightarrow$ 100x = 35.353535.............

$\Rightarrow$ 100x = 35 + 0.35353535.............

$\Rightarrow$ 100x = 35 + x

$\Rightarrow$ 99x = 35

$\Rightarrow x = \dfrac{35}{99}$

∴ The required fraction is $\dfrac{35}{99}$.

Hence, the correct option is (A).

49. The ozone layer is an area or a continuous region in the stratosphere of the earth that includes high concentrations of ozone(O3) and protects the earth from the sun's harmful ultraviolet radiation. It has the ability to absorb the sun's harmful ultraviolet radiation, which can damage life on Earth.

UV radiation, which is made up of various types of photons, is found in sunlight. UVA and UVB rays are the two forms of UV radiation you're probably most familiar with.

These rays can have a variety of effects on our skin.

Hence, the correct option is (D).

50. The sting of an ant contains formic acid. When an ant bites it injects the acidic liquid into the skin. Formic acid is the common name for methanoic acid (HCOOH).

Hence, the correct option is (C).

51. Carbon dioxide reacts with limewater (a solution of calcium hydroxide, $Ca(OH)_2$, to form a white precipitate (appears milky) of calcium carbonate, CaCO$_3$. Adding more carbon dioxide results in the precipitate dissolving to form a colorless solution of calcium hydrogen carbonate.

Hence, the correct option is (A)

52. Biogas is also known as Gobar Gas.

It is produced through the anaerobic decomposition of organic wastes from animals and plants.

It is primarily a mixture of mainly methane and carbon dioxide and methane is a major component of biogas.

Hence, the correct option is (B).

53. The smallest organelle in a cell is the ribosome it has a diameter of about $20nm$ only.

Ribosomes are membranous granular structures present in the cytoplasm.

They were first observed under an electron microscope as dense particles by George Palade in the year $1953.$

Ribosomes are the site for protein synthesis so they are also called the "protein factory" of the cell.

Hence, the correct option is (D).

54. Both longitude and latitude are angles measured with the center of the earth as an origin. Longitude is an angle from the prime meridian, measured to the east (longitudes to the west are negative). Latitudes measure an angle up from the equator (latitudes to the south are negative).

- The line joining the north and south pole is called Prime Meridian.

- A (geographic) meridian (or line of longitude) is half of an imaginary great circle on the Earth's surface.

- It is a coordinate line terminated by the North Pole and the South Pole, connecting points of equal longitude, as measured in angular degrees east or west of the Prime Meridian.

Hence, the correct option is (A).

55. The given sentence is grammatically incorrect.

- Here, 'Suresh has neither' should be used instead of 'Suresh have never'.

- 'Neither' is used in the negative sense when we are presenting things that aren't true or valid. Neither...nor gives a negative meaning to verbs.

- And we also know that 'Neither' is always followed by 'nor'.

- Hence, 'never' should be replaced with 'neither' to form a grammatically correct sentence.

- We know that 'Suresh' is singular and it should be followed by a singular helping verb. Hence, 'has' should be used instead of 'have'.

Hence, the correct option is (A).

56. The given sentence is grammatically correct.

- The given sentence is talking about a past event. Hence, the use of second form of verb (intended) is grammatically correct.

- The word 'intended' means 'to have as a plan or purpose'.
  - Example: The course is intended for intermediate-level students.

Hence, the correct option is (D).

57. Kheer Bhavani Mela is a popular fair held in Jammu and Kashmir. This Mela is one of the biggest religious festivals of Kashmiri Pandits, it is held annually on Jyeshtha Ashtami.
Hence, the correct option is (C).

58. This festival celebrated in the state of Telangana between 28 September to 6 October 2019 is also known as the 'Festival of Flowers'.
Hence, the correct option is (D).

59. On the basis of the above figure we found the image as below:

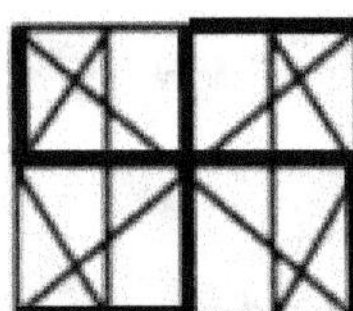

Hence, the correct option is (D).

60. On the basis of the above figure we found the image as below:

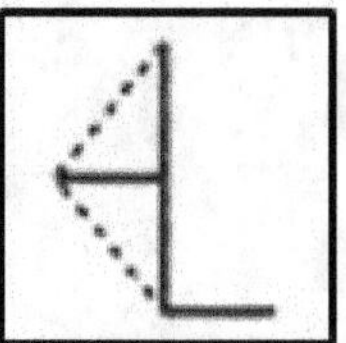

Hence, the correct option is (B).

61. On close observation, we find that the question figure is embedded in option (D) as shown below:

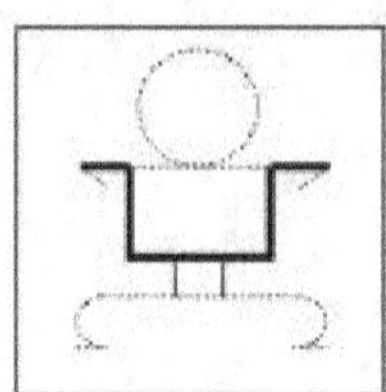

Hence, the correct option is (D).

62. On close observation, we find that the question figure is embedded in option (B) as shown below:

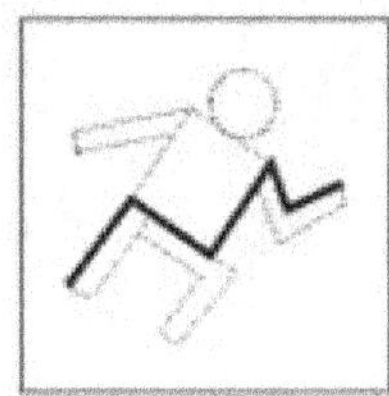

Hence, the correct option is (B).

63.

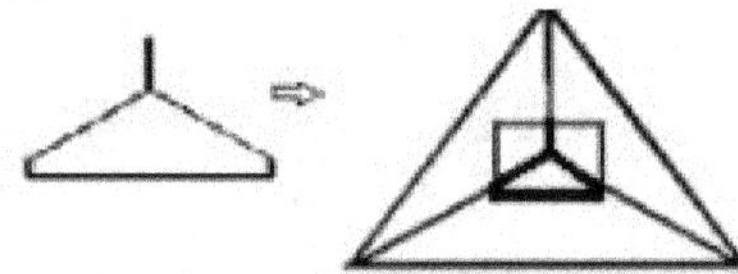

Hence, the correct option is (B).

64.

Only in figure (4), the black triangle and the black circle lie at the two ends of the same diameter.

Hence, the correct option is (C).

65.

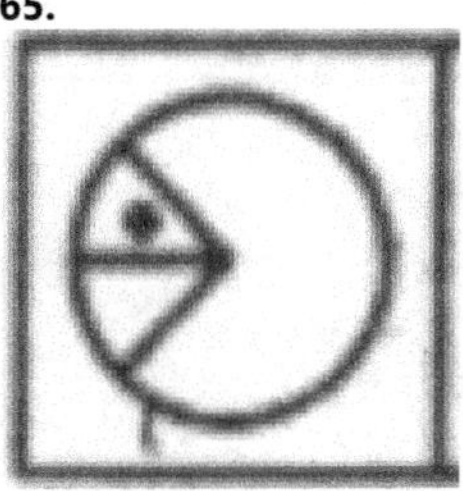

Except for figure (1), all other figures can be rotated into each other.

Hence, the correct option is (A).

66. In figure (1), (2) and (4), the two lines are parallel to each other but in figure (3), the two lines are intersecting.

Figure (3) is different from the rest.

Hence, the correct option is (C).

67. In figure (1), (3) and (4), the lines outside the circle are uniformly distributed along the circumference whereas in figure (2), the lines outside the circle are not uniformly distributed along the circumference.

Figure (2) is different from the rest.

Hence, the correct option is (B).

68. In figure (2), (3) and (4), the pins that are equal to the number of sides of the figure are attached to a side of the figure whereas in figure (1), the pins equal to the number of sides are attached to a vertex of the figure.

Figure (1) is different from the rest.

Hence, the correct option is (A).

69. According to the question, the Ratio of the initial mixture will be the same as the ratio of the mixture after taken out:

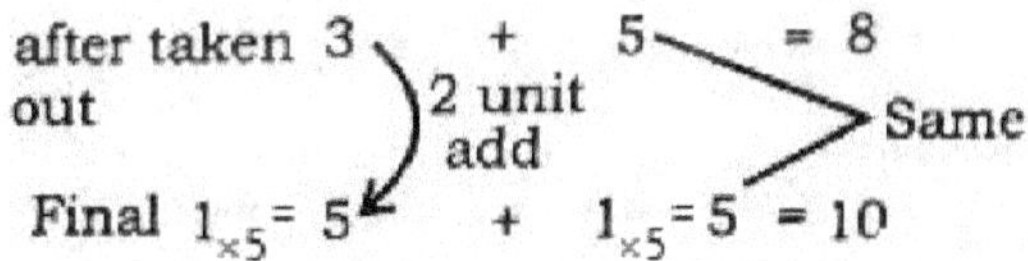

Initial mixture = 8+2 =10

Taken out = 2

$$\Rightarrow \frac{2}{10} = \frac{1}{5}$$

Hence, the correct option is (B).

70. Given:

Initial ratio of apples and oranges $= 7 : 5$

Let number of apples $= 7a$ and oranges $= 5a$

According to the question:

When 25 apples were rotten and when 25 new oranges were bought the new ratio becomes $\dfrac{(7a - 25)}{(5a + 25)} = \dfrac{1}{5}$

$$\Rightarrow 35a - 125 = 5a + 25$$

$$\Rightarrow 30a - 125 = 25$$

$$\Rightarrow a = 5$$

$\therefore$ Number of apples left after rotten apples $= 7a - 25 = (7 \times 5) - 25 = 10$

Hence, the correct option is (D).

71. Total students $= 640$

Ratio of boys to girls $= 5: 3$

Number of boys $= \left[\dfrac{5}{8}\right] 640 = 400$

Number of girls $= 640 - 400 = 240$

Let x boys admitted in the school.

According to the question

$$\frac{(400+x)}{(240+30)} = \frac{14}{9}$$

$$\Rightarrow 400 + x = \left[\dfrac{14}{9}\right] \times 270$$

$$\Rightarrow x = 420 - 400$$

$$\Rightarrow x = 20$$

$\therefore$ 20 students admitted in the school.

Hence, the correct option is (A).

72. Ratchanok Intanon, the Badminton player of Thailand, defeated Spain's Carolina Marin in the women's singles final match of the Indonesia Masters tournament in Jakarta, held recently. This is her second win in the Indonesian Masters event after her triumph in 2010.

Ratchanok Intanon became world champion in women's singles in 2013 and became the first Thai player to become No.1 in women's singles. Carolina Marin is the present Olympic Champion and three-time World Champion.

Hence, the correct option is (B).

73. A single person can be an advocate, gardener, and cook at the same time.

The correct Venn diagram representation is,

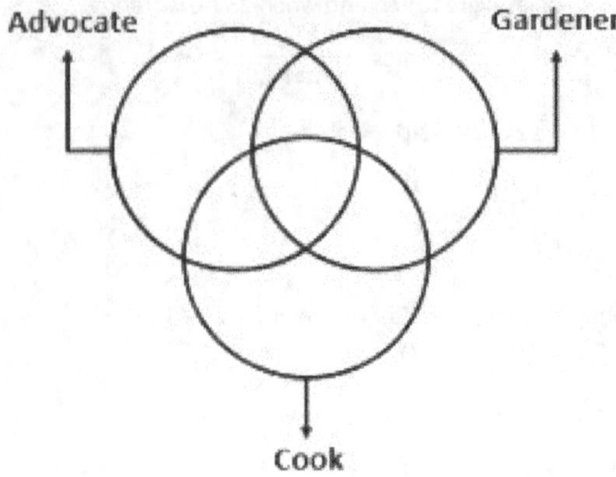

Hence, the correct option is (A).

74. Summer and Winter both are seasons but not related to each other.

The correct Venn diagram representation is,

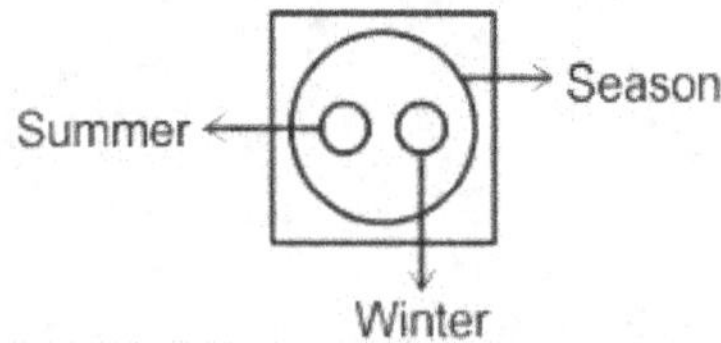

Hence, the correct option is (C).

75. The Venn diagram that best illustrates the relationship between Engineers, Professionals and Doctors is shown below:

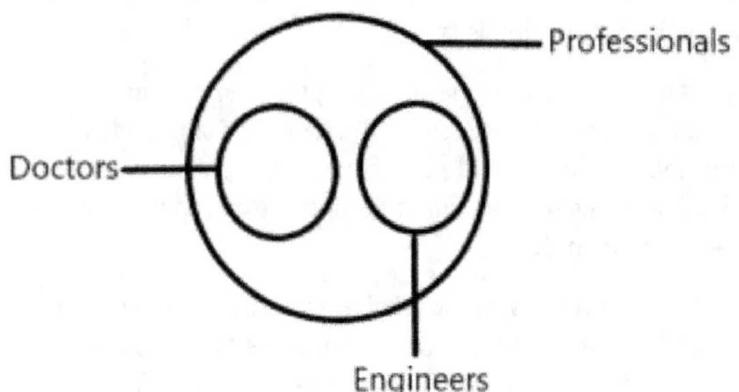

Engineers and Doctors belong to the Professionals class and there are no common things between Engineers and Doctors.

Hence, the correct option is (D).

76. Jackfruit and Pumpkin are entirely different. But, both are vegetables.

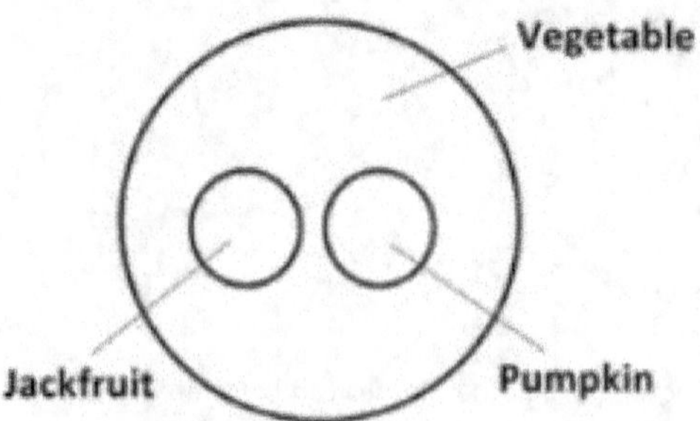

Hence, the correct option is (B).

77. An year consists of weeks, and a week consists of days.

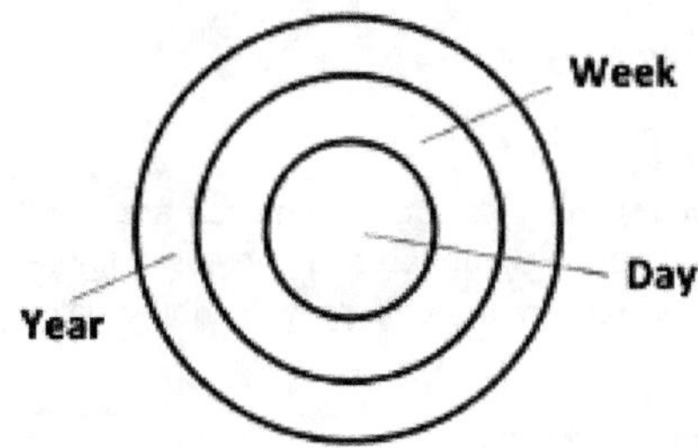

Hence, the correct option is (A).

78. The correct order is based on the selection process from start to end for any post or exam.

3. Form fill up

2. Preliminary examination

4. Mains examination

1. Interview

5. Final result.

Therefore, the logical order is 3, 2, 4, 1, 5.

Hence, the correct option is (B).

79. The correct sequence is B, D, A, E, C. Population > Unemployment > Poverty > Disease > Death as they are related in this manner, huge population will cause unemployment which results in poverty then diseases due to lack of money for food and medicines and ultimately death.

Hence, the correct option is (B).

80. Contempt of court, as a concept that seeks to protect judicial institutions from motivated attacks and unwarranted criticism, and as a legal mechanism to punish those who lower its authority.

There are two types of Contempt of court.

- Civil contempt of court is the willful disobedience of a court order or judgment or willful breach of an undertaking given to a court. So, Statement 1 is not correct.

- Criminal contempt of court is written or spoken words or any act that scandalizes the court or lowers its authority or prejudices or interferes with the due course of a judicial proceeding or interferes/obstructs the administration of justice. So, Statement 2 is not correct.

Hence, the correct option is (C).

81. The correct answer is 'modern'.

- The word 'Archaic' means very old or old-fashioned.
- The antonyms of the word 'Archaic' are "modern, recent, current".
- From the antonym of the given word, we can say that the word 'Modern' is the opposite in meaning.
- The word 'Modern' means relating to the present or recent times as opposed to the remote past.

Hence, the correct option is (D).

82. The correct answer is 'concentrate'.

- The word 'Diffuse' means to spread out over a large area; not concentrated.
- The antonyms of the word 'Diffuse' are "concentrate, converge, meet".
- From the antonym of the given word, we can say that the word 'Concentrate' is the opposite in meaning.
- The word 'Concentrate' means to gather (people or things) together in a common location.

Hence, the correct option is (A).

83. The correct answer is 'Calm'.

- The word 'Unrest' means a disturbed or uneasy state.
- The antonyms of the word 'Unrest' are "calm, ease, peace".
- From the antonym of the given word, we can say that the word 'Calm' is the opposite in meaning.
- The word 'Calm' means the absence of violent activity in a place.

Hence, the correct option is (D).

84. Since the shopkeeper sells the article for $Rs.\,7,500$ and changes sales tax at the rate of 12%

A tax charged by the shopkeeper $= 12\%$ of Rs. 7500

$$= \frac{12}{100} \times 7500 = 900$$

$VAT = $ Tax charge $-$ Tax paid

$\Rightarrow Rs.180 = Rs.\,900 - $ Tax paid

Tax paid by the shopkeeper $= Rs.\,900 - Rs.\,180 = Rs.\,720$

If the shopkeeper buys the article for Rs. x,

Tax on it $= 12\%$ of Rs. $x = Rs.\,720$

$\Rightarrow x = Rs.\,6{,}000$

The price (inclusive of tax) paid by the shopkeeper $= $ Rs. $6000 + $ Rs. $720 = $ Rs. 6720

Hence, the correct option is (A).

85. Let the salary of Mohan be a.

Given:

Ramesh gets 10% more salary than Mohan.

Ramesh's salary = Mohan's salary $+10\%$ of Mohan's salary

$\Rightarrow$ Ramesh's salary $= a + 0.1 \times a = 1.1a$

Mohan's salary is less than Ramesh by an amount $= 1.1a - a = 0.1a$

% of Mohan's salary lesser than Ramesh $= \frac{0.1a}{1.1a} \times 100\%$

$\Rightarrow$ % of Mohan's salary lesser than Ramesh $= \frac{100}{11}\%$

$$= 9\frac{1}{11}\%$$

Hence, the correct option is (C).

86. Previous salary $= $ Rs. 50000

10% of Rs. 50000

$$= \frac{10}{100} \times 50000$$

$$= Rs.\,5000$$

New salary = Rs. $50000 + $ Rs. 5000 $= $ Rs. 55000

Hence, the correct option is (A).

87. This is the boy who scored the highest marks.

The most suitable pronoun for the given blank is 'who'. A pronoun is a word that replaces a noun to avoid its repetition.

A relative pronoun is one which is used to refer to nouns mentioned previously, whether they are people, places, things, animals, or ideas" (i.e. Who, whom, that, which, etc.). Who should be used to refer to the subject of a sentence.

For example: Jack is the one who wants to go.

Hence, the correct option is (D).

88. Correct sentence: Giving money to the poor is a/an **benevolent** act of service to the poor.

Benevolent: kind and helpful, giving money or help to people or organizations that need it.

According to the given sentence, giving money to the poor is an act of charity. Therefore, we need a word whose meaning is close to kind/helpful.

So, according to the context of the sentence, 'benevolent' fits appropriately in the given blank.

Hence, the correct option is (A).

89. Correct sentence: When I met Ram yesterday, it was the first time I met him since my graduation.

The first part of the given sentence is in the Past Tense. Since the principal clause of the sentence is in the past tense, the following clause will also be in the past tense.

For example: When I went for the interview on Monday, I saw Kiya for the first time since my college.

So, 'met' is the appropriate word to be used.

Hence, the correct option is (A).

90. Correct sentence:

a. What's your skirt made from? It feels like wool.

b. I won't be coming to work today. I don't feel very well.

We commonly use the pronoun it as both a subject and an object pronoun.

It always takes a singular verb.

- For example: It is too expensive for us.

I is a singular pronoun but it always takes a plural verb.

- For example: I don't want to go there.

Hence, the correct option is (B).

91. The correct answer is 'Looking back to renewable sources to reduce the changes in climate'.

Let's have a look at the third line of the first paragraph:

Returning to renewables to help mitigate climate change is an excellent approach that needs to be sustainable in order to meet the energy demand of future generations.

It can be concluded from the above line that the magnificent perspective that needs to be maintained is looking back to renewable sources to reduce the changes in climate.

Hence, the correct option is (B).

92. The correct answer is 'These are the challenges that create obstructions to reduce climatic changes'.

Let's have a look at the first and second lines of the second paragraph:

'Despite these opportunities, there are challenges that hinder the sustainability of renewable energy sources towards climate change mitigation. These challenges include Market failures, lack of information, access to raw materials for future renewable resource deployment, and our daily carbon footprint.'

It can be concluded from the above lines that Market failures, lack of information, access to raw materials for future renewable resource deployment, and our daily carbon footprint as used in the passage are the challenges that create obstructions to reduce climatic changes.

Hence, the correct option is (A).

93. The correct answer is 'Because it is helpful for the development of human beings that further leads to productivity'.

Let's have a look at the first line of the third passage:

'Energy is a requirement in our everyday life as a way of improving human development leading to economic growth and productivity. '

It can be concluded from the above lines that energy is required in our day-to-day life because it is helpful for the development of human beings that further leads to productivity.

Hence, the correct option is (B).

94. The correct answer is 'Energy Security, Energy Access, Social and Economic Development, Climate Change Mitigation, and reduction of environmental and health impacts'.

Let's have a look at the fourth, fifth, and sixth lines of the first paragraph:

The study reviewed the opportunities associated with renewable energy sources which include: Energy Security, Energy Access, Social and Economic Development, Climate Change Mitigation, and reduction of environmental and health impacts. '

It can be concluded from the above lines that the opportunities which are connected to renewable sources of energy are Energy Security, Energy Access, Social and Economic Development, Climate Change Mitigation, and reduction of environmental and health impacts.

Hence, the correct option is (D).

95. We can infer that the main purpose of the passage is to 'inform'.

The passage provides us information regarding how world is becoming a global village due to the increasing daily requirement of energy, studies that have been done, suggestions, need of the hour, and much more.

Thus, we can infer that the main purpose of the passage is to 'inform'.

Hence, the correct option is (A).

96. The answer figure that will complete the pattern in the given question figure is as follows:

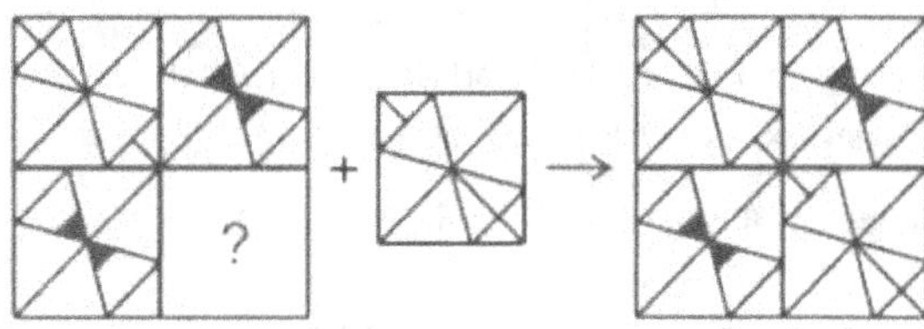

Hence, the correct option is (B).

97.

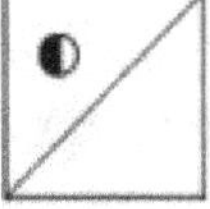

figure inside the box moves 90 degree in clockwise direction each time. So if you move the 3rd box figure in clockwise direction with 90 degree, we will get the option (a) is right figure to complete.

Hence, the correct option is (A).

98. The next figure is:

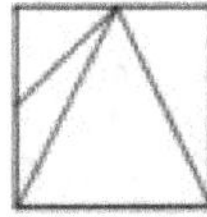

Hence, the correct option is (B).

99. The next figure is:

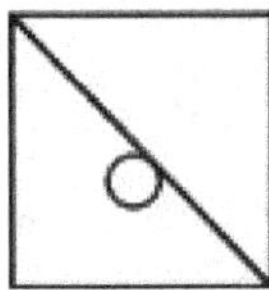

Rod is moving 90 degree in clockwise direction. Move the Rod from 3rd box by 90 degree in clockwise direction.

Hence, the correct option is (B).

100. The next figure is:

Option B figure will complete the circle and will show the correct arrow marks on the line also.

Hence, the correct option is (B).

Mock Test 08

Q.1 Who has won the Best Male actor award in the International Indian Film Academy Awards 2022 held in Abu Dhabi?

A. Salman Khan
B. Shah Rukh Khan
C. Vicky Kaushal
D. Varun Dhawan

Q.2 Who has been appinted as the Chief Executive Officer (CEO) of Indigo in September 2022?

A. Sanjay Kumar Verma
B. Adille Sumariwalla
C. Pieter Elbers
D. Anuj Poddar

Q.3 Fengyun-4B, the New-Gen Meteorological Satellite, has been launched by which country?

A. Japan
B. China
C. Israel
D. UAE

Q.4 Which company has signed a Memorandum of Understanding (MoU) with SIDBI to accelerate e-commerce for small industries in August 2022?

A. Flipkart
B. Zomato
C. Myntra
D. ONDC

Q.5 Who among the following became the Chief Minister of Uttarakhand in March 2021?

[SSC CGL, 2022]

A. Madan Kaushik
B. Dhan Singh Rawat
C. BC Khanduri
D. Tirath Singh Rawat

Q.6 What would be the interest accrued in two years on Rs. 300 if the sum is invested at 10% interest compounded annually?

[UP Police Constable, 2018]

A. Rs. 60.50
B. Rs. 60
C. Rs. 61.50
D. Rs. 63

Q.7 What will be the compound interest on a sum of ₹ 9000 at compound interest compounded annually at 8% per annum in two years?

A. Rs. 1498.76
B. Rs. 1497.6
C. Rs. 1597.6
D. Rs. 1480.60

Q.8 A sum becomes five times of itself in 8 years at simple interest. What is the rate of interest per annum?

A. 37.5%
B. 25%
C. 62.5%
D. 50%

Q.9 1.27 is equal to:

A. $\frac{127}{100}$
B. $\frac{73}{100}$
C. $\frac{14}{11}$
D. $\frac{11}{14}$

Q.10 If $\frac{10}{7}(1 - 2.43 \times 10^{-3})$ = 1.417 + x, then x is equal to:

A. 0.0417
B. 0.417
C. 0.0081
D. 0.81

Q.11 Find the value of: $\dfrac{(1.569\times1.569\times0.431)+(1.569\times0.431\times0.431)}{(1.569+0.431)^2-(1.569-0.431)^2}$

A. 1.5
B. 2
C. 0.5
D. 1

Q.12 Which of the following statement is/are correct?

1. Non-Aligned Movement(NAM) was established in 1961 in Belgrade, SR Serbia Yugoslavia.

2. Indian Prime Minister Jawaharlal Nehru also contributed to the established NAM.

A. 1 only
B. 2 only
C. Both 1 and 2
D. Neither 1 nor 2

Ques (13-14):Direction: Choose the option which best expresses the meaning of the idiom/phrase given below.

Q.13 "Let the grass grow under one's feet"
[SSC Sub Inspector (CPO), 2018], [SSC Sub Inspector (CPO), 2017]

A. To accept responsibility
B. To engage in a project
C. To remain idle
D. To grow grass at home

Q.14 "Be in the same boat"
[SSC Sub Inspector (CPO), 2018], [SSC Sub Inspector (CPO), 2017]

A. To ask someone to travel on the same boat
B. To be in the same difficult situation
C. Willing to do something immediately
D. To force an issue that has already ended

Q.15 What will be the impact of the absence of ants on the Earth?

A. No effect
B. Destroys life
C. A little adverse impact
D. Decrease in termites

Q.16 Arrange the following words in a logical and meaningful order.

1. Blue
2. Red
3. Yellow
4. Indigo
5. Orange

A. 4-1-5-2-3
B. 2-5-3-1-4
C. 2-5-1-3-4
D. 4-1-3-2-5

Q.17 Arrange the following words in a logical and meaningful order.

1. Throat
2. Bladder
3. Pupil
4. Liver
5. Pinna

A. 5-3-1-2-4
B. 5-3-1-4-2
C. 3-5-1-4-2
D. 3-5-1-2-4

Q.18 Choose the option that is the passive form of the sentence.

The tennis ball hit Dhiraj on the head.

[SSC Sub Inspector (CPO), 2019]

A. Dhiraj had been hit on the head by the tennis ball.
B. Dhiraj was hit on the head by the tennis ball.
C. The tennis ball was being hit by Dhiraj.
D. Dhiraj was being hit on the head by the tennis ball.

Q.19 Choose the option that is the passive form of the sentence.

They found her guilty of theft.

[SSC Sub Inspector (CPO), 2019]

A. She found them guilty of theft.
B. She was found guilty of theft.
C. She had been find guilty of theft.
D. She is find guilty of theft by them.

Q.20 In the following question, select the related number from the given alternatives.

95 : 106 :: 87 ?

A. 136 **B.** 113 **C.** 101 **D.** 183

Q.21 In the following question, select the related word from the given alternatives.

Lion : Cub :: Kangaroo : ?

A. Fawn **B.** Joey **C.** Kitten **D.** Calf

Q.22 Select the related letter /number from the given alternatives.

XY : 2425 : : ? : 1213

A. LM **B.** NL **C.** ML **D.** LN

Q.23 In the following question, select the related word from the given alternatives.

Sardar Sarovar Dam : Gujrat :: Tehri Dam : ?

A. Uttarakhand **B.** Odisha
C. Andhra Pradesh **D.** Telangana

Q.24 Direction: In the following question, select the related letter/word from the given alternatives.

THEFT : SUGIDFEGSU : : PULSE : ?

A. OQTVKMRTDF **B.** QOVTKMTRFD
C. OQTVMKRTDF **D.** OQTVKMTRFD

Q.25 Points 'A' and 'B' are 70 km apart on a highway and two cars start at the same time. If they travel in the same direction, they meet in 7 hours, but if they travel towards each other they meet in one hour. Find the speed of the two cars (in km/hr).

A. 20, 30 **B.** 40, 30 **C.** 30, 50 **D.** 20, 40

Q.26 A boy rides his bicycle 10 km at an average speed of 12 km/hr and again travels 12 km at an average speed of 10 km//hr. His average speed for the entire trip is approximately:

A. 10.4 km/hr **B.** 10.8 km/hr
C. 11 km/hr **D.** 12.2 km/hr

Q.27 A walk at a uniform rate of 4 km/hr, and 4 hr after his start, B bicycles after him at the uniform rate of 10 km/hr. How far from the starting point will B catch A?

A. 16.7 km **B.** 18.6 km **C.** 21.5 km **D.** 26.7 km

Q.28 A thief escapes in a car driving at 60 km/h towards a city 400 km away. Only after 30 minutes, the police start to chase at 80 km/h. What distance will the police have covered when the thief is caught?

A. 120km **B.** 70 km **C.** 90 km **D.** 85 km

Q.29 Direction: In question, find the odd number pair from the given alternatives.

A. 24 – 76 **B.** 12 – 39 **C.** 16 – 52 **D.** 19 – 61

Ques (30-33):Direction: Find the odd one out:

Q.30 Onlookers, Theatre -goers, Queue, Spectators

[CLAT UG, 2019]

A. Onlookers **B.** Theatre goers
C. Queue **D.** Spectators

Q.31 Heart, Lungs, Kidney, Skin, Liver

[CLAT UG, 2019]

A. Skin **B.** Lungs **C.** Heart **D.** Kidney

Q.32 Find the odd-man-out:

[CLAT UG, 2019]

A. http://www.scholar.google.com
B. http://www.manupatra.com
C. http://www.lexisnexis.com
D. http://www.westlawindia.com

Q.33 Symphony, Orchestra, Guitar, Mob

[CLAT UG, 2019]

A. Guitar **B.** Orchestra
C. Mob **D.** Symphony

Q.34 The average salary of all the workers in a factory is Rs. 15000. The average salary of 12 technicians is Rs. 18000 and the average salary of the rest is Rs. 12000 Then, what is the total number of workers in the factory?

[Telangana Police Constable, 2018]

A. 22 **B.** 24 **C.** 28 **D.** 20

Q.35 The ratio of number of employees in the technical section and the management section of company 7 : 2. The average salaries of employees in the technical section and the management section are Rs. 25000 and Rs, 47500 respectively. The average salary of employees of these two sections together is (in rupees):

[Telangana Police Constable, 2018]

A. 37500 **B.** 35000 **C.** 30000 **D.** 40000

Q.36 The average weight of A, B and C is 65 kg. If the person D joins them then the average of weights of those four persons becomes 70 kg. The average weight of B, C and D is 75 kg. then the weight of A is (in kgs):

[Telangana Police Constable, 2018]

A. 60   **B.** 65   **C.** 70   **D.** 55

Q.37 A and B together can do a piece of work in 10 days, B and C together can do it in 15 days while C and A together can do it in 20 days. They work together for 8 days. C alone will complete the remaining work in:

A. 12 days   **B.** $3\frac{1}{5}$ days   **C.** 16 days   **D.** $5\frac{1}{3}$ days

Q.38 Two printing machines A and B can print 2400 high-quality pages working 5hrs in 5 days. Machine A can print as many pages in 2.5hrs as machine B can print in 1.5 hrs. How many pages can machine B print in 1 hour?

A. 80 pages   **B.** 70 pages   **C.** 50 pages   **D.** 60 pages

Q.39 Anil can do a piece of work in 16 days which Shashi can finish in 24 days. If they work on alternate days with Anil starting. In how many days the work will be finished?

A. 15 days   **B.** 17 days   **C.** 18 days   **D.** 19 days

Ques (40-41):Directions: In each of the following questions, choose the option which can be substituted for the given words/sentence.

Q.40 A person who does not express himself freely.
[NCHM JEE (Hotel Mgmt & Catering), 2019]

A. Insolvent   **B.** Invincible
C. Introvert   **D.** Impostor

Q.41 One who specialises in the study of birds.
[NCHM JEE (Hotel Mgmt & Catering), 2019]

A. Naturalist   **B.** Zoologist
C. Ornithologist   **D.** Biologist

Q.42 Consider the following statements regarding Decomposers.

1. By the process of leaching, water-soluble inorganic nutrients go down into the soil horizon and get precipitated as unavailable salts.

2. Humification leads to the accumulation of a dark-coloured amorphous substance called humus that is highly resistant to microbial action and undergoes decomposition at an extremely slow rate.

Which of the statements given above is/are correct?

A. 1 only   **B.** 2 only
C. Both 1 and 2   **D.** Neither 1 nor 2

Q.43 Which of the following statements is/are correct about COVID-19?

1. It is an RNA virus with ribonucleic acid (RNA) as its genetic material leading to mutations.

2. RNA viruses are single-stranded.

3. RNA replication takes place in the cytoplasm.

A. 1 and 2 only   **B.** 2 and 3 only
C. 1 and 3 only   **D.** All of the above

Q.44 Which of the following statements is/are incorrect about Gene therapy?

1. It is a collection of methods that allows correction of a gene defect that has been diagnosed in a child/embryo.

2. ADA deficiency cannot be cured by bone marrow transplantation.

A. 1 only   **B.** 2 only
C. Both 1 and 2   **D.** Neither 1 nor 2

Q.45 Which of the following statements is/are correct regarding PCR (Polymerase Chain Reaction)?

1. In this reaction, multiple copies of the gene (or DNA) of interest is synthesized in vitro using two sets of primers (small chemically synthesized oligonucleotides that are complementary to the regions of DNA) and the enzyme DNA polymerase.

2. Real-time RT–PCR is a nuclear-derived method for detecting the presence of specific genetic material in any pathogen, including a virus (COVID-19).

A. 1 only   **B.** 2 only
C. Both 1 and 2   **D.** Neither 1 nor 2

Q.46 Which of the following is/are correctly matched?

1. Genetic engineering: Techniques to alter the chemistry of genetic material (DNA and RNA), to introduce these into host organisms and thus change the phenotype of the host organism.

2. Bioprocess engineering: Maintenance of sterile (microbial contamination-free) ambience in chemical engineering processes to enable the growth of only the desired microbe/eukaryotic cell in large quantities for the manufacture of biotechnological products

A. 1 only   **B.** 2 only
C. Both 1 and 2   **D.** Neither 1 nor 2

Q.47 On 29th April, DRDO successfully test-fired the Python Missile, Python missile belongs to which generation?

A. 6th generation   **B.** 4th generation
C. 7th generation   **D.** 5th generation

Q.48 In which city is the summer Olympic Games 2024 to be held?

A. Los Angeles   **B.** London
C. Beijing   **D.** Paris

Q.49 In which time is the raga des sung?

A. Dead of night
B. Morning
C. First stroke of the night
D. Second stroke of night

Q.50 Which of the following is well-known in singing?

A. Shobhana Narayan
B. Pandit Yuraj
C. M. S. Gopalakrishnan
D. M. S. Subbulakshmi

Q.51 Identify the segment in the sentence, which contains the grammatical error.

Sunita is senior to me in this office and know all the rules.
[SSC Sub Inspector (CPO), 2019]

A. Sunita is senior to me
B. all the rules

C. and know
D. in this office

Q.52 Identify the segment in the sentence, which contains the grammatical error.

One should be careful to re-read what they has written.

A. to re-read what
B. be careful
C. One should
D. they has written

Q.53 Choose the odd one out from the given alternative:

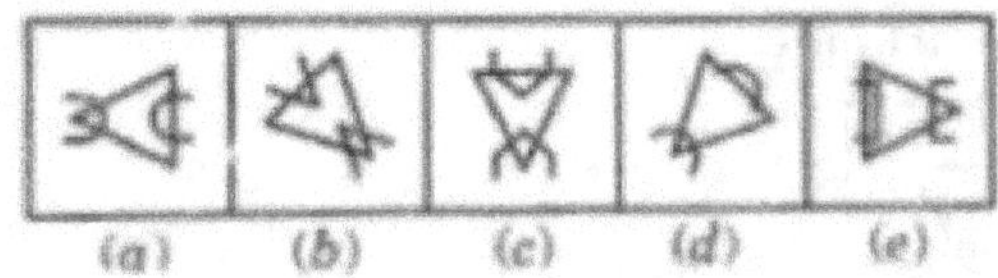

A. (a)
B. (b)
C. (c)
D. (d)

Q.54 Choose the odd one out from the given alternative:

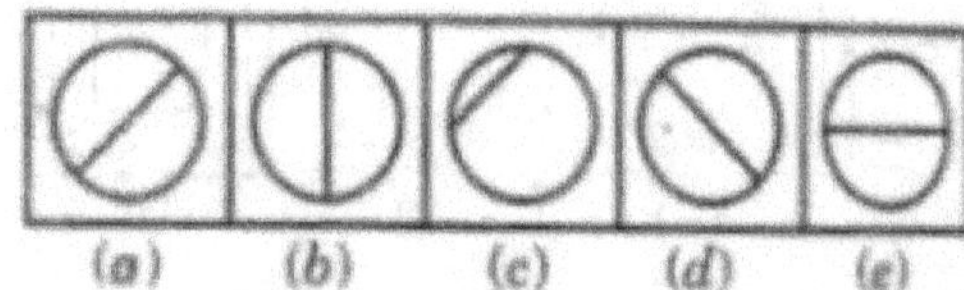

A. (a)
B. (b)
C. (c)
D. (e)

Ques (55-57):Direction: The following question consists of some Problem Figures followed by other figures marked 1, 2, 3, 4 called the Answer Figures.

Find out the correct answer figure that should come next in the sequence of problem figures.

Q.55

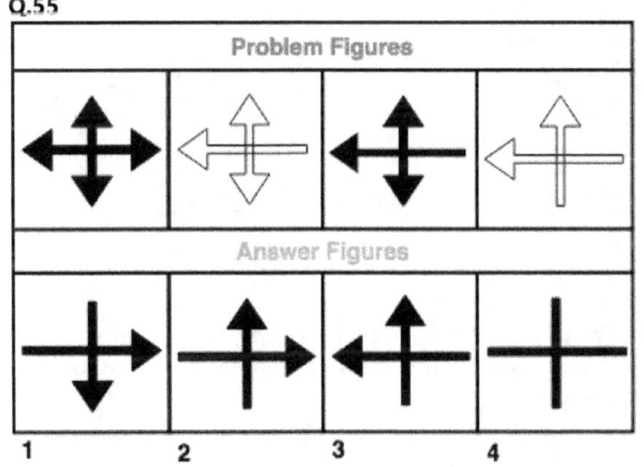

[Telangana Police Constable, 2015]

A. 1
B. 2
C. 3
D. 4

Q.56

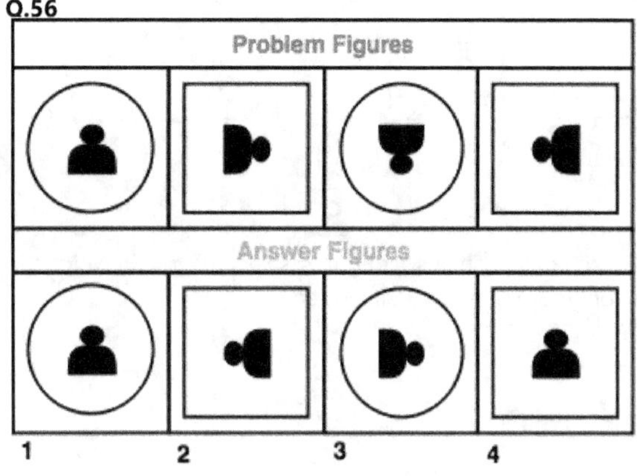

[UP Police Sub Inspector, 2021]

A. 1
B. 2
C. 3
D. 4

Q.57

[SSC Sub Inspector (CPO), 2020]

A. 1
B. 2
C. 3
D. 4

Q.58 Some amount of money is divided between Harsh and Nikhil in the ratio $8:17$. They go for shopping and Harsh spent $\frac{3}{4}$th of his money. Nikhil spent 20% of his money and is left with Rs. 6528. How much money do both spent altogether?

A. Rs.2832
B. Rs.4816
C. Rs.2880
D. Rs.4512

Q.59 A bag contains $Rs.\,1,50$ paisa and 25 paisa coins, and the ratio of no. of coins is $\frac{1}{2}:\frac{1}{3}:\frac{1}{5}$. If the total value of all coins is $Rs.\,860$. Find the numbers of 50 paisa coins.

A. 400
B. 600
C. 500
D. 300

Q.60 The ratio of story books in a library to other books is 1: 7. The total number of story books is 800. Find the total number of books in the library.

A. 5600
B. 5500
C. 6000
D. 5560

Q.61 Direction: In the following question, you are given a figure (X) followed by four alternative figures (1), (2), (3), and (4) such that figure (X) is embedded in one of them. Trace out the alternative figure which contains fig. (X) as its part.

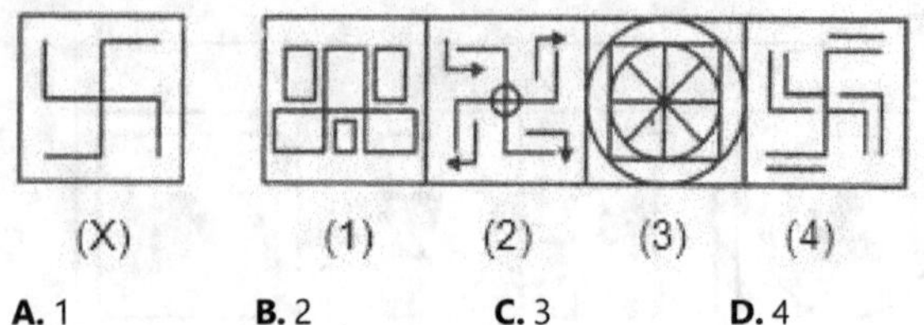

(X)　　(1)　　(2)　　(3)　　(4)

A. 1　　　**B.** 2　　　**C.** 3　　　**D.** 4

Q.62 From the given answer figures, select the one in which the question figure is hidden/embedded.

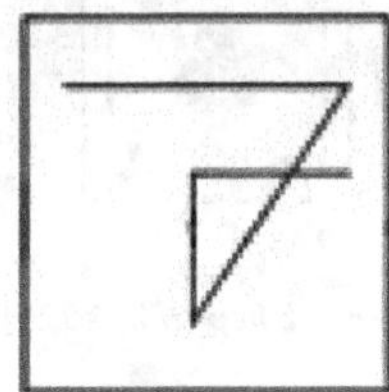

[SSC Constable (GD), 2019], [UP Police Constable, 2019], [SSC MTS, 2017]

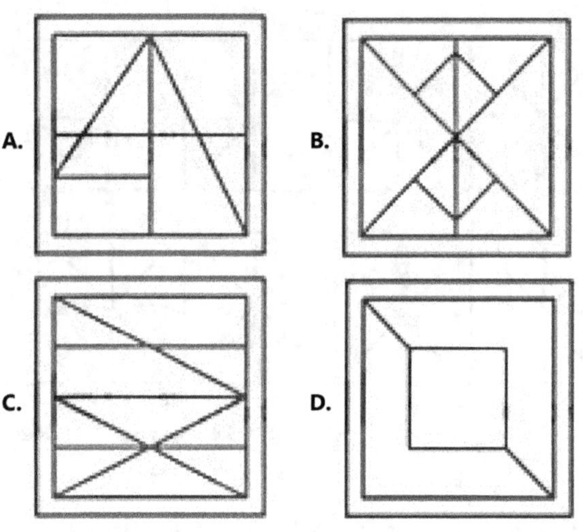

A.　　　　　B.

C.　　　　　D.

Q.63 Find out the alternative figure which contains figure (X) as its part.

(X)

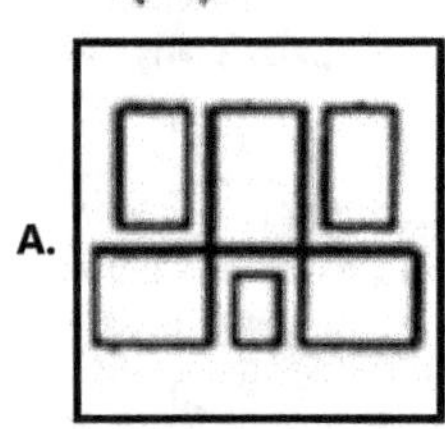

A.

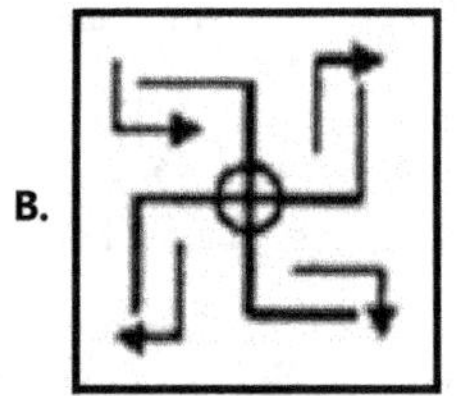

B.

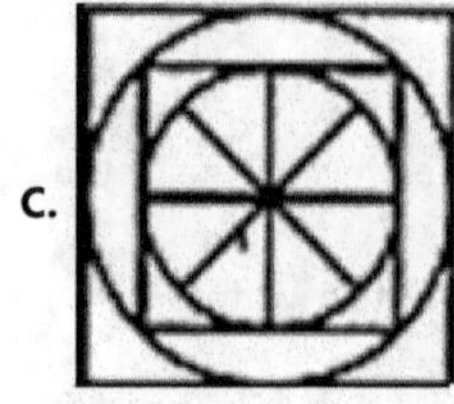

C.

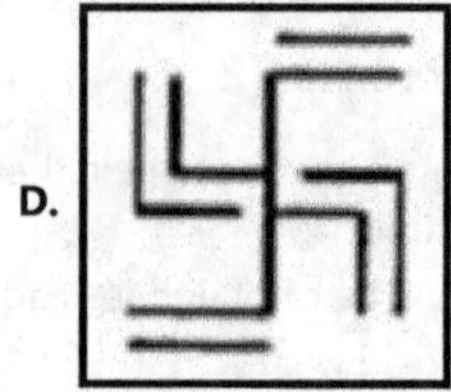

D.

Q.64 From the given answer figure, select the one in which the question figure is embedded.

Question figure

Answer figure

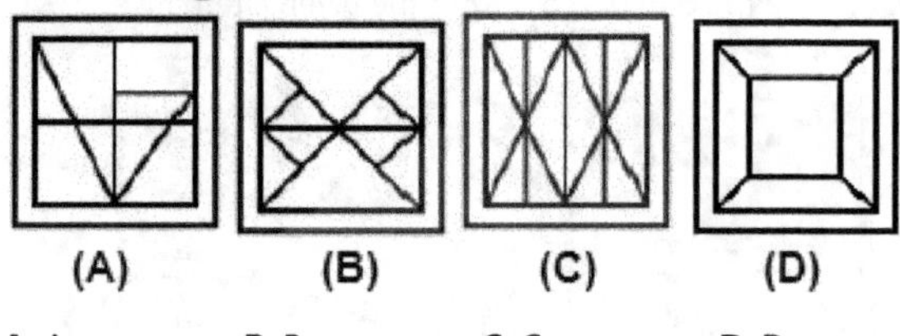

(A)　　　　(B)　　　　(C)　　　　(D)

A. A　　　**B.** B　　　**C.** C　　　**D.** D

Q.65 Choose the alternative figure which contains the given figure as its part.

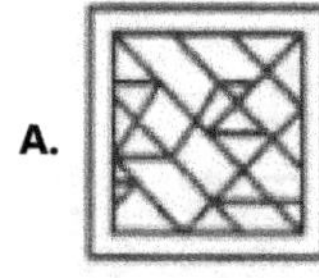

A.

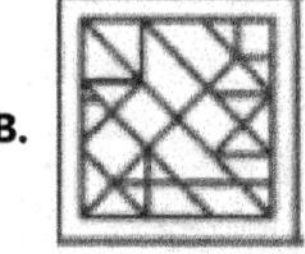

B.

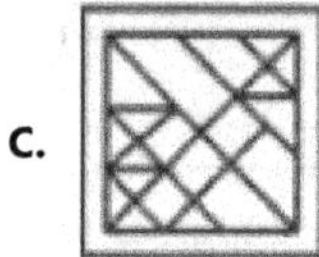

C.

D.

Q.66 The cost price of a shirt is Rs. 262.40, At what price should it be marked so as to gain 14% after allowing a 18% discount on the market price?

[SSC Selection Post Phase IX, 2020]

A. Rs. 364.80　　　　**B.** Rs. 356

C. Rs. 358.40　　　　**D.** Rs. 352

Q.67 Rina bought 24 kg sugar for Rs. 1,056. She sold it at a profit equal to the selling price of 4 kg of it. The selling price of sugar, per kg, was:

[SSC Selection Post Phase IX, 2020]

A. Rs. 54.50　　　　**B.** Rs. 54.20

C. Rs. 55.40　　　　**D.** Rs. 52.80

Q.68 An article is sold for Rs. 1,683, after giving three successive discounts of 15%, 10% and 12% on its marked price. The marked price of the article is:

[SSC Selection Post Phase IX, 2020]

A. Rs. 2,400
B. Rs. 2,640
C. Rs. 2,500
D. Rs. 2,560

Q.69 Direction: In the following diagram, the square represents the male, the triangle represents the manager, and the circle represents the engineer. Which numbered section represents men who are managers but not engineers?

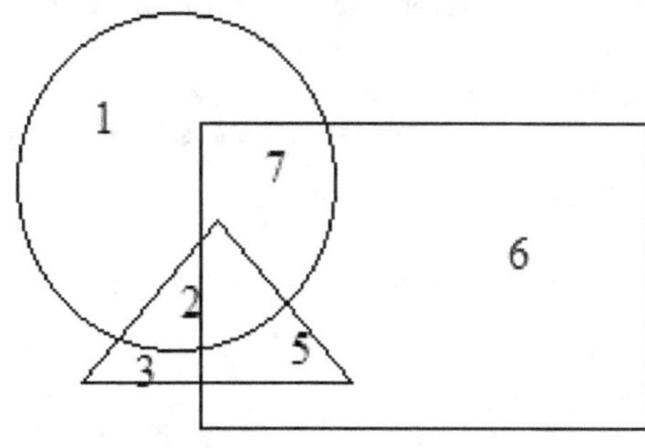

A. 5
B. 6
C. 2
D. 1

Q.70 Direction: Study the statements/statements given in the question and two conclusions carefully and answer that (A) if only I follow. (B) If only II follows. (C) If neither I nor II follows. (D) If both I and II follow.

Statement:

All towers are doors.

All doors are temples.

conclusion:

I. Some temples are towers.

II. Some towers are doors.

A. (A)
B. (B)
C. (C)
D. (D)

Ques (71-72):Direction: In the following figure small square represents the persons who know English, triangle to those who know Marathi, a big square to those who know Telugu, and a circle to those who know Hindi. In the different regions of the figures from 1 to 12 are given.

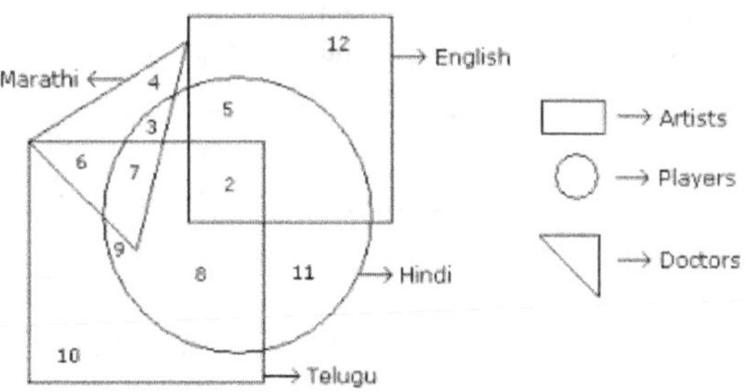

Q.71

How many persons can speak Marathi and Telugu both?

A. 10
B. 11
C. 13
D. None of these

Q.72 How many persons can speak all the languages?

A. 1
B. 8
C. 2
D. None

Q.73 Direction: Identify the diagram which best represents the relationship among the classes given below.

Mountains, Rivers, Ganga, Kanchenjunga

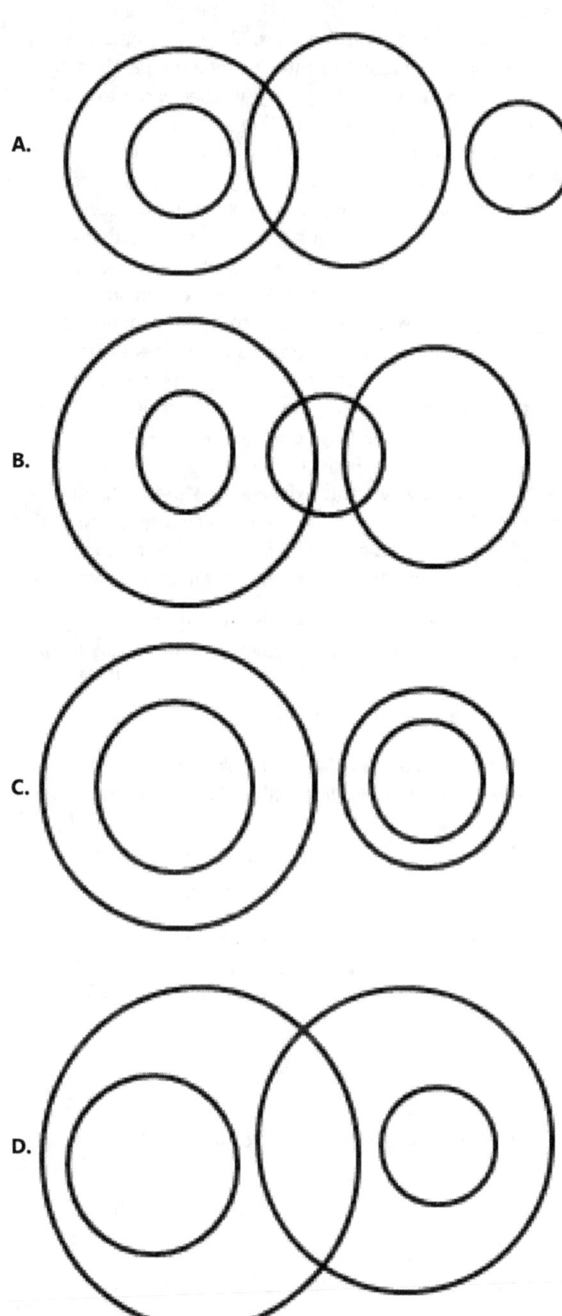

Ques (74-78):Direction: Each of the following sentences in this section has a blank space with four-word or a group of words given. Select whichever word or group of words you consider the most appropriate for the blank space and indicate your response on the answer sheet accordingly.

The difficult thing about (1)_______the science of habits is that most people when they hear about this field of research

(2)______ to know the secret formula for quickly changing any habit. If scientists have discovered how (3)______ patterns work, then it stands to reason that they (4)_______ have also found a recipe for rapid change, right? if only it (5)________ that easy. It's not (6)_______ formulas don't exist. The problem is that there isn't one formula for (7)________ habits. There are thousands. Individuals and habits are (8)________ different and so the specifics of diagnosing and changing the patterns in our lives differ from person to (9)_______ and behaviour to behaviour. Giving up cigarettes is different (10)_______ curbing overeating, which is different from changing how you communicate with your spouse, (11)______ is different from how you prioritize tasks at work. What's more, each person's habits are (12)_____ by different cravings. As a result, this book does not (13)_______ one prescription, Rather, I hoped to deliver something else: a framework for understanding (14)________ habits work and a guide to experimenting with how they (15)_______ change. Some habits yield easily to analysis and influence. Others are (16)_____ complex and obstinate and require prolonged study. And for others, change is a (17)______ that never fully concludes. But that does not (18)______ it can't occur. Each chapter in this book explains a different aspect of why habits exist and how they function. The framework (19)_________ in this section is an attempt to distill, in (20)________ very basic way, the tactics that researchers have found for diagnosing and shaping habits within our own lives.

Q.74 What would come in place of blank (11)?

[Indian Military Academy (IMA), 2020], [Officers Training Academy (OTA), 2020]

A. it   **B.** this   **C.** what   **D.** which

Q.75 What would come in place of blank (12)?

[Indian Military Academy (IMA), 2020], [Officers Training Academy (OTA), 2020]

A. broken   **B.** given
C. driven   **D.** prescribed

Q.76 What would come in place of blank (13)?

[Indian Military Academy (IMA), 2020], [Officers Training Academy (OTA), 2020]

A. contain   **B.** contains
C. contained   **D.** containing

Q.77 What would come in place of blank (14)?

[Indian Military Academy (IMA), 2020], [Officers Training Academy (OTA), 2020]

A. how   **B.** what   **C.** where   **D.** whose

Q.78 What would come in place of blank (15)?

[Indian Military Academy (IMA), 2020], [Officers Training Academy (OTA), 2020]

A. might   **B.** would   **C.** will   **D.** must

Q.79 Which one of the following is fundamental in the governance of the country?

A. Fundamental Rights   **B.** Fundamental Duties
C. Preamble   **D.** None of the above

Q.80 Give the antonym of Protects.

A. Defends   **B.** Deprives   **C.** Deserts   **D.** Devises

Q.81 Give the antonym of Terrible.

A. Soothing   **B.** Frightening
C. Horrible   **D.** Delectable

Q.82 Give the synonym of Busy.

A. Active   **B.** Occupied
C. Preoccupied   **D.** Diligent

Q.83 Statement A): Only one side of the moon is visible to us on Earth.

Statement B): The moon moves around the Earth in about 27 days and takes exactly the same time to complete 1 spin.

Select the correct option from the given alternatives.

[CTET Paper-II (Social Science), 2019]

A. Both A) and B) are true and B) is the correct explanation of A)

B. Both A) and B) are true, but B) is not the correct explanation of A)

C. A) is true, but B) is false

D. A) is false, but B) is true

Q.84 What percent of 1 day is 37 minutes 45 sec?

A. 2.62%   **B.** 2.1%   **C.** 2.69%   **D.** 0.25%

Q.85 40 litres of 60% concentration of acid solution is added to 35 litres of 80% concentration of acid solution. What is the concentration of acid in the new solution?

A. 66%   **B.** $66\frac{2}{3}\%$ **C.** $69\frac{1}{3}\%$ **D.** 69%

Q.86 A dishonest vendor professes to sell fruits at the cost price but uses a weight of 800 grams in lieu of 1 kg weight. Find the percentage gain.

A. 20%   **B.** 24%   **C.** 25%   **D.** 30%

Q.87 Direction: The following question has two blanks. In blank, a preposition has been omitted. Choose the set of prepositions for each blank that best fits in the context of the sentence.

Pakistan Prime Minister Imran Khan's bluster ________ Kashmir and the implied threat of a nuclear war were irresponsible and _______ the top.

A. among, from   **B.** on, over
C. at, above   **D.** on, among

Q.88 Direction: Fill in the blank with the most appropriate word.

The city was plunged _____ darkness due to sudden power failure.

[Punjab Patwari, 2016]

A. through   **B.** to   **C.** into   **D.** under

Q.89 She liked to be with him _________ than with the others, and when alone with him she sometimes laughed.

A. Good   **B.** Better   **C.** Best   **D.** Over

Q.90 You haven't many teeth left, but _______ few you have are sharp enough to make me shudder.

A. A   **B.** An   **C.** Very   **D.** The

Ques (91-95):Direction: Select a suitable figure from the four alternatives that would complete the figure.

Q.91

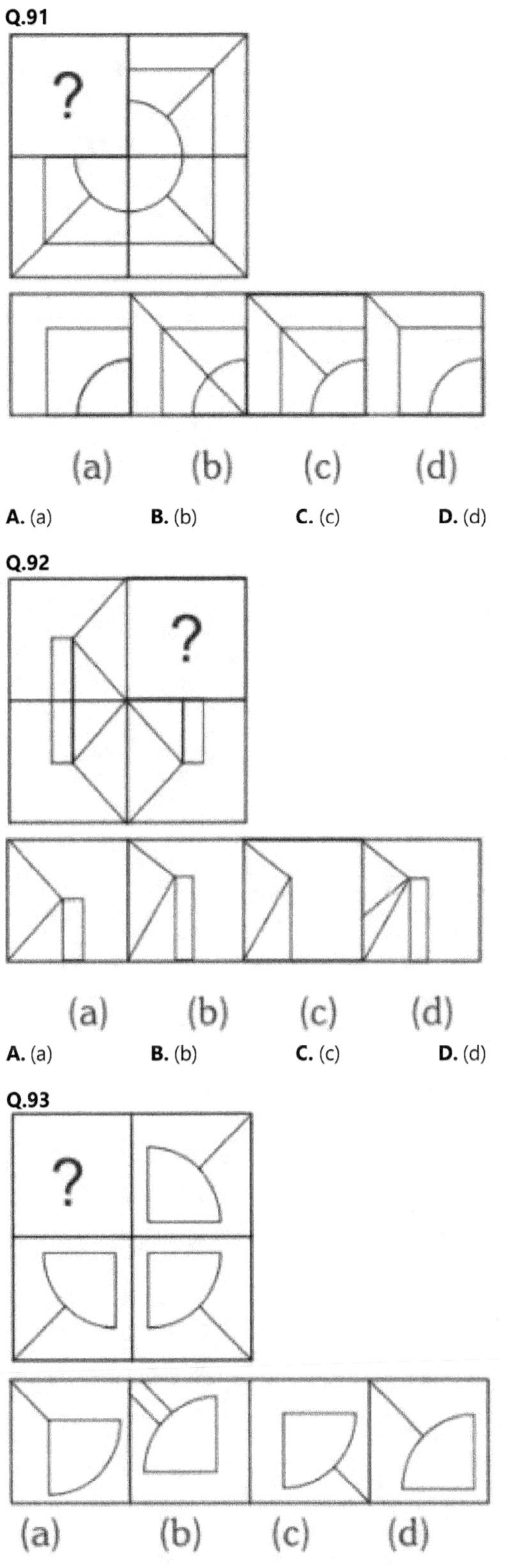

(a)   (b)   (c)   (d)

A. (a)   **B.** (b)   **C.** (c)   **D.** (d)

Q.92

(a)   (b)   (c)   (d)

A. (a)   **B.** (b)   **C.** (c)   **D.** (d)

Q.93

(a)   (b)   (c)   (d)

A. (a)   **B.** (b)   **C.** (c)   **D.** (d)

Q.94

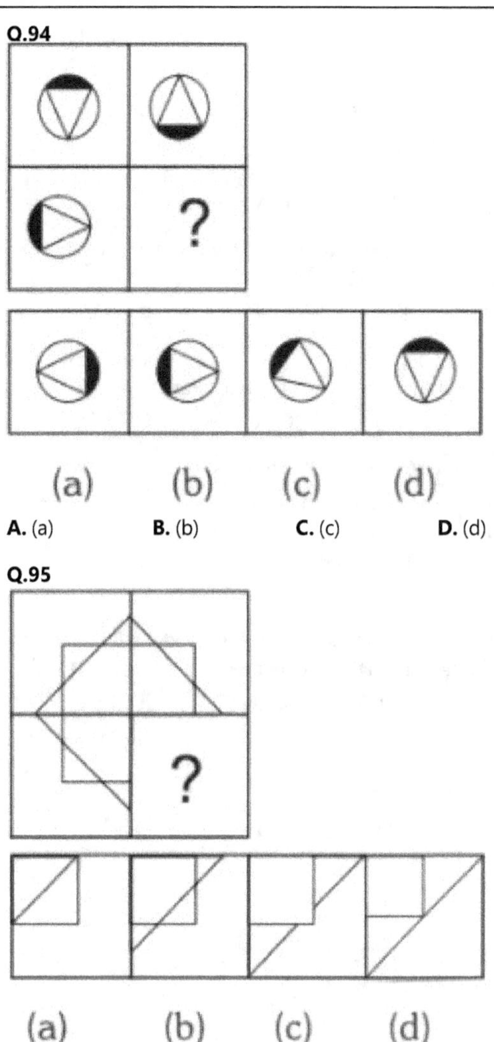

(a)   (b)   (c)   (d)

A. (a)   **B.** (b)   **C.** (c)   **D.** (d)

Q.95

(a)   (b)   (c)   (d)

A. (a)   **B.** (b)   **C.** (c)   **D.** (d)

Ques (96-100):Direction: Read the passage carefully and answer the following questions:

Huge attention and resources have been placed on the youth mental health crisis in recent years. Yet, the crisis is getting worse, not better. Existing solutions have assumed that today's youth have a resilience deficit, thus creating programmes to 'build' or 'create' resilience. Knowing this would completely change the approach needed for today's youth – and this is exactly what iheart has achieved. Our innovative, evidence-based mental wellbeing educational programme challenges current practices and outlooks and has already improved the lives of over 15,000 young people in twenty countries. Our role is to educate young people that they do NOT have a resilience deficit. Rather, we empower them with the confidence that they CAN uncover their built-in mental health, wellbeing and resilience so that they can overcome their challenges and realise their extraordinary potential. When we focus on solving the right problem – educating our children about their innate resilience –the evidence speaks for itself. 98% of children noticed a positive change in themselves at the end of the iheart programme. 95% would recommend the programme to a friend. 90% saw increased emotional resilience for dealing with adversity.

Q.96 Select the word that could replace the word resilience as used in the passage:

A. Rigidity
B. Flexibility
C. Fragility
D. Weakness

Q.97 How many saw percent of increased emotional resilience for dealing with adversity?

A. 89%   **B.** 90%   **C.** 98%   **D.** 76%

Q.98 How many per cent of children noticed a positive change in themselves at the end of the iheart programme?

A. 85%   **B.** 98%   **C.** 90%   **D.** 75%

Q.99 What is the suitable title for the passage?

A.   Solving physical health crisis
B.   Solving economic health crisis
C.   Solving mental health crises
D.   None of these

Q.100 Our innovative practices have improved the lives of over _____ young people in twenty countries.

A. 15000   **B.** 16000   **C.** 18000   **D.** 2000

// Smart Answer Sheet //

Correct — Percentage of students who answered correctly. **Skipped** — Percentage of students who skipped.

Q.	Ans.	Correct / Skipped	Q.	Ans.	Correct / Skipped	Q.	Ans.	Correct / Skipped	Q.	Ans.	Correct / Skipped	Q.	Ans.	Correct / Skipped	Q.	Ans.	Correct / Skipped
1	C	57.4 % / 33.74 %	18	B	27.15 % / 71.67 %	35	C	69.44 % / 30.41 %	52	D	41.63 % / 51.77 %	69	A	53.97 % / 40.32 %	86	C	67.07 % / 32.02 %
2	C	67.45 % / 30.71 %	19	B	43.73 % / 38.49 %	36	D	45.65 % / 50.0 %	53	D	67.86 % / 30.58 %	70	D	58.56 % / 32.36 %	87	B	40.65 % / 52.11 %
3	B	69.83 % / 30.03 %	20	B	42.35 % / 43.19 %	37	C	65.53 % / 31.54 %	54	C	58.36 % / 35.97 %	71	C	89.52 % / 10.28 %	88	C	66.78 % / 32.4 %
4	D	59.13 % / 40.18 %	21	B	81.65 % / 11.05 %	38	D	47.57 % / 43.06 %	55	C	80.53 % / 13.16 %	72	D	48.83 % / 43.98 %	89	B	85.11 % / 13.14 %
5	D	55.35 % / 31.68 %	22	A	19.48 % / 76.16 %	39	D	51.04 % / 46.9 %	56	A	79.04 % / 16.87 %	73	C	41.66 % / 42.18 %	90	D	82.92 % / 12.92 %
6	D	81.58 % / 10.42 %	23	A	84.96 % / 13.64 %	40	C	40.2 % / 37.5 %	57	D	78.47 % / 11.02 %	74	D	19.67 % / 67.09 %	91	C	44.15 % / 46.53 %
7	B	40.13 % / 46.53 %	24	A	32.32 % / 67.67 %	41	C	63.43 % / 30.82 %	58	D	85.8 % / 12.4 %	75	C	65.99 % / 30.78 %	92	B	56.89 % / 37.42 %
8	D	88.67 % / 10.22 %	25	B	47.79 % / 51.99 %	42	C	46.29 % / 45.19 %	59	A	68.63 % / 30.47 %	76	A	67.71 % / 31.05 %	93	D	41.6 % / 35.11 %
9	C	62.79 % / 34.88 %	26	B	43.41 % / 39.18 %	43	D	60.93 % / 38.85 %	60	A	64.3 % / 34.3 %	77	A	11.21 % / 76.55 %	94	A	47.83 % / 43.66 %
10	C	77.54 % / 17.08 %	27	D	47.26 % / 40.4 %	44	B	67.85 % / 32.08 %	61	C	59.88 % / 36.87 %	78	A	55.2 % / 31.47 %	95	B	65.17 % / 33.43 %
11	C	61.25 % / 37.08 %	28	A	58.83 % / 35.24 %	45	C	57.16 % / 40.62 %	62	A	55.14 % / 41.74 %	79	D	86.62 % / 10.21 %	96	B	46.98 % / 38.83 %
12	C	30.93 % / 67.04 %	29	B	62.47 % / 32.92 %	46	C	11.86 % / 70.21 %	63	C	84.5 % / 13.76 %	80	C	87.45 % / 11.91 %	97	B	58.36 % / 38.89 %
13	C	65.32 % / 31.28 %	30	C	68.27 % / 30.51 %	47	D	56.49 % / 30.45 %	64	A	47.1 % / 31.21 %	81	A	88.89 % / 10.65 %	98	B	69.2 % / 30.74 %
14	B	55.95 % / 40.44 %	31	A	61.54 % / 31.82 %	48	D	40.62 % / 57.24 %	65	A	56.17 % / 30.91 %	82	B	85.62 % / 14.01 %	99	C	63.67 % / 30.53 %
15	B	46.96 % / 52.19 %	32	A	51.79 % / 38.05 %	49	D	60.82 % / 37.63 %	66	A	40.06 % / 53.29 %	83	A	47.56 % / 32.44 %	100	A	64.96 % / 30.74 %
16	B	67.43 % / 32.19 %	33	C	52.5 % / 31.28 %	50	D	58.1 % / 30.32 %	67	D	77.98 % / 10.79 %	84	A	66.63 % / 32.68 %			
17	C	48.96 % / 42.43 %	34	B	57.03 % / 31.72 %	51	C	53.57 % / 33.14 %	68	C	63.48 % / 32.6 %	85	C	83.28 % / 14.16 %			

//Hints and Solutions//

1. Vicky Kaushal has won the Best Male actor award in the International Indian Film Academy Awards held in Abu Dhabi. He has bagged the award for the best performance for a leading role (Male) at the IIFA 2022 held in Abu Dhabi. He won the award for the film Sardar Udham, directed by Shoojit Sircar.

Hence, the correct option is (C).

2. Pieter Elbers has been appinted as the Chief Executive Officer (CEO) of Indigo in September 2022.

Pieter Elbers has joined IndiGo as the Chief Executive Officer (CEO). Elbers replaced Ronojoy Dutta who is set to retire on 30 September 2022. Elbers has previously served as the President and Chief Executive Officer of KLM Royal Dutch Airlines since 2014 and is also a member of the Executive Committee of the Air France-KLM Group.

Hence, the correct option is (C).

3. China launched into orbit a new-generation weather satellite named Fengyun-4B (FY- 4B) successfully.

The Fengyun-4B satellite was launched aboard a Long March 3B rocket into the geostationary orbit, to join the network of Fengyun satellites. The first of the Fengyun series, a low-Earth orbit satellite testing machine – FY-1A, was launched in 1988. Hence, the correct option is (B).

4. ONDC has signed a Memorandum of Understanding (MoU) with SIDBI for the coordination of functions of institutions engaged in similar activities in August 2022.

- The partnership is aimed to change the landscape of MSMEs by bringing them into the ONDC network and accelerating their participation in eCommerce.
- The MoU was signed by Sivasubramanian Ramanan, Chairman & MD of SIDBI and T Koshy, MD & CEO of ONDC.

Hence, the correct option is (D).

5. Tirath Singh Rawat became the Chief Minister of Uttarakhand in March 2021.

- He is a former Chief Minister of Uttarakhand and a serving Member of Parliament in India.
- In the 2019 Indian general election, he was elected to the 17th Lok Sabha from the Garhwal constituency as a member of the Bharatiya Janata Party.
- From 9 February 2013 until 31 December 2015, he was the party head of the Bharatiya Janata Party Uttarakhand and a former member of the Uttarakhand Legislative Assembly from the Chaubattakhal constituency from 2012 to 2017.
- He was also Uttarakhand's first Education Minister.

Hence, the correct option is (D).

6. Given,

Principal = Rs. 300

Rate of interest = 10%

Time = 2 years

As we know,

Compound interest = Principal[1 + ($\frac{rate}{100}$)]^{time} - Principal

Compound Interest for 2 years = 300[1 + ($\frac{10}{100}$)]^2 - 300

= 363 - 300

= 63

∴ The compound interest for 2 years is Rs. 63.

Hence, the correct option is (D).

7. Given, $P = $ Rs. $9000; R = 8\%; n = 2$ years

We know that, $CI = A - P$

$$\Rightarrow CI = P \left(1 + \frac{R}{100} \right)^n - P$$

$$= 9000 \left(1 + \frac{8}{100} \right)^2 - 9000$$

$$= 9000 \left(\frac{27}{25} \right)^2 - 9000$$

$$= 9000 \left(\frac{729}{625} - 1 \right)$$

$$= 9000 \times 104 = \text{Rs. } 1497.6$$

Hence, the correct option is (B).

8. Given:

The sum becomes five times itself in 8 years at simple interest.

Time = 8 years

Let the sum of money be x.

After 8 years it becomes 5 times.

So it becomes 5x,

∴ The simple interest is 5x – x = 4x

Let, the rate of interest be y.

$$4x = \frac{(x \times y \times 8)}{100}$$

$$y = \frac{400}{8} = 50\%$$

Hence, the correct option is (D).

9. In the given recurring decimal, the non-recurring digit is 1, recurring digits are 27.

Let x = $1.\overline{27}$ = 1.272727..... (i)

100x = 127.272727..... (ii)

Subtraction eqution (i) from (ii) we'll get

99x = 126

$$\Rightarrow x = \frac{126}{99} = \frac{14}{11}$$

$1.\overline{27}$ is equal to $\frac{14}{11}$

Hence, the correct option is (C).

10. Given:

$$\frac{10}{7}(1 - 2.43 \times 10^{-3}) = 1.417 + x$$

$$\Rightarrow \frac{10}{7}(1 - 0.00243) = 1.417 + x$$

$$\Rightarrow \frac{10}{7} \times 0.99757 = 1.417 + x$$

$$\Rightarrow 1.4251 = 1.417 + x$$

$$\Rightarrow x = 1.4251 - 1.417$$

$$\therefore x = 0.0081$$

Hence, the correct option is (C).

11. Given:

$$\frac{(1.569\times1.569\times0.431)+(1.569\times0.431\times0.431)}{(1.569+0.431)^2-(1.569-0.431)^2}$$

$$= \frac{(1.569\times1.569\times0.431)+(1.569\times0.431\times0.431)}{4\times1.569\times0.431}$$

$$= \frac{(1.569\times0.431)\times(1.569+0.431)}{4 \times 1.569 \times 0.431}$$

$$= \frac{(1.569+0.431)}{4}$$

$$= \frac{2}{4} = 0.5$$

Hence, the correct option is (C).

12.

- Non-Aligned Movement (NAM) was established in 1961 in Belgrade, SR Serbia Yugoslavia.

- Indian Prime Minister Jawaharlal Nehru also contributed to the established NAM.

- The Non-Aligned Movement (NAM) is a forum of 120 developing world states that are not formally aligned with or against any major power bloc. After the United Nations, it is the largest grouping of states worldwide.

- Drawing on the principles agreed at the Bandung Conference in 1955, the Non-Aligned Movement was established in 1961 in Belgrade, SR Serbia, Yugoslavia through an initiative of the Indian Prime Minister Jawaharlal Nehru, Ghanaian President Kwame Nkrumah, Indonesian President Sukarno, Egyptian President Gamal Abdel Nasser and Yugoslav President Josip Broz Tito.

Hence, the correct option is (C).

13. The meaning of the given idiom 'Let the grass grow under one's feet' is 'To remain idle'

- Examples,

    - I used to let the grass grow under my feet, and I missed out on a lot of opportunities.

    - Mary doesn't let the grass grow under her feet. She's always busy.

- The word 'idle' means 'unemployed or unoccupied; inactive'.

- Therefore, from the given explanation and examples, option (C) is the correct answer.

Hence, the correct option is (C).

14. The meaning of the given idiom 'Be in the same boat' is 'be in the same unfortunate or unpleasant situation as others'.

- Examples,

    - My sister failed her driver's test, and I'll be in the same boat if I don't practice parallel parking.

    - None of us could pass the maths exam, so we're all in the same boat.

- From the explanation and examples that are given above, option (B) is the correct answer.

Hence, the correct option is (B).

15. The ants play an essential role in existence of life on Earth. The absence of ants may increase the population of termites. Ants introduce air into the soil that allows the water and oxygen to reach the roots in the soil. Therefore, the absence of ants may destroy life on the Earth.

Hence, the correct option is (B).

16. The given colors are arranged in increasing order of their frequency. So, the logical and meaningful order is:

2. Red

5. Orange

3. Yellow

1. Blue

4. Indigo

Hence, the correct option is (B).

17. The logical and meaningful order is:

3. Pupil

5. Pinna

1. Throat

4. Liver

2. Bladder

The given words are arranged from the parts of upper body to lower body.

Hence, the correct option is (C).

18. The above-given sentence is in the active voice.

We need to change it in the passive voice.

The following steps are required to change the given sentence into passive voice:

- The subject 'the tennis ball' of the active voice will become the object of the passive voice.
- The object 'Dhiraj' of the active voice will become the subject of the passive voice.
- The tense(simple past tense) will change according to the following structure:-
    - Active Voice - Subject + did + V₁ or V₂ + Object.
    - Passive Voice - Object + was/were + V₃ + by + Object.
- Thus, 'hit' will be converted to 'was hit'.

Hence, the correct option is (B).

19. The correct answer is:

She was found guilty of theft.

The voice of a verb tells whether the subject of the sentence performs or receives the action.

In active voice, the subject (agent) acts upon the verb; while in passive, the verb acts upon the subject (agent).

Rules of Conversion from Active to Passive Voice:

1. Identify the subject, the verb and the object: S+V+O.
2. Change the object into subject.
3. Put the suitable helping verb or auxiliary verb.
4. Change the verb into past participle of the verb.
5. Add the preposition "by".
6. Change the subject into object.

Option (B) follows all the proper conversion rules.

Hence, the correct option is (B).

20. The pattern follow is;

$95 = 9^2 + 5^2 = 106;$

Similarly,

$87 = 8^2 + 7^2 = 113$

Hence, the correct option is (B).

21. The baby of Lion is called Cub. Similarly, the baby of Kangaroo is called Joey.

Hence, the correct option is (B).

22. Given:

XY → 2425 (X → 24 and Y → 25)

Let's check the options,

(A) LM → L → 12, M → 13, LM → 1213

(B) NL → N → 14, L → 12, NL → 1412

(C) ML → M → 13, L → 12, ML → 1312

(D) LN → L → 12, N → 14, LN → 1214

Hence, the correct option is (A).

23. The Sardar Sarovar Dam is in Gujrat.

Similarly,

Tehri Dam is in Uttarakhand and is the biggest dam of India.

Hence, the correct option is (A).

24. Here the pattern followed is:

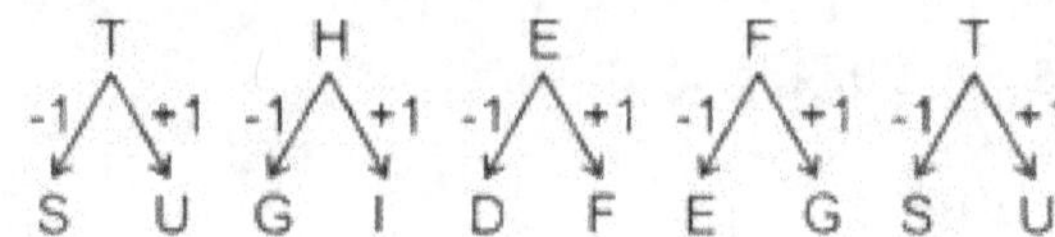

Similarly;

Thus, "PULSE" can be written as "OQTVKMRTDF".

Hence, the correct option is (A).

25. Given,

Distance = 70 km and time taken to meet:

If travel in same direction = 7 hours

If travel towards each other = 1 hour

Let the speed of the cars be S_1

and S_2 And $S_1 - S_2 = \dfrac{70}{7} = 10$ ... (i)

Also $S_1 + S_2 = \dfrac{70}{1} = 70$ ... (ii)

From equation (i) and (ii)

$$S_1 = \frac{10 + 70}{2} = 40 \ km/hr$$

And $S_2 = \dfrac{70 - 10}{2} = 30 \ km/hr$

$\therefore$ Required speeds are $40 \ km/hr$ and $30 \ km/hr$

Hence, the correct option is (B).

26. Given,

Total distance travelled:

$$= (10 + 12) km$$

$$= 22 \ km$$

And speed is 12 km/hr and 10 km/hr

Total time taken :

$$= \left(\frac{10}{12} + \frac{12}{10} \right) hrs$$

$$= \frac{61}{30} hrs$$

∴ Average speed :

$$= \left(22 \times \frac{30}{61}\right) km/hr$$

$$= 10.8 \ km/hr$$

Hence, the correct option is (B).

27. Given,

Speed of A = 4 km/hr and speed of B = 10 km/hr.

Distance covered by A in 4 $hrs = (4 \times 4)km = 16 \ km$

Relative speed of B and $A = (10 - 4)km/hr = 6 \ km/hr$

$$Speed = \frac{Distance}{Time}$$

Time taken to cover $16 \ km$ at relative speed:

$$= \left(\frac{16}{6}\right) hrs$$

$$= \frac{8}{3} hr$$

Distance covered by in $\frac{8}{3}$ hrs

$$= \left(10 \times \frac{8}{3}\right) km$$

$$= \left(\frac{80}{3}\right) km$$

$$= 26.7 \ km$$

Hence, the correct option is (D).

28. Speed of the thief = 60 km/hr

Speed of police = 80 km/hr

Thief and police running in the same direction, then effective speed = 80 – 60 = 20 km/hr

Distance covered by thief in (30 min or $\frac{1}{2}$ hr) = 60 × $\left(\frac{1}{2}\right)$ = 30 km

Time taken by police to catch the thief = $\frac{30}{20} = \frac{3}{2}$ hrs

Distance covered by the police in $\frac{3}{2}$ hrs = 80 × $\left(\frac{3}{2}\right)$ = 120 km.

Hence, the correct option is (A).

29. The pattern is as follows:

76 = 24 x 3 + 4

39 = 12 x 3 + 3

52 = 16 x 3 + 4

61 = 19 x 3 + 4

Thus the odd number is 12 – 39.

Hence, the correct option is (B).

30. Onlookers, Theatre goers, and spectators are all people who are there to watch something whereas a queue does not necessarily refer to people who are there to watch something. That makes queue the odd one out.

Hence, the correct option is (C).

31. Except for skin, Heart, Lungs, and Kidney are internal parts of a human body.

Hence, the correct option is (A).

32. Manupatra, pioneer in online legal research in India since 2001, is India's premier legal information resource. It is the largest content aggregator of Indian and International material, linking primary information, secondary material and proprietary analytical content.

LexisNexis provides customers with access to billions of searchable documents and records from more than 60000 legal, news and business sources. Westlaw India is the first online legal information resource combining Indian and International Law.

Whereas http://www.scholar.google.com is not an authentic one.

Hence, the correct option is (A).

33. Symphony, orchestra and guitar are related to music but Mob is an electronic device.

Hence, the correct option is (C).

34. Given:

The average salary of all the workers in a factory = Rs.15000

Average salary of 12 technicians = Rs. 18000

Average salary of the Rest of the workers = Rs. 12000

Formulae used:

$$Average = \frac{Sum \ of \ observations}{Number \ of \ observations}$$

Calculation:

Let the number of employees be "x"

Total salary of all workers = 15000x

Total salary of 12 technicians = 18000 × 12 = 216000

Total salary of rest of the workers = 12000(x - 12) = 12000x - 144000

According to question

15000x = 12000x - 144000 + 216000

x = 24

∴ Total number of workers in the factory is 24
Hence, the correct option is (B).

35. Given,

The ratio of the number of employees in the technical section and the management section of the company = 7 : 2.

The average salaries of employees in the technical section = Rs. 25000

The average salaries of employees in the management section = Rs. 47500

Formulae used:

$$\text{Average} = \frac{\text{Sum of observations}}{\text{Number of observations}}$$

Calculation:

The total number of employees be 9

Total salary of Technical section = 25000 × 7 = 175000

Total salary of the management section = 47500 × 2 = 95000

$$\text{Average salary} = \frac{270000}{9}$$

∴ The average salary of employees of these two sections together is Rs. 30000
Hence, the correct option is (C).

36. Given:

$$\frac{(A+B+C)}{3} = 65$$

$$\frac{(A+B+C+D)}{4} = 70$$

$$\frac{(B+C+D)}{3} = 75$$

Formulae used:

$$\text{Average} = \frac{\text{Sum of observations}}{Number of observations}$$

Calculation:

(B + C + D) = 75 × 3 = 225

Now,

$$\frac{(A+225)}{4} = 70$$

A + 225 = 280

∴ A = 55
Hence, the correct option is (D).

37.

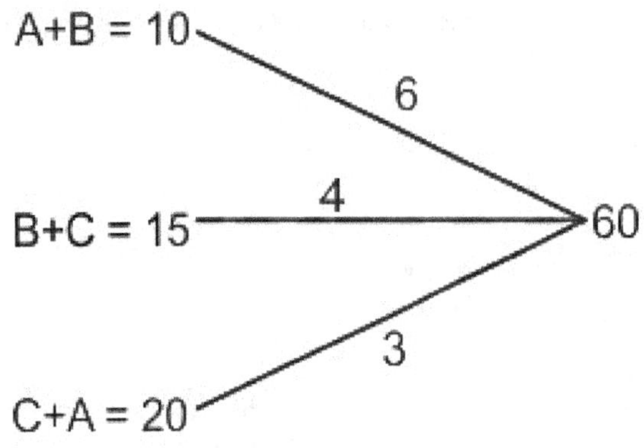

2(A + B + C) = 6 + 4 + 3

⇒ 2(A + B + C) = 13

⇒ A + B + C = 6.5

If A, B and C work together for 8 days, the work done = 8 × 6.5 = 52 units

Remaining work = 60 − 52 = 8 units

Efficiency of C = Efficiency of (A + B + C) − Efficiency of (A + B)

⇒ Efficiency of C = 6.5 − 6 = 0.5

∴ The remaining work will be completed by C in $\frac{8}{0.5}$ = 16 days

Hence, the correct option is (C).

38. Given:

Pages printed by A and B = 2400

Hours of work = 5

Days of work = 5

A's 2.5 hrs work = B's 1.5 hrs work

We know that,

Total unit of work = Work done by (A + B) in 1 hour × No of hours of work in 1 day × No of days of work

∵ A's 2.5 hrs work = B's 1.5 hrs work

⇒ A × 2.5 = B × 1.5

⇒ $\frac{A}{B} = \frac{1.5}{2.5}$

⇒ $\frac{A}{B} = \frac{3}{5}$

Let, A's one hour's work = 3x

B's one hours work = 5x

∴ (5x + 3x) × 5hr × 5 days = 2400 pages

⇒ 8x × 5 × 5 = 2400

⇒ x = $\frac{2400}{(8×5×5)}$

⇒ x = 12

∴ Pages printed by B in 1 hour = 5x = 5 × 12 = 60 pages.

Hence, the correct option is (D).

39. Given:

Anil and Shashi took 16 and 24 days respectively to complete a piece of work.

Anil and Shashi worked for a day alternately and Anil begins the work.

We know that,

$$\text{Efficiency} = \frac{Work}{Time}$$

Total work = LCM

Total work = LCM(16, 24) = 48

Person	Time taken	Total work	Efficiency

| Anil | 16 | 48 | $\dfrac{48}{16} = 3$ |
| Shashi | 24 | 48 | $\dfrac{48}{24} = 2$ |

∵ Anil begins the work and Anil and Shashi are working alternately

∴ Work done by Anil and Shashi in 2 days = 3 + 2 = 5

So, In every 2 days, Anil and Shashi can complete 5 units of work

Now, 2 days = 5 unit

$\Rightarrow 9 \times 2$ days $= 9 \times 5$ unit

$\Rightarrow 18$ days = 45 units.

Remaining work = 48 - 45 = 3 units

Anil will do 3 units in one day.

Total days = 18 + 1 = 19 days

∴ P and Q completed the work in 19 days if they work on alternate days.

Hence, the correct option is (D).

40. Introvert: A person who does not express himself freely.

Insolvent: Not having enough money to pay what you owe.

Invincible: Too strong or powerful to be defeated.

Impostor: A person who deceives others by pretending to be someone else.

Hence, the correct option is (C).

41. 'Ornithologist' is a person "who specializes in the study of birds".

'Biologist' is a person who studies biology.

'Naturalist' is a person who studies and knows a lot about plants and animals.

'Zoologist' is a person who scientifically studies animals.

Hence, the correct option is (C).

42. Decomposers break down complex organic matter into inorganic substances like carbon dioxide, water, and nutrients and the process is called decomposition.

Dead plant remains such as leaves, bark, flowers, and dead remains of animals, including faecal matter, constitute detritus, which is the raw material for decomposition.

The important steps in the process of decomposition are fragmentation, leaching, catabolism, humification, and mineralization.

Detritivores (e.g. earthworms) break down detritus into smaller particles. This process is called fragmentation.

By the process of leaching, water-soluble inorganic nutrients go down into the soil horizon and get precipitated as unavailable salts. Therefore, statement 1 is correct.

Bacterial and fungal enzymes degrade detritus into simpler inorganic substances. This process is called catabolism.

It is important to note that all the above steps in decomposition operate simultaneously on the detritus.

Humification and mineralization occur during decomposition in the soil.

Humification leads to the accumulation of a dark-coloured amorphous substance called humus that is highly resistant to microbial action and undergoes decomposition at an extremely slow rate. Therefore, statement 2 is correct.

- Being colloidal in nature it serves as a reservoir of nutrients.
- The hummus is further degraded by some microbes and the release of inorganic nutrients occurs by the process known as mineralization.

Hence, the correct option is (C).

43. Coronaviruses belong to a family of viruses called Coronaviridae and the order Nidovirales.

- It gets its name from its crown-like shape.
- They are found in animals and birds.
- They are Zoonotic in nature.
- They are Zoonotic in nature.

Some types of coronavirus are dangerous for humans and result in severe diseases such as respiratory syndromes (MERS – Middle East Respiratory Syndrome and SARS – Severe Acute Respiratory Syndrome).

A new strain of the coronavirus that has not been identified previously is called a novel coronavirus (nCov).

Coronavirus disease 2019 is an infectious disease caused by Severe Acute Respiratory Syndrome Coronavirus 2 (SARS-CoV-2).

Coronavirinae can be further subdivided into alpha, beta, gamma, and delta coronaviruses.

It is an RNA virus with ribonucleic acid (RNA) as its genetic material that means the virus blends with its host's DNA and can mutate rapidly. Therefore, statement 1 is correct.

- RNA viruses are single-stranded. Therefore, statement 2 is correct.
- The RNA mutation rate is higher than the DNA.
- RNA replication takes place in the cytoplasm. Therefore, statement 3 is correct.
- RNA viruses are unstable.

Hence, the correct option is (D).

44. Gene therapy is a collection of methods that allows correction of a gene defect that has been diagnosed in a child/embryo. Therefore, statement 1 is correct.

Here genes are inserted into a person's cells and tissues to treat a disease.

Correction of a genetic defect involves the delivery of a normal gene into the individual or embryo to take over the function of and compensate for the non-functional gene.

The first clinical gene therapy was given in 1990 to a 4-year old girl with adenosine deaminase (ADA) deficiency.

This enzyme is crucial for the immune system to function.

- The disorder is caused due to the deletion of the gene for adenosine deaminase.

- In some children, ADA deficiency can be cured by bone marrow transplantation. Therefore, statement 2 is not correct.

- in others, it can be treated by enzyme replacement therapy, in which functional ADA is given to the patient by injection.

- But the problem with both of these approaches that they are not completely curative.

As a first step towards gene therapy, lymphocytes from the blood of the patient are grown in a culture outside the body.

A functional ADA cDNA (using a retroviral vector) is then introduced into these lymphocytes, which are subsequently returned to the patient.

However, as these cells are not immortal, the patient requires a periodic infusion of such genetically engineered lymphocytes.

However, if the gene isolate from marrow cells producing ADA is introduced into cells at early embryonic stages, it could be a permanent cure.

Hence, the correct option is (B).

45. PCR (Polymerase Chain Reaction):

- In this reaction, multiple copies of the gene (or DNA) of interest is synthesized in vitro using two sets of primers (small chemically synthesized oligonucleotides that are complementary to the regions of DNA) and the enzyme DNA polymerase. Therefore, statement 1 is correct.

- The enzyme extends the primers using the nucleotides provided in the reaction and the genomic DNA as a template.

- If the process of replication of DNA is repeated many times, the segment of DNA can be amplified approximately a billion times, i.e. 1 billion copies are made.

- Such repeated amplification is achieved by the use of a thermostable DNA polymerase (isolated from a bacterium, Thermus aquaticus), which remain active during the high temperature-induced denaturation of double-stranded DNA.

- The amplified fragment if desired can now be used to ligate with a vector for further cloning.

RT-PCR (Real-time Polymerase Chain Reaction):

- Reverse transcription PCR, or RT-PCR, allows the use of RNA as a template. An additional step allows the detection and amplification of RNA.

- The RNA is reverse transcribed into complementary DNA (cDNA), using reverse transcriptase.

- The quality and purity of the RNA template are essential for the success of RT-PCR.

- The first step of RT-PCR is the synthesis of a DNA/RNA hybrid.

- Reverse transcriptase also has an RNase H function, which degrades the RNA portion of the hybrid.

- The single-stranded DNA molecule is then completed by the DNA-dependent DNA polymerase activity of the reverse transcriptase into cDNA.

- The efficiency of the first-strand reaction can affect the amplification process.

- The standard PCR procedure is used to amplify the cDNA. The possibility to revert RNA into cDNA by RT-PCR has many advantages.

- RNA is single-stranded and very unstable, which makes it difficult to work with.

- Most commonly, it serves as the first step in qPCR, which quantifies RNA transcripts in a biological sample.

- Real-time RT–PCR is a nuclear-derived method for detecting the presence of specific genetic material in any pathogen, including a virus (COVID-19). Therefore, statement 2 is correct.

Hence, the correct option is (C).

46.

- Biotechnology deals with techniques of using live organisms or enzymes from organisms to produce products and processes useful to humans.

- In this sense, making curd, bread, or wine, which are all microbe-mediated processes, could also be thought of as a form of biotechnology.

- However, it is used in a restricted sense today, to refer to such processes that use genetically modified organisms to achieve the same on a larger scale.

- Further, many other processes/techniques are also included under biotechnology.

- For example, in vitro fertilization leading to a 'test-tube' baby, synthesizing a gene and using it, developing a DNA vaccine, or correcting a defective gene, are all part of biotechnology.

- Among many, the two core techniques that enabled the birth of modern biotechnology are:

1. Genetic engineering: Techniques to alter the chemistry of genetic material (DNA and RNA), to introduce these into host organisms and thus change the phenotype of the host organism. Therefore, Statement 1 is correct.

2. Bioprocess engineering: Maintenance of sterile (microbial contamination-free) ambience in chemical engineering processes to enable the growth of only the desired microbe/eukaryotic cell in large quantities for the manufacture of biotechnological products like antibiotics, vaccines, enzymes, etc. Therefore, Statement 2 is correct.

- The techniques of genetic engineering which include the creation of recombinant DNA, use of gene cloning,

and gene transfer, overcome this limitation and allows us to isolate and introduce only one or a set of desirable genes without introducing undesirable genes into the target organism.

- The piece of DNA would not be able to multiply itself in the progeny cells of the organism. But, when it gets integrated into the genome of the recipient, it may multiply and be inherited along with the host DNA.

This is because the alien piece of DNA has become part of a chromosome, which has the ability to replicate.

- In a chromosome, there is a specific DNA sequence called the origin of replication, which is responsible for initiating replication.
- Therefore, for the multiplication of any alien piece of DNA in an organism, it needs to be a part of a chromosome(s) that has a specific sequence known as the 'origin of replication'.
- Thus, an alien DNA is linked with the origin of replication, so that, this alien piece of DNA can replicate and multiply itself in the host organism.
- This can also be called cloning or making multiple identical copies of any template DNA.

Hence, the correct option is (C).

47. The Defence Research and Development Organization (DRDO), successfully test-fired the 5th generation Python-5 missile from Tejas aircraft, at Goa.

The Python-5 missile is an Air-to-Air missile (AAM). Python-5 is powered by a solid propellant rocket engine. The propulsion system provides a speed of Mach 4 and an operational range of more than 20km.

Hence, the correct option is (D).

48. The summer Olympic Games 2024 to be held in Paris.

- Paris will become the second city to host the Olympics three times, after London (1908, 1948, and 2012).
- It was previously the host in the year 1900 and 1924. The year 2024 will mark the centenary of the Paris Games of 1924.
- These will be the sixth Olympic Games hosted by France (three summers and three winters).
- Paris was elected as the host city on September 13, 2017, at the 131st IOC Session in Lima, Peru.
- Paris is the capital of France.
- Currencies: Euro, CFP franc.

Hence, the correct option is (D).

49. The raga des originates from Kafithat. All the vowels are made in its descent. Playing time is considered to be the second hour of the night.

Hence, the correct option is (D).

50. 'Madurai Shanmukhavadivu Subbulakshmi' or M.S. Subbulakshmi is considered synonymous with Carnatic music and was the first singer in India to be awarded the highest civilian award of Bharat Ratna. His sung songs, especially bhajans, are still very popular among the people.

Hence, the correct option is (D).

51. The correct sentence is:

'Sunita is senior to me in this office knows all the rules.'

The preposition 'to' correctly shows the relation between the two people.

Option (B) uses 'the' before 'rules' which is correct.

Option (D) uses the preposition 'in' which is correct.

Instead of 'know', 'knows' should be used as the subject is in the third person singular form.

Hence, the correct option is (C).

52. In option (D), the usage of 'they' is incorrect.

'One' will be used instead of 'they'.

Whenever the subject of the sentence is 'one' the pronoun should be used according to the subject of the sentence i.e., 'one'.

Let's see an example:

One should do one's duty sincerely.

The correct sentence will be:

One should be careful to re-read what one has written.

Hence, the correct option is (D).

53.

Only in fig. (d), the two similar elements intersection the triangle opens up in the same direction.

Hence, the correct option is (D).

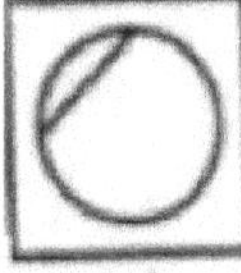

54.

In fig (c), the arrow indicates an ACW motion while in each of the other figures the arrow indicates a CW motion.

Hence, the correct option is (C).

55. In the first step, triangle element is deleted and shallow figure is obtained.

In the second step, shallow figure is replaced by filled one. This pattern is followed and repeated. Thus, the answer figure should be figure 3.

Hence, the correct option is (C).

56. Circle and square outlines are alternatively changed and the figure inside is rotated through 90 degrees in clockwise direction. The answer figure should be figure 1.

Hence, the correct option is (A).

57. The bold bar is rotated through 180 degrees in first step and then through 45 degrees in anti-clockwise direction. The same step is repeated in a set order. The answer figure should be figure 4.

Hence, the correct option is (D).

58. Let the total amount which is divided be ' x '

$\Rightarrow$ Harsh's money $= \dfrac{8x}{25}$

$\Rightarrow$ Nikhil's money $= \dfrac{17x}{25}$

Harsh spent $\dfrac{3}{4}^{th}$ of his money

$\Rightarrow$ Money left with harsh $= \dfrac{1}{4}^{th}$ of $\dfrac{8x}{25} = \dfrac{2x}{25}$

Nikhil spent 20% of his money; 80% is thus left.

$\Rightarrow$ Money left with Nikhil $= 6528$

$\Rightarrow 6528 = \left(\dfrac{80}{100}\right) \times \left(\dfrac{17x}{25}\right)$

$\Rightarrow x = 12000$

$\therefore$ Money spent by Harsh $= \dfrac{3}{4}^{th}$ of $\dfrac{8}{25} = 3 \times 8 \times \dfrac{12000}{100} =$ Rs. 2880

And, Money spent by Harsh $= 20\%$ of $\dfrac{17}{25} =$

$20 \times 17 \times \dfrac{12000}{2500} = Rs.\,1632$

$\Rightarrow$ Total money spent by both $= Rs.\,2880 + Rs.\,1632 = Rs.\,4512$

Hence, the correct option is (D).

59. The total value of all coins $= Rs.\,860$

The ratio of coins of $Rs.\,1, 50$ paisa, and $\dfrac{1}{2} : \dfrac{1}{3} : \dfrac{1}{5}$

Formula:

Value of coins $=$ number of coins $\times$ per coin value

Calculation:

We know that

$Rs.\,1 = 100$ paisa

The ratio of value per coin $= 100 : 50 : 25 = 4 : 2 : 1$

The ratio of number of coins $= \dfrac{1}{2} : \dfrac{1}{3} : \dfrac{1}{5} = 15 : 10 : 6$

$\Rightarrow$ The total value of coins $= 60 : 20 : 6 = 30 : 10 : 3$

$\Rightarrow 43x = 860$

$\Rightarrow x = 20$

So,

Value of 50 paise coins $= 10 \times = 10 \times 20 = Rs.\,200$

$\Rightarrow$ Number of 50 paise coins for $Rs.\,200 = 200 \times 2 = 400$ coins

$\therefore$ The required answer is 400 coins

Hence, the correct option is (A).

60. Given,

Number of storybooks = 800

The ratio of storybooks in a library to other books = 1 : 7

Let,

Number of storybooks = x

= 800

$\therefore$ Number of other books = 7 x

= 7(800)

= 5600

Hence, the correct option is (A).

61.

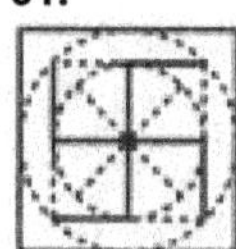

Hence, the correct option is (C).

62.

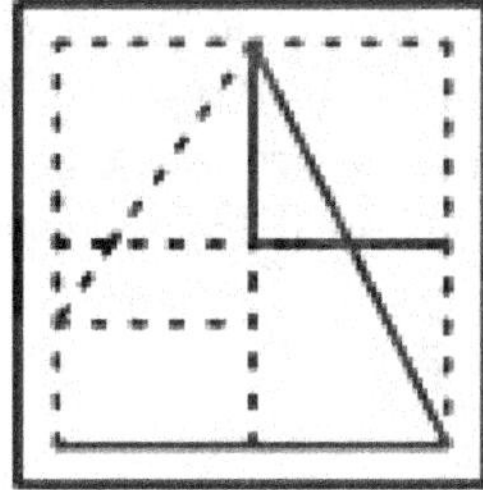

So, option (A) has the given figure embedded in it.

Hence, the correct option is (A).

63.

On close observation, we find that figure (X) is embedded in option (C) as shown below:

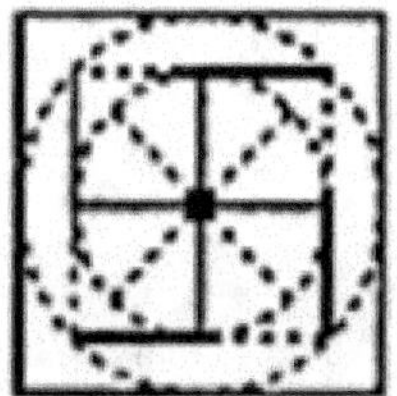

Hence, the correct option is (C).

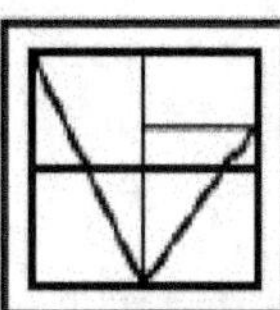

64. Hence, the correct option is (A).

65. On close observation, we find that the given figure is embedded in option (A) as shown below:

Hence, the correct option is (A).

66. Given:

Cost price = Rs.262.40

Formula:

$$\text{Selling price} = \text{Cost price} \times \frac{(\text{Profit\%}+100)}{100}$$

Let the marked price of a shirt be Rs. a

$$\text{Selling price after discount} = a \times \frac{(100-18)}{100} = \text{Rs.} \frac{82a}{100}$$

Accordingly,

$$\frac{82a}{100} = 262.40 \times \frac{(100+14)}{100}$$

$$\Rightarrow \frac{82a}{100} = \frac{262.40 \times 114}{100}$$

$$\Rightarrow a = 364.80$$

∴ The marked price of a shirt is Rs. 364.80.

Hence, the correct option is (A).

67. Given:

Cost price of 24 kg sugar = Rs. 1056

Let selling price of sugar per kg be Rs. a.

Profit = selling price - cost price (As we know)

$\Rightarrow$ 4a = 24a - 1056

$\Rightarrow$ a = 52.80

∴ The selling price of a sugar per kg is Rs. 52.80.

Hence, the correct option is (D).

68. Given:

Selling price = Rs.1683

Concept Used:

If a%, b% are two different discounts then the selling price is calculated as -

$$\text{Selling price} = \text{marked price} \times \frac{(100-a)}{100} \times \frac{(100-b)}{100}$$

$$\text{Marked price} \times \frac{85}{100} \times \frac{90}{100} \times \frac{88}{100} = 1683$$

∴ Marked price $=$ Rs. 2500

Hence, the correct option is (C).

69. The common area for the square and triangle represents male managers who are not engineers. The required field number is 5.

Hence, the correct option is (A).

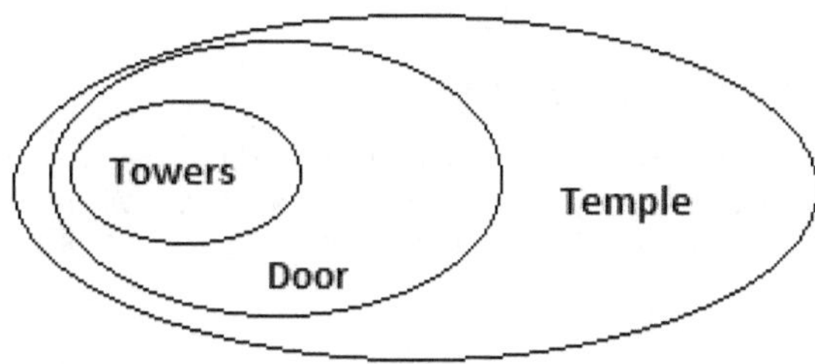

70.

Both I and II follow.

Hence, the correct option is (D).

71. Number of persons can speak Marathi = 6

Number of persons can speak Telugu = 7

Persons can speak Marathi and Telugu both

= 6 + 7

= 13

Hence, the correct option is (C).

72. There is no such person who can speak all the languages. Hence, the correct option is (D).

73. Ganga is a river and Kanchenjunga is a mountain. Rivers and mountains are different.

Hence, the correct option is (C).

74. The correct answer is 'which'.

Parallelism in grammar is defined as two or more phrases or clauses in a sentence that have the same grammatical structure.

It is used to balance nouns with nouns, prepositional phrases with prepositional phrases, participles with participles, infinitives with infinitives, clauses with clauses.

Example:

- My brother likes cooking and to read novels.
- My brother likes cooking and reading novels.

Since the previous clause in the sentence (which is different from...) starts with the pronoun 'which', 'which' will be used in the eleventh blank of the sentence as per the given rule.

Hence, the correct option is (D).

75. The correct answer is 'driven'.

Let's look at the meanings of the given options:-

- broken- to terminate
- given- to cause to have, in the abstract sense or physical sense
- driven- the act of applying force to propel something
- prescribed- to issue commands or orders for

As per the possible context of the sentence, a person's habits are propelled by various desires.

Therefore, from the given meanings, we find that the 3rd option i.e. driven is the correct choice in the twelfth blank.

Hence, the correct option is (C).

76. The correct answer is 'contain'.

The simple present tense is used when an action is happening right now, to state or ask about things in general, or when it happens regularly or unceasingly.

The structure is given below:

- Subject + V1 + object.
- Subject + do/does not + V1 + object. (negative sentence)

The verb will take 's/es' (except the negative sentences) if the given noun/pronoun (3rd person) is singular.

Example:

- He plays badminton daily.
- He does not play badminton daily.

Since the given sentence is in the present tense (negative sentence structure), the plural verb 'contain' will be used in the thirteenth blank.

Hence, the correct option is (A).

77. The correct answer is 'how'.

An adverb is a word or phrase that modifies or qualifies an adjective, verb, or other adverb or a word group, expressing a relation of place, time, circumstance, manner, etc.

The adverb 'how' most commonly means 'in what way' or 'to what extent'. We often use it with verbs such as tell, wonder and know in indirect questions:

Example:

- I just don't know how she manages to cook so well in such a small kitchen.

The former part of the given sentence talks about understanding the way habits work and the latter part talks about experimenting with a possible change in the habits.

In the given condition, the adverb 'how' will be used in the fourteenth blank.

Hence, the correct option is (A).

78. The correct answer is 'might'.

An auxiliary verb is a verb that adds functional or grammatical meaning to the clause in which it occurs, so as to express tense, aspect, modality, voice, emphasis, etc.

A modal or a modal auxiliary is a word such as 'can' or 'would' which is used with the main verb (the 1st form of the verb) to express ideas such as possibility, intention, or necessity.

Example:

- I have taken my breakfast. (have- auxiliary verb)
- One should obey one's elders. (should- modal)

The former part of the given sentence talks about understanding the way habits work and the latter part talks about experimenting with a possible change in the habits.

In the given condition, the modal verb 'might' will be used in the fifteenth blank of the cloze test as it provides the required tone of uncertainty.

Hence, the correct option is (A).

79. Directive Principles of state policy are fundamental in the governance of the country. Article 37 states the duty of the state to apply these principles in the making of laws. Part IV of the Constitution deals with the Directive principles for the states. These are incorporated to ensure a "Welfare state" and hence considered fundamental in governance.
Hence, the correct option is (D).

80. The antonym of Protects is Deserts.

Protects: Keep safe from harm

Deserts: To abandon that is to stop supporting or looking after

Defends: Protect from harm or danger

Deprives: Prevent (a person or place) from having or using something

Devises: Plan or invent (a complex procedure, system, or mechanism) by careful thought

Hence, the correct option is (C).

81. The meanings of the given words are,

Terrible: Very unpleasant, causing great shock or injury

Soothing: Having a gently calming effect

Horrible: Bad or unpleasant

Frightening: Making you feel afraid or shocked

Delectable: Delicious or humorous extremely attractive

Therefore, 'Soothing' is the antonym of 'Terrible'.

Hence, the correct option is (A).

82. Busy: Having a lot of work or tasks to do

Occupied: Busy and active

Active : (Of a person) Engaging or ready to engage in physically energetic pursuits

Preoccupied: Restless, nervous, fidgety, feverish, disquieting, preoccupied

Diligent: Having or showing care and conscientiousness in one's work or duties

Hence, the correct option is (B).

83. The Moon is the natural satellite of the Earth. The Moon is the second brightest object in the sky after the Sun.

- We can see only one side of the Moon from the Earth because the Moon rotates on its axis at the same rate that the Moon orbits the Earth. Also, the moon rotates on its axis at the same time that it takes to orbit the Earth i.e. approximately 27 days. So, Statement A is correct.

- The above-mentioned situation is known as tidal locking which slows the moon's rotation to the point where it always keeps the same side towards Earth. Thus it allows only one side of the moon's surface to be viewed from the Earth.

- The Moon orbits Earth once every 27.3 days and spins on its axis once every 27.3 days.

From the above-mentioned points, it becomes clear that it reveals that both statements (A) and (B) are true and (B) is the correct explanation of (A).

Hence, the correct option is (A).

84. $37 \text{ min } 45 \text{ sec } = \dfrac{151}{4} \text{ min}$

$1 \text{ days } = 24 \text{ hrs } = 24 \times 60 \text{ min}$

$\Rightarrow \dfrac{151}{4 \times 24 \times 60} \times 100 = 2.62\%$

Hence, the correct option is (A).

85. The concentration of new solution is

$$\dfrac{40 \times \frac{60}{100} + 35 \times \frac{80}{100}}{75} \times 100$$

$$= \dfrac{24 + 28}{3} \times 4$$

$$= 69\dfrac{1}{3}\%$$

Hence, the correct option is (C).

86. Percentage gain $= \dfrac{1000 - 800}{800} \times 100$

$$= 25\%$$

Hence, the correct option is (C).

87. 'Bluster' means 'loudly boastful or threatening speech' and the only preposition that should follow it is 'on'. This eliminates options (A) and (C).

For the blank 2, the preposition 'over' is the most appropriate choice as the phrase 'over the top' must have been used here in the given context of the sentence.

Over the top (Adverbial phrase): To an excessive or exaggerated degree

The the sentence is, "Pakistan Prime Minister Imran Khan's bluster **on** Kashmir and the implied threat of a nuclear war were irresponsible and **over** the top."

Hence, the correct option is (B).

88. In the above-given sentence, 'into' will be used.

It is so because 'Plunged in/plunged into' is a phrasal verb meaning to suddenly start doing something actively or enthusiastically.

For Examples:-

Two months before his exams, he suddenly plunged into his studies.

He took a deep breath and plunged into his speech.

In the given sentence, the city suddenly was in darkness due to the power cut which is aptly expressed by the phrasal verb 'plunged into'.

Thus, 'into' will be used.

Hence, the correct option is (C).

89. The word 'than' after the blank is a major hint that a comparative degree should be filled in the blank. Therefore, 'better' is the only appropriate choice here.

She liked to be with him better than with the others, and when alone with him she sometimes laughed.

Hence, the correct option is (B).

90. A few means some. It has a positive meaning. The few means not many, but all of those. Here we are talking about all the teeth that are left, so 'the' is the correct choice here.

Hence, the correct option is (D).

91. The missing figure is:

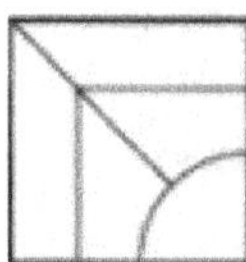

Hence, the correct option is (C).

92. The missing figure is:

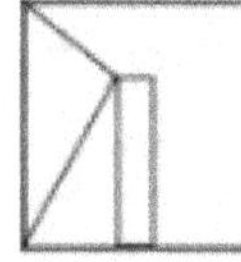

Hence, the correct option is (B).

93. The missing figure is:

Hence, the correct option is (D).

94. The missing figure is:

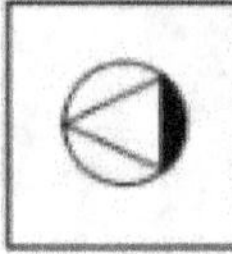

Hence, the correct option is (A).

95. The missing figure is:

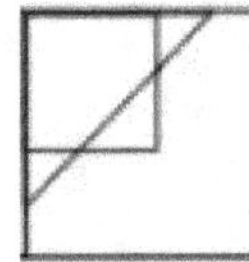

Complete the square and cross the line in middle. Answer B will correct option to complete the figure.

Hence, the correct option is (B).

96. The meaning of the word 'resilience' is the quality of being able to return quickly to a previous good condition after problems.

Let us see the meaning of the following words:

- Rigidity: inability to be changed or adapted.
- Fragility: the quality of being easily damaged or broken.
- Weakness: the state or condition of being weak.
- Flexibility: the ability to change or be changed easily according to the situation.

It can be concluded that the word 'flexibility' could replace the word 'resilience' as used in the passage.

Hence, the correct option is (B).

97. Let's have a look at the tenth sentence of the first paragraph of the passage:

'90% saw increased emotional resilience for dealing with adversity.'

It can be concluded from the above line that 90% saw increased emotional resilience for dealing with adversity.

Hence, the correct option is (B).

98. Let's have a look at the ninth sentence of the first paragraph of the passage:

'98% of children noticed a positive change in themselves at the end of the iheart programme.'

It can be concluded from the above line that 98% of children noticed a positive change in themselves at the end of the iheart programme.

Hence, the correct option is (B).

99. The passage explains how different methods and techniques to solve mental health crises.

It can be concluded from the passage that 'Solving mental health crises' would be the most suitable title for the passage.

Therefore, the correct option is 'Solving mental health crises.'

Hence, the correct option is (C).

100. Let's have a look at the fifth sentence of the passage:

'Our innovative, evidence-based mental wellbeing educational programme challenges current practices and outlooks and has already improved the lives of over 15,000 young people in twenty countries.'

It can be concluded from the above line that our innovative practices have improved the lives of over 15000 young people in twenty countries.

Hence, the correct option is (A).

Q.1 Who is the head of the Labour Ministry's commission, which recommended a basic living wage?

A. Santosh Kumar Gangwar
B. C V Ananda Bose
C. Apurva Chandra
D. Alok Kumar Mathur

Q.2 Where was the International Conference on Climate Change held in December 2018?

[Super TET Paper - I, 2019]

A. Kankun (Mexico)
B. Durban (South Africa)
C. Katowice (Poland)
D. Doha (Qatar)

Q.3 Who among the following has been awarded for Ramon Magsaysay Award, 2018?

[Super TET Paper - I, 2019]

A. Bharat Vatwani
B. Bruce Rittmann
C. Robert Langlands
D. Richard H. Thaler

Q.4 Which of the following won the Pulitzer Prize 2022 in the fiction category?

A. Netanyahus
B. Book of Numbers
C. People Love Dead Jews
D. French Braid

Q.5 Which one of the following Indian Ocean island nations has recently declared a state of environmental emergency due to oil spill from a grounded ship?

[Indian Military Academy (IMA), 2020], [Officers Training Academy (OTA), 2020]

A. Maldives
B. Mauritius
C. Madagascar
D. Sri Lanka

Q.6 A man wants to invest Rs. 8400 in his two sons bank account in such a way that when they become 18 years old they get equal interest. Present age of his 2 sons is 13 years and 15 years. If the Rate of simple interest. is 5% p.a. . Find the investment in younger son account?

A. 4050
B. 3650
C. 3150
D. 4500

Q.7 A person invests Rs. 30000 as a fixed deposit at a bank of 10% p.a. S.I. But due to some problem, he has to withdraw the entire money after 3 yrs for which the bank allowed him a lower rate of interest. If he gets Rs. 7800 less than what he would have got at the end of 5 yrs; Find R.O.I allowed by the bank?

A. 2%
B. 5%
C. 4%
D. 8%

Q.8 A sum of Rs. 1000 is increased by 100% of its original after 7 years at compound interest. What will be the time period when the amount will be increased by 700% of the principal at the same rate of interest compound interest?

A. 14 years
B. 21 years
C. 28 Years
D. 35 years

Q.9 Field Marshal is the highest rank in _____.

A. Territorial army
B. Air force
C. Navy
D. Army

Q.10 If the numerator of a fraction be increased by 15% and its denominator be diminished by 8%, the value of the fraction is $\dfrac{15}{16}$. Find the original fraction.

A. $\dfrac{1}{2}$
B. $\dfrac{3}{2}$
C. $\dfrac{3}{4}$
D. $\dfrac{4}{3}$

Q.11 When 36 is written in simplest fractional form, the sum of the numerator and the denominator is:

A. 34
B. 45
C. 114
D. 135

Q.12 Students asked many questions to their teacher.

A. Many teachers were asked questions by the students.
B. The teacher was asked many questions by their students.
C. Their teacher was asked many questions by the students.
D. Their teachers were asked many questions by the students.

Q.13 Your mother called you many times.

A. You was called many times by your mother.
B. You were being called many times by your mother.
C. You called many times by your mother
D. You were called many times by your mother.

Q.14 Period of geopolitical tension between the Soviet Union and the United States said to be Cold War Era, in which duration?

A. $1914 - 1919$
B. $1939 - 1945$
C. $1947 - 1991$
D. $1991 - 2001$

Ques (15-19):Direction: Complete the sentence with the most appropriate word.

Q.15 Dolphins are _____ humans and are able to understand and talk among themselves with a particular sound.

A. intelligent
B. more intelligent
C. most intelligent
D. as intelligent as

Q.16 Coconut water is the ____ and most hygienic water found on the earth.

A. pure
B. purer
C. purest
D. as pure as

Q.17 The company in order to make up for its loss, had to lay ____ many workers.

A. off
B. of
C. to
D. at

Q.18 The tradition of having yogurt and sugar before leaving home has been ____from father to son.

A. handed up
B. handed down

C. handed   **D.** told

Q.19 If I win the jackpot, I _____ an orphanage cum old age home, so that the older and younger generation could thrive together.

A. had opened   **B.** will open
C. would open   **D.** opened

Ques (20-21):Directions: Given below idioms/phrases followed by four alternative meaning to each. Choose the response which is the most appropriate expression and mark your response.

Q.20 Get the jitters

[Indian Military Academy (IMA), 2020], [Officers Training Academy (OTA), 2020]

A. Feeling anxious   **B.** Feeling happy
C. Stammering   **D.** Feeling exposed

Q.21 French leave

[Indian Military Academy (IMA), 2020], [Officers Training Academy (OTA), 2020]

A. Absent from work without asking for permission in French
B. Asking for permission before leaving work
C. Work for permission to get leave
D. Absent from work without asking for permission

Q.22 Azolla increases soil fertility for-

A. Maize cultivation   **B.** Wheat cultivation
C. Barley cultivation   **D.** Rice cultivation

Q.23 An article is sold for Rs.799.50 after allowing two successive discounts of 18% and 22% on its marked price. The cost price of the article is Rs.1,000. If it is sold at the marked price, then the gain is:

[SSC Selection Post Phase IX, 2020]

A. Rs. 250   **B.** Rs. 240   **C.** Rs. 300   **D.** Rs. 220

Q.24 Anu gains 18% on selling an article of Rs.265.50. If she sells it for Rs. 231.30, then her gain or loss percentage is:

[SSC Selection Post Phase IX, 2020]

A. Gain: 2.4%   **B.** Loss: 2.4%
C. Loss: 2.8%   **D.** Gain: 2.8%

Q.25 A trader earns 20% profit by selling an article. If he increases the price of the article by Rs.130, his gain percentage increases to 28%. What is the cost price of the article?

[SSC Selection Post Phase IX, 2020]

A. Rs. 1,620   **B.** Rs. 1,650
C. Rs. 1,600   **D.** Rs. 1,625

Q.26 A train ran at a speed of 35 km /hr in the first 10 minutes and the speed of 20 km /hr in the next 5 minutes. What is the average speed of the train in 15 minutes?

A. 30 km /hr   **B.** 23 km /hr
C. 31 km /hr   **D.** 29 km /hr

Q.27 How many seconds a 120 m long caravan running at the rate of 10 m /s will take to pass a standing boy?

A. 10 seconds   **B.** 12 seconds
C. 11 seconds   **D.** 14 seconds

Q.28 If a boat walks smoothly along the streamline, the distance of 36 km is completed in 3 hours. While returning, it completes the same distance in 9 hours. So what is the speed of the boat?

A. 8 km /hr   **B.** 12 km /hr
C. 14 km /hr   **D.** 10 km /hr

Q.29 A wheel makes 1000 revolutions in covering a distance 88 km. The radius of the wheel is:

A. 7 m   **B.** 12 m
C. 14 m   **D.** None of these

Q.30 Direction: Find out the alternative figure which contains figure (X) as its part.

    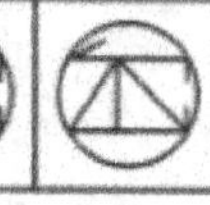

  (X)   (1)   (2)   (3)   (4)

A. (1)   **B.** (2)   **C.** (3)   **D.** (4)

Q.31 From the given answer figure, select the question in which the question figure is hidden/embedded.

Question figure:

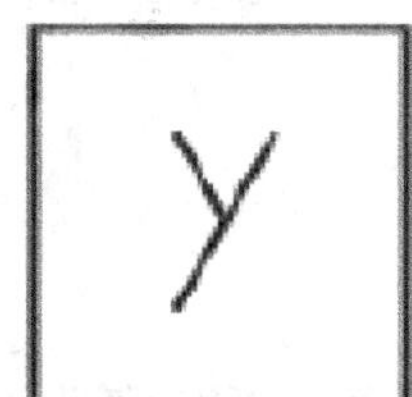

Answer figure:

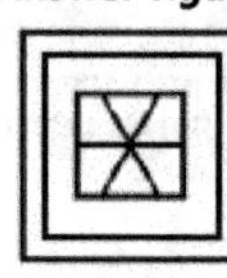 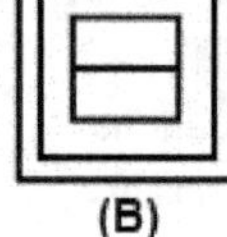 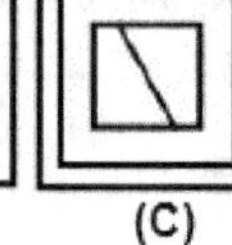 

  (A)   (B)   (C)   (D)

A. (A)   **B.** (B)   **C.** (C)   **D.** (D)

Q.32 Direction: Complete the following figure:

Question figure

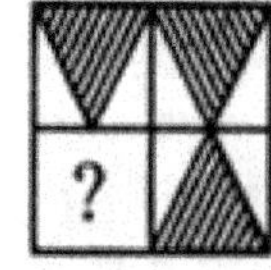

Answer figure

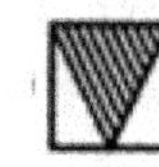 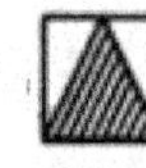  

  (A)   (B)   (C)   (D)

A. (A) **B.** (B) **C.** (C) **D.** (D)

Q.33 Find the answer figure in which the question figure is embedded?

Question Figure:

Answer Figure:

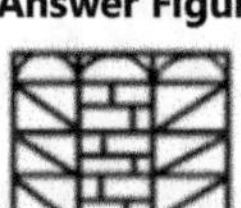  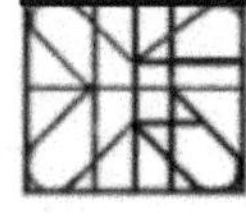 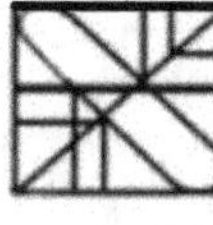

A   B   C   D

A. A **B.** B **C.** C **D.** D

Q.34 From the given answer figures, select the one in which the question figure is hidden/embedded.

Question Figure:

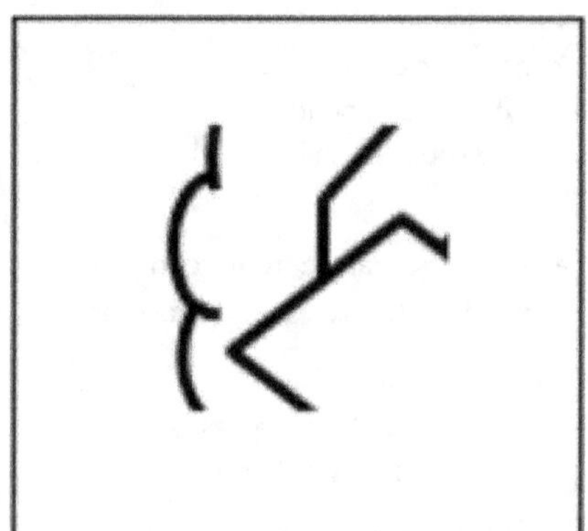
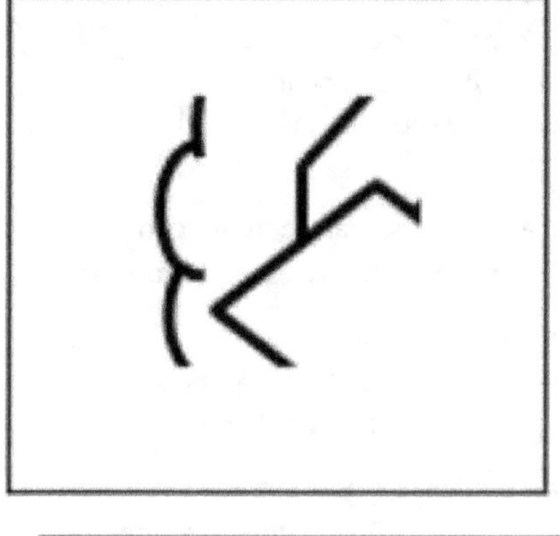

A.

B.

C.

D.

Q.35 The average of 10 numbers is 15.2 is added to each number. What is the new average?

A. 16 **B.** 30 **C.** 32 **D.** 17

Q.36 A cricket player scores 20, 30, and 40 runs each in different matches. Find the average score of the player?

[MP Police (Constable), 2017]

A. 40 runs   **B.** 50 runs   **C.** 45 runs   **D.** 30 runs

Q.37 Find the average.
29, 34, 39, 44, 49 & 57

[MP Police (Constable), 2017]

A. 42   **B.** 39   **C.** 37   **D.** 46

Q.38 Rahul is twice as good at building a wall as Shiv. Together they can build the wall in 12 days. In how many days can Rahul alone build the wall?

A. 36 days   **B.** 16 days   **C.** 18 days   **D.** 14 days

Q.39 Two pipes can fill an empty tank separately in 24 minutes and 40 minutes respectively and a third pipe can empty 30 gallons of water per minute. If all three pipes are open, empty tanks become full in one hour. The capacity of the tank (in gallons) is:

A. 800 gallons   **B.** 600 gallons
C. 500 gallons   **D.** 400 gallons

Q.40 A cistern can be filled by two pipes in 20 and 30 minutes respectively. Both pipes being opened, when the first pipe must be turned off so that the cistern may be filled in 10 minutes more.

A. After 10 minutes   **B.** After 12 minutes
C. After 20 minutes   **D.** After 8 minutes

Q.41 Direction: In the question given below out of four alternatives, choose the one which can be substituted for the given sentence.
That which cannot be avoided

A. Inevitable   **B.** Irreparable
C. Incomparable   **D.** Indisputable

Q.42 Direction: In the question given below out of four alternatives, choose the one which can be substituted for the given sentence.
One who able to use the right and left hands equally well

A. Sinister   **B.** Ambidextrous
C. Ambivalent   **D.** Amateur

Q.43 Direction: Choose the figure which is different from the rest.

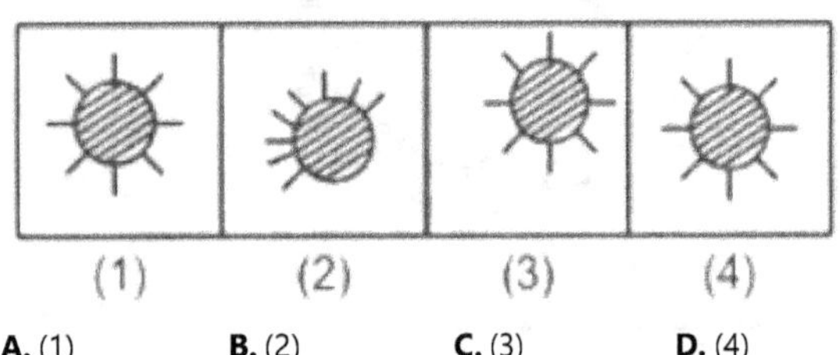

A. (1)   **B.** (2)   **C.** (3)   **D.** (4)

Q.44 Arrange these letters of each group to make a meaningful word and then find the odd one out.

A. ORFU   **B.** VIDEID   **C.** GHIET   **D.** VEENS

Q.45 Identify which one of the given alternatives will be another member of the group of that class.
Lucknow, Patna, Bhopal, Jaipur?

A. Pune   **B.** Indore   **C.** Shimla   **D.** Mysore

Q.46 Four of the following five are alike in a certain way and so form a group. Which is the one that does not belong to that group?

A. Water   **B.** Juice   **C.** Petrol   **D.** Sugar

Q.47 Select the one which is different from the other three responses.

A. Mayor   **B.** Lawyer
C. Governor   **D.** Legislator

Q.48 Which hydrocarbons are the constituents of LPG?

A. Methane and Ethane
B. Propane and Butane
C. Pentane and Benzene
D. Only Methane

Q.49 Which one of the following statements is correct about camphor and ammonium chloride?

A. Both of them are inorganic compounds
B. Both of them are organic compounds
C. Both of them undergo sublimation
D. Both (A) and (B)

Q.50 Which man-made fiber is obtained from wood pulp?

A. Nylon   **B.** Rayon   **C.** Silk   **D.** Polyster

Q.51 Kepler's second law is also known as:

A. Law of periods   **B.** Law of areas
C. Law of rules   **D.** Law of orbits

Q.52 Excess fluoride in drinking water causes:

A. Lung disease   **B.** Intestinal infection
C. Fluorosis   **D.** Rickets

Ques (53-54):Direction: In the following question, the given sentence has four parts marked P, Q, R, and S. Choose the part of the sentence with the error and mark it as your answer. If there is no error, mark 'No error (S)' as your answer.

Q.53 The government need to adopt (P) / a multi-year expenditure outlook (Q) / while preparing the budget. (R) / No error (S)

[SSC Sub Inspector (CPO), 2018], [SSC Sub Inspector (CPO), 2017]

A. P   **B.** Q   **C.** R   **D.** S

Q.54 Tickle is (P) /one of the broadest and deepest (Q) / subject in science. (R) / No error (S)

[SSC Sub Inspector (CPO), 2017]

A. P   **B.** Q   **C.** R   **D.** S

Ques (55-59):Direction: In the following question, select the related number from the given alternatives.

Q.55 $1511 : 2 :: 6554 : ?$

A. 3   **B.** 4   **C.** 5   **D.** 6

Q.56 $56:72::90:?$

A. 96 **B.** 97 **C.** 100 **D.** 110

Q.57 $967:386::542:?$

A. 762 **B.** 812 **C.** 763 **D.** 982

Q.58 $6:72::8:?$

A. 94 **B.** 96 **C.** 74 **D.** 92

Q.59 VERMIN :? :: ORDERS : ERSORD

A. MNIVER **B.** MINERV
C. MINVRE **D.** MINVER

Q.60 Select the correct figure that replaces the (?) symbol from the given options:

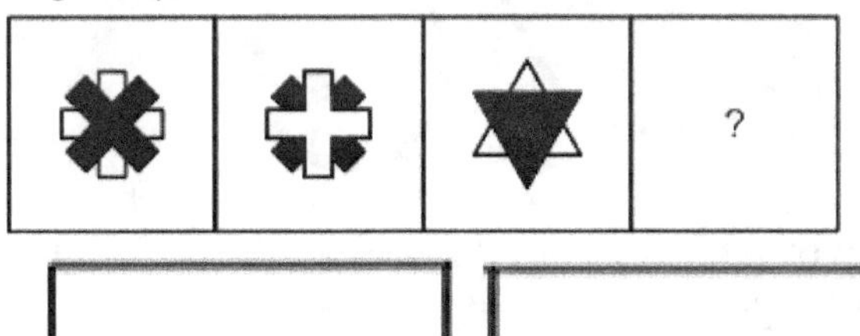

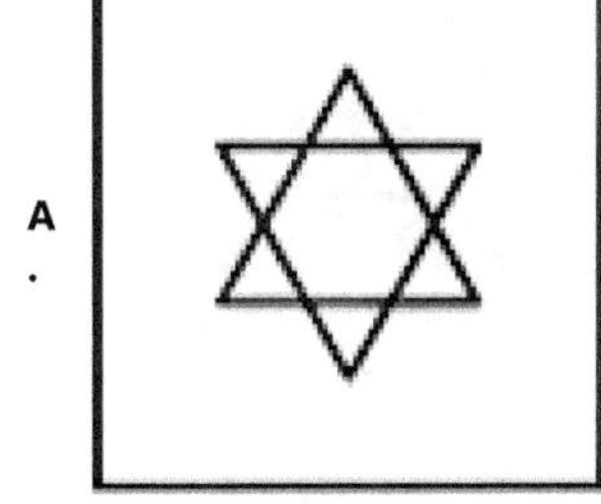
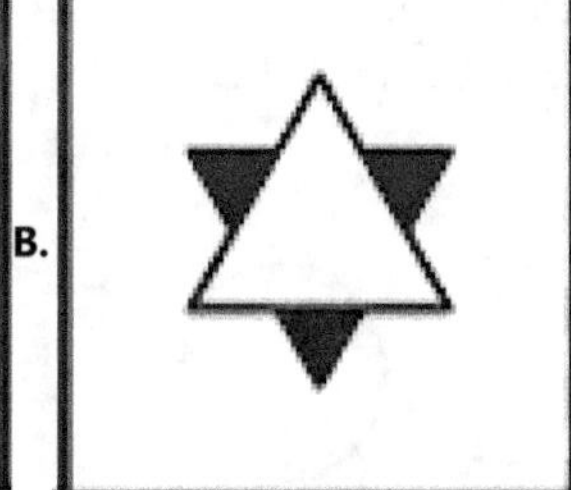

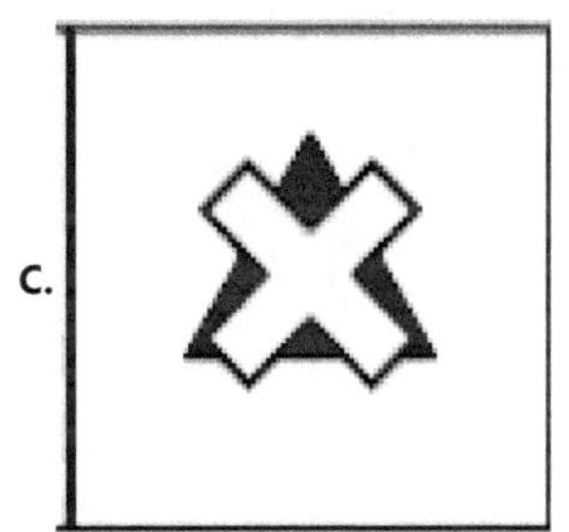
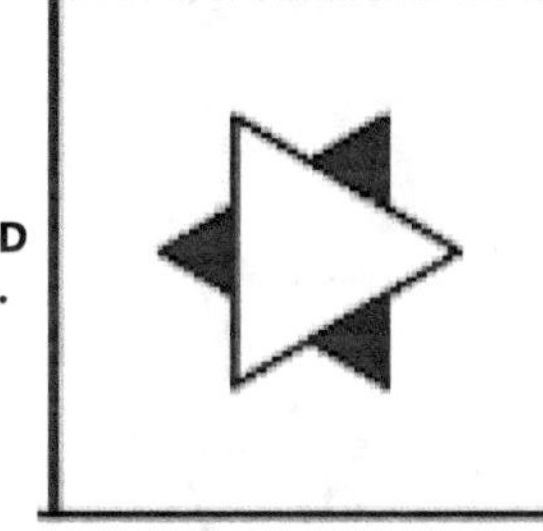

Q.61 Select the figure that will come next in the following series.

[AFCAT, 2021], [SSC MTS, 2019], [SSC Constable (GD), 2019]

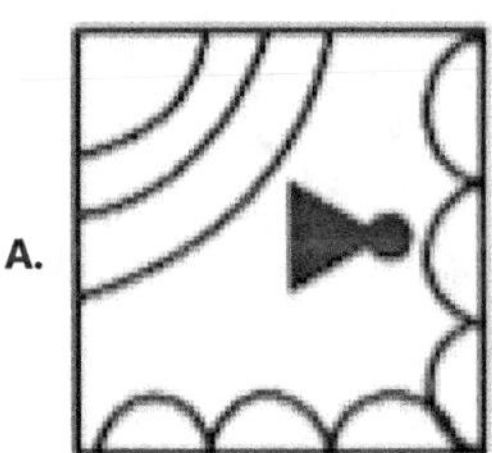
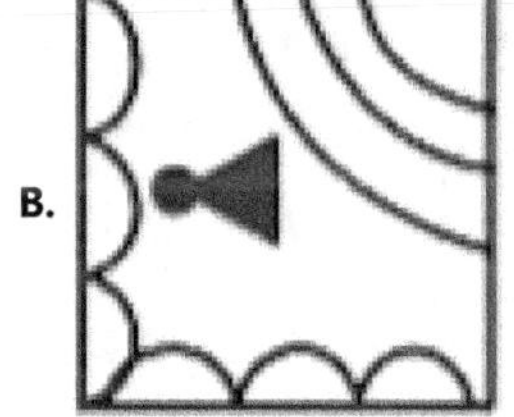

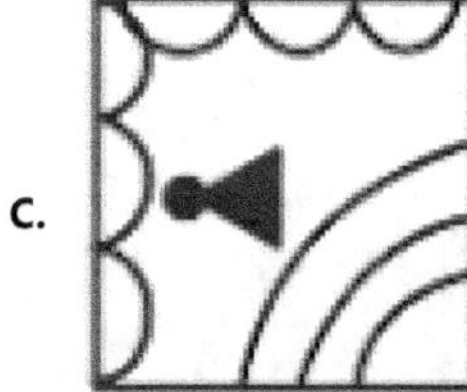
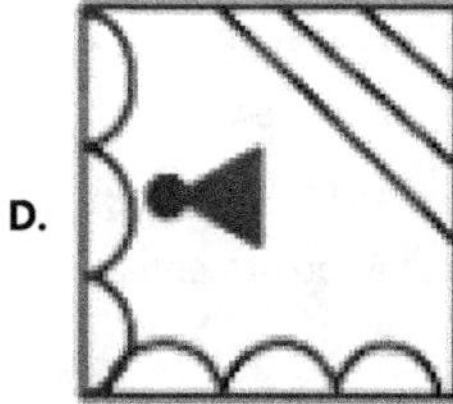

Q.62 A dice with six faces is marked with six numbers 1, 2, 3, 4, 5 and 6 respectively. The dice is rolled three times and three positions are shown as:

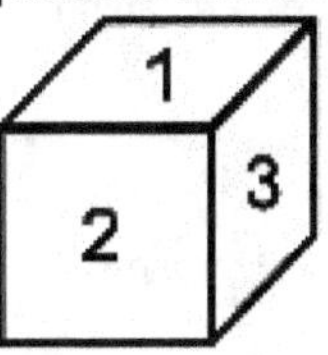
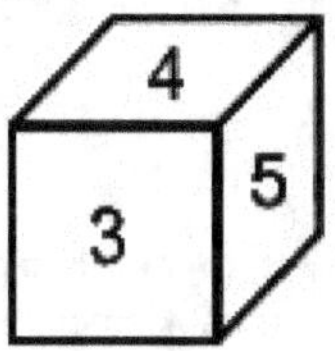
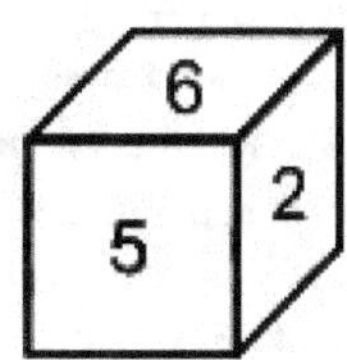

Find the number opposite to 1?

A. 2 **B.** 6 **C.** 5 **D.** 4

Q.63 Choose the figure which is different from the rest.

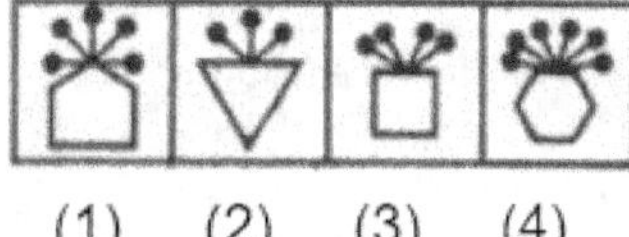

(1) (2) (3) (4)

A. (1) **B.** (2) **C.** (3) **D.** (4)

Q.64

Choose the figure which is different from the rest.

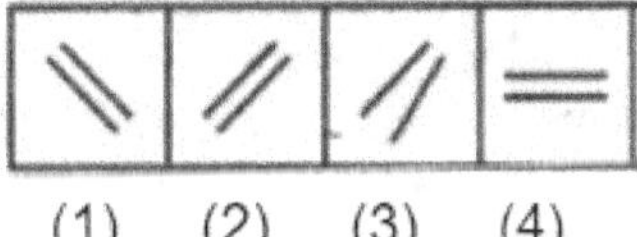

(1) (2) (3) (4)

A. (1) **B.** (2) **C.** (3) **D.** (4)

Q.65 If $A:B=7:3$, find the value of $\frac{AB+B^2}{A^2-B^2}$.

A. $\frac{3}{4}$ **B.** $\frac{4}{3}$ **C.** $\frac{7}{3}$ **D.** $\frac{3}{7}$

Q.66 If $X^2+4Y^2=4XY$, find the value of $X^3:Y^3$.

A. $27:1$ **B.** $1:64$ **C.** $8:1$ **D.** $1:8$

Q.67 If $A:B=\frac{1}{2}:\frac{1}{5}$ and $C:B=\frac{1}{4}:\frac{1}{5}$, find the value of $\frac{A^2+B^2}{C^2-B^2}$.

A. $12\frac{8}{9}$ **B.** $14\frac{1}{7}$
C. $12\frac{7}{8}$ **D.** None of these

Q.68 Who among the following cricket player has won the ICC men's ODI player of the decade award, one of the ICC Awards of the Decade?

A. Virat Kohli **B.** Brett Lee
C. Chris Gayle **D.** Stuart Broad

Q.69 Arrange the words given below in a meaningful sequence.

1. Probation
2. Interview
3. Selection
4. Appointment
5. Advertisement
6. Application

A. 5, 6, 3, 2, 4, 1   **B.** 5, 6, 4, 2, 3, 1
C. 5, 6, 2, 3, 4, 1   **D.** 6, 5, 4, 2, 3, 1

Q.70 Which one of the given responses would be a meaningful order of the following?

1. Add oil in the frying pan.

2. Peel the potatoes.

3. Remove and place the potato fries on a plate with paper towels to absorb the leftover cooking oil.

4. Add the sliced potatoes to the oil in the frying pan.

5. Cut potatoes into thin straw-like pieces.

A. 4, 1, 5, 3, 2   **B.** 2, 5, 1, 4, 3
C. 1, 2, 5, 3, 4   **D.** 4, 2, 1, 5, 3

Ques (71-72):Direction: Choose which of the following diagrams represents the relationship among the given elements in a much logical way.

Q.71 Eyewear, Sunglass, mercury sunglass

A.    **B.** 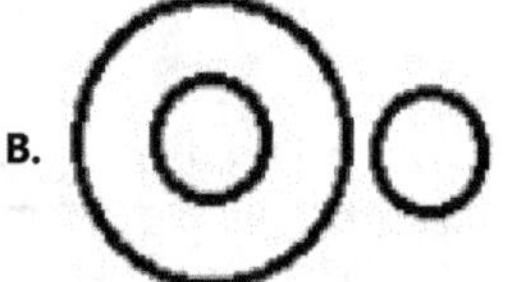

C.    **D.** 

Q.72 Brinjal, Meat, Vegetables

A. 

B. 

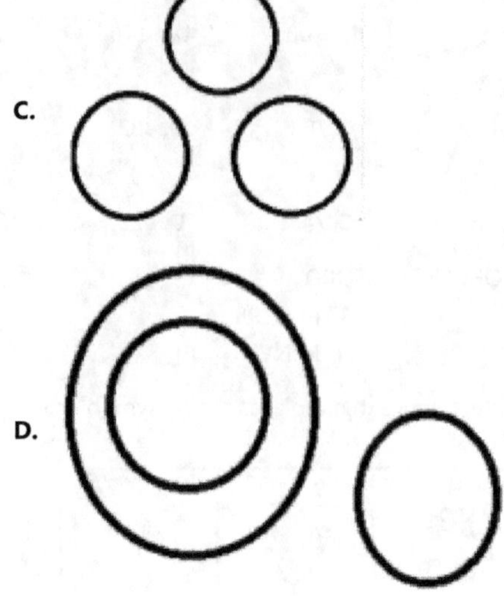

C.

D.

Q.73 Direction: Identify the diagram which best represents the relationship among the classes given below.

Surat, Gujarat, India

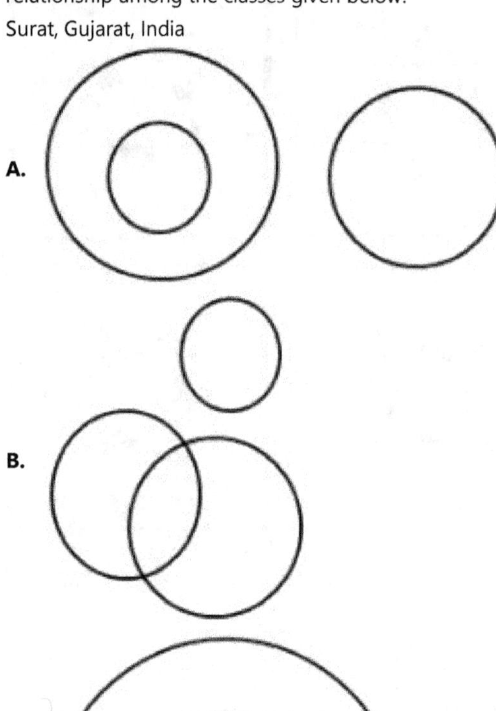

A.

B.

C.

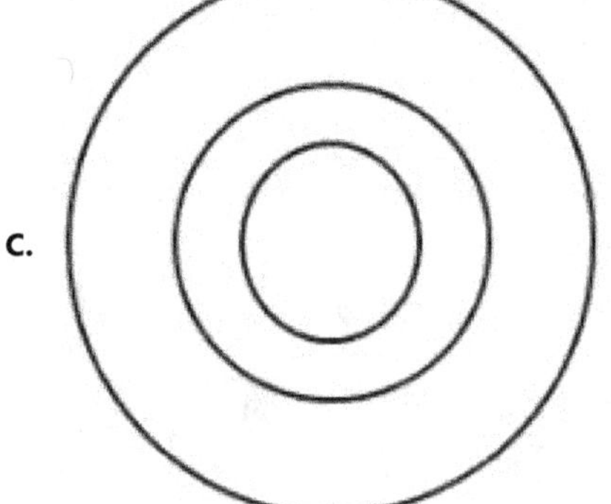

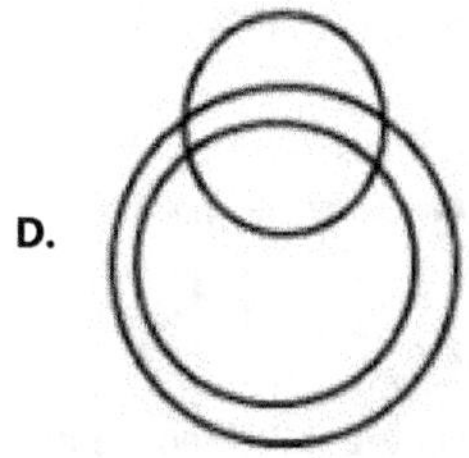

D.

Q.74 Identify the diagram which best represents the relationship among the classes given below.
Brinjal, Jasmine, Rice, Mango.

A.

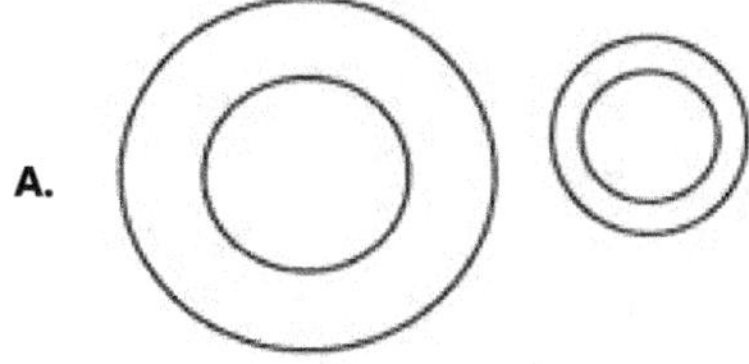

B.

C.

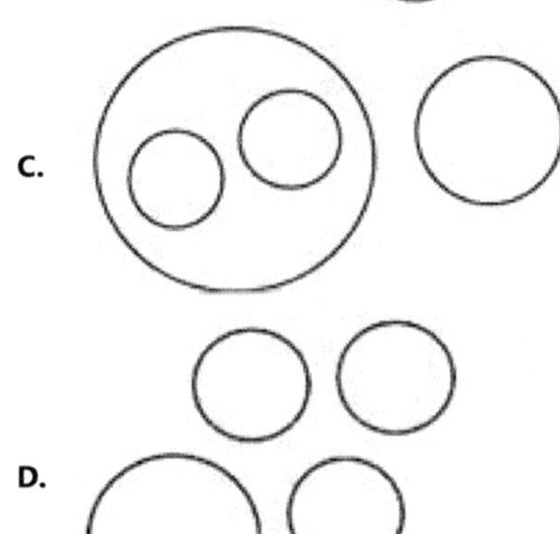

D.

Q.75 Identify the diagram which best represents the relationship among the classes given below.
Body, Digestive system, Excretory system, Stomach.

A.

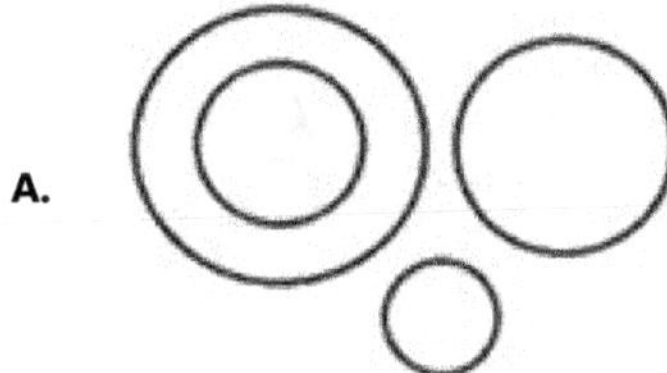

B.

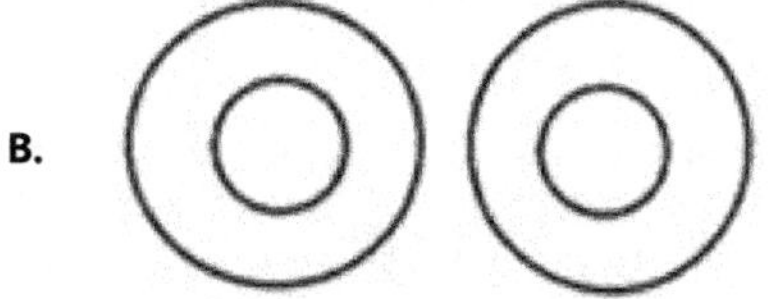

C.

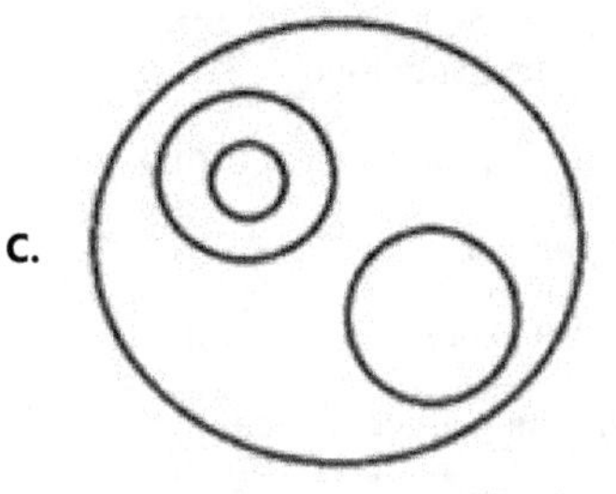

D.

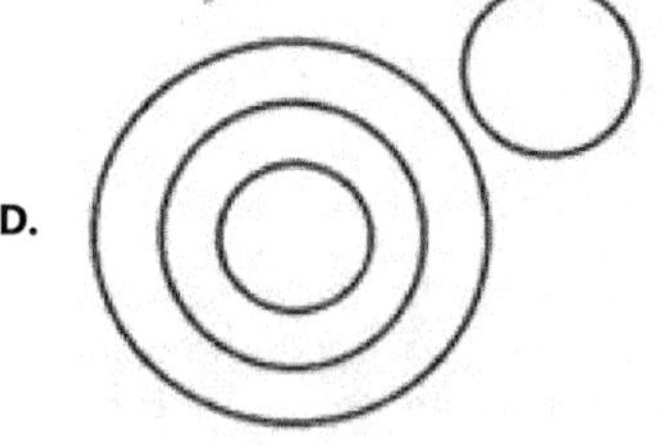

Q.76 Consider the following statements:

1. According to this philosophy, Vedas are eternal and possess all knowledge.

2. Religion means the fulfillment of duties prescribed by the Vedas.

3. This philosophy encompasses the Nyaya-Vaisheshika systems and emphasizes the concept of valid knowledge.

The above statements are related to?

A. Vedanta School   **B.** Samkhya School
C. Mimamsa School   **D.** Yoga School

Q.77 Consider the following statements regarding Khyal:

1. The origin of this style was attributed to Amir Khusrau.

2. Alap is given more room in the Khyal music as compared to Dhrupad.

3. Usually, the theme for Khyal bandish is romantic in nature.

Which of the above statements is/are correct?

A. 1 only   **B.** 1, 2   **C.** 1, 3   **D.** 1, 2, 3

Q.78 The doctrine of harmonious construction was propounded by Supreme Court in which of the following cases?

A. Kerala Education Bill (1957) Case
B. Venkataraman vs State of Madras (1966) Case
C. Golaknath & Ors vs State Of Punjab (1967) Case
D. Kesavananda Bharati vs the State of Kerala (1973) Case

Q.79 Direction: Select the most appropriate synonym of the given word.
ACCURATELY

A. Moderately   **B.** Correctly
C. Promptly   **D.** Partially

Q.80 Direction: Select the most appropriate synonym of the given word.
CONDESCENDING

A. Stimulating   **B.** Accusing
C. Creating   **D.** Patronising

Q.81 Direction: Select the most appropriate antonym of the given word.
AMBIGUOUS

A. Unclear   **B.** Clear   **C.** Bright   **D.** Faded

Q.82 Equinox is a state in which the duration of day and night is equal. It falls on:

A.   22th March and 31st September
B.   10th March and 13th September
C.   21st March and 23rd September
D.   21th June and 22nd December

Q.83 In an election, there were two candidates Arvind and Manoj. If 20% of votes were declared invalid and Arvind got 20% more votes than Manoj. Then find the total number of people who voted if Arvind won by 480 votes.

A. 3000   **B.** 30000   **C.** 2400   **D.** 9600

Q.84 If a number is subtracted from three-seventh of itself, the value so obtained is -48. Then, Find 75% of the number.

A. 84   **B.** 63   **C.** 36   **D.** 27

Q.85 A child spends 25% of her pocket money on chocolates and 20% of the rest on toys. She is now left with INR 1080. Find her pocket money.

A. INR 1800   **B.** INR 1600
C. INR 1880   **D.** INR 1860

Q.86 Direction: Choose the appropriate word to fill in the blank.
Complete the notice with the right word. Use of cell phones is _____ within the premises.
[Allahabad High Court Review Officer (RO), 2017]

A. avoided   **B.** disallowed
C. prevented   **D.** suspended

Q.87 Direction: Use the correct question tag to complete the sentence.
Suicide is not a solution to life's problems, ____?
[Allahabad High Court Review Officer (RO), 2017]

A. are they   **B.** isn't it   **C.** is it   **D.** aren't it

Q.88 Direction: Choose the appropriate word to fill in the blank.
A mix of decayed wood, leaves and manure is known as ______.
[Allahabad High Court Review Officer (RO), 2017]

A. compose   **B.** composed
C. composite   **D.** compost

Q.89 Direction: Choose the appropriate word to fill in the blank.
He _____ goodbye to his friends before leaving.
[Allahabad High Court Review Officer (RO), 2017]

A. was bidding   **B.** bidding
C. bid   **D.** bode

Ques (90-94):Direction: Which answer figure will complete the pattern in the following question figure?

Q.90

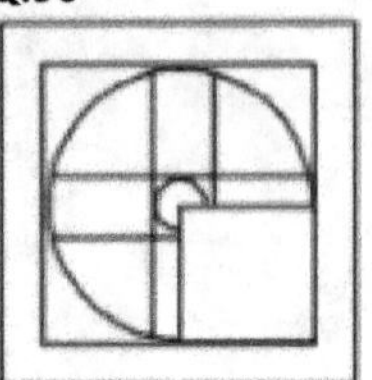

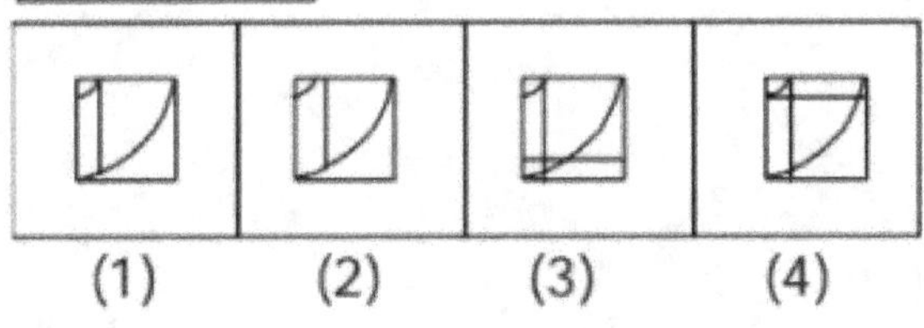

(1)   (2)   (3)   (4)

[SSC Sub Inspector (CPO), 2020]

A. 1   **B.** 2   **C.** 3   **D.** 4

Q.91

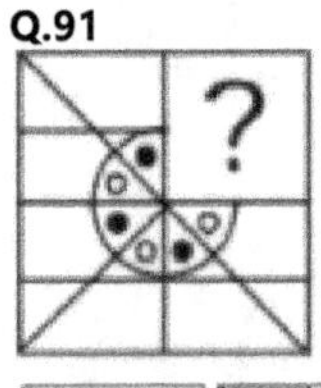

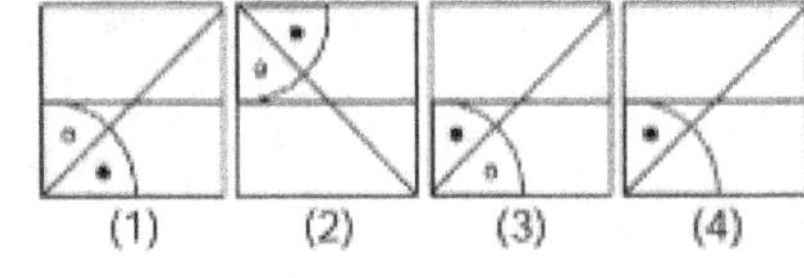

(1)   (2)   (3)   (4)

[UP Police Sub Inspector, 2021]

A. 1   **B.** 2   **C.** 3   **D.** 4

Q.92

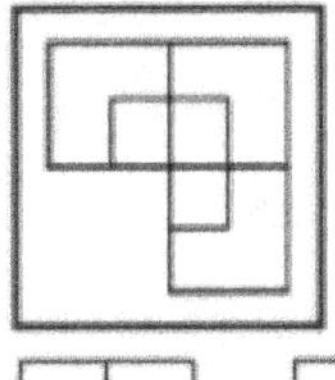

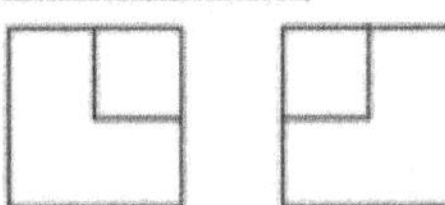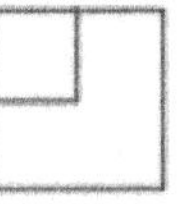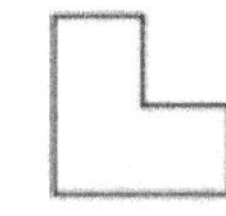

(1)   (2)   (3)   (4)

[UP Police Sub Inspector, 2021]

A. 1   **B.** 2   **C.** 3   **D.** 4

Q.93

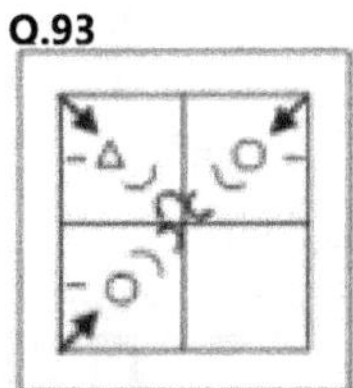

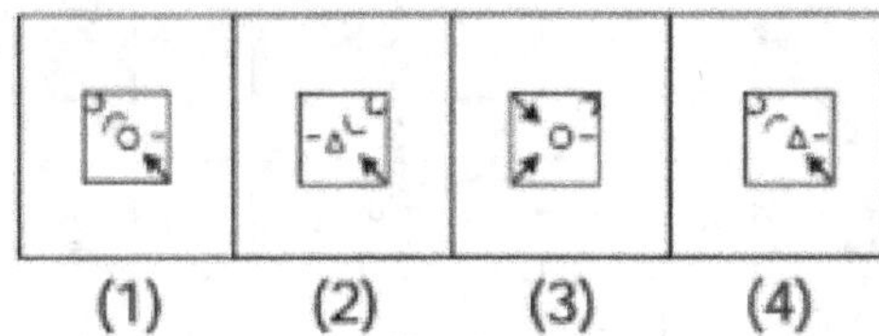

(1)   (2)   (3)   (4)

[SSC Sub Inspector (CPO), 2020]

A. 1   **B.** 2   **C.** 3   **D.** 4

Q.94

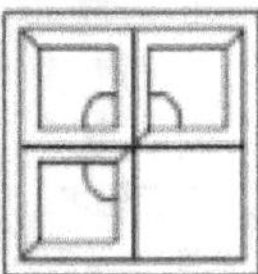

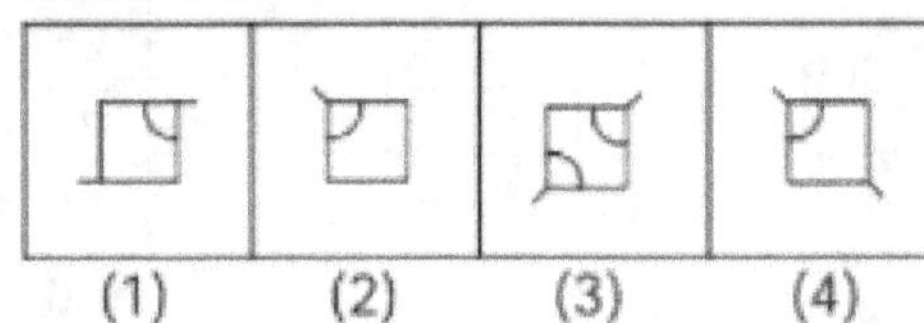

(1)   (2)   (3)   (4)

[SSC Sub Inspector (CPO), 2020]

A. 1   **B.** 2   **C.** 3   **D.** 4

Ques (95-99):Direction: A passage is given with 5 questions following it. Read the passage carefully and choose the best answer to each question out of the four alternatives and click the button corresponding to it.

Without breakfast, all of us irrespective of age are likely to experience the late morning slump; tiredness, sleepiness and the urge to sit back. Our efficiency goes down even further as the day progresses. Moreover, skipping the first meal of the day leads to intense hunger pangs by late morning and we end up eating chips, samosas, burgers or other highfat unhealthy foods. Breakfastskippers are more likely to be overweight. A good breakfast leads to a more active, productive day. Research has found a definite connection between skipping breakfast and memory impairment in both young and older adults. Moreover, breakfast is directly linked to performance in school and college. Breakfast should contribute at least one--fourth of our daily requirement of nutrients. An ideal breakfast should contain adequate amounts of carbohydrates, proteins, and fats in addition to minerals and vitamins. Essentially this means including most of our food groups in the morning meal. Whole grain cereals like atta in parathas and puris, dalia, suji, etc. are an integral part of the traditional Indian breakfast. Their high fiber and protein content provide a feeling of satisfaction, which lowers the urge to snack before lunch. On the other hand, high-sugar foods actually make people sleepier, not active. Milk, cheese, eggs or dals (as sprouts in idli or dosas or as sambhar) are other protein sources. A serving of milk (one

cup) provides B-complex vitamins and also minerals like zinc, magnesium, and calcium. Fruits or vegetables provide valuable vitamin C and keep constipation away.

Q.95 We eat unhealthy food when:
A. We suffer from hunger
B. We have become overweight
C. We have skipped the first meal
D. We love chips, burgers etc.

Q.96 We experience sleepiness in the morning because:
A. We eat breakfast
B. We miss breakfast
C. Efficiency goes down
D. We feel tired and sleepy

Q.97 A good breakfast:
A. Makes you lethargic
B. Causes memory loss
C. Causes hunger pangs
D. Keeps you active; boosts performance

Q.98 An ideal breakfast should contain:
A. Carbohydrates, proteins, fats, minerals and vitamins
B. Some food groups
C. Only high fibre and protein
D. Foods of our choice

Q.99 Breakfast is satisfying when
A. It is rich in fatty foods
B. It contains high protein and fibre content
C. It is rich in carbohydrates, proteins and fats
D. We eat to our heart's content

Q.100 If the fractions $\dfrac{7}{13}, \dfrac{2}{3}, \dfrac{4}{11}, \dfrac{5}{9}$ are arranged in ascending order, then the correct sequence is ?

A. $\dfrac{2}{3}, \dfrac{7}{13}, \dfrac{4}{11}, \dfrac{5}{9}$ **B.** $\dfrac{7}{13}, \dfrac{4}{11}, \dfrac{5}{9}, \dfrac{2}{3}$

C. $\dfrac{4}{11}, \dfrac{7}{13}, \dfrac{5}{9}, \dfrac{2}{3}$ **D.** $\dfrac{5}{9}, \dfrac{4}{11}, \dfrac{7}{13}, \dfrac{2}{3}$

// Smart Answer Sheet //

Correct — Percentage of students who answered correctly. **Skipped** — Percentage of students who skipped.

Q.	Ans.	Correct / Skipped	Q.	Ans.	Correct / Skipped	Q.	Ans.	Correct / Skipped	Q.	Ans.	Correct / Skipped	Q.	Ans.	Correct / Skipped	Q.	Ans.	Correct / Skipped
1	B	12.51 % / 79.04 %	18	B	77.26 % / 21.87 %	35	D	78.22 % / 21.54 %	52	C	54.07 % / 40.07 %	69	C	20.99 % / 69.71 %	86	B	40.51 % / 38.05 %
2	C	32.4 % / 67.36 %	19	B	48.1 % / 32.56 %	36	D	84.82 % / 10.8 %	53	A	49.7 % / 39.43 %	70	B	68.77 % / 30.61 %	87	C	52.51 % / 45.93 %
3	A	64.66 % / 32.46 %	20	A	29.95 % / 70.03 %	37	A	79.28 % / 18.08 %	54	C	68.15 % / 31.51 %	71	C	46.31 % / 46.45 %	88	D	29.89 % / 69.44 %
4	A	47.27 % / 52.25 %	21	D	58.34 % / 40.62 %	38	C	82.9 % / 10.49 %	55	C	22.42 % / 73.24 %	72	D	87.57 % / 11.78 %	89	C	40.46 % / 39.27 %
5	B	65.84 % / 30.52 %	22	D	46.28 % / 44.25 %	39	B	82.57 % / 15.6 %	56	D	76.44 % / 21.09 %	73	C	87.18 % / 12.02 %	90	D	59.24 % / 32.25 %
6	C	43.68 % / 47.87 %	23	A	68.64 % / 30.35 %	40	D	60.22 % / 30.75 %	57	C	11.83 % / 68.07 %	74	D	77.44 % / 15.27 %	91	A	51.46 % / 30.05 %
7	D	41.28 % / 43.27 %	24	D	66.99 % / 31.71 %	41	A	86.41 % / 10.84 %	58	B	87.75 % / 10.75 %	75	C	78.61 % / 17.12 %	92	A	60.7 % / 30.9 %
8	B	41.12 % / 53.52 %	25	D	69.09 % / 30.43 %	42	B	62.77 % / 33.93 %	59	D	18.59 % / 74.84 %	76	C	56.1 % / 43.05 %	93	D	40.6 % / 42.64 %
9	D	52.13 % / 35.74 %	26	A	65.54 % / 32.69 %	43	B	83.85 % / 11.64 %	60	B	65.56 % / 33.73 %	77	C	26.53 % / 70.87 %	94	D	40.77 % / 58.69 %
10	C	58.07 % / 31.71 %	27	B	82.16 % / 12.59 %	44	B	77.08 % / 20.27 %	61	B	55.1 % / 32.55 %	78	A	85.58 % / 13.15 %	95	C	58.13 % / 36.04 %
11	A	80.59 % / 14.06 %	28	A	58.45 % / 35.05 %	45	C	84.57 % / 13.37 %	62	C	40.58 % / 41.72 %	79	B	81.88 % / 12.1 %	96	B	64.67 % / 32.34 %
12	C	66.32 % / 31.15 %	29	C	47.76 % / 34.84 %	46	D	89.24 % / 10.64 %	63	A	54.86 % / 31.9 %	80	D	84.43 % / 14.13 %	97	D	46.57 % / 46.96 %
13	D	59.76 % / 35.12 %	30	B	60.69 % / 38.95 %	47	B	44.14 % / 47.51 %	64	C	82.23 % / 12.52 %	81	B	49.24 % / 32.42 %	98	A	55.48 % / 38.51 %
14	C	66.74 % / 31.63 %	31	A	82.65 % / 15.48 %	48	B	51.62 % / 39.72 %	65	A	53.25 % / 36.5 %	82	C	63.36 % / 33.47 %	99	B	59.36 % / 34.28 %
15	D	41.65 % / 55.01 %	32	C	65.04 % / 32.75 %	49	C	80.2 % / 13.8 %	66	C	23.22 % / 74.62 %	83	A	27.93 % / 72.02 %	100	C	66.27 % / 30.1 %
16	C	48.58 % / 40.32 %	33	C	85.8 % / 12.17 %	50	B	44.63 % / 39.14 %	67	A	31.91 % / 68.03 %	84	B	86.91 % / 12.43 %			
17	A	56.27 % / 35.08 %	34	A	60.02 % / 39.85 %	51	B	59.69 % / 35.68 %	68	A	86.85 % / 12.74 %	85	A	49.37 % / 34.39 %			

//Hints and Solutions//

1. A one-member commission was created under the Labour Ministry's Central Advisory Contract Labour Board (CACLB), to prepare an action plan for the welfare and development of guest and contract workers during the COVID-19 pandemic.

Veteran IAS officer C V Ananda Bose, who was in-charge of the commission, has recommended payment of a basic living wage in the event of employment loss. He also sought to establish Labour Authority of India as a nodal body.

Hence, the correct option is (B).

2. The International Conference on Climate Change held in December 2018 was held at Katowice in Poland.

The 2018 United Nations Climate Change Conference, more commonly referred to as the Katowice Climate Change Conference or COP24, was the 24th Conference of the Parties to the United Nations Framework Convention on Climate Change. It was held between 2 and 15 December 2018 in Katowice, Poland. The conference was held in the International Congress Centre. The president of COP24 was Michał Kurtyka. The conference also incorporated the fourteenth meeting of the parties for the Kyoto Protocol (CMP14), and the third session of the first meeting of the parties for the Paris Agreement (CMA1-3 or CMA1.3) which agreed on rules to implement the Agreement. The conference's objective was to have a full implementation of the Paris agreement.

Hence, the correct option is (C).

3. Bharat Vatwani has been awarded for Ramon Magsaysay Award, 2018.

Bharat Vatwani is an Indian psychiatrist in Mumbai. He was awarded Ramon Magsaysay Award in 2018 for leading the rescue of thousands of mentally ill street paupers to treat and reunite them with their families. Bharat Vatwani and his wife established Shraddha Rehabilitation Foundation in 1988, aimed at rescuing mentally-ill persons living on the streets; providing free shelter, food, and psychiatric treatment; and reuniting them with their families.

Hence, the correct option is (A).

4. Netanyahus won the Pulitzer Prize 2022 in the fiction category.

Winners of the Pulitzer Prize 2022 were announced in May 2022. The Netanyahus by Joshua Cohen won in the fiction category.

Frank sonnets by Diane Seuss won in the poetry category. First awarded in 1917, the Pulitzer Prize recognizes excellence in journalism, literature, and musical composition.

Hence, the correct option is (A).

5. Mauritius island has recently declared a state of environmental emergency due to oil spill from a grounded ship.

Effects:

- The oil spill threatens the ecology of the coastline of Mauritius and the marine life in the Indian Ocean.

- It endangers the already endangered coral reefs, seagrasses in the shallow waters, mangroves, fishes, and other aquatic fauna.

Hence, the correct option is (B).

6. Let the amount invested be ' x ' on younger and ' y ' on elder son respectively.

When they will be of 18 years age, they will get equal amount

Time when age of son is 13 years $= 18 - 13 = 5$ years

Time when age of son is 15 years $= 18 - 15 = 3$ years

According to question:

$$\frac{(x \times 5 \times 5)}{100} = \frac{(y \times 3 \times 5)}{100}$$

$$\Rightarrow \frac{25x}{100} = \frac{15y}{100}$$

$$\Rightarrow \frac{x}{y} = \frac{3}{5} \text{ or } x : y = 3 : 5$$

Given that he invested total $(3 + 5) = 8$ unit $=$ Rs. 8400

∴ Younger son is 13 years and amount invested on him

$$= \left(\frac{8400}{8}\right) \times 3 \text{ unit}$$

$$= \text{Rs. } 3150$$

Hence, the correct option is (C).

7. Given:

Principal $=$ Rs. 30000

Rate $= 10\%$

Time $= 5$ years

Let the rate of interest allowed by bank be r%

According to question

$$7800 = \left(\frac{30000 \times 10 \times 5}{100}\right) - \left(\frac{30000 \times r \times 3}{100}\right)$$

$$7800 = 15000 - 900r$$

$$r = 8\%$$

∴ rate of interest allowed by bank is 8%.

Hence, the correct option is (D).

8. Given:

A sum of Rs. 1000 is increased 100% of its original after 7 years at compound interest.

Let the amount be A and principal be P.

$$\text{Amount} = \text{principal} \times \left(1 + \frac{rate}{100}\right)^n$$

After 7 years,

$$A = P \times \left(1 + \frac{\text{rate}}{100}\right)^7 = 2P \quad (\because P \text{ is increased by } 100\%)$$

$$\Rightarrow \left(1 + \frac{\text{rate}}{100}\right)^7 = 2$$

Amount will be increased by 700%

$\Rightarrow$ A will be $8P$

$$\Rightarrow A = 2^3 \times P = \left(\left\{\left(1 + \frac{\text{rate}}{100}\right)^7\right\}\right)^3 \times P$$

$$= \left(1 + \frac{\text{rate}}{100}\right)^{21} \times P$$

$\Rightarrow$ time $= 21$ years

$\therefore$ After 21 years the amount will be increased by 700% of its initial value / Principal.

Hence, the correct option is (B).

9. Field Marshal is the highest rank in Army.

It has been abolished by the present army. At present, General is the highest rank of the army of India. The highest rank attainable in the Indian Army is Field Marshal. Ranked as a Five Star General Officer, a Field Marshal is ranked above a General. A Field Marshal's insignia comprises the national emblem over a crossed baton and saber in a wreath of lotus flowers. Till date this rank has been conferred on only two individuals. One was Sam Manekshaw. He was known for his bravery, which also earned him the nickname of Sam Bahadur. The other was K.M. Cariappa who was also the first Indian Commander-in-Chief of the Indian Army.

Hence, the correct option is (D).

10. Given,

The numerator of a fraction be increased by 15% and its denominator be diminished by 8%, the value of the fraction is $\frac{15}{16}$.

Let the original fraction be $\frac{x}{y}$.

According to the question,

$$\frac{115\% \text{ of } x}{92\% \text{ of } y} = \frac{15}{16}$$

$$\Rightarrow \frac{115x}{92y} = \frac{15}{16}$$

$$\Rightarrow \frac{x}{y} = \left(\frac{15}{16} \times \frac{92}{115}\right)$$

$$\Rightarrow \frac{x}{y} = \frac{3}{4}$$

Hence, the correct option is (C).

11. Given number is 0.36.

$$= \frac{36}{100}$$

$$= \frac{9}{25}$$

Sum of the numerator and the denominator $= 9 + 25$

$$= 34$$

Hence, the correct option is (A).

12. Basic rules to be followed for Active/Passive conversions are:
1. The object of the active verb becomes the subject of the passive verb.
2. The finite form of the verb is changed (to be+ past participle).
3. The subject of the active sentence becomes the object of the passive sentence (or is dropped).
4. Preposition "by" is used before the object.
The given sentence is in the active form of simple past tense. The structures for active/passive voices are:

Active: Subject + verb (IInd form) + object.

Passive: Object + was/were + verb (IIIrd form) + by + subject.

So, with the help of the above structures, we can convert the given sentence into passive voice:

Their teacher was asked many questions by the students.

Hence, the correct option is (C).

13. The given sentence is in the active form of simple past tense. The structures for active/passive voices are:
Active: Subject + verb (IInd form) + object.

Passive: Object + was/were + verb (IIIrd form) + by + subject.

So, with the help of the above structures, we can convert the given sentence into passive voice:

You were called many times by your mother.

Hence, the correct option is (D).

14. Period of geopolitical tension between the Soviet Union and the United States said to be Cold War Era, in 1947-1991.

- The Cold War was a period of geopolitical tension between the Soviet Union and the United States and their respective allies, the Eastern Bloc and the Western Bloc, after World War II.

- The period is generally considered to span 1947 to the 1991 dissolution of the Soviet Union.

- The term "cold" is used because there was no large-scale fighting directly between the two superpowers, but they each supported major regional conflicts known as proxy wars.

- The West was led by the United States as well as the other First World nations of the Western Bloc that were generally liberal democratic but tied to a network of authoritarian states, most of which were their former colonies.

Hence, the correct option is (C).

15. The adjective required for the blank is 'as intelligent as' as it qualifies the dolphins and shows a comparison with the humans.

Complete Sentence:

Dolphins are **as intelligent as** humans and are able to understand and talk among themselves with a particular sound.

Hence, the correct option is (D).

16. The attribute 'the' denotes that a superlative adjective follows it.

Complete Sentence:

Coconut water is the **purest** and most hygienic water found on the earth.

Hence, the correct option is (C).

17. The preposition 'off' means separation, removing and here it is 'laying off' means removing them from service, 'of' is used to show belonging, 'to' shows the place, and 'at' is used for time.

Complete Sentence:

The company in order to make up for its loss had to lay **off** many workers.

Hence, the correct option is (A).

18. Handed down – the preposition means to give to someone younger, hence the other options are inapt.

Complete Sentence:

The tradition of having yogurt and sugar before leaving home has been **handed down** from father to son.

Hence, the correct option is (B).

19. According to the rule, when the subordinate clause i.e. 'if clause' is written in the present tense the principal clause should be in the future tense.

The structure will be: If+present tense+object, Subject+will+main verb+Object.

Complete Sentence:

If I win the jackpot, I **will open** an orphanage cum old age home so that the older and younger generation could thrive together.

Hence, the correct option is (B).

20. Let's look at the meaning of the given idiom:

Get the jitters- to experience a temporary state of nervous anxiety or anticipation

Example:

Lo Jill always gets the jitters before exams.

Thus, from the explanation given above, we find that the first option is the correct choice.

Hence, the correct option is (A).

21. Let's look at the meaning of the given idiom:

French leave- without permission; go away without telling anyone

Example:

I think I might take French leave this afternoon and go to the cinema.

Thus, from the explanation given above, we find that the fourth option is the correct choice.

Hence, the correct option is (D).

22. Azolla is an efficient Nitrogen fixer. The use of Bio-fertilizers like Azolla not only increases the rice productivity but also improves the long term soil fertility.

Hence, the correct option is (D).

23. Given:

SP of the article $=$ Rs. 799.50

Successive discount rates $= 18\%$ and 22%

CP of the article = Rs. 1,000

We know that:

Successive discount $= x + y - \left(\dfrac{xy}{100}\right)$

Let the MP of the article $= a$

Net effective discount rate $= 18 + 22 - \left[\dfrac{(18\times22)}{100}\right]$

$= 36.04\%$

$\therefore SP$ of the article ater discount $= a - \left(\dfrac{a\times36.04}{100}\right)$

$= \dfrac{(100a-36.04a)}{100}$

$= \dfrac{63.96a}{100}$

$\therefore$ SP of the article $=$ Rs. 799.50

$\therefore \dfrac{63.96a}{100} = 799.50$

$\Rightarrow a = \dfrac{(799.5\times100)}{63.96}$

$\Rightarrow a = 1250$

$\therefore$ MP of the article $=$ Rs. 1,250

$\therefore$ Profit if article sold at $MP = MP - CP$

$= 1250 - 1000$

$=$ Rs. 250

Hence, the correct option is (A).

24. Given:

Initial SP of article = Rs. 265.50

Gain % = 18%

New SP = Rs. 231.30

We know that:

$$CP = SP \times \left[\frac{100}{(100 + Profit\%)}\right]$$

Profit $\% = \frac{(Profit \times 100)}{CP}$ Profit $= SP - CP$

CP of the article $= 265.50 \times \left[\frac{100}{(100+18)}\right]$

$= 265.5 \times \left(\frac{100}{118}\right)$

$= \frac{26550}{118}$

$= 225$

$\therefore$ CP of the article $=$ Rs. 225

$\because$ The New $SP =$ Rs. 231.30

$\therefore$ There will be a profit.

Profit $= SP - CP$

$= 231.3 - 225$

$=$ Rs. 6.3

$\therefore$ Profit $\% = \frac{(6.3 \times 100)}{225}$

$= 2.8\%$

Hence, the correct option is (D).

25. Given:

Initial Profit $\% = 20\%$

Increased in $SP =$ Rs. 130

Final Profit $\% = 28\%$

Let the CP of the article $= 100a$

$\therefore$ Initial $SP = CP + 20\%$ of CP

$= 100a + \left[\left(\frac{20}{100}\right) \times 100a\right]$

$= 100a + 20a$

$= 120a$

Final $SP = CP + 28\%$ of CP

$= 100a + \left[\left(\frac{28}{100}\right) \times 100a\right]$

$= 100a + 28a$

$= 128a$

$\because$ Final SP $-$ Initial $SP = 130$

$\Rightarrow 128a - 120a = 130$

$\Rightarrow 8a = 130$

$\therefore 1a = \frac{130}{8}$

$\Rightarrow 100 \times 1a = \left(\frac{130}{8}\right) \times 100$

$\Rightarrow 100a = 1625$

$\therefore CP$ of the article $=$ Rs. 1,625

Hence, the correct option is (D).

26. Given that,

Distance covered by train in first 10 minutes $= 35$ km /hr

$= \frac{35 \times 10}{60} = \frac{35}{67}$ km

Distance covered by train in next 5 minutes $= 20$ km /hr

$= \frac{20 \times 10}{60} = \frac{20}{6}$ km

So, total distance covered by train is:

$$\Rightarrow \left[\left(35 \times \frac{10}{60}\right) + \left(20 \times \frac{5}{60}\right)\right]$$

$$\Rightarrow \left(\frac{35}{6} + \frac{10}{6}\right)km = \frac{45}{6}km$$

Given that, total time $= 15$ minutes $= \frac{1}{4}$ hr

$\therefore$ average speed of the train $= \frac{total\ distance}{time\ spent} =$

$\frac{45}{6} \times 4 = 30$km/hr

Hence, the correct option is (A).

27. Given that,

Length of caravan $= 120$ m

Speed of caravan $= 10$ m /s

So, time taken $= \frac{distance}{speed}$

$\Rightarrow$ time taken $= \frac{120}{10} = 12$ seconds.

Hence, the correct option is (B).

28. Let the speed of the boat be c and the speed of the current is v.

So we have,

Speed of the boat with the stream $= c + v = \frac{36}{3} = 12$ km/hr

Speed of the boat against the stream $= c - v = \frac{36}{9} = 4$ km /hr

By adding the above result obtained and removing v, we get,

$\Rightarrow 2c = 16$ km /hr

$\Rightarrow c = 8$ km /hr

Hence, the correct option is (A).

29. Given:

A wheel makes a number of revolutions = 1000

Distance covered = 88 km

Formula required:

The perimeter of circle = 2πr

Calculations:

88 km = 88 × 1000

Distance covered in one revolution = Distance travelled/number of revolutions

$\Rightarrow 88 \times \dfrac{1000}{1000} = 88$ m

Perimeter of a wheel = 88 m

2πr = 88

$\Rightarrow r = \dfrac{88}{(2\pi)}$

$\Rightarrow r = \dfrac{88}{\left(2 \times \dfrac{22}{7}\right)}$

$\Rightarrow r = 7 \times 2$

$\Rightarrow r = 14$ m

∴ The radius of the wheel is 14 m.

Hence, the correct option is (C).

30.

Hence, the correct option is (D).

31. By observing all the figures we find that the question figure is hidden in the answer figure (A).

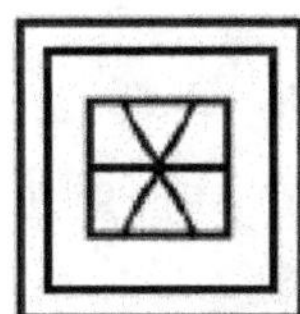

Hence, the correct option is (A).

32.

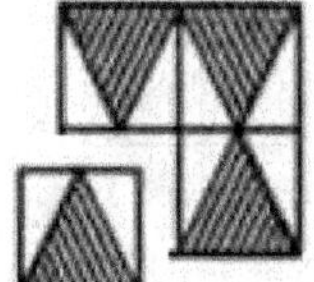

Hence, the correct option is (C).

33. We can easily observe that in option (C) the question figure is embedded.

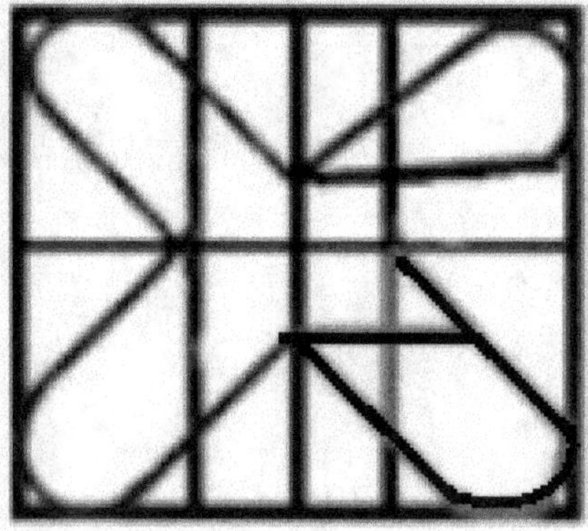

Hence, the correct option is (C).

34. After carefully observing the figure given in the question, it is very clear that the question figure is embedded in the answer figure (A). It is shown as given below:

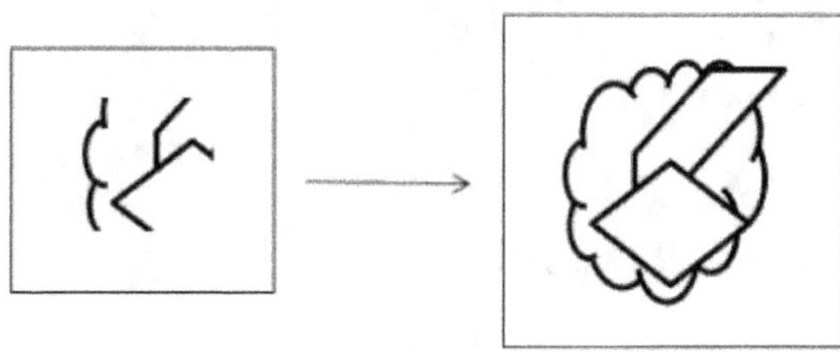

Hence, the correct option is (A).

35. Given,

The average of 10 numbers $= 15$

The average $= ($ The sum of all items $)/($ The total items $)$

$\Rightarrow$ The sum of all 10 number $= 10 \times 15 = 150$

$\Rightarrow$ When 2 is added then sum of all number $= 150 + (2 \times 10) = 150 + 20 = 170$

$\Rightarrow$ The new average $= \dfrac{170}{10} = 17$

∴ The required result will be 17.

Hence, the correct option is (D).

36. Given:

He scores three different runs 20, 30, 40.

$$\text{Average} = \frac{\text{Sum of all scores}}{\text{Number of scores}}$$

$$\frac{(20+30+40)}{3}$$

$$= \frac{90}{3} = 30 \text{ runs}$$

∴ The required result will be 30 runs.

Hence, the correct option is (D).

37. Given:

The numbers is 29, 34, 39, 44, 49 and 57.

$$\text{Average} = \frac{(29+34+39+44+49+57)}{6}$$

$$= \frac{252}{6} = 42$$

∴ The required result will be 42.

Hence, the correct option is (A).

38. The efficiency of Rahul : Shiv $= 2:1$

time taken by Rahul : Shiv $= 1:2$

Let time taken by Rahul be x and by Shiv be $2x$.

∴ their one day work together $= \dfrac{1}{x} + \dfrac{1}{2x} = \dfrac{3}{2x}$

Their actual one day work is $\dfrac{1}{12}$.

So, $\dfrac{3}{2x} = \dfrac{1}{12}$

$\Rightarrow 2x = 36$

$x = 18$ days

Hence, the correct option is (C).

39. Let capacity of the tank be x gallons.

Part of the tank filled in 1 minute $= \dfrac{x}{24} + \dfrac{x}{40} - 30$

$\Rightarrow \dfrac{x}{24} + \dfrac{x}{40} - 30 = \dfrac{x}{60}$

$\Rightarrow \dfrac{x}{24} + \dfrac{x}{40} - \dfrac{x}{60} = 30$

$\Rightarrow \dfrac{10x+6x-4x}{240} = 30$

$\Rightarrow 12x = 30 \times 240$

$\Rightarrow x = 600$ gallons

Hence, the correct option is (B).

40. % Cistern is filled by 1st pipe in one minute $= \dfrac{100}{20} = 5\%$

% Cistern is filled by 2nd pipe in one minute $= \dfrac{\overline{100}}{30} = 3.33\%$ %

Cistern filled by 1st and 2nd pipes in one minute $= 8.33\%$

According to question, Cistern is totally filled by 2nd pipe in last 10 minute.

That means 2nd pipe filled 33.3% of the cistern in last 10 minute and 66.66% of cistern is filled by 1st and 2nd pipe together in $= \dfrac{66.66}{8.33} = 8$ minutes

Thus, after 8 minute, 1st pipe must be turned off.

Hence, the correct option is (D).

41. The one-word substitution is Inevitable.

Inevitable: certain to happen, unavoidable.

Irreparable: impossible to rectify or repair.

Incomparable: without an equal in quality or extent, matchless.

Indisputable: unable to be challenged or denied.

Hence, the correct option is (A).

42. Ambidextrous: able to use the right and left hands equally well.

Sinister: One who able to use the left hand well.

Ambivalent: having mixed feelings or contradictory ideas about something or someone.

Amateur: a person who is contemptibly inept at a particular activity.

Hence, the correct option is (B).

43. In all the figures except figure (2), outer lines are fully covering the circle.

Figures (1), (3) and (4) are symmetric about any axis but Figure (2) is not showing any symmetry.

Hence, the correct option is (B).

44. Arranging the letter in meaningful order, we get

ORFU - FOUR

VIDEID - DIVIDED

GHIET - EIGHT

VEENS – SEVEN

So, Except DIVDED, all others are numbers.

Hence, the correct option is (B).

45. All the places given in the question are capitals of states.

So, the asked place would be Shimala beacuse it's a capital of Himachal Pradesh.

Hence, the correct option is (C).

46. Except Sugar, all others are liquid.

Hence, the correct option is (D).

47. Except for Lawyer, all others are elected government officials.

Hence, the correct option is (B).

48. LPG stands for liquefied petroleum gas. Like all fossil fuels, it is a non-renewable source of energy.

It is extracted from crude oil and natural gas. LPG is composed hydrocarbons containing three or four carbon atoms. The normal components of LPG thus, are propane (C_3H_8) and butane (C_4H_{10}).

Hence, the correct option is (B).

49. Both camphor and ammonium chloride are solid at room temperature. But they are vaporized (gas phase) when heat is applied. This property is called Sublimation.

The heat of sublimation - Heat required to change a unit mass of solid directly into vapour, at a given temperature, is called the heat of sublimation at that temperature.

Hence, the correct option is (C).

50. Rayon is obtained from the wood pulp. Rayon is a regenerated cellulose fiber. It is made from natural sources such as wood and agricultural products.

There are two types of man-made fibers.

Synthetic fibers: Synthetic fibers are made only from polymers found in natural gas and the by-products of petroleum. Examples: Nylon, Acrylics, Polyurethane, and Polypropylene

Regenerated fibers: Regenerated fibers are made from cellulose polymers that occur naturally in plants such as cotton, wool, hemp, and flax. Examples: Rayon and Acetate.

Hence, the correct option is (B).

51. Kepler's second law states that an imaginary line joining a planet and the sun sweeps out an equal area of space in equal amounts of time i.e. the areal velocity of the planet around the sun is constant. It is also known as Law of areas.

Hence, the correct option is (B).

52. Ingestion of excess fluoride, most commonly in drinking water, can cause Fluorosis which affects the Bones and Teeth.

Fluorine is a chemical element, denoted by the symbol (F) and atomic number (9). It is the lightest Halogen element and exists as a Highly Toxic Pale Yellow Diatomic Gas. In 1529, Georgius Agricola discovered this element.

It is the most electronegative element, and extremely reactive, as it reacts with all other elements, except for Neon, Helium, and Argon gases (Nobel gases).

Hence, the correct option is (C).

53. The given sentence is grammatically incorrect.

- Here, 'The government needs to adopt' should be used instead of 'The government need to adopt'.
- 'Government' is followed by a singular verb.
- Hence, 'need' must be replaced with 'needs' to form a grammatically correct sentence.

Hence, the correct option is (A).

54. The given sentence is grammatically incorrect.

- Here, 'subjects in science' should be used instead of 'subject in science'.

- The noun following the phrase "one of the" is always a plural noun.
- Therefore, 'subject' must be replaced with 'subjects' to form a grammatically correct sentence.

Hence, the correct option is (C).

55. Here, the second number can be represented as the Average of digits of the first number.

In $1511 : 2 \Rightarrow \dfrac{(1+5+1+1)}{4} = 2$

In a similar way,

In $6554 \Rightarrow$ Average of $\dfrac{(6+5+5+4)}{4} = 5$

Hence, the correct option is (C).

56. The given question follows the following pattern:

$7 \times 8 = 56$

$8 \times 9 = 72$

$9 \times 10 = 90$

$10 \times 11 = 110$

Hence, the correct option is (D).

57. As, The sum of the digits of 967 = 9 + 6 + 7 = 22

The sum of the digits of 386 = 3 + 8 + 6 = 17

Similarly the sum of the digits of 542 = 5 + 4 + 2 = 11

Sum of the digits of 763 = 7 + 6 + 3 = 16

Difference of both digits are $\Rightarrow$ (22 - 17) = (11 - 16) = 5

Hence, the correct option is (C).

58. As 6: 72

$72 = 6 \times 12$

Similarly

8:?

$? = 8 \times 12 = 96$

? = 96

8: 96

Hence, the correct option is (B).

59. The words are reversed from the middle.

ORDERS = ERSORD

The first 3 letters come after the last 3 letters.

So doing the same for VERMIN gives us: MINVER.

Hence, the correct option is (D).

60. The logic is:

The common shaded portion of both the shape in 1st image in unshaded in the 2nd image.

Similarly,

The bigger triangle will be unshaded and the three small triangles will be shaded.

Hence, the correct option is (B).

61.

The figure has been rotated through 90 degrees in the clockwise direction.

Hence, the correct option is (B).

62. From figure (2) and (3) we can conclude that the numbers 2, 4, 3 and 6 appear adjacent to the letter 5. Therefore the number 1 appears opposite to 5, In other words, we can say that 5 appear opposite to 1.

Therefore, the correct answer is 5.

Hence, the correct option is (C).

63. The pins, equal in number to the number of sides in the main figure are attached to the midpoint of a side of the main figure in case of figures (2), (3) and (4). In figure (1), these pins are attached to a vertex of the main figure.

Hence, the correct option is (A).

64. In all other figures, the two line segments are parallel to each other.

Hence, the correct option is (C).

65. Given-

$$A:B = 7:3$$

Let $A = 7k, B = 3k$.

On putting the values of A and $B,$

$$\frac{AB+B^2}{A^2-B^2}$$

$$= \frac{(7k \times 3k)+(3k)^2}{(7k)^2-(3k)^2}$$

$$= \frac{21k^2+9k^2}{49k^2-9k^2}$$

$$= \frac{30k^2}{40k^2}$$

$$= \frac{3}{4}$$

Hence, the correct option is (A).

66. Given-

$$X^2 + 4Y^2 = 4XY$$

$$\Rightarrow X^2 + 4Y^2 - 4XY = 0$$

$$\Rightarrow (X - 2Y)^2 = 0$$

$$\Rightarrow X - 2Y = 0$$

$$\Rightarrow X = 2Y$$

$$\Rightarrow \frac{X}{Y} = \frac{2}{1}$$

On cubing both the sides,

$$\Rightarrow \left(\frac{X}{Y}\right)^3 = \left(\frac{2}{1}\right)^3$$

$$\Rightarrow \frac{X^3}{Y^3} = \frac{8}{1}$$

$$\Rightarrow X^3:Y^3 = 8:1$$

Hence, the correct option is (C).

67. Given-

$$A:B = \frac{1}{2}:\frac{1}{5}$$

$$\Rightarrow A:B = 5:2$$

$$\Rightarrow A:B = 10:4$$

$$C:B = \frac{1}{4}:\frac{1}{5}$$

$$\Rightarrow C:B = 5:4$$

$$\Rightarrow B:C = 4:5$$

On combining $A:B$ and $B:C$ we get,

$$A:B:C = 10:4:5$$

Let $A = 10k, B = 4k, C = 5k$.

On putting the values of $A,$ B and C in $\frac{A^2+B^2}{C^2-B^2},$

$$= \frac{(10k)^2+(4k)^2}{(5k)^2-(4k)^2}$$

$$= \frac{100k^2+16k^2}{25k^2-16k^2}$$

$$= \frac{116k^2}{9k^2}$$

$$= \frac{116}{9}$$

$$= 12\frac{8}{9}$$

Hence, the correct option is (A).

68. Virat Kohli has been awarded the ICC men's ODI player of the decade Award.

He also won Sir Garfield Sobers award for the best male cricketer of the past decade.

Other ICC awards of the decade:

Mahendra Singh Dhoni won the ICC Spirit of Cricket Award of the decade.

Ellyse Perry a female all-rounder cricketer from Australia won the following awards:

- ICC female cricketer of the decade.
- ICC women ODI cricketer of the decade.
- Women's T20 Cricketer of the decade.

Hence, the correct option is (A).

69. The correct order is:

5. Advertisement

6. Application

2. Interview

3. Selection

4. Appointment

1. Probation

Hence, the correct option is (C).

70. The logical order of cooking potato fries are as follows:

2. Peel the potatoes.

5. Cut potatoes into thin straw-like pieces.

1. Add oil in the frying pan.

4. Add the sliced potatoes to the oil in the frying pan.

3. Remove and place the potato fries on a plate with paper towels to absorb the leftover cooking oil.

So, the meaningful order is 2, 5, 1, 4, 3

Hence, the correct option is (B).

71. Mercury sunglass is a part of sunglass and both come under the eyewear section.
Hence, the correct option is (C).

72. Brinjal is a vegetable. But, Meat is entirely different.

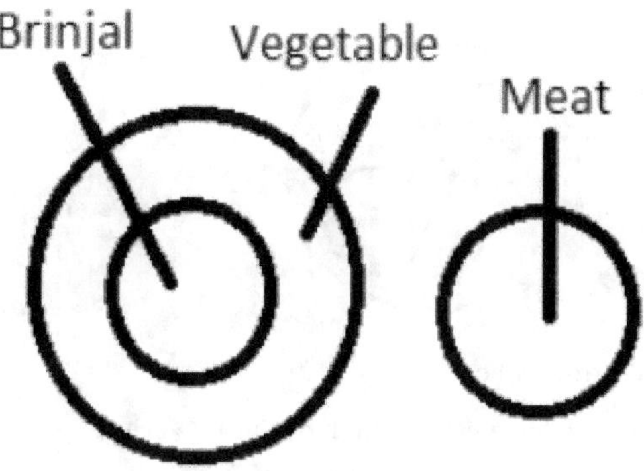

Hence, the correct option is (D).

73. Surat is a city in Gujarat and Gujarat is a state in India.

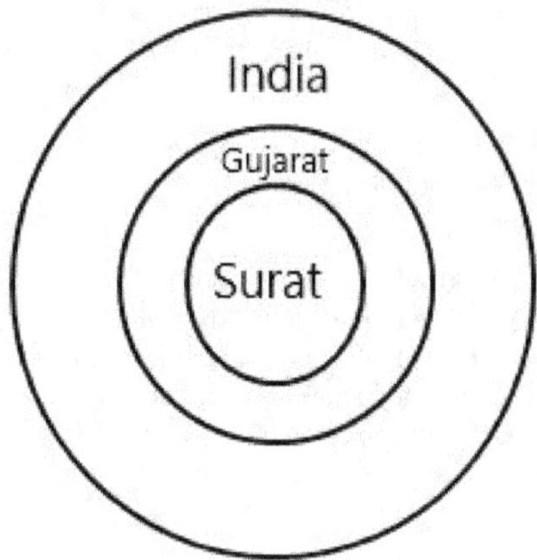

Hence, the correct option is (C).

74. Here, we know that brinjal is a vegetable, jasmine is a flower, rice is a grain and mango is a fruit. So, there is no relation between these four. So, it can be represented by option (D) as shown below:

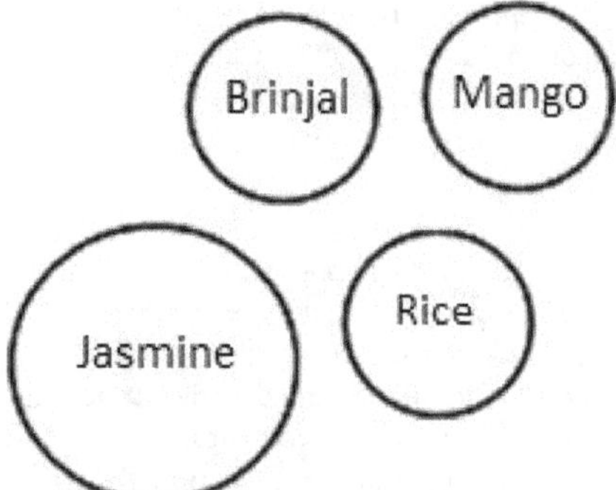

Hence, the correct option is (D).

75. The digestive system and excretory system are parts of the body and the stomach is a part of the digestive system. This relation can be shown by the given figure below:

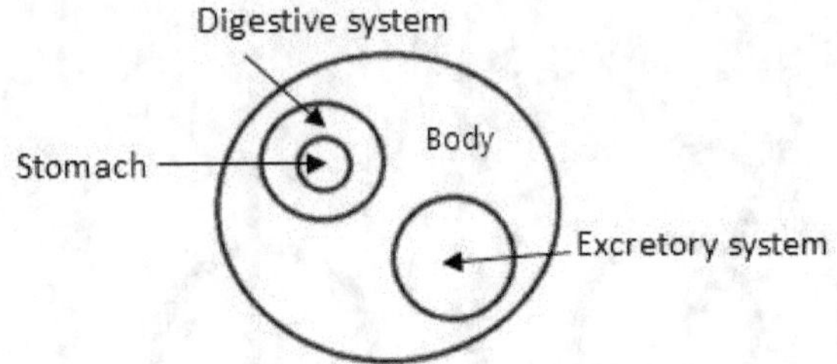

Hence, the correct option is (C).

76. The above statement are related to Mimamsa School.

Mimamsa philosophy is basically the analysis of interpretation, application, and the use of the text of the Samhita and Brahmana portions of the Veda.

According to Mimamsa philosophy, Vedas are eternal and possess all knowledge, and religion means the fulfillment of duties prescribed by the Vedas.

This philosophy encompasses the Nyaya-Vaisheshika systems and emphasizes the concept of valid knowledge.
Hence, the correct option is (C).

77. Statement 1: The word 'Khyal' is derived from Persian and means "idea or imagination". The origin of this style was attributed to Amir Khusrau. This form is popular amongst the artists as this provides greater scope for improvisation. Khyal is based on the repertoire of short songs ranging from two to eight lines. Generally, a Khyal composition is also referred to as a 'Bandish'.

Statement 3: In most cases, every singer renders the same bandish differently, while keeping the text and raga constant. Usually, the theme for these Khyal bandishes is romantic in nature. They sing about love, even if they are related to the divine creatures. It may be praising God or a particular king. Exceptional Khyal compositions are composed in the praise of Lord Krishna.

Statement 2: Sultan Mohammad Sharqi gave the biggest patronage to Khyal in the 15th century. One of the most unique features of Khyal is the use of taan in the composition. Because of this, Alap is given much less room in the Khyal music as compared to Dhrupad.

Hence, the correct option is (C).

78. In Kerala Education Bill (1957), the Supreme Court said that in case of a conflict between Fundamental Right and Directive Principles, the principle of harmonious construction should be applied. The court observed that: "though the directive principles can not override the fundamental rights, nevertheless, in determining the scope and ambit of fundamental rights the court could not entirely ignore the directive principle but should adopt the principle of harmonious construction and should attempt to give effect to both as much as possible".

Hence, the correct option is (B).

79. Accurately: in a way that is correct, exact, and without any mistakes

Correctly: in a way that is in agreement with the true facts or with what is generally accepted

Moderately: in a way that is neither small nor large in size, amount, degree, or strength

Promptly: done quickly and without delay

Partially: not completely
Hence, the correct option is (B).

80. Condescending: showing or characterized by a patronizing or superior attitude toward others

Patronizing: speaking or behaving towards someone as if they are stupid or not important

Stimulating: encouraging or arousing interest or enthusiasm

Accusing: indicating a belief in someone's guilt or culpability

Creating: bringing something into existence
Hence, the correct option is (D).

81. Ambiguous means open to more than one interpretation; not having one obvious meaning.

The meanings of the given words-

Clear means easy to perceive, understand, or interpret.

Unclear means not easy to see, hear, or understand.

Bright means giving out or reflecting much light, shining.

Faded means gradually grow faint and disappear.
Hence, the correct option is (B).

82. An equinox is an event in which a planet's subsolar point passes through its Equator. The equinoxes are the only time when both the Northern and Southern Hemispheres experience roughly equal amounts of daytime and nighttime.

- There are two equinoxes every year: one around March 21 and another around September 23.

- Sometimes, the equinoxes are nicknamed the "vernal equinox" (spring equinox) and the "autumnal equinox" (fall equinox).

- During the equinoxes, solar declination is 0°. Solar declination describes the latitude of the Earth where the sun is directly overhead at noon.

- The subsolar point is an area where the sun's rays shine perpendicular to the Earth's surface at a right angle.

- Only during equinox is the Earth's 23.5° axis not tilting toward or away from the sun: the perceived center of the Sun's disk is in the same plane as the Equator.

Hence, the correct option is (C).

83. Given:

Invalid votes = 20% of the total votes

Arvind won by 480 votes.

And Arvind got 20% more votes than Manoj.

Let total votes be x.

Invalid votes = 20% of x = 0.2x

Valid votes = x – 0.2x = 0.8x

Arvind and Manoj gets 0.8x votes.

Arvind got 20% more votes than Manoj.

⇒ Arvind gets 60% of valid votes and Manoj gets 40% of valid votes.

⇒ Votes received by Arvind $= 0.8x \times \dfrac{60}{100} = 0.48x$

⇒ Votes received by Manoj = 0.8x – 0.48x = 0.32x

Votes of Arvind – Votes of Manoj = 480

⇒ 0.48x – 0.32x = 480

⇒ 0.16x = 480

⇒ x = 3000

∴ Total number of people who voted are 3000.

Hence, the correct option is (A).

84. Given:

A number is subtracted from three-seventh of itself = -48

Let the number be x.

According to the question,

$$\left(\dfrac{3x}{7}\right) - x = -48$$

$$\Rightarrow \dfrac{(3x-7x)}{7} = -48$$

$$\Rightarrow (-4x) = (-48 \times 7)$$

$$\Rightarrow x = 12 \times 7$$

$$\Rightarrow x = 84$$

Now, 75% of number $= 84 \times \dfrac{75}{100}$

$= \dfrac{(84 \times 3)}{4} = 63$

∴ 75% of the number is 63.

Hence, the correct option is (B).

85. Given:

Child spends 25% of her pocket money on chocolates.

Child spends 20% of the rest on toys.

Let child's pocket money be 100x.

⇒ Amount spent on chocolates = 25% of 100x $=$ $\dfrac{25}{100} \times 100x = 25x$

⇒ Amount left with child = 100x – 25x = 75x

Also, Amount spent on toys = 20% of rest = 20% of 75x $=$ $\dfrac{20}{100} \times 75x = 15x$

⇒ Amount left with child = 75x – 15x = 60x

Given, amount left with child = INR 1080 = 60x

⇒ x = INR 18

Child's pocket money = 100x = 100 × 18 = INR 1800

∴ Child's pocket money is INR 1800.

Hence, the correct option is (A).

86. Complete the notice with the right word. Use of cell phones is **disallowed** within the premises.

The use of Verb 'disallowed' (to prohibit, retaliate) is appropriate in the blank space of the sentence.

Hence, the correct option is (B).

87. The above question is based on Question Tag format. The first part of this type of English sentence is Assertive or Imperative and the second part is Interrogative. This second part is called Question Tag. It is a rule that the question tag of Affirmative (Affirmative) Sentences is Negative. That is, the question tag of Auxiliary Verb $+n't +$ subject $+?$ and Negative Sentences is Affirmative (Affirmative) i.e. Auxiliary Verb + Subject + ? Is used. Therefore, the use of 'is it' in the blank space is appropriate.

Ex. This novel is not interesting, is it?

Hence, the correct option is (C).

88. A mix of decayed wood, leaves and manure is known as **compost**.

The use of the word 'compost' (compound manure, vegetable manure, litter manure) in the blank space of the sentence is appropriate. The term 'compost' means- 'a mixture of various decaying organic substances, as dead leaves or manure, use for fertilizing soil, decayed organic material used as a fertilizer for growing plants.

Hence, the correct option is (D).

89. He **bid** goodbye to his friends before leaving.

Bid means to greet, command.

The given sentence is a simple indefinite sentense so use of bid is appropriate here.

In the simple present, most regular verbs use the root form, except in the third-person singular (which ends in -s).

Hence, the correct option is (C).

90. The missing figure is:

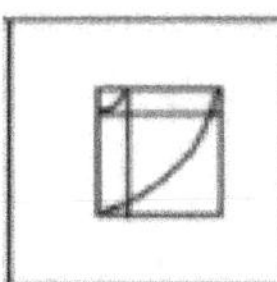

Hence, the correct option is (D).

91. The missing figure is:

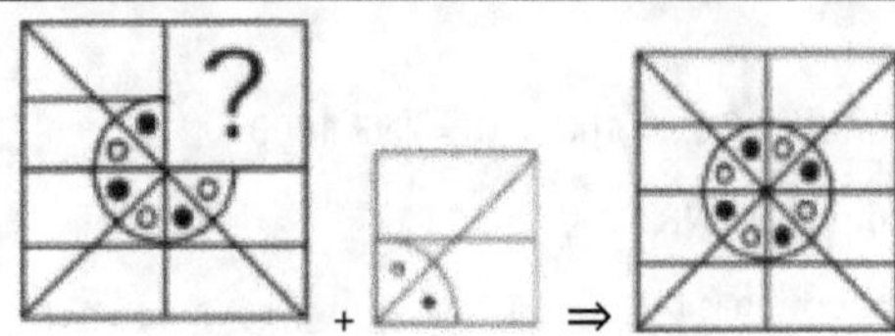

Hence, the correct option is (A).

92. The missing figure is:

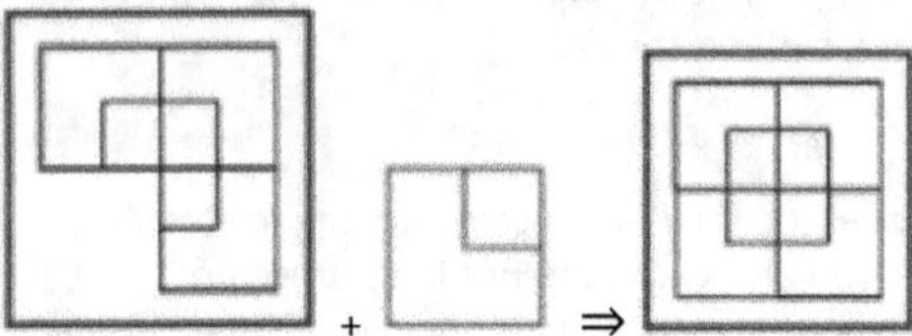

Hence, the correct option is (A).

93. The missing figure is:

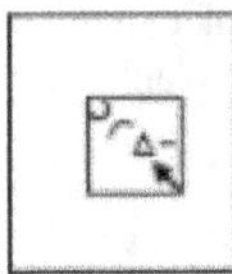

Hence, the correct option is (D).

94. The missing figure is:

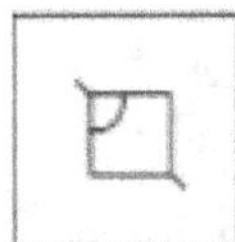

Hence, the correct option is (D).

95. In the 2nd and 3rd line, it is clearly mentioned that 'Moreover, skipping the first meal of the day leads to intense hunger pangs by late morning and we end up eating chips, samosas, burgers or other high fat unhealthy foods.'

This means that because of skipping our breakfast we feel a urge to eat something which drags us to the unhealthy foods like chips, samosas, burgers which increase our weight and leads to obesity.

Therefore the correct answer will be 'We have skipped the first meal'.

Hence, the correct option is (C).

96. In the first line it is clearly mentioned that 'Without breakfast, all of us irrespective of age are likely to experience the late morning slump; tiredness, sleepiness and the urge to sit back.'

This happens because if we do not have breakfast then our body does not get the nutrients and energy it needs to perform the daily activities.

This is the reason why we feel sleepy and tired.

Therefore, the correct answer will be 'We miss breakfast'.

Hence, the correct option is (B).

97. In the 3rd and 4th line it is clearly mentioned that 'A good breakfast leads to a more active, productive day'.

It is so because if we have quality breakfast then our body gets the desired energy from the food and therefore we are able to perform our daily activities with a lot more energy and enthusiasm.

Therefore, the correct answer will be 'keeps you active; boost performance'.

Hence, the correct option is (D).

98. In the 6th and 7th line, it is clearly mentioned that ' An ideal breakfast should contain adequate amounts of carbohydrates, proteins, and fats in addition to minerals and vitamins.Essentially this means including most of our food groups in the morning meal.'

In this way the body will get all the required nutrients and we will not feel sleepy and tired.

Therefore, the correct answer will be 'carbohydrates, proteins, fats, minerals and vitamins.

Hence, the correct option is (A).

99. In the 7th,8th and 9th line it is clearly mentioned that ' Whole grain cereals like atta in parathas and puris, dalia, suji, etc. are an integral part of the traditional Indian breakfast. Their high fiber and protein content provide a feeling of satisfaction, which lowers the urge to snack before lunch. On the other hand, high-sugar foods actually make people sleepier, not active'.

This means that if we eat healthy breakfast containing high fiber and protein, it provides us with satisfaction and we do not feel the urge to snack before lunch.

Therefore, the correct answer will be 'It contains high protein and fibre content'.

Hence, the correct option is (B).

100. $\left(\frac{7}{13}\right) = 0.538$

$\left(\frac{2}{3}\right) = 0.666$

$\left(\frac{4}{11}\right) = 0.3636$

$\left(\frac{5}{9}\right) = 0.5555$

Out of $\frac{2}{3}, \frac{7}{13}, \frac{4}{11}\frac{5}{9}$

$\frac{2}{3}$ is the largest number followed by $\frac{5}{9}$ then $\frac{7}{13}$ and the smallest is $\frac{4}{11}$.

∴ The ascending order will be $\frac{4}{11}, \frac{7}{13}, \frac{5}{9}, \frac{2}{3}$.

Hence, the correct option is (C).

Q.1 India's first 'Amrit Sarovar' has come up in which state?
A. Gujarat
B. Punjab
C. Odisha
D. Uttar Pradesh

Q.2 Which is the venue of the 11th World Urban Forum held in 2022?
A. Spain
B. Poland
C. Australia
D. France

Q.3 In which state, India's first lithium-ion cell factory was inaugurated in September 2022?
A. Mizoram
B. Andhra Pradesh
C. Goa
D. Gujarat

Q.4 The term "Levant" often heard in the news roughly corresponds to which of the followingregions?

[UPSC Prelims, 2022]

A. Region along the eastern Mediterranean shores
B. Region along North African shores stretching from Egypt to Morocco
C. Region along Persian Gulf and Horn of Africa
D. The entire coastal areas of Mediterranean Sea

Q.5 In which city, Union Minister Sarbanand Sonowal has inaugurated the Chabahar Day conference in July 2022?
A. Chennai
B. Chabahar
C. Gandhinagar
D. Mumbai

Q.6 What is the compound interest on a sum of Rs. 8000 at the rate of 10% per annum for 1.5 years when interest is compounded half-yearly?
A. Rs. 1282
B. Rs. 1241
C. Rs. 1241
D. Rs. 1261

Q.7 What would be the simple interest accrued in 4 years on a principal of Rs. $16,500$ at the rate of 16 percent per annum? (in Rs.)
A. 11,560
B. 10,250
C. 12,500
D. None of these

Q.8 At what rate of compound interest per annum will a sum of Rs. 1200 become Rs. 1348.32 in 2 years?
A. 6%
B. 6.5%
C. 7%
D. 7.5%

Q.9 Which Indian State/ UT has won the Khelo India Youth Games Champions trophy, 2020?
A. Haryana
B. Maharashtra
C. Gujarat
D. Karnataka

Ques (10-14):Direction: In the following question, select the related word from the given alternatives.

Q.10 RST : QPO :: MNO : ?
A. YZA
B. GHI
C. BAC
D. LKJ

Q.11 APPEAR : FUUJFW : : GRIND : ?
A. LWNSI
B. ISNWL
C. LNWSI
D. LINWS

Q.12 AMERICA : BPFUJFB : : INDIA : ?
A. JQLEA
B. QJELB
C. JQLEB
D. JQELB

Q.13 Fan : Electricity :: Generator : ?
A. Kerosene
B. Diesel
C. Petrol
D. Hydraulic Liquid

Q.14 Flower : Fragrance :: Bulb : ?
A. Switch
B. Electricity
C. Light
D. Holder

Ques (15-16):Direction: Select the most appropriate word for the given group of words.

Q.15 The practice or art of choosing, cooking, and eating good food:
A. Idolatry
B. Horticulture
C. Hydrophobia
D. Gastronomy

Q.16 A person or thing living or existing at the same time as another:
A. Cynic
B. Predator
C. Fanatic
D. Contemporary

Q.17 Which of the following statement is/are correct?
1. The eastern alliance North Atlantic Treaty Organisation (NATO), which came into existence in April 1949.
2. The western alliance, known as the Warsaw Pact, was led by the Soviet Union, which was created in 1955.
A. 1 only
B. 2 only
C. Both 1 and 2
D. Neither 1 nor 2

Ques (18-22):Direction: In the following passage, some of the words have been left out. Read the passage carefully and select the correct answer out of the four alternatives for the given blanks.

The other day I visited a refugee _____ (1) where the victims _____ (2) the Gujarat Earthquake _____ (3) in very_____ (4) conditions. I was particularly _____ (5) by an old woman who was determined to give her grandchildren a better future.

Q.18 Find out the appropriate word for the case 1.
A. House
B. Camp
C. Home
D. Nest

Q.19 Find out the appropriate word for case 2.
A. Of
B. To
C. In
D. At

Q.20 Find out the appropriate word for the case 3.
A. Was living
B. Are living
C. Were living
D. Have lived

Q.21 Find out the appropriate word for the case 4.
A. Apathetic
B. Sympathetic
C. Pathetic
D. Empathetic

Q.22 Find out the appropriate word for case 5.

A. Cornered
C. Worked
B. Collected
D. Moved

Q.23 The average salinity of oceans is _____ parts per 1000.
A. 5   **B.** 15   **C.** 25   **D.** 35

Ques (24-25):Direction: In the following question, a sentence has been given in Active/Passive Voice. Out of the four alternatives suggested, select the one which best expresses the same sentence in Passive/Active Voice.

Q.24 He was not given the information he needed.
A. Somebody was not given the information he needed.
B. The information he needed wasn't given to him.
C. He needed the information he wasn't given.
D. They didn't give him the information he needed.

Q.25 Bipin was not told about the meeting.
A. Somebody did not tell Bipin about the meeting.
B. There was nobody who could tell Bipin about the meeting.
C. Nobody told Bipin about the meeting.
D. The meeting was not told about Bipin.

Q.26 An object travels 10 m in 4 s and then another 14 m in 2 s. What is the average speed of the object?

[RRB/RRC Group D, 2018]

A. 4.5 ms $^{-1}$
C. 4 s $^{-1}$
B. 4 m
D. 4 ms $^{-1}$

Q.27 One person travels on through the sides of an equilateral triangle at a speed of 12 km/h 24 km/h, and 8 km/h, Find the average speed of it. (In km/h)
A. 14   **B.** 13   **C.** 12   **D.** 11

Q.28 In a race of 900 meters, Shreya beats Rahul by 15 seconds or 225 meters. Find the time in which Shreya finished the race?
A. 30 seconds
C. 60 seconds
B. 45 seconds
D. 40 seconds

Q.29 The distance between two countries P and Q which are joined by land route is $5000\ km$. A train starts from country P at $6:00\ am$ and travels towards country Q at the speed of $250\ km/hr$. Another train starts from country Q at $10:00\ am$ and travels towards country P at the speed of $150\ km/hr$. At what time they will meet each other?
A. $8:00\ pm$
C. $10:00\ pm$
B. $9:00\ pm$
D. $11:00\ pm$

Q.30 Four pairs of numbers have been given, out of which three are alike in some manner, while one is different. Choose out the odd one.
A. 4, 12   **B.** 8, 4   **C.** 4, 8   **D.** 16, 2

Q.31 Select the odd number pair from the given alternatives.
A. 136, 17   **B.** 152, 19   **C.** 160, 20   **D.** 148, 18

Q.32 Three of the following four letter-clusters are alike in a certain way and one is different. Pick the odd one out.
A. FILO   **B.** QTWZ   **C.** POWZ   **D.** KNQT

Q.33 Four words have been given, out of which three are alike in some manner and one is different. Select the odd word.
A. Chennai
C. Hyderabad
B. Gangtok
D. Aurangabad

Q.34 In the following question, select the odd word from the given alternatives.
A. Iron   **B.** Mercury   **C.** Silver   **D.** Gold

Q.35 The average temperature for Wednesday, Thursday and Friday was 40°C. The average for Thursday, Friday and Saturday was 41° C. If temperature on Saturday was 42° C, what was the temperature on Wednesday?
A. 39° C   **B.** 44° C   **C.** 38° C   **D.** 41° C

Q.36 Ram got 20 marks in Hindi. In English, Ram got double of Hindi. Ram got 20 marks more in Science than English. He got 50 marks in Math. Find his average marks.
A. 42   **B.** 42.6   **C.** 42.5   **D.** 43

Q.37 If the average age of three students is 15 and two students are of the same age 16. Find the age of the third student.
A. 12   **B.** 13   **C.** 15   **D.** 16

Q.38 Direction: Find the odd one out from the given figures.

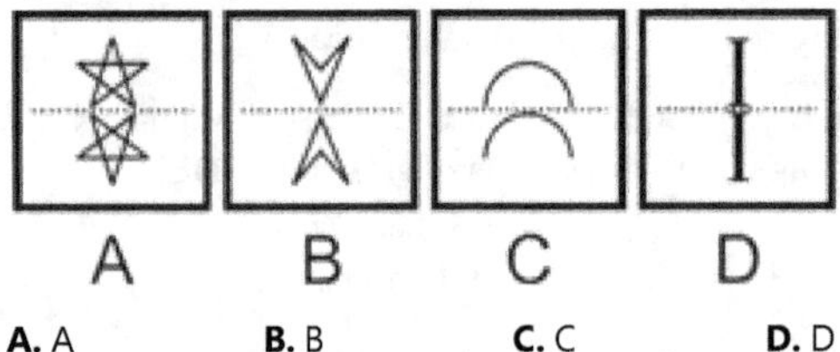

A. A   **B.** B   **C.** C   **D.** D

Q.39 Choose the figure which is different from the rest.

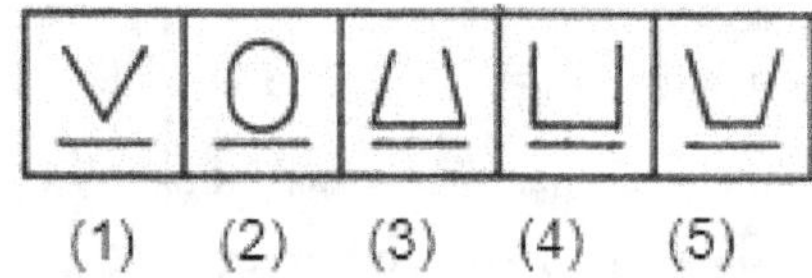

A. (1)   **B.** (2)   **C.** (3)   **D.** (4)

Q.40 Direction: Given below are four figures, out of which three are similar in some manner, and find the figure which differs from all other figures.

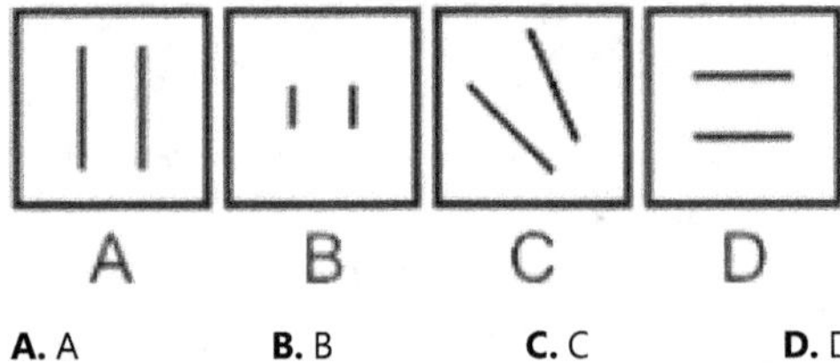

A. A   **B.** B   **C.** C   **D.** D

Q.41 Direction: Given below are four figures, out of which three are similar in some manner, and find the figure which differs from all other figures.

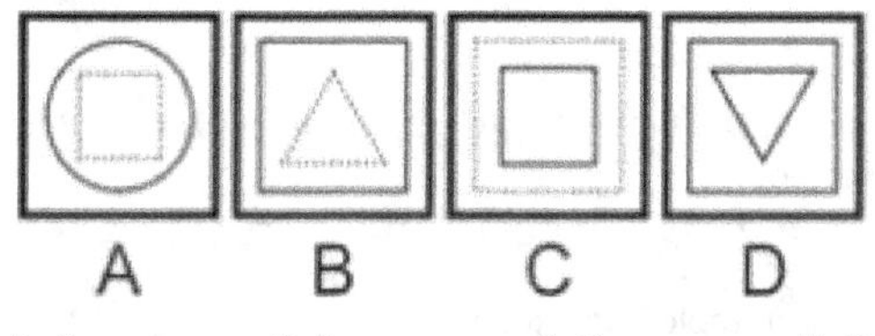

A	B	C	D

A. A   **B.** B   **C.** C   **D.** D

Q.42 Select the correct option which is related to the third term in the same way as second term related to the first.

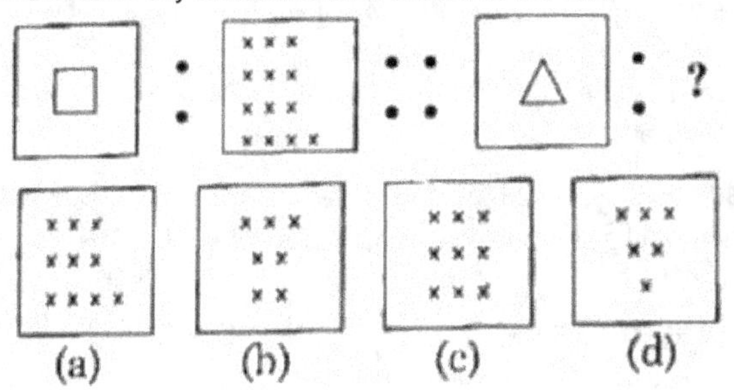

[KVS Trained Graduate Teacher, 2018]

A. (a)   **B.** (b)   **C.** (c)   **D.** (d)

Q.43 What will come in the place of question mark (?).

$$3\frac{18}{57} \times 48\frac{54}{63} \times 6\frac{1}{9} + 2\frac{1}{2} = ?$$

A. 792.5   **B.** 852.5   **C.** 1092.5   **D.** 992.5

Q.44 What will come in the place of question mark (?).

$$3\frac{1}{6} + 7\frac{2}{3} - 4\frac{1}{4} = ? + 2\frac{1}{6}$$

A. $8\frac{7}{15}$ **B.** $5\frac{4}{11}$

C. $7\frac{3}{10}$ **D.** None of these

Q.45 If the numerator of a fraction is increased by 150% and the denominator of a fraction increased by 200%, the fraction becomes $\frac{10}{19}$. Find the fraction.

A. $\frac{12}{17}$ **B.** $\frac{10}{16}$ **C.** $\frac{12}{19}$ **D.** $\frac{9}{11}$

Q.46 Which of the following statements is/are correct regarding Magnetic Resonance Imaging (MRI)?

1. Magnetic field inside our bodies is similar and equal in magnitude to that of earth.
2. Heat generated by our body parts can be traced by an electromagnetic field.

A. 1 only   **B.** 2 only
C. Both 1 and 2   **D.** Neither 1 nor 2

Q.47 You observe a fire nearby your house with lots of black smoke and a dazzling yellow flame. The fire has been caused most likely due to the burning of:

A. Vegetable oil that is used for cooking
B. A large propane cylinder
C. A natural gas pipeline
D. Any of the above

Q.48 Manganese can be used in the manufacturing of:

1. Insecticides
2. Paints
3. Bleaching powder
4. Atomic force microscopy

A. 1 and 2   **B.** 3 and 4
C. 1, 2 and 3   **D.** 1, 2 and 4

Q.49 The Source of Ocean Thermal Energy is:

A. Molten Magma at the base of Ocean
B. Frictional force among the tides
C. Plate movement near mid-oceanic ridges
D. None of the above

Q.50 A mixture of oxygen and ethyne is burnt for welding. Which of the following statements is correct about NOT using a mixture of ethyne and air?

1. Ethyne may not burn completely with air as with pure oxygen.
2. Without mixing oxygen, it is difficult to reach high temperatures needed for welding.

A. 1 only   **B.** 2 only
C. Both 1 and 2   **D.** Neither 1 nor 2

Q.51 IN-EUNAVFOR exercise was held in which of the following place?

A. Gulf of Mexico   **B.** Gulf Of Aden
C. Labrador Sea   **D.** English Channel

Q.52 Which of the following soil is transported by gravity?

[Allahabad High Court ARO, 2020]

A. Aeolian soil   **B.** Colluvium soil
C. Alluvium soil   **D.** Glacial soil

Q.53 Study the given pattern carefully and select the figure that will complete the pattern given in the question figure.

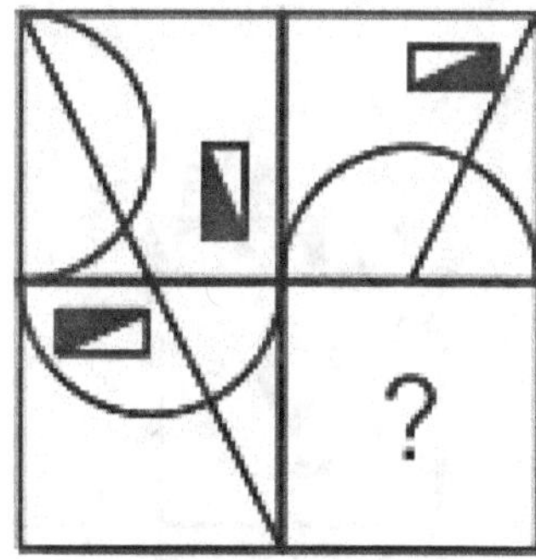

[SSC MTS, 2019]

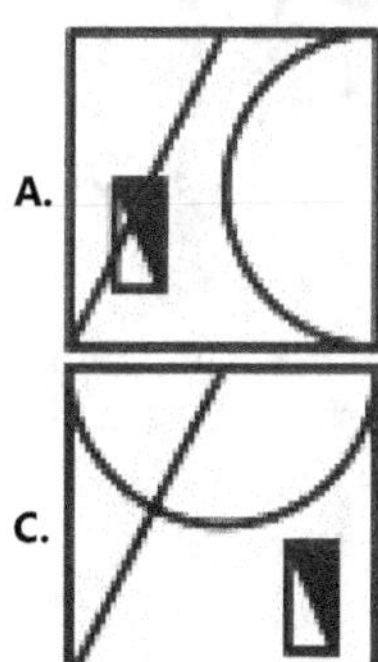

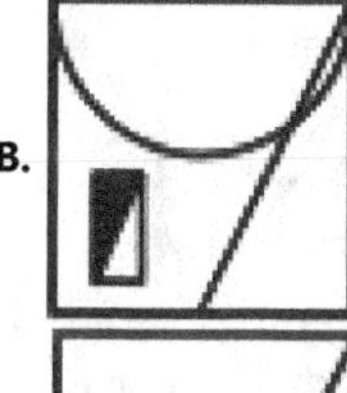

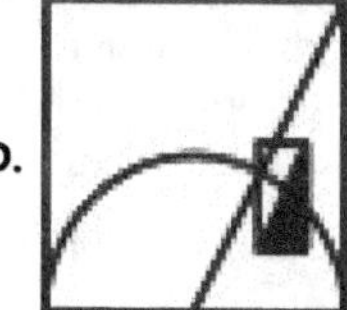

A.   B.   C.   D.

Q.54 Study the boxes of images carefully and choose appropriate option to replace the question mark.

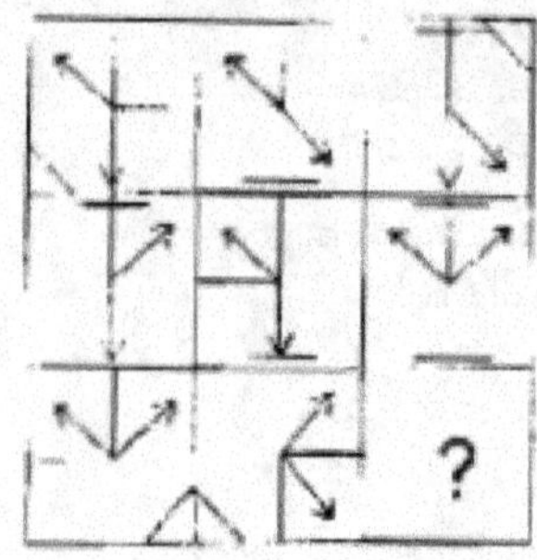

[Maharashtra Public Service Commission, 2019]

A. 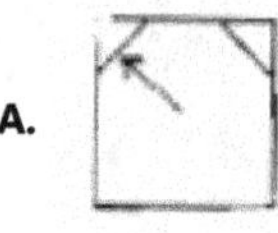   **B.** 

C.    **D.** 

Q.55 Direction: Study the given pattern carefully and select the figure that can replace the question mark (?) in it.

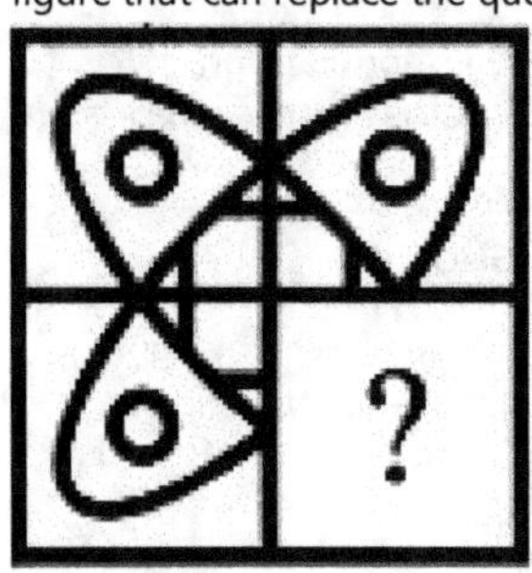

[SSC MTS, 2019]

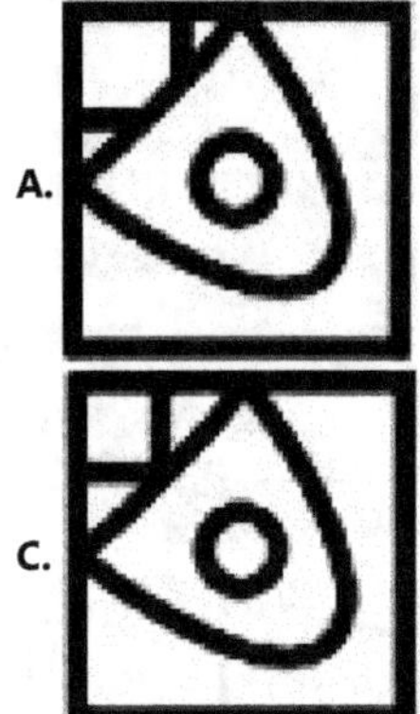

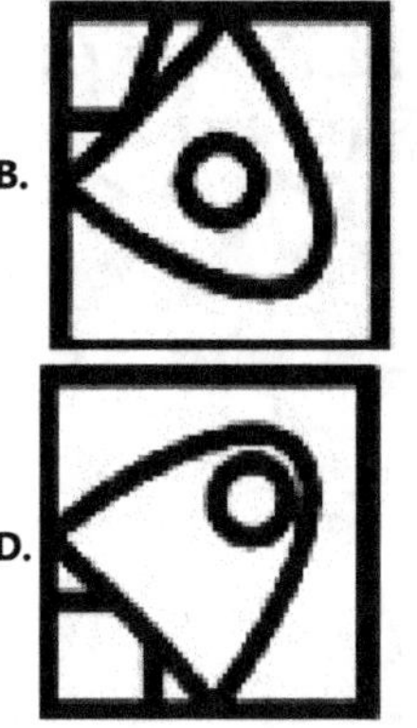

Ques (56-57):Direction: In the following question, one part of the sentence may have an error. Find out which part of the sentence has an error and click the button corresponding to it. If the sentence is free from error, click the "No error" option.

Q.56 Rohan had been playing (1) for his club since fifteen years, (2) but then his elbow got injured. (3) No error (4)

A. 1   **B.** 2   **C.** 3   **D.** 4

Q.57 The principal (1) started his lecture (2) with a pessimistic note. (3) No error (4)

A. 1   **B.** 2   **C.** 3   **D.** 4

Q.58 Sabarimala Temple is located:

A. Kerala   **B.** Karnataka

C. Tamil Nadu   **D.** Odisha

Q.59 Which state is associated with the "Chaitra Jatra Festival" held annually?

A. Chhattisgarh   **B.** Andra Pradesh

C. Karnataka   **D.** Odisha

Q.60 Two pipes, when working one at a time can fill a cistern in 2 hours and 3 hours, respectively while a third pipe can drain the cistern empty in 6 hours. All three pipes were opened together when the cistern was $\frac{1}{6}$ full. How long will it take for the cistern to be completely full?

A. 1 hour   **B.** 1 hour 20 minutes

C. 1 hour 30 minutes   **D.** 1 hour 15 minutes

Q.61 Person B is 50% more efficient than person A and the time taken by person A alone to do work are 6 days more than that taken by B alone, then in how much time the work will be finished if both A and B together started working?

A. 7.2 days   **B.** 8 days

C. 9.6 days   **D.** 10.8 days

Q.62 A boat goes 15 km in an hour in still water and takes thrice the time to cover the same distance upstream. The speed of the current (in km/hr) is –

A. 10 km/hr   **B.** 12 km/hr   **C.** 13 km/hr   **D.** 14 km/hr

Q.63 The salaries of X, Y and Z are in the ratio of 10:12:15. They are awarded increments of 40%, 50% and 60% respectively. What is the new ratio of their salaries?

[Delhi Forest Guard, 2021]

A. 7 : 9 : 14   **B.** 7 : 9 : 12

C. 7 : 10 : 12   **D.** 8 : 9 : 12

Q.64 In a bag, there are coins of 25 paise, 50 paise and Rs 1 in the ratio of 8:4:1. In there is 30 in total, how many 50 paise coins are there?

[Delhi Forest Guard, 2021]

A. 48   **B.** 6   **C.** 12   **D.** 24

Q.65 If Rs 1120 is to be divided into 3 proportions of $\frac{4}{5} : \frac{5}{4} : \frac{3}{4}$, then how much is second proportion worth?

[Delhi Forest Guard, 2021]

A. Rs 300   **B.** Rs 400   **C.** Rs 320   **D.** Rs 500

Q.66 From the given answer figure, select the option in which the question figure is hidden / contained.

Question Figure:

Answer Figure:

(A)  (B)  (C)  (D)

A. (A) **B.** (B) **C.** (C) **D.** (D)

Q.67 Direction: A figure is given below which is embedded inside a figure out of the four figures given in the options. Choose the appropriate option which contains the figure given below as the answer.

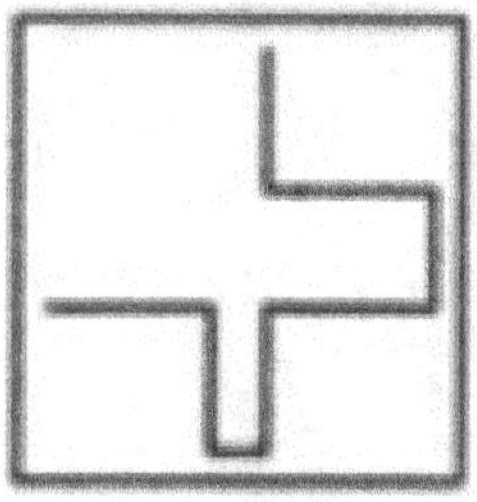

A.

B.

C.

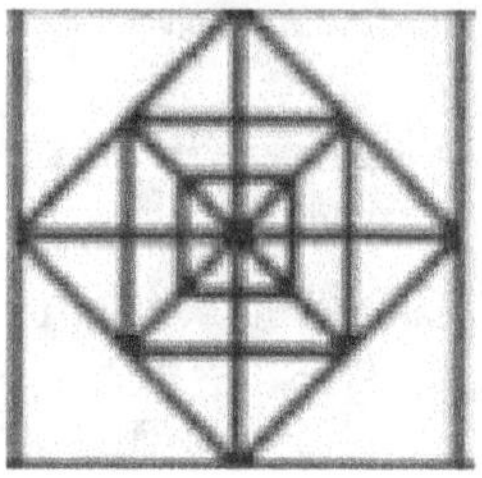

D.

Q.68 Select the option in which the question figure is hidden/vested.

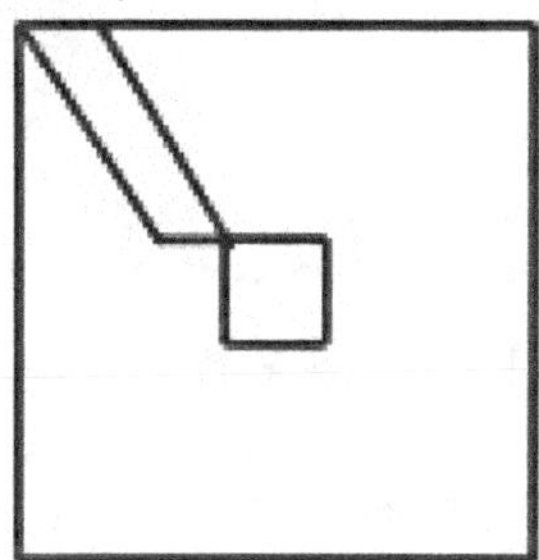

[UP Police Sub Inspector, 2017]

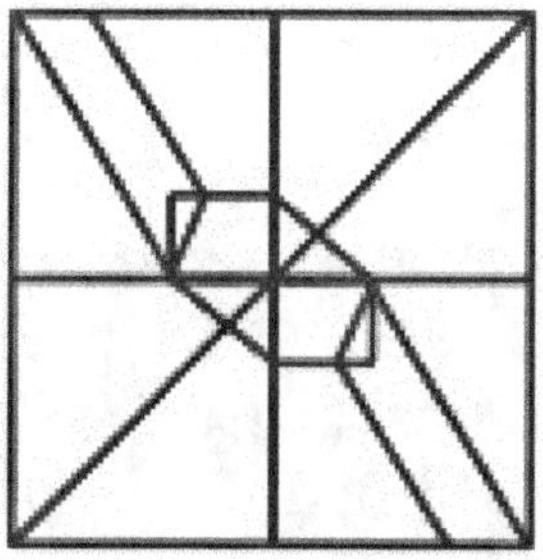

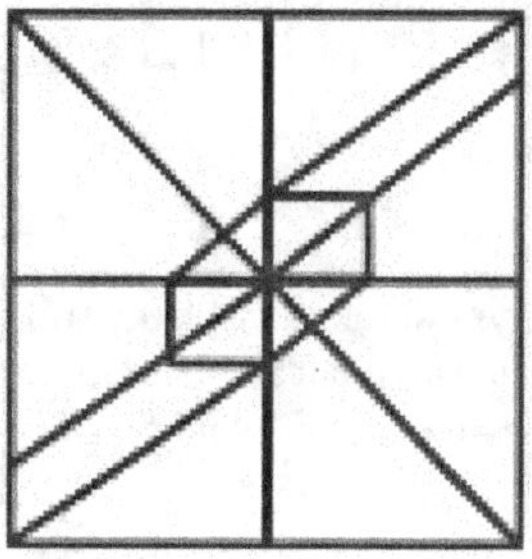

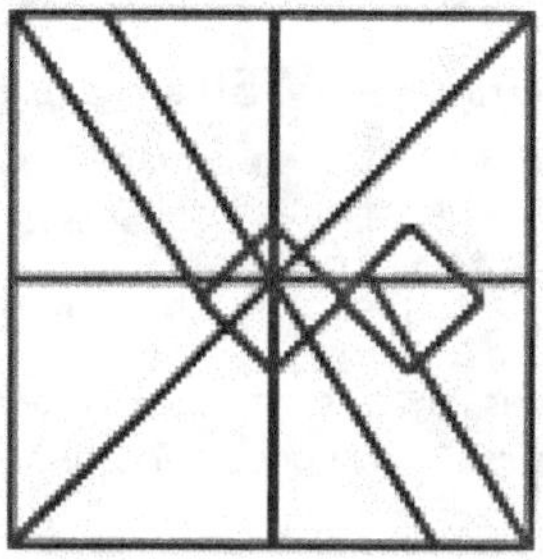

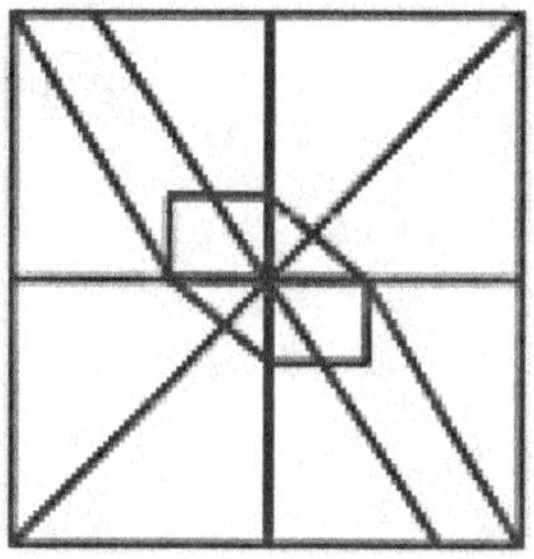

Q.69 Direction: From the given options, select a figure in which the Question Figure is hidden/embedded.

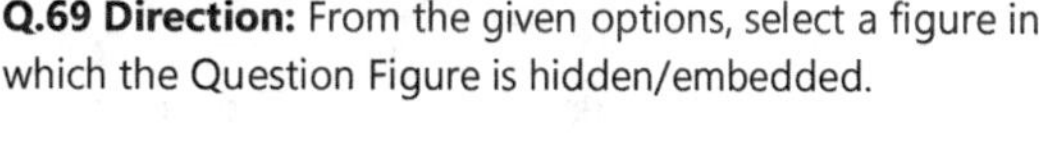

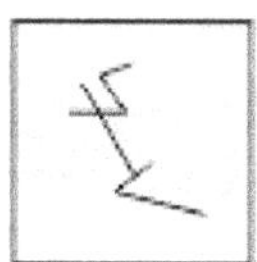

A.

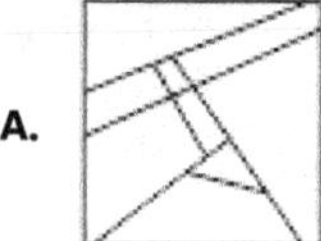

B.

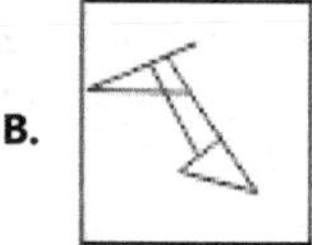

C.

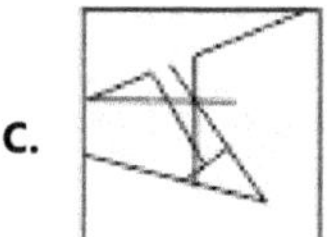

D.

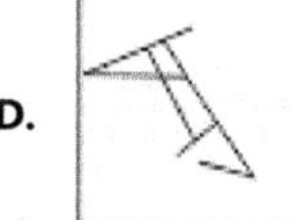

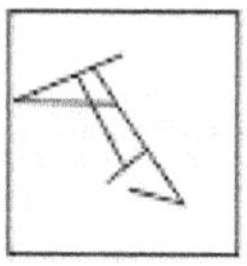

Q.70 Find the answer figure in which the question figure is embedded?
Question Figure:

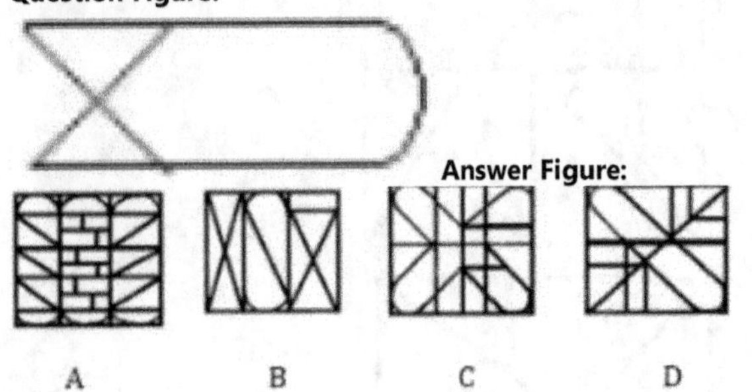

Answer Figure:

A   B   C   D

A. Figure A   **B.** Figure B   **C.** Figure C   **D.** Figure D

Q.71 A man purchased an old typewriter at Rs 19200, and spent some amount on its repair. He sold it for Rs 24150, and earned a profit of 15%. Find the amount he spend on the repair of the old typewriter.

A. Rs 1200   **B.** Rs 1800   **C.** Rs 2100   **D.** Rs 1500

Q.72 The marked price of an article is Rs. 750 and a customer pays Rs. 600 for it. What is the discount percentage?

[SSC MTS, 2017]

A. 20%   **B.** 30%   **C.** 15%   **D.** 10%

Q.73 The cost price of a chair is 25% less than the cost price of a table. If a man sells 5 chairs at the cost price of 7 tables, then what is his profit percentage?

A. 33.33   **B.** 45   **C.** 86.66   **D.** 96

Ques (74-77):Direction: Fill in the blank with the appropriate option given below.

Q.74 Sakshi _______ in this company for the past 10 years.
A. is working   **B.** has been working
C. has been worked   **D.** has worked

Q.75 The boss, as well as his wife _______, invited.
A. were   **B.** were also
C. was   **D.** were being

Q.76 Parul had to resign from the college union committee on the ground that she does not get on very well ___ the other members and abuses them.
A. with   **B.** among   **C.** along   **D.** by

Q.77 He knew more about the culture and philosophy _______ any man living.
A. than   **B.** then   **C.** as   **D.** or

Q.78 Direction: You are required to identify the words that are contextually similar to the idiom/phrase given sentence.
All in all
A. Every person
B. Particular thing same in all
C. Call all at once
D. Most important

Q.79 Directions: In the following question given below a/an idiom/phrase is given in bold which is then followed by five options that try to decipher its meaning as used in the sentence. Choose the option which gives the meaning of the phrase most appropriately in the context of the given sentence.
They go to the beach when they should be **hitting the books** and then they wonder why they get low marks.
A. Scrutinizing   **B.** Studying
C. Reflecting   **D.** Exploring

Q.80 Choose the word which will occur second when arranged in the sequence in which they occur in the dictionary.
A. People   **B.** Petal   **C.** Pencil   **D.** Peahen

Q.81 Arrange the following words in a logical and meaningful order.
(i) Vegetable
(ii) Market
(iii) Cutting
(iv) Cooking
(v) Eat
A. (i), (ii), (iii), (iv), (v)
B. (iii), (i), (ii), (v), (iv)
C. (ii), (i), (iii), (iv), (v)
D. (v), (ii), (i), (iii), (iv)

Q.82 What is the tenure of individual Rajya Sabha members?
A. 3 years   **B.** 4 years   **C.** 5 years   **D.** 6 years

Q.83 Select the most appropriate synonym of the given word
Accorded
A. Solitary   **B.** Aloof   **C.** Give   **D.** Crowded

Q.84 Select the most appropriate synonym of the given word:
Assertions
A. Grow   **B.** Reproduce
C. Breed   **D.** Declaration

Q.85 Directions: Choose the word nearest in the meaning to the italicized words:
Few actors are as versatile as he is; he writes scripts, directs, and produces.
A. multi-purpose
B. greedy
C. having no specific interest
D. ambitious

Q.86 Find a quarter of 40% of the square of 40.

[UP Police Constable, 2019]

A. 120   **B.** 140   **C.** 160   **D.** 180

Q.87 A man spends 75% of his income. If his income increases by 28% and his expenditure increases by 20%, then what is the increase or decrease percentage in his savings?

[SSC Sub Inspector (CPO), 2020]

A. 13% increase   **B.** 52% decrease
C. 13% decrease   **D.** 52% increase

Q.88 If 40% of a number is 112. Then, find the 15% of a number.

A. 42   **B.** 21   **C.** 54   **D.** 56

Ques (89-90):Direction: Study the following questions carefully and choose the right answer:

Q.89 Identify the diagram that best represents the relationship among classes given below:

Police, Thief, Criminal

A.    **B.** 

C.    **D.** 

Q.90 House, Storeroom, Bedroom

A.    **B.** 

C.    **D.** 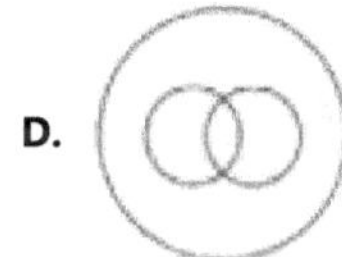

Ques (91-92):Direction: In the question given below contains three elements. These elements may or may not have some inter linkage. Each group of elements may fit into one of these diagrams at (A), (B), (C), (D).

Q.91 Which of the following diagrams indicates the best relation between Factory, Product and Machinery?

A.    **B.** 

C.    **D.** 

Q.92 Which of the following diagrams indicates the best relation between Author, Lawyer and Singer?

A.    **B.** 

C.    **D.** 

Q.93 Direction: Observe the following information carefully and answer the Questions:

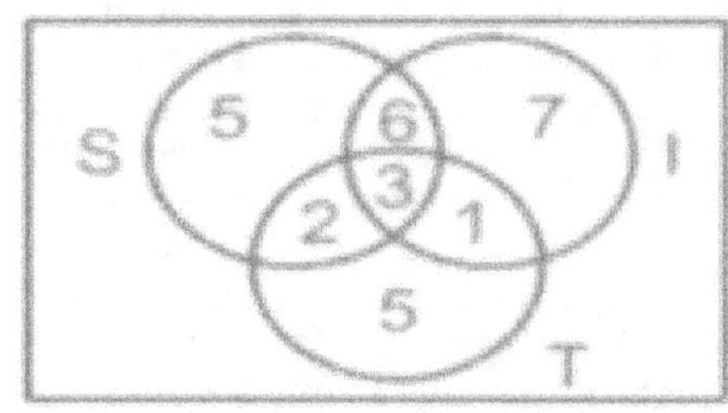

The circle S indicates strict officers, T indicates tall officers and I indicates IAS officers.

The number of strict IAS officers who are not tall is:

[Telangana Police Constable, 2015]

A. 4   **B.** 5   **C.** 6   **D.** 7

Ques (94-95):Direction: Study the given pattern carefully and select the figure that will complete the pattern given in the question figure.

Q.94

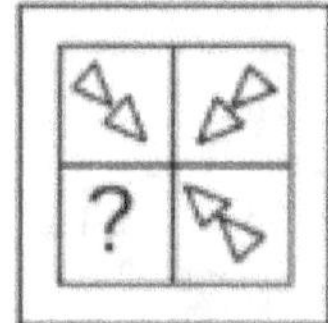
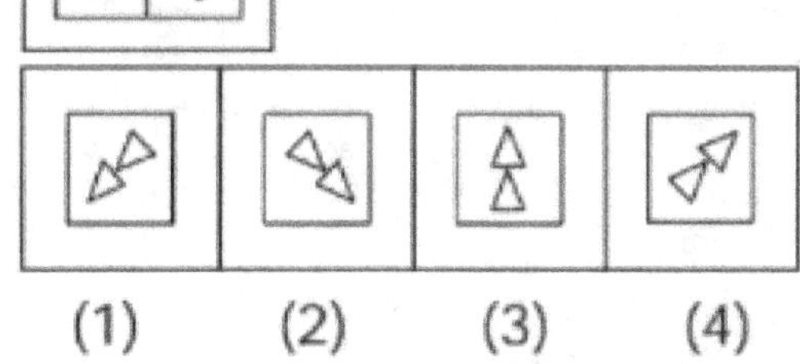

(1)   (2)   (3)   (4)

[SSC Sub Inspector (CPO), 2020]

A. 1   **B.** 2   **C.** 3   **D.** 4

Q.95

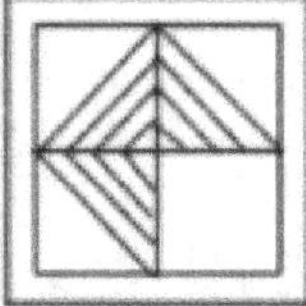

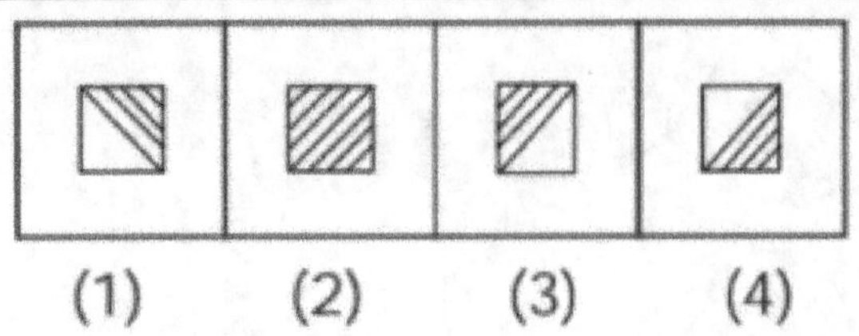

(1)　　　(2)　　　(3)　　　(4)

[Telangana Police Constable, 2015]

A. 1　　　**B.** 2　　　**C.** 3　　　**D.** 4

Ques (96-100):Directions: Read the following passage carefully and answer the questions given below it.

It is an old saying that knowledge is power. Education is an instrument that imparts knowledge and, therefore indirectly controls power. Therefore, ever since the dawn of civilization persons in power have always tried to control education. It has been the hand-maid of the ruling class. During the Christian era, the ecclesiastics controlled the institution of education and diffused among the people the gospel of the Bible. These gospels were no other than a philosophy for the maintenance of the existing society. This religious education taught the poor man to be meek and to earn his bread with the sweat of his brow, while the priests and the landlords lived in luxury and fought duels for the slightest offence.

During the Renaissance, education passed more from the clutches of the priest into the hand of the prince. In other words, it became more secular. It was also due to the growth of the nation - stale and powerful monarchs who united the country under their rule. Thus, under the control of the monarch, education began to devise and preach the infallibility of its masters. It also invented and supported fantastic theories like the Divine Right Theory and that the king can do no wrong' etc.

With the advent of the industrial revolution, education took a different tum and had to please the new masters. It now no longer remained the privilege of the baron class but was thrown open to the newly rich merchant class of society. Yet education was still confined to the few elite. The philosophy which was in vogue during this period was that of 'Laissez Faire' restricting the function of the State to a mere keeping of law and order while, on the other hand, in practice, the law of the jungle prevailed in the form of free competition and the survival of the fittest.

Q.96 Which of the following is chronologically arranged?

A. Renaissance period, Christian period, Period of Industrial Revolution

B. Christian period, Renaissance period, Period of Industrial Revolution

C. Period of Industrial Revolution, Christian period. Renaissance period.

D. Christian period, Period of Industrial Revolution, Renaissance period

Q.97 What does 'Laissez - Faire' mean ?

A. Joint control on the means of production by the state and private enterprise

B. Individual freedom in the political field

C. State control on the means of production

D. None of these

Q.98 Why have persons in power always tried to control education?

A. Because they wanted to educate the whole public

B. Because they wanted to deprive the common man of the benefits of education

C. Because it involved a huge burden on the state exchequer

D. Because it is an instrument of knowledge and power

Q.99 Who controlled the institution of education during the Christian era?

A. The church and the priests

B. The monarchs

C. The secular leaders of society

D. The common people

Q.100 What did the ruling class in the Christian era think of the poor man ?

A. He is the beloved of God

B. He deserves all sympathy of the rich

C. He should be strong

D. He is meant for serving the rich

// Smart Answer Sheet //

Correct — Percentage of students who answered correctly. **Skipped** — Percentage of students who skipped.

Q.	Ans.	Correct / Skipped	Q.	Ans.	Correct / Skipped	Q.	Ans.	Correct / Skipped	Q.	Ans.	Correct / Skipped	Q.	Ans.	Correct / Skipped	Q.	Ans.	Correct / Skipped
1	D	64.9 % / 33.02 %	18	B	76.54 % / 17.86 %	35	A	11.38 % / 86.39 %	52	B	52.35 % / 44.48 %	69	B	57.5 % / 36.98 %	86	C	83.63 % / 11.81 %
2	B	40.31 % / 58.9 %	19	A	77.56 % / 15.76 %	36	C	81.1 % / 15.86 %	53	A	14.5 % / 72.21 %	70	C	67.75 % / 31.64 %	87	D	55.31 % / 38.03 %
3	B	65.99 % / 31.68 %	20	C	66.78 % / 31.93 %	37	B	68.08 % / 30.56 %	54	C	13.83 % / 82.04 %	71	B	50.4 % / 47.81 %	88	A	66.86 % / 31.88 %
4	A	88.8 % / 11.09 %	21	C	48.01 % / 40.37 %	38	C	50.91 % / 31.31 %	55	A	82.35 % / 17.26 %	72	A	67.99 % / 31.9 %	89	A	85.32 % / 11.51 %
5	D	68.65 % / 30.1 %	22	D	87.37 % / 12.0 %	39	B	80.09 % / 10.17 %	56	B	44.79 % / 33.09 %	73	C	54.29 % / 35.55 %	90	B	80.0 % / 16.3 %
6	D	29.26 % / 69.52 %	23	D	47.31 % / 31.19 %	40	C	82.64 % / 10.25 %	57	C	62.4 % / 36.9 %	74	B	88.37 % / 11.14 %	91	D	80.31 % / 14.82 %
7	D	41.69 % / 40.76 %	24	D	15.83 % / 68.1 %	41	D	50.14 % / 30.88 %	58	A	48.23 % / 31.47 %	75	C	83.31 % / 11.71 %	92	B	88.03 % / 11.46 %
8	A	63.46 % / 34.23 %	25	C	14.56 % / 70.51 %	42	C	50.69 % / 32.71 %	59	D	48.64 % / 31.97 %	76	A	76.55 % / 11.76 %	93	C	25.47 % / 67.07 %
9	B	32.52 % / 67.36 %	26	D	87.8 % / 10.13 %	43	D	57.92 % / 36.45 %	60	D	14.18 % / 85.4 %	77	A	62.06 % / 36.85 %	94	D	64.45 % / 30.17 %
10	D	58.88 % / 36.29 %	27	C	25.74 % / 71.93 %	44	D	42.66 % / 35.17 %	61	A	49.86 % / 47.4 %	78	D	47.74 % / 48.0 %	95	C	58.47 % / 33.34 %
11	A	49.15 % / 42.08 %	28	B	64.76 % / 31.1 %	45	C	59.43 % / 39.88 %	62	A	61.26 % / 36.44 %	79	B	53.02 % / 43.57 %	96	B	64.63 % / 33.51 %
12	D	54.66 % / 32.77 %	29	A	25.44 % / 70.29 %	46	D	79.6 % / 13.76 %	63	B	67.34 % / 31.96 %	80	C	88.62 % / 10.45 %	97	D	44.77 % / 48.38 %
13	B	49.55 % / 45.77 %	30	A	77.73 % / 21.48 %	47	A	81.95 % / 11.35 %	64	D	62.92 % / 31.84 %	81	C	51.18 % / 35.29 %	98	D	54.91 % / 43.16 %
14	C	48.32 % / 30.33 %	31	D	69.7 % / 30.02 %	48	C	86.91 % / 12.59 %	65	D	68.72 % / 30.25 %	82	D	42.53 % / 32.51 %	99	A	46.67 % / 51.01 %
15	D	68.15 % / 30.79 %	32	C	55.47 % / 31.94 %	49	D	85.46 % / 11.79 %	66	C	19.1 % / 78.81 %	83	C	83.55 % / 16.2 %	100	D	45.26 % / 31.34 %
16	D	56.43 % / 34.99 %	33	D	53.79 % / 40.2 %	50	C	86.81 % / 12.11 %	67	D	48.42 % / 36.83 %	84	D	83.33 % / 16.45 %			
17	D	61.25 % / 33.29 %	34	B	51.55 % / 33.75 %	51	B	67.3 % / 32.45 %	68	D	86.18 % / 10.19 %	85	A	48.4 % / 49.24 %			

//Hints and Solutions//

1. India's first 'Amrit Sarovar' has come up in Uttar Pradesh's Rampur.

India's first "Amrit Sarovar" was inaugurated by the Union Minister for Minority Affairs Mukhtar Abbas Naqvi on 13 May 2022.

PM Narendra Modi had called for having at least 75 ponds in every district in the 75th year of India's Independence, calling them 'Amrit Sarovar'.

Hence, the correct option is (D).

2. The 11th World Urban Forum was held in Poland. The National Institute of Urban Affairs' (NIUA) Climate Centre for Cities (NIUA C-Cube), World Resources Institute India (WRI India) and their partners launched India's first national coalition platform for urban nature-based solutions (NbS).

'India Forum for Nature-Based Solutions' aims to create a collective of NbS entrepreneurs, government entities and like-minded organisations, to aid in scaling urban nature-based solutions.

Hence, the correct option is (B).

3. MoS for Electronics & Information Technology, Rajeev Chandrasekhar on 16 Sept 2022 launched the pre-production run of India's first lithium cell manufacturing facility at Tirupati, Andhra Pradesh.

- This state-of-the-art facility has been set up by Chennai-based Munoth Industries Ltd with an outlay of Rs165 crores.
- Currently, India imports lithium-ion cells primarily from China & South Korea.

Hence, the correct option is (B).

4. Levant is an approximate historical geographical term referring to a large area in the region along the eastern Mediterranean shores.

In its narrowest sense, which is in use today in archaeology and other cultural contexts, it is equivalent to a stretch of land bordering the Mediterranean in southwestern Asia, i.e., the historical region of Syria, which includes present-day Syria, Lebanon, Jordan, Israel, Palestine and most of Turkey southwest of the middle Euphrates.

Hence, the correct option is (A).

5. Union Minister Sarbanand Sonowal inaugurated the Chabahar Day conference in Mumbai on 31 July 2022.

Union Shipping & Waterways Ministry organized this conference on the occasion of 'Chabahar Day'. This day is celebrated to mark the beginning of the International North-South Transport Corridor (INSTC).

Hence, the correct option is (D).

6. Given:

Principal, $(P) = Rs8000$

Rate, $(R) = 10\%$

Time, $(t) = 1.5$ years

We know,

$$A = P\left(1 + \frac{R}{100}\right)^t$$

Amount, $(A) = P + CI$

For half yearly, $R = \frac{10}{2} = 5\%$ and $t = 1.5 \times 2 = 3$ years

$$A = P\left(1 + \frac{R}{100}\right)$$

$$\Rightarrow 8000 \times \left(1 + \frac{5}{100}\right)^3$$

$$\Rightarrow 8000 \times \left(\frac{21}{20}\right)^3$$

$$= 9261$$

$$CI = A - P = 9261 - 8000 = Rs.\,1261$$

$\therefore$ The CI is $Rs.\,1261$

Hence, the correct option is (D).

7. Given,

Principal $= Rs.\ 16,500$

Time $= 4$ years

Rate $= 16\%$

$$\text{Simple Interest} = \frac{\text{Principal} \times \text{Time} \times \text{Rate}}{100}$$

$$= \frac{16500 \times 4 \times 16}{100}$$

$$= Rs.\ 10,560$$

Hence, the correct option is (D).

8. Let, the rate be $R\%$ per annum

$$\text{Then, } 1200 \times \left(1 + \frac{R}{100}\right)^2 = 1348.32$$

$$\Rightarrow \left(1 + \frac{R}{100}\right)^2 = \frac{134832}{120000} = \frac{11236}{10000}$$

$$\therefore \left(1 + \frac{R}{100}\right)^2 = \left(\frac{106}{100}\right)^2$$

$$\Rightarrow 1 + \frac{R}{100} = \frac{106}{100}$$

$$\Rightarrow R = 6\%$$

Hence, the correct option is (A).

9. The Team of Maharashtra dominated the Khelo India Youth Games by clinching the overall trophy for the second time with a huge haul of 256 medals, including 78 gold and 77 silver. Last year, Maharashtra topped the table with 228 medals. The trophy

was presented to Maharashtra by the Chief Minister of Assam Sarbananda Sonowal in the presence of Union Sports Minister Kiren Rijju, during the closing ceremony.

The second place was bagged by the state of Haryana with 200 medals and Delhi with 122 medals. Khelo India Youth games has been organised in Assam's Guwahati for the last 13 days.

Hence, the correct option is (B).

10.

Alphabet	A	B	C	D	E	F	G	H	I	J	K	L	M
Position value	1	2	3	4	5	6	7	8	9	10	11	12	13
Alphabet	Z	Y	X	W	V	U	T	S	R	Q	P	O	N
Position value	26	25	24	23	22	21	20	19	18	17	16	15	14

R − 1 = Q

S - 3 = P

T - 5 = O

Likewise, M - 1 = L, N - 3 = K & O - 5 = J

Therefore, LKJ is the required word.

Hence, the correct option is (D).

11.

Alphabet	A	B	C	D	E	F	G	H	I	J	K	L	M
Position value	1	2	3	4	5	6	7	8	9	10	11	12	13
Alphabet	Z	Y	X	W	V	U	T	S	R	Q	P	O	N
Position value	26	25	24	23	22	21	20	19	18	17	16	15	14

A+4=F Similarly, G+4=L

P+4=U R+4=W

P+4=U I+4=N

E+4=J N+4=S

A+4=F D+4=I

R+4=W

So we can see the pattern that is being followed above.

Therefore the answer to the problem is LWNSI.

Hence, the correct option is (A).

12.

Alphabet	A	B	C	D	E	F	G	H	I	J	K	L	M
Position value	1	2	3	4	5	6	7	8	9	10	11	12	13
Alphabet	Z	Y	X	W	V	U	T	S	R	Q	P	O	N
Position value	26	25	24	23	22	21	20	19	18	17	16	15	14

A+1=B Similarly, I+1=J

M+3=P N+3=Q

E+1=F D+1=E

R+3=U I+3=L

I+1=J A+1=B

C+3=F

A+1=B

Hence, the correct option is (D).

13. A fan is an electrical device that runs on electricity. Similarly, the generator runs with diesel.

Thus Generator is related to Diesel.

Hence, the correct option is (B).

14. The flower gives Fragrance. Similarly, Bulb gives Light.

Thus Bulb is related to Light.

Hence, the correct option is (C).

15. Gastronomy is the practice or art of choosing, cooking, and eating good food.

Idolatry is extreme admiration and love for something or someone.

Horticulture is the practice of garden cultivation and management.

Hydrophobia is an extreme fear of water especially because of a symptom of rabies.

Hence, the correct option is (D).

16. A person or thing living or existing at the same time as another is known as contemporary.

A cynic is a person who questions whether something will happen or whether it is worthwhile.

A predator is a person who ruthlessly exploits others.

A fanatic is a person filled with excessive and single-minded zeal.

Hence, the correct option is (D).

17. The western alliance North Atlantic Treaty Organisation (NATO), which came into existence in April 1949.

So, statement 1 is not correct.

- The eastern alliance, known as the Warsaw Pact, was led by the Soviet Union which was created in 1955.

So, statement 2 is not correct.

The North Atlantic Treaty Organization, also called the North Atlantic Alliance, is an intergovernmental military alliance between 30 European and North American countries.

- The organization implements the North Atlantic Treaty that was signed on 4 April 1949.
- Founded: 4 April 1949, Washington, D.C., United States
- Headquarters: Brussels, Belgium

Hence, the correct option is (D).

18. The given passage talks about a scenario after the Gujarat Earthquake. At such places, the government set up refugee camps for the victims to stay there. Words like "home, house or nest" cannot be used in this scenario.

Hence, the correct option is (B).

19. The correct preposition to be used in the sentence is "of" as it connects the relationship of the victims to the Gujarat Earthquakes.

Hence, the correct option is (A).

20. The given passage describes a past scenario. Therefore, only past tense can be used here. Since the subject is "victims" which is plural in case, it should also carry a plural verb.

Hence, the correct option is (C).

21. In order to find the correct word, let's understand their meanings first:

apathetic = showing or feeling no interest, enthusiasm, or concern.

sympathetic = feeling, showing, or expressing sympathy.

pathetic = arousing pity, especially through vulnerability or sadness.

empathetic = showing an ability to understand and share the feelings of another.

The passage describes a scenario where the author was feeling pity and sadness at the condition of the earthquake victims. So, the correct emotions are described by the adjective "pathetic".

Hence, the correct option is (C).

22. The author mentions a woman who though being old was determined to give her children a bright future. The correct phrasal verb here is "to be moved by" which means to have strong feelings of sadness or sympathy because of something someone has said or done.

Hence, the correct option is (D).

23. The average salinity of oceans is 35 parts per 1000.

Salinity is the amount of salt present in 1000 grams of water. The Dead Sea of Israel has a salinity of 340 grams per litre. Earth is the main source of ocean salinity. The main means of collecting salts are rivers, ocean waves, winds, volcanic eruptions, etc.

Hence, the correct option is (D).

24. The given sentence is in passive form and its structure is:

Passive: Object + was/were (not) + verb (IIIrd form) + (by + subject).

Its active structure would be:

Active: Subject + did not + verb (Ist form) + object.

It is optional to include the part (By + subject) in the passive voice. In sentences where the subject is hidden or not given, we need to create a subject accordingly.

The active form of the given sentence would be:

They didn't give him the information he needed.

Hence, the correct option is (D).

25. The sentence is in passive form and needs to be changed into active voice. The structure for passive/active voice has been shown below:

Passive: Object + was/were + verb (IIIrd form) + (by + subject).

Active: Subject + verb (IInd form) + object.

So, according to the above structure, the active voice of the given sentence would be:

Nobody told Bipin about the meeting.

Hence, the correct option is (C).

26. As we know,

$$\text{Average speed} = \frac{\text{Total Distance}}{\text{Total Time}}$$

$\Rightarrow$ Total distance $= 10 + 14 = 24$ m

$\Rightarrow$ Total time $= 4 + 2 = 6$

$\Rightarrow$ Average Speed $= \frac{24}{6} = 4$ ms^{-1}

Hence, the correct option is (D).

27. Given:

The speed of the man is $12\ km/h, 24\ km/h$ and $8\ km/h$

Concept Used:

$$Average speed = \frac{total distance}{total time}$$

The sides of an equilateral triangle are equal.

Calculation:

Let, the side of the triangle be $x\ km$.

As we know,

Time to cover $x\ km$ distance at a speed of $12\ km/hr = \dfrac{x}{12}\ hrs$

Time to cover $x\ km$ distance at a speed of $24\ km/hr = \dfrac{x}{24}\ hrs$

Time to cover $x\ km$ distance at a speed of $8\ km/hr = \dfrac{z}{8}$ hrs

Total distance covered by the man $= (x + x + x) = 3x$

Total time to cover the distance $\left(\dfrac{x}{12} + \dfrac{x}{24} + \dfrac{z}{8}\right)$

$\therefore$ Average speed $= \dfrac{3x}{\frac{x}{24}+\frac{x}{12}+\frac{z}{8}}$

$\Rightarrow \dfrac{3x}{\frac{x+2x+3x}{24}}$

$\Rightarrow \dfrac{3x}{\left(\frac{6x}{24}\right)}$

$\Rightarrow \dfrac{1}{2} \times 24 = 12\ km/h$

$\therefore$ The average speed of the person is $12\ km/h$.

Hence, the correct option is (C).

28. Given,

In a race of 900 meters, Shreya beats Rahul by 15 seconds or 225 meters.

As Rahul lost by 15 seconds or 225 meters, that means he would have covered 225 meters in 15 seconds only.

So, Speed of Rahul $= \dfrac{225}{15} = 15\ m/s$

So,

Time in which Rahul covers 900 meters $= \dfrac{900}{15} = 60$ seconds

Therefore,

Time in which Shreya finished the race $= 60 - 15 = 45$ seconds

Hence, the correct option is (B).

29. Given,

Distance between two countries P and $Q = 5000\ km$

A train starts from country P at $6{:}00\ am$ at the speed $= 250\ km/hr$

Second train B starts from country Q at $10{:}00\ am$ at the speed $= 150\ km$

Formula:

If the speed of the two trains be $x\ km/hr$ and $y\ km/hr$ respectively if $x > y$.

Relative speed, if opposite directions $= (x + y)\ km/hr$

$Speed = \dfrac{Distance}{Time}$

Distance cover by train A in $4hrs = 250 \times 4 = 1000\ km$

Remaining distance between two countries P and Q which is to be covered by both trains

$= 5000 - 1000 = 4000\ km$

Relative speed of both train if they running opposite direction $= 250 + 150 = 400\ km/hr$

Time taken after $10am$ to meet $= \dfrac{4000}{400} = 10\ hrs$

$\therefore$ Required time $= 10{:}00\ am + 10\ hrs = 8{:}00\ pm$

Hence, the correct option is (A).

30. The pattern followed is,

Option (A) $\Rightarrow 4 \times 12 = 48$

Option (B) $\Rightarrow 8 \times 4 = 32$

Option (C) $\Rightarrow 4 \times 8 = 32$

Option (D) $\Rightarrow 16 \times 2 = 32$

All other pairs when multiplied give 32 as a result, except '4, 12'.

Hence, the correct option is (A).

31. The pattern followed is,

Option (A)

$\Rightarrow \dfrac{136}{17} = 8$

Option (B)

$\Rightarrow \dfrac{152}{19} = 8$

Option (C)

$\Rightarrow \dfrac{160}{20} = 8$

Option (D)

$\Rightarrow \dfrac{148}{18} = 8.22$

All the options give 8 as remainder, when first number is divided with second number, except '148, 18'.

Hence, the correct option is (D).

32. F + 3 = I

$\Rightarrow$ I + 3 = L

$\Rightarrow$ L + 3 = O

Q + 3 = T

⇒ T + 3 = W

⇒ W + 3 = Z

P - 1 = O

⇒ O + 8 = W

⇒ W + 3 = Z

K + 3 = N

⇒ N + 3 = Q

⇒ Q + 3 = T

So, 'POWZ' is the odd one out.

Hence, the correct option is (C).

33. Chennai is the capital of Tamil Nadu.

Gangtok is the capital of Sikkim.

Hyderabad is the capital of Telangana.

Whereas,

Aurangabad is a city in Maharashtra.

Hence, the correct option is (D).

34. Mercury is found in liquid form at the normal temperature, while others are found in the solid form.

Hence, the correct option is (B).

35. Average temperature for Wednesday, Thursday and Friday = 40° C

Total temperature = 3 × 40 = 120° C

Average temperature for Thursday, Friday and Saturday = 41° C

Total temperature = 41 × 3 = 123° C

Temperature on Saturday = 42° C

Now,

(Thursday + Friday + Saturday) - (Wednesday + Thursday + Friday) = 123 - 120;

Saturday - Wednesday = 3

Wednesday = 42 - 3 = 39° C

Hence, the correct option is (A).

36. Ram's Hindi marks = 20

Ram's English marks = 2 × Hindi

Ram's English marks = 2 × 20 = 40

Ram's Science marks = 20 + English

Ram's Science marks = 20 + 40 = 60

Ram's Math marks = 50

Ram's total marks = 20 + 40 + 60 + 50 = 170

Total subject = 4

Average marks = $\dfrac{170}{4}$ = 42.5

Hence, the correct option is (C).

37. Let age of third student is x

$$\Rightarrow \frac{(x + 16 + 16)}{3} = 15$$

$$\Rightarrow x + 32 = 45$$

$$\Rightarrow x = 13$$

∴ Third student's age is 13

Hence, the correct option is (B).

38.

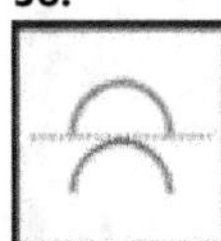

Except (C) all other figures are inverted images of each other.

Hence, the correct option is (C).

39. Each one of the similar figures is composed of straight lines only.

Hence, the correct option is (B).

40.

Only in this figure, the two lines are not parallel.

Hence, the correct option is (C).

41.

In all other cases, One of the two figures is made of dotted lines.

Hence, the correct option is (D).

42.

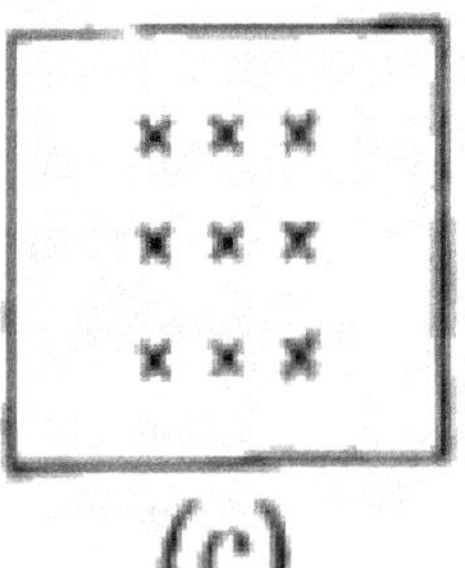

Hence, the correct option is (C).

43. Given that,

$$\Rightarrow 3\frac{18}{57} \times 48\frac{54}{63} \times 6\frac{1}{9} + 2\frac{1}{2} = ?$$

$$\Rightarrow \frac{189}{57} \times \frac{3078}{63} \times \frac{55}{9} + \frac{5}{2} = ?$$

$$\Rightarrow 18 \times 55 + 2.5 = ?$$

$$\Rightarrow ? = 990 + 2.5 = 992.5$$

Hence, the correct option is (D).

44. Given,

$$\Rightarrow 3\frac{1}{6} + 7\frac{2}{3} - 4\frac{1}{4} = ? + 2\frac{1}{6}$$

$$\Rightarrow 3\frac{1}{6} + 7\frac{2}{3} - 4\frac{1}{4} - 2\frac{1}{6} = ?$$

$$\Rightarrow ? = (3 + 7 - 4 - 2) + \left(\frac{1}{6} + \frac{2}{3} - \frac{1}{4} - \frac{1}{6}\right)$$

$$\Rightarrow ? = 4 + \frac{2+8-3-2}{12}$$

$$\Rightarrow ? = 4 + \frac{5}{12}$$

$$\Rightarrow ? = 4\frac{5}{12}$$

Hence, the correct option is (D).

45. Let fraction $= \dfrac{x}{y}$

According to the question,

$$\Rightarrow \frac{x \times 250\%}{y \times 300\%} = \frac{10}{19}$$

$$\Rightarrow \frac{250x}{300y} = \frac{10}{19}$$

$$\Rightarrow \frac{x}{y} = \frac{10}{19} \times \frac{300}{250}$$

$$\Rightarrow \frac{x}{y} = \frac{12}{19}$$

Hence, the correct option is (C).

46. The magnetic field inside the body forms the basis of obtaining the images of different body parts. This is done using a technique called Magnetic Resonance Imaging (MRI). But, these fields are very weak and are about one-billionth of the earth's magnetic field. MRI is not based on tracing heat patterns.

Hence, the correct option is (D).

47. Saturated hydrocarbons will generally give a clean flame while unsaturated carbon compounds will give a yellow flame with lots of black smoke. Vegetable oil is normally unsaturated oil, i.e., if it burns it gives black smoke and yellow flame. Propane and natural gas (mostly methane) are saturated hydrocarbons (single bond carbon chains). So they give a clear flame.

Hence, the correct option is (A).

48. Sheet Mica is used for atomic force microscopy (a very high resolution of microscoping). So, statement 4 is not correct.

Manganese dioxide has been used since antiquity to oxidatively neutralize the greenish tinge in the glass caused by trace amounts of iron contamination. MnO_2 is also used in the manufacture of oxygen and chlorine, and in drying black paints. Manganese is mainly used in the manufacturing of steel and ferromanganese alloy. Nearly 10 kg of manganese is required to manufacture one tonne of steel. It is also used in preparing insecticides and bleaching powder.

Hence, the correct option is (C).

49. The water at the surface of the sea or ocean is heated by the Sun while the water in deeper sections is relatively cold. This difference in temperature is exploited to obtain energy in ocean-thermal-energy conversion plants. These plants can operate if the temperature difference between the water at the surface and water at depths up to 2 km is 293 K (20C) or more. The warm surface- water is used to boil a volatile liquid like ammonia. The vapours of the liquid are then used to run the turbine of generator. The cold water from the depth of the ocean is pumped up and condense vapour again to liquid. The energy potential from the sea (tidal energy, wave energy and ocean thermal energy) is quite large, but efficient commercial exploitation is difficult.

Hence, the correct option is (D).

50. When ethyne is burnt with air, it gives a yellow sooty flame which has much lower temperatures. This is because ethyne is not burnt completely. So, statement 1 is correct.

When pure oxygen is used, the flame is cleaner, the combustion of ethyne is complete, and much higher temperatures can be used with lesser quantities of ethyne. So, statement 2 is correct.

Hence, the correct option is (C).

51. The maiden Indian Navy European Union Naval Force (IN-EUNAVFOR) Exercise is being conducted in the Gulf Of Aden.

Along with the Indian Navy, other naval forces are from Italy, Spain and France. The naval exercise included advanced air defence and anti-submarine exercises, tactical manoeuvres, Search & Rescue, and other maritime security operations.

The objective of the IN-EUNAVFOR naval exercise is to enhance the combat prowess and capability of navies as an integrated force to promote peace, security and stability in the Indian Ocean.

Hence, the correct option is (B).

52. The correct answer is Colluvium soil.

- Colluvium soil is transported by gravity.
- Colluvium is a type of parent material that moved downslope due to gravitational forces (in some cases water may play a role in initiation of the movement).
- Colluvium is heterogeneous, unsorted material of all particle sizes (from boulders to clay) with relatively little abrasion to round the particles.
- Colluvium consists of very sharp, angular rock fragments accumulated at the base of steep slopes.

Hence, the correct option is (B).

53. When the question figure is merged with the figure in option (A), the complete pattern can be seen.

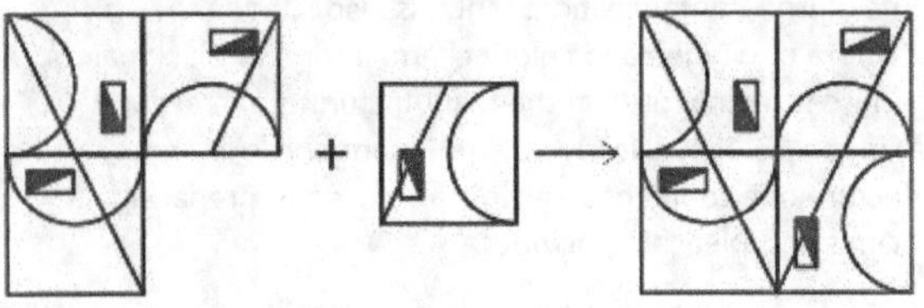

Thus, the figure in option (A) will complete the pattern.

Hence, the correct option is (A).

54. The correct image that will complete the question figure will be:

Hence, the correct option is (C).

55.

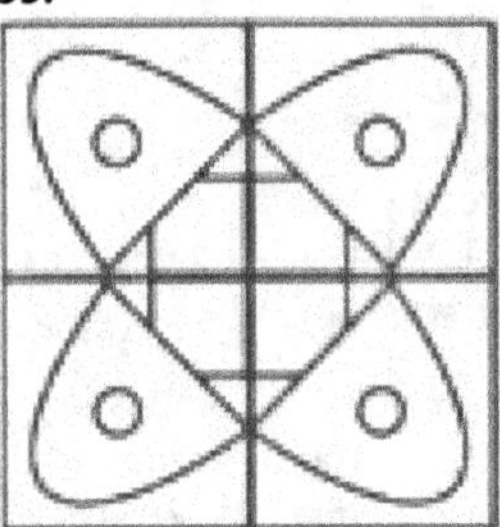

Hence, the correct option is (A).

56. Here 'since' is used to denote time duration (15 YEARS) which is incorrect. 'For' must be used to denote time duration.

E.g. two years, months, weeks etc. 'since' is used to denote the point of time. E.g. since childhood,1992, etc. Thus, the error is in part 2.

The correct sentence will be:

'Rohan had been playing for his club for fifteen years but then his elbow got injured.'

Hence, the correct option is (B).

57. There is a prepositional error in the third part of the sentence. Instead of 'with' the preposition 'on' should be used. For example, we say 'on a serious note'.

Thus, the correct sentence will be:

The principal started his lecture on a pessimistic note.

Hence, the correct option is (C).

58. Sabarimala is a famous Hindu temple located in the Periyar Tiger Sanctuary in Kerala. It has the largest annual pilgrimage in the world, which attracts about 2 crore devotees every year.

Sabarimala is a wonderful link between Shaivites and Vaishnavites. In Malayalam, 'Shabarimala' means mountain.

There is a temple of Lord Ayyappan in Sabarimala. Hence, the correct option is (A).

59. The Chaitra Jatra festival is held every year at the "Tara Tarini hill temple" on the Tuesday of the Hindu month of Chaitra. Tara Tarini Pahari Temple is located in Kumari Pahari on the banks of river Rushikulya. It is a major center of Shakti Puja in Odisha. Tara Tarini hill temple is one of the four major ancient Tantra Peeths and Shakti Peethas in India.
Hence, the correct option is (D).

60. Two pipes can fill a cistern in 2 hours and 3 hours, while a third pipe can drain the cistern empty in 6 hours,

When three pipes opened then their 1 hour's work $= \dfrac{1}{2} + \dfrac{1}{3} - \dfrac{1}{6} = \dfrac{2}{3}$

Total cistern full $= \dfrac{1}{6}$

$\Rightarrow$ Remaining part to filled $= 1 - \dfrac{1}{6} = \dfrac{5}{6}$

$\Rightarrow$ time taken by three to fill $\dfrac{5}{6}$th of the cistern is $= \dfrac{\left(\frac{5}{6}\right)}{\left(\frac{2}{3}\right)}$

$= 1.25$

$\therefore$ It will take 1 hour and 15 minutes to fill the cistern.

Hence, the correct option is (D).

61. Since B is 50% more efficient than A.

Ratio of efficiency of A to B $= 100 : 150 = 2 : 3$

The ratio of time taken by A to B to finish the work $= \left(\dfrac{1}{2}\right) : \left(\dfrac{1}{3}\right)$
$= 3 : 2$

Let the time taken by A and B alone to do work be 3x and 2x respectively.

According to the question:

$3x - 2x = 6$

$x = 6$

Time taken by A and B alone to do work is 18 days and 12 days respectively.

The efficiency of A and B when they work together $= \dfrac{1}{8} + \dfrac{1}{12}$
$= \dfrac{5}{36}$

The required time is taken when both A and B together started working $= \dfrac{36}{5} = 7.2$ days

Hence, the correct option is (A).

62. Let the speed of the stream be 'a' and speed of boat be 'b'.

In still water, speed of boat = b

In the upstream speed of boat relative to stream = b − a

Given, the boat goes 15 km an hour in still water and takes thrice the time to cover the same distance upstream.

$$\text{Speed} = \frac{distance}{time}$$

$$b = \frac{15}{1}$$

$$\Rightarrow b = 15 \text{ km/hr}$$

$$b - a = \frac{15}{3}$$

$$\Rightarrow b - a = 5$$

$$\Rightarrow a = b - 5 = 10 \text{ km/hr}$$

Hence, the correct option is (A).

63. Given,

The ratio of the salaries of X, Y and $Z = 10:12:15$

$$\text{Percentage} = \frac{\text{Actual}}{\text{Total}} \times 100$$

Salaries after increments

$$\Rightarrow X = 10x + 40\% \text{ of } 10x = 14x$$

$$\Rightarrow Y = 12x + 50\% \text{ of } 12x = 18x$$

$$\Rightarrow Z = 15x + 60\% \text{ of } 15x = 24x$$

The ratio of new salaries of X, Y and $Z = 14x:18x:24x$
$$\Rightarrow 7:9:12$$

$\therefore$ The Required Answer is $7:9:12$

Hence, the correct option is (B).

64. Given,

Total Money in bag = Rs 30

Total value = no. of coins × value per coin

Value per coin:

25 p = 1

50 p = 2

Rs 1 = 4

No. of coins:

25 p = 8

50 p = 4

Rs 1 = 1

Total Value:

25 p = 8

50 p = 8

Rs 1 = 4

Total Value = 30

$\Rightarrow 20x = 30$

$\Rightarrow x = 1.5$

Value of 50p coins = 8x = 8 × 1.5 = Rs 12

No. of coins = 12 × 2 = 24

$\therefore$ No. of 50 paise coins are 24.

Hence, the correct option is (D).

65. Given,

Total amount = Rs 1120

$$I : II : III = \frac{4}{5} : \frac{5}{4} : \frac{3}{4}$$

$I : II : III = 16 : 25 : 15$

Total = 1120

$\Rightarrow 56x = 1120$

$\Rightarrow x = 20$

so, 2nd part = 25x = 25 × 20 = Rs 500

$\therefore$ The required answer is Rs 500.

Hence, the correct option is (D).

66.
Hence, the correct option is (C).

67. The figure given in the question is embedded in the fourth figure as shown below-

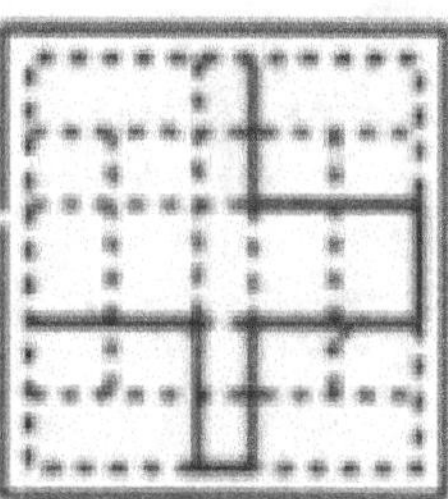

Hence, the correct option is (D).

68. On close observation, we find that the question figure is embedded in option (D) as shown below:

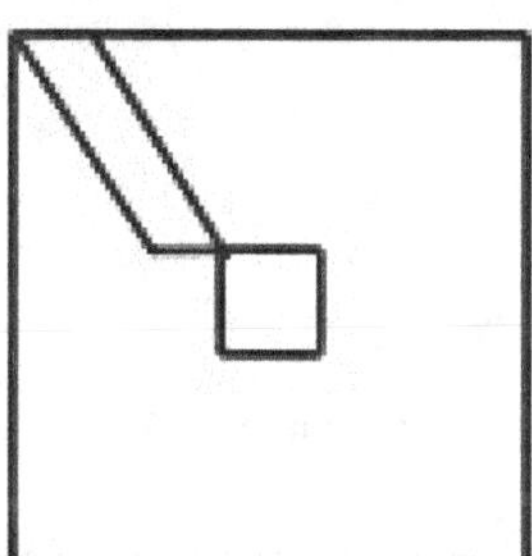

Hence, the correct option is (D).

69.

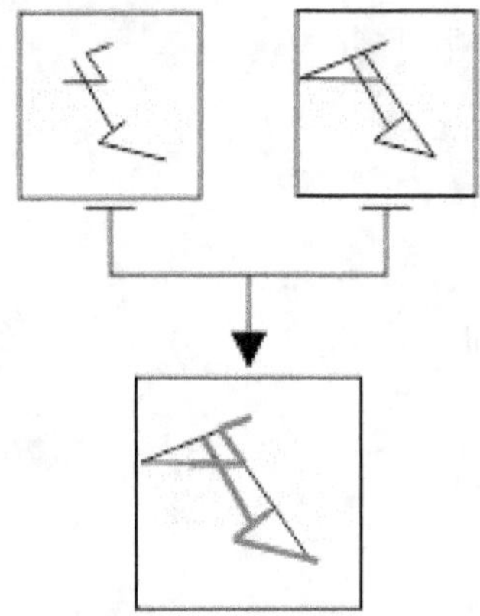

Hence, the correct option is (B).

70. We can easily observe that in option C the question figure is embedded.

Hence, the correct option is (C).

71. As we know,

Selling price = (Cost price + amount spend on repairing)

$$\times \frac{(100 + profit\ \%)}{100}$$

$$\Rightarrow 24150 = (19200 + x) \times \frac{(100 + 15)}{100}$$

$$\Rightarrow 24150 = (19200 + x) \times \frac{115}{100}$$

$$\Rightarrow 19200 + x = 24150 \times \frac{100}{115}$$

$$\Rightarrow 19200 + x = 21000$$

$$\Rightarrow x = 21000 - 19200$$

$$\Rightarrow x = 1800$$

$\therefore$ The amount spend on repairing of old typewriter is Rs 1800.

Hence, the correct option is (B).

72. Given:

Marked price, M.P. $=$ Rs. 750

Selling price, S.P. $=$ Rs. 600

From formula,

Discount $=$ M.P. $-$ S.P.

Discount $\% = \dfrac{\text{Discount}}{\text{M.P.}} \times 100$

Discount $\% = \dfrac{(750-600)}{750} \times 100$

$$= \frac{150}{7.5}$$

$$= 20\%$$

Hence, the correct option is (A).

73. Let the cost price of a table = Rs. 100

The cost price of a chair = Rs. 75

The selling price of 5 chairs at the cost price of 7 tables

Cost price of 5 chairs = 75 x 5 = Rs. 375

The selling price of 5 chairs = 7 x 100 = Rs. 700

Profit % = $\dfrac{700-375}{375} \times 100$

$$= \frac{325}{375} \times 100$$

= 86.66 %

Hence, the correct option is (C).

74. Here, the concept of the present perfect continuous is brought under consideration. When, words like since and for are used in a sentence to represent time and continuation of action is being shown Then, following patten is followed :- Sub + has/have + been + v4 (verb + ing) + since + rest of the sentence.

Complete sentence:

Sakshi has been working in this company for the past 10 years.

Hence, the correct option is (B).

75. Here, the concept of conjunction is brought under consideration. Conjunction like as well as follows the verb according to the number of nouns that is used before the verb. Her, a noun used is wife which is a singular noun. Hence, according to subject-verb agreement, the verb should also be singular.

Complete sentence:

The boss, as well as his wife, was invited.

Hence, the correct option is (C).

76. The sentence tries to state that Parul does not behave well with the other members of the committee and therefore she had to resign. The phrasal verb 'get on with' means sharing a good relationship with others.

Complete sentence:

Parul had to resign from the college union committee on the ground that she does not get on very well with the other members and abuses them.

Hence, the correct option is (A).

77. 'Than' is a conjunction that is used for making comparisons between elements, objects, people, etc.

'Then' is commonly used to express a sense of time or what comes next or used to be.

'As', 'Or', and 'Of' are idiomatically and grammatically incorrect.

Complete sentence:

He knew more about the culture and philosophy than any man living.

Hence, the correct option is (A).

78. All in all- Most important

As she is only girl in a big family, so she is all in all in her home.

Hence, the correct option is (D)

79. "Hitting the books" means to study especially in time of tests and exams. Here the sentence means implying the meaning of the idiom as "They go to the beach when they should be studying really hard and then they wonder why they don't get good marks."

Hence, the correct option is (B).

80. According to the sequence in the dictionary:

Peahen

Pencil

People

Petal

Pencil will come in the second position.

Hence, the correct option is (C).

81. Given:

(i) Vegetable, (ii) Market, (iii) Cutting, (iv) Cooking, (v) Eat

The logical order will be:

(ii) Market → We go to market first.

(i) Vegetable → We buy vegetables.

(iii) Cutting → We cut the vegetables.

(iv) Cooking → We cook the vegetables.

(v) Eat → We eat the cooked vegetable.

Hence, the correct option is (C).

82. Rajya Sabha has an indefinite term and not subject to dissolution (Article 83.1). The term of an Individual Rajya Sabha member is 6 years and one third of its members retire every two years, in accordance with the rules as prescribed by the parliament of India.

Hence, the correct option is (D).

83. The most appropriate synonym of the given word 'Accorded' is 'Give'.

Let's look at the meaning and examples of the given options:

Therefore, as per the points mentioned above, we find that the correct answer is Option C.

Hence, the correct option is (C).

84. The most appropriate synonym of the given word 'Assertions' is 'Declaration'.

Let's look at the meaning and examples of the given options:

Hence, the correct option is (D).

85. Let's see the meaning of the given word:

Versatile- able to adapt or be adapted to many different functions or activities.

Let's see an example:

A leather jacket is a timeless and versatile garment that can be worn in all seasons.

So the correct answer is Option 1 i.e., multi-purpose.

Hence, the correct option is (A).

86. Calculations :

Square of 40 = $(40)^2$

= 1600

A quarter of 40% of 1600 = 25% of 40% of 1600

$$\left(\frac{1}{4}\right) \times \left(\frac{2}{5}\right) \times 1600$$

$$\Rightarrow 1600 \times \left(\frac{2}{20}\right)$$

$$\Rightarrow 160$$

∴ The result will be 160

Hence, the correct option is (C).

87. Given:

Man spends 75% of his income.

Income increases by 28%

Expenditure increases by 20%

Formula Used:

Saving = Income – Expenditure

Calculation:

Let the Income of a man = 100

Expenditure = 75% of 100

$$\Rightarrow \left(\frac{75}{100}\right) \times 100 = 75$$

Saving = Income – Expenditure

Initial Saving $\Rightarrow 100 - 75 = 25$ ----(1)

Now as per the question,

His income increased by 28%

His new income = Old income + 28% of Old income

$\Rightarrow$ His new income = $\left(\dfrac{128}{100}\right) \times 100 = 128$

Similarly, his expenditure increased by 20%

His new expenditure = $\left(\dfrac{120}{100}\right) \times 75$

$\Rightarrow$ His new expenditure = 90

$Saving_{(new)} = Income_{(new)} - Expenditure_{(new)}$

$Saving_{(new)} = 128 - 90 = 38$ ----(2)

Now, % increase in savings = $\left\{\dfrac{(38-25)}{25}\right\} \times 100$ ----(from 1 and 2)

$\Rightarrow 13 \times 4 = 52\%$

$\therefore$ The % increase in saving is 52%

Hence, the correct option is (D).

88. Given:

40% of a number is 112.

Calculation:

Let the number is x.

$\left(\dfrac{40}{100}\right) \times x = 112$

$x = \dfrac{(112 \times 100)}{40}$

x = 280

So, 15% of 280 = 42

$\therefore$ 15% of a number is 42.

Hence, the correct option is (A).

89. All thieves are criminals. But police is different.

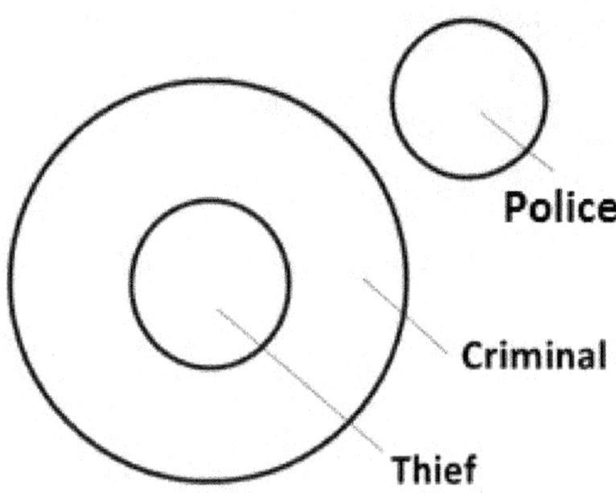

Hence, the correct option is (A).

90. Storeroom and Bedroom are entirely different. But both are of a house.

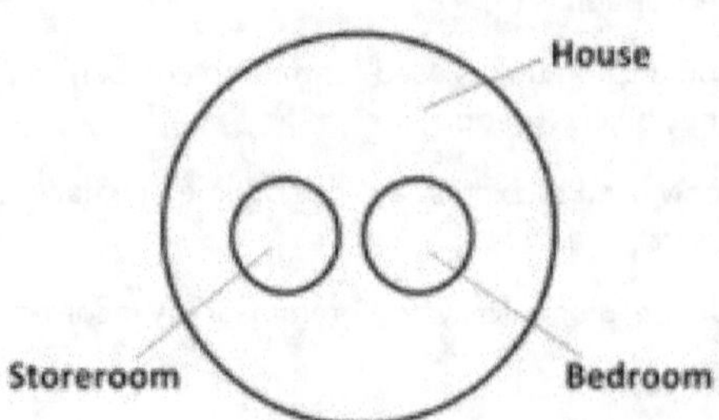

Hence, the correct option is (B).

91. From the information given in the question, we analyse,

Product and Machinery are different from each other but both are found in Factory.

Hence, the correct option is (D).

92. From the information given in the question, we analyse,

All three are different professions.

Hence, the correct option is (B).

93. Given:

S indicates strict officers.

T indicates tall officers.

I indicates IAS officers.

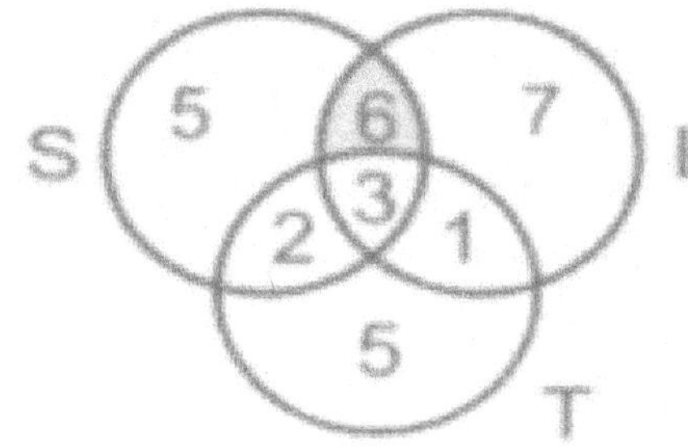

Officers	Number of officers
S	5
S and T	2
T	5
T and I	1
I	7
I and S	6
S, T, and I	3

Therefore, the total number of strict IAS officers who are not tall is 6.

Hence, the correct option is (C).

94. The missing figure is:

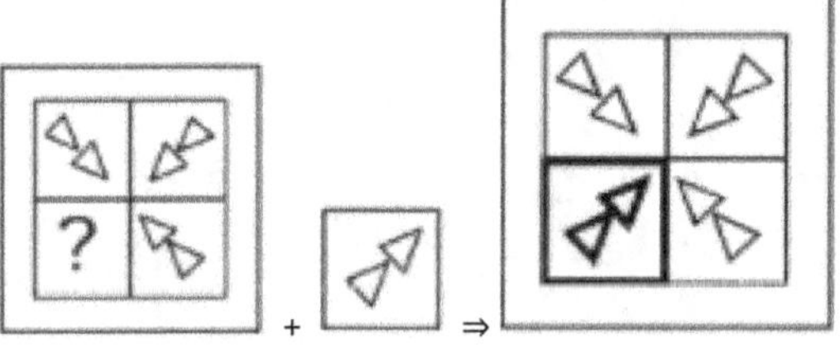 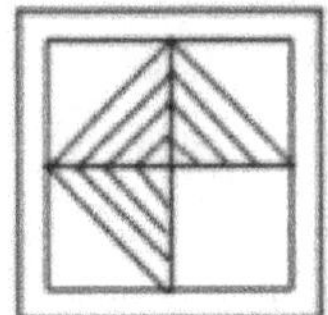 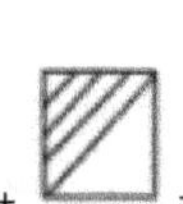 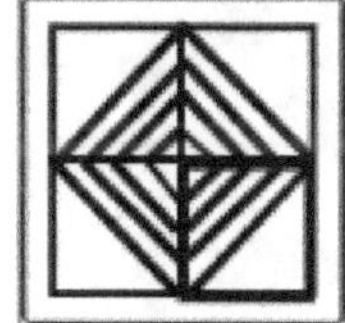

Hence, the correct option is (D).

95. The missing figure is:

Hence, the correct option is (C).

96. The first paragraph mentions that During the Christian era, the ecclesiastics controlled the institution of education and diffused among the people the gospel of the Bible.

In the second paragraph, it has been mentioned that During the Renaissance, education passed more from the clutches of the priest into the hand of the prince.

And finally, in the last i.e. third paragraph, it has been mentioned that With the advent of the industrial revolution education took a different turn and had to please the new masters.

Thus, the chronological order is Christian period, Renaissance period, Period of Industrial Revolution.

Hence, the correct option is (B).

97. Refer to the lines: The philosophy which was in vogue during this period was that of 'Laissez Faire' restricting the function of the State to a mere keeping of law and order.

Upon the perusal of the above line, it can be deduced that 'Laissez - Faire' relates to restricting the function of the State to a mere keeping of law and order.

Hence, the correct option is (D).

98. Refer to the lines: It is an old saying that knowledge is power. Education is an instrument which imparts knowledge and, therefore indirectly controls power. Therefore, ever since the dawn of civilization persons in power have always tried to control education.

Thus, it can be concluded that the persons in power always tried to control education because it is an instrument of knowledge and power.

Hence, the correct option is (D).

99. Refer to the lines: During the Christian era, the ecclesiastics controlled the institution of education and diffused among the people the gospel of the Bible.

During the Renaissance, education passed more from the clutches of the priest into the hand of the prince.

Upon the perusal of the above lines, it can be concluded that the education before Renaissance i.e. in the Christian era, was controlled by priests.

Thus, we can conclude that The church and the priests controlled the institution of education during the Christian era.

Hence, the correct option is (A).

100. Refer to the lines: During the Christian era, the ecclesiastics controlled the institution of education and diffused among the people the gospel of the Bible. These gospels were no other than a philosophy for the maintenance of the existing society. This religious education taught the poor man to be meek and to earn his bread with the sweat of his brow.

Upon the perusal of the above lines, it can be concluded that the poor man was meant to earn his bread by working too hard for the rich class during the Christian era.

Hence, the correct option is (D).

// Notes //

www.ingramcontent.com/pod-product-compliance
Lightning Source LLC
LaVergne TN
LVHW080550200726
843510LV00008B/1067

* 9 7 8 9 3 5 5 5 6 2 5 2 4 *